Ford F-Series Pickup

OWNER'S BIBLE™

By Moses Ludel

A Hands-on Guide to Getting the Most From Your F-Series Pickup

RB

BENTLEY PUBLISHERS

Ford
F-Series Pickup

OWNER'S BIBLE™

Ford F-Series history, see Chapter 1

Operator's tips, see Chapter 3

Servicing your F-Series, see Chapter 4

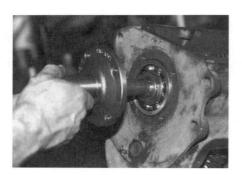

Transmission rebuilding, see Chapter 9

TABLE OF CONTENTS

PREFACE **V**

1 EVOLUTION OF THE FORD F-SERIES **1**

V-8 Era: A New Truck Emerges 1 • 1942: Ford Trucks Forge Their Own Way 2 • 1948: A Truck With A Firm Identity 2 • 1953–56: A Marque Emerges 4 • 1957–64: The Pragmatic Years 8 • 1965: The Advent Of Twin I-Beam 10 • 1967–79: Years Of Bold Refinement 12 • 1980: An Advanced 4x4 Chassis 15 • Poised for the Future 17

2 BUYING AN F-SERIES TRUCK **19**

Selecting The Right Truck 20 • Anatomy of a Half-ton 20 • F-250 Virtues 21 • One-ton 22 • Shopping for the Right Components 23 • The Ten Best Picks In Used Ford F-trucks 24 • Inspecting A Used Truck 24 • Buying A New F-Series Truck 28 • 1994 Ford F-Series Specifications 30

3 OPERATING YOUR F-SERIES **33**

Learning To Drive Your F-Series Truck 35 • Operating A 4x4 F-truck 36 • Off-pavement Four-wheel Drive 38 • Tread Lightly Four Wheeling 41 • Special Uses For Your 4WD Truck 43 • 4WD Clubs 45

4 WORKING ON YOUR F-SERIES **47**

The F-truck Chassis 48 • Front Axle Types 48 • Steering Gear and Linkage 49 • Drum and Disc Brake Systems 50 • A Glance At F-truck Engines 51 • Transmissions and Transfer Cases 55 • Driveshafts 58 • Repairs On Your F-Series Truck 59 • The F-truck Owner's Toolbox 61 • Sourcing Ford Truck Parts 68 • Assigning Work to a Shop 69

5 LUBRICATION AND MAINTENANCE **73**

Maintenance Overview 73 • Selecting Lubricants and Fluids 74 • Service Intervals 75 • Building a Maintenance Schedule 76 • Do Your Own Maintenance 78 • Storing Your Truck 86

6 TROUBLESHOOTING AND MINOR ADJUSTMENTS **89**

Guide To Troubleshooting 91 • Engine and Electrical Problems 91 • Cooling System Troubles 96 • Clutch and Manual Transmission 97 Driveshaft and Axle Woes 99 • Steering and Tire Troubles 100 • Brake Problems 102

7 COOLING SYSTEM SERVICE **105**

Safety Precautions 105 • Cooling System Basics 106 • Finding Leaks 108 • Overheating Problems 111 • Water Pump Service 112

8 ENGINE TUNE-UP AND EMISSION CONTROLS **117**

Emission Controls and Tune-up 118 • Engine Applications 118 • A Closer Look At EFI/MFI Engines 121 • Ignition Tune-up 122 • Carburetor Tune-up 133 • Major Engine Diagnosis 139 • Valve Adjustment 141 • Emission Controls 144

9 CLUTCH AND TRANSMISSION SERVICE **153**

Troubleshooting 153 • Clutch Service 156 • Transmission Adjustments 164 • Rebuilding The Warner T-98/T-18 Ford Truck Transmission 165

Brake fluid changing, see Chapter 12

Winches and accessories, see Chapter 15

Engine upgrades, see Chapter 16

Traction devices, see Chapter 17

Suspension lift kits, see Chapter 18

10 TRANSFER CASE, DRIVESHAFTS, AXLES AND HUBS   177

Transfer Cases 177 • Troubleshooting 178 • Driveshafts 180 • U-joint Service and Repair Tips 180 • Driveshaft Lubrication 182 • Driveshaft Angularity 183 • U-joint Installation 184 • Axle Assemblies 185 • Differential Action 186 • Axle Types 187 • Axle Troubleshooting 188 • Axle Seals 189 • Closed-knuckle Steering Rebuild 190 • Locking Hubs 195 • Hub Rebuilding 196

11 SUSPENSION AND STEERING   201

Springs 201 • Installing New Springs 202 • Frame Damage 204 • Shock Absorbers 204 • Gas Shocks 205 • Selecting Shocks 205 • 4x4 Steering and Front End 206 • Rebuilding A Ball-joint Steering Knuckle 206 • Steering System 208 • Power Steering 210 • Inspecting the Steering System 212 • Wheel Alignment 213

12 BRAKES AND WHEEL BEARINGS   217

Wheel Bearings 217 • Front Wheel Bearing Fundamentals 217 • Wheel Bearing Service 218 • The Braking System 220 • Pedal Warning Signals 221 • Brake Fluid Precautions 221 • Brake Service Tips 223

13 BODY AND DETAILING   229

Battling Rust 229 •Body Detailing 232 • Quick Tips to a Better Detail Job 235 • Pickup Bed and Tub Liners 237

14 ELECTRICAL SYSTEM BASICS   239

The Electrical System 239 •Electrical Troubleshooting 242 • Testing Battery and Charging System 246 • Starter Motor 248 • Starter Troubleshooting 249 • Starter Overhaul 250

15 ACCESSORIES   253

Winches 254 • Electrical System Upgrades 261 •Roll Bars 267 • Seat Belts and Safety Harnesses 269 •Trailering 270

16 FORD ENGINE PERFORMANCE: MILD TO WILD!   273

Engine Performance and Smog Legal Modifications 273 • Ford F-truck Power: An Overview 275 • Valvetrain Modifications 275 • Ignition Modifications 278 • Performance Carburetion 280 • Lubrication and Engine Oil Cooling 283 • Supercharging 284 • Flathead to FE F-truck Power 287 • 460 V-8: The Ultimate Racing and Tow Engine 290 • 351 Windsor V-8 Buildup 292 •302/5.0L V-8 Tips 294 • Engine Overhaul 300

17 DRIVETRAIN UPGRADES   311

Performance Transmissions 312 • Four-speed Changeover 313 • The Clutch 314 • Clutch Types 314 • Aftermarket Clutches 315 • Traction Differentials 317 • Conversion Axles 321 • Driveshaft Footnotes 322

18 CHASSIS AND SUSPENSION UPGRADES   323

Chassis Modifications 323 • State Lift Laws 325 • Off-pavement Suspension Tuning 325 • Upgrading Shocks 327 • Urethane Bushings 328 • Installing An Upgraded Suspension 329 • Steering Gear Conversions 336 •Tires 337 • Tire Glossary 339 • Brake System Upgrades 342

APPENDICES   343

Sources, Hardware Grading, Toolbox, Engine Break-in, 4x4 Trials

INDEX   357

ACKNOWLEDGMENTS, ABOUT THE AUTHOR   363

BENTLEY PUBLISHERS | AUTOMOTIVE BOOKS & MANUALS

1734 Massachusetts Avenue
Cambridge, MA 02138 USA
800-423-4595 / 617-547-4170

Information that makes
the difference®

www.bentleypublishers.com

WARNING—Important Safety Notice

In this book we have attempted to describe repairs, modifications and accessories which may be used with Ford vehicles, using examples and instructions which we believe to be accurate. However, the examples, instructions, and other information are intended solely as illustrations and should be used in any particular application only by personnel who are experienced in the repair and modification of Ford vehicles and who have independently evaluated the repair, modification or accessory. Implementation of a modification or attachment of an accessory described in this book may render the vehicle, attachment, or accessory unsafe for use in certain circumstances.

Do not use this book unless you are familiar with basic automotive repair procedures and safe workshop practices. This book illustrates procedures required for some service and modification work; it is not a substitute for full and up-to-date information from the vehicle manufacturer or aftermarket supplier, or for proper training as an automotive technician. Note that it is not possible for us to anticipate all of the ways or conditions under which vehicles may be serviced or modified or to provide cautions as to all of the possible hazards that may result.

The vehicle manufacturer and aftermarket suppliers will continue to issue service information updates and parts retrofits after the editorial closing of this book. Some of these updates and retrofits will apply to procedures and specifications in this book. We regret that we cannot supply updates to purchasers of this book.

We have endeavored to ensure the accuracy of the information in this book. Please note, however, that considering the vast quantity and the complexity of the information involved, we cannot warrant the accuracy or completeness of the information contained in this book.

FOR THESE REASONS, NEITHER THE PUBLISHER NOR THE AUTHOR MAKES ANY WARRANTIES, EXPRESS OR IMPLIED, THAT THE EXAMPLES, INSTRUCTIONS OR OTHER INFORMATION IN THIS BOOK ARE FREE OF ERRORS OR OMISSIONS, ARE CONSISTENT WITH INDUSTRY STANDARDS, OR THAT THEY WILL MEET THE REQUIREMENTS FOR A PARTICULAR APPLICATION, AND WE EXPRESSLY DISCLAIM THE IMPLIED WARRANTIES OF MERCHANTABILITY AND OF FITNESS FOR A PARTICULAR PURPOSE, EVEN IF THE PUBLISHER OR AUTHOR HAVE BEEN ADVISED OF A PARTICULAR PURPOSE, AND EVEN IF A PARTICULAR PURPOSE IS INDICATED IN THE BOOK. THE PUBLISHER AND AUTHOR ALSO DISCLAIM ALL LIABILITY FOR DIRECT, INDIRECT, INCIDENTAL OR CONSEQUENTIAL DAMAGES THAT RESULT FROM ANY USE OF THE EXAMPLES, INSTRUCTIONS OR OTHER INFORMATION IN THIS BOOK. IN NO EVENT SHALL OUR LIABILITY WHETHER IN TORT, CONTRACT OR OTHERWISE EXCEED THE COST OF THIS BOOK.

Your common sense and good judgment are crucial to safe and successful automotive work. Read procedures through before starting them. Think about how alert you are feeling, and whether the condition of your vehicle, your level of mechanical skill or your level of reading comprehension might result in or contribute in some way to an occurrence which might cause you injury, damage your vehicle, or result in an unsafe repair or modification. If you have doubts for these or other reasons about your ability to perform safe work on your vehicle, have the work done at an authorized Ford dealer or other qualified shop.

This book is only intended for persons who are experienced in repairing automobiles and who are seeking specific information about Ford vehicles. It is not for those who are looking for general information on automobile repair. REPAIR AND MODIFICATION OF AUTOMOBILES IS DANGEROUS UNLESS UNDERTAKEN WITH FULL KNOWLEDGE OF THE CONSEQUENCES.

Before attempting any work on your Ford, read the Warnings and Cautions on the inside front cover and any warning or caution that accompanies a procedure or description in the book. Review the Warnings and Cautions each time you prepare to work on your Ford.

The publisher encourages comments from the reader of this book. These communications have been and will be considered in the preparation of this and other manuals. Please write to Robert Bentley Inc., Publishers at the address listed on the top of this page.

This book was published by Robert Bentley, Inc., Publishers. Ford has not reviewed and does not warrant the accuracy or completeness of the technical specifications and information described in this book.

Library of Congress Cataloging-in-Publication Data

Ludel, Moses.
    Ford F-series pickup owner's bible : a hands-on guide to getting
the most from your F-series pickup / by Moses Ludel.
        p.   cm.
    Includes index.
    ISBN 0-8376-0152-5 (alk. paper) : $29.95
    1. Ford trucks--Maintenance and repair.   2. Ford trucks-
-performance.   I. Title.
TL230.5.F57L84   1994
629.223--dc20   94-35251
                                                      CIP

Bentley Stock No. GOWF

03 02 01 00   10 9 8 7 6 5 4

The paper used in this publication is acid free and meets the requirements of the National Standard for Information Sciences-Permanence of Paper for Printed Library Materials. ∞

Ford F-Series Pickup Owner's Bible™: A Hands-on Guide to Getting the Most From Your Ford F-Series Pickup, by Moses Ludel

Preface

I had just turned fifteen, barely old enough for a learner's driving permit, when my brother-in-law towed a well-worn early Ford V-8 pickup into our yard and handed me the title. Complete with barnyard smells, weather-cracked tires and welded tears in the fenders, my first Ford truck was home.

The '38 half-ton wore a coat of red oxide primer, which blended nicely with the changing autumn leaves. Beneath the side-lift hood, a later 8BA flathead V-8 refused to start, its gummed piston rings and waxy oil now stiff from years of dormancy. And so the project began.

Beneath the ladder and X-member frame of that '38, my initiation to truck mechanics unfolded. I scrutinized the early Ford chassis, poring over details of the transverse leaf spring suspension that characterized early Ford passenger cars and light trucks. 1938 was the last V-8 pickup with mechanical brakes, but my truck had an upgrade to the more modern hydraulic system. By Thanksgiving, the scent of fallen cottonwood leaves mixed with pungent gear oil odors from the disassembled torque tube "banjo" rear axle and aged three-speed manual transmission.

During the spring of 1967, I bought my first Ford F-Series truck, a 1951 F-3 pickup, and quickly discovered the balky nature of its spur gear four-speed transmission. Fortunately, my previous Ford pickup's non-synchromesh first gear had provided ample practice at double clutching.

The heavy duty F-3 boasted thirteen leafs at each rear spring stack and featured Ford's slow speed 226-cubic-inch flathead six-cylinder. Were it not for the 4.86:1 final drive gearing, the lean 95 horsepower would have succumbed early to the truck's unabashed bulk. These gears permitted heavy hauling with ample crawl speed performance in first gear and a practical cruise speed of 45–50 mph.

The rounded body lines of the original 1948–52 F-models gave hint to Ford's second generation design. Among America's most popular light trucks, the F-100 to F-350 models built from 1953 to 1956 have provided unparalleled aesthetic appeal coupled with a pragmatic chassis design and ample powertrain. F-trucks of that era, which sold in unprecedented numbers, still hold a premium value.

My appreciation for the versatility of Ford's early F-100 marque began with a high mileage 1955 pickup. Between 1968 and 1974, the truck underwent three personality changes, twice emerging as a potent street rod before receiving a full chassis rebuild and restoration to its original appearance.

Preface

Later, my family needed a safe and reliable multi-purpose vehicle while I attended the University of Oregon. Our choice was a very clean 1964 F-100 long bed pickup. The truck's odometer had nearly turned over, but the Y-block 292 V-8, T-98 four-speed and Ford 9-inch rear axle were still full of life. When the situation called for economy and utility, a used F-100 met our demands. The appeal of early F-100s was their pleasurable ride, great looks, ample performance and ease of service, themes reflected in today's F-Series trucks.

By the mid-1980s, my role as an automotive journalist included road tests and evaluations of new four-wheel drive trucks. In an intensive comparison, I ran three distinctly different 1989 Ford F-Series 4x4 trucks through a range of tests.

The first truck was a base F-150 4x4 model with a five-speed and the familiar 4.9L six, which had gained electronic fuel injection (MPI) in 1987. Utilitarian and easy to maneuver, the no frills truck stood boldly against the competition, with workhorse willingness, a sturdy stance and a rugged profile—much like the original 1948 F-1.

Next up the Gross Vehicle Weight (GVW) scale was a 351-Windsor V-8 F-250 XLT Lariat with a full complement of power options. F-250 Twin-Traction Beam suspension gave the 3/4-ton 4x4 an unrivaled ride. Ford's renowned workhorse, now four decades into production and a long list of luxury appointments.

At the top of the test sequence was Ford's quintessential trailer puller, a fully equipped one-ton capacity F-350 4x4 with the Navistar 7.3L V-8 diesel engine option. Even this model offered the ride quality, occupant comfort and ergonomics of a sportier truck. The yeoman's workhorse of 1948, Ford F-Series trucks had evolved into highly versatile multi-purpose vehicles.

For the do-it-yourself owner, the *Ford F-Series Truck Owner's Bible* serves as a hands-on technical guide, model review and data source for performing light service work. If you prefer delegating repair work to a capable shop, this book offers valuable troubleshooting tips that can help you assess your service and repair needs.

Within these chapters, I share my experience as a truck mechanic, shop instructor, technical columnist and seasoned journalist in the light truck and sport utility 4x4 field. Equipped with this book and a genuine Ford factory service manual for your F-truck model, you can accomplish quality repairs or a complete mechanical restoration.

Exceptional value is the hallmark of F-Series Ford models. For the first time owner or loyal repeat buyer, a Ford truck can provide durability, utility, safety and performance. I have written and illustrated the *Ford F-Series Pickup Owner's Bible* as a tribute to America's most enduring and popular line of light trucks.

Chapter 1

Evolution of the Ford F-Series

FORD MOTOR COMPANY'S original light truck was a passenger car chassis with a cab and pickup bed. Beginning with the Model T era and ending after the 1941 model run, light trucks and passenger cars shared chassis, powertrain and body components. This helped keep the purchase price and maintenance costs of light trucks low, but the limitation of this strategy was that truck advances depended upon passenger car engineering, and Ford made long term commitments to each chassis platform and powertrain design.

Model T production ran from 1908–1927, with few changes in the intrinsic chassis design of these cars and Ford's earliest trucks. The Model A, built from 1928–31, also provided a universal chassis and powertrain with various body options. While the canvas top Model A roadster pickup reflected Model T roots, the metal cab Model A pickup served as Ford's first light truck.

Although Ford had built a larger one-ton load capacity Model TT truck and a 1-1/2-ton Model AA truck (each featuring heavier axles, a stronger gearbox, a stouter frame, and beefier spring package than lighter cars and trucks), even these vehicles relied on passenger car engines and components. Ford was years away from a truck division with full engineering autonomy.

V-8 Era: A New Truck Emerges

Ford's all-new 1932 Ford Model B four-cylinder and V-8 trucks still shared chassis and powertrain pieces with passenger cars. Although larger in size and curb weight than the Model A, and boasting a healthy 65 horsepower 221-cubic-inch flathead V-8 engine option, the new half-ton pickup and cab-and-chassis trucks looked much like a Ford coupe or two-door sedan from the doors forward.

0012000

Fig. 1-1.   1959 Ford F-100 and F-250 four-wheel drive models were Ford's first factory built 4x4s. A ladder frame and leaf springs made the front axle and transfer case fitup easy.   *System uses a Spicer 44 front axle and a two-speed transfer unit. (Photo courtesy of Ford Motor Company)*

0012001

Fig. 1-2.   Ford's L-head (flathead) V-8 revolutionized the automobile and light truck industry. 1932–42 221-cubic-inch V-8s ranged from 65 to 90 horsepower. In 1946, Ford increased the flathead V-8 to 239.4 cubic inches and raised horsepower to 100. A revised version of this engine and the 226H inline L-head six powered the first F-Series trucks in 1948.

The new mass production V-8 engine, which developed 85 horsepower by the mid-1930s, provided a solid value for the Depression years. Built around a stronger chassis with Ford's familiar transverse mounted front and rear leaf springs, the light truck satisfied a variety of uses.

Although Ford cars and light trucks retained mechanical brakes longer than competitor's models, overall quality and dependability made the early V-8 Fords successful. Good looks prevailed through the mid-1930s, and for 1938 the commercial car/light truck cab reflected the classic 1938–40 passenger car profile.

1939 was a milestone year as Ford passenger cars and light trucks acquired hydraulically actuated brakes and subtle improvements in the V-8 engine. A tiny 136-cubic-inch 60 horsepower V-8, introduced in 1937, was a light truck economy option, while other powertrain components were similar to earlier years. The 221-cubic-inch flathead V-8 now boasted 90 horsepower.

When the 1940 models emerged, subtle differences separated Ford cars and half-ton trucks. Car transmissions now featured a steering column shifter, while trucks continued to offer a floor shift. Half-ton truck front sheet metal was similar to the standard 1940 car grille and hood, the last year that passenger cars used this styling.

For 3/4- and one-ton Ford trucks, 1939 and '40 body styling began to differ strongly from half-ton models, and

in 1940 these larger trucks opted for an open drive-line Hotchkiss rear axle and four semi-elliptic springs. The half-ton maintained its passenger car-type chassis with transverse leaf springs, radius support rods and a torque tube rear axle.

In 1941, Ford cars acquired a fresh look, more in step with the bold styling of General Motors and Chrysler models. Although the 221 V-8 had offered 90 horsepower since 1939, performance of the heavier '41 and '42 Ford cars fell short of models like the Buick OHV straight eight. Even the 226G inline L-head six, Ford's new engine option, could match the horsepower rating of the 221 V-8.

Large Ford trucks began using the new Mercury line V-8 in 1939. These 239.4-cubic-inch engines produced 95 horsepower and provided better performance. For 1941, the lighter truck models offered an austere four-cylinder Ford tractor economy engine, the all-new inline 226G six or the 221 V-8. The 1941 half-ton pickup looked intrinsically the same as 1940 models and served as Ford's last pickup with a passenger car face.

1942: Ford Trucks Forge Their Own Identity

1942 chassis changes forever separated Ford light trucks from passenger cars. New front sheet metal gave a utility look to the '42 truck models, and the ladder chassis featured fore-and-aft mounted semi-elliptic leaf springs with the first open driveshaft rear axle in a light Ford truck. The stark body profile lasted through 1947.

World War II halted Ford's production of civilian trucks. Light truck assembly resumed in late 1945 with virtually a continuation of the 1942 model. The notable improvement for 1946 Ford cars and lighter trucks was the introduction of Mercury's 239.4-cubic-inch displacement 59A-type flathead V-8 with a rating of 100 horsepower. Hop-up potential of the 59-series flathead engines became legendary among Forties and Fifties hot rodders.

The 90-horsepower 226 flathead six, introduced in 1941 pickups, continued as an option. The new V-8 provided more power, and an optional four-speed spur gear (non-synchromesh) transmission, archaic with its demanding double clutch shifts, widened the versatility of these trucks.

1942–47 Ford truck owners were familiar with some of the powertrain features that characterized the all-new F-Series light truck models. Introduced in January of 1948, the badges F-1, F-2 and F-3 signified a new and easy to understand Gross Vehicle Weight Rating (GVWR) system. The F-1 rated a half-ton capacity, while the F-2 could carry a 3/4-ton load. F-3s, like my first Ford F-truck, ranked as a heavy duty 3/4-ton hauler, by today's standards more like a full one-ton load chassis. This nomenclature carries through the 1990s in respective F-150, F-250 and F-350 models.

1948: A Truck With A Firm Identity

The new 1948 F-Series truck featured far more than a facelift. Ford Motor Company, recognizing the post-WWII consumer demand for light trucks, gave the new models a bold chassis and distinctive personality. The interior was distinctly truck-oriented. Dashboard instrumentation and a utility profile separated the '48 F-Series cab from passenger cars. New styling cues and the in-

0012003

Fig. 1-3. *The F-1, F-2 and F-3 trucks rated one-half, three-quarter and heavy duty 3/4-ton load capacities. A new cab distinguished F-Series trucks from previous models. Ford now had a truck with distinctive styling and engineering autonomy. This 1948 F-1 is first year model. Reminiscent of the* early Ford era, F-Series trucks featured an engine crank hole through the grille. Crank starting a flathead V-8 or six is possible, but use extreme caution. Even a balky Model T four-cylinder engine could break an arm or wrist.

creased cab size of F-trucks met the demands of American buyers who now wanted trucks with that full-bodied look of post-WWII automobiles.

Early F-trucks were available as either a cab-and-chassis for stake bed use or with a conventional pickup bed and fenders. A panel truck body for delivery work also was popular, and many users preferred the superior stamina of a true truck chassis to the passenger car platform of the Sedan Delivery models.

Half-ton F-1 models had a Spicer-type integral rear axle plus a column-shift three-speed transmission. The F-2 and F-3 used more traditional split housing differentials, carried over from earlier heavy duty trucks.

Ride quality and chassis safety improved dramatically with the 1948–52 F-models as Ford built a basic platform that served through the 1953–56 F-100, F-250 and F-350 models. The F-1 and early F-100 chassis, in particular, shared large numbers of components.

The new Ford trucks boasted better braking and steering. A distinctive steering wheel, knobs and levers defined Ford truck styling, and many features of the 1948 F-Series models lasted for the next decade and a half. Consumer acceptance of the new Ford F-trucks reflected in the largest number of sales since 1929, when sales of Model A and AA steel cab trucks shattered all records.

0012005

Fig. 1-4. *F-1 featured a popular Spicer 44 rear axle. The base transmission was a column or floor shift three-speed. Optional floor shift heavy duty three- or four-speed transmissions gave buyers choices. Unlike synchromesh Chevrolet and GMC four-speeds, Ford's spur gear transmission had no synchromesh and required double clutch shifts.*

Consistent with Ford production methods and parts policy, 1948–52 F-1 to F-3 models had a high level of interchangeable pieces. Even with the projected body change for 1953, familiar geartrain and engine offerings continued.

Early Engine and Geartrain Developments

Ford mechanics know that interchangeable parts mean ease of service. The 1948 F-trucks came on line with a new "R" version of the 239.4-cubic-inch flathead V-8 and the 226H inline L-head (flathead) six. In the various models, these engines were backed by three transmission types: a column shifted light duty three-speed, a heavy duty floor shift three-speed, or the spur gear heavy duty four-speed transmission.

Although the V-8 option was common for heavy hauling, the 95-horsepower 226H six also drew a following. The 226 six produced an impressive 180 lb/ft of torque at 1200 rpm. The improved 239.4-cubic-inch flathead V-8 boasted 194 lb/ft of torque at 1900 rpm and 106 horsepower at 3500 rpm. Like the 1948 8BA passenger car engine, the R engine was also easier to service.

These flathead engines each had low 6.80:1 compression ratios, tolerant of the poor octane levels in early fuels. The crank handle hole in the grille of early F-trucks was more than decorative: with patience and extreme caution, you can actually crank start these engines by hand.

Fig. 1-5. Popular 8BA flathead V-8 powered 1949–53 Ford cars. 1948-52 F-Series trucks from F-1 to F-6 models used a similar "R" engine. "R" engines also served in 1953 F-100 through F-600 models. At a modest 106 horsepower, Ford's last flathead gave way to modern OHV V-8s in 1954.

The first overhead valve (OHV) or valve-in-head six, a 7:1 compression 215-cubic-inch inline design, replaced the flathead 226H in 1952. With 101 horsepower at 3500 rpm and 185 lb/ft torque at 1300 rpm, the new six nearly matched the R-type V-8 for usable power. 215 OHV sixes were also available in 1952 Ford cars.

That same year, Lincoln introduced the OHV 317 V-8, Ford's first over-square (bigger bore diameter than stroke length) higher compression engine. This engine benefited from advances in gasoline blending, particularly the use of such additives as Tetra-Ethyl lead (TEL), which substantially raised octane and allowed the use of higher compression ratios.

The 317 actually served in medium and heavy duty F-trucks from 1952–55. The 215, found in many 1952–53 light duty F-trucks, was a near square design at 3.56-inch bore and 3.60-inch stroke.

The 239 flathead V-8 survived the first generation F-trucks. The familiar dual inlet, dual outlet radiator hoses and double water pump engine, a basic design that had served successfully since 1932, lasted slightly longer than Ford's Model T. Fundamental engineering had taken Ford trucks from the era of commercial cars to the age of F-Series trucks.

1953–56: A Marque Emerges

The greatest honor a vehicle manufacturer can receive is recognition for a classic design. As Ford Motor Company prepared for its 50th Anniversary Year, the 1953 F-Series trucks gained a striking new look.

American society had entered an unprecedented period of prosperity, a time that created the highest standard of living in history. Gasoline prices were as low as the Great Depression era, and national funding for a massive interstate highway system was underway. Cars and trucks had become larger, with more powerful engines and better handling to match the high speed roadways.

Passenger cars now boasted optional power assist steering, vacuum assisted brakes, power window lifts and even air conditioning that strained under six-volt electrical systems. Automatic transmissions were popular by 1953, and Ford realized that truck owners were also interested in these technological advances.

In the onrush of the high compression, high-octane, high-speed technological revolution, Ford's legendary flathead V-8 engine met its end. 1954 brought a new valve-in-head (OHV) V-8 engine for Ford passenger cars and light trucks, bearing the familiar 239-cubic-inch displacement. Unlike the flathead V-8's under-square 3-3/16-inch bore and long 3-3/4-inch stroke, the new 130 horsepower Y-block V-8 had a modern 7.2:1 compression ratio and over-square 3.5-inch bore by 3.10-inch stroke.

That same year, the fuel-thrifty 215 six increased to 223 cubic inches with a slightly over-square 3.62-inch bore and 3.60-inch stroke. At 7.2:1 compression ratio, the engine produced an impressive 115 horsepower at a brisk 3900 rpm and a remarkable 193 lb/ft peak torque at 1000 rpm. Both the Y-block V-8 and six-cylinder overhead valve engine designs served Ford light trucks for the next decade.

In 1954 and '55, Ford light trucks also offered the 256-cubic-inch V-8, essentially the Mercury passenger car en-

Fig. 1-6. *1953–56 Ford F-100 is a classic and collectible model. Prized for alluring looks and functional engineering, these trucks command a premium price today. '53–'55 bodies show subtle differences in grille design and trim. 1956 Custom Cab (shown) has squarer cab. Short bed '56 pickup with wrap-around rear window holds highest value.*

gine introduced in 1954. This Y-block had a larger 3.62-inch bore and in 1954 produced 138 horsepower at 3900 rpm. The 1955 increase to 7.5:1 compression added two horsepower and a considerable boost in torque.

The horsepower race warmed up when Chevrolet introduced the lightweight 265 V-8 in its second series 1955 light trucks. Pontiac supplied the 288-cubic-inch OHV V-8 muscle for GMC trucks that same year, while Dodge trucks experimented with several Red Ram hemi-head V-8s. Ford responded in 1956 with the 272 Y-block, an engine more akin to the potent Thunderbird 292 and 312 Y-block engines.

Fig. 1-7. *The 215-cubic-inch OHV six was a high torque fuel miser. Ford's first OHV six, these engines met many buyers' needs. The 215 increased to 223 cubic inches in 1954, a size that attracted fleet and utility users through 1964. On the highway, a 223 with a three-speed overdrive transmission could deliver as much as 25 m.p.g. in an F-100 pickup.*

Fig. 1-8. *Popular 239, 256, 272 and 292-cubic-inch V-8s shared Y-block design with Ford's legendary 300 horsepower 312 Thunderbird Special. In two-barrel form, the 272 and 292 relied on torque to compete with Chevrolet's 265 and 283 small-block V-8s. For 1956, Ford F-truck owners were happy with 272 V-8 performance.*

In two-barrel form, the 272 boasted 8:1 compression and a longer 3.30-inch stroke to produce a stump pulling 260 lb/ft of torque at 2400 rpm. 167 horsepower at a brisk 4400 rpm actually surpassed Chevrolet's 1956 265 V-8 truck ratings. Despite the wide interest in the new high-revving Chevy engines, Ford held an edge in peak power and brute strength.

Even in subsequent years, when the larger Chevrolet 283 small block gained popularity, the Ford Y-blocks proved substantial for truck use. A crankshaft well-supported by cast block material plus a valvetrain with sturdy rocker shafts and rocker arm assemblies kept Ford truck owners satisfied. Low maintenance, strong performance and rugged durability characterize the 1954–64 light F-Series trucks with the 223 six or 239/256/272 and 292 Y-block V-8s.

Modern Geartrains

Transmission options improved for the '53–'56 models, with the spur gear four-speed replaced by an efficient and durable T-98 Warner four-speed unit. The Warner transmission featured synchromesh on second through fourth gears and a compound low gear with a reduction ratio of over 6:1 for severe duty use.

The standard three-speed transmission was a popular Ford design: a nine-bolt/straight bottom side cover unit found in passenger cars and light duty trucks since the 1940s. Still fitted with the early Ford style 1-3/8-inch spline input shaft, three-speed transmissions were available with an optional overdrive. My 1955 F-100 had a 256 two-barrel V-8 and the rare three-speed overdrive transmission.

Fig. 1-10. *A nine-bolt, straight bottom side cover indicates Ford's light duty three-speed transmission. A gearbox common to passenger cars and light duty trucks, this transmission type served from the 1940s through 1962.*

Y-block era Ford trucks also used several Warner three-speed transmissions. Like the standard Ford unit, these T-86, T-87 and T-89 gearboxes had synchromesh only on second and third gear. The transition to full synchromesh gearboxes was slow for all manufacturers, and Ford buyers did best with the four-speed T-98, designed for easy starts in second gear and downshifts to second without completely stopping the truck.

During the '53–'56 era, the Ford-O-Matic three-speed iron case automatic transmission also entered the light truck option list. A three-element torque converter gave the automatic some degree of performance credibility, but it lagged considerably in comparison to manual transmission models. A rear pump assembly allowed push starting of the engine. Transmission service was minimal and limited to periodic linkage and band adjustments, fluid changes, cleaning of the filter and general inspection. Ultimately, overhaul costs and vulnerability to seal and gasket leaks kept many consumers away from early automatic transmissions, and few buyers ordered light F-trucks with this option.

Last Classic Chassis

The 1953–56 truck chassis carried many features of early Fords. Restorers find that these trucks offer a strong blend of traditional technology and modern efficiency. Easy to service and repair, these popular chassis prove fertile for a frame-up restoration.

'53–'56 F-Series models were the last Ford trucks to use chassis-mounted clutch and brake pedal assemblies and through-the-floorboard pedals. This classic touch is legend, and even street rod builders make great efforts to preserve the familiar round pedals. The greaseable pedal pivot bushings carry back to the earliest Ford trucks.

Fig. 1-9. *T-98 Warner four-speed (top) was the transmission breakthrough of 1953. Ford F-trucks now offered a four-speed with synchromesh on second, third and fourth gears. Compound first gear ratio was over 6:1, excellent for heavy hauling.*

The '53 F-trucks introduced a stable new engine mounting system that incorporates a stout frame member beneath the bellhousing. For flathead V-8s, two front engine mounts and two side bellhousing mounts support the engine firmly and isolate vibration. '54–'56 OHV V-8s and '53–'56 sixes use one mount beneath the engine timing cover and two sturdy bellhousing mounts.

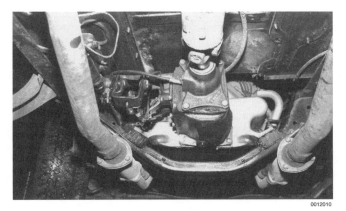

Fig. 1-11. Major service like a clutch replacement was easiest with 1953–64 F-Series trucks. The rear motor mounts support the bellhousing and engine during this operation. With the transmission and clutch cover bolts removed, the clutch slides out the lower opening in the bellhousing.

This style of mounting the engine simplifies repairs. By carefully supporting the transmission, the engine and clutch assembly can be detached from the bellhousing and removed as a unit, leaving the bellhousing, clutch linkage, transmission and driveline in place.

Likewise, with the bellhousing mounted in place, you can easily replace the clutch or transmission without disturbing the engine assembly. In the seven years that I worked on my '55 F-100, I altered the entire powertrain design twice, changed transmission types four times and installed so many clutch assemblies that I had the operation down to just under one hour.

Ford's use of the popular Spicer 44 rear axle in 1953–56 F-100 models was smart. Parts were readily available, although these axles seldom require service. The 4.27:1 ratio axle unit in my '55 had at least 250,000 miles on it when I finally sold the truck, and the only repair necessary was a pinion seal replacement! Remarkably, even the semi-floating style axle bearings were original, despite subjection to shock loads from transplant engines that produced 300-plus horsepower.

The extensive use of bronze bushings at kingpins, spring hangers, shackles, pedal pivots and other strategic wear points contributed to the long lifespan of these classic trucks. 1956 was the last year that Ford used greaseable chassis pivots, and by 1957, the only remaining grease fittings were on kingpins, steering linkage and driveline U-joints.

Steering linkage on the 1953–56 trucks was also a throwback to earlier models, with a rebuildable spring and ball seat draglink assembly. The Gemmer worm-and-roller steering gear, although less efficient than GM's recirculating-ball-type gear, continued through 1964. Worm-and-roller gears wear and require service much sooner than recirculating ball-and-nut types.

A Cab For Comfort

Despite the narrower cab width inherent to trucks with running boards, the '53–'56 cab interior felt more spacious and featured an easy view of the road. A large and curving windshield glass, doors with windows and wind wings, and plenty of headroom made these cabs attractive.

Instrumentation on '53–'56 models shows a distinctive style that carries into later F-trucks. The reshaped '56 cab took on a squarer profile that distinguishes this model from other second generation F-Series trucks. Restorers and collectors prize the 1956 F-100 Custom Cab model with wrap-around rear window.

1956 also offered several other changes. Cosmetically, the instrumentation and steering wheel became stylized, reflecting the sporty image of Ford passenger cars and the classic Thunderbird. Introduction of a 7.6:1 compression ratio 272 Y-block V-8 demanded more starting power than a standard six-volt battery could offer, and the Ford F-trucks, like other Ford models, switched to 12-volt electrics for 1956. New components included a 12-volt starter, heater motor and wiper motor. A re-shaped F-truck cab placed the wiper motor on the engine bay side of the cowl, more accessible than previous models and easier to service. The battery box remained beneath the right side floorboard, the last F-Series light truck to use this mounting location.

Fig. 1-12. Instrumentation of 1956 F-truck is distinctly different from all previous or later models. Customized unit features painted script and highlights.

Like other trucks of the era, the single reservoir brake master cylinder still mounted beneath the floorboard. An archaic design, these master cylinders were difficult to access and susceptible to brake fluid contamination. Despite this drawback, the 1953–56 F-Series light trucks rank among the easiest models to service. They were also safer and more pleasurable to drive than all previous Ford trucks.

1957–64: The Pragmatic Years

As Ford Motor Company tooled for the next generation of F-trucks, the U.S. economy was shaken by recession. Many believed that prosperity would end and that new trucks should adhere strictly to cost effective production methods, offer less frills and remain price competitive. Like the staggering change to a four-passenger Thunderbird in 1958, Ford trucks abandoned the casualness of the post-WWII years. Utility and value were salient marketing tools for the new F-trucks.

Fig. 1-13. *1957–60 body style was a significant change. Wider cab and bed offered roominess and utility. Austerity of these models made earlier '53–'56 F-trucks more appealing. '57 had two headlamps while '58–'60 trucks have four.*

Changes included a broader new cab with no running boards, and the first use of a full cab-width Styleside pickup box. The standard utility Flareside box remained, not so much to retain the pleasing aesthetics of the '53–'56 rear fenders but rather as an offering for the traditional truck buyer who wanted easier side access for loading.

Bold changes on the '57 chassis streamlined the assembly process and substantially reduced maintenance. Gone was the bevy of grease fittings. The new light truck featured low-maintenance, replaceable rubber bushings at spring ends and shackles.

In step with quick and simple maintenance was the new hydraulic clutch linkage. Rather than wrestle with elaborate chassis-mounted pedals, Ford placed the brake and clutch master cylinders at the upper firewall in the engine bay. '57 light F-trucks became the first to use hanging brake and clutch pedals. A hydraulic slave cylinder attached to the bellhousing actuated the familiar clutch release fork. Hydraulic linkage provided smooth, easy clutch operation and eliminated the erratic and shaky engagement inherent to mechanical linkage. The new square pedal pads were easy to grip.

As a truck fleet mechanic who serviced several '57–'60 Ford F-Series light and medium duty work trucks, I have an appreciation for the ease of service and utility that these models offered. After a year of intimate work with each chassis, I could perform a lube job, check all fluid levels, change oil and replace filters in less than half an hour. It took that long just to service the oil bath air cleaner of an earlier F-truck.

New Y-Block Powerplant

Ford offered the 272 V-8 through 1958 models. The more potent 292 Y-block came on line in 1959. Two years earlier, passenger cars had benefitted from a 9.10:1 compression ratio 212 horsepower four-barrel version of this engine.

The light truck 292 kept the 2300-Series Holley two-barrel carburetor that Ford had introduced on 1957 272 V-8s. At a milder 7.6:1 compression, the truck engine earned a 186 horsepower rating at 4000 rpm. Peak torque, an important part of truck performance, was a respectable 269 lb/ft at 2200 rpm.

Fig. 1-14. *Ford used this two-barrel carburetor (top) with the flathead and early Y-block V-8. For V-8s, 1957 engines introduced the modern 2300-Series Holley two-barrel (bottom). These carburetors are reliable and easy to service.*

Y-block 292 V-8s carried F-100, F-250 and F-350 models through 1964. The 223 six-cylinder engine received a heavy duty 262-cubic-inch counterpart in 1961. Many of these rugged Y-block V-8s and sixes are still in service, and the popularity of high horsepower 292 and 312 Thunderbird engines of the mid-'50s has nurtured an aftermarket performance market around the 272, 292 and 312 V-8s.

The most enduring powertrain innovation of 1957 was Ford's own non-integral rear axle assembly. Commonly referred to as the "9-inch" axle (based on ring gear diameter), this drop-in center section introduced a unique pinion shaft design. Unlike other axles, the pinion shaft receives its bearing support from each side of the gearhead. So advanced was the 9-inch design that Ford produced this unit into the 1980s. These rugged axles are found in two- and four-wheel drive F-100s, F-150s and 4x4 Broncos.

0012016

Fig. 1-15. A new look for 1961 and time for special option packages. 1961–63 "Styleside" bed was integral with the cab.

Look was highly original, however, 4x4 models required more flexibility. Concept ended with 1963 models.

0012015

Fig. 1-16. Ford's 9-inch rear axle, introduced in 1957 trucks, was an engineering milestone. The rugged design served in heavy cars and light F-trucks into the 1980s. Main advantage is superior pinion gear support, with bearings mounted at each end of pinion shaft.

9-inch Ford semi-floating rear axles on F-100s and a Spicer 60 full-floating axle on the F-250 models made identification of third generation F-models simple. F-350s, with their one-ton load rating and single or dual rear wheel applications, used various axle types during this period.

In 1959, the F-100 and F-250 introduced Ford's first factory four-wheel drive models. Although Ford light trucks had four-wheel drive conversions from Marmon-Harrington and NAPCO prior to this time, the increasing demand for all-wheel drive trucks encouraged Ford to incorporate 4x4 systems as a factory option.

The ladder frame, leaf springs and I-beam front axle found in Ford F-trucks of that era made the factory task easy. These early 4x4s, equipped with a popular Spicer 44 live front axle and a rugged two-speed transfer case, shared engines and other components with two-wheel drive models.

A New Look For 1961

The styling of '57–'60 F-trucks carried austerity to the limit. For 1961, F-Series models once again demonstrated that form and function could coexist. A fresh look found ready acceptance, while the chassis remained much the same through the 1964 models.

Significant changes in '61 light trucks included a retreat to mechanical clutch linkage, although this time the system involved swinging pedals, a relay rod and a cross-shaft between the frame and bellhousing. Service procedures were otherwise similar to '57–'60 F-trucks.

The slow ratio Gemmer worm-and-roller steering gears continued to serve light F-trucks. Low maintenance remained a popular theme, and spin-on oil filters made oil changes quicker and less messy. The bellhousing side mount engine support method carried forward to 1964.

Transmission offerings were largely the same through 1962, and the automatic transmission was not a wide-scale option until the new 1965 chassis platform. Popular transmissions of this era were the light duty Ford three-speed, a number of Warner three-speed designs and the heavy duty T-98 four-speed transmission.

1961–64 Ford F-Series trucks competed well with the GM, Dodge and I-H offerings of that era. Ford, Dodge and I-H retained four-wheel leaf spring suspension with

I-beam front axles, while GM made a bold change to independent front suspension in 1960. For 1965, Ford challenged the ride quality of GM trucks with an all-new chassis design.

1965: The Advent Of Twin I-Beam

Heavier trucks, faster roads and a broader base of truck buyers sparked a revolution in U.S. truck design. While the utility profile of trucks built through 1964 reflected a primary market of commercial and agricultural users, by the mid-1960s, Ford recognized the growing number of recreationalists buying trucks for campers and other multi-purpose uses. A mid-Sixties consumer was as likely an urban family with plans for a cabover camper or pulling a ski boat. For 1965, Ford took a bold step forward, developing an entirely new F-Series chassis platform and revamping the powertrain.

Although body sheet metal looked largely like the '64 models, the new chassis featured the first use of front coil springs on an F-Series Ford truck. F-100 and F-250 models incorporated the ride quality of coils with the rugged dependability of twin half-beam axles, essentially of the same stamina as the earlier I-beams.

The new design, called "Twin I-Beam" suspension, coupled the strengths of a traditional I-beam front axle with the flexibility and ride found in independent suspension systems. Twin I-Beam allowed the front wheels to move independently, a reasonable match for GM's coil spring and dual A-arm suspension.

Fig. 1-17. Twin I-Beam coil spring front suspension was Ford's major change for 1965. Independent front suspension (IFS) improved ride quality and handling. Twin I-Beam has served light F-Series trucks into the 1990s.

Steering control was more concise, as Ford added an improved recirculating ball-and-nut manual steering gear to the new front end package. By 1966, power assisted steering became a light truck option on two-wheel drive models, the first in Ford history.

Four-wheel drive models also changed in 1965, with a much lower body profile on F-100 models that resulted from the use of the two-wheel drive style chassis and coil springs. The front axle was still a solid Spicer/Dana 44 unit, however, the lower center-of-gravity and improved suspension tuning provided buyers with a durable, low-maintenance and easy riding 4x4.

Fig. 1-18. 1965 F-100 4x4s had lower chassis and body profile than previous models. Front coil springs and radius arms were like Twin I-Beam design, although Ford half-ton 4x4s stayed with a solid front axle through 1979, as shown on this late 1970s model.

In the bargain, unfortunately, the two-speed transfer case was dropped for F-100 models, and in its place was a Dana 21 power divider. 1965–76 Dana 21 equipped trucks work best with the optional four-speed truck transmission and its compound low gear for heavy hauling and rock crawling.

The 3/4-ton rated F-250 4x4 retained its high chassis profile, a two-speed transfer case and the conventional four-wheel leaf spring suspension. This distinction between the '65-up F-100 (later the F-150) and an F-250 chassis gave buyers some clear choices when selecting a four-wheel drive truck.

Two-wheel drive F-250s continued to offer a heftier chassis, heavier springs, bigger brakes, eight-lug wheels, a full-floating rear axle and typically lower axle gearing. By 1966, the F-100 and F-250 popularized power steering, the Cruise-O-Matic automatic transmission and a long list of options that satisfied weekend recreationalists and traditional truck buyers. Ford light F-Series trucks had a new identity.

For heavy hauling, the F-350 remained an important component in Ford's lineup. Still offering a solid front axle and leaf springs through 1966, the F-350 benefited from the powertrain and other changes introduced with the 1965 F-100 and F-250 models. In 1967, along with a major body style change, the F-350 one-ton added Twin I-Beam suspension.

Two New Engine Families

Despite the widely recognized stamina of the Y-block V-8s and 223/262 inline sixes, Ford understood the horsepower race. For high performance passenger cars, the Y-block had lost ground since 1957. The larger displacement FE big-block engines had supplanted even the famed 312 Thunderbird Special V-8.

Beneath the now familiar hood of 1965 Ford F-trucks were two distinctly new engine approaches. For a standard six-cylinder engine, the all-new 240- and 300-cubic-inch engines provided Ford's first seven main bearing crankshaft and the assurance of rugged pulling torque and massive stamina.

Fig. 1-19. *300-cubic-inch inline six, introduced in 1965, still proves its worth in the 1990s. Seven main bearings contribute to remarkable durability, while balance and smoothness of in-line six design is legend. Properly maintained and serviced, a 240- or 300-cubic-inch six can run 200,000 or more miles. The 300 six has proven unbeatable, hailing into the 1990s as the base engine in full-size Broncos and F-Series light trucks. In its original 1965 form, the big displacement engine developed 170 horsepower at 3600 rpm with a one-barrel carburetor. Also impressive, the relatively high 8.4:1 compression ratio developed 213 ft/lb peak torque at a highly useful 2000 rpm.*

For V-8 muscle, Ford captured buyers' attention with the popular 352 FE V-8, one version of which had served as a Police Interceptor powerplant in 1959 and 60 passenger cars. The race for horsepower had since produced the 390, 406 and 427 versions of the FE engine, and the 352 now took a milder two-barrel form as the only F-truck V-8 powerplant available in 1965 and '66.

Rated 206 horsepower at 4400 rpm with 315 lb/ft of torque at 2400 rpm, the 8.6:1 compression ratio 352 big

block was a heavyweight powerplant. Even the substantial mass of Y-block V-8s tipped the scales at less weight than the two-barrel 352.

The new engines required less maintenance than previous designs. Both the 352 V-8 and 240/300 inline sixes featured hydraulic valve lifters. Earlier Y-block and 223/262 sixes had solid tappets and adjustable rocker arms that required periodic valve lash adjustments. From 1965 forward, all F-Series light truck gasoline engines have hydraulic lifters.

Chevrolet's high revving 283 and 327 small-block V-8s, potent performers in passenger cars and light trucks of the mid-'60s, were a viable competitor for stoplight drag races, yet Ford opted for a truck oriented engine. The adage, "no substitute for cubic inches" made even more sense for trucks, where a large displacement automobile engine, de-tuned for truck use, promised long service and substantial muscle for hauling.

110-plus octane gasoline cost less in 1965 than a gallon of bottled drinking water in the 1990s. Fuel economy became a token issue, and Ford's bigger 300-cubic-inch inline six and 352 V-8 proved popular. Each were larger than counterpart mid-'60s Chevrolet and GMC truck offerings, with the exception of GMC's 305-cubic-inch V-6, a medium duty truck engine that GMC used in light trucks from 1960–69.

During this period, as truck image shifted, Ford and other light truck manufacturers began niche marketing, especially Camper Special packaging. The best suited Ford F-truck was the 3/4-ton F-250. Its long bed and heavy duty chassis could easily carry a slide-in cabover camper. Buyers could order Ford's F-250 Camper Special with a rugged full-floating Spicer/Dana 60 rear axle, the T-98 (later the T-18) Warner truck four-speed or a rugged Cruise-O-Matic automatic. A stout spring package, big drum brakes, durable steering and heavy front and rear axle weight ratings supported the forward weighted campers and also allowed for towing.

Fig. 1-20. *352- and 390-cubic-inch FE engines proved their worth in Ford passenger cars. A 1960 Police Interceptor 352 rated 300 horsepower, while the 1962 Thunderbird 390 with three two-barrel carburetors developed 401 horsepower. These high torque FE engines were de-tuned for F-trucks, with a lower compression ratio and two-barrel carburetion.*

Fig. 1-21. *Full-floating Dana 60 rear axle distinguished F-250 models from lighter trucks. A full-floating axle (lower) has inner and outer wheel hub bearings that support a very heavy load. Unlike lighter duty semi-floating axles with one outer axle bearing, a full-floating hub/wheel assembly will remain in place and allow braking if the axle shaft fails.*

Gone was the austerity and utility profile of earlier trucks. Buyers of mid-'60s Ford F-models could have a real workhorse plus trendy new improvements in upholstery, the cab headliner, the dashboard, floorboard design and ergonomics. Burgeoning light truck sales generated options and accessories once found only in luxury cars.

The '61–'66 F-truck body style proved popular, but a distinctive body style change was due. For 1967, Ford F-Series trucks blended their contemporary powertrain and chassis technology with a notable cab update.

1967–79: Years Of Bold Refinement

The 1967 body style ended the utilitarian look that began in 1957. While earlier F-truck cab changes allowed for some carryover parts, the 1967 cab exterior looked dramatically different than previous models. For the interior, the streamlined dashboard and changes in switches and controls created a totally new image. Familiar shapes remained at knobs and some manual controls, but many features took aesthetic cues from Ford cars. Overall, F-trucks were roomier, with a growing list of options.

Beneath the sheet metal stood a rugged chassis, now tuned to please first-time suburban truck buyers with aims for recreation and multi-purpose use. At the same time, Ford maintained reserve on 4WD models, holding back on power options and promoting the agricultural, fleet and commercial sales of these trucks.

1967 saw no engine changes as the 352 entered its last year of production. Still remaining was the iron cased three-speed Cruise-O-Matic (iron FMX), introduced in 1965. The quickest distinction between F-100 and F-250 models was still the number of lug nuts per wheel and the rear axle design: semi- vs. full-floating.

Ford kept the familiar 5-on-5-1/2-inch wheel bolt pattern for F-100s, a tradition since the early Ford cars and light trucks. This pattern survives into the 1990s on the F-150 and full-size Broncos. F-250 (3/4-ton) and many F-350 (one-ton) models have featured eight-lug wheels, even after the introduction of the heavy duty semi-floating rear axles in the 1980s. Heavy duty F-350s with dual wheels have offered a variety of lug patterns.

The 352 engine yielded to a 360-cubic-inch FE family engine in 1968. That same year, Ford also brought a popular passenger car engine into the light F-truck lineup, the 390 FE design.

Ford's 360 V-8 was a two-barrel carbureted engine akin to the 361-cubic-inch medium duty truck powerplant. A higher 8.4:1 compression ratio gave the 360 a 215-horsepower rating at 4400 rpm and 327 ft/lb of torque at 2600 rpm. By contrast, the truck tuned 390 with an 8.6:1 compression ratio boasted a whopping 255 horsepower and 376 ft/lb of torque! The 390 became the logical choice for Camper Special models and trailer pulling.

In the wake of high horsepower engines, Ford added an additional automatic transmission to the lineup, the now legendary C-6 aluminum case unit. This transmission, a match for the Muscle Era horsepower of the 1960s, has proven superior to all other Ford light truck units and carries into the 1990s as a companion for heavy duty F-350 hauling and the massive torque of diesel power.

0012023

Fig. 1-22. *Body style change for 1967 was distinctive and enduring. Ford F-trucks kept this popular look from 1967–79,* *an exceptional length of time. This style established Ford truck's marketing supremacy.*

0012022

Fig. 1-23. Introduction of C-6 automatic transmission into light F-trucks is a milestone. Legendary ruggedness, smooth shifts and longevity make this transmission popular. Increased use of heavy campers and broader towing demands made the C-6 automatic the right choice.

By 1968, Ford's 240- and 300-cubic-inch sixes had earned a loyal following. But light truck buyers were infected with high horsepower expectations. By 1969 the small-block 302 V-8, popularized by Mustang and Bronco in its earlier 289-cubic-inch form, now provided standard V-8 power for the F-100 pickup. Standard in 1969 meant an 8.6:1 or 9.5:1 compression ratio, depending upon application. Horsepower was an impressive 205 or 210, respectively, with either 295 or 300 ft/lb torque. The ultralight weight 302 Ford shares pertinent bore/stroke dimensions with the Chevy 302, each having a 4.00-inch bore and 3.00-inch stroke.

The 302, even in de-tuned two-barrel carbureted truck form, is a dramatically over-square engine with peak horsepower and torque at a relatively high rpm. For pure truck-type lugging power, the 300 inline six with 8:1 compression ratio and 4.00-inch bore by 3.98-inch stroke held an edge. Despite its lower 165 horsepower, the 300 six produced 294 ft/lb of peak torque at a workable 2000 rpm. Users who valued strong lugging power and thrifty performance under load opted for the 300. The 302, noted for its peppy cruise speed performance, served well with lighter cargos and for highway commuting. A quarter century later, that same choice remains.

0012025

Fig. 1-24. 302 two-barrel V-8 shared features with Mustang 289 and other Ford small-block engines. Although the 302 V-8 offered greater torque than the one-barrel 300 six, the big six delivered far more torque at low rpm.

The 360 and 390 two-barrel carbureted V-8s were the choice for serious hauling. In the wake of increasing demand for camper and trailer pullers, 1970 and onward would have likely seen a steady horsepower progression in Ford F-Series truck engines, but the high-octane-fueled Muscle Era ceased abruptly after 1971.

The Muscle Era Ends

At the peak of America's enthusiasm for performance, a time when buyers shopped for the highest horsepower rating, new Federal and California emission standards changed the priorities. Beginning in 1971, vehicle manufacturers faced stringent anti-pollution requirements. In addition to the containment or recycling of gasoline fumes, new emission control laws aimed at further reductions in hydrocarbons (HC), carbon monoxide (CO) and oxides of nitrogen (NOx).

To comply, Ford dropped engine compression ratios by four-tenths of a point between 1971 and 1972, effecting a similar decrease in performance. Other smog reduction measures included adding emission controls, evaporative loss control systems, and modifying the ignition spark timing and carburetor tune.

Clean air and energy conservation measures followed with the ban on lead in gasoline in 1975. Required fuel tank inlet restrictors assured use of unleaded only gas. Ford also installed catalytic converters on many light GVWR trucks. Simultaneously, standards for fuel mileage increased, compelling Ford and other truck manufacturers to offer economy gear ratios. The tall (numerically lower) ratios meant that engines needed peak horsepower at much lower rpm.

By 1976, a Ford 300 six in a California bound F-100 chassis produced 100 horsepower. The 302 V-8 made a paltry 134 horsepower, and the 360 a mere 145 horses. Even the huge 390 FE V-8, a top F-Series light truck engine, packed a scant 156 horsepower.

> **NOTE —**
> After 1971, the industry gave horsepower ratings as net instead of gross. During the Muscle Era, horsepower was often described in gross engine output or flywheel measured. 1972-up ratings reflect the engine-as-installed horsepower.

For needed muscle, Ford fitted special F-Series trucks with an emission-constrained version of the massive 460 big-block engine. The 460, sharing design features with the 429-cubic-inch passenger car engine, began replacing Lincoln and Mercury FE engines in 1968 and '69. In its original 1968 form, the 460 offered 365 gross horsepower at 4600 rpm with a 10.25:1 compression ratio and four-barrel carburetor. Torque was a phenomenal 500 ft/lb at 2800 rpm. These ratings lasted through the 1971 engines.

For the 1974 F-100 light duty emissions truck, a 460 with 8.0:1 compression ratio managed 238 net horsepower at 4200 rpm and 380 ft/lb of torque at 2600 rpm. By contrast, Chevrolet's 8.25:1 compression ratio 454 big block truck engines netted between 230 and 245 installed horsepower and 350 to 365 ft/lb of torque.

Overall, trucks suffered far less from emission constraints than passenger cars. The compression losses were less drastic, and most light trucks, especially over 8500

Fig. 1-25. *The four-barrel carbureted 460 V-8 gave F-Series Ford trucks a big block engine for heavy pulling. Many consider the 460 superior to both Chevrolet's 454 and the Dodge 440 V-8s. The high torque 460 has established itself as a reliable muscle engine.*

pounds GVWR, demanded far less smog equipment than passenger cars. Federal/49-State trucks over 8500 pounds GVWR required the least restrictions.

Second Generation 4x4 Chassis

The 1967–72 Ford F-Series 4x4s saw few changes. Spartan F-100 models continued to offer a single-speed power divider, four-wheel drum brakes and a manual transmission. Growing numbers of buyers opted for the improvements and advances in competitive GM, Jeep, I-H and Dodge 4x4s of that period.

Ford 4x4 F-trucks first offered power steering in 1969. Unlike 2WD trucks with integral power steering gears, the 4x4 trucks used a manual steering gear with linkage attached power assist. These systems placed hydraulic lines below the chassis on F-100 trucks and just above the draglink on F-250s. While these systems did provide owners with easier steering, they were vulnerable to damage from brush and debris. Other drawbacks of linkage power steering are higher maintenance costs and susceptibility to wear and breakage.

Fig. 1-26. *1969 linkage power steering option eased driving effort, although hoses, the hydraulic power cylinder, a control valve and other hardware were vulnerable to damage. GM's integral type power steering, a better design for 4x4 trucks, was years away for Ford F-models. Shown here is F-250 linkage type power steering on a 4x4.*

Ford offered linkage power steering through 1975 on F-100 4x4 models and into early 1977 on F-250 4x4s. Several improvements came on line in 1976 with the introduction of the new heavy duty half-ton F-150.

While GM had incorporated open knuckle front axles and disc front brakes on 1971 4x4s, Ford waited until 1976 for a front disc brake system on the 4x4 trucks. Although drum front brake sizing had matched the load capacity of F-100 and F-250 4x4 models, more modern disc brakes were a substantial upgrade.

Another area where GM, Dodge, Jeep and I-H 4x4s advanced more rapidly was the use of automatic transmissions. In 1973, Ford first offered the automatic on 4x4s. F-100s with the 302 V-8 used the lighter duty C-4 unit with an attached and high quality New Process 205 part-time 4x4 transfer case. Part time 4x4 with free wheeling lockout hubs enabled full disengagement of the front axle drive in 2WD mode.

The F-250 4x4 with a big-block V-8 offered a divorced (separately mounted) NP205 transfer case and a rugged C-6 automatic. The C-6 transmission and an NP205 part-time transfer case were well worth the wait. From 1973–79, GM committed to a gas guzzling full-time 4x4 NP203

Fig. 1-27. *Disc front brakes marked another milestone. Ford's 4x4 F-Series light trucks waited longer than comparable GM models for this valuable feature. Disc brakes assure better all weather performance and safer stopping.*

0012563

Fig. 1-28. 1976–79 F-150 and late-1970s F-250 models rank among the best 4x4s ever built. Stylish trucks with durable components, advanced steering and braking systems and a smart profile, these trucks remain exceptional buys. This F-250 features 390 V-8 option and rugged four-wheel drive system.

system on automatic transmission models, while Dodge made the same commitment on both automatic and manual transmission 4x4s built from 1975–79.

Although late in offering an automatic transmission option, Ford gained an edge by offering customers the choice of a full- or part-time 4x4 system. Most Ford light F-Series models built from 1973–79 feature the rugged NP205 part-time transfer case, while some use the full-time NP203 system.

As a used vehicle prospect, a Ford equipped with the NP205 gear drive part-time transfer case unit reigns supreme. The NP205 ranks among the most rugged transfer cases offered in light trucks. NP203 full-time units, although durable, feature a chain drive system and differential mechanism that can wear over time.

As the 1970s ended, Ford light 4x4 trucks featured a refined four-wheel drive system and front disc brakes on all models. F-250 and F-350 4x4 models boasted a lower chassis profile with tapered front leaf springs, while F-100 and F-150 trucks maintained their easy riding coil front springs.

A two-speed transfer case was now standard, and many 4x4 buyers purchased integral power steering and the automatic transmission option. Air conditioning was now a common feature, and a variety of stylish trim and paint packages allowed buyers a wide range of personal choices.

Ford's 1979 F-Series 4x4 lineup included the F-350 one-ton for the first time. This 4x4 proved popular for heavy towing and carrying severe loads. There were now three distinct platforms of 4x4 trucks, each targeted for different levels of work and play.

A Ford F-150 4x4 with a 300 six, heavy duty cooling and a Warner T-18, T-19 or rugged New Process 435 four-speed manual transmission was likely to win a telephone company or commercial fleet bid. The family seeking an ideal hauler for their cabover camper or pulling a pleasure boat could opt for the F-250 Explorer Camper Special 4x4 with a big V-8, a C-6 automatic, air conditioning, power steering and a stereo sound system.

1980: An Advanced 4x4 Chassis

By 1980, stiffer regulations around fuel savings compelled light truck manufacturers to drop the full-time 4x4 systems. Rather than continue using the NP205 transfer case, however, most 1/2- and 3/4-ton truck builders switched to lighter chain drive units like the New Process 208 and Warner 1345 designs. An advantage of chain drive cases was a lower (numerically higher) reduction ratio for low range mode. While axle gearing remained taller (numerically lower) in the pursuit of gas savings and lower tailpipe emissions per mile, severe hauling and rock crawling performance improved.

1980 hails as a milestone change year for Ford F-Series trucks. More contemporary body styling defined the next generation look, and the 4x4 chassis platform revealed the largest engineering change since 1965.

Fig. 1-29. *1980 was a major change year. Aside from a sleeker body style, the 4x4 platform added Twin-Traction Beam IFS suspension on trucks through the F-250. F-150 maintained coil front springs, while F-250 uses leaf front springs with the pivoting front axle. IFS engineering has carried into the 1990s.*

For 1980, Ford moved toward a smoother ride in F-150, F-250 and F-350 4x4 models. The F-150 gained a pivoting front axle system that coupled an element of independent front suspension (IFS) travel with traditional durability. Built by Dana and dubbed the IFS 44, this axle and its F-250 counterparts, the IFS HD 44 and IFS 50, gave Ford an edge over GM and Dodge 4x4 truck chassis.

The F-150 4x4 version of this platform, which hails into the 1990s, boasts the coil spring and radius arm suspension common in Ford half-tons since 1965. 1980 F-250s introduced a novel combination of tapered leaf front springs with a pivoting two-section axle. The F-250 retained its rugged four-wheel leaf spring suspension while incorporating an IFS front axle. Both systems improve handling and ride.

The 1980 F-350 4x4 retained four-wheel leaf spring suspension and a massive Dana 60 solid (non-IFS) front axle. With recommended tow equipment and chassis options, an F-350 4x4 could pull as much as 13,700 pounds Gross Combination Weight (GCWR). At the same 133-inch wheelbase as an F-250, this F-350 earned a 9,100 pound Gross Vehicle Weight Rating (GVWR) with single drive rear wheels.

Fig. 1-30. *Into the 1980s and '90s, F-350 4x4 has kept heavy duty Dana 60 solid front axle with full-floating wheel hubs. Four-wheel leaf springs and rugged chassis components make the F-350 popular among heavy haulers.*

Ford had dropped the 360 and 390 FE engines by 1980, opting for the 351-Windsor (5.8L) and a 351-Modified/400 (6.6L) powerplants. The lighter weight 351W engine shares many of Ford's small-block 289/302 features. For increased stamina, the 351W has larger main bearing journals and a more rugged block than the 302/5.0L V-8.

Ford's 351M/400 modified engines were a unique stop gap design, an attempt to create a large powerplant around the 351W. The 351M/400 had a short history in F-Series models. As a truck engine, the 400 could not rival the big block design of the 460 V-8, and Ford soon dropped the 400 from its light truck engine list.

Fig. 1-31. *Carbureted 460 V-8 proved superior to Ford's 351M/400 engine. After a quarter century of production, the 460 still reigns among large displacement gasoline engines.*

The 300/4.9L inline six, 302/5.0L V-8, 351W/5.8L V-8 and the 460/7.5L V-8 have satisfied Ford buyers from the early 1980s into the 1990s. This gas engine lineup, plus the addition of Navistar's proven 6.9L and 7.3L diesel options, have contributed to Ford's remarkable sales record.

Electronic Fuel Injection: 'Ford Tough' Power

Between 1972 and the mid-'80s, consumers chose their F-Series trucks by fuel economy ratings, GCWR/GVWR capacity, and wheelbase preferences. Emission constraints continued to dictate horsepower output and engine options. During that period of gasoline embargoes, a 55-mph federal speed limit, recession and gross inflation, Ford concentrated on chassis improvements, safety upgrades, convenience features, style packages and luxury options. The most significant breakthrough in engine technology during this period was electronic fuel and spark management. Early 1980s Ford cars boasted Central Point Injection (CPI), while Multi-Point Injection (MPI) was under development. Ford took advanced MPI technology into the 302 V-8 truck engines in 1986. By 1987, the 351W, 460 V-8 and 300 six also benefitted from electronic fuel injection.

Each engine developed more torque and better horsepower, yet compliance with emission standards was easier than at any time since 1970. Tailpipe pollutants came in at less than 1/20th the output of an early 1970s model truck, and these engines could tolerate low octane fuels.

0012032

Fig. 1-32. MPI gave Ford truck engines wider market appeal. A refined induction system capable of substantial fuel savings, radical reduction of emissions and higher compression ratios, MPI brought horsepower and torque figures back into the high output realm.

Like the impact of EFI in the passenger car market, the mid-'80s Ford MPI truck engines started a Second Muscle Era. As automatic overdrive units and manual five-speed overdrive transmissions developed popularity and stamina, their acceptance by truck buyers permitted use of lower (numerically higher) axle ratios. Now economy meant an overdrive gear with an axle capable of pulling.

MPI has assured the success of these popular Ford truck engines. The 300/4.9L six, long noted for durability and torque, now has lower tailpipe emissions, a snappier throttle response and excellent fuel economy.

Ford's 302/5.0L MPI V-8 is the first choice for F-150 light hauling and highway commuting. Geared right, this engine delivers good torque and horsepower on a miserly fuel bill. An overdrive automatic and lower (numerically higher) axle ratio really make the 302 perform.

The 351W/5.8L V-8 has become an F-truck mainstay, with notable stamina, light weight and brisk response. MPI has cranked up the horsepower and torque, and like the later 302 V-8s, roller valve lifters and other improvements make the 351W engine perfect for lighter towing.

Like other big displacement V-8 engines, the 460 V-8, with its 4.36-inch bore and 3.85-inch stroke, had difficulty meeting emission standards. MPI quickly turned that around, and Ford engineering continues to refine the 460/7.5L gasoline engine with improvements in plenum design, injector efficiency and spark timing.

Today's 460 burns cleaner than ever before, although fuel consumption remains the perennial pricetag for big horsepower and torque. An effective way to offset this tendency is taller (numerically lower) axle gearing, although heavy hauling usually demands a lower (numerically higher) ratio gearset.

The trailering solution from the mid-1980s onward has been Ford's effective use of the Navistar medium duty truck diesels in the F-250 and F-350 chassis. Heavyweight engines with a reputation for substantial torque at very low rpm, these fuel efficient diesels have a loyal following among trailer pullers and commercial users.

Poised For The Future

Ford's truck evolution has been methodical, with each F-Series light truck platform lasting many years. Incorporating reasonable changes at a conservative pace has contributed to the success of Ford trucks.

In today's market, Ford's strategy has many advantages. Safety standards, emissions requirements and constraints on materials can change daily. So do consumer trends and tastes. The step side bed introduced with the '53 F-100 barely survived as the power company's utility box of 1957. By the late 1970s, this same Flareside bed became a sensation, as buyers seized on its classic profile and aesthetic appeal.

For the 1990s, a stylized version of that same Flareside bed became the touted look for boulevard street truckers.

0012033

Fig. 1-33. At the mid-'90s, the F-Series XLT package now offers style with a practical flare, like the optional 40/20/40 front bench seat. Head restraints for the driver and right side passenger provide safety, while seats adjust, recline and provide lumbar support. The 20-percent center seat doubles as an armrest when folded forward, with storage space and cup holders providing an ideal "office" for the portable worksite of the '90s.

A milestone 1953 styling cue has satisfied Ford F-Series buyers for over four decades.

Passenger car safety advancements are reflected in mid-'90s F-trucks. Beginning with 1994 models, a driver's side air bag supplemental restraint system (SRS) was fitted to vehicles with gross vehicle weight ratings (GVWR) under 8,500 pounds. Doors now boast impact-protection beams. The brake pedal must be applied when pulling the transmission out of Park position, and a center high-mount stop light shines above the bed cargo light.

F-Series trucks also reflect concern for the environment and a TREAD LIGHTLY philosophy. Air conditioning systems in new F-Series trucks use refrigerant free of chlorofluorocarbons (CFCs). A change in piston design and roller tappets now accounts for one more mile per gallon in the 351W/5.8-liter EFI V-8 engine.

The growing ranks of first time truck buyers appreciate Ford F-Series ride quality, performance and multipurpose value. Refinements in chassis and powertrain engineering keep pace with consumer demands.

At the mid-'90s, the 7.3L Navistar V-8 diesel, available in F-250, F-350 and the heavier F-Super Duty chassis, benefits from indirect injection (IDI) and turbocharging. The turbocharged 7.3L diesel engine produces 190 horsepower at 3000 rpm and 395 ft/lb torque at a low 1400 rpm. A turbocharged diesel will outperform naturally aspirated engines at higher altitudes, realms where trailer pullers need brute muscle.

Mid-'90s 460/7.5L EFI V-8s rate 245 horsepower at 4000 rpm with an impressive 400 ft/lb torque at 2200 rpm. The 351W/5.8L V-8 makes 200 horsepower at 3800 rpm and 310 ft/lb torque at a brisk 2800 rpm, making this engine a prime candidate for lower (numerically higher) axle gearing and an overdrive transmission like the durable E4OD automatic.

The 302 also gains performance, producing 195 to 205 horsepower in various F-Series truck applications. Torque of 270–275 ft/lb reaches peak by a high 3000 rpm, classifying the 302 as a light hauler. By contrast, the spunky 300/4.9L inline six, a truck option dating to 1965, can make 265 ft/lb of torque at a stump pulling and more useful 2000 rpm.

Despite the preponderance of luxury features and appointments, Ford F-Series light trucks maintain their traditional stamina and rugged chassis design. The 1980 platform, which began with a basic 116.8-inch F-150 Regular Cab wheelbase, continues today. A 138.8-inch and 155-inch F-150 SuperCab are also available, plus the longer Styleside bed F-150, F-250 and F-350 Regular Cab pickup models with a 133-inch wheelbase.

0012034

Fig. 1-34. *Despite full range of passenger car luxury items, latest Ford F-trucks retain traditional stamina. 1980 chassis design has provided durability and continued value well into the 1990s, while growth of comfort and convenience options continue to attract first time truck buyers.*

The mid-'90s F-350 wheelbases also include a 136.8- and 160.8-inch Regular Chassis/Cab, a 155-inch Super-Cab, plus the ever popular 168.8-inch Crew Cab, available in both 2WD and 4x4 versions. Today's Ford F-Series light trucks feature long range fuel tanks, power steering as a standard item, hefty disc front brakes and self-adjusting drum rear brakes. Disc rear brakes are available on special applications.

Basic twin I-beam 2WD coil spring suspension has evolved since 1965, with the current design offering adjustable caster, camber and toe-in. Twin-Traction Beam IFS on F-150 and F-250 4x4s allows for camber and toe-in adjustment. At the mid-'90s, the solid Dana 60 live front axle remains a mainstay of F-350 4x4 dependability.

F-250 and F-350 4x4s continue to offer leaf front springs, while all 2WD and 4x4 Ford trucks use variable rate leaf rear springs. Ford trucks still satisfy utility and commercial users, delivering exceptional service while requiring a minimum of maintenance. Versatility and continuing quality have made Ford the number one selling American truck since the late 1970s.

For the new or used truck buyer, Ford means durability and a wide selection of options. The right chassis and powertrain choices can provide years of trouble-free service and truck value. The *Ford F-Series Pickup Owner's Bible* can help you choose the right chassis, powertrain and options for a "Ford Tough!" truck.

Chapter 2

Buying an F-Series Truck

POST-WORLD WAR II AMERICA was a society on the move. Years of rationed vehicle sales had created a huge need for light trucks, with buyers ranging from farmers, mining operations and ranchers to utility companies, delivery services and even a few suburban commuters. By 1947, both General Motors and Dodge were making serious bids for light truck market share, with new trucks featuring larger cabs and far more style. Ford trucks kept their staid pre-War look through 1947, but by early 1948, the all new F-Series truck answered the competition resoundly.

Beginning with the 1948–52 F-trucks, Ford light truck engineering and style have been a formidable force. Continued quality and technological advances have ranked Ford F-trucks among the most popular vehicles built. For the buyer of a new truck, the Ford F-Series models keep pace with consumer demands for safety, comfort, load carrying capacities and value.

The resale value of Ford trucks is legend. While 1953–56 F-100 models hold collectible status for their classic body style and engineering, a well maintained 1979 F-350 4x4 can still haul massive loads or deliver years of rugged service.

Ford truck appeal continues, and the overwhelming numbers of Ford F-Series light trucks sold from 1980 to the present provides buyers with the widest selection of quality two- and four-wheel drive used truck models in history. Parts are readily available, and Ford dealerships have access to an extensive line of truck parts, while the aftermarket and NOS sources provide both maintenance and full restoration pieces.

For the new truck buyer, Ford F-150 through F-350 models offer a broad range of chassis platforms and powertrain options. New Ford trucks provide commercial and private users with exceptional work, play and multipurpose vehicles.

Fig. 2-1. *Ford F-trucks serve a multitude of uses. This mid-'70s F-250 pickup offers ample GVWR (Gross Vehicle Weight Rating) and GCW (Gross Combination Weight), beautifully matching this stylish two-horse trailer.*

While the interior and luxury appointments of these late Ford F-trucks rival upscale passenger cars, the chassis and powertrain maintain their traditional stamina and rugged work profile. Ford's marketing success results from an ability to give buyers true truck value in a stylish and comfortable package.

1. SELECTING THE RIGHT TRUCK

A successful truck buy begins with understanding your needs and finding a truck with the right stamina and equipment to meet your goals. Even the earliest F-truck could deliver service if you matched the chassis and powertrain with your hauling plans.

Aside from a vehicle flawed with mechanical defects, the greatest source of dissatisfaction among new and used truck buyers is ill-suited equipment. Whether the truck provides multi-purpose transportation or must haul a massive cargo over rough roads, the chassis, powertrain and options determine a vehicle's worth.

Advertising jingo aside, a Ford F-Series truck is tough. How tough? Well, that's a matter of choosing a properly rated chassis. Remember that with the F-Series, model designation has its corollary in chassis stamina or Gross Vehicle Weight Rating (GVWR).

Fig. 2-2. Model identification plates play an important role when ordering parts or determining load carrying capacity. Check the model code and GVWR rating when shopping for a used truck.

The earliest F-1, F-2 and F-3 models were distinct. In 1948, simple classification characterized these F-trucks as a half-ton, 3/4-ton and heavy duty 3/4-ton, respectively. Actually, the F-3 was to replace the earlier Ford "One-Tonner," but the story goes that Ford could not match GM's one-ton pickup truck features and, therefore, attached a lighter rating to the early F-3.

By 1953, with the introduction of the F-100 to F-350 light truck badges, Ford was clear in its intent. The F-100 was a half-ton class truck, while the F-250 rated 3/4-ton and the F-350 indicated full one-ton load capacity.

Although users sometimes challenge light truck engineering standards, the significance of load capacity goes far beyond how much weight a set of springs can carry. If heavier springs alone could make a one-ton F-350 truck from an F-150, the cost of heavy haulers would drop dramatically. While the wheelbase, and even body parts, sometimes match, a half-ton truck offers substantially less chassis and powertrain stamina than a one-ton. If

Fig. 2-3. 1948–52 F-Series trucks have gained a following among restorers. However, the all-time classic is still the 1956 F-100 short bed model. A 110-inch wheelbase 1953–56 F-100 in restorable condition fetches a good price and makes an excellent investment.

you can identify your hauling needs and cargo carrying demands, a particular F-truck can match that goal. The significant differences in load capacity center around the frame and geartrain.

Fig. 2-4. The popularity of four-wheel drive gives new and used Ford truck buyers a wide variety of choices. For light hauling chores, the F-150 4x4 has offered solid construction and exceptional value since 1976.

Anatomy Of A Half-Ton F-Truck

At the most basic level, both the 1948 F-1 and current F-150 have ladder frames, Hotchkiss-style open driveline rear axles, and semi-elliptic rear springs. Although the F-150 Twin I-Beam front suspension offers a smoother ride than the F-1's mono-beam front axle and leaf springs, the stamina of each design is exceptional.

Each of these trucks offers the choice of a six cylinder inline or V-8 engine. Economical manual transmissions, in the same sense as early F-truck offerings, can still be had, with today's overdrive popularity an additional bonus. Four-wheel drum brakes on the early truck were adequate and impressive for their time, while the F-150 enjoys the benefit of power assisted disc front brakes.

Fig. 2-5. 1948–62 F-Series light GVWR models offer this three-speed transmission. Common feature is nine-bolt straight bottom shifter cover. Available with an overdrive option during several model years, this transmission is easy to rebuild but too light for heavy hauling needs.

Although integral power steering, dual safety braking systems with anti-lock, high tech EFI, safety features, and unimaginably comfortable interiors characterize the newer trucks, a new half-ton F-150 pickup is still a hauler with a big view of the road.

Ford F-Series buyers want size and content in a truck. The very success of the F-trucks rests with their determination to remain a real truck. While Ford's smaller Ranger compact or mid-size truck has its own loyal following, the two- or four-wheel drive F-150 buyer would rather have a traditional full-size truck.

F-250 Virtues

The late-'40s F-2 and F-3 models established some long term rules for 3/4-ton Ford light trucks. Although the F-3 metamorphosed as the one-ton F-350, its earliest form was a Heavy Duty 3/4-ton. Both the F-2 and F-3 shared engine and cab components with the F-1, but the cargo demands resulted in a much heavier frame, axles and springs.

Fig. 2-6. Engines must match the load. The 460 V-8, here in 1985 carbureted form, serves well with the F-250's GVWR capacity. When loads increase, fuel economy drops, yet the added horsepower means less engine stress and wear.

Ford engineering tradition placed the 3/4-ton models well beyond the lighter duty half-ton, yet still lower in curb weight and load capacity than a one-ton rated truck. The F-2 and F-3 set a trend for several generations of F-Series 3/4-ton models with the use of full-floating rear axles.

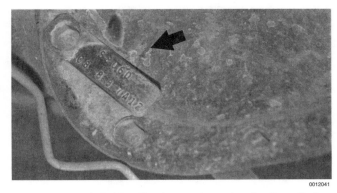

Fig. 2-7. Axle identification tag (arrow) codes the ratio for the ring-and-pinion gears. Lower gearing (higher numerically) means better pulling power and crawling ability. For F-250s, lower gearing means a 4.10, 4.27, 4.56 or 4.86 ratio. Tall gearing, for economy and primarily highway cruising, would be 3.50-3.73:1 range.

In the 1930s, large trucks popularized full-floating axles. This design provides for a separate rear wheel hub assembly and axle shaft. The design is described more fully in Chapter 11, but the bottom line is that this design is well-suited to trucks that carry severe loads. Ford light trucks like the F-2, F-3, F-250 and F-350 have used the full-floating axle for this reason. A full-floater is easy to identify, and until 1980, you could readily spot an F-250 truck.

Beginning in 1980, Ford F-250 3/4-ton trucks turned to a heavy duty semi-floating rear axle, a trend that other domestic truck manufacturers followed. These axles are much larger than Ford's 9-inch and later 8.8-inch (integral) rear axle units found in half-ton F-150 models. Since the earliest F-trucks, 3/4-ton models have used 8-stud wheels, and this industry-wide standard carries forward, even with these later semi-floating axles.

Fig. 2-8. 1980 and newer F-250 rear axle has a semi-floating axle shaft and bearing design. Although many users prefer the added stamina and safety of a full-floating axle, Ford and other truck manufacturers have switched to heavy duty semi-floating types.

Fig. 2-9. *Truck type synchromesh four-speed transmissions have been popular in F-truck models. Rugged T-98, T-18 and T-19 Warner gearboxes, and the severe duty New Process NP435 unit shown here, deliver excellent service for heavy hauling.*

A 3/4-ton F-2/F-3 or F-250 model has also meant beefier springs, a heavier front axle (twin axle beams since 1965), and a stronger frame to support more cargo. The powertrain of an F-250 also matches payload, and this means a heavy duty transmission, whether automatic or manual design. Whether trailer pulling or lugging a camper, the 3/4-ton Ford provides substantially more stamina than a half-ton. This can translate as a better cooling system, much larger brakes, power options, axle gear ratios for a higher GVWR and tires that can withstand the added weight

Many buyers opt for a larger truck to assure safety and provide for adequate load capacity. The only downside is fuel economy, the higher cost of tires and shorter engine life if axle gearing is much lower (numerically higher). Were it not for these issues, everyone wanting a long-bed pickup would choose the F-2/F-3 or F-250 over an F-1, F-100 or F-150 (heavy duty) half-ton model.

One-Ton Only If You Mean Business

The irony of common body shells is that an F-350 can be purchased with the same cab and bed as a long wheelbase F-150. Since 1956, Ford has offered an F-100 (later the F-150) with an optional eight-foot bed length. While earlier F-2/F-250 and F-3/F-350 trucks were the only models with beds of 8-foot length or longer, the half-ton bed could now match the bigger F-models.

Prior to 1956, a quick glance could distinguish an F-100 with its 6-1/2 foot bed from other Ford pickups. The optional long half-ton bed length has confused some buyers, who assume that the longer bed means more load ca-

Fig. 2-10. *F-350 remains the premier hauler for a multitude of uses. Super Camper Special edition blended convenience options and safety features with a rugged workhorse. Since* the 1973 introduction of the Super Camper Special option, recreationalists have taken advantage of the F-350's supreme stamina and exceptionally high GVWR/GCW ratings.

pacity. These are separate issues, and the F-350 models prove this point even more.

The F-350's roots were the "Tonner" models that Ford once built to satisfy heavy haulers. As the F-Series emerged, Ford made the F-4 a one-ton truck and relegated it to heavy duty use. Until the advent of the F-350, these models wore stake beds and other cargo berths, while the F-350 introduced the long pickup bed version to compete with other one-ton rated pickups of the '50s.

The popularity of these one-ton pickups waned in the 1960s, and the F-350 served mostly as a dual-rear-wheeled carrier for stake beds, cargo boxes, tow hoists and other special equipment. Some still ordered the over-sized pickup models, but the mass popularity of an F-350 pickup waited until 1973, when Ford introduced the Super Camper Special two-wheel drive model.

From this point forward, F-350 meant as much versatility as any other light F-Series truck. The model line, which formerly held fast to commercial use, now could serve as the heaviest duty pickup available for multi-purpose use. Even Crew Cab models evolved, and by the end of the 1970s, hardcore recreationalists had welcomed the F-350 Crew Cab into their campsites.

Today, when the load calls for maximum strength and safety, the F-350 two- and four-wheel drive models provide front and rear full-floating axles and a massive frame. Available in a variety of wheel bases, including the popular 133-inch length found on lighter duty F-Series pickups, the F-350 is Ford's supreme pickup.

Consistent with F-350 standards, mid-'90s 4x4 models continue to offer a Dana 60 solid front axle. Leaf springs with stabilizer bars, and computer tuned springs and shock absorbers now make the F-350 as manageable as other light F-trucks.

Buyers looking for maximum stamina, safety and durability, coupled with the highest GVWR and GCW ratings available in light Ford trucks, find the F-350 and the Super Duty models attractive. The diesel engine option provides more affordable fuel bills, while buyers of gasoline models can expect high fuel costs with these haulers.

2. SHOPPING FOR THE RIGHT COMPONENTS

In the many column questions that I field, my recommendation is always "buy the heaviest components available." While a new truck buyer can actually build an F-Series truck to suit, buyers of used vehicles must understand the various packages and options available during past model years.

Fuel economy is a valid concern, but you need components that match your usage needs and safety demands. As one example, if you want reasonable economy but plan to pull a 29-foot travel trailer up and down steep mountain passes, then an economy axle ratio, which might help when driving without a load, is both a nuisance and a hazard for towing the hefty trailer.

While towing, your truck needs maximum power and good compression braking. An economy axle will not provide either. Late model trucks with an overdrive option can deliver reasonable fuel economy in overdrive (seldom used while pulling a load) while tolerating a towing or numerically lower axle ratio. If fuel economy is

Fig. 2-11. *Heavy duty options cost a good deal when new. At resale, add-ons like heavy duty suspension or cooling return maximum value. Four-wheel drive is one option that holds high resale value over the entire life of the truck. If the 4x4 system is in good condition, consider four-wheel drive an excellent investment.*

an issue, this kind of compromise enhances the versatility of your Ford truck.

Likewise, certain components can serve better and last much longer. In the 1960s, when Ford experienced brisk sales of Camper Special models, a column shifted three-speed transmission was standard on lighter F-models. While this transmission was reasonably durable, the T-98 and T-18 Warner four-speeds afforded much higher stamina plus the greater versatility of a compound low gear.

On earlier model F-trucks, I fully recommend heavy duty four-speed truck transmissions. 1980s and '90s models with iron case New Process NP435 and T-18/T-19 Warner gearboxes provide a better margin of stamina than the lighter aluminum three-, four-, and five-speed types. The four-speed truck transmission option usually comes with a heavy duty or larger diameter clutch assembly.

If a five-speed overdrive is essential, the latest heavy duty units can match the service of earlier truck four-speeds. As a rule, if a particular transmission is available with larger engines, like the 460 gas or 7.3L diesel, odds suggest that this same transmission will hold up very well behind a smaller engine.

For automatic transmissions, the C-6 aluminum cased unit is Ford's best for stamina and a rugged life. From the late 1960s onward, these units find their way into heavy duty chassis applications and trucks with the optional high output engine, like the 460. In the 1980s, overdrive automatics emerged, and the E4OD currently holds the best track record.

The only time that a heavy duty chassis becomes a liability is when a unit repair or overhaul is necessary. Larger engines, transmissions and axles cost more to service than light duty units. Here the trade-off is that the heavy duty components may outlast lighter equipment by as much as 100,000 miles! Again, if well maintained F-150 and F-350 trucks carried exactly the same loads for identical distances, the F-350 should go far further before major service is necessary.

Unless you have no need for a larger truck, find such models cumbersome to operate, or prefer the ride of a light duty model, take the big truck or model with heavy duty options. These components cost a good deal when new and are terrific savings when passed along at resale.

For real hauling, the best used buys include heavy duty suspension, heavy duty factory cooling add-ons, larger brakes, a heavy duty transmission and drive axle(s), a factory chassis mounted towing package (including mirrors) and a high factory GVWR/GCW rating. Keep in mind, though, that a towing package can mean severe use, so make sure you know the history of such a used prospect.

3. INSPECTING A USED TRUCK

As a used truck buyer, the fear of waking to a pile of scrap iron in your driveway is real. Gloomy repair expenses create anxiety about buying any used vehicle. Insight, however, can demystify the process. Add to this the conviction that no matter how much you want a truck, desire won't override good judgement. This may be tough, as the search for a quality used truck often leads to junk. When you finally find a presentable piece of iron, the impulse is to buy it. That's when you need to be wary!

Ten Best Picks In Used Ford F-trucks

My top ten choices in F-Series light trucks span a wide range of model years. These selections take aesthetics, stamina, available equipment and driveability into account. Features described for a given truck may also apply to other F-models that you find more attractive or affordable.

1. 1953–56 110-inch wheelbase F-100: Who wouldn't want one of these classic beauties? Although the 1956 style holds the highest value (plus the advantage of 12-volt electrics), '53–'55 F-100s have strong appeal and are equally easy to service or restore. The most durable stock powertrain is a '54–'56 Y-block V-8 or 223 six with a T-98 four-speed. The more factory options, the rarer the truck, so watch for Magic-Aire heaters, OEM radios and Custom Cab trim packages. '56 cab with wrap-around rear window is prized.

2. 1957–60 and 1961–64 F-100 or F-250: Utility and some aesthetic appeal, especially Custom Cab models and those with unusual trim packages. Rarer models include 1961–63 Styleside beds with bed attached to cab section. 4x4 available from '59-up, but these early versions prove very utilitarian and cumbersome to operate. Y-block V-8s are big muscle for this era, boasting lots of torque and dependability. Best transmission is T-98 four-speed.

3. 1965–66 2WD F-100 and F-250: Continuation of '61–'64 styling with all new Twin I-Beam suspension and 352 FE big-block V-8. Many accessories available, including options like a rugged automatic or T-98 and T-18 Warner four-speed transmission. First F-trucks with modern convenience options and good looks make this an appealing model. 4x4 F-100 rates poorly with its single speed Dana 21 power divider, but F-250 4x4 has strong appeal if your forearms can handle the manual steering.

4. 1967–79 two-wheel drive models: This period represents steady development of two-wheel drive F-trucks. Within these years, F-Series 2WD trucks popularize a wide range of options, including integral power steering, disc brakes and handling improvements. Refinements accelerate during the 1970s as option packages match user needs.

1966 F-250 was a tall workhorse. This FE powered 4x4 features a rugged chassis and two-speed transfer case. Four-speed transmission and Dana 60 (Spicer-type) rear axle can handle a massive load.

5. 1976–79 F-150 4x4: Designated a "heavy duty half-ton," these models feature some of the best components available in a 4x4 light truck. Powertrain and chassis are especially durable, with disc front brakes, a two-speed transfer case, integral power steering and a rugged automatic or truck four-speed transmission on the shopping list. Rear axle is a rugged 9-inch Ford.

6. Late-1977–79 F-250 4x4: Well equipped, these models rank among the best built Ford 4x4 trucks. Integral power steering, a lower chassis profile (transfer case attaches to the transmission) and some outstanding GVWR/GCW ratings characterize these trucks. Look for Camper Special or heavy duty chassis versions, models that include the heavier duty 3800- and 4500-pound front axle option.

continued on next page

The Chassis

The condition of the frame is the most important aspect of a used truck. You can recondition cosmetic areas and mechanical assemblies, but a twisted, broken or fatigued frame means severe trouble. I always begin looking at a used truck by crawling under it and checking for obvious signs of wear and abuse.

Damage is easy to spot: bent springs, spring hangers, or frame crossmembers; torn cables or hoses; a twisted skid plate on a 4x4 or damaged frame horns at the bumper attachment points. Axle misalignment presents

itself as worn tires. If you have suspicions about a truck's frame condition, suggest that the seller accompany you to a reputable frame and alignment shop. Have the frame checked for straightness on a four-wheel alignment rack.

Taking critical measurements between points on the frame will indicate whether the truck has sustained damage or suffers from fatigue and cracks. The frame specialist can also check for wear at the steering linkage, the steering gearbox, spring hangers, bushings and steering joints.

Ten Best Picks In Used Ford F-trucks (continued)

7. 1979–up F-350 4x4: Available as a single rear wheel pickup for heavy camper use, many of these trucks have convenience and power options. Geartrain is virtually indestructible under normal use, and the heavier duty Dana 60 full-floating front axle ranks as the best ever in light trucks. Looking much like an F-250, added stamina lies in the frame, axles and powertrain. Crew Cab is available.

8. 1986 and up F-Series models with EFI/MPI: The gains from MPI are dramatic, and the 4.9L six or 5.0L, 5.8L and 7.5L V-8 engines each benefit. Trucks of this era are well built and full of convenience items. 302/5.0L V-8 made EFI switch in 1986, other engines followed in 1987.

Electronic fuel and spark management has revolutionized the automotive industry. F-Series light trucks from the mid-1980s onward feature EFI/MPI, the key to better fuel economy and improved performance

9. Late Navistar 7.3L diesel models: Any two- or four-wheel drive model equipped with this rugged engine has superior chassis and geartrain features to match. Many diesel trucks have a full complement of convenience and power options and deluxe trim packages. For trailer pulling, hauling a serious load, or simply to benefit from the improved fuel economy of diesel power, the 7.3L engine is a proven choice.

10. Camper Special packages: Overall, trucks equipped with this package have upgraded powertrain and chassis components that, if properly cared for and not abused, will provide the truck with a longer service life and added stamina. Earlier packages were oriented toward spring and load capacity enhancements, while late-'60s and newer equipment often includes improved engine and transmission cooling plus a list of heavy duty chassis items. Factory trailer wiring and a quality platform/frame mounted hitch are often found with this package.

The most dependable F-Series light truck V-8 engines include the 292 Y-block, 302, 351W, 352/360/390 FE types and the 460. Top six cylinder designs are the 240 and 300 inlines with seven crankshaft main bearings. Better performance on today's lower octane fuels, improved fuel economy, precise tune and easier routine service make the later EFI/MPI engines a great choice. Navistar 6.9L and 7.3L diesels have an excellent track record, the latter offering more power and other improvements.

The strongest light F-Series truck transmissions are iron case four-speed types with synchromesh, including the Warner T-98, T-18 and T-19 gearboxes or a New Process NP435. Ford's C-6 aluminum three-speed automatic ranks highest for durability and efficiency. Later five-speed manual overdrives and electronically shifted four-speed automatic overdrive units offer dramatic gains in fuel economy.

Best rear axles, depending upon model choice and GVWR needs, are the semi-floating 9-inch Ford and Dana/Spicer 60 and 70 full-floating types. Best 4x4 front axles are the late '70s-up open knuckle, disc-brake-equipped Dana 44 and 60 types. Many owners prefer the rugged design and lower maintenance costs of pre-'80 solid front axles. The '80-up F-150 and F-250 IFS Twin-Traction Beam axles have more moving parts and an increased number of wear points. F-350 4x4s continue to offer the Dana 60 solid front axle, the strongest unit available for light trucks.

Fig. 2-12. *Frame damage is a serious problem, sometimes impossible to repair safely. If in doubt about the condition of a used truck prospect, take the vehicle to a reputable frame and alignment shop for closer inspection.*

Inspecting Drivelines And Axles

Jack and support the truck safely off the ground, and check the steering bearings (called knuckle/kingpin bearings or ball joints on a 4x4 model). Grab each front wheel at six and twelve o'clock and rock the wheel in and out. Play shows inboard of the wheels at the kingpins or ball joints.

On a 4x4 truck, note whether the knuckle seals or axle tubes leak grease or gear lube. With all trucks, check for loose wheel bearings and any signs of bearing, front and rear axles, or universal joint damage. For 4x4 models, water is the primary destroyer of wheel assembly parts, steering knuckle pieces and axle components.

Fig. 2-13. *Front wheel driving axle trouble can mean expensive repairs. Check for wear at steering knuckle bearings, wheel bearings and axle joints. (See service chapter for details.) Water in an axle housing can ruin expensive gears and bearings.*

Any indication of water in an axle housing, transfer case or transmission assembly should raise concern. These components make up the high cost repair areas of the geartrain.

Check for excess play at the ring and pinion gears by rotating each driveshaft back and forth. Distinguish U-joint looseness from gear problems. While driveshafts cost plenty, axle assembly overhauls are even more expensive.

When you test drive the truck, listen for whining, clunks or growling. Axle noises telegraph during acceleration, coasting and deceleration. U-joint or driveshaft play sounds like a metallic clicking or snapping noise when you change speed or jerk the throttle open and shut, especially at a steady road speed in a higher gear.

Checking The Clutch and Transmission

The clutch can be a difficult assembly to access, especially on 4x4 models. Owners often sell their truck rather than replace a worn clutch! Official flat-rate labor to replace a clutch can run in excess of five hours on some 4x4s. Add clutch parts and flywheel machining, and the job can cost as much, or more, than a good used engine.

Check the clutch by moving the transmission shifter to high gear at 20 mph. With the clutch pedal depressed, bring the engine speed to 2000 rpm and hold the throttle steady, then quickly let the clutch pedal go. Listen carefully.

If the engine speed drops immediately to a near idle, the clutch cover (pressure plate) assembly and disc are likely okay. A gradual decrease in speed usually indicates that the clutch either slips or needs adjustment. Also make certain the clutch does not shudder during engagement.

Often the clutch needs minor adjustment, but when clutch mis-adjustment is bad enough to allow slippage, major damage is well underway. Slippage generates heat and friction, which translates as wear and fatigue.

Transmission woes telegraph unique noises. While test driving the truck, listen for crunch and gear clash. In each gear, pull gently on the shifter while accelerating lightly. If the synchronizers and shifter detents are okay, you'll feel resistance in the lever. When the transmission immediately slides out of gear, suspect a weak synchronizer assembly.

Synchronizer wear also shows up on a downgrade, as deceleration causes the transmission to jump out of gear. Bearing or gear tooth wear will also cause the transmission to slip out of gear.

Automatic Transmission

An automatic transmission may slip or chatter on take-off. Harsh shifts are another sign of trouble. A shuddering sensation, much like a bad manual clutch or weak motor mounts, also means real problems. Burnt fluid, leaks or erratic shifts suggest that an automatic transmission is in bad shape.

For automatics, repairs generally involve a major overhaul. Again, tough access to some transmissions, especially on 4x4s, raises repair costs considerably. If you suspect transmission troubles, get a transmission overhaul estimate before making an offer on the truck.

Labor to remove, overhaul and install an automatic transmission in a 4x4 truck runs upward of 10 hours. Add to this the expensive parts involved, and your used truck buy has a whole new price perspective!

Engine

A common misconception about used vehicles is that the engine is most important. Especially on larger trucks and 4x4s, an axle, transmission or major brake system rebuild can exceed the cost of an engine overhaul! Installing a complete engine is often easier and quicker than removing and overhauling the transmission or an axle assembly.

Before buying a used truck, you'll still want to make sure the engine is sound. An engine's basic requirements include: 1) normal and even compression, 2) accurate valve timing, 3) correct valve lift at each valve, and 4) normal bearing clearances and oil pressure. If you can borrow the truck or encourage the owner to comply, have the engine oscilloscope analyzed or tested on a chassis dynamometer.

Fig. 2-14. *A leakdown tester and engine oscilloscope are quick means for determining engine condition. Find weakest cylinder with scope analysis, then run a leakdown test to determine source of compression loss. (See service chapter for details.)*

On a scope, a quick check of dynamic compression can compare cylinder spark loads and help determine approximate compression. Check the weakest cylinder with a compression gauge or, better yet, a cylinder leakdown tester. (You will find a complete explanation of engine troubleshooting in the service chapters.)

If you find signs of overheat, look further. Excess rust or chronic boil over can indicate aeration caused by cylinder gases leaking into the cooling system from a cracked block or head casting, a blown head gasket or a defective water pump. Run a cooling system pressure test, and also check for normal coolant circulation. (See the cooling system chapter for troubleshooting details.)

Engine Oiling System

Engine bearing and lubrication problems are tricky to diagnose. On trucks with an oil pressure gauge, it's far easier to observe oil pressure under load. Check the consistency of the engine oil to make sure that heavy additives do not alter the oil pressure.

Listen for knocks at cold start-up, after the engine has set for some time. Warm the engine completely, watching the oil pressure during this period. Drive the truck under load, up hills and such, and constantly monitor the oil pressure.

An automotive stethoscope or even a long hollow tube makes an excellent diagnostic tool for finding internal engine noises. Get used to the amplified sound, though, or the engine will resonate like a metallic thrashing machine! Learn to isolate various noises, such as the normal clicking of a mechanical fuel pump.

Isolate loose piston pin noise or a cracked piston by shorting or disconnecting each spark plug wire and seeing whether the knock is still there. Rod and main bearing noises will also decrease by eliminating spark.

If you lack the equipment or skill to do the job, consider paying a professional mechanic to check the engine, geartrain or cooling system. If you find that the truck is not in good shape, you can either negotiate a better price or consider your money well spent in that you did not buy a worn-out truck.

Body and Accessories

Sheet metal, body mounts and rubber body seals also take abuse. The effects of sun, rain, snow and salted roads beat trucks mercilessly. Rubber rots, hinges twist and windows rattle in worn channels. The degree of wear can be a barometer of the overall abuse the truck has suffered.

Radio, heater and air conditioning systems are costly and time-consuming to repair. Don't accept suggestions that the air conditioner simply needs a recharge. Especially with today's changing laws concerning A/C refrigerants, ask the seller to have the system charged before you agree to buy the truck.

Belts, hoses, wiring, the battery, filters and routinely serviced items speak for the truck's maintenance. Look thoroughly under the hood, and assess the kind of re-

Fig. 2-15. *Body rust is the most expensive and difficult of repairs. Inspect sheet metal with a magnet if you suspect that plastic filler has concealed large areas of rust or collision damage. Routing out rust and a restoration paint job can cost more than any other repair on the truck.*

placement parts that the owner has used. Ultra-cheap parts usually mean a neglected truck.

Other signs of trouble are a broken speedometer and vague records of mileage. This isn't really important on a 1948 model, but it sure should color your thinking about a late '80s truck! No lube stickers, missing pedal pads, bald tires and a poor paint finish are ominous signs. You want a well kept truck, one that received regular maintenance.

Pollution Controls and Vehicle Registration

Since 1971, pollution controls on light truck engines have proliferated. The emission control era started in the early '60s with a PCV valve and closed crankcase. Next came the smog pump, followed by the exhaust gas recirculation (EGR) valve and evaporative systems for fumes. The mid-'70s brought on catalytic converters and unleaded fuel, and more recently, electronic fuel injection and spark management have become part of the emission program. (See the emission controls chapter.)

Smog laws, enforced by individual states and the federal government, mean that your used truck purchase must have a functional and complete OEM emission control system. If equipment is missing, non-operative or malfunctioning, you will have a problem registering the truck. Mandatory inspection programs have become common, with California serving as a model for the entire United States.

Fig. 2-16. *In most states, emission control restoration is necessary for registration of a used vehicle. To pass visual inspection, all pollution control hardware must be in place, including the OEM air cleaner, correct carburetion and approved manifolds. If you doubt the legality of a system, consult an inspection facility before buying the truck.*

A truck engine stripped by the previous owner of its emission hardware, or an engine transplant unauthorized by your state's smog laws, means real trouble. Replacing items like original equipment intake and exhaust manifolds, a smog pump, electrical and vacuum controls, the catalytic converter, an EGR valve and a host of other pieces can run way beyond the cost of a good used engine!

A modified engine with non-approved aftermarket headers, intake manifold, carburetor, air cleaner, ignition

and other components is a prime candidate for failing the visual portion of an emission control test.

To meet legal demands, make the seller responsible for the restoration of the smog system. Otherwise, reduce the vehicle's price enough to cover the equipment necessary for compliance. If you have questions about necessary equipment or its cost, get an estimate from a licensed smog shop, authorized dealership or your state motor vehicle pollution control agency before you buy the truck.

4. BUYING A NEW F-SERIES TRUCK

Light trucks, once regarded strictly as utility or work vehicles, have metamorphosed from beasts of burden into modern multi-purpose transportation. Over the years, buyers and sales personnel have also changed. Years ago, truck and farm equipment sales often took place at the same outlet. Today, more car buyers find themselves first-time truck buyers at a truck dealership.

Whether or not you are new to light truck ownership, four-wheeling or recreational vehicles, you can still take charge of selecting and ordering your new truck. Buyer's remorse, due mainly to winding up with the wrong options and equipment, is too common. Everyone wants to get a good deal, yet many buyers shop for a vehicle solely on the basis of price, with only a vague sense for what equipment to buy.

Fig. 2-17. *New Ford F-Series trucks have refinements and fresh styling. Bought properly, a Ford truck provides years of quality service and an excellent investment. Identify your needs, then tailor your new truck's equipment to meet the demand. If necessary, make a special order purchase.*

Dealer showroom literature often does not explain the full range of available options; further research is likely necessary. Truck dealers have detailed specification and equipment ordering books, and the fleet sales manager has expertise at how to spec out a new truck.

Such order books describe far more items than you will find in glossy point-of-sale materials. A complete, factory-tailored new truck always makes better sense than hastily selecting that random "nice color" truck on the lot. For a special order, see the dealership's sales manager or fleet manager.

Selecting The Right Chassis

Veteran truck buyers learn equipment needs from pounding over highways and dirt roads with a full load of cargo. Four-wheelers find places where studio lamps and advertising props can't reach. Begin your truck selection by determining whether a standard chassis has enough stamina for your needs. If not, the order and pricing books describe heavy duty options that will better meet your requirements.

By reviewing the equipment listed in the dealer's order book, you can buy factory engineered and installed components that serve your needs. Understand truck chassis and suspension ratings. Even if a light duty frame and springs can support a weight of 1000-plus pounds, an axle gear ratio or transmission designed for passenger car-type fuel economy will not meet continuous hauling demands. It's not just load capacity but also the life-span of powertrain and chassis pieces that distinguish a truck's toughness.

Factory Upgrades

Boost your truck's load carrying capacity with a heavy duty spring option, heavy duty shock absorbers, a better wheel and tire combination and a trailer towing package. The cost of heavy duty OE springs is a fraction of what aftermarket springs will cost later. Remember that the manufacturer credits back the cost of standard parts when you order heavy duty factory-installed upgrades.

When ordering springs, many buyers assume that if heavier is good, the heaviest available springs must be better. This is not always true, especially with full size trucks. The order catalog, for example, lists snow plow front springs as an option for 4x4s. Without the massive weight of a snow plow, these springs can jar your bones or cause kidney trauma!

Unless you run snow plow equipment or have an overhanging load that bears heavily on the front axle, stick with the regular heavy duty suspension package. Always opt for the heaviest gear and axle components available. For full-size trucks to the mid-'80s, simply ordering a four-speed transmission was the difference between a passenger car type three-speed and a 2-ton capacity four-speed truck gearbox.

When available, a heavier front or rear axle assembly is equally valuable, and so is a heavy duty clutch or brakes. When ordering these components, despite the initial added cost, you buy years of extra service.

Heavy duty factory shocks are a must. Often, you will end up replacing worn-out standard shocks in 12,000–15,000 miles of normal on- and off-pavement use. Another important item is an optional heavy duty anti-sway bar (front and rear if available). This will enhance cornering and stability of your truck. Often, the anti-sway bar(s), heavy shocks, heavy duty charging and upgrade cooling system come as part of the trailer towing or Camper Special package.

Engine and Transmission Choices

One of the worst fates in the aftermath of a new truck purchase is the discovery that the vehicle does not meet your towing or cargo load needs. This often occurs when

Fig. 2-18. *Factory upgrades, like this engine oil cooler on a Navistar diesel, can enhance engine life and improve performance. Cost of such factory options is competitive with aftermarket devices. Ford has carefully engineered these parts and their installation.*

you pick the wrong engine, transmission and axle ratio combination or when the pursuit of fuel economy overrides all other considerations.

Many of today's trailer towing gear ratios were considered economy ratios twenty years ago. These axles may work fine for breezing down the highway unloaded, but with a heavy camping trailer in tow, the strain is just too much! You snail crawl up grades, while serious engine or transmission damage develops. A trailer of 2500 or more pounds, if towed often, requires a larger V-8 option and heavy duty cooling for the engine and transmission.

As a rule, a lighter half-ton truck chassis cannot hold up under constant trailering loads. In addition to frame and suspension shortcomings, the engine cooling capacity, braking ability, and smaller tires compromise your safety. For heavy hauling, economy must yield to a larger chassis. Turn your attention toward a 3/4-ton or larger truck with a heavy duty frame and a healthy V-8. .

Transmission Options

Automatic transmissions have become increasingly popular. They sometimes meet special physical needs of drivers but most often satisfy those with no desire to work a shift lever and clutch. During the 1980s, three-speed automatics with an overdriving fourth gear came into the truck market. The demand for fuel savings and improved gear ratios have increased the popularity of late model electronically shifted overdrive automatics.

For full-sized light trucks, the most durable manual transmissions have been iron-cased, heavy duty truck four-speeds with a compound low gear. Although automatics can offer good control in sand, a manual transmission and low axle ratios remain the safest approach for downgrades and pulling massive loads.

American truck manufacturers have moved away from the iron truck transmissions, a shift that has popularized five-speed aluminum-cased overdrive gearboxes. Aiming toward weight reduction and maximum fuel economy, the trend has produced lighter transmissions that bridge the needs of hauling and economy with a rea-

Fig. 2-19. When continuous trailering is the plan, opt for an F-250 or F-350 chassis. The frame, springs, brakes, axle stamina and powertrain will match your towing needs. Check GVWR and GCW ratings carefully, and know your cargo and trailer weights before selecting a chassis package or powertrain. Ford offers gross load guidelines for determining the right truck and necessary options.

sonably low first gear ratio, synchromesh on all forward speeds and an overdriving fifth gear for fuel savings.

Accessories For Survival

Look for factory extras that will increase your truck's life expectancy. For example, air conditioning or a heavy duty charging (electrical) system may include items like a heavy duty alternator, a larger battery, and harnesses for trailer wiring. The factory-installed air conditioning option usually includes a heavy duty radiator and engine cooling upgrade. Again, the factory provides heavy duty options for merely the cost difference between standard pieces and these heavier components.

You can often order upgrade brakes. A heavy duty brake system may come as a stand alone option or with a towing package. Heavy duty brakes might include a heavier master cylinder, bigger vacuum booster, even larger brake shoes, disc pads, drums or rotors.

Factory equipment must meet high quality standards. Always consider factory-installed tow hooks, tow hitches and wiring harnesses. Consider tire options. A few dollars extra can provide a major gain. Look over the factory tire options and compare them in the marketplace. Avoid getting stuck with short-lived, undercapacity standard tires. Match your new truck's tires to your turf!

Consider Special Ordering Your New Truck

Your factory authorized dealer may have just the truck you want in stock. Check the dealer's inventory first. You might get lucky and drive home immediately with a new vehicle. If, however, the stocked vehicles fall short of your needs, avoid buying someone else's truck. Ask your local dealer to trade with another dealer or special order your truck. Although it's fun to get something new while you're in a buying mood, waiting for the right truck assures years of satisfaction and pleasure. The trade-off is worth the wait!

5. 1994 FORD F-SERIES SPECIFICATIONS

Dimensions (Inches) And Capacities

Wheelbases

F-150	Reg. Cab	116.8, 133.0
	SuperCab	138.8, 155.0
F-250	Reg. Cab	133.0
	HD SuperCab	155.0
F-350	Reg. Cab	133.0
	Reg. Chassis Cab	136.8, 160.8
	Crew Cab	168.4
	SuperCab	155.0
	F-Super Duty	136.8, 160.8, 184.8

Cargo capacity (cu.ft.)

SuperCab . . . . .29.9 [a]

[a] Behind front seat with standard rear bench seat folded; 30.2 with optional rear jump seats folded

Chassis

Steering:

Recirculating ball, power

Ratio . . . . 17.0:1 (power)

Brakes:

Front disc/rear drum; rear anti-lock brake system (except F-Super Duty); Four-wheel disc (F-Super Duty)

Front disc diameter:

F-150 . . . . 11.72"

F-250/250HD/350 . . . . 12.56"

F-Super Duty (front and rear) . . . . 12.8"

Rear drum diameter:

F-150 . . . . .11-1/32"

F-250/250HD/350 SRW models . . . . .12"

F-350 DRW models (except F-Super Duty) . . . . . .12-1/8"

Wheels:

F-150 . . . . 5-hole, steel disc

F-250/250HD/350 . . . . 8-hole, steel disc

F-Super Duty . . . . 10-hole, steel disc

Frame:

Ladder-type with up to eight cross-members, 36,000 psi low carbon steel

Front Suspension:

Twin-I-Beam IFS with adjustable camber and caster (F-150/250/250HD/350 4x2 models)

Twin-Traction Beam IFS with adjustable camber (F-150/250/250HD 4x4 models)

Monobeam solid front axle with kingpin steering knuckles (F-350 4x4/F-Super Duty)

Springs:

Coil, computer-selected (F-150/250/250HD/350 4x2 and F-150 4x4

Leaf, single-stage constant-rate (F-250/250HD/350 4x4/F-Super Duty)

Rear Suspension:

Leaf, 2-stage variable-rate springs (All models except F-350 136.8" and 160.8" WB Chassis-Cab and F-Super Duty; F-350 133-wheelbase models also include 710 lb. nominal rating auxiliary rear spring)

Leaf, single stage constant-rate springs (F-350 136.8" and 160.8" WB Chassis-Cab and F-Super Duty; also includes 900 lb. nominal rating auxiliary rear spring)

Tires

F-150 4x2 Regular Cab: P215/75R-15SL steel-belted radial-ply

F-150 4x2 SuperCab, F-150 4x4: P235/75R-15XL steel-belted radial-ply

F-250: LT215/85R-16D steel-belted radial-ply

F-350 4x2 dual rear wheel models: LT215/85R-16D steel-belted radial-ply

F-250 HD/350 single rear wheel models, F-350 4x4 dual rear wheel Chassis-Cab and F-Super Duty: LT235/85R-16E steel-belted radial-ply

Powertrain Availability

Engine	Transmissions	Horsepower @ RPM	Torque @ RPM
4.9L EFI I-6	5-sp. Man. OD	145 @ 3400(a)	265 @ 2000(a)
	5-sp. Man. OD - HD	150 @ 3400	260 @ 2000
	3-sp. Auto.	150 @ 3400	260 @ 2000
	4-sp. Auto. OD (E4OD)	145 @ 3400(a)	265 @ 2000(a)
5.0L EFI V-8	5-sp. Man. OD	205 @ 4000	275 @ 3000
	4-sp. Auto. OD (4R70W)	195 @ 4000	270 @ 3000
	4-sp. Auto. OD (E4OD)	195 @ 4000	270 @ 3000
5.8L EFI V-8	5-sp. Man. OD - HD	200 @ 3800	310 @ 2800
	3-sp. Auto	200 @ 3800	310 @ 2800
	4-sp. Auto. OD (E4OD)	200 @ 3800	310 @ 2800
7.3L V-8 IDI Diesel	5-sp. Man. OD	185 @ 3000(b)	360 @ 1400(b)
	3-sp. Auto	185 @ 3000(b)	360 @ 1400(b)
	4-sp. Auto. OD (E4OD)	185 @ 3000(b)	360 @ 1400(b)
7.3L V-8 IDI Turbo Diesel	5-sp. Man. OD	190 @ 3000	395 @ 1400
	4-sp. Auto. OD (E4OD)	190 @ 3000	395 @ 1400
7.5L EFI V-8	5-sp. Man. OD	245 @ 4000(c)	395 @ 2400(c)
	3-sp. Auto	245 @ 4000(c)	395 @ 2400(c)
	4-sp. Auto. OD (E4OD)	245 @ 4000(c)	400 @ 2200(c)

(a) Ratings are with 2.73/3.08 rear axle ratio on F-150 only or F-150-250 (below 8500# GVWR) with 4-speed Automatic OD (E4OD). All others use 150 hp @ 3400 and 260 lb.-ft. @ 2000.
(b) High altitude ratings are 165 hp @ 3000 and 325 lb.-ft. @ 1600.
(c) F-Super Duty ratings are 255 hp @ 4000 and 405 lb.-ft. @ 2400.

Chapter 3

Operating Your F-Series Truck

M Y APPRECIATION FOR LIGHT TRUCKS began in 1963, when our family moved to Carson Valley, Nevada. Here, surrounded by the majestic Sierras and a lesser range of desert juniper and pinion pine, sprawled forty square miles of alfalfa fields and cattle grazing land. Criss-crossing the Valley, a host of paved and gravel roads linked the sagebrush covered foothills, broad pastures and willow-lined irrigation ditches.

Southern California, which quickly became a memory, had offered an entirely different climate and culture. By the early '60s, a high-octane freeway lifestyle flaunted factory muscle cars, vintage hot rods and surfers' woody station wagons. At Carson Valley, the principle rolling stock was trucks, and "high horsepower" meant a good cutting horse that stood fifteen hands or taller.

Ford Truck Country

Carson Valley was surely truck country, the kind of terrain and inclement weather that sharpens wits and compels good driving skills. During harsh winters, when the ground froze hard and mean Sierra storms threatened livestock, pickup and stake bodied trucks lugged implements and hauled bales of cattle fodder.

By early summer, when the first hay cuts came, the ranchers and their trucks still labored hard. The scorching heat of August had the ranchers up before dawn, often weary by mid-morning, and headed for Minden to get a friendly cup of coffee at the pharmacy next to the Post Office. Their pickups were lined up in front, cattle racks looped with twine ropes, the tube-type traction tires caked with mud. Two- and four-wheel drives, these iron workhorses helped raise productivity, ferried bulky goods and battled the seasonal challenges of high altitude cattle ranges.

Behind The Wheel

My earliest Ford truck was a '38 half-ton that required considerable work. When the powertrain finally ran, I needed to register the vehicle. As Nevada based truck registration fees on the vehicle's actual weight, my first drive involved a trip to the local lumber yard for an official weight slip.

Quite happily, and thoroughly ignoring the safety risk, I drove to the scales on a hastily fabricated seat, more accurately, an old wooden orange crate. With the floorpan above the transmission removed, the whining flathead V-8

0012056

Fig. 3-1.   Cattle country, Western Nevada's high valleys offer majestic views, bitter winters and hot, dry summers. Ford   F-Series light trucks have served rural life well. Rugged 4x4s remain the most popular models.

Fig. 3-2. *As a trailer puller, hauler or recreational vehicle, your F-Series truck has plenty of personality. Make a place in your family photo album for this rig.*

and worn transmission countergear bearings sounded much like a muffled hay thresher, a noise that thrilled me.

That engine and other distinctly Ford sounds were familiar when I later bought my first F-Series truck, a '51 F-3 pickup with the flathead 226 six and a spur gear transmission. The F-3 powertrain provided a wealth of insight into driving a truck. Much like a large over-the-road tractor-trailer puller, the F-3's slow revving, high torque engine had a distinct feel and attention span. The transmission, sans the synchronizers that we now take for granted, demanded double clutching and careful synchronizing of the throttle setting between each shift. Unlike the sleek muscle cars and 1955–57 Chevys that filled the other half of the high school parking lot, my truck was a spartan ox, austere, cumbersome and committed to utility.

More Modern Truckin'

Since 1965, I have owned, worked on, or tested an exorbitant number of trucks. As a recreationalist, truck fleet mechanic, heavy equipment operator, and automotive journalist, I've driven full-size trucks built by Jeep, International Harvester, Chevrolet, GMC, Ford, Dodge, and even Studebaker.

In retrospect, one of my favorite models was Ford's first effort at a modern light truck. In 1968, the Muscle Era infected my truck tastes, and I bought a 1955 F-100 pickup. The truck had a yellow re-paint, a rough orange peel finish that barely covered the stock green color. Already high in mileage, the short bed F-100 was free of rust with a very straight body.

Beneath the hood was a smaller Y-block V-8, the 256 odd-ball that few know existed. Originating with the '54 Mercury car line, the 256 shared features with the later passenger car 272, 292 and 312 V-8s. As the 256 OHV V-8 was a relative to Y-block muscle engines like the Thunderbird Special 312 V-8, I was certain that this two-barrel carbureted engine could stand some hopping up.

I worked for Grand Auto Stores in Oakland, California at the time, and a wrecking yard on East 14th near San Leandro had a set of the famous ECZ casting cylinder

heads from a '57 312 engine. In my optimistic view, the 312 heads were just what a mediocre utility engine needed. Huge intake and exhaust valves, intended to keep a 300-horse 312 breathing, would surely help the '55 pickup keep up with the Hayward Strip's muscle machines on Friday night!

Fig. 3-3. *The Y-block V-8s share many features. For '57 Thunderbirds, a supercharged version of the 312 rated 300 horsepower. My first F-100 had a two-barrel 256 V-8, and many parts interchanged with the more popular 272, 292 and 312 engines.*

Once installed, the heads complemented the truck's light curb weight and left impressive patches of rubber on the pavement. Intoxicating like a child's new toy, the high mileage engine got pounded like a '57 Ford 312-powered NHRA championship drag car. Over fueled, seeping coolant, and over tired, the 256 soon ran itself to death, and I learned how raising compression can ruin an old and weary engine.

In subsequent years, the '55 F-100 served as every possible object lesson. I changed engine types several times, tried three different transmission approaches and altered the wheel and tire scheme in so many ways that I eventually replaced a full set of worn lug studs.

Ultimately, the lesson was clear and simple: Ford trucks, built tough, deliver great service when driven wisely and maintained in accord with factory engineering and service guidelines. In its final stage of refinement, the F-100 featured a complete restoration to OEM standards and was then preserved on a fastidious preventive maintenance schedule.

Today, keeping your Ford F-truck alive and operating well is as important as ever. Foremost is the use of original equipment quality replacement parts and regular, preventive-type maintenance. Such an approach will help the powertrain and chassis deliver maximum service and also preserve your truck's value.

Equally important, the ways in which you use and operate your Ford F-truck will determine the degree and quality of service. I believe that true "lemons" are virtually non-existent among Ford trucks, although any production vehicle can require warranty repairs—or even a recall for potential safety hazards. Overall, a quality new or used Ford F-Series light truck can deliver tremendous value in a multitude of capacities.

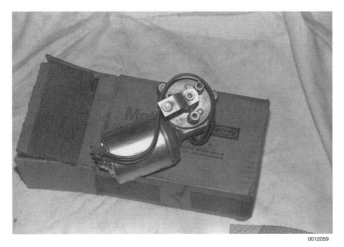

Fig. 3-4. *Use of OEM quality replacement parts is one assurance that your Ford F-Series truck will deliver maximum performance over a long service life.*

F-Series Trucks And Your Lifestyle

Two- or four-wheel drive trucks complement an active lifestyle. Individually suited for family recreation, foul weather security, and off-pavement chores, Ford F-truck models have special talents. Worked within their broad design limits, the powertrain and chassis can deliver many years of dependable service.

In our family, the children have grown up with various pickups and sport utility vehicles. 4x4s have been the family's access to hunting, fishing, hiking, firewood and some of North America's most rugged and picturesque back country. As a local Search-and-Rescue volunteer, my 4x4 vehicles double at service to the community.

Trucks hold a special place in our household. As a source of recreation and cornerstone for wholesome family fun and community involvement, four-wheel-drive trucks have served us particularly well. Any Ford truck, whether a new or good used model, can provide you and your family with a rich outdoor life and year around motoring safety.

1. LEARNING TO DRIVE YOUR F-SERIES TRUCK

Although technology has changed both the appearance and creature comfort levels of F-trucks, operating techniques remain much the same. Especially with 4x4 models, irregular road surfaces always pose a challenge. Although knowing your Ford's equipment and controls proves important, understanding the truck's handling characteristics is an even greater concern.

Light trucks, designed to carry a cargo, generally suffer from poor weight distribution. Running empty, the back end of your truck may feel loose and unpredictable in its handling, especially on icy, wet or muddy roads. Fortunately for F-Series trucks, the overall curb weight is high, which offsets these liabilities to a degree.

If your truck handles strangely, first rule out any chassis-mechanical or tire related problems. (See the service

chapters of the book for details.) You may find the root of your concern by running the vehicle over a set of truck scales that weigh each axle's load separately. Note the weight distribution.

Fig. 3-5. *A higher center-of-gravity and stiff spring rates characterize most light trucks. With the bed empty, weight bias shifts toward the front, leaving a lightened rear end susceptible to spinout on icy, off-camber highways. Under such road conditions, the rear axle can slip sideways and start the spin. Without a cargo, positive traction rear differentials exaggerate side-slip tendencies.*

Since light weight at the back of your truck can become trouble, many F-truck owners install a shell (cap or canopy) or permanently store useful items in the bed. A tool box is another method of adding ballast to better distribute weight.

During winter months, some owners carry an extra load in the bed, items like snow chains or even sacks of aggregate rock laid above or rearward of the axle. A heavy step rear bumper also helps. Late model F-trucks have anti-lock rear brakes, which dramatically reduce the risk of spinout and dangerous loss of directional stability when braking hard with a light load. Beyond this, you need to familiarize yourself with the handling characteristics of the truck.

Not A Mustang GT

Driving a full-size F-Series truck can be fun. However, truck and car handling differs dramatically in the areas of center-of-gravity, weight distribution and suspension responsiveness. As a result, your truck cannot respond or handle like a well tuned car suspension.

CHAPTER 3

The need to carry a substantial cargo over rough roads, which requires a relatively long wheelbase, means that truck bodies ride higher than a car. With the body mounted above a driveable chassis (ladder frame), the cab and bed set considerably taller than a car. For ground clearance and wheel travel, the frame rides higher than a car frame.

Fig. 3-6. *Compared to a Mustang GT, F-150 pickup has a robust chassis and much stouter components. In a tight corner, however, Mustang squats low and hugs the road. Higher center-of-gravity, stiffer springs and tall chassis height give the truck an unfair disadvantage. 4x4s ride even higher than 2WD truck models.*

Larger diameter tires, a higher frame and body height, and a powertrain that rides further above the ground mean that an F-Series truck has a higher center-of-gravity. In simple terms, this translates as more vulnerability to roll over, although the F-truck's relatively wide track width offsets risk to a degree.

Coupled with the higher center-of-gravity is a spring package designed for a cargo hauler. The high load capacity means that the truck's springs are stiffer than a car, especially when the truck has no cargo. As a consequence, trucks respond much differently on corners. Simply put, on any comparison point you choose—cornering ability, resistance to roll over, likelihood of spinout, ability to drift, lateral force reaction—trucks handle differently than cars.

Moreover, a given truck will even handle differently when loaded or unloaded. Be aware of these factors when orienting yourself to a light truck. When you can predict the handling of your truck under a wide variety of driving circumstances, loads and tire types, you will find comfort in the fact that a Ford F-truck can be as stable as any other truck in its class.

Two- Vs. Four-wheel Drive

Two- and four-wheel drive trucks also handle differently. The 4x4 F-trucks ride higher than comparable 2WD models, with a higher center-of-gravity and even more awkward weight distribution. The front wheel drive system places additional weight forward of the truck's mid-

line, while the need for ground clearance demands a taller ride height.

Older 4x4s have very high ride heights, and these trucks, naturally, are more susceptible to handling quirks and roll over. Models like the pre-'78 high-boy F-250 4x4s or a '64 and earlier F-100 4x4 epitomize the high center-of-gravity issue in 4x4 trucks. For these models, an increase in track width can, to a degree, offset an obvious safety risk. (See chapters on suspension modifications and tire/wheel changes.)

Another concern is the use of a tall cabover-type camper. Later Camper Special packages increase spring rates, add axle capacity and even provide necessary stabilizer bars for handling the extra load. Cabover campers radically alter the roll center and center-of-gravity of a truck, and safety equipment is a must.

If you decide that a cabover camper is a necessity, use caution when driving with a full load. Allow adequate stopping distances, take corners at reasonable speeds and observe road conditions. Avoid crisis situations that demand fast moves—such maneuvers could end in a roll over. (See suspension and accessories chapters for tips on trailering or hauling heavy cargo and a camper.)

Whether your F-truck has two- or four-wheel drive, the driving techniques for four-wheeling can help any truck operator. For this reason, I have devoted the balance of the current chapter to 4x4 and off-pavement driving concerns. Owners of two-wheel drive trucks will find much of this information relevant.

Operating A 4x4 F-Truck

The main difference between a 4x4 truck and a rear drive two-wheel drive truck or automobile is the live front axle and transfer case; a 4x4 truck's transmission and transfer case have separate shift levers. The 4x4 transfer case usually provides modes for high range, low range and two- or four-wheel drive.

Since 1959, manually shifted Ford 4x4s have utilized a single lever transfer case. Some late models offer electronic shift control switches. Most F-100 4x4s built from 1965–

Fig. 3-7. *'66 Ford F-250 4x4 is a classic truck from the era of high-boy 4x4s. Note tall frame height and low hanging transfer case. In late 1977, Ford lowered the F-250 4x4 with a modified chassis design and reverse arch, progressively rated (tapered) front leaf springs.*

76 featured a one-speed power divider instead of a two-speed transfer case. 4x4 F-250s have always offered high and low range 4WD modes.

The single-stick transfer case control modes include 2WD high, 4WD high, neutral and 4WD low ranges. Neutral mode on earlier units can operate a Power Take Off (PTO) component of the transfer case. 1970s models equipped with the NP203 full-time 4x4 system offer 4WD high, 4WD low, 4-high-lock and 4-low-lock modes to serve various driving conditions.

For safety sake and powertrain survival, consult your Ford F-Series truck owner's handbook or the 4WD instruction decal located in the cab for directions on operating the four-wheel drive system. This is a complex gear mechanism with very expensive components.

Two-wheel drive high range is much like driving a comparable two-wheel drive Ford truck. Power flows only to the rear axle, and the transfer case operates at a 1:1 ratio. The rear driveshaft spins at the same speed as the transmission output shaft.

In 4WD high or high-lock range, both the front and rear driveshafts spin at the same speed as the transmission output shaft. High range 2WD is useful for hard surface highways and most civilized driving conditions. In high range, the front and rear drive axle gear ratios determine the overall gear reduction.

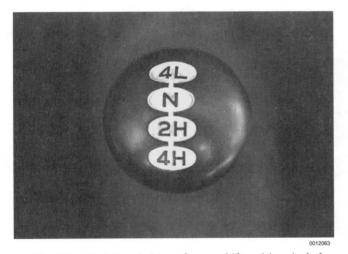

Fig. 3-8. *Part-time 4x4 transfer case shift positions include 2-High, 4-High, Neutral, 4-Low. (Shift patterns may vary or your late truck might use electronic controls with manual dash mounted switches.) Become familiar with these modes and their locations. For safety sake, be able to shift into any position without looking at the floorboard or knob.*

When in four-wheel drive high range, your truck offers substantially better traction, with the front axle pulling while the rear axle pushes the truck. 4x4 powertrains, with the exception of full-time 4x4 systems in non-lock mode, cannot tolerate four-wheel drive use on hard surfaced roads. On these surfaces, front axle pull and rear axle push will not take place in full synchronization, and the result is gear bind. This condition, characterized by a frozen transfer case lever or free-wheeling hubs, can damage the powertrain. (A differential within the transfer case of the full-time 4x4 units prevents gear bind.)

Front axle engagement on hard surfaced roads also affects steering. The axle shafts transmit torque, which jacks the steering assemblies as the front wheels strive for traction. On a loose surface road, these problems are seldom noticeable. Dirt, snow, mud or ice provide a margin of slip for safe four-wheel drive operation.

All Ford F-trucks with part-time 4x4 have a two-wheel drive mode for running on hard surfaces. Preserving your powertrain means using four-wheel drive only when the road surface will allow some degree of slip. This also limits use of 4WD low range to ice, snow, mud and off-pavement surfaces.

On steep pavement pulls like a boat ramp, I will use 4x4 mode as a means of safely moving the trailer. Since the pull is straight, risk of gear bind is minimal. At the top of the ramp, on flat ground, you can relieve bind by rocking the truck gently forward and back as you shift the transmission from reverse to drive (forward gear) and then neutral. With the transmission in neutral ("Park" mode with an automatic), move the transfer case shifter to 2WD mode, then turn hubs to FREE.

Free-wheeling Front Hubs

Most Ford 4x4 F-trucks spend the majority of their service life on the highway or well graded gravel roads. The front axle assembly on a part-time 4x4 system seldom sees use. Here, free-wheeling hubs can reduce wear at the front axle shafts, U-joints and the differential assembly.

Fig. 3-9. *During foul weather, leaving hubs in LOCK mode with the transfer case in 2WD will permit easy engagement of 4WD high range as road conditions worsen. On occasion, engaging the free-wheeling hubs for a few miles is actually valuable. This will keep seals from becoming brittle and reduces risk of condensation damage in the axle housing.*

The first Ford factory 4x4s came without free-wheeling hubs, and unless the dealer or owner installed aftermarket hubs, the front axle shafts and differential spun and created fuel-robbing drag for the life of the truck. Now a common component on 4x4s, free-wheeling hubs reduce parts wear and increase fuel economy. If your truck has free-wheeling hubs, use FREE mode while in two-wheel drive for sustained periods.

In the early 1980s, many truck models introduced the use of automatic locking hubs that engage when you shift

CHAPTER 3

to 4WD mode. As the torque flows to each front wheel, the hub assembly has an internal clutch mechanism that automatically locks the hub. In this mode, the hub functions much like a conventional (manual) hub in LOCK position. An exception is those automatic hub designs that fail to provide compression braking and simply free wheel on downgrades.

Although automatic locking hubs eliminate the need for manual operation, they do require backing up the truck to disengage the lock mechanisms. When road conditions once again permit use of 2WD mode, you must stop the truck, make sure the transfer case is in 2WD mode, then safely back the truck up (usually fifteen feet) to disengage the automatic hubs.

Shifting A 4WD Transfer Case

During intermittent icy highway conditions, you can leave your manual or automatic locking hubs in lock mode. During stretches of hard-surfaced road, simply shift out of front axle drive mode (4WD) with the transfer case lever. When the mountain pass or snow zone is past, stop the truck, make certain the transfer case is in 2WD mode, and either manually unlock your front hubs or, if equipped with automatic locking hubs, safely back your truck up about fifteen feet to free the hubs.

Some later model transfer cases boast shift-on-the-fly. These gear units allow the operator to move from 2WD high to 4WD high without effort. Under no circumstance, however, can you shift any transfer case to low range without stopping the vehicle. Although some transfer cases will tolerate engagement of low range gears at a very low vehicle speed, the safest method of low range engagement is at a complete stop.

WARNING —
When you downshift between transmission gears in low range, slow down first. The low range gear reduction will exaggerate the speed drop between gears. The result is like slamming on the brakes.

For engaging the front axle drive at any speed, you will find that unloading torque from the gears helps ease the shift. If your truck has a manual transmission, you can leave the transmission in gear and momentarily depress the clutch pedal. Move the transfer case lever from 2WD high to 4WD high as if you were shifting gears in the transmission. For automatic transmission models, leave the transmission in drive range, but release the throttle as you pull the transfer case lever from 2WD to 4WD high range.

Consult your Ford truck owner's handbook or the instructional decals before engaging low range 4WD. An automatic transmission may require placing the transmission in neutral or park range before you move the transfer case lever to 4WD Low Range. Otherwise, the transmission will spin the gears at speed as the transfer case shift lever passes through its Neutral mode. Severely abusive gear clash will result if you attempt to engage the low range gears while the transfer case input shaft is spinning at speed.

When To Use Four-wheel Drive

Faced with the perils of sleet and dropping temperatures, owners appreciate their 4x4 trucks. When the highway surface is wet, temperatures continue to drop, and it's still a few degrees above treacherous black ice, the time is right to lock your manual hubs.

Early readiness is your best hedge against trouble. Lock your hubs before visibility decreases and traffic begins to stagger. Leaving the pavement when the visibility worsens could cause a collision. The driver of the next vehicle might see your brake lamps, mistake your motive for leaving the road and over react by making a dangerous move.

If the weather clearly calls for ice and snow, lock your manual hubs before you leave home. You can drive for many miles with the hubs locked and the transfer case in 2WD high range without damaging the front axle system.

With hubs locked, you can engage 4WD high range while moving. As highway conditions worsen, or if a stretch of ice lies ahead, engage 4WD and stay in this mode until you pass the hazard. At that point, simply shift the transfer case lever back to 2WD high mode. You'll likely repeat this procedure several times on long stretches of intermittent ice, snow and dry pavement.

If a dry, straight section of pavement lasts for a very short spell (1/8th mile or less), I leave the transfer case in 4WD mode, stay very light on the throttle to reduce torque application and work the steering carefully. When the road is straight, geartrain stress and risk of binding are minimal. I believe that under these conditions, shifting the transfer case in and out of 4WD places far more strain on components and creates unnecessary demands for the driver.

2. OFF-PAVEMENT FOUR-WHEEL DRIVE

When the pavement ends and the dirt begins, consider your truck's traction needs. Since a softer roadway allows some slip and eliminates the risk of gear bind, it's wise to engage your hubs, whether you're using 4WD mode or not. Spinning the front axle system places a light load on the powertrain, while the benefit of locking the hubs is that four-wheel drive is available at the flip of the transfer case lever.

Commonly, before entering a gravel trail, four-wheelers will lock the hubs and drop tire pressures for increased traction and to lessen chassis bounce on irregular road surfaces. Lowered tire pressures can also reduce risk of tread and sidewall damage from rocks.

Many four-wheelers, however, get carried away with airing down tires. Each tire design and vehicle load has a minimum safe inflation pressure. Lower pressures also increase the risk of unseating the bead. Unseating a bead or driving with severe sidewall flexing can ruin your expensive tires or cause tire failure and loss of control.

My rough guideline for airing down is that a tire with a 32–35 psi maximum load pressure will tolerate no lower than 22–24 psi pressure, and this for only short distances at slow speeds. As pressure drops, so does a tire's load capacity. You trade greater traction for higher heat buildup and more risk of tire fatigue and failure. (See tire details in other chapters.)

0012065

Fig. 3-10. *Airing down is common vernacular for off-pavement trail runners. While ride and traction improve, airing down reduces load carrying capacity. Dropping pressures to run in sand makes sense. Always air back up to normal when you've passed the hazards. Re-check pressures when tires are cold. (See chapter on tires.)*

Concentrate on good driving habits and minimize your wheelspin. Wheelspin loses traction, places tires at risk and can cause environmental damage. Good driving techniques will take your truck much further than excessively low tire pressures.

The number one cause of environmental damage, and the surest sign of an inexperienced four-wheeler, is unnecessary tire spin. Your best traction is a tire tread surface that makes full contact with the road. You can minimize wheelspin by reducing throttle pressure or shifting to a higher gear in the transmission. This will apply less torque to the wheels and lessen the likelihood of tire spin.

> **WARNING —**
>
> *A spinning tire is dangerous. General Tire suggests, "AVOID excessive tire spinning when your vehicle is stuck in snow, mud or sand. Never exceed 35 mph indicated on the speedometer. The centrifugal forces generated by a free spinning tire/wheel assembly may cause a sudden tire explosion resulting in vehicle damage and/or serious personal injury. Use a gentle backward and forward rocking motion to free your vehicle for continued driving. Never stand near or behind a tire spinning at high speed while attempting to push a vehicle that is stuck."*

The Terrain

Terrain dictates when to use four-wheel drive. Experience teaches that it's always better to engage 4WD before entering a hazard than once you commit your truck. Negotiating mud and snow requires steady pulling traction, and stopping in the middle of a muddy trail courts disaster. Trying to regain traction can result in spinning tires and damage to a fragile environment. Wherever possible, keep moving while minimizing tire spin and chassis bounce.

The Steepest Hills

If the trail gets rocky or steep and your truck begins bouncing, it's time for low range. Low range will reduce throttle effort and drastically lower the vehicle's speed. The gear reduction in low range will allow your vehicle to idle through rocky or rough stretches.

In 4WD high range, your truck might idle at 3 to 5 mph in first gear. Placing the transfer case in low range drops speed to nearly one mile per hour. This allows far more control of the truck and reduces risk of damage. Low range stopping and starting is also simpler, especially on inclines. Use of lighter throttle pressure and less braking action reduce risk of wheelspin or dangerous skidding.

When top speed on a rough trail is 10 to 20 miles per hour, I place the transfer case in low range 4WD and leave it there. This allows use of all forward transmission gears to keep up with the crowd and also provides crawl speeds and excellent compression braking for moving slowly through rocky obstacles. This is the key to safety and a long service life for your truck.

Low range is a valuable braking mechanism. When facing a very steep decline, select the transmission gear that will control your truck's speed. Always minimize the use of wheel brakes on slick or poor traction surfaces. If a wheel(s) lock up with application of the brakes (which they do readily on ice or sand covered granite boulders), skidding will result.

The best traction is a tire that continues to rotate. At the slowest imaginable speeds, in low range first gear, your 4x4 truck's tires can still provide traction over the entire area of the tread surface. If possible, avoid skidding. Keep your tires rotating under engine compression braking to provide the highest traction.

The reduction ratio of low range also provides exceptional pulling power. Assuming that your truck can get traction, 4WD low range will permit even the most modestly powered six-cylinder 4x4 F-model, which by itself weighs 4000 or more pounds, to move a stalled 8000 lb. flatbed truck! Freeing another vehicle from a ditch can easily be performed if your 4x4 can get traction.

If you need to move a heavy vehicle for more than a few feet, avoid using 4WD lock mode on a hard surfaced road. Never hook the chain or strap to a trailer ball, driveshaft, spring hanger, steering components or an axle housing that has brake pipes or hoses running along its surface.

There are many situations where four-wheeling is unsafe or will cause damage to the environment. When your 4x4 truck totters on the edge of disaster, winching is far more practical than driving. A properly angled winch cable can function as both the motive force and a safety anchor for your delicately balanced truck. If losing traction means poor vehicle control, use a winch. (See winching instructions in the accessories chapter.)

Uphill and Downhill

Negotiating steep hills causes more adrenaline flow than any other four-wheel drive maneuver. Angles, especially downslopes, appear distorted and ominous. This is just as well, as the real threat of losing control on a descent deserves all of your attention. When going uphill in four wheel drive, the front wheels claw for traction and tend to pull your truck into line. Downward, these same wheels want to skid, slip sideways and search awkwardly for traction.

Fig. 3-11. When approaching an uphill section or downslope, line the truck up squarely and avoid driving sideways across the hill. Driving sideways on a slope is a roll over about to happen. Stay straight and move steadily.

On ascents, minimize wheelspin. When descending, use the correct gear to minimize skidding and the need to apply your truck's brakes. Moderation has never had a better mentor than four-wheeling.

In rough and angled terrain, excess movement courts disaster. Oversteering and understeering can cross the vehicle up at just the wrong moment. On both ascents and descents, if your truck loses directional stability, the risk of roll over increases.

> **WARNING —**
> • *Never drive sideways across a hill. If side tilt overcomes your truck's roll center and center-of-gravity, the vehicle is likely to turn over.*
>
> • *If your 4x4 turns completely sideways on a steep sideslope, prepare to roll over. Always wear a seatbelt/harness and install a full roll cage if you intend to climb risky slopes. If you must get out of the vehicle, do so only on the uphill side.*

If you find your truck beginning to turn sideways on a loose traction downslope, keep your foot off the brake pedal. Steer into the skid, as if the vehicle were on ice or snow. If safe and timely, accelerate very gently to pull the vehicle straight. Either of these techniques require nerves of steel, acute sensitivity and your conviction that the truck cannot straighten out any other way.

Hair-raising Hill Climb Techniques

During the Sixties, four-wheeling competitive events became popular. Organized hill climbs attracted large crowds, and the winning formula was traction, torque and solid driving skill. Typically, a 4x4 needed enough muscle to claw its way up a rocky shale slope. Exotic traction tires and axle locking devices increased the chances of a win. Here, many of us learned the finer points of high-horsepower traction.

Most hill climb courses were remarkably steep. In some of my archival photos from that era, course judges stand with one leg a foot and a half higher than the other, leaning into the hillside to stay upright. Walking these hills was nearly impossible. Most slopes were simply crude cuts made by a D-8 Caterpillar tractor at its maximum approach angle. Some courses were even more primitive.

Modified short wheelbase Jeeps, Scouts, early Broncos and an occasional 4x4 pickup screamed at redline as they charged the hill. The winner was the truck in each class (four-cylinder, six-cylinder or V-8) that reached the highest point on the hill.

Axles, clawing through paddle tires and spinning mercilessly, grabbed what meager traction the rocky hillside could furnish. Judges leaped out of the path of airborne 4x4s that left the ground under full power, landing forty feet off the course with their nose ends still aimed uphill. Often, with the engine throttled wide open as the tires bit, the frame jerked into line, gaining the truck an even greater height on the hill.

The risk of getting sideways was extreme. Of all the driving techniques I gleaned from hill climbs, the most significant was how to maintain control of a 4x4 that loses traction while climbing a steep slope. The trick is a rapid shift to reverse gear before backing down, then descending under compression braking while avoiding the use of hydraulic wheel brakes.

Fig. 3-12. Competitive hill climbs and sand drags demand nerves of steel and lightning reflexes. High horsepower drag racing in loose sand requires four-wheel drive. At Sand Lake, Oregon, Eda Ward wins another victory with "Orange Crate."

This is a critical maneuver that demands quick hands and feet. As soon as the truck reaches its furthest point on the hill and traction becomes futile, you must depress the clutch pedal quickly, simultaneously shift the transmission to reverse and release the clutch pedal before the truck starts to roll backward.

Timing is all important. If you miss reverse and the transmission is in neutral, you will roll backward out of control. (The non-synchromesh reverse gear in a manual transmission will not permit a shift to reverse with the truck moving.) Stuck in neutral, the only option is to use the brakes. Applied on a steep and loose slope, the brakes want to lock the wheels, which usually throws the truck into a skid, then sideways into a roll over.

The important steps are to: 1) shift your manual transmission to reverse just as the truck peaks its forward momentum, 2) release the clutch pedal immediately and steer straight backward with the engine idling, and 3) rely on engine compression braking with minimal, if any, application of the wheel brakes. These steps must take place in rapid succession, and if your coordination and the engine tune is right, the truck's engine should keep the tires creeping in reverse.

WARNING —

Competitive 4x4 hill climbing is a hazardous sport. Damage to your vehicle and personal injury are real possibilities. Like other forms of competition, rules and safety regulations apply. Never attempt these competitive maneuvers without the benefit of a full roll cage, approved safety equipment, emergency medical personnel, close supervision and full acceptance of the risks involved.

Pitfalls Of an Automatic Transmission

4x4 hill climbs place trucks with automatic transmissions at a disadvantage. Although a torque converter helps multiply torque for successful hill and sand assaults, backing down slopes with an automatic in reverse can prove hazardous. With the engine idling or stalled, the torque converter slips, acting much like neutral. This encourages use of the brakes as vehicle speed increases, and that's when trouble begins. The wheels can lock, and when the tires skid, the truck may turn sideways and roll over.

An automatic transmission has many advantages, including good throttle control and torque application in sand, predictable pulling in mud and tremendous torque for going up reasonable hills that don't require backing down. If, however, your plans include negotiating serious downslopes under compression or backing down hills in reverse, consider the superior control of a manual transmission and clutch.

Low Environmental Impact

The popularity of four-wheeling has an effect on the environment. TREAD LIGHTLY, Inc. and other organizations encourage low impact four-wheeling and respectful use of public lands. Although the concept is new to some recreationalists, many of us have been treading lightly for decades.

In the summer of 1964, I attended Nevada Range Camp, a 4-H/USDA Extension Service project for high school students. Fifteen miles south of U.S. Highway 50 near Austin, Nevada, our base was the Reese River Valley at Big Creek. We studied erosion and soil conservation, witnessed the planting of wild wheat over a vast semi-

Tread Lightly Four Wheeling

Through the efforts of Clifford G. Blake, a U.S. Forest Service manager and advocate of multiple-use policy, TREAD LIGHTLY, Inc. became the first joint public/private sector venture aimed at wise recreational use of public lands.

As National Coordinator of the U.S. Forest Service Tread Lightly program, Cliff's vision encouraged the major manufacturers of motor vehicles and outdoor recreational equipment to take a direct role in serving consumers by promoting environmentally sound use of public lands.

Charter members of TREAD LIGHTLY, Inc., a non-profit organization, include domestic and import vehicle manufacturers, OHV and power sport equipment manufacturers, aftermarket component builders, the outdoor and four-wheel drive media, tire producers and a number of concerned groups, including the Izaak Walton League. I am a charter member and currently instruct TREAD LIGHTLY driving clinics throughout the U.S.

Ford Motor Company, a charter member of TREAD LIGHTLY, Inc., has been among the major contributors of funds. Jim Trainor with F-Series Truck Public Relations and other Ford staff have provided their valuable time and resources. The national TREAD LIGHTLY office also works closely with the U.S. Forest Service, the BLM and other agencies at promoting sensible multiple use of public lands. It is the aim of members to use, and not abuse, the environment.

As an OHV writer and recreationalist, I have joined with other concerned four-wheel drive enthusiasts in supporting TREAD LIGHTLY, Inc. Through education and low impact land use advocacy, TREAD LIGHTLY, Inc., helps preserve our access to trails that generations of four-wheeling families have enjoyed. As an active member, I encourage public land users to join TREAD LIGHTLY, Inc., and make a difference. (For membership information, phone 1-800-966-9900.)

The TREAD LIGHTLY Creed

T–ravel only where motorized vehicles are permitted. Never blaze your own trail.

R–espect the rights of hikers, skiers, campers, and others to enjoy their activities undisturbed.

E–ducate yourself by obtaining travel maps and regulations from public agencies, complying with signs and barriers and asking owner's permission to cross private property.

A–void streams, lakeshores, meadows, muddy roads and trails, steep hillsides, wildlife and livestock.

D–rive responsibly to protect the environment and preserve opportunities to enjoy your vehicle on public lands.

When it comes to trail etiquette, remember hikers and horses. Your truck kicks up dust, makes noise and raises terror in the eyes of unsuspecting people and horses. Show courtesy, slow down, pass with caution and be considerate. The only way we'll all maintain access to North America's grand and scenic outdoors is through sharing and cooperation. There's plenty of fun and land for everyone— and you know, sometimes it's fine to walk or hike.

Fig. 3-13. In a semi-arid high desert environment, we must vitally protect the land from soil erosion and loss of topsoil. Three decades ago, Nevada ranchers and Indians dealt severely with city slick recreationalists who made tire ruts in precious soil, tore up sagebrush, meandered from designated roads, chased cattle and knocked down stream banks.

Fig. 3-14. Should you cross? Not if there's a bridge nearby! Aware four-wheelers always take the easiest route, one that leaves the least impact on the land. There's plenty of opportunity for high adventure along primitive trails. Save your 4x4 truck for those places.

Fig. 3-15. Restore soil when you've been stuck. Treading lightly requires back filling holes to leave the path intact for future four-wheelers and other users.

arid mountain range, and learned about the fragile nature of desert environments.

If only the whole four-wheeling crowd could experience such a school. At the Reese River Reservation ranches, we learned firsthand how indigenous people apply their knowledge of the land to cattle ranching. Near our camp, we teased untamed fourteen-inch trout from a yardstick wide stream that feeds melted spring snow into the Reese River.

For my strong belief in low impact four-wheeling, I am indebted to Nevada ranchers, the Bureau of Land Management, the USDA/U.S. Forest Service and American Indians. Neither I nor any of my four-wheeling friends have torn up sagebrush, damaged stream eco-systems, left livestock gates open or blazed our own trails across a fragile landscape.

Beyond the few bad apples, many 4x4 truck owners simply have no knowledge of how to four-wheel. Unaware of either the natural environment or the dynamics of their four-wheel drive trucks, naive recreationalists can abuse both their expensive equipment and our land.

3. SPECIAL USES FOR YOUR 4WD TRUCK

Your F-Series 4WD truck can perform a multitude of useful chores. One of the most gratifying aspects of four-wheel drive trucks is their utility value and ability to serve the community. When hazardous weather strands motorists and emergency vehicles are the only stock still rolling, 4x4 trucks lead the way. You will greatly enrich your four-wheeling experience by helping other motorists. A 4x4 truck owner is duty bound to serve, much like a Canadian Royal Mounted Police officer.

Many 4x4 owners carry this responsibility further, joining local Search-and-Rescue (SAR) organizations. Likewise, most volunteer firefighters who live at rough climate zones own 4x4 trucks. When responsibilities demand readiness, regardless of weather conditions, a 4x4 truck serves best.

SAR Volunteerism

I am an SAR volunteer through our local 4WD club. In hazardous weather and during the summer months when campers flow into the Cascade Range for recreation, our telephones can ring at the wee hours. A number of us roll out of sound sleep and into our ready 4x4 trucks. I feel that this kind of volunteer work, wake-up calls for helping fellow human beings, epitomizes the worth of a four-wheel drive vehicle.

Here, a 4x4 truck serves best. On one occasion, we pulled a 4x4 pickup, with a fifth wheel trailer in tow, from a roadway covered by 18-inches of snow. A paved road, cleared to a point, had suddenly turned into a snow field. The driver continued, winding up 150 yards out in the slushy snow. Equipped with ham and CB radios, he called for help. We responded.

On another occasion, we searched for two 10-year-old boys who had ridden their bicycles into the Waldo Wilderness and couldn't find their way out. By two in the morning, both youngsters were safe in their families' campsites.

Typically, your local sheriff's department heads up SAR activities. If you have an interest in learning survival skills and acquiring the many tools necessary to effectively find and assist lost hikers, hunters, recreationalists and travelers, consider volunteering for SAR. The work is highly rewarding.

Snow Plowing and Other Utility Uses

Commercial users have always appreciated Ford 4x4 trucks. A front-mounted snowplow is a common accessory for parking lot owners, ski lodges and even private residences where steep driveways become a hazard during the winter months.

F-Series 4x4s are frequently seen on construction and mine sites, at American farms and ranches. In many of these environments, a 4x4 truck has become the standard vehicle, capable of moving heavy materials along remote and hazardous roads. For modern society, the 4x4 truck has effectively replaced our four-legged beasts of burden.

Some of the more popular accessories that have developed for industrial and agricultural uses of 4x4 trucks are PTO and electrically operated winches, posthole dig-

Fig. 3-16. *4WD trucks can be valuable emergency vehicles. Equipped with a C.B. radio, a winch, winch accessories, a Hi-Lift jack and a Max tool kit, your Ford F-truck can assist stranded motorists. If you enjoy community service and own a 4WD truck, consider joining a local Search-and-Rescue unit.*

gers, boom hoists, plows, harrow discs and auxiliary lighting. On-board welders can provide a complete repair shop at the most remote station. The shift toward recreational uses has made 4x4 F-trucks easier to drive and more comfortable, with factory and aftermarket accessories that enhance handling, increase stowage capacity, provide comfortable seating and personalize your truck to meet recreational needs.

Advanced Trail Running

Faced with temptation, a hill that rises into the pastel sky or a washed out trail that accesses a favorite fishing hole, my friend Al Herndon simply shrugs his shoulders and says, "You use two-wheel drive until you get stuck... Then you lock your hubs, shift into four-wheel drive, and back out!"

Sage advice, Al. Four-wheelers, however, often scorn such practicality. Sometimes Nature provides her very own surprises. Sand that appears hard packed suddenly swallows your 4WD truck to its frame. Your frozen tracks through a bog at dawn give no hint of the underlying mud soup that will churn like homemade butter by mid-morning. Last year's solid road, now ripped by torrential flooding and muddy rock slides, lies ahead—you still need to get through safely, with your cargo intact.

Wise four-wheelers all agree, the best route is the easiest one. Long before trails had fashionable difficulty classifications, experienced four-wheelers scanned hillsides, washes, streams, and rock piles, sizing up the terrain. A dozen mountaintops and desolate valleys from home, the challenge is to not get stuck. A C.B. radio and winch make essential traveling companions.

Plan your trip in advance. Read road and trail conditions on a map or call the local Forest Service or BLM office for road reports. Aside from getting stuck, the number one fear of all four wheelers, and justifiably so, is a roll over. Twisty, off-camber hillsides and slippery mountain trails have totalled many 4x4s. The best means for avoiding a roll over at some remote place is careful consideration of terrain.

Three conditions characterize most roll overs: 1) too much side angle, which overcomes the center-of-gravity and equilibrium; 2) a weight shift upsets equilibrium on an otherwise negotiable sideslope; or 3) exaggerated speed. This last point relates to off-camber side slopes, speeding around curves, or flirting with danger on casual 4x4 terrain by adding excess speed.

Unfortunately, many four-wheelers, especially newcomers to the art of off-pavement driving, confuse sport with speed. These two terms are not synonymous. Safe recreational trail driving is a far cry from desert racing. My friends Ivan "Ironman" Stewart and Rod Hall have each mastered fast desert travel on four wheels. Like other professional racers, however, they quickly discourage

0012072

Fig. 3-17. Lock your manual hubs and flip the transfer case lever into four-wheel drive before entering a water crossing. If in doubt about loose, slippery, or muddy terrain, always use four-wheel drive. Low range serves in rocky or dangerously steep terrain. Low range 4WD provides compression braking and far more control of the truck. Here's a typical place for 4WD low range and use of the lower transmission gears.

fast driving in uncertain environments, especially in a production type truck.

For most recreationalists, safe and methodical trail driving is challenging enough. This includes driving over rocky, slippery, sandy, snow-covered or mountainous terrain. The winning objective is to get your family, friends and 4x4s through tough trails in one piece.

Driving Through Sand Traps

Imagine a road, not just your ordinary fire road or graded gravel road, but a trail that winds through rugged high desert country. Ahead looms a sandy wash, likely a dry riverbed of deep, loose sand. In flood season, a race of water tears through the steep walled canyon, swirling around tall rocks that now bake under a summer sun....

Since the ancients first rotated stone wheels, the number one obstacle to travel has been sand. Granular, loose and deceptive, sand operates by its own rules. When monsoons or summer rains saturate the ground, sand can be hard, packed, and tractable. In dry weather, however, the same material defies even the best floatation tires.

For traveling loose sand, your best bet is steady forward momentum, while keeping wheelspin at a minimum. The slightest amount of traction loss and sand wins. Once wheels lose their grip, especially at both axles, disaster lurks.

Traveling in sand begins with basics. Lock your front hubs before entering the wash. Engage your four-wheel drive system, and if the load feels heavy, use low range. High floatation tires also make a difference in sand. (See chapter on tires and wheels.)

Moving forward, you can feel the traction and load by listening to the engine. When I was an apprentice heavy equipment operator, the older hands taught us that the cutting depth of a dozer or grader blade translated to various levels of tension at the seat of our pants! Maintain steady progress, and concentrate on constant throttle pressure and a firm control of the steering wheel.

If your engine coughs as you bump a smooth rock and the truck momentarily bogs, watch out! As the clutch engages or you bump the throttle, the truck is highly susceptible to tire spin. Too much throttle pressure now and your 4x4 could quickly become buried to the frame at the rear wheels and down to the springs at the front.

What now? If you're alone without a winch, the tool of choice is the multi-purpose (Handyman or Hi-Lift) type jack. These tall, industrial strength setups can be used for a variety of chores: pushing, pulling or lifting. In combination with a chain or cable, a multi-purpose jack can also serve as a come-along.

A hefty board is usually necessary for a firm jack foot. Jack up each wheel and safely back fill the holes with sand or rocks. Place pieces of brush beneath and in front of the tires. When you attempt to move the truck, avoid spinning the tires and apply power smoothly.

Fig. 3-18. Plan ahead! What was solid frozen ground in the morning may be impassable mud by the time you return in the afternoon.

4. 4WD CLUBS

As bats darted through the treetops, silhouetted by trailing twilight, our youngest son slept soundly in his bedroll. A pair of coyotes howled as my wife stared warily across the campfire. "Moses," she asked, "why do we persist in traveling alone? Isn't there some way to have four-wheel drive fun without mimicking a Paleolithic vision quest?"

Why Go It Alone?

Group travel on a 4x4 run into the wilderness can provide more resources and the safety of numbers. Aside from safer passage, traveling as a group adds several other benefits: social activities, fun sporting activities and a place to build life-long friendships with those who share your appreciation for outdoor recreation. Additionally, local, state, and national 4x4 groups serve as lobbyists for access to public recreational lands.

My wife, Donna, is a prolific reader who often shoves clippings and news briefs under my nose. "Look at this copy of *IN GEAR* that you grabbed at the SCORE Show. Every off-road thing that we're interested in doing is covered here!" she exclaimed, rifling through California Association of 4WD Clubs' monthly publication. "The calendar of events lists several of the runs and family outings that we've talked about."

CA4WDC's *IN GEAR* and publications like *United's Voice*, printed quarterly by United Four-Wheel Drive Associations (UFWDA), brim with calendar events and reports of 4x4 club activities throughout the United States and Canada. These and other four-wheel drive publications can broaden your 4WD contacts.

Regional publications include activities suited to entire families, off road survival tips, equipment ads, vehicle classifieds, accounts of trail rides, poker runs, 4x4 breakfast runs and group barbecues. A calendar of fundraising benefits, public interest projects, social functions and future runs can help members organize free time.

How To Find A 4WD Club

For newcomers to four-wheeling, clubs are an ideal way to learn safe driving skills and how to tread lightly on the land. Regional sanctioning associations promote family recreation, publish newsletters and encourage clubs to protect trails and sponsor local activities.

If four-wheeling with a group of outdoor enthusiasts sounds like your kind of good time, contact the nearest state or regional association of 4x4 clubs. The better organized local clubs usually belong to regional and national sanctioning bodies.

The umbrella over all regional, state and locally sanctioned clubs is United Four-Wheel Drive Associations (UFWDA). UFWDA can provide guidelines for forming your own four-wheel drive group or provide referrals to regional associations and local clubs.

There are liabilities that accompany any vehicle owners' association. If you plan to form a local club, charters and by-laws should follow established guidelines. State and regional associations or UFWDA can furnish advice.

Anatomy Of A Club Run

Sponsored by the Central District of CA4WDC, the Molina Ghost Run near Coalinga, California draws folks from as far away as Nevada and Oregon. Local legends and mining lore encourage a "Fright Night" headlamp run on opening night each year.

Most four-wheelers enter the dry camp (situated just below New Idria and halfway between Hernandez Reservoir and Coalinga) by way of Los Gatos Road. Some drive from the Highway 101 side of the mountains, winding down from Hollister, California.

Those arriving early enough on Friday can join the Fright Night trek through the surrounding hills. Hundreds of participants arrive late Friday, setting up their camps after registering. Motorhomes and camper pickups serve as tow vehicles for shorter wheelbase Jeep, Landcruiser, Bronco and Scout 4x4s. For tight and twisty trail running, these shorter models hold an edge. 4x4 pickups do well on the poker run and other daylight trails.

Friday night, as the dry camp fills, a live band plays. Most avoid partying, though, preferring to prepare for the post-dawn run on Saturday morning. Sleep will be elusive, as a steady flow of late arrivals rumble noisily into camp until the wee hours.

Saturday morning, staff lines the registered vehicles up for the day run. A poker game ensues en route. Each checkpoint provides a playing card, and drivers build a poker hand as the run proceeds. A huge procession of vehicles eventually snakes the hills, while everyone shares in a spectacular view and the excitement of the trail.

As scenes from higher peaks reveal a breathtaking California spring landscape, participants unwind. The Molina Run's main attraction is the Saturday tour through the hills west of the San Joaquin Valley. These same hills inspired the early California settlers and, in the Twentieth Century, the pioneering prose of John Steinbeck. Tall grass and brush sweep the region from February through April. Traditionally, the Molina Run takes place in mid-March.

CHAPTER 3

As the sky darkens, the last vehicles return to camp, their occupants ready for the best tasting dinner a herd of trail beaten and hungry four wheelers can imagine. Steak, beans, corn-on-the-cob, rolls, Haagen Daz ice cream and hot or cold beverages put smiles on everyone's face.

CA4WDC's Central District chefs and staff spend the whole day preparing this meal, and it shows. The hoard of altitude-teased appetites appreciate the effort. CA4WDC volunteers serve selflessly to assure the success of the Molina event. Certainly, anyone who's eaten a Molina Run barbecue dinner, or the hot eggs and sausage on Sunday morning, has gone home happy.

Saturday night is sheer fun and relaxation. After a long trip to reach Molina and pounding the hills all day, four wheelers are ready for the live band. With liquor sanctions lifted for the evening, many adults imbibe the spirits, yet everyone follows the rules faithfully: NO DRINKING AND DRIVING ALLOWED! Most dance and enjoy the music, then meander back to their campsites, where campfire tales provide the late night entertainment.

Sunday breakfast precedes a vehicle show and the 4x4 Trials Competition. The trials event is new to West Coast four wheelers and has begun to attract a following through the efforts of the Molina Run staff. (See appendix for more information on 4x4 trials.) Central District folks see that everyone remembers these contests, presenting the winners with impressive trophies.

Fig. 3-19. *How do you feed 600 hungry four-wheelers? In style! CA4WDC/Central District clubs serve steak, corn on the cob, chili, beverages and—What? Haagen Daz ice cream in a dry camp? Now that's roughin' it.*

The Molina Run takes all ages into consideration. Each participant, including the smaller children, has plenty of fun. New friendships develop, campfire camaraderie runs high and next year's event becomes the main topic of discussion before the weekend winds to an end.

Chapter 4

Working on Your F-Series Truck

Y OU WILL FIND YOUR FORD F-SERIES TRUCK easy to service. Quick access to components and sub-assemblies helps simplify routine maintenance, while a light truck's utilitarian design makes field fixes possible. Many owners learn the basics of automotive repair by working on their truck.

All F-Series light truck models feature a relatively uncomplicated chassis, a conventional powertrain layout and familiar accessory sub-assemblies. Although 1971–up trucks have more engine emission controls and power options, the chassis and powertrains remain easy to identify.

Since the early 1980s, the introduction of automatic and manual overdrive transmissions, plus changes in the automotive industry's methods of complying with EPA and CAFE standards, has widened F-truck engine and geartrain distinctions.

Light truck emission control requirements have always fit particular GVWR categories. Tiers include trucks up to 6,000 pounds GVWR (light duty emissions), 6,001–8,500 pounds GVWR, trucks between 8,501–10,000 pounds GVWR (heavy duty emissions) and trucks over 10,000 pounds. Over the years, the 6,001–8,500 pound GVWR category has bounced between light and heavy duty emission control requirements.

As these categories and regulations change continually, your main concern is requirements for your particular year and model engine and chassis. When ordering replacement parts, the GVWR, vehicle identification number and the information on the underhood emission decal are each significant.

The decal notes the engine type, family and whether 49-State (Federal) or 50-State (California) requirements apply. California engines, although typically demanding more emission controls than federal engines, must also comply with EPA/Federal emission standards. Emission equipment is summarized on the decal.

0012076

Fig. 4-1. A conventional ladder-type frame has assured Ford F-Series truck stamina. Often described as a "driveable chassis" design, a rugged ladder frame can support the suspension, body and powertrain.

47

1. THE F-TRUCK CHASSIS

The Ford light F-truck ladder frame chassis covered within these service chapters fit into six categories:

1. I-beam front axle models with leaf springs: 1948–64 2WD, plus the '65–'66 F-350
2. Twin I-beam models with coil front springs: 1965–up 2WD
3. Mono-beam or solid front drive axle models with leaf front springs: 1959 and newer 4WD
4. Solid front axle models with coil front springs: 1965–79
5. Twin Traction-Beam front drive axle models with coil springs: 1980 and newer
6. Twin Traction-Beam front drive axle models with leaf front springs: 1980 and newer

To date, all Ford F-trucks feature semi-elliptic leaf rear springs. Front spring designs change from traditional semi-elliptic leaf type to either coil springs (beginning in 1965) or reverse arch tapered/progressive rate leaf type (4WD models only) beginning with late 1977 F-250 4x4s.

Commonly described as a driveable chassis, the Ford truck's ladder frame has several advantages. As with other full-size American trucks, these strong chassis help off-set the effects of body rust and fatigue. A restorer will often replace the entire cab of a rusted '53–'56 F-100 yet find the vintage frame intact and fully functional.

From a service standpoint, the ladder frame requires little maintenance. Support members, such as spring and shock absorber anchor mounts, attach solidly to the frame. Although early model F-truck spring shackles require periodic lubrication, the frame rails and crossmembers are maintenance-free. Aside from periodic power washing and brushing away surface scale and debris, an undamaged frame seldom needs more than occasional paint and undercoating.

Leaf springs anchor at one end with a pivot bolt and bushings. During suspension travel, a swinging shackle at the opposite end of the main leaf permits fore and aft spring movement. All 1956 and earlier F-truck spring shackles and anchor bolts feature grease fittings and replaceable bronze bushings. Those later trucks equipped with leaf springs and rubber spring bushings require less periodic maintenance.

Mono-Beam and Twin I-Beam Front Axles

Unlike Ford passenger cars with transverse leaf springs and wishbones, the 1948 Ford F-Series light trucks offered semi-elliptic front and rear leaf springs. This conventional and proven layout, used by most competitive truck builders of that era, continued through 1964 on F-100 and F-250 trucks and last appeared on 1966 F-350 models. (The late Super Duty models have returned to this design.)

The solid front axle, called an I-beam or mono-beam type, attaches to the springs with U-bolts and offers a high degree of stamina. Steering knuckles pivot on king-pins, and the steering linkage is a simple and efficient design. Kingpins, recognized for their stability and durability, have remained a mainstay with light Ford F-trucks, long after other manufacturers abandoned this engineering.

In 1965, Ford switched to a quasi-independent front suspension system on 2WD light trucks. Although respected for its rugged dependability, Twin I-Beam suspension allows only a limited range of wheel motion and far less geometric flexibility than GM and Dodge truck models with double A-arm suspension systems.

Twin I-Beam borrows much of its design from earlier I-beam models. (The supportive radius arms even mimic Ford's earliest wishbone suspension.) However, coil springs provide a smoother ride, and two beams, moving independently, legitimize the term "independent" suspension. The recognized stamina of I-beams with kingpin steering pivots makes Ford's Twin I-Beam system popular into the 1990s.

Live Front and Rear Driving Axles

At the mid-1990s, Ford F-Series 4x4s continue to offer a live front axle of full-floating design. Rear axles for various models are either full-or semi-floating type. Half-ton F-1/100/150 models use semi-floating rear axles, while early F-2 and F-3 trucks, and the F-250 models through 1979, use full-floating axles.

Beginning in 1980, F-250 trucks introduce the first semi-floating 8-lug wheel rear axles to the Ford truck line. F-350 heavy duty models, which have always used a full-floating rear axle, still offer full-floating rear axles and solid front driving axles on 4x4 models after 1980.

Ford truck models feature three distinct live front axle designs. Early solid axle models have closed-knuckle steering joints. Sealed, ball-shaped castings extend from the axle tubes, providing a cavity for oiling the enclosed axle shafts and steering knuckle joints. Later models feature open-knuckle live axles, with ball-stud steering knuckle pivots. Here, the axle shaft, visible between the end of the axle tube and the steering knuckle, features a cross-type U-joint to permit steering.

The open-knuckle joint requires less maintenance, provides less trouble, and affords tighter turner angles than a closed knuckle axle. Earlier closed knuckle axles often develop seal leaks and weep grease. Also, the shimmed kingpin bearings on early axles require a precise pre-load adjustment, making service more complex. (See service section for details.)

0012077

Fig. 4-2. 1948–56 Ford F-trucks provide plenty of grease fittings. Use of bronze spring-shackle bushings requires periodic service with chassis lubricant. Newer models have rubber bushings and require less maintenance.

Fig. 4-3. *Full-floating axle provides wheel support in the event of an axle shaft failure. F-2, F-3 and F-250 models through 1979 boast full-floating rear axles. F-350, rated at one-ton capacity, continues full-floating tradition.*

Fig. 4-4. *Ford 4x4s had closed knuckle front axles for many years. These axles resemble Willys/Jeep design (top photo). By mid-'70s, various open knuckle style Dana 44 axles serve F-100, F-150 and F-250 models. F-350 4x4s use a larger, heavy duty open knuckle Dana 60 axle (bottom).*

Ford truck engineering aims for long service and parts integrity. F-Series live front axles with full-floating hubs serve as one example of superior strength in design. Many competitive trucks have fallen to semi-floating front axles and even the use of passenger car type half-shafts, C.V. joints, and failure prone boot seals. At the mid-'90s, Ford continues to offer rugged full-floating front wheel hub assemblies on F-Series 4x4 trucks, even with Twin Traction-Beam axles.

Twin Traction-Beam is a conservative approach to an independent front end (IFS) design for 4x4s. Introduced with 1980 F-150 and F-250 models, these axles feature a two-section pivoting front axle housing assembly. Like Twin I-Beam 2WD front ends, the 4x4 IFS axle allows independent movement of each wheel yet retains the stamina and major advantages of a solid live front axle.

F-150 IFS 4x4 models retain front coil springs, while the '80–up F-250 IFS trucks continue to offer leaf springs. Ford trucks with IFS/Twin Traction-Beam suspension provide a smoother ride, improved handling and the kind of reliability that Ford buyers expect.

Semi- and full-floating rear axles are of conventional Hotchkiss design, and Ford F-trucks all use semi-elliptic leaf-type rear springs. All F-Series trucks feature open propeller/driveshafts, which permit quicker service and easier removal of the transmission or rear axle and center member assemblies.

Rear axles require little periodic maintenance beyond oil level checks and changing oil. Axle shaft bearings or full-floating hub bearings offer a long service life, and the overall stamina of Ford light truck axles is excellent. Ford has used integral, carrier, and split housing type axles assemblies in various light F-truck models.

2. STEERING GEAR AND LINKAGE

Early F-trucks feature very basic steering systems. A Gemmer/worm-and-roller type steering gear, with a fore and aft pivoting pitman arm, attaches to the frame. The drag-link connects this pitman arm with a steering arm at the left steering knuckle (left hand drive models).

On non-independent front suspension (IFS) F-truck models, a single tie-rod connects the left and right steering knuckle arms, simultaneously turning the steering knuckles and wheel spindles. This fundamental layout is common to all non-IFS models with solid I-beam front axles.

Beginning with the 1965 IFS/Twin I-Beam front axles, the steering linkage and location of the gear change. An improved recirculating ball-and-nut steering gear comes on line in 2WD models. (F-100 4x4 and F-250 4x4 models retain worm-and-roller manual gears until well into the 1970s.).

Fig. 4-5. *Recirculating ball-and-rack integral power steering has a reputation for superior service and durability. Many Ford trucks benefit from these gears. Linkage type power steering, found on 4x4 models from late '60s to mid-'70s, is more complex and vulnerable to damage.*

Much improved integral power steering of recirculating ball-and-nut design first came on line in '66 2WD trucks, and ultimately replaced the optional linkage-type power steering in 4x4 models. Integral power steering offers major gains in stamina, safety and efficiency. A linkage power steering option came on line for '71 model 4x4s. The F-100/F-150 4x4s gained integral power steering in 1976, followed late in 1977 by the introduction of an integral power unit on F-250 4x4s.

Fig. 4-6. *GM's Saginaw-type recirculating ball-and-nut manual steering is superior to Gemmer worm-and-roller type. Precisely machined worm shaft groove acts as an inner half of the ball bearing race, while the nut provides the matching groove. Reduced friction means easier steering and longer service life. Here, GM led Ford trucks in switch to recirculating ball-and-nut type manual steering gears.*

Steering linkage varies on half-ton (F-100 and later the F-150) 4x4s from 1965–up, the two types being inverted-Y and inverted-T. By design, the inverted-Y type is much like the 2WD Twin I-Beam style linkage. (See service and upgrade chapters for details.) F-250 4x4s have two basic linkage arrangements: solid axle models with a one-piece tie-rod (1959–79) and the '80–up IFS 4x4 style with its Y-type linkage.

Fig. 4-7. *1948–64 light 2WD Ford F-trucks and 4x4 models into the mid-1970s use worm-and-roller type steering gear. The weakness of this design is high friction between the roller teeth and worm shaft groove. These gears wear more rapidly, resulting in wander and reduced steering control.*

WARNING —
Worm-and-roller manual steering gears fatigue at high mileage and become dangerous when wear is excessive. Adjusting out play on these steering units can prove futile and often ignores hazardous wear on the roller teeth or worm bearings. If sector, worm or roller shaft play feels excessive on any type of steering gear, replace or completely overhaul the steering gear unit.

3. DRUM AND DISC BRAKE SYSTEMS

Ford F-truck braking systems consist of a hydraulic master cylinder feeding brake fluid through pipes and high strength brake hose to each wheel cylinder or disc caliper. Pedal pressure actuates the master cylinder piston (dual pistons on tandem master cylinders), causing brake fluid to flow.

Typical Ford drum brake systems have one hydraulic cylinder per wheel. These cylinders have twin, opposing pistons that move outward as fluid enters the cylinder. Depending upon the model and brake type, Ford drum brakes apply pressure via several methods, each design described generically as self-energizing.

Overall, earlier four-wheel drum brake systems are inferior to disc front/drum rear designs. Although Ford engineered drum brake sizes to match chassis and advertised load capacities, drum type brakes simply cannot offer the braking efficiency, resistance to fade and performance of disc brakes.

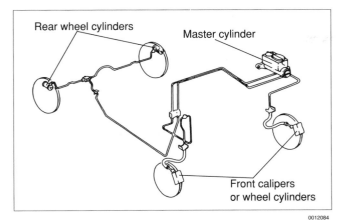

Fig. 4-8. The Ford truck braking system is similar to most other American truck designs. A pedal actuated master cylinder forces fluid into each of the hydraulic wheel cylinders or disc brake calipers. Friction brake shoes or pads act against metal drums or rotors.

Fig. 4-9. Self-energizing brakes, with both shoes sharing a common anchor bolt or pin, utilize the rotational force of the drum to force the brake shoes more firmly against the braking surface of the drum. Added force enhances braking without need for additional hydraulic pressure.

All Ford F-Series trucks use drum front and rear brakes through 1972. 2WD models introduce disc front brakes in 1973, while 4x4 F-trucks began using disc front brakes in 1976. Disc brakes provide superior stopping force, quicker recovery from exposure to water, straighter stops, a wider safety margin and ease of service. Simpler maintenance and overhaul make disc brakes popular with truck owners. Recent F-trucks feature anti-lock braking systems.

Emergency/Parking Brake

The Ford F-truck parking brakes come in two versions: rear brake shoe application type and transmission output shaft type. Rear brake apply types force the brake shoes against the drums by way of mechanical linkage and cables that attach to a handle or foot operated lever in the cab.

Earlier models with heavy duty transmissions and high cargo capacities depend upon an emergency brake assembly (drum with an external band lining) that mounts just outboard of the transmission tail housing. When applied, this brake helps prevent rotation of the rear propeller shaft, differential and axle shafts.

Fig. 4-10. A mechanical shoe-and-drum mechanism at the transmission output flange provides emergency braking on heavier duty early F-trucks. When wet, muddy, oil soaked or glazed, these brake mechanisms offer marginal service at best. Later trucks use the rear wheel brakes, applied mechanically, for emergencies and parking.

These transmission mounted parking brake assemblies are notoriously vulnerable to seeping oil from transmission or engine leaks and even road debris. Contamination of lining plus the relatively small surface area of the emergency brake drum/lining each limit the braking efficiency. Chock blocks make a good backup.

4. A Glance At F-truck Engines

Beginning with the earliest F-models, Ford has built its light truck sales successes around high torque engines that can haul a severe load and last a long time.

Early Six-cylinder and V-8s

The earliest six-cylinder F-Series light truck engine was the 226H inline design. This powerplant is a durable L-head engine rated 95 horsepower. Used from 1948–51, the one-barrel carbureted L-head six can be found in many F-1 to F-3 models. I had such an engine in my '51 F-3 and found it reliable, miserly on fuel and very happy to perform a hard day's work. Compared to flathead V-8s of that era, this engine runs cooler and requires less attention.

A 239.4-cubic-inch V-8 was also available from 1948–53. These R-designated engines have the distributor mounted much like a modern V-8, upright at the right side of the engine, with ignition wires and the distributor cap accessible.

Fig. 4-11. Last of Ford's famous flathead V-8s was a 239.4-cubic-inch design with a more modern and accessible distributor. Dual water pumps, much like the original 1932 V-8 design, continued to last flathead V-8 of 1953.

Fig. 4-12. 215, 223 and 262 inline OHV sixes were very durable and launched Ford trucks into the modern era. These sixes, standard equipment in many light F-trucks, delivered excellent torque and fuel economy.

The 239 V-8 is much like the passenger car 8-BA engine of that era. These flathead V-8s feature a traditional three-bolt mount, two-barrel carburetor with an oil bath air cleaner. To date, all of Ford's light truck gasoline engines have roots in passenger car engines.

In 1952, Ford's first light truck engine with a valve-in-head (OHV) design broke new ground. The 215 and later 223 and 262 inline sixes impressed commercial and fleet users for years. Durable and capable of outperforming both the older flathead sixes and V-8s, these engines were on their way to redefining light truck performance standards when consumers began pressing for high horsepower modern V-8s.

In the late 1960s, I worked on a fleet of trucks, many with Ford 223 six-cylinder engines. These four-main bearing engines were well engineered and remarkably easy to service, with subtle features like a flat oil pan for quick access to the crankshaft and oil pump. Tune-up, valve adjustment and quick service were simple and rewarding.

After 1964, the sequel to the 223/262 sixes is the 240 and 300-cubic-inch inline design, the latter engine still offered today. The 240 and 300 sixes, with seven main bearings, provide the most versatile kind of power. High torque at low rpm makes the 300/4.9L six popular with a variety of users.

I am particularly impressed by the durability these engines demonstrate. Properly maintained, an easy task in this case, a 240 or 300 six can run 200,000 miles without a whimper. For the owner of a 300 six, maintenance is simple, with ready access to components.

The 300 six makes a wonderful "first engine" for the aspiring mechanic, an easy to understand assembly of parts that like to perform with a scant amount of support. Upkeep is easier than any other currently built Ford truck engine, with only six spark plugs, each easy to find and replace, contributing to lower service costs and efficiency.

Fig. 4-13. Ford's 240- and 300-cubic-inch sixes offer seven main bearings for exceptional durability. 300/4.9L inline engine ranks among the best light truck engines ever built, surviving in today's EFI/MPI era as a high torque standard powerplant. Commercial/fleet users rave about this engine.

OHV V-8 Engines

The first modern V-8s in Ford's light F-trucks were OHV engines referred to affectionately as Y-blocks. Introduced in 1954, the block casting located the crankshaft high up in the block, which gave the front view of the engine a "Y" shape. Various Y-block engines (239, 256, 272 and 292) dominated Ford light truck and passenger car engine bays through 1964.

When I worked on these engines years ago, they were comparable in performance and tuning requirements to other early OHV engines. These are rugged and industrious engines that earn their keep, delivering exceptionally long service when maintained properly. For their era, they require minimal service: oil/filter changes, periodic valve adjustment, breaker points installation, setting point dwell, adjusting spark timing and servicing the oil bath air cleaner if so equipped.

By today's standards, these vintage Y-block engines best serve the hobbyist or restorer with sound mechanical skills and a good deal of time on his or her hands. Unless your truck requires a precise OEM restoration for maintaining its value, you might consider a later engine transplant, one prospect being the 351-Windsor V-8. (See performance chapter.)

Engine developments during the late 1950s and early 1960s revolutionized the automotive industry. High octane meant high compression, and the result was high horsepower. Heavy Fords and models like the Edsel, Mercury and Lincoln demanded large displacement engines. The FE family of powerplants emerged in 1958 as a formidable challenge to GM and Chrysler big displacement, high output engines.

Fig. 4-15. Owner swears that this '57 Ford F-100's Y-block 272 has gone well over 300,000 miles without an overhaul or removal of the cylinder heads! High torque of Y-block engines made them popular with Ford light truck owners.

The popular 352 Ford V-8 of that era, closely related to the subsequent 390 engine design, showed good truck potential. In 1965, this low maintenance engine became the choice for light F-Series trucks.

Aside from reliability and excellent performance, the 352 and later 360 and 390 FE V-8s feature zero maintenance hydraulic valve lifters, an ignition distributor at the front of the engine for easy access, a spin-on oil filter, dry-paper air cleaner and a readily serviceable block assembly.

The only drawback to the FE design is its weight. Some refer to these bulky engines as "boat anchors." I

Fig. 4-14. Ford's famous FE family of passenger car engines has also scored well among Ford F-Series light truck users. 352, 360 and 390 V-8s are especially popular with camper haulers and those who pull hefty trailers.

downplay this negative connotation, especially for truck applications. Here, the only negative element to bulk is poor weight distribution, a dilemma that generally plagues light trucks. (See engine performance and suspension chapters for ways to offset these problems.) For heavy hauling, the massive torque of a big-block FE engine more than compensates for weight liabilities.

FE engines can provide users with a powerful high torque powerplant. Although fuel economy has never been a strong card with either two- or four-barrel versions of these engines, the FE delivers long service and tremendous reliability. FE V-8s serve a variety of Ford F-Series light trucks from 1965 until the mid-1970s.

To date, the grandest V-8 of all F-Series light truck engines is the 460 big-block. Although the 460 has a healthy appetite for fuel, you will surely admire its performance and ease of service. This is a modern engine that has survived the heavy constraints of emission controls and fuel economy standards.

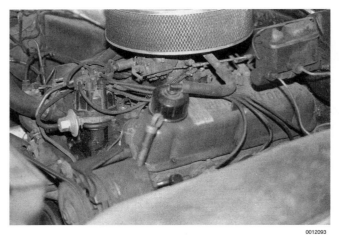

Fig. 4-17. 302 and 351-Windsor small-block Ford V-8s have an excellent reputation for performance and reliability. The 351W offers more torque and horsepower, plus larger diameter main bearings and crankshaft main journals. 351s make a good compromise for the annual trailer puller and daily commuter.

Fig. 4-16. 460 Ford big-block V-8 ranks as the undisputed big hauler. If the load calls for massive torque and high horsepower at a usable rpm, the 460 will deliver. Fuel economy, however, corresponds to the performance output. Carbureted versions of this engine spend a good deal of time at the gas pumps. EFI/MPI 460s fare somewhat better.

Since its 1968 introduction in Lincoln-Mercury cars, owners of 460 V-8s have enjoyed the high torque and high horsepower output of this engine. In Ford F-truck form, they require little attention beyond routine service and offer a long service life. The addition of EFI/MPI in 1987 made this engine even better.

The small block 302 and 351-Windsor V-8s have also satisfied many Ford light truck owners. I especially like the 351W engine (not to be confused with the 351M) and devote considerable space to this engine in the performance section of the book. The 351W with EFI has become a mainstay powerplant in Ford's popular light trucks, providing owners with low maintenance costs, good performance and exceptional longevity.

Although the 302/5.0L small-block V-8 ranks among the worthiest pound-for-pound engines in automotive history, I find this engine overworked in many truck applications. This is a fine commuter engine or light duty hauler for carrying a few bales of hay on occasion. When

pressed to pick a serious economy engine with enough flexibility to haul a load without complaint, however, my choice is the 300-cubic-inch/4.9L inline six with EFI/MPI. For more muscle, I recommend the 351W or a 460 V-8.

Not overlooked among Ford's F-Series engines is the odd 351M/400 that appears in light trucks from the mid-'70s until 1980. I am very reticent to recommend these engines, although some owners have gotten good service from them. The design is derivative of the highly dependable 351W, however, the need to establish a big-block powerplant by inflating the 351-Modified engine to 400 cubic inches has dramatically lowered the reliability of these engines.

I discuss the weaknesses of this engine design in the performance chapters of the book. Suffice to say here, the 351-Modified/400 powerplants require special consideration before re-boring the block, as core shift is an issue.

Fig. 4-18. 351M/400 engines have satisfied some Ford F-truck owners, while many of us find the engine lacking in power and overtaxed with emission controls. Essentially a small-block trying to do a big job, some of these engines were even pressed into F-350 service.

The heat generated by emission constraints places these engine castings at severe stress and risk. Many 351M/400 blocks and heads have been through major overhauls or landed in the scrap pile.

The consolation is that 351M/400 car and truck engines are plentiful at recycling yards, so inexpensive and rebuildable cores exist for those who wish to stay with the design. Better yet, there are emission legal ways to replace a 351M/400 engine with a later 351W carbureted or EFI equipped engine—or even a 460 V-8. (See performance and emissions chapters for discussion of engine transplants.)

For diesel buffs, the Navistar V-8 engine is reliable and worthy. Although users find the 7.3L and newest 7.3L DI factory turbocharged engines a considerable improvement, even the 6.9L engine provides the longevity and favorable torque expected of a quality medium duty truck powerplant. You will find the Navistar engines free of major flaws and easy for routine service.

Fig. 4-19. *Navistar's 6.9L and 7.3L V-8 diesel is a real stump puller, respected for its lively low speed torque and smart fuel efficiency. The best of these engines is the DI factory turbocharged versions, available in Ford F-trucks from 1995 on.*

5. TRANSMISSIONS AND TRANSFER CASES

A wide range of manual and automatic transmissions have been coupled to Ford light truck engines. For four-wheel drive, the geartrain requires an additional member, the transfer case or power divider, which delivers power to each driving axle.

The standard Ford clutch assembly is common to other trucks and automobiles. Spring-type clutch covers of several designs have been used in F-truck models. Each clutch provides the clamping force necessary to press the clutch disc between an engine-driven steel flywheel and the clutch cover's face or pressure plate.

A pilot bearing at the rear of the engine crankshaft supports the nose end of the manual transmission input shaft/gear, while the clutch release or throwout bearing rides on the front bearing retainer of the transmission.

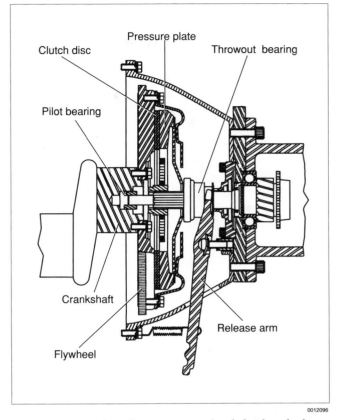

Fig. 4-20. *Ford trucks use a conventional clutch and release mechanism. The throwout bearing rides on the transmission front bearing retainer and presses against the clutch release fingers during disengagement. A crankshaft pilot bearing centers and supports the input shaft.*

Clutch Linkage

Ford trucks use a variety of clutch linkage types. 1948–56 trucks have through-the-floor pedal assemblies attached to the frame, and the clutch linkage operates from below the cab floor. This is a good arrangement, as the frame, linkage and engine move along the same plane. Trucks like my '55 F-100, with two solid motor mounts on the bellhousing, offer very smooth mechanical linkage.

Since 1957, the two linkage designs have been hydraulic (a master cylinder, hose and slave cylinder) and mechanical linkage (a cross-shaft and series of link rods). These designs vary in reliability.

Poor linkage design is a weakness on some Ford truck models, especially where cross-shafts move with the engine and cause vibration and rough clutch engagement. When working properly, the smoothest clutch linkage is a hydraulic design. This type of linkage is not affected by chassis twist or engine torque flexing.

Clutch linkage requires close periodic inspection. Worn parts usually fail when your truck is under load or off-pavement. For this reason, clutch linkage is a vital part of preventive care. (See the service section for preventive maintenance of your truck's clutch linkage.)

Fig. 4-21. Ford truck clutch linkage design has varied. Below-the-floor pedal-and-rod system (shown) was a mainstay from '48–'56. Hydraulic linkage was big change for 1957, then ends after 1960. Mechanical linkage carries from here to later Ford trucks, which return to hydraulic linkage.

Rugged Automatic Transmissions

Ford realized early that automatic transmissions suited many light truck owners. In 1953, the F-100 introduced the option of a three-speed Fordomatic transmission unit. General Motors soon promoted the use of the now legendary dual range (band type) four-speed Hydramatic as an option in 1954 light trucks.

The Ford automatic offered a durable transmission with a three-segment torque converter for reasonable breakaway performance. Some buyers, already familiar with the Fordomatic drive in passenger cars, were willing to try this new technology. Unfortunately, coupled to a small displacement OHV six or the last flathead V-8, which rated a meager 106 horsepower, the Fordomatic could hardly prove its worth.

Word soon circulated that these transmissions were expensive to service and offered sluggish performance. I once had the opportunity to drive a '53 F-100 with the

Fig. 4-22. Iron case Borg-Warner three-speed automatic was popular in many Ford cars and trucks. Earliest light F-truck Cruise-O-Matic was a durable version of this transmission, which became an option with the 352 FE V-8 in 1965.

Fordomatic drive. Frankly, the truck could barely get out of its own way. Worse yet, the owner lamented the poor fuel economy.

Despite the slow acceptance of automatic transmissions, Ford F-Series truck engineers continued research. Particular successes in passenger cars, mostly with large displacement engines, encouraged Ford to offer an iron case Cruise-O-Matic with the new light truck 352 FE V-8 engine option in 1965.

This unit was actually a spin-off of Borg-Warner's popular three-speed iron case design. Highly durable, these transmissions saw use in many Ford cars and light trucks of the 1950s and well into the '60s.

In the late 1960s, as a truck fleet mechanic, my first automatic transmission overhaul experience was a similar Borg-Warner three-speed automatic. I followed the service manual to the letter and marveled when the unit worked flawlessly after re-assembly. Particularly impressive was the minimal number of specialty tools needed to service and overhaul these units.

Iron case automatics require little maintenance beyond periodic fluid changes, a filter cleaning, and minor band adjustments as mileage accumulates. You can perform this kind of service with the guidance of a factory or professional level service manual that covers your year and model truck. You can readily find the tools needed for such service.

1965 F-trucks with the new 240 and 300 sixes featured an optional light duty aluminum three-speed automatic transmission, Ford's own C-4 unit. Close in design to the larger C-6 unit that began replacing iron case three-speed units during the late 1960s, the C-4 is a reliable transmission that has seen service in many F-Series trucks with six-cylinder and small V-8 engines.

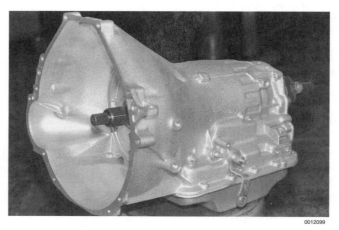

Fig. 4-23. Best Ford F-truck transmission offering to date is Ford's own C-6. Aluminum housed and full of stamina, these transmissions serve in trucks up to F-600 size. Here's the margin of strength a heavy hauler needs.

The aluminum case C-6, introduced as a three-speed automatic for large engine applications, is generally regarded as the best automatic transmission Ford has ever offered in light trucks or passenger cars. Rugged and durable, the C-6 requires little maintenance and willingly serves under the most severe duty. These units have been coupled behind Cobra Jet and Boss Mustang big-blocks, behemoth cars with 460 V-8s during the high horsepower era, and in F-Series trucks through the F-600 model.

If you want reliability in an automatic transmission and easy maintenance that you can perform with the guidance of a factory level service book, the C-6 makes an ideal choice. Ford has offered these transmissions in F-Series light truck models built from the late '60s into the '90s. The C-6 even serves willingly behind engines like Navistar's 7.3L V-8 diesel. This is my best pick in Ford automatics.

The emergence of automatic overdrive transmissions as a fuel saving device and means for lowering per-mile tailpipe emissions carries into the light F-Series truck line. In the early 1980s, Ford introduced a number of AOT automatics, four-speed overdrive types with planetary geartrains.

These early AOT transmissions have a mixed service record. Field service and overhaul shops have turned up many problems that Ford later corrected. If you find yourself with a troubled early AOT type transmission, see a quality transmission shop or your Ford dealer for an overhaul. Once upgraded, the AOT can provide a long service life in a lighter duty truck.

The improvements in automatic overdrive units have led to Ford's later E4OD units. These transmissions have a much better service record and hold up well in a wider range of applications. Overdrive technology continues to develop, and both manual and automatic overdrive transmissions have higher survival rates now than they did in the 1980s.

Transfer Cases

Ford F-truck transfer case units attach in one of two ways: 1) either directly to the rear of the manual or automatic type transmission via an adapter, or 2) mounted separately (divorced) with a short driveline between the transmission and transfer case.

The common two-speed transfer unit serves as both a power divider (directing power flow to the front axle) and a means for achieving exceptionally low gearing (models equipped with low range) in 4WD mode.

Gear driven part-time 4x4 systems, like the original Ford transfer case designs, offer a distinct two-wheel drive mode. In this mode, power flows from the engine through the transmission to the transfer case, then rearward to the rear axle. Here, the front propeller shaft receives no power from the transfer unit.

In 4-Wheel High or 4-Wheel Low, power flows through the front and rear driveshafts to both axles. Low range provides a reduction gearset, with a ratio factor between 2:1 and nearly 3:1 (depending upon the year and transfer case model application). The transfer case is a crucial part of the Ford four-wheel drive system.

Ford F-trucks have offered several transfer case designs, including gear and chain drive types. Chain drive emerged in the '70s, when full-time 4x4 popularity peaked. Part-time 4x4 transfer cases, with aluminum-housings and chain drive, are currently popular. Aluminum-housed transfer cases are lighter and more energy efficient. For some applications, however, the earlier gear drive units serve better.

Fig. 4-24. Original two-speed transfer case in F-100 and F-250 4x4s was a Spicer 24. This durable through-drive design mounts separately from the transmission in divorced style. In 1965, Ford F-100s went to a single speed power divider, the Dana 21, which places a limit on hauling capacity and off-highway utility.

The earliest Ford transfer cases were two-speed Spicer 24 types, used on both F-100 and F-250 4x4 models. In 1965, as Ford lowered the F-100 4x4 chassis and switched to coil front springs, the Spicer/Dana 21 single speed power divider replaced the two-speed transfer case on F-100 models. The F-250 retains the two-speed Spicer 24 unit through 1972.

Both of these transfer units are high quality types, although the two-speed variety has far more flexibility than the single speed Model 21. By 1973, the overwhelming popularity of competitive New Process transfer cases encouraged Ford's switch to the two-speed NP205 gear drive unit. Both 1973 F-250 models and F-100s with automatics benefit from this high quality design, offered as an option through 1979.

In 1974, Ford followed other truck manufacturers and offered optional full-time 4x4 systems with the chain drive NP203 transfer case. (The F-100 4x4 manual transmission models kept the Dana 21 single speed unit through 1976. All F-150 4x4s offer two-speed transfer cases.) The NP203 is also a rugged transfer case, although many owners have converted such units to part-time operation through the use of aftermarket kits.

The NP203 and NP205 were high quality transfer cases and served under the most adverse conditions. The iron cased NP205 unit, in my opinion, is the best transfer case ever offered in a light duty truck. Some manufacturers continued using these units with one-ton truck applications into the '90s, also installing the NP205 unit behind turbocharged diesels. Ford discontinued use of the NP205 transfer case after 1979.

In 1980, Ford and other manufacturers, insisting that they needed lighter transfer case units with lower (numerically higher) gearing in low range, began using a variety of aluminum housed two-speed transfer cases. Ford, like others, experimented with the New Process NP208 unit, which features a planetary gear reduction system and a chain drive for the output shaft that serves the front axle.

Like Ford's subsequent choices, the Borg-Warner 1345 and 1356 chain drive units, these NP208 transfer cases

Fig. 4-25. Ford has used several part-time chain drive transfer cases since 1980. The NP208, Borg-Warner 1345 and Warner 1356 have served many F-truck owners. 1356 unit (shown) has refinements and a reasonably good track record.

perform well but lack the long and trouble-free lives offered by NP205 part-time 4x4 units.

All chain drive transfer case units have light aluminum cases and an increased number of wear points. On the bright side, the reduction ratios for low range are very low (numerically high), which offers great crawl paces, heavy lugging ability, and less overall load on the powertrain during 4WD low range operation.

If your Ford truck has an NP208 or any of the Borg-Warner transfer cases, whether manual or electrically shifted, routine service is crucial. Many of these later transfer cases use automatic transmission fluid (ATF) or light oil as a lubricant. Watch for seal leaks and seepage at case halves, where anaerobic sealers sometimes fail. Change fluid regularly, and pay close attention to the color of oil or ATF.

Driveshafts

Power flow between the transfer case and axles on Ford four-wheel drive models is through conventional propeller shafts. Two-wheel drive trucks use a similar rear driveline. Most often, Ford trucks have Spicer cross-type U-joints with a single tube and slide coupler or a two-piece (splined) driveshaft.

Larger F-trucks or models with longer wheelbases often employ a mid-shaft or carrier support bearing, which incorporates a two-piece driveline. Slide couplers and

Fig. 4-26. Mid-shaft/carrier bearing (arrow) is common on long wheelbase trucks. Many Ford F-Series models use such a setup. Bearing and two-section driveline reduce vibration and the need for one excessively long driveshaft tube.

splined sections compensate for axle movement by lengthening or shortening the overall driveshaft length as the axle moves with suspension travel.

Driveline service usually consists of required routine lubrication and inspection of the U-joints and spline sections. At high mileage and when damage occurs, the driveline will need repairs or overhaul. (For details on driveshaft overhaul and construction, see service chapters.)

6. REPAIRS ON YOUR F-SERIES TRUCK

Your Ford F-Series truck's serviceable components fit into several sub-groups. The common chassis and powertrain layout provides an easy orientation. Once familiar with your truck's design, you can readily make repairs.

Unless you must remove the crankshaft, engine work is possible in the chassis. The engine bays of F-trucks are broad and designed to facilitate service. An exception to this rule is a large V-8-powered truck with a full complement of power accessories.

Powertrain Orientation

You can quickly become familiar with your Ford's features. Servicing propeller shafts, cables, the brakes, shock absorbers (airplane type removable units) and wheels is fast and straightforward. On 4x4 models, the transfer case is either divorced or detaches from the transmission, making it easier to remove each of these units. Reducing the weight of the transmission/transfer case assembly permits safer handling of parts and reduced risk of damage.

Axle service, generally performed in the truck, follows standard guidelines for Spicer-type (integral) and Ford carrier type housings. Spicer/Dana axles have been widely used on American trucks. They have an excellent reputation for reliability.

Like a trained Ford mechanic, you'll find the factory service manual very valuable. By following factory recommended procedures for disassembly and installation of parts, you can perform professional level work. Your Ford F-Series truck deserves your highest work standards and competency.

0012103

Fig. 4-27. Factory Ford truck service manual is your assurance of a job that meets OEM standards. If you plan to keep your truck and do your own service work, invest in a service book(s) for your particular Ford model and year. (See appendix for sources of older factory guidebooks.)

The Workplace

When servicing your truck, a clean and safe workspace is essential. Ford geartrain and chassis parts are expensive. Losing parts can create lengthy delays, as many components have special order status.

By establishing neat work habits at the beginning of a repair or restoration project, you will speed up the work process and assure success. Each part has its place. Before starting a repair, lay out labelled coffee cans or similar non-breakable containers to hold the nuts and bolts.

Parts illustrations, either from this book or the detailed unit repair section of your factory F-truck service and repair manual, should accompany the job. Especially on an older F-Series truck, which may have suffered years of mediocre repairs, you should account for each part illustrated in the guidebook.

Use Correct Tools

Before starting any repair, review the tools required. Ford F-trucks, in some cases, need specialty wrenches or other devices to complete a diagnosis or repair. You will find references to such tools in this book or your Ford truck service and overhaul manual. Avoid loss of time and knuckle tissue by using the proper tools.

Some basics apply to work on any F-truck. Repairs to the undercarriage and wheel service frequently require chassis hoisting. The use of safe floor jacks and jackstands is a must. The ideal jackstands for light truck work have four-cornered platforms and a minimum of five-ton rating per stand. Stay away from light duty tube type stands. They provide too small margin of safety for wrestling with a transmission or transfer case.

Jacks and Lifting

Quality hydraulic floor jacks are another safety requirement. Minimally, your floor jack must be of 1-1/2 ton or greater capacity. Whenever possible, avoid lifting the entire front or rear of the truck with a single jack. Never rely upon a hydraulic jack to support the truck while you work beneath the body or chassis. Insert jack stands immediately to avoid overloading your jack. When lifting the truck for wheel and tire removal, take extra time and use jackstands. Safety is primary.

To safely position your jackstands, note the design of the chassis. (Your Ford owner's handbook or factory service manual outlines the safe points for lifting and positioning stands.) Common support points on the F-trucks are the frame rails and beneath the axle housing tubes or I-beams. Space jacks evenly, as near to the spring mounting points as possible. These locations are engineered to support the truck.

Avoid placing a jackstand in any area of the chassis where rocking might result. Never place a floor jack or jackstand under steering linkage, brake pipes/hoses, exhaust system parts or body sheet metal. Note the reinforced chassis sections and axle points recommended for positioning a jack. If you are uncertain about the lift points for your chassis, consult your local Ford dealership service representative or refer to the factory repair manual covering your model.

Fig. 4-28. *Assure a margin of safety when working on your truck. These 1-1/2 ton rated floor jacks offer features found in professional equipment. Invest in quality. Your safety is at stake.*

Fig. 4-29. *As a rule, you can position floor jacks safely beneath the front axle beam(s) or an axle housing. Allow room to place jackstands at the frame rails or other safe locations. Leave work room and space to remove stands.*

> **WARNING —**
> *Never work under a lifted vehicle unless it is solidly supported on stands designed for the purpose. Keep the jackstands well spaced and secure. Allow ample and unobstructed space to work. Do not work under a vehicle supported solely by a jack.*

Hoisting Equipment

Powertrain and axle unit repairs involve very heavy sub-assemblies. If service involves the removal and replacement of the axles, engine, transmission or transfer case, be prepared to handle these heavy units. Consider renting the correct hoisting tool(s) or a portable engine hoist. Rental firms often have transmission/transfer case jacks as well. When performing heavy work, always ask a robust friend for assistance.

Hoists and specialty tools help prevent personal injuries and damage to your truck. The manhandling of parts, such as attempts to install a weighty transmission by hand, can lead to broken components and severe bodily injury.

Failure to detach all of the hardware before hoisting can result in major damage. Take time to envision the sub-assembly standing alone. Check the step-by-step service procedures and parts diagrams to make sure that you have disconnected all necessary hardware and linkages. Ask an assistant to watch progress from a different vantage point.

Fig. 4-30. *Inline sixes are long and require care during removal. A cherry picker hoist provides the angle and control to safely lift an engine. Use a tilt cable for added safety, and avoid swinging the engine or damaging parts.*

In the case of engine removal, always secure the engine with suitable chain or cables. Find balance points to assure the stability of the engine as you raise it, and also pay attention to the angle of pull. Use strong, high grade attachment hardware and, if available, an engine tilt cable that allows angle adjustments as you hoist.

Special Safety Considerations

For work around coil suspension springs, like those found on '65–up 2WD Ford light trucks and 4x4 F-100 and F-150 models, be extra careful. Before changing springs, either allow the spring to safely extend and fully unload its force or constrain the spring with a special coil spring compressor. (Consult your service manual for the safest and recommended method for your model.)

Compressed coil force exceeds a ton, and an unrestrained spring can come loose and cause severe physical injury or damage to the truck.

Always account for the size of the transmission or transfer case assembly when placing the chassis on stands. If you intend to slide the transmission from beneath the truck, be certain that there is sufficient room. A disconnected transmission or axle, laying trapped beneath the truck, is like the story of the man who built a boat in his basement.

7. THE F-TRUCK OWNER'S TOOLBOX

On-and off-pavement driving environments are full of hazards and mechanical threats. The prepared truck owner carries an on-board complement of hand tools and simple diagnostic equipment.

At home, for the F-truck owner who performs maintenance and repairs on his or her vehicle, a variety of tools make up the workshop. If you plan to work on your own truck, your tool selection must meet a wide range of service needs, including periodic maintenance, light repairs, troubleshooting, and diagnosis.

Reference Books: The Literary Tools

This book serves as your orientation and reference guide for preventive care, tune-up and diagnosis of mechanical troubles. If your skill level and ambitions include sub-assembly repairs and overhaul, I highly recommend a Ford F-Series truck factory service manual, available through your local Ford dealership.

Between the factory level service manual and your owner's handbook, you will find concise information on tune-up specifications, tolerances and fluid capacities. For overhaul of the engine, geartrain and electrical sub-assemblies, a factory level service manual provides the necessary details and those specifications considered essential by the vehicle manufacturer.

Filling Your Toolbox

Your light truck garage requires a full assortment of U.S. size wrenches to cover all but the most recent metric hardware. Ford trucks, for the most part, have adhered to domestic tooling, despite U.S. auto industry attempts to shift toward the metric standard.

Hand tools should include open and box ended wrenches, sockets in 1/4", 3/8" and 1/2" square drive sets and special sockets for spark plugs, wheel lugs and the front wheel bearing adjuster and lock nuts on 4x4s.

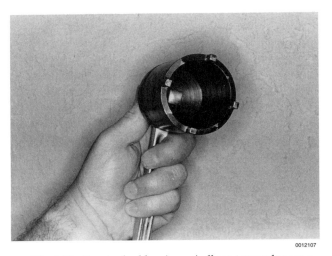

Fig. 4-31. Front wheel bearing spindle nut wrenches are a must. This specialty socket, available through NAPA and other auto supply retailers, is for later model 4x4s. Such sockets are also available for earlier hex nuts. Never use a hammer and punch to remove or tighten spindle nuts.

The wheel bearing nut wrench is a necessity. Many pre-owned Ford trucks show signs of severely abused front wheel bearing nuts. Instead of using the correct socket, unequipped mechanics apply a hammer and chisel to the corners of the hex or round type locking nuts. This not only ruins the nut but also eliminates any chance of accurately measuring torque on either the bearing adjusting nut or the lock nut.

4x4 front axle spindle nut wrenches are available in most retail auto parts stores. OTC, Snap-On and others produce flat-walled, 1/2" square drive sockets for precisely this purpose. The large nut size and small space between the nut and inner face of the hub makes use of a conventional socket or wrench impossible.

Many Ford 4x4 models utilize special wheel bearing nuts that require a special four-lug socket. The steering knuckle upper ball-joint stud seat on Dana open-knuckle axles adjusts with a similar tool. A special socket is available for accurately positioning these ball-joint stud seats and setting correct ball-joint preload.

Additional Chassis And Powertrain Tools

Your other chassis service tools should include tie-rod and Pitman/steering arm pullers, a pickle fork and those tools commonly used for working on any other domestic truck. For earlier Ford F-truck owners, both the 4x4 king-pin bearings and the steering gear adjustments require an accurate pull-type spring scale.

Fig. 4-32. Specialty pullers will ease steering linkage disassembly. Use of the right tool prevents damage to expensive safety components.

Cross-type U-joint service, a frequent truck repair procedure, may be performed successfully with a bench vise and some sockets, although more elaborate specialty tools are available. Some types of driveshaft work and other service operations may demand access to a hydraulic press, bearing or gear pullers and fixtures.

You can assign such tasks to an automotive machine shop or rent equipment at a local rental yard. The cost of equipment and frequency of use will dictate whether you should buy a hydraulic press.

For transmission and clutch work, a dummy input shaft for alignment is practical, as transmissions and at-

Fig. 4-33. *Many jobs require use of a hydraulic press. If a press is beyond your budget, send your heavy bearing, gear or bushing work to an automotive machine shop. Attempts to improvise with a hammer are wasteful and dangerous.*

Fig. 4-34. *A dial indicator and magnetic stand are very useful. For adjusting wheel bearing end play and runout on shafts, use a dial indicator. You can also detect camshaft lobe wear with a dial indicator.*

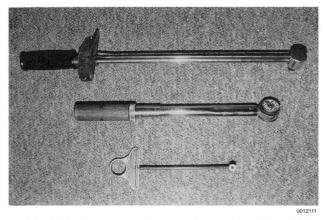

Fig. 4-35. *Torque wrenches come in a variety of sizes. This assortment serves every need from companion flange nuts to ultra-sensitive automatic transmission band adjustments.*

tached transfer cases are heavy and awkward—especially with four-speed, iron case truck transmissions.

You can fabricate transmission locating dowels by removing the heads from long bolts. Thread the bolts into the bellhousing's upper transmission mounting holes. These simple guide pins can prevent clutch disc damage during transmission installation.

Spicer/Dana axle and differential work requires use of a spreader to relieve tension on the carrier bearing cups during removal of the differential carrier. (Although axle overhaul is often a shop repair, you can perform this kind of work with the right tools and proper service data.) Removing axle shafts and wheel hubs on full-floating axles may require a special puller.

Precise Measurements

Competent truck repairs require precise adjustments and measurements. Shimming bearings, checking shaft end float, adjusting backlash of gears, setting wheel bearing endplay and other chores require a dial indicator and magnetic stand. The stand or a gooseneck holding fixture will help with awkward measurements. You will also need a precision micrometer(s) for measuring shaft diameters and checking shim thickness.

Ford truck service and overhaul work demand a wide range of torque wrenches: 1/4" drive inch-pound, 3/8" drive inch/foot-pound, 1/2" square drive foot-pound and even a 3/4" square drive heavy duty type. If cost is prohibitive, rent or borrow a quality torque wrench. Make sure the calibration is correct.

Nitty Gritty Tools

Your basic hand tools should include a hacksaw, a variety of chisels, punches and drifts (both hard steel and malleable brass), Allen hex wrenches, and in the case of later model trucks, Torx-type drivers. Seal and bearing cup driver sets are optional, as careful improvisation often works satisfactorily. Wear safety goggles whenever you work with air impact tools, sharp cutting tools, hammers, chisels or punches.

Brake Work Tools

For brake tubing nuts and fuel pipe fittings, a flare nut wrench set is mandatory. (Open end wrenches will damage compression and flare nuts.) Other brake work tools include adjuster spoon wrenches, spring pliers, retainer/hold down tools, wheel cylinder piston clamps and bleeder hose.

Disc brake work requires a pad/caliper piston spreader and a micrometer for checking disc thickness/variance. There are special hones for wheel cylinder, master cylinder and disc caliper rebuilding.

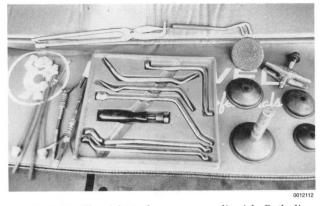

Fig. 4-36. The right tools assure a quality job. Both disc and drum brake systems require specialty tools. If you intend to perform brake work, invest in quality brake tools.

Air Tools: Speed and Efficiency

Air wrenches are a major timesaver. A wide range of pneumatic tools quickly tame difficult repair jobs. In addition to time savings, air impact wrenches enhance the quality of high torque, heavy duty repairs.

This is especially true with older sub-assemblies suffering from semi-seized hardware and rust accumulation. (Specially hardened, impact quality sockets should always be used with air wrenches.) Also, hardware like transmission output yoke nuts and U-joint/pinion flange nuts require high torque settings. Air tools for the removal and installation of these large nuts can eliminate the awkward use of a breaker bar and special holding fixtures.

When using air tools, avoid over tightening. Always check final torque with a torque wrench. Avoid using a pneumatic impact gun to fully tighten or torque precision fasteners.

Fig. 4-37. Air wrenches and other pneumatic tools save time and ease truck repair work, especially the removal and installation of shaft nuts on the transmission, transfer case or axles.

Engine Overhaul: Tools For Hardcore Repairs

In-the-chassis engine overhaul requires common tools like a valve spring compressor, cylinder ridge reamer, hone, and ring compressor. For a major out-of-chassis rebuild, you will assign re-boring the block, grinding the crankshaft and valves, fitting piston pins, installing cam bearings and other machine shop procedures.

Tune-up and Engine Diagnostic Equipment

The tune-up needs of your Ford truck engine depend upon the model and engine type. Various fuel, spark and ignition systems have different tool requirements.

Early F-trucks provide the arguable simplicity of a breaker point primary ignition, supported by remote ignition coil and high tension spark cables. A common misunderstanding is that breaker points are easier to service. The contemporary Ford electronic distributor is equally easy to troubleshoot and repair. (See repair and troubleshooting procedures in service chapters.)

Servicing earlier Ford breaker point distributors requires traditional tune-up tools. A point feeler gauge set helps adjust the point gap. (Tappet feeler gauges are for

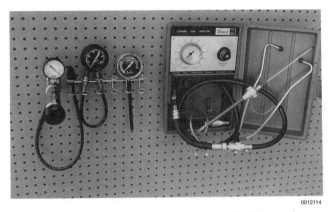

Fig. 4-38. A vacuum pump or gauge tests ignition, carburetor and emission devices. A compression gauge and cylinder leakdown tester can diagnose internal engine troubles.

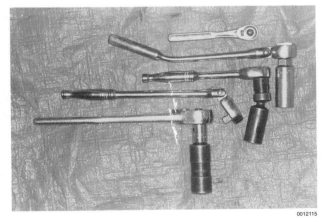

Fig. 4-39. A variety of handtools ease your truck work. These ratchets and sockets serve specific needs, including spark plug changes and removal of wheel lug nuts.

Fig. 4-40. *Ignition tune-up tools should match your truck's requirements. Some of these automotive tools date back thirty years. Ignition wrenches, point files, breaker cam lubricant and feeler gauges were common to the breaker point distributor era.*

Fig. 4-41. *A dwell meter, timing light and volt-ohmmeter help with tuning and troubleshooting. Volt-ohmmeter has become the most important electronic and electrical troubleshooting tool.*

engine valve stem clearance adjustments.) For accurate, parallel spark plug gaps, use a gapping pliers. Simpler wire-type feeler gauges also work fine on used plugs and fit in your on-board tool kit.

A dwell-meter provides precise breaker point adjustment, while a timing light verifies timing after you have set the point dwell angle. The volt/ohm meter is an ideal companion for your electrical troubleshooting and tune-up work, offering quick, concise diagnosis of everything from shorts and open circuits to testing alternator or generator current and battery voltage.

For precise performance, setting the breaker point spring tension assures accurate spark at all engine speeds while extending point life. Today, this is rarely necessary. Modern, high quality replacement points have pre-set tension.

Carburetor tuning requires a float height gauge and needle/seat removal tool. A complete assortment of quality screwdrivers (straight slot, Phillips and Torx) is necessary for repairs and tuning chores on your Ford truck.

Fig. 4-42. *Round out your tune-up tools with a fuel pump tester, vacuum gauge, float height gauge, needle/seat driver, assorted screw drivers, Torx sockets and a distributor terminal brush. During heyday of flathead and Y-block Ford V-8s, breaker point spring gauge served as a high performance tuning tool.*

Ignition wrenches are versatile for breaker point replacement and other electrical system repairs. A continuity tester is helpful, although the volt/ohmmeter surpasses the effectiveness of any test lamp. Although pinpoint tester probes allow testing through wire insulation, I avoid use of these testers. They can damage insulation, weaken your wiring and make the circuit susceptible to shorts.

Fig. 4-43. *Ford starter solenoids allow easy use of remote starter switch. For quickly aligning timing marks or checking compression, the remote switch is an asset.*

Electrical System Tools

When working alone, I find a remote starter switch handy. This permits cranking the engine from beneath the hood. A remote starter tool is very helpful for compression testing. With all spark plugs removed and the high tension spark current safely isolated or eliminated (check your factory service manual for recommended procedure), you can hold the throttle open, crank the engine and watch the compression gauge—all from beneath the hood.

Regular battery maintenance, a critical need for all trucks, requires tools for cleaning the cable terminals and posts. A battery hydrometer test is useful when you suspect a dead cell while simpler voltmeter tests answer most battery questions.

Another quick diagnostic tool for starter and charging systems is the induction meter. These meters sense magnetic current flow through the starter or charge circuit cable, showing the approximate output in amperes. In seconds, you can determine current flow rate or draw.

Fig. 4-44. *Induction meters provide a quick view of starter current draw or generator/alternator output. Held over the starter cable or charge wire, meter reads magnetic field or current flow.*

Engine Compression Versus Cylinder Leakdown

Although the compression gauge registers cranking compression (a quick reference to overall engine condition), a more reliable test is cylinder leakdown percentages. The leakdown tester pressurizes a cylinder through the spark plug hole, with the piston at top-dead-center (TDC) of its compression stroke. If the valves, rings, head gasket or castings fail to seal normally, the tester indicates the volume or percentage of the leak.

The advantage of the leakdown test is two-fold. First, the piston rests at the point of greatest cylinder wear (maximum taper). With parts immobile, leakage and piston ring blowby show up readily. It is not uncommon for an engine to display normal cranking compression yet have 30% or higher leakdown due to poor ring seal. Eight to ten percent leakage means an engine in top condition.

Second, the leakdown tester immediately indicates the area of the leak. If an intake valve leaks, air will blow back through the carburetor or EFI throttle body. A leak-

ing exhaust valve sends an audible signal out the tailpipe. Piston ring wear telegraphs through the dipstick tube, oil filler hole or crankcase vent.

If a professional quality leakdown tester is unavailable or more costly than your budget allows, the traditional substitute is an air-hold fitting designed for changing valve springs. Screw the fitting into a spark plug hole. With the piston at TDC on its compression cycle, adjust air line pressure to a point between 60 and 80 psi. Attach the air hose coupler to the fitting. Listen for leaks and pinpoint where leakage occurs.

Electronic Ignition/Emission Control Service Tools

Later Ford truck models bring computer-triggered electronic spark and fuel management into play. Beginning in the mid-'80s, Ford switched gasoline truck engines to Multi-Point Injection (MPI/EFI). Starting in the mid-'70s, all Ford truck engines feature electronic ignitions with an electronic module eliminating the use of breaker points.

Fig. 4-45. *Electronic ignitions have reduced service requirements. This late Motorcraft six-cylinder distributor with DuraSpark components is easily accessible and serviceable. For these ignitions, best troubleshooting tool is a volt-ohmmeter.*

From a service standpoint, the electronic distributor has actually reduced truck maintenance. Electronic ignitions eliminate the need to gap points and set dwell. Instead, troubleshooting now consists of ohmmeter and voltage tests. Here, a precision digital-type volt/ohmmeter proves invaluable, a must tool for your later Ford truck toolbox.

Timing Light

The timing light has remained an important element of ignition tuning, as normal wear to the camshaft timing chain and distributor drive mechanism still require periodic tests of spark timing. The ideal timing light has a built-in advance, which allows testing the vacuum advance function and the mechanical (centrifugal) advance. Better timing lights are inductive variety. This means that you may hook the connector to the insulation of number-one cylinder's spark cable without disconnecting the cable from the spark plug.

Distributor machines, once popular for testing a distributor unit off the engine, have nearly become obsolete. I still prefer this method for programming distributor spark advance mechanisms. Unfortunately, few shops can provide such services any more.

Timing lights with built-in advance now use the engine as a test stand for spinning the distributor safely to 1000–1250 rpm (2000–2500 crankshaft rpm—See specifications in your factory shop manual). The timing light's advance mechanism allows zeroing the timing to the factory TDC mark or any other degree setting within the timing light's range. This allows an accurate readout of the distributor's total spark advance.

Stay clear of the fan when using the engine to increase distributor rpm. Avoid standing above the fan, as fan separation or water pump shaft failure could cause severe bodily injury, even death. Limit rpm as much as possible. If you can perform tests with a cool engine, consider temporarily removing the fan belt(s) and other belts. Closely watch engine temperature. Discontinue testing if the engine begins to overheat.

Many of the Ford F-truck engines have distributor vacuum advance mechanisms. (The late engines with EFI/MPI use the computer to adjust all timing functions.) The use of a hand held vacuum pump aids in testing vacuum ignition spark advance mechanisms.

Tools For Checking Emission Controls

A vacuum pump/pressure tester also serves as a tune-up tool for emission control devices. You can test the exhaust gas recirculation valve (EGR), found on most Ford truck engines built since the early 1970s, with a vacuum pump. Additionally, applying vacuum to various emission control parts, like the thermal vacuum switch and bi-metallic air cleaner switch, helps locate leaks and troubles.

As many emission switches rely on coolant temperature, an accurate temperature gauge is necessary. To test the opening point for a thermal vacuum switch, for example, requires both a thermometer and vacuum test tool. Emission control tests are far less intimidating when these tools are available.

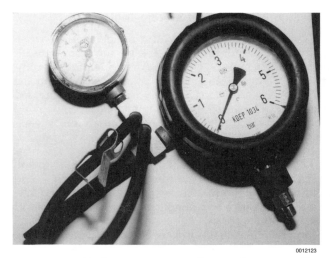

Fig. 4-47. Fuel pump pressure affects carburetor needle and seat action. Electronic fuel injection systems require higher, precisely regulated fuel pressure. These gauges pinpoint trouble.

On a pre-owned Ford truck, emission control devices and hoses may be missing. For restoring the system, I strongly recommend Mitchell's *Emission Control Manual* or your Ford F-Series truck factory shop manual. Either will provide diagrams and illustrations of the original equipment components. Your local Ford dealership's parts department is the best source for emission legal replacement parts.

Cooling System Tools

Ford truck engines depend on their cooling systems for survival. Radiator cleanliness, the correct thermostat, the right coolant mixtures and a properly working fan provide the backbone of engine cooling efficiency.

For both radiator cap and cooling system tests, a hand pump tester provides quick results. Locating head gasket seepage or a cracked engine casting is also within the scope of a cooling system pressure tester.

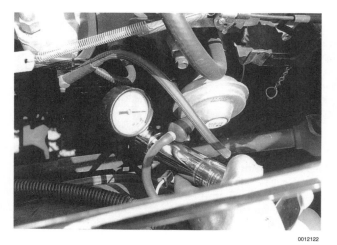

Fig. 4-46. A quality hand vacuum pump/pressure gauge is valuable. Emission control devices like this EGR valve can be tested easily with a vacuum pump.

Fig. 4-48. STANT pressure tester can verify cooling system pressure, find leaks and determine overall condition of the cooling system. This gauge has served for fifteen years, saving a considerable amount of diagnostic time and effort.

For anti-freeze and coolant protection tests, inexpensive radiator hydrometers are available. The reliability of your Ford truck's radiator cap and the concentration of coolant/anti-freeze play a vital role in boil-over protection. Radiator cap pressure also raises the boiling point of the coolant mix.

It is therefore essential to maintain correct pressure in your truck's cooling system. STANT and other companies provide pressure testers for both radiator cap and radiator/cooling system diagnosis. (See the service chapter for more information.)

Soft Tools

Conventional composition gaskets leak from the effects of heat (embrittlement), shrinkage or their inability to fill minute gaps and voids. The gap need not be very large, like a valve cover with a few thousandths of an inch of gasket gap. Such a leak, however, could easily spill an entire crankcase of oil along a remote back country trail! Aging, fatigue and oxidation can affect neoprene, rubber, cork, and even steel gaskets.

Chemical products and sealants, known in the automotive trade as "soft tools," make the ideal companion for your Ford truck's traveling toolbox.

0012125

Fig. 4-49. FoMoCo and aftermarket suppliers offer sealants and chemical soft tools that meet OEM guidelines for your Ford truck. Specialized items, such as rubber bonder, mirror adhesive, thread locking liquids and gasket forming materials, meet rigid standards and assure a quality repair.

RTV silicone sealants are unlike conventional gaskets. Rather than deteriorate when exposed to corrosive oils, products like Permatex/Loctite's Ultra Blue actually become more flexible, pliant and oil resistant. During engine assembly, you should use silicone products at the oil pan gasket corners, especially between cork and neoprene junctions, such as those found with intake manifold gaskets. Along the trail, Ultra Blue can create a thermostat housing gasket, valve cover gasket, oil pan gasket or timing cover gasket.

When selecting an RTV high temperature silicone for exhaust system joints and flanges, make sure the volatility level of the sealant is correct. For applications involving emission control oxygen sensors, use low-volatility

sealant. Higher volatility sealants can seriously damage the sensor. Most factory warranties on emission hardware will not cover the replacement of an oxygen sensor damaged by the use of high-volatility RTV sealant.

Never use a non-automotive silicone sealant, like bathtub caulk, on your Ford engine or geartrain parts. On manual gearboxes and axle housings, the correct RTV silicone sealant provides a sturdy, permanent fit up of parts. For some parts assemblies, Ford now uses anaerobic sealers that cure in the absence of air. Mechanisms like gasketless transfer cases and alloy transmission housings often require anaerobic type sealants.

Many mechanics use silicone sealants to replace conventional gaskets, but there are some geartrain parts that use a pre-cut gasket as a selective fit spacer. Unless otherwise specified in your factory service manual, avoid the use of RTV with selective fit gaskets.

For axle differential covers and all oil exposed seals, automotive RTV silicone can help eliminate seepage. Ford trucks, especially 4x4s, flex and distort paper gaskets, and the older transmission and transfer case cut gaskets are notorious for leaking. Many late powertrain components no longer use cut gaskets, substituting the more flexible silicone products.

RTV sealant allows a more direct fitup of parts, which reduces flexing, keeps hardware from loosening and helps prevent parts misalignment. Although neoprene-lipped seals still serve on many shaft surfaces, the outer jacket of these seals should also be lightly coated with automotive RTV silicone before driving the seal into place. This includes timing cover seals, transmission front shaft and output shaft seals and axle shaft seals. Although coating the jacket of a seal will not prevent the lip portion from failing, you can reduce the likelihood of housing bore-to-seal seepage.

Once you become familiar with the properties and proper uses of these sealants and adhesives, they prove as handy as your screwdrivers and wrenches. Often, soft tools provide faster, more permanent repairs than conventional gaskets—especially when your makeshift garage is in remote back country.

Miscellaneous Chores

There are other tasks that you may want to perform on your Ford truck. In particular, front end alignment is a relatively easy job on a solid I-beam or solid hypoid front driving axle. Adjusting toe-in may be within your abilities. The setting of caster and camber, however, involves more skill, special tools and sometimes special parts. A solid front axle with springs in good shape seldom requires caster or camber adjustment.

Toe-in changes caused by normal wear of steering linkage takes place over time. Inexpensive toe-set alignment bars serve the home mechanic. These toe bars can be used on most 2WD I-beam and Twin I-Beam models and also with solid axle 4x4 trucks. Performing your truck's toe-set provides savings in both service costs and longer tire life. Your F-truck shop manual should have the specifications and details.

A variety of miscellaneous tools serve your truck's needs. Body work and paint, detailing chores and repair of upholstery are often part of a complete restoration.

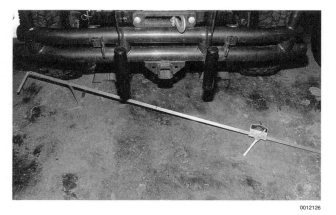

Fig. 4-50. *For front wheel alignment at home, Eastwood Company offers this inexpensive toe-set bar. Toe-in is easy to calculate and adjust on a solid front axle truck.*

With proper maintenance or restoration, your Ford F-truck will deliver years of rugged service.

8. SOURCING FORD TRUCK PARTS

For many Ford F-Series truck models, your local Ford dealer remains the most reliable parts source. Ford's genuine FoMoCo parts provide a high quality standard and your assurance of quality fit-up. When restoring your truck to OEM standards, the local Ford dealership can assist.

The indomitable nature of Ford F-trucks, the massive numbers of older Ford trucks still on the road and the collectible value of particular models has encouraged aftermarket suppliers to provide replacement parts. The popularity of '53–'56 F-100 pickups alone assures a brisk niche market for remaining "new original stock" (NOS) FoMoCo parts and accurate replica or rebuilt parts for models built over four decades ago.

Chassis components are available through quality lines like MOOG and TRW, even for the earliest model F-trucks. For Ford light truck engines, many with passenger car ties, repair parts remain readily accessible. The sheer numbers of Ford engines built assures the likelihood of parts for many years. Even the flathead V-8 engines remain popular enough for new, reproduction or rebuilt parts.

Automotive parts outlets and machine shops throughout the U.S. and Canada are very familiar with all Ford F-Series light truck engines. "Perishable" and fast moving items like shock absorbers, ignition parts, filters, shock absorbers, belts and hoses are available through local parts outlets, especially national retailers like NAPA. Whether a new or vintage model, your Ford F-truck will always be among the most popular and roadworthy vehicles in its class.

Aftermarket Geartrain Sources

Axle, transmission, driveshaft and transfer case pieces are available from a number of sources. Many geartrain pieces have industry-wide use. Dana, Spicer, Borg-Warner (Warner Gear Division), New Process, ZF,

Tremac and other manufacturers have produced a variety of gear components for Ford and other American truck manufacturers.

In some instances, interchangeability of parts between makes is possible. Often, though, the Ford truck version of a gear or powertrain component is unique, which will make parts sourcing more complicated. For older models, aftermarket parts sources often have easier access to parts than the modern Ford dealership, including engine rebuilding, re-wiring sources, fuel system repair parts, suspension pieces and even some body panels.

Mail-order Aftermarket

The brisk aftermarket of 4WD and off-highway vehicle parts also services Ford F-Series trucks. Businesses like Dick Cepek and Four-Wheel Parts (Wholesalers) do a huge mail-order and retail business. Product lines range from tires and off-road accessory items to winches and utility products for 4x4 trucks. Geartrain and traction devices are also available.

J.C. Whitney and other mail order retailers have kept suburban and rural Ford truck owners in parts for many years. J.C. Whitney and Eastwood Company serve restorers of vintage trucks, and J.C. Whitney now caters to the burgeoning recreational truck market. (For details on a variety of parts sources, see the appendix. In the accessories chapter of the book, I delve into the many products available.)

Local Parts Outlets

Your local auto parts store can help with tune-up and routine service parts. Choose the best available tune-up components for your Ford F-truck. Trucks demand flawless ignition performance. Bargain hunting for replacement parts is unwise. When genuine FoMoCo parts are not available, I have four aftermarket preferences (starting with my top choice): NAPA/Echlin, Autolite, Bendix, Delco-Remy or Standard-Blue Streak.

Water crossings and foul-weather driving conditions require a much higher standard of performance from your Ford truck. Especially with 4x4 models, water-proofing is a practical goal for your ignition distributor, coil and secondary spark cables. (See tune-up and performance chapters for details on ignition service and upgrades.)

Quality Filtration

For consistent performance, use genuine FoMoCo replacement air and fuel filters. You will find high performance filtration systems in the Ford SVO or Motorsport Catalog and also through the performance aftermarket. (See performance chapter for details.)

Any Ford truck exposed to poor quality fuels or water contamination, especially diesels, needs an add-on fuel filtration system. This includes water trap filters for diesels or when driving in regions where gasoline has a high water content.

9. ASSIGNING WORK TO A SHOP

For many consumers, nurturing a second career as an automotive/truck mechanic is impractical. You may find that performing hands-on mechanical work has no appeal. Perhaps your lifestyle or work space is too busy for servicing your own vehicle. Sometimes, the cost of special tools or the sheer scope of a repair job ranges beyond your capacity. Chasing parts and tying up your vehicle for unreasonable periods can be costly and stressful.

Assigning such jobs to a specialist can save considerable time and assure quality workmanship. You'll save in the long run by setting your ego or the challenge aside and simply recognizing that you would be better off assigning the work elsewhere.

Fig. 4-52. Your local Ford dealership's service department can perform factory level repairs and diagnostic work. Assess the repair steps and decide whether you want to tackle the job yourself. If not, with a knowledge of the work involved, you will be a better informed consumer with respect for the mechanic who does this job.

Fig. 4-51. An automatic transmission or axle assembly overhaul requires special tools and skills. Unless you are building a career around light truck mechanics, consider sending these types of jobs to a specialist.

Assess The Job

Whether you enjoy servicing your vehicle or saving the cost of labor on repairs, each task has its challenges. My approach to mechanics always begins with a thorough review of the job, starting at the factory service guidebook for my vehicle. The factory manuals assist at troubleshooting problems and give step-by-step instructions for performing mechanical tasks. Each repair includes a list of specialty tools required.

The factory shop manual can even serve truck owners who plan to assign repairs. If you can pinpoint the actual problem, or at least narrow the field of possibilities, you have a distinct advantage when approaching a shop or dealership service facility.

The Well-informed Customer

If you assign work to an independent shop or Ford dealership's service department, your sense for the repairs needed can help the staff. When your diagnosis is accurate, the mechanic can focus on the actual trouble and save time—and your money—by not having to troubleshoot the job. If you suspect that extra service is being sold, your own shop manual can verify whether such service is warranted for the kind of troubles and repairs in question.

Having written and worked from repair orders within a truck dealership environment, I suggest that you approach the service department with diplomacy. Surveys often reveal that American consumers mistrust auto repair facilities. Surely, there are unscrupulous shops or service operations that set profit above all other considerations, but the current trend has been toward improved customer relations.

Your best safeguard is information, becoming a well-informed consumer who has a sense for the task at hand and reasonable costs. In fairness, remember that the shop staff has more experience at troubleshooting and repairs. If you insist that a certain repair be done, you will pay whether that was the problem or not. When there is a gray area, you are wiser to pay for further diagnostic work and an opinion from the professional mechanic.

Flat-rate Cost Estimating

In some cases, you will find that shopping around (phoning different shops, asking friends where they do business, etc.) is an effective way to determine a fair cost for repairs. When you know the exact work needed and are certain that the truck will perform properly once a competent shop does these tasks, then you can do your own cost estimation work.

The standard practice for billing automotive service in the United States and Canada is by "flat rate." This provides a basis for estimating repair costs and paying the mechanic. Flat-rate work differs substantially from clock or hourly labor billing, the latter varying greatly on a given job due to different mechanics' skill levels, obstacles in a given job, or tools available in the shop.

As a former fleet and dealership truck mechanic, my personal library includes flat-rate labor and parts estimating guidebooks offered by Chilton, Motor and Mitchell. These books are the professional trade variety found in independent repair shops and dealerships. Automotive/truck dealerships also use new vehicle warranty labor time schedules.

The flat-rate guidebook lists specific labor operations and the recognized fair time to perform tasks. You can acquire such books, new or used, and actually do your own labor estimating before shopping for repairs. It is also reasonable to ask the service writer/salesperson to provide a labor time guidebook.

Become familiar with the guide's format and how to read an estimate. For example, many procedures overlap. The overhaul of an engine will say whether the overhaul includes removal-and-replacement (R & R) of the engine from its chassis. If so indicated in the guidebook, the shop should not charge for R & R of the engine plus the overhaul. Tune-up procedures may include diagnosis. If so indicated, you should not pay for diagnosis as a separate procedure.

I also find the parts estimating section of my books valuable, although in fairness, parts pricing changes frequently.

Ethics and The Flat-rate System

Flat-rate pays minimal (if any) time for diagnostic work. Most vehicles brought into the shop for repair focus only on a current trouble symptom. Flat-rate time does not include preventive maintenance or inspection. If you want thorough service and inspection of your truck, that is a separate labor procedure, which bears an additional cost.

The flat-rate mechanic must make quick and accurate assessment of a problem and propose a repair procedure. When the paid repair fails to make a difference, a credibility gap develops. The shop likely contends that you should pay for the first repair, especially if an observable improvement occurred. You, on the other hand, may feel that the shop failed to cure the symptoms yet took your hard earned money.

0012129

Fig. 4-53. Repair personnel in advanced industrial societies commonly replace, rather than overhaul, a sub-assembly. The argument is often cost effectiveness, even with the extreme of replacing entire commodities. Cheaper goods and cost competitive rebuilt parts have denigrated the role of field service technicians and mechanics who once took responsibility for actually fixing a worn or defective product or sub-assembly.

If no change in the original symptom took place, the flat-rate system (when ethically applied) says that your mechanic has earned a "come back." This means the mechanic absorbs the labor cost of the first repair, and sometimes the shop absorbs the parts cost. This punishment of the mechanic supposedly serves as an incentive to prevent hasty or inaccurate diagnosis.

The largest complaint that consumers have about the flat-rate system is its emphasis on parts replacement. Unfortunately, since a hard hourly flat-rate program can only apply to repairs entailing R & R of parts, the system does encourage outright parts replacement.

The flat-rate system implies that automotive troubleshooting and repair estimating are an exact science. In fact, jobs like troubleshooting a late model electronic fuel and spark management system can become ensnared in the mysteries of systems overlap—or mired in the complexities and idiosyncratic nature of computer programming. Such engineering issues often reach beyond the control of a service technician.

In my view, many automotive labor procedures can fall within consistent time frames—R & R operations like a transmission overhaul, differential rebuild, engine overhaul, alternator replacement or brake system overhaul. However, I also believe that mechanics deserve more time for diagnostic work. This would encourage more thorough repairs and increase the likelihood of long term, preventive remedies.

Knowledge Is Your Best Friend

In the automotive flat-rate system, here is how the R & R incentive works: You approach the service shop with a complaint that your truck's engine has a misfire. The ethical mechanic in a well-equipped shop will put the engine on an oscilloscope and analyze the exhaust content and ignition performance.

Let's say your six cylinder engine shows that #2 cylinder's spark firing line is weak. As a fleet mechanic, I would check resistance of the plug wire at #2 cylinder and compare this reading with other wires. The air filter and other parts would deserve a quick look, but once the ignition system was isolated as a problem, I'd focus on restoring the plug firing line for #2 cylinder. If I found that other wires, the distributor components or spark plugs looked marginal, some of those parts would also be replaced.

A flat-rate mechanic, wanting to avoid a costly comeback and recognizing that the parts department likes additional sales, decides to cover all possibilities. The parts list soon includes a fuel filter, air cleaner, six new platinum spark plugs, a distributor rotor, a full set of spark plug wires and the PCV valve.

The service estimator/writer/salesperson usually calls the customer and gains approval for installation of these parts. Here is how the dialog might go: "Ms. Jones, your engine's misfire is ignition related, but the mechanic feels that the engine shows other wear points, and he would like to perform a complete tune-up. When was the engine tuned last?"

To the salesperson, this question is critical. If you had such work done recently, there would be no basis for buying all these parts and service. The mechanic would simply replace the one spark plug wire and bill accordingly.

As a consumer, you need to make decisions based upon your knowledge of the vehicle's service history and the factory recommended service guidelines. Your factory level shop manual describes the normal intervals between tune-ups and other routine maintenance. Keeping a trail of maintenance work orders helps you prevent an overly zealous service writer from re-selling work recently done.

Ask, nicely, how the mechanic arrived at the conclusion that all of these parts need replacement. Since the diagnosis involves ignition or fuel problems, ask what diagnostic equipment aided the conclusions. Did the equipment suggest that all of these parts needed replacement to end the symptoms and restore reliable and economical operation of the engine?

Unless a problem is obvious, request thorough diagnostic procedures. Dealerships have extensive resources for diagnosing problems, everything from a special "customer flight recorder" that detects and records problems away from the dealership, under real-world conditions. Ford's Service Bay Diagnostic System (SBDS) is a highly advanced diagnostic tool that can service the latest fuel and spark management and electronically controlled transmission programming. If a service facility like your local Ford dealership has such equipment, you can radically reduce the risk of engine or powertrain mis-diagnosis and unnecessary repair work. Money spent here is spent wisely.

Remember that the adage "too much knowledge is dangerous" applies. Don't flaunt your wisdom and insight. You will find that an ethical mechanic or service writer will happily share information and engage in dialog. Such an exchange is valuable, as there are many diagnostic gaps that only a mechanic's experience can overcome.

0012130

Fig. 4-54. Diagnostic equipment can save time and provide detailed insight into problems. If a shop has high quality diagnostic equipment, you can expect more reasonable and accurate estimates. Such shops should expect to pay for equipment with satisfied customers and repeat business.

Chapter 5

Lubrication and Maintenance

REGULAR MAINTENANCE is the most important way to attain maximum service from your Ford F-Series light truck. Preventive care proves cost effective and assures safety and reliable performance when your truck needs it. Preventive maintenance can reduce the risk of hazardous and costly breakdowns. As a truck fleet mechanic and heavy equipment operator, I trained at visualizing potential weaknesses in a chassis, engine and geartrain. The best place for making these observations was during routine lubrication and service.

Although much of the maintenance on your Ford truck will be routine, such care has a direct effect on your safety. For 4x4 trucks that travel to remote and nearly inaccessible places, regular maintenance could prevent a serious breakdown or equipment related accident. Even simple fluid or filter changes will help ensure good engine performance and fuel efficiency when the going gets tough.

1. DO YOUR OWN "FULL-SERVICE" MAINTENANCE!

Most modern gasoline stations fail to meet motorists' needs. Drivers at Full Service pumps pay up to two-fifths more per gallon for fuel, expecting genuine vehicle care. Perhaps their windshield receives attention or the attendant will ask if the oil needs checking. After several minutes beneath the hood, some attendants return to inquire, "Where's the oil dipstick?"

When I was a high school student in the mid-Sixties, there was Bud Berrum's Chevron, across the highway from the C.O.D. Garage at Minden, Nevada. I worked after school and summers for Bud, and he ran a real service station. As attendants, we catered to customers' needs, and that meant thorough service.

If you drove into Bud's Chevron while I was on shift, your cares were over. I'd pump 94–110 octane gas into your tank, check your oil, drive belts, hoses, automatic transmission fluid, brake fluid, battery and windshield washer fluid.

Without leaving a streak, I'd whisk away the summer bugs or January ice from your windshield, wipe your sideview mirror and even clean the back window glass. If your truck's tires were cool enough, I'd check pressures at all four corners plus the spare if accessible.

Fig. 5-1. Chassis lubrication provides an excellent opportunity to inspect your truck's undercarriage. By performing such chores, you become intimately aware of your F-truck's needs. This is a vital part of preventive care.

0012132

Fig. 5-2. Mini-Lube unit from C.D.U. Services in Visalia, California is a professional quality portable greasing system, ideal for the home workshop. High pressure gun makes quick chore of lubrication.

What did this cost? Nothing more than your gasoline business and, if you felt like it, you could say, "Thanks!"

The lube room was always busy, with a grease job for two dollars and fifty cents, and a lube, oil and filter running near five dollars, depending upon the filter's cost. A thorough wheel bearing repack, even on a Ford 4x4 truck, was less than six dollars, including the price of new seals.

For these services, I'd take out Standard Oil's lubrication chart and look up your truck model. The guide listed each grease fitting, gear case check point and fluid type. It also noted how frequently each service procedure should be performed, and at the last service, I put a dated mileage sticker on the door jamb as a reminder.

All fittings greased, the engine oil drained, gearbox and axle oil levels checked, rubber bushings dressed with rubber lube, I inspected the clutch free-play, exhaust system and chassis. After installing a new oil pan drain plug gasket, I lowered your truck carefully and headed for the hood latch.

Armed with special data for your Ford truck, I'd remove and service the oil bath air cleaner (if so equipped), check the radiator coolant with a hydrometer, inspect the steering gearbox fluid level, and carefully check brake fluid—only after vacuuming the dirty floorboard around the inspection plate ('48–'56 F-trucks) and brushing all dirt away from the master cylinder fill plug or cap.

Next, I'd clean the battery case, check its water and wire brush the terminals. Since early trucks had generators and wick-oiled distributors, a squirt can of motor oil was always handy. Careful not to overfill the wicks, I'd apply oil with a light squeeze of the trigger. Then, as the engine crankcase filled from the station's five-quart copper down spout can, I would test all lights and the turn signals (if your truck was originally equipped with them!).

Finally, I'd spray lube each hood, door and tailgate hinge, the parking brake handle mechanism and even the ball bearing in your ash tray. Before the truck rolled out

the door, I would vacuum the cab, clean all of the windows (inside and out), and check tire air pressures for all four tires and your side-mounted or under chassis spare.

Was this all that our customers came to expect? Oh, no. A free wash job went with each lube and oil change. Winter or summer, searing heat or low teens temperatures (complete with a frozen water bucket and wash mitten), I'd wash your truck thoroughly and be thankful for the $1.50 per hour that Bud paid me!

Well, times have changed. Now, I'm recommending that you do your own service. You'll be better off for it. Not only will you learn more about your favorite truck, you'll also be better equipped to handle problems afield.

Bud Berrum's training gave me a darn good foundation. My first stint as a truck fleet mechanic yielded a zero breakdown record for the organization's twenty-two vehicles. I had entered the job with a thorough grasp of preventive maintenance. If you take this whole thing half as seriously as Bud and I, your Ford truck will give its all.

Defining Chassis Maintenance

Your Ford truck's chassis, though durable and designed for longevity, requires regular maintenance. Earlier F-trucks demand more chassis service than later models, and '48–'56 models, in particular, have grease fittings at the kingpins, shackle bushings, spring anchor bolts, pedal pivots, steering linkage, shift linkage and several other wear points.

Later models use zero-maintenance nylon and rubber bushings at most wear points. Such pieces still require periodic inspection and need replacement when they wear out. According to Ford's maintenance schedules, most greaseable joints demand lubrication at 1000-mile intervals. They, too, wear out, which means time for new bushings.

Minimizing wear at friction points is the overall goal of chassis maintenance. In your Ford factory service manual or owner's handbook, you will find a chassis lubrication chart for your model. Pay close attention to the greases specified.

As a home mechanic, you will likely use a hand grease gun, which minimizes grease seal damage. U-joints, in particular, require hand gun lubrication. High pressure equipment can destroy delicate seals, leaving a U-joint exposed to debris and abrasive contaminants.

Selecting Lubricants and Fluids

Various lubricants, oils, greases and fluids serve your Ford truck. Proper oils and fluids are crucial to the safety and reliability of your vehicle. Compatibility of oils, correct quantities and proper viscosities are each essential to proper maintenance.

Earlier Ford trucks require conventional lubricants. Typically, 90-weight gear oil fills the differentials, manual steering gearbox, manual transmission and transfer case. With the advent of chain-drive full-time 4x4 systems, automatic transmission fluid (ATF) has become common for both the automatic transmission and transfer case. Many late model Ford manual gear cases also call for lighter lubricants.

Mixing oil brands and types is a mistake. Even when viscosity and type (GL or API rating) are the same, oil producers use different chemical additives with their

Synthetic oils have generated controversy. Synthetic lubricants will outperform conventional crude oil base stocks under heavy duty/severe service use. Regardless of your choice, beware of compatibility. Avoid mixing stocks of synthetic oil with either conventional oils or other synthetic brands.

Note your vehicle's warranty requirements as they relate to lubricants, oil types and ratings. When uncertain about the correct lubricant for a given area of your truck, refer to the owner's handbook or a factory service manual.

Proper Greases

Lubrication greases have become simpler in recent years. Many vehicle manufacturers use a common, multi-purpose grease for all chassis, steering linkage and wheel bearing needs. I still prefer precise greases for each application: a specified chassis/steering linkage and U-joint grease or a specific wheel bearing lubricant. Use the highest grade grease (usually designated as a wheel bearing grease for disc brake models) when servicing wheel bearings.

Wheel bearing greases and chassis lubes have various base stocks. A major concern is compatibility of greases. Do not mix brands or types of grease. If you have just begun servicing your wheel bearings, thoroughly remove all old grease before repacking with fresh grease. (See other chapters for wheel bearing service details.)

On steering linkage and chassis joint grease fittings, simply pump fresh grease through the assembly until only new grease squeezes out. Wipe away excess with a rag. This will prevent abrasive dirt from accumulating around the joint.

Gear Oil

For gear case lubricants and oils, use a slightly different strategy. Ideally, especially if your truck has higher mileage, the gear units should be drained and refilled with a high grade gear oil. As with engine oil, gear oil viscosity and type must correspond to climate and the load on your vehicle.

Once you've selected an oil brand/type, periodic inspection and topping off will be simple. If you drive your truck extensively off-pavement or to remote reaches, squeeze bottle containers are practical, easy dispensers. Major oil companies distribute gear lube in pint or quart size plastic bottles, ideal for stowage on board.

Service Intervals

The tight factory service recommendations for early Ford F-trucks, such as chassis lubrication each 1,000 miles, assume that users will give their vehicles a real workout. When subjected to severe environments, older Ford trucks, and especially 4x4s, demand closer care than later models.

Longer oil change intervals allow oil to deteriorate. The contemporary 7,500-mile oil change recommendations of many vehicle manufacturers mean that combustion contaminants will find their way into the crankcase oil for even longer periods. At recommended oil change points, with crude stock oils, crankcase contamination can reach ten percent.

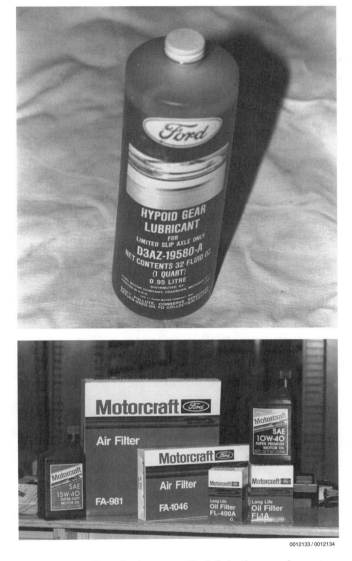

0012133 / 0012134

Fig. 5-3. F-trucks have specific lubrication requirements. Ford offers special FoMoCo gear oils, power steering fluid, wheel bearing grease and filters. Your best assurance of long service life is quality lubrication at recommended intervals. When planning a long trip over dusty roads or trails, carry extra air cleaner elements. A clogged air filter drastically reduces fuel economy and performance. Carbon buildup and internal engine damage can result from long-term neglect.

base stocks. Strange chassis/wheel bearing greases, engine oils or gear oils may react adversely with your truck's existing lubricants. For this reason, the Ford truck owner who maintains his or her own vehicle has a distinct advantage: the ability to assure consistent use of compatible fluids, greases and oils.

When changing engine oil, select a brand and stay with it. Carry a spare can or bottle of this type oil to assure availability in the field. Likewise, when draining and refilling the gearboxes or differential(s), adhere to a specific type and brand of lubricant.

4x4 Ford trucks have their special needs. Few vehicles submerge their wheel hubs and axle housings in swift running streams. If your 4x4 sees this kind of use, regular wheel bearing service and axle housing inspection is mandatory. If you stall in a fast moving stream or suspect water seepage into the wheel hubs, repack the wheel bearings immediately.

Recognizing the superior quality of modern chassis and wheel bearing greases, you can usually extend the intervals between wheel bearing and axle shaft service. Be certain that wheel hub seals, gaskets, axle and gear unit vent hoses and the one-way vent check valves can each do their job.

Your Ford F-truck demands the best. For maximum service life and performance, adjust oil and filter change intervals to 2,000–3,000 miles with premium grade conventional (crude or mineral base) oil. Even with synthetic oil, light truck driving demands call for oil change intervals at 7,500–10,000 miles.

For synthetic oil, I install a new, high-quality oil filter each 3,000 to 3,500 miles, and top off the oil level. I also replace the oil filter with each routine oil change. The goal is reliability. Superior lubricants and filtration are a truck's most basic need.

Building A Maintenance Schedule For Severe Service

Common sense should dictate your truck's service intervals. Years ago, service intervals were more frequent. Industrial and agricultural F-truck users changed gear lube each 300 hours, flushed the cooling system twice a year and fussed constantly over the amazing number of chassis lubrication points.

In industrial or farm work, oil bath air cleaner service takes place every 100–150 hours. (As always, dust conditions affect these figures.) If your truck has gone through twenty miles of alkaline gravel road, or at a snail's pace in high dust conditions, service the oil bath air cleaner (early F-trucks) or change the later Ford truck's dry paper element.

Fig. 5-5. *During stream fording, water drawn through the air intake snorkel can quickly pass through a paper element and into engine cylinders. If sufficient in volume, this water can act like a hydraulic ram, bending connecting rods or breaking other vital engine parts. Protect your intake system from exposure to water, and avoid use of an open faced paper filter air cleaner.*

Likewise, for 4x4 trucks, stalling the vehicle for several minutes in a thirty-inch deep, fast flowing stream raises several concerns. You will immediately need to inspect the hubs, wheel bearings, each gear unit and the engine oil for water contamination. Grease all fittings to flush out water.

Similarly, a day's play in dusty sand dunes begs a complete chassis lube and careful air cleaner service. (Keep sand from the intake area when you remove the filter.) Before performing this service, wash the chassis with a high pressure approach, like the local car wash.

Fig. 5-4. *For the Ford 4x4 truck that makes stream crossings, consider extending the axle housing or transmission and transfer case vents upward onto the body. Using pipe thread nipples, oil resistant hose and insulated clamps, mount these vents well above the frame height. This reduces the risk of water entering important geartrain parts during water crossings.*

Synthetic Versus Mineral Oil Products

When Ford flathead and early Y-block V-8s reigned, few oil choices existed. Viscosity and detergent levels were the major considerations when picking an oil. Until the 1960s, multi-viscosity oil was virtually non-existent.

Until the advent of synthetic oils, the fundamental difference between one brand of oil and another was the additive package. Generally, we accept that a modern, multi-viscosity, high-detergent/dispersant oil will offer broader engine protection under the widest variety of engine operating conditions.

Over the last two decades, a newer debate has surfaced around mineral versus synthetic based oils and greases. This controversy will likely reign through the 1990s, but on the basis of currently available information, a higher quality synthetic oil or grease is superior to a conventional mineral or crude stock product.

A major engine killer is sludge. Plugged or restricted oil screens mean scored bearings and engine failure. Poor oil circulation always accompanies sludge. Although changing oil is the best way to resist sludge buildup, other factors also play a role. The composition of an oil, regardless of the oil drain intervals, can contribute to sludge buildup.

High temperatures also encourage sludge buildup. Teardown of a worn truck engine generally reveals sludge in the valve covers, timing cover, and lower block or oil pan. It is easy to spot the engine's highest temperature areas; they show the greatest sludge deposits.

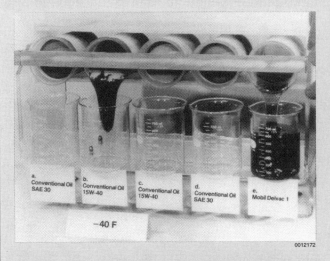

The typical gasoline automotive engine, for each 100 gallons of fuel burned, produces a horrifying 1/4 to 4 pounds of nitrogen and sulfuric acid, 1 to 2 ounces of hydrochloric acid, 90 to 120 gallons of water, and 3 to 10 gallons of unburned gasoline. For the once popular lead-additive gasolines, add 6 to 10 ounces of lead salts to this medley of pollutants. At the typical 3,000-mile drain interval, petroleum oils in the crankcase have reached a contamination level of four percent.

How, then, do synthetic oil manufacturers extend oil change intervals to as high as 25,000 miles? Mobil and others claim that longer term viscosity stability (due to superior control of hydrocarbon volatility), plus greater resistance to sludge formation, contribute to these longer service cycles. Superior ingredients reduce engine heat, friction and oxidation. Higher film strength and lower volatility allow many synthetic oils to last longer and protect an engine far better than any mineral base oil currently available.

The lubrication quality, engine cooling and the cleansing action of synthetics is exceptional. Even at minus 40° F (pictured) Mobil Delvac 1 still pours. Typical mineral based oils have already solidified. More importantly, the piston ring sealing properties of an oil largely determine the amount of contaminants that will find their way into the crankcase.

Test results show Mobil 1 can operate an engine 50° F cooler than a premium mineral based oil. As oil is responsible for cooling pistons, rings, the valvetrain, the crankshaft assembly and other critical running parts, oil temperature reduction represents a significant gain.

Under laboratory tests, high grade synthetic oils drastically reduce sludge, piston varnish, wear of metal parts and oil consumption. Prominent race engine builders confirm the merits of synthetic oils.

Notably, Smokey Yunick, quoted from a *Popular Science* interview, comments about his Indianapolis 500 engine and polyol synthetic. Upon teardown after the race, Yunick observed, "When you disassemble an engine that's been run on petroleum oil, if you examine the rings and cylinder bores with a glass, you'll see ridges and scratches—that's wear going on. With polyol (a variety of synthetic), when you take the engine apart, everything has the appearance of being chrome plated. In the engine we ran at Indianapolis, we used a polyol synthetic. When we tore the engine down, you could still see the original honing marks on the bearings...no wear at all. We put the same bearings back in because the crankshaft never touched the bearings. I've never seen that before."

Is such protection necessary for your truck? Recognizing the stresses of heavy hauling, off-road driving and harsh climates, any oil product faces hard work in a Ford F-truck engine.

On the downside, many owners switching to synthetic oil on high mileage engines have trouble. Worn, varnish-coated seals and gaskets, suddenly faced with the high cleansing action and superior lubricity of synthetic oil, sometimes begin to leak. The synthetic oil has washed away the false sealing surfaces of built-up varnish and deposits.

Seals and gaskets may require upgrading before your truck's gear units or engine will adequately hold synthetic oil. Once seals meet normal standards, however, a synthetic oil could actually increase seal and gasket life.

Weigh the information available. If your Ford truck powertrain is relatively new or recently restored, consider use of high grade synthetic lubricants. The added protection, probability of longer component life and extension of service intervals will usually offset the higher cost of these products.

2. YOU CAN LUBE YOUR OWN TRUCK

Many truck owners have developed a better knowledge of their vehicles by performing routine service. Aside from saving labor costs, you can learn about how your truck works and contribute to its reliability.

The greatest benefit of routine service is that you can find a problem before it becomes costly to repair or causes an inopportune breakdown. You can inspect safety areas and assure that the truck's vital components are intact and properly lubricated. This, basically, is what quality preventive maintenance is all about.

You should keep an accurate account of the service you perform on the truck. Over time, patterns emerge, and the routine begins to pay off. By keeping these records and holding onto receipts for parts purchases, you will enhance the value of your truck for resale.

Since the best way to learn routine service is by watching close-up, I have constructed a pictorial guide for basic lubrication work. (See troubleshooting and service chapters for specific details on mechanical/safety inspection.) Compare these steps with recommended procedures found in your Ford F-truck owner's handbook or a factory service manual.

If you follow the manufacturer's service interval guidelines, your truck will have a long and reliable life. Use the right tools to protect your hands and eyes, and always recycle or dispose of your drained fluids and other hazardous materials properly.

Engine Oil and Filter Change

Begin service by placing a drain pan beneath the engine's oil pan, then remove the drain plug. Whether oil is warm or hot, wear an industrial rubber glove for protection. Drain oil is caustic and contains carcinogenic agents.

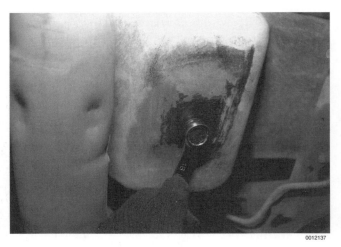

Fig. 5-6. *It is better to drain engine oil when the engine is warm. To make sure all old oil drains, leave the plug out while you perform other lube chores.*

Oil filters differ depending on the year of your F-Series. Ford's older L-head (flathead) engines have cartridge type by-pass oil filters. A replacement cartridge fits securely within the canister. See Fig. 5-7. Some Ford engines use a full-flow type canister oil filter that mounts to the engine block.

Remove the canister's top and disassemble the filter. Note parts layout. Discard the cartridge and wipe sludge and debris from the interior of the housing. Install a new cartridge, making certain that the oil seal(s) are in place and seat squarely. Re-install the mounting bolt. Install a new gasket under the bolt head if wear is evident.

Fig. 5-7. *If your filter mounts separately from the engine block, with oil lines connected to the engine block, you have a by-pass oil filter.*

Ford introduced spin-on oil filters with later 223 sixes and 292 Y-block V-8s. See Fig. 5-8. Remove the oil filter carefully, using a special filter wrench. Use a clean shop rag to wipe the area where the filter mounts. Keep debris away from oil passages. Apply a small film of clean engine oil to filter gasket before installing filter. Follow directions on filter, and tighten new filter securely. Avoid overtightening, or you will have a very difficult time removing the filter next time.

Fig. 5-8. *Ford introduced spin-on oil filters with later 223/262 sixes and Y-block V-8s. If your Ford truck engine has a spin-on oil filter, replace the unit with each oil change.*

Clean and inspect oil pan drain plug gasket. See Fig. 5-9. If the gasket is damaged or worn, replace with a new gasket. Be cautious when threading the drain plug, and tighten to specification.

Fig. 5-9. *It's wise to stock some new gaskets if you plan to perform your own lube and oil change services. Be careful not to cross-thread the drain plug when you reinstall it.*

Topside in the engine bay, wipe the oil fill cap/hole and remove the cap. Make sure that dirt cannot enter the engine during service. Pour the new oil in carefully and avoid spilling by using a spout can or funnel. After filling crankcase with specified amount of oil, replace cap and start the engine at an idle. Check for oil leaks around the filter and drain plug. Shut off the engine, let it set for several minutes, then re-check oil level on dipstick. Make sure oil reaches FULL mark. Add oil as needed.

Air Cleaner

F-trucks through the years used two types of oil filters. Older Ford trucks use an oil-bath air cleaner, where dirt in the intake air is filtered through oil-soaked metal mesh. See Fig. 5-11. The second type of air cleaner is the more familiar paper element.

Whichever the type, it is important to regularly service the air filter. A very dirty oil bath-type air filter, unlike a paper element, will still allow reasonable engine performance. This can create the impression that the filter is okay. For maximum service and economy, always service the filter more often if you operate your truck in dusty conditions.

To service an oil bath air cleaner, remove the assembly completely from the engine, then separate the filtering element from the oil cup. Clean both of these components

Fig. 5-10. *It's important to make sure that no dirt enters the engine through the oil filler hole. Clean the area before removing the filler cap.*

Fig. 5-11. *If your earlier Ford F-truck engine has an oil bath air cleaner, you should service the unit every few thousand miles or at the same time that you change engine oil.*

thoroughly in a suitable solvent and allow them to air dry. Do not use compressed air, as it may damage the element. Note the oil fill level, which is indicated on the inside of oil cup section. See Fig. 5-12. Use clean engine oil of the recommended viscosity (usually straight 30-wt. or a 20-wt. for cold temperature operation).

Fig. 5-12. *Oil fill level for oil bath air cleaner is indicated on the inside of the filter housing.*

If your engine uses a dry paper element, you must check it regularly. Once impacted with dirt, the dry paper element starves the engine for air. The result is similar to operating your engine with the choke on, and the rich mixture can eventually damage the engine.

Fig. 5-13. *Later model F-trucks all have dry paper air filtration. Although dry paper elements offer exceptionally good air filtration, they quickly clog when exposed to high dust levels.*

It is virtually impossible to clean a dry paper element. Most manufacturers caution against reverse blowing (inside to outside) with compressed air as this can damage the paper matrix. If you are uncertain whether the air cleaner will flow enough air, remove the filter and gently tap its base on a clean, flat surface until loose debris has fallen free. Then aim the filter toward bright sunlight or a flashlight. See Fig. 5-14. (Keep away from heat or flame—the air cleaner element contains flammable gasoline fumes!) Look from the center toward the light source. A new or functional dry paper filter will show light through its wafered layers. (Compare light flow of a new filter.) If no light is visible, or light seems scarce and intermittent, assume that filter element needs replacement.

Fig. 5-14. *Check paper air filters by seeing how much light passes through. If in doubt, replace the element—it's cheap insurance for your engine.*

Make certain the air cleaner cover seals properly. Abrasive dust, seeping into the engine through an air cleaner mounting gasket leak, can quickly destroy piston rings. If the air cleaner seals look weak or seat poorly, replace them immediately. Clean and ample air supply is vital to an engine's survival.

Fig. 5-15. *For paper element air cleaners, also check the sealing gasket for the cover.*

Fuel, Spark, and Emission Controls

Engine service includes the fuel, spark and emission control systems. (For details on tune-up, troubleshooting and emission controls, refer to service chapters.) Closed crankcase ventilation eliminated the open road draft tube. Check the positive crankcase ventilation (PCV) valve during routine service. See Fig. 5-16. Periodically clean or replace the valve.

Fig. 5-16. *The positive crankcase ventilation (PCV) valve is just one part of emission control maintenance. For more information see the engine chapter.*

Steering Gear

While beneath the hood, check the steering gear fluid. Begin by clearing away debris from the inspection plug on a manual steering gear or the power steering pump dipstick. Check fluid level and top off, if necessary, with recommended lubricant. If you find fluid level very low, look for leaks and make repairs.

Manual steering gears usually use conventional gear lubricant. SAE 80-wt. or equivalent was standard on many older trucks. (In a hotter climate, 90-wt. gear lube works fine in a manual steering gear.) Power steering systems require the ATF fluid type recommended on the power steering reservoir or in your Ford owner's manual.

Fig. 5-17. *Steering gear lubricant needs to be checked regularly.*

Other Lubrication Points

On an earlier F-truck, the generator, ignition distributor and even the starter motor may require periodic oiling. Several drops of oil, applied regularly to oil wicks, assure long service. See Fig. 5-18. Add clean engine oil with a squirt can. Ford recommended oiling every 1,000 miles. Avoid excess oil. Simply saturate the wicks.

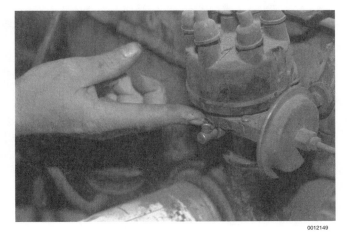

Fig. 5-18. *Earlier F-trucks require periodic lubrication of the generator, ignition distributor and even the starter motor. Look for spring-loaded oil caps at these locations.*

Chassis and Driveline Lubrication

Move next to the underside of your F-truck. You may need to raise the vehicle. Always use jackstands for support.

> *WARNING —*
> *Always use jackstands to support the vehicle when raised. Never use just a jack, cinder blocks, wooden blocks, or other makeshift supports.*

Chassis and driveline lubrication includes spring pivots (early models), ball joints, U-joints, steering knuckles, transmission, and differential(s).

If your Ford F-truck is an early model, the leaf spring shackles and anchor pivot bushings require grease. Grease the steering linkage, tie-rod ends, the drag link and Pitman arm joints. Wipe each fitting with a clean rag or shop towel, then apply fresh lubricant through the grease fitting. See Fig. 5-19. Watch for grease to exit the opposite end of bushing. Wipe away excess.

On leaf spring models with rubber or synthetic bushings, spray each bushing with rubber or silicone lubricant. See Fig. 5-20. This will reduce both friction and formation of surface oxidation, which will maximize the life of these materials. Avoid use of lubricant that contains petroleum distillates or other mineral/petroleum based solvents and oils. They harm rubber and cause premature wear.

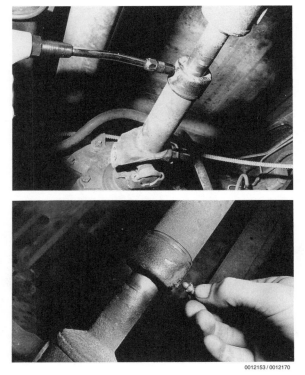

Fig. 5-21. *Avoid overgreasing driveshaft joints, especially the splined slip collars.*

Fig. 5-19. *Early models require more greasing than later models. Check the leaf spring shackles, anchor pivot bushings, steering linkage, tie-rod ends, the drag link and Pitman arm joints for grease fittings.*

Move toward the rear springs and driveshaft. On an earlier Ford F-truck, you will find additional grease fittings that need attention, including the clutch/brake pedal linkage, transfer case lever pivot (4WD) and column shift linkage.

Fig. 5-20. *"Maintenance-free" rubber or synthetic bushings, can still benefit from a spray of rubber or silicone lubricant.*

Once you have greased the front spring ends and steering linkage, begin lubing all driveshaft components, including slip collars and U-joints. See Fig. 5-21. If the slip collar is extended, add grease modestly. Otherwise, compression of the driveshaft will displace grease.

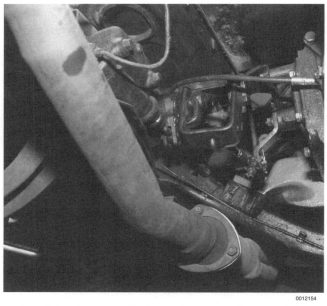

Fig. 5-22. *On an earlier F-truck, additional grease fittings need attention, including the clutch/brake pedal linkage, transfer case lever pivot (4WD) and column shift linkage.*

On an earlier 4x4 with closed-knuckle steering joints, the fill hole appears much like a gear oil check point. See Fig. 5-23. Some guides recommend 90-wt. while others call for 140-wt. gear oil. At high mileage, a mix of gear lube and light chassis/U-joint grease works fine and is less likely to leak past seals. When lubing closed steering knuckles, add enough grease to lightly fill the cavity. Avoid pressurizing the knuckle, which could stress seals. Closed steering knuckles are notorious for seal leaks, anyway, especially at the large inner grease seal. This seal, exposed to road debris and ice, fatigues over time.

Fig. 5-23. Early closed-knuckle steering joint.

Steering knuckle lubrication assures that axle shaft joints and kingpin bearings receive grease. Periodic engagement of free-wheeling hubs is necessary to supply adequate lube for upper kingpin bearings. If your closed-knuckle Ford 4x4 model has manual hubs, engage LOCK mode for a few miles each month. This will circulate grease for axle shaft joints and kingpin bearings and also reduce the effects of condensation. After running on slush or ice in freezing weather, swing the front wheels to each extreme before parking your closed-knuckle equipped 4x4 truck. Knuckle wipers will sweep away debris that could otherwise freeze and damage components.

Ford 4x4 front axles with closed knuckles call for periodic steering knuckle/axle shaft grease or fluid changes. Front wheel bearings call for a repack at 6,000 miles, more often if you run through water. If your Ford truck is a newer model with open knuckles (See Fig. 5-25), you will find that intervals have been extended.

Fig. 5-24. Inadequate lubrication of closed knuckles can cause seal failure and expensive damage.

Fig. 5-25. For both new and older 4x4s, modern greases can lengthen periods between bearing and joint service.

On all Ford 4x4 models, the axle differentials, transfer case and manual transmission each have oil fill plugs. See Fig. 5-26. Fill hole also indicates the oil full mark with vehicle stationary and level. Recommended interval for changing hard working 4x4 gear and differential lubricant is 10,000–15,000 miles. You should check fluid level with each oil change or at 2,500–3,000 miles, more often if seepage is apparent.

Your kind of driving and periods that the truck remains idle, which contributes to condensation and corrosion, also govern fluid change intervals. Before multi-viscosity gear oils, SAE 80-wt. (cold weather) or 90-wt. was commonly recommended for front and rear differentials. Positive traction differential units require special lubricant and/or additives. Periodic flush-and-clean can slow clutch deterioration. Contemporary multi-viscosity gear lubricants, like this synthetic line, are much more resilient. These products enable Ford trucks to go way beyond 10,000 miles between gear lube changes.

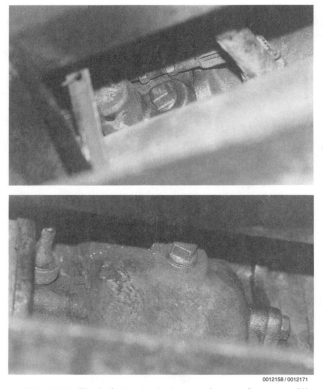

Fig. 5-28. *Since the introduction of improved, multi-viscosity lubricants, 75/90-wt. and even 80/140-wt. gear oils (designed for both wide temperature range and limited slip use) have become popular. Later chain drive transfer cases, and even some manual transmissions, rely on lighter viscosity (weight) gear lubricants. Some even specify an engine oil or automatic transmission fluid (ATF). For late model transmissions and chain drive transfer cases, consult your Ford owner's manual for recommended fluid types.*

Fig. 5-26. *Typical transmission and transfer case fill plugs.*

country. Cleanliness assures reliability. With your truck on level ground, fluid should not be above lower edge of inspection/fill hole. See Fig. 5-29. If gear unit is over full, drain it down to the lower edge of fill hole. (Make sure your truck's chassis is level and that fluid has settled before making this determination.)

Fig. 5-27. *Contemporary multi-viscosity gear lubricants, like this synthetic line, enable Ford trucks to go way beyond 10,000 miles between gear lube changes.*

Fig. 5-29. *Checking differential lubricant level.*

Before removing any fill/inspection plug, clean the surrounding area. Keep debris and abrasive contaminants away from openings. These are expensive gear units, responsible for taking your truck into remote back

Overfilled gear cases can raise havoc, especially on 4x4 vehicles that operate on steep angles. Excess oil can cause a leak or drive a seal loose from the gear housing. See Fig. 5-30. If this occurs, expensive parts can starve for oil or gear lube can find its way into the clutch lining, ruining friction material.

Fig. 5-30. Watch for loose seals on transmission case. Overfilling lubricant can dislodge seals.

Final Lubrication Details

Several other service points require attention. Clean the battery case and cable ends, then check and add distilled water as necessary. The manifold heat riser valve found on many Ford truck engines, requires penetrating oil. With engine cold, apply a solvent/penetrant oil, like WD-40, to the riser shaft, then test to see that it moves freely and opens smoothly as engine warms.

Fig. 5-31. Exhaust heat riser should be checked for free movement.

Remove the speedometer cable occasionally, wipe it down and dress with speedometer cable lubricant. On early F-trucks, treat all control cables (steel conduit sleeve type) with a penetrating oil such as WD-40. Some lithium

sprays work equally well. (Always wipe off excess to avoid attracting dirt.) If cables still balk, remove and clean them thoroughly, then lubricate with a suitable graphite or lithium based grease.

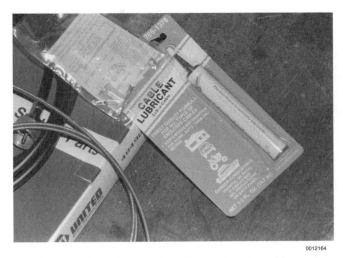

Fig. 5-32. Even items such as the speedometer cable require periodic lubrication.

White lithium and silicone sprays work well on hood and tailgate hinges, latches, strikers and locks. Lithium acts more like a grease, while silicone penetrates and frees up sticky mechanisms. For rubber parts and seals, use silicone based products that are free of solvents or petroleum distillates. (303 Protectant is an exceptional antioxidant for trim, dashpads, tires, chassis rubber and door edge seals.) Read labels carefully to understand a product's intended use. Choose a protectant that will dry completely. Wipe off excess and keep these products away from painted surfaces.

Fig. 5-33. Use other specialty lubricants for the small details.

3. STORING YOUR TRUCK

Many trucks, especially camper and trailer pulling models that serve seasonally, park for long periods of time. Some 4x4 models are strictly for snowplowing, idle for the other three seasons of the year. Arctic trucks often hibernate through deep freeze periods, immobile from early fall to the beginning of summer. Even a collectible '56 F-100 pickup might undergo long storage to protect its value.

When storing your Ford F-Series truck for long periods, consider the temperature, air quality and humidity. Major areas of concern are the engine, geartrain, cooling and electrical systems, the body and interior, fuel system, tires and brakes.

Body and Upholstery

Preserving your truck's body and upholstery involves many of the chemicals used for detailing work. For exterior painted surfaces, a heavy coat of wax, preferably buffer applied for even distribution, will help protect the finish. For long storage, apply two coats of a carnauba-base wax, buffing lightly. (A coat of cosmoline has been the long-term approach for severe climate storage or salty air.)

Vinyl upholstery, along with the dash pad, tire sidewalls and all other plastic and rubber areas, requires a liberal coating of a protectant/anti-oxidant treatment like 303. Professional rustproofing treatment, hot wax, and spray undercoatings can help protect the underside of the body and chassis.

You can apply some products at home, like rubberized spray undercoating. Whenever your truck faces exposure to corrosive environments, especially salted roads or sea air, take every precaution to eliminate oxidation of bare metal.

Once the body, frame/chassis, wheels and tires have been thoroughly protected, you should blanket the truck with a fitted cover. An enclosed garage, barn or storage shed will further protect your truck from elemental damage. Prevent exposure to bird droppings, tree sap and other corrosive hazards that might impair wax protection and destroy paint.

Engine Protection

Before storing your truck, change the engine oil and install a new oil filter. Run the engine to warm up and assure clean oil flow throughout the system. Install a new air filter element (paper-type), and make sure that it fits securely. If your older F-truck has an oil bath air cleaner, thoroughly clean the unit and change the oil. Be sure belts and hoses are in top condition and apply a quality belt dressing or protectant to each drive belt.

If the engine will set for a very long period, or if high humidity and varied temperatures are a factor, protect the engine's cylinder walls, valve guides, valve seats, valves and piston rings. Remove the spark plugs and squirt approximately two tablespoons of Marvel Mystery Oil or a similar fine lubricant into each cylinder.

Reinstall the spark plugs, and with the coil wire disconnected or ignition rotor removed, crank the engine just a few revolutions. This will coat the cylinder walls and other bare metal in the upper cylinders with a film of highly

Fig. 5-34. *Removal of coil wire and rotor during storage discourages theft. After long storage period, you can crank the engine without start-up to circulate oil.*

refined oil. Leave the rotor out or ignition coil wire disconnected as a safety and anti-theft measure during storage.

After the storage period, before attempting a start up, crank the engine over (with the coil wire or rotor still removed). This will pump the fine oil from the cylinders. Remove and clean the spark plugs in solvent or install a fresh set of plugs.

Reinstall the ignition rotor or coil wire. Start the engine, maintaining the lowest possible rpm during start-up and initial warm-up. Oil pressure should appear immediately upon start-up, quickly registering normal on the gauge.

Protect The Fuel System

If water contamination in the fuel is a concern, run a can of fuel system de-icer through the fuel tank before storing your truck. Carburetor cleaners with alcohol or other water bonding dispersants may be sprayed directly into the float bowl through the carburetor bowl's vent opening. A teaspoonful is plenty.

Cooling System and Storage

The cooling system requires fresh anti-freeze/coolant (ethylene glycol type or equivalent) with a 50/50 mixture that tests, minimally, to minus -34° F or lower on a hydrometer. Coolant must be thoroughly mixed, with a quality water pump lubricant/anti-rust agent added. An alternative to water pump lubricant is traditional soluble oil, a vegetable based, non-mineral (non-petroleum) oil that can help preserve rubber parts.

Unless the vehicle will be subject to temperatures below -34° F, avoid heavier concentrations of anti-freeze. Pure anti-freeze has an insufficient expansion rate and can actually cause engine castings to crack at temperature extremes. An overly concentrated coolant mixture can also boil over. Follow the mixture chart and manufacturer's recommendations described on the anti-freeze container.

Tighten all hose clamps, inspect hoses for cracking or weather checking and consider installing a new thermostat if the system requires flushing or draining. When

Fig. 5-35. *Radiator hydrometer tests specific gravity of coolant/anti-freeze. Weak concentrations allow freeze-up and also lower the boiling point. Excess concentration adversely impacts the expansion rate of coolant mix.*

Fig. 5-36. *When greasing steering linkage, suspension or driveline parts, grease fittings sometimes fail. These fittings are replaceable. Take care not to overfill joints, as seals may rupture. Ruptured seals allow contamination of joint or bushing.*

running the engine and circulating new coolant, be certain to turn on and operate the heater. Coolant/anti-freeze of proper mix must fill the heater and all hoses, or damage from freezing could result.

Chassis and Geartrain Preservation

Several powertrain items require attention. Lubricate the U-joints and all other grease fittings on your truck. Force out old chassis lube and make certain new grease squeezes from each joint. Wipe off excess. Dress rubber shock absorber, spring and sway bar bushings with rubber lubricant to prevent surface oxidation and dehydration.

If you haven't repacked the wheel bearings recently, buy new front wheel hub seals and fresh grease. Remove the wheels and hubs, and inspect for any signs of moisture damage. Thoroughly clean, closely inspect and repack the bearings. Fit new seals during installation. (For details on front wheel bearing repack, see the service chapter.)

Check fluid levels in each gear case and the axle/differential units. Note the smell and appearance of gear oil. (A burnt, acrid odor indicates older and likely worn gear lube.) Signs of damaging moisture are a milky, greyish appearance either in the fluid or around the housing cavity.

If signs of moisture appear in a gearcase, drain and flush the unit with a specified flushing oil, an appropriate solvent or clean kerosene. (During the flushing operation, drive the truck at minimal load for a very short distance to thoroughly wash the gear housing walls. Do not pull a load or allow gearcase to get hot.) Drain unit immediately and completely. Refill with fresh, proper grade gear oil.

Major damage to expensive bearings, gears and shafts will result from unchecked water or condensation in the gear cases. Check all vents from the axle housings, trans-

fer case and transmission. One-way check valves must be clean and seat properly to prevent moisture from entering gearcase during storage period.

If you are storing an automatic transmission equipped F-truck for a lengthy period, change the transmission fluid and filter. Operate the truck long enough to fully circulate new fluid. ATF is a high detergent oil, and fresh fluid purges older, acidic lubricant that might otherwise act on seals. Fresh fluid also helps flush varnish forming agents from the valve body.

Fig. 5-37. *One-way type check valves (arrow) allow transfer case, transmission and axle housings to vent pressure. Make sure these valves are clean and seating properly to prevent moisture from entering the gear unit.*

Prepping The Electrical System

Disconnect the battery cables to eliminate any drainage from the clock or other items. Clean the outer battery case thoroughly with a solution of warm water and baking soda. Use an inexpensive nylon paint brush.

WARNING —
Avoid splashing cleaning solution on painted surfaces or into your eyes. Wear protective goggles. Make certain that the cleaning solution does not enter any of the battery cells. Rinse away all cleaning solution with a stream of clean water.

If you remove the battery, make sure it rests on a non-conductive surface, with a full charge at the time of storage. Remember that a fully discharged battery, at low enough specific gravity, can freeze and crack.

Battery specialists recommend storage of batteries in a temperate setting. If at all possible, avoid exposing the battery to extremes of heat or cold, and always store away from spark or flame sources. After storage, bring the battery slowly up to full charge with a low amperage trickle charger. (Make certain that the charger has a built-in voltage regulator to prevent overcharging.)

Brake System and Storage

Hydraulic brake fluid is hygroscopic and readily bonds with water. On domestic trucks built prior to 1967, the master cylinder vents directly to atmosphere. These brake systems are especially vulnerable to moisture contamination. Eventually, especially if you store the vehicle for long periods, moisture can seep into the system, lowering the boiling point of the brake fluid, causing oxidation damage and pitting or corroding the hydraulic brake cylinders.

As a minimal precaution you should routinely flush fresh brake fluid through the hydraulic system. (A power bleeder speeds up this procedure.) The aim is to force old fluid, and any contaminants suspended in that fluid, out of the system.

The traditional, more involved method is to flush the system with denatured alcohol or a specially formulated hydraulic brake system flushing compound, then disassemble each wheel cylinder, caliper and the master cylinder. Air dry the lines and cylinders. Coat cylinder bores with special brake/rubber parts assembly lube or brake fluid, then install new rubber cups and seals. Fill/bleed the system with clean DOT 3 or higher grade brake fluid. (See service chapters.)

Along with a thorough flushing and installation of new rubber parts, you might consider switching to silicone brake fluid. Although expensive, silicone brake fluid nearly eliminates the water absorption problem. If you store your truck regularly, for long periods, silicone brake fluid could be practical.

When converting from conventional brake fluid to silicone, the system must be entirely purged of conventional brake fluid. (Use the silicone brake fluid during assembly of cylinder rubber parts.) Follow instructions carefully to avoid mixing incompatible chemistry. Make sure silicone brake fluid meets your vehicle's DOT brake fluid requirements.

WARNING —
Silicone fluid and conventional brake fluid are incompatible. Do not mix or blend these substances.

Fortunately, Ford F-truck brake systems built since 1967 are less prone to absorbing moisture. These trucks have master cylinder covers with bellows-type gaskets that offer far more protection from atmospheric contamination. Even with these models, I recommend periodic purging of old brake fluid using the pressure bleeding method. This will at least reduce moisture content in the brake fluid and help maintain a normal boiling point for safe braking.

Tires and Climate

If your truck will be dormant for more than a few months, raise the chassis and place the frame safely on jack stands. (See your owner's handbook or Ford F-truck shop manual for jacking locations and where to place stands.) Tires suffer from long storage periods, which can cause sidewall distortion and damage plies or radial belts. Raise the truck enough to take the weight off tires.

Climate plays a role in the precautions you take. In desert environments, the concern is ultraviolet damage and dehydration of rubber seals and bushings. Arctic regions require protection from freezing. Moist and salt air regions call for anti-rust measures. Consider the environmental stresses that your truck will face, and prepare accordingly.

Chapter 6

Troubleshooting and Minor Adjustments

TYPICALLY, A FORD F-TRUCK can take a lot of abuse, especially when equipped with four-wheel drive and forced to convey severe loads on bad roads. While routine maintenance and inspection will enhance any truck's reliability, your talent at making emergency field repairs could mean the difference between walking or driving back to civilization.

After three decades of working with four-wheel trucks, I cannot overstate the need for preventive care, to turn up potential problems. Your truck will provide signs and symptoms before most parts fail, so the best tactic for preventing a breakdown is periodic inspection of the chassis and powertrain.

The off-pavement work truck stretches over rocks and logs, stressing its chassis to the limit. Springs and shackles twist in every direction, bushings and joints in awkward angles. As the dust settles after a hard day on the trail or pulling a fifth-wheel trailer, kneel under the truck and take a physical inventory of the chassis and powertrain.

Aftermath Of A Hard Day's Work

Look beneath the front bumper at the axle, steering linkage, leaf springs (radius arm/C-bushings and coil springs on 2WD models or the F-100 and F-150 4x4s) and front shackles. Vulnerable items on off-pavement 4x4s include the tie-rod assembly, steering stabilizer shock and axle housing(s). Look for oil seepage and cracks along the axle unit, especially gear lube leaking where the axle housing tubes press into the center member. Extreme jarring and twisting can dislodge, bend or crack an axle housing.

Note the condition of the springs. Look for broken or out-of-line leafs and bent U-bolts. If a leaf spring appears offset from its axle perch, suspect a broken center bolt. Leafs out of alignment mean loose U-bolts or distorted spring clamps. Extreme flexing and twisting is the usual cause.

The tie-rod and steering stabilizer damper are especially vulnerable on 4x4 trucks. Due to available space

Fig. 6-1. *When work or recreation takes you to the open spaces, a thorough knowledge of your truck's powertrain and chassis will assure a safe return. Troubleshooting skill is vital in remote country.*

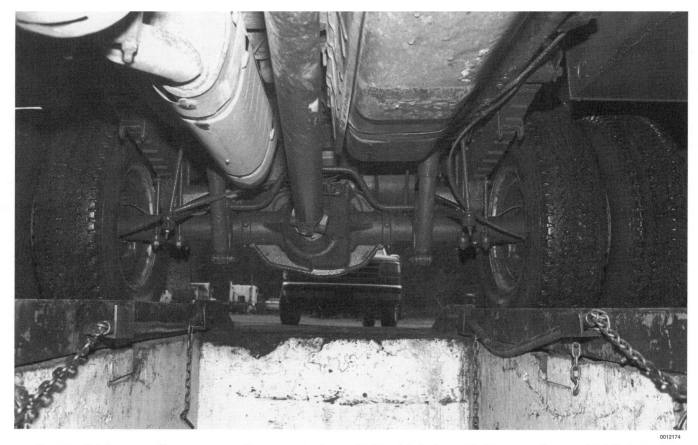

Fig. 6-2. *While severe off-pavement pounding or overloading can loosen axle tubes at the housing center section, that* likelihood is far less with this extremely rugged F-350 dual-wheel full-floater axle.

and the necessary position of the front driveshaft, the steering linkage mounts forward of the axle housing. This makes the long tie-rod and hydraulic stabilizer/damper susceptible to damage from obstacles like rocks, tree stumps and debris. The later 2WD Twin I-Beam models use a similar steering linkage layout.

Veteran four-wheelers know where this tie-rod rides. Aware driving involves a sense for low hanging and vulnerable chassis parts. When knocking around on boulder strewn trails, protect your truck's axle housing(s), suspension, steering, driveshafts, brakes, fuel system and

Fig. 6-3. *Spring flexing loosens U-bolts and clamps. Look for misaligned leafs, broken plates and spring sag. All Ford F-trucks have leaf-type rear springs. Leaf springs have also been popular with many 4x4 front axles.*

Fig. 6-4. *Steering linkage, stabilizer shock and tie-rods require close inspection. On 4x4s and later Twin I-Beam 2WD models, tie-rods mount in front of the axle housing, vulnerable to rocks, stumps and debris. 2WD mono-beam axle and earlier Twin I-Beam trucks have the advantage of a tie-rod mounted behind the axle.*

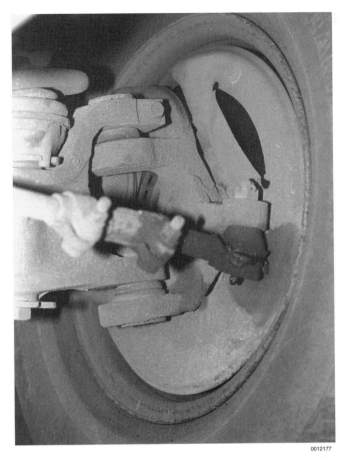

0012177

Fig. 6-5. Steering knuckles and kingpin (pivot pin) or ball joint pivotal supports are vulnerable to impact damage. Inspect these safety components regularly, along with brake pipes and hoses.

other chassis/powertrain components. Become familiar with exposed, expensive pieces.

Check the stabilizer bar (if so equipped), support links and bushings. These parts really flex, especially off pavement. Look closely at the brake hoses and other brake hardware. Brush, tree limbs and loose rock can damage sensitive safety items. Learn to scan along brake and fuel lines; watch for kinks or rock damage. In the worst cases, it is possible to rip whole sections of brake pipe loose from the frame or rear axle housing. Accidently backing into a rock or tree stump can crush the rear axle housing brake piping and impair brake action.

Before finishing your front end inspection, pay close attention to the steering knuckle joints on earlier 4x4s. A broken or loose knuckle joint will impair steering and place your safety at extreme risk. Severe off-pavement impact can break a kingpin bearing race, crack a knuckle casting or damage a steering knuckle ball joint. On closed knuckle 4WD front ends, watch for spindle separation from the knuckle casting and for cracks at the spindle, especially if your truck has aftermarket wide wheels and big tires. (Later in this chapter, you will find the procedure for checking knuckle joint/kingpin play and identifying damage.)

Inspect the rear axle housing for leaks, cracks or broken welds. Springs and spring supports demand close at-

tention. Look for emergency brake cable damage, signs of water in the axle housing and evidence of mud or sand in the brake drums. Inspect the exhaust system for leaks, dents, kinks or any other damage that might impair flow or create unsafe and noxious fumes.

The driveshafts, flexing and moving constantly, are also susceptible to wear and damage. If your Ford truck wallows constantly along rocky trails and through creek beds, keep U-joint flanges and driveshaft tubes away from rocks and stumps. It is relatively easy to spring (bend) a driveshaft tube.

Memorize the safe, original appearance of your truck's undercarriage. When inspecting the chassis, use that image as your standard. Especially when subject to off-pavement hazards, Ford truck reliability depends on good driving habits, the willingness to pick sensible travel routes and unrelenting chassis inspection. Skid plates are not enough.

1. GUIDE TO TROUBLESHOOTING

Engine failure is intimidating, especially if you use your Ford truck in remote country or pull a heavy horse trailer or fifth wheel. Your engine can quit for many reasons, and if unprepared while in the back country, you can burn as much shoe leather over a shorted ignition module as a seized connecting rod bearing.

Servicing your Ford F-truck includes troubleshooting savvy and the means to remedy common problems. Whether you perform repairs or send the work to a qualified shop, troubleshooting skill increases self-sufficiency and heightens your understanding. (For additional details on service work, see service chapters.)

> **NOTE —**
> Overhaul of individual powertrain and chassis components is beyond the aims of this book. For detailed overhaul and unit repair guidelines, refer to your Ford F-Series factory shop manual.

Lack Of Power

Low Compression can result from a pressure leak at one or more cylinders. Loss of compression suggests several possibilities: Leaking or misadjusted intake or exhaust valves, worn or defective piston rings, a blown head gasket, casting cracks, a severely worn camshaft and timing chain or gear set. Coolant loss into the engine oil (turning it milky) indicates a cracked cylinder head or engine block—or a leaking head gasket.

Diagnosing low compression requires a compression gauge or cylinder leakdown tester. (See other chapters for these test procedures.) A field testing method involves shorting each cylinder's spark lead and noting the engine rpm drop.

Internal Friction indicates major engine trouble. If the engine will not crank easily, first rule out the obvious battery or starter/electrical problems. Place the transmission in neutral. Remove all spark plugs and rotate the crankshaft with an appropriate socket and ratchet. The engine should turn freely, with only the moderate resistance of the valvetrain.

Fig. 6-6. *A compression test reveals loss of cylinder pressure. When only two adjacent cylinders show low pressure, suspect a warped cylinder head or a head gasket failure.*

Fig. 6-7. *Remove the spark plugs and rotate the crankshaft. High resistance indicates internal damage.*

To rule out transmission damage as a possible cause, have a helper disengage the clutch (depress the pedal) while you rotate the crankshaft. If the engine will not turn freely, suspect bearing, piston, connecting rod or valve damage. When water (either drawn through the intake system or originating as an internal leak) prevents engine rotation, removing the spark plugs allows liquid to escape. Water exiting the cylinders suggests severe damage, even bent connecting rods or damaged rod bearings.

Overheat/Seizure means serious trouble. If the engine will not crank or rotate after a severe overheat or running without oil, major damage has occurred. Pistons can distort from heat, gall the cylinder walls and destroy crankshaft bearings. Lubrication generally fails during a severe overheat, causing glazing and scoring as the piston rings drag on cylinder walls. Valve stems can seize in their guides, and the camshaft may seize in its bearings. Casting cracks are common, especially near exhaust valve seats and along cylinder walls.

The least gloomy prospect is that a cylinder head (possibly both heads on a V-8) has warped, resulting in a head gasket failure. Coolant fills the cylinders, locking up the engine. Even here, the risk of bent connecting rods and other crankshaft assembly damage remains.

Fig. 6-8. *Radiator damage, overheat and loss of coolant are more than an inconvenience. Piston/cylinder wall galling and engine bearing damage result from extreme heat. Amount of heat involved will determine the extent of damage.*

Fuel Starvation results from low fuel supply pressure or volume. In addition to fuel pump malfunctions and restrictions in the supply or return lines, EFI/MPI-equipped engines suffer from pressure regulator defects or fouled/defective injectors. A sticking carburetor float needle, although rare, is another source of trouble for carbureted engines.

Testing fuel pump pressure requires a special gauge. Pump flow volume is easier to determine. Before suspecting the fuel pump volume, flow rate or carburetion/injection troubles, consider the fuel filter(s) or the fuel line inlet filter in the gas tank. Especially with a paper element fuel filter, a single fill-up with watery gasoline is enough to stop fuel flow.

Fig. 6-9. *A fuel pump pressure gauge quickly determines pressure output. Before condemning the pump or other expensive items, look to the simpler causes, like a plugged fuel filter.*

Weak Ignition creates hard-starting problems and a lack of power. On older engines with breaker points, rubbing block wear retards ignition timing, and the points resistance increases with pitting and arcing. Condenser, rotor, distributor cap and spark cable defects each weaken spark output.

Check the distributor shaft for excess runout (sideplay), a common cause of erratic spark output and errant ignition timing. Dwell angle variance of more than 2° is a sign of distributor defects. Mechanics often condemn the coil, although a coil is far less likely to fail than the breaker points, condenser, primary or secondary wiring or a high mileage set of distributor bushings.

Breaker point and electronic ignitions are vulnerable to wire failures and poor connections (due to corrosion or dirt). Consider this a major cause of poor ignition performance. Check carefully for insulation breakdown and shorts to ground. Especially on early trucks with cloth type insulation, wire failures and shorts are a very common source of trouble.

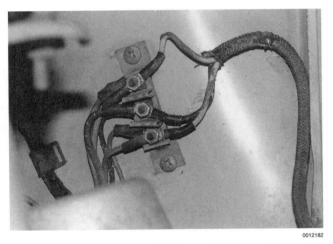

Fig. 6-10. *Wiring shorts, fraying and bad grounds cause the majority of field failures. Look closely at routed wires and connections.*

Test wires between junctions. (You will find a wiring diagram for your Ford F-truck in the factory shop manual.) If an electrical or ignition problem is not readily apparent, test circuits with your volt-ohmmeter or have it done by a local service garage that has special testing equipment.

Vacuum Leaks, if severe, will prevent the engine from running. A sufficient leak creates low manifold pressure, stalling, lean air-fuel mixtures and backfire. Even small vacuum leaks can lean the air-fuel mixture, cause idle speed to drop and prevent smooth performance.

The engine's sudden inability to idle indicates a vacuum leak. Check the PCV valve, all vacuum hoses, the distributor advance diaphragm and the transmission vacuum modulator and hoses, if so equipped. Intake manifold bolts loosen over time, resulting in poor gasket sealing and possible vacuum loss. Torque manifold bolts and the carburetor mounting nuts. As the engine idles, spray a mist of fine penetrating oil (non-volatile) along the gasket sealing edges. Listen for a change in engine speed. This indicates a leak.

Fig. 6-11. *A non-volatile spray solvent or penetrating oil helps detect engine vacuum leaks. With the engine idling, spray toward the intake manifold sealing edges and the carburetor base. If rpm changes, a leak exists.*

WARNING —
Always keep volatile solvents away from hot engine parts. Use a spray substance that will not ignite if it contacts a hot surface or spark.

Clutch Slippage and related troubles are relatively easy to detect. Before testing, check and adjust the clutch at the release arm. (See service chapter for proper clutch adjustment). Make certain that the clutch disengages and engages properly. Through the release arm opening in the bellhousing, observe whether the throwout bearing actually moves the clutch release fingers (levers).

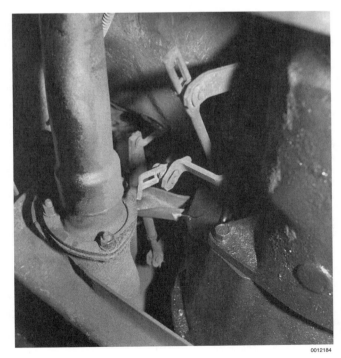

Fig. 6-12. *Always check clutch adjustment at the release arm. Pedal play alone is misleading, as linkage wear can masquerade as clutch free play.*

Keep your fingers away from moving linkage while an assistant depresses the clutch pedal. The force of the clutch linkage could easily crush a finger. The bellhousing's release arm opening has sharp edges that could cut your hands.

If the clutch release arm has insufficient movement, check the linkage from the pedal all the way to the release arm. Note excessive play and correct the cause. In the case of a hydraulic linkage system, inspect the fluid level and bleed any air from the system. Repair or replace defective parts.

Now drive down a deserted road at 15–20 mph. Depress the clutch pedal, and place the transmission in high gear. Raise engine speed to 2500 rpm and rapidly release the clutch pedal. Engine rpm should drop immediately. If rpm decreases gradually, the clutch unit is probably weak. Sources of trouble could include worn clutch cover springs; a worn or glazed clutch plate; a glazed or worn flywheel face; or oil on the friction disc.

Engine Will Not Run

Tune-up Problems include faulty ignition, inadequate fuel supply, flooding, or vacuum leaks. On breaker point ignitions, verify point dwell angle and resistance. Both breaker point and electronic distributors require spark timing adjustment. Fuel system troubles involve dirty filters, plugged carburetor passages, a sticky needle/seat assembly in the carburetor, a defective float or a defective fuel pump. (See service chapters for details on ignition timing procedures and other tune-related tasks.)

Isolate problems. Verify the strength of the ignition spark, check timing, and ensure that the engine has an adequate fuel supply. Check vacuum circuits. Make certain that the emission control system functions, especially the PCV and EGR valves. If indicated, remove and overhaul the carburetor with a quality rebuild kit. You will find instructions for the carburetor overhaul within the kit or a professional level service manual.

Engine Problems reach beyond tune-up fixes. There are three essentials for optimal engine performance: normal compression, correct valve lift and proper valve timing. Make certain your engine meets these three requirements.

Measure compression with a compression gauge or cylinder leakdown tester. (See tune-up/service chapters for details.) If compression registers normal for each cylinder, verify valve lift by removing the valve cover (and side cover on L-head and OHV inline sixes). Measure the height of each valve stem tip from its closed position to fully open. This is the total valve lift produced by each camshaft lobe. Compare this figure to specifications found in your Ford F-Series truck shop manual.

In addition to valve lift, make note of valve timing variances that result from a severely worn timing chain mechanism or gearset. If ignition timing has suddenly become retarded, yet the distributor housing remains securely clamped to the engine block, suspect excess slack in the timing chain or bad sprockets, which can allow valve timing to jump one or more teeth.

Fig. 6-13. *A worn camshaft lobe or improper valve adjustment will affect valve lift. Always check valve adjustment or tappet clearance before testing valve lift.*

Exhaust System Restriction has vexed plenty of troubleshooters. Check the exhaust system! Off-pavement or construction site pounding can flatten the tailpipe or muffler. Restricted exhaust can prevent the engine from starting or developing full power. A muffler or catalytic converter may show no external damage yet have broken baffles or internal restrictions.

Fig. 6-14. *Exhaust system restriction is a possible cause of power loss. Off-pavement use leaves tailpipes, mufflers and catalytic converters vulnerable to damage. Tap muffler gently with a rubber or sand filled plastic hammer to test for loose baffles.*

Engine Will Not Crank

Poor Battery Maintenance/Charge Circuit Troubles remain the primary sources of starting problems. The simplest cause is dirty or corroded battery posts. Regular cleaning of the posts and battery case prevent hard starts and a stranded truck. Make certain that cables are clean and connections tight, especially on an early 6-volt electrical system with high amperage demands and a low output generator.

Generator or alternator troubles are easy to identify. using a charge current induction meter or a simple volt-ohmmeter. Begin with the voltmeter OFF. Take care not to generate a spark near the battery. Securely attach the negative (black) probe to a good chassis or engine ground point. Attach the positive (red) probe to a battery current source some distance from the battery, such as at the fender well mounted solenoid switch. Switch the voltmeter to DC.

NOTE —
On six-volt F-truck positive ground systems, reverse the voltmeter DC probes for proper reading.

Measure the voltage level before cranking, during cranking and after starting the engine. Make certain that the maximum charge voltage reads within the regulator's normal charging range as listed in your Ford F-Series shop manual or a professional guide.

Dead Battery Cell(s) present a difficult diagnostic problem. A high capacity battery can limp along with a dying cell for months. It takes a deep overnight freeze to bring out the worst in a battery. To avoid walking home from a chilly mountain top, test each of your battery's cells with a hydrometer. Specific gravity should be normal and uniform at each cell.

Fig. 6-16. *A safety precaution, even for a battery that shows no sign of weakness, is the hydrometer test. Specific gravity of a fully charged battery should read uniformly at each cell. Perform this test before cold weather begins.*

Fig. 6-15. *Battery maintenance is the best preventive care for the starting circuit. Don't buy a new starter, generator or alternator before thoroughly cleaning the battery and cables and testing specific gravity.*

Starter Motor Problems generally give warning. A solenoid switch or starter drive unit often shows signs of weakness before it fails. Run-on, clicking and erratic cranking are signs of starter and solenoid troubles.

Ford truck engines use a variety of starter and solenoid designs, but starter principles remain universal: The solenoid acts as a relay to handle heavy amperage flow. In some designs, the solenoid actually moves the starter drive. On all but the latest Ford engines, starter motors are

a series-wound design with brushes. Periodically inspect for water damage, clutch drive fatigue and brush wear.

Poor cranking when hot is often due to worn brushes or armature bushing wear that allows drag on the field coils. Exhaust headers passing too close to the starter may also cause hard starting when hot. To diagnose whether your starter draws too much amperage, test the draw with an induction meter on the starter cable or measure the voltage drop at the solenoid switch battery cable while cranking the engine.

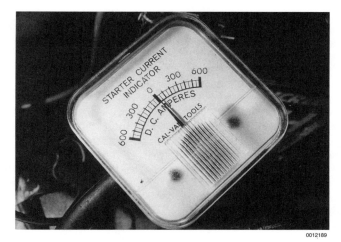

Fig. 6-17. *Starter defects often give warning. A clicking solenoid or erratic, dragging motor indicates trouble. An amperage draw test helps determine the condition of the starter.*

Geartrain Friction Or Drag can prevent cranking. (Also see section on "Lack of Power.") Among geartrain items that can prevent engine cranking are seizures of a transmission input shaft bearing, a gear set or the crankshaft pilot bearing. A seized pilot bearing will not allow power to disengage between the engine and transmission. However, the engine will crank in neutral.

Seized transmission components also allow the engine to crank with the clutch disengaged, but the engine will stall when you engage the clutch. (Before suspecting a damaged transmission, check clutch adjustment and operation.) A seized transmission can result from poor lubrication, severe parts stress or excessive wear.

Cooling System Troubles

Engine cooling presents a challenge, especially with high horsepower conversion engines or trips through hot desert environments. Rock crawling in the desert at high noon is the ultimate test for any truck's cooling system.

Before troubleshooting common cooling system problems, clarify your truck's needs. For years, the two most popular buzzwords around cooling system upgrades have been "four row" and "cross-flow" radiators. These terms are meaningless without an understanding that horsepower equals BTUs. The more horsepower, the more heat your radiator and fan system must handle.

Back in 1968, I installed a 270-horsepower conversion V-8 in my '55 Ford F-100 pickup. The stock Ford down flow radiator had a huge tank on top and looked very adequate. However, the high gallon-per-minute (gpm) coolant flow rate of the new engine, plus its horsepower figure of more than twice the original V-8's output, thoroughly overtaxed the radiator.

A knowledgeable radiator specialist gave me an education, showing me the gpm flow needed for the new engine. He found a larger radiator core that easily fit the original top and bottom tanks. The engine ran cool ever after....

Sometimes the issue is fan air flow through the radiator core. A radiator may have plenty of flow capacity, tube size and fin surface area, but the fan draws too little air through the core. The cure in this case is a heavy duty mechanical fan. Well-pitched blades and a shroud may solve the cooling problem completely. (If the radiator core surface is too small, both a larger radiator core and a mechanical fan might be necessary.)

Heavy-pitched truck type or high performance aftermarket mechanical fans draw far more CFM air flow than an automobile type or light duty fan. Check your truck's engine fan for blade count and pitch. Upgrade if necessary.

Make certain a shroud captures the fan's full draft without creating an air block. (See the cooling chapter for further details.) Fortunately, most F-truck models have large grill openings, which makes the fan's job easier.

An air conditioning-type radiator provides a good design for the basically stock Ford truck engine. For higher horsepower transplant engines, evaluate the heaviest duty replacement radiator available for your chassis. Order that radiator or have an adequately sized radiator built. Install a hefty mechanical (engine driven) fan. A fan clutch unit, which lessens engine load at speed, is often advisable.

Engine Overheat At Low Speeds suggests an undercapacity or restricted fan or radiator. Overheat can also re-

Fig. 6-18. A high performance engine and heavy duty radiator benefit from aftermarket stainless steel flex fan. This setup keeps engine within 5° F of thermostat setting, even under load in the hottest climates.

sult from insufficient water pump volume, cavitation or aeration problems. Air, either trapped within the cooling system or siphoned through a pinhole leak or defective water pump seal, can cause cavitation (air gaps and blocks) and drastically lower cooling efficiency.

Another source of air in the cooling system is a slight head gasket leak that allows pressurized combustion gases to seep from a cylinder into an adjacent cooling port. This rapidly creates rust or oxidation, visible in the upper radiator and coolant recovery tank. As preventive care, you should periodically check torque of the cylinder head bolts, tighten all hose clamps, watch the water pump bleed hole for seepage and pressure check the cooling system.

Fig. 6-19. Pressure tester checks hoses, water pump, engine block, gaskets and heater core. Radiator pressure cap must also seal properly, or boiling point will drop.

NOTE —
Restrictions in air flow through the radiator core, like from a tall winch, will cause overheating.

Engine Overheat At High Speeds involves incorrect coolant flow (either too fast or too slow) through the radiator, restrictions in the radiator core or an undercapacity water pump. Many of the symptoms for low speed overheat apply, so first follow those troubleshooting guidelines. Always check the thermostat, which regulates the coolant flow rate and temperature.

If coolant actually pushes from the radiator overflow at higher speeds, the water pump generates more coolant than the gallon-per-minute (gpm) capacity of the radiator core. (The core is either too small or plugged with scale.) Freeze plug failure and hose leaks are not uncommon under such conditions, as excess pressure backs through the entire cooling system.

Coolant Boil-over requires careful diagnosis. Is the coolant erupting from extreme engine heat? This means the radiator and fan cannot cool the liquid sufficiently—or that the engine/powertrain produces very high temperatures due to abnormal friction, spark timing error, improper air-fuel mixtures, automatic transmission overheat or other cooling system overloads.

NOTE —
An under-capacity radiator flow rate will cause coolant overflow from the radiator—even at normal engine temperatures.

Fig. 6-20. *A relatively inexpensive item like the thermostat can cause major heating problems. Replace the thermostat during your periodic flush and refill of the cooling system.*

Observe when the overflow occurs. Monitor the temperature gauge closely. If the engine runs consistently hot, suspect a sticky thermostat, plugged radiator core, obstructive block mud (accumulated rust and scale in an older engine), a defective water pump or other factors that raise coolant temperature.

Clutch and Manual Transmission

Clutch Noises forebode bad tidings. Fatal clutch noises include the abrasive whirring of the throwout bearing during disengagement, the grinding of clutch plate rivets as the clutch engages, or the rattle of broken clutch disc torsion springs. Expect that any new, persistent sound from the clutch means trouble.

A defective pilot bearing makes noise with the transmission in gear and the clutch disengaged. Clutch disc or cover assembly noises occur during engagement and disengagement. (Broken clutch cover springs cause uneven engagement and severe chatter.) Throwout or release bearing noise becomes apparent with light pressure against the clutch pedal, just enough pressure to start the bearing spinning.

Fig. 6-21. *Clutch plate (disc) torsion springs and rivets make distinct noises. Rivets grind against the flywheel or clutch cover face while torsion springs rattle in the hub.*

CAUTION —
Continued vehicle operation with a defective clutch can damage motor mounts, the flywheel and components of the transmission.

Gearbox noises grate and amplify according to load on the gear teeth. Coast and acceleration noises differ. Transmission bearing troubles give distinct cues, with countergear or counter bearing noises evident in the lower gears. Input or output bearing noises correspond to shaft or road speeds. Any clutch or transmission noise requires immediate repairs.

Gear Clash in a manual transmission or transfer case has several possible causes. Before condemning the trans-

Fig. 6-22. Shift linkage binding or failure can prevent gear engagement or power flow. In an emergency, it may be necessary to free a 4x4's transfer case linkage by manually moving the shift rails beneath the floorboard.

mission, check the clutch adjustment at the release arm and note any slack in the linkage. Complete travel of the linkage is necessary for disengagement of the clutch. A partially disengaged clutch causes difficult shifting and rapid wear of parts.

Another source of clash is hasty shifting to a non-synchromesh first or reverse gear. You must allow gears to quit spinning (or double-clutch on a first gear downshift) before engaging gear teeth. A defective synchromesh assembly will also produce this metallic clashing noise during gear shifts.

Use of the wrong gear lube can cause synchronizer balkiness and also make shifting difficult under various climate conditions. As such, gear clash and hard shifting will occur when using an overly stiff gear lube viscosity in winter months.

A well-driller friend from Idaho attests that STP Oil Treatment allowed his surplus deuce-and-a-half (2-1/2-ton capacity 6x6) to operate in -40-degree F weather. Prior to adding STP to the gear cases, the engine stalled as the clutch engaged in neutral—even while revving the engine at a high rpm. Heavier gear and engine oils become rigid in extremely cold environments. Multi-viscosity synthetic gear lubricant is another cure for cold weather problems.

Synchronizers, which act much like a friction brake mechanism, wear over time. A patterned gear clash or jumping out of gear (especially first or second on a light duty Ford truck three-speed unit) usually indicates bearing, shift housing, shift fork or synchronizer damage. These troubles require a transmission overhaul.

The Vehicle Will Not Move means several possibilities. A failed clutch is the first consideration. A clutch permanently disengaged (linkage extended and binding,

disc worn completely or clutch cover springs broken) may still allow shifting of gears.

The opposite situation is damaged clutch linkage or bad contact between the throwout bearing and clutch cover fingers, which prevents disengagement of the clutch. With the truck in an open area and the engine shut off, place the transmission in low gear (also low range if a 4x4). Click or crank the starter. This should move the truck.

> *WARNING —*
> *Make sure nothing is in the truck's way, as the engine may start! Be ready to shut the ignition switch off immediately.*

If the clutch works, check the transmission and, on a 4x4 model, the transfer case. On a 4x4, begin by locking the front hubs and engaging four-wheel drive. Now shift gears and try to move the truck. If your truck still will not move, power flow has stopped at the transmission or transfer case input. If the truck moves in four-wheel drive mode, suspect a broken rear transfer case output, a failed rear driveline or rear axle troubles.

When power fails to reach the axles, defective transfer case shift linkage is a common cause. The linkage may bind or catch between gear ranges, creating a neutral effect. As an emergency repair, block the wheels carefully, crawl beneath the vehicle and shift the transfer case manually at its shift rails.

> *WARNING —*
> *Stop the engine and place safety blocks at each wheel before attempting to engage the transfer case. The vehicle can roll with the transfer case in neutral.*

Poor Traction/Erratic Wheel Spin is usually an axle/differential problem. On Ford 4x4s with full-time NP203 transfer cases (an option from 1973–79), the transfer case's differential mechanism is much like an axle differential. Before condemning a part-time 4x4 transfer case or axle system, rule out the much simpler possibility of a defective front axle free-wheeling hub(s).

To check free-wheeling hubs, first engage/lock the wheel hubs and the 4x4 drive system. (Roll forward in 4WD mode to engage automatic free-wheeling hubs.) Jack each front wheel, one at a time, safely off the ground. By hand, rotate the raised wheel assembly with the opposite wheel still on the ground. The axle shaft should spin the front differential and cause the front driveshaft to rotate. (If your Ford 4x4 has a front axle positive-traction device, the wheel assembly should rotate only slightly in each direction.)

If your F-truck has a limited slip differential at the rear, erratic handling and odd traction are often caused by wear in the differential's clutch unit. Lurching, clicking and snapping noises indicate trouble here. A failing limited slip unit shows obvious signs: poor traction with audible symptoms of trouble, most notable as the vehicle negotiates turns.

Gear bind is a common phenomenon with any 4x4 truck. If you attempt to operate your 4x4 F-truck on a dry,

Fig. 6-23. On a 4x4 truck, power flow includes front hubs that work properly. While the engine, clutch, transmission, transfer case, driveshafts, differentials and axle shafts may work fine, a defective free-wheeling hub can prevent front axle traction.

Fig. 6-24. U-joints fail at inopportune times. Off-pavement, radical driveshaft angles and high torque loads place maximum stress on these components.

hard road surface with the front hubs locked and the transfer case in either 4WD high or low range (or lock mode on full-time 4x4 systems), the rotational speed differences between the front and rear axles will act as a counterforce within the geartrain.

Gear bind prevents disengagement of the transfer case. To overcome the binding force, gently rock your truck forward and in reverse while maintaining gentle, steady pressure on the transfer case lever. There is a point of free load, somewhere between forward and reverse power flow, at which the bind loosens. At that moment, the transfer case lever will slide into the two-wheel drive position. Never apply excess force to the transfer case lever.

Driveshaft and Axle Woes

A common driveline problem on Ford 2WD trucks and 4x4s is U-joint and constant velocity joint failure. Especially, in rough and rocky terrain, the radical change angles place major loads on driveshaft U-joints and live front axle steering joints. Massive torque applied under high stress driving conditions can destroy a U-joint.

The loud, metallic snap of a breaking U-joint is hard to forget. Back country veterans of hardcore trails carry spare U-joints for such occasions. Although proper driving habits prevent the majority of mishaps, U-joint failure is still a major concern.

Another source of driveshaft trouble is torque twisting the tubes. A properly built driveshaft, operating at normal angles and in correct phase, will withstand tremendous abuse. If, however, a shaft sustains impact damage or operates at an abnormal posture, the tube and welds may fail. Inspect your truck's driveshafts regularly, and note any shake or vibration at road speeds. A bent or sprung driveshaft will create havoc, most apparent as vehicle speed increases.

If your truck has a conventional, non-positive traction differential(s), an axle shaft or joint failure means an immediate loss of power flow. Although a truck equipped with four-wheel drive may still move when the front or

rear differential fails, if a semi-floating rear axle shaft breaks, do not drive the truck.

On a semi-floating rear axle, like those found on Ford half-ton and later 3/4-ton F-models, a broken axle shaft offers no stability to the wheel, tire and brake drum. If the axle shaft breaks outboard of the outer bearing, or if the bearing and its pressed-on lock collar loosen from the shaft, or if the inner C-lock dislodges, the wheel and brake drum assembly can separate from the axle housing!

With a full-floating rear axle, common to pre-'80 F 250s and most F-350 models, it is possible to move the truck with a broken rear axle shaft. If the full-floating axle has a positive traction device, you can remove the inner section of the broken axle shaft, reinstall the outer flange section, and carefully drive the truck.

On 4x4s, front axle shaft or steering joint failure is another safety risk. A broken shaft, cross-type joint or constant velocity joint may wedge in the housing or steering knuckle cavity. This could prevent rotation of the steering knuckle and wheel spindle, causing loss of vehicle control. If the axle shafts are still safely in line and supported, you may place the transfer case in two-wheel drive mode and turn the hubs to FREE. Drive cautiously and make certain that the steering knuckles continue to pivot freely.

CAUTION —
If you believe the defective axle shaft/joint could cause a lock-up of steering, and you must get home, remove the axle shaft. (See service chapter covering front axle work or your Ford F-Series truck shop manual.) Leave the transfer case in 2WD mode and the front hubs on FREE. This is a temporary fix for a "must" trip home. Once home, immediately make a thorough repair.

In any instance where your truck must operate with failed axle components, understand the extent of damage. If necessary, remove the inspection cover from the differential to locate the source of trouble. (In the field, catch drain oil in a clean container and save for refilling the differential if necessary.) Raise each wheel/tire from the ground and rotate the wheel (with both front hubs engaged) to determine whether the axle shafts and joints are

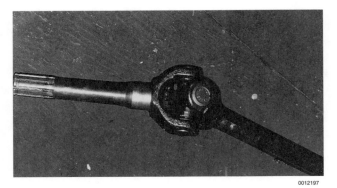

Fig. 6-25. *Front axle joint failure is a dangerous situation. A broken shaft or joint can wedge in the steering knuckle and prevent the wheels from turning. Before driving the truck, check closely for such damage. If necessary, remove the axle shaft.*

intact. On an open steering knuckle axle, watch joint and driveshaft rotation.

If your 1973–79 Ford truck has a full-time 4x4 system and no free-wheeling front hubs, axle shaft damage poses several driving threats, including steering impairment, risk of losing a wheel assembly, loss of braking or the possibility of increased damage to the truck. If an inner component in the axle breaks, exercise extreme caution if you must move the truck at all. Do not attempt to drive the truck if the steering knuckle, outer axle shaft, steering knuckle U-joint or wheel bearings have become severely damaged.

On such a truck, the full-floating front wheel hubs permit removal of a broken front axle shaft in an emergency. If you must move a full-time 4x4 model that has an unsafe, broken front axle shaft or joint, first remove the broken shaft, then the front driveshaft assembly. Set the transfer case in 4-Loc. (See axle service chapter or your Ford F Series shop manual for details on front axle shaft removal.)

During axle oil changes, with the differential cover removed, clean and inspect all parts. Look closely for abnormal tooth contact patterns on the ring and pinion gears. Check the pinion shaft for any end play or radial movement. Inspect the seals, observe side gear/pinion backlash (play) and note the condition of the carrier bearings that support the ring gear and differential carrier housing. Preventive maintenance and careful inspection remain your best safeguards against axle troubles.

Differential Troubles include clutch failure on positive traction units, broken differential side gears or small pinions and the stripping of teeth from the ring and pinion gears. Bearing failures, seal leaks and thrust washer wear are other trouble areas.

Steering and Tire Troubles

Wander, the tendency for steering to either drift or follow road irregularities, is a common complaint with both two- and four-wheel drive models. The usual causes are front end misalignment, cupped tires (mostly bias-ply type), a loose steering gear, defective steering linkage, or suspension wear. Steering linkage and radius arm bushing wear are other problem spots for many F-truck models.

When aligning the front wheels, service should include a caster check. Insufficient positive caster angle can cause shimmy and loss of steering control. If your Ford truck needs coaxing to steer straight after a turn, check caster and toe-in. Sagging suspension or aftermarket lift kits can also affect caster angle.

For earlier 4x4 axles, if slight caster and camber correction is necessary and no safety problem exists, adjustment is possible through the use of shims. Later model 4x4 and 2WD light duty F-trucks have factory adjustment provisions for caster, camber and toe-in. (See your F-Series shop manual for details on your truck's front end design and adjustment/alignment.)

Loose steering gear and linkage result from high mileage and wear, severe loads and the rigors of off pavement pounding. Excess play translates as wander. Inspect for wear at tie-rod end(s), the steering gear, spring bushings and shackles, the center link assembly, draglink, steering arm, kingpin bearings and all ball-joints.

Fig. 6-26. *Ring and pinion gears, side gears and differential pinions can each fail. Remove the axle inspection cover to check these parts. Excess play at the pinion shaft or axle shafts can mean trouble.*

Fig. 6-27. *Limited slip, like a Spicer axle's Powr-Lok traction unit, feature multi-plate clutches. Wear occurs over time, and traction diminishes.*

Fig. 6-28. On Ford F-trucks with either a 2WD or 4WD mono-beam front axle, and on earlier kingpin-type Twin I-Beam 2WD systems, camber is only a concern when a spring sags, an axle housing/beam fatigues or becomes bent, or if C- or radius arm bushings wear.

Front End Shimmy usually results from looseness in the steering knuckle (kingpin) bearings or ball-joints. A contributing factor is looseness in the steering linkage, front wheel spindles or wheel bearings. Sagging springs and improper wheel alignment (especially caster angle) can also cause front end shimmy. Oversize tires exaggerate shimmy and so does severe tire imbalance. Any vibration can set off this potentially violent shaking of the front wheels. With manual steering, kingpin shimmy is a wrist-wrenching experience.

Perform a quick check of spindles, wheel bearings, kingpins or ball-joints by raising front wheels safely from the ground and installing jack stands beneath the axle housing(s) on 4WD models or the 2WD axle beam(s). Grab each front wheel and tire firmly at 6 and 12-o'clock. Rock the tire in and out with a lifting motion. Note the amount of movement.

If play exists, have a helper watch the backside of the wheel and steering knuckle. Determine whether the play is at the wheel hub (loose wheel bearings or spindle) or the knuckle support (kingpin bearings or ball-joints). When wheel bearing play is excessive, adjust the wheel bearings to specification, then repeat the inspection. (See service chapters for further details.)

Wheel Run-out and **Tire Imbalance** is another area of concern. Especially with oversize mud-and-snow tires, the weight mass at each wheel becomes excessive. Cleated truck tires, unlike conventional passenger car types,

Fig. 6-29. Use of a quality tire gauge is essential. Your truck requires specific pressures for on- or off-highway use. Off-highway pressures below 20 psi will reduce load capacity drastically and possibly damage the tires. Always check tire pressures cold, and follow the manufacturer's recommended inflation rates for your F-truck model.

fall out of balance with normal wear. Periodic re-balancing and rotation are essential. (Switch in cross with bias ply, non-radial tires; ask your tire dealer for manufacturer's recommendations on new radial tires.)

Hard-core 4x4 rock crawling can dislodge wheel weights or cause them to rotate on the rim. Tire damage, including internal belt separation of radial tires, causes vibration and shake. Bent wheel rims (runout) creates a wide range of handling and tire wear problems. The best preventive measure is periodic spin balancing of each tire and wheel. Have the technician pay close attention to rim run-out and distortion. Replace rims that show excess run-out.

Traditionally, heavy duty bias-ply tires have benefitted from truing, a procedure that trims out-of-round material from the new tread surface. Radial tires sometimes

Fig. 6-30. Spin balancing is the best safeguard against vibration and abnormal tire wear. In some cases, tires require truing, matching or balancing on the truck. Rotate tires every 5,000–7,500 miles and check balance as needed.

require tread and sidewall matching, a procedure that contributes to uniform tread pressure over the full circumference of the tire.

Tire imbalance usually becomes noticeable between 45 and 55 mph. Sometimes a set of tires and wheels may balance perfectly, yet the symptoms of imbalance remain. This situation may call for balancing the tires on the vehicle, with the brake drum or rotor and hub included in the rotating mass. Balancing on the truck requires re-balancing the tires each time you rotate them.

Brake Problems

Brake Pull and Grab occurs when you apply the brakes. Defects in hydraulic or mechanical parts of the brake system cause these problems. A pitted or corroded wheel cylinder or disc caliper piston bore can cause erratic piston action, while a sticking piston prevents normal movement of the brake shoes or disc pads.

An incorrectly adjusted master cylinder pushrod or dirty and corroded fluid reservoir can affect brake performance. If brake fluid cannot return to the master cylinder reservoir through the compensation port, fluid trapped in the system will keep pressure on the brakes. This can cause drag, fade and erratic braking action.

Several mechanical factors contribute to brake pull and grab. Oil on the brake lining, binding linkage, a broken shoe return spring, warped brake shoes and drums (bell mouthed or out-of-round), distorted rotors and pads, hard spots on drums or rotors and excessive lining wear each contribute to erratic braking. Poor lining quality, which leads to fade and undercapacity braking, is another source of trouble.

Slipshod brake jobs, without turning drums and rotors or rebuilding (sometimes replacing) hydraulic cylinders, can lead to problems. With exposure to water, mud and drastic climate changes, your brakes deserve quality care. Restore your brakes properly, then protect the brake system by periodically cleaning debris from shoes, backing plates, brake drums or rotors. Inspect the dust boot seals regularly.

> *WARNING —*
>
> *All older brake linings contain harmful asbestos. Brake vacuum equipment and special parts washers are available to prevent exposure to harmful asbestos brake dust. If you cannot safeguard yourself from asbestos, leave brake work to a professional shop. When performing brake work, inquire whether a non-asbestos lining is available for your truck.*

Failure To Stop has two symptoms: no pedal pressure or an extremely hard pedal. No pedal pressure generally means a hydraulic system failure, especially on pre-'67 trucks with single master cylinder systems. Also, if you use your truck off-pavement, it faces environmental hazards that can damage brake pipes or hoses. If fluid loss has occurred, carefully repair the hydraulic system, bleed air out, and check for leaks before driving the vehicle.

Mechanical problems like a broken brake shoe, drum, actuating linkage or defective self-adjuster mechanism will cause the master cylinder piston to fully exhaust its

Fig. 6-31. Master cylinder pushrod clearance is crucial to safe braking. Insufficient clearance at the tip of the pushrod will prevent the piston from retracting completely.

stroke before the brakes apply. (Actually, this too is a hydraulic failure, although a mechanical cause underlies the problem.)

Under extreme circumstances, misadjusted brake shoes, combined with major lining wear, will create the same effect. The brake pedal reaches the floor before lining reaches the drums. If your truck's brakes have no self adjusters, you must periodically adjust the shoe-to-drum clearance and monitor lining wear.

Normal lining wear lowers the level of fluid in the master cylinder reservoir. Check brake fluid at regular intervals to assure an adequate reserve. The master cylinder must displace a full stroke of fluid to actuate the wheel brakes. (See chapters on maintenance and brake service.)

An extremely hard pedal is usually the result of contaminated lining (oil, dirt or water), glazed brake lining or warped drums and/or rotors. Poor brake shoe seating, often a consequence of improper shoe arc, can prevent lining from making full contact with the drums. Binding of linkage, actuating hardware or hydraulic cylinder pistons will also increase brake pedal pressure.

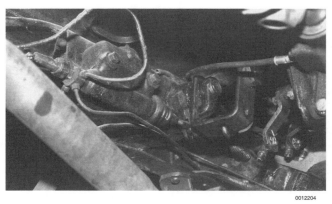

Fig. 6-32. Early F-truck master cylinders mount below the floorboard. Exposed to moisture, debris and ice, the master cylinder's dust boot must seal properly. Otherwise, rust and corrosive road salts will attack the cylinder.

0012205

Fig. 6-33. *Glazed or contaminated brake lining, rotors and drums will increase pedal pressure. A defective outer axle shaft seal permits gear lube to saturate and ruin the brake lining.*

In freezing weather, always check your brakes before driving the truck. Wet hardware may ice up—another cause of hard pedal. Additionally, hard pedal can result from overheated lining or fade.

There are several causes of fade: improper fitup of brake parts; hydraulic fluid trapped in the lines (due to a misadjusted master cylinder pushrod, bent pipe or kinked brake hose); extensive use or abuse of the brakes; excess load on the brake system; a misadjusted wheel-type emergency brake system; incorrect brake shoe-to drum clearance (too tight); and glazed or contaminated lining.

Chapter 7

Cooling System Service

YOUR FORD F-SERIES TRUCK places a high demand on its cooling system. The engine must maintain normal operating temperatures, whether the air outside is -60° Fahrenheit or 130° above. Dusty roads pack dirt and abrasive material into a radiator core, and rocks and debris from the tires of other vehicles can damage the radiator core just as easily as they break a windshield.

For 4x4 models, a twisting back country trail, where tires hang suspended in air, can loosen a weak radiator core support. Hose flex fatigues the radiator inlet and outlet tubes. Hard impact force can drive the fan into the radiator or fan shroud.

Add to this the burden of air conditioning and an automatic transmission. Many Ford truck owners consider creature comfort a valid part of driving. Why suffer with 120° heat inside your vehicle? The installation of a factory or aftermarket air conditioner introduces another obstacle to the cooling system, as the air conditioning condenser restricts air flow through the radiator core.

Many Ford trucks have an automatic transmission. Ford and Borg-Warner automatic transmissions each cool ATF at the engine's radiator. This places an even greater load on the radiator, coolant and fan system. Likewise, an auxiliary engine or transmission oil cooler mounts within the fan's air flow. This adds extra heat that the cooling system must handle.

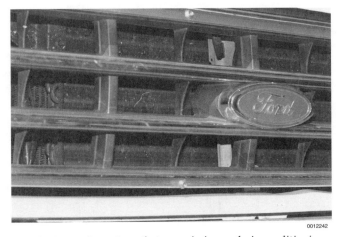

Fig. 7-1. *An automatic transmission and air conditioning place an added load on the engine's cooling system. The air conditioning condenser and auxiliary transmission cooler each block air flow through the radiator core.*

Another factor that increases the risk of overheat is a forward mounted winch. Often, 4x4 truck models have such an assembly or other accessories mounted just forward of the grill. Today's better winch mounting kits place the winch behind or in line with the bumper, below the grill opening. This allows vital air to flow through the radiator.

Since many light truckers pull trailers, higher horsepower engines are popular in Camper Special Ford F-Series models. The ultimate cooling challenge for any truck is a high horsepower engine, which places a tremendous load on the radiator and fan system.

The simplest way to explain this equation is that each horsepower equals a certain number of British Thermal Units (BTUs). More horsepower means a higher BTU output or engine heat. The cooling system must adequately dissipate this thermal load.

Sufficient cooling requires maximum transfer of heat from the engine to the air. The radiator, comprised of coolant tubes and fins, handles the majority of this task. For those who like engineering formulas, here's the actual equation for engine cooling: Draw off at least 42.5 BTUs of heat per minute for each horsepower.

Since BTU heat dissipation relates directly to the area of radiator tube and fin exposure, core size is very important. Air flow and radiator core size (reflected by the number and size of the coolant tubes plus the area of the fins) will determine cooling capacity.

Safety Precautions: An Overheated Engine

WARNING —
- *Never remove the radiator cap when your truck's engine is hot. Hot coolant under pressure leaves the radiator with extreme force and spews in all directions. This scalding hot liquid could cause severe burns.*

- *Always use extreme caution when removing a radiator cap. (Use a heat resistant rubber glove or stack of shop rags.) Always shield yourself from the fill neck when removing the cap. Safely relieve all pressure by first releasing the latch or holding the cap at its safety notch, if so designed.*

- *Never add coolant to the engine when it is hot or overheated. If you must add coolant, leave the engine running.*

- *Coolant is poisonous to pets. Use extreme care when draining and disposing of engine coolant.*

Fig. 7-2. *If a hot engine has a good amount of coolant still in the system, run the engine while pouring a light stream of water over the radiator core and tanks. (Avoid hitting a hot engine with cold water, as this could crack a block, cylinder head or other castings.) The temperature will drop quickly. Allow the engine and radiator to cool completely before removing the radiator cap.*

1. COOLING SYSTEM BASICS

Chronic cooling system problems usually originate at the radiator. Often, especially with larger engines, an undercapacity or clogged radiator creates trouble. Several factors apply when choosing the correct radiator, but the main issue is horsepower. Higher horsepower equates to a greater need for heat transfer, your truck radiator's principle job.

Engineers see horsepower output as the main variable when determining the capacity of a radiator or fan system. Your truck's engine loses approximately one-third of its thermal energy as heat dissipating from the radiator, the heater core and surfaces of the engine. Another one-third of the thermal energy goes out the tailpipe as hot exhaust. (This valuable energy, when harnessed to power an exhaust turbocharger, produces considerable extra horsepower.)

The actual ignition process and combustion of fuel consume the other third of this thermal energy, as the hot gases expand and drive the pistons. Moving pistons rotate the crankshaft and propel the vehicle.

Matching Cooling System Components

Whether you are restoring an earlier model truck, retrofitting a higher horsepower engine into your truck's chassis or increasing an engine's performance, you must accurately determine the horsepower level. It's better to guess high than low, as a thermostat can regulate coolant temperatures if you install a slightly oversize radiator that cools too well. With an undersize radiator core, the engine will never run cool.

Also consider water pump volume and coolant flow rate. If the engine pumps more water into the radiator than the tubes can flow, the coolant will overflow the filler neck as engine speed increases. This is a common symptom of an inadequate radiator flow rate.

Lastly, the radiator's ability to rapidly transfer or dissipate heat must be sufficient. The engine fan plays a

large role here. As an absolute minimum, you need a fan that creates an air flow rate of 725 to 1150 feet per minute through the radiator core.

Excess loads, high ambient temperatures, air restriction or unusually slow road speeds require additional fan capacity and a higher radiator flow rate.

Flow rate is the amount of coolant that can move through the radiator in a given interval of time. The industry standard of measurement is gallons-per-minute flow (gpm). If your truck's original radiator won't cool a transplanted bigger engine, the cause is either a deficiency in gpm flow or too little surface area.

The usual cure for flow rate weaknesses is a larger radiator or radiator core. Popular four- or five-row radiators offer a thicker core with more rows of tubes. If you must adhere to the original radiator's height and width dimensions, and that radiator has two or three rows of tubes, the addition of a four-row core may provide the necessary gpm flow level.

The size of each tube is actually more important than the number of rows. Many three row cores, with larger tubes, offer higher BTU dissipation ratings than a four-row core with small tubes. When in doubt, consult flow and BTU charts at a local radiator shop.

Fig. 7-3. *Here is the difference between a late model Ford V-8 cross-flow radiator (top) and an early F-truck down-flow unit (bottom). A big V-8 with air conditioning requires far more overall radiator size, more tubes and a larger core surface area than the radiator for a smaller V-8 or inline six.*

Fig. 7-4. A four-row core is not always bigger than a three row. Tube size also contributes to flow rate and surface area. Pay attention to gpm flow ratings and various engine/chassis applications when selecting a high output radiator. Recyclers and radiator shops offer information.

Fan Air Flow

If, despite adequate coolant flow and proper thermostat action, your truck's engine overheats, air flow or fan shrouding could be at fault, especially at slow speeds. With a narrow grill opening, fan draw becomes a major part of cooling. Poor fan location, a defective clutch-fan unit, or an improperly shaped shroud can prevent air from passing through the radiator core.

Some truck owners make the mistake of eliminating the clutch fan unit and trying to run a non-flexing metal fan. This can actually create a blockage of air flow at high road speeds. Here, air moving through the grill and radiator can travel much faster than the draw speed of the fan. For this reason, and to reduce horsepower drain, either a fan clutch assembly or an aftermarket flexible-blade fan are frequently found on high performance engines.

The shroud must capture the entire core area of the radiator. Ideal fan location will have half the thickness of the blades inside the shroud, the other half just rearward. (Aftermarket flex fans alter this formula slightly, so read instructions that come with any conversion fan.) This allows the fan to draw under all circumstances and prevents turbulence or an air blockage to occur within the shroud.

The last area of concern is coolant or air blockage within the cooling system. Beware of improperly installed engine gaskets, especially the head gasket(s), or an upside down thermostat! When performing a valve grind or complete engine overhaul, follow engine assembly instructions carefully. On many Ford truck engines, the water pump and timing cover plate/gasket placement is critical.

Fig. 7-5. Flex-A-Lite aftermarket flex fan and spacers replace a factory fan clutch and fan. Stainless steel blades will flatten at higher engine speeds to prevent air blockage. Note reverse fan rotation, required on many late engines with serpentine drive belts.

Fig. 7-6. The location of the fan and shroud are important to cooling. Factory fan blade lies approximately halfway into the shroud opening. Shroud captures air from the entire radiator core. Late 300 six-cylinder F-trucks have reverse rotation engine driven fan.

Finding Leaks

Coolant leaks can ruin your drive or vacation. As a safeguard, check your cooling system regularly with a pressure tester. External leaks are easiest to find. With the engine shut off and cool, simply pump the tester to the cooling system's normal pressure, and watch the gauge. It should not drop. If it does, look for leaks at hoses, the intake manifold, the thermostat housing, freeze plugs, or the radiator and heater core.

If no external leaks are present, suspect an internal engine leak, including a seeping or blown head gasket, casting cracks, or an interior intake manifold/cooling passage leak. A blown head gasket or cracked casting will either leak coolant into a cylinder or create low compression in two adjacent cylinders.

When coolant can enter a cylinder, compression gases also leak into the engine's cooling ports. Rapid overflow at the radiator filler neck or coolant recovery tank results when high pressure cylinder gases enter the cooling system.

Intake manifold gaskets leaking at the coolant crossover passages on Ford V-8 engines will drain coolant into the crankcase. So will a leaking timing cover casting or gaskets. Block or cylinder head cracks cause coolant leaks into the upper cylinders and/or crankcase, depending upon the crack's location in the casting.

There are several tests for an internal coolant leak. Securely attach a pressure tester to the radiator fill neck. Have someone start the engine while you watch the gauge. If pressure rises rapidly and pegs at the high side of the gauge, shut the engine off. This indicates that cylinder pressure has entered the cooling system and pressurized the radiator. A casting crack or blown head gasket is the cause.

CAUTION —

Cylinder gases in the cooling system will create an abrupt and dangerous rise in pressure. (Imagine 100-plus psi of pressure within a cooling system designed for 17 psi!) Shut the engine off immediately if pressure starts to rise rapidly. Use extreme care when working around a cooling system. Do not remove the cap if the engine has warmed or if the tester gauge reads high. Allow time for the system to cool and pressure to drop.

The appearance of bubbles in the radiator often indicates the presence of cylinder gases and a head gasket or casting leak. This can be deceptive, though, since other causes of aeration, including water pump malfunctions, can also introduce air bubbles into the cooling system.

An infra-red exhaust analyzer can quickly confirm whether bubbles in the radiator are from leaking combustion gases. By holding the analyzer probe just above an open radiator fill neck or coolant recovery tank, a reading of carbon monoxide and hydrocarbons is possible. If you find these gases present, suspect cylinder leakage.

Fig. 7-7. A cooling system pressure tester is quickest check for leaks. Pump tester to normal cooling system pressure, then watch gauge. Sealing properly, no drop should occur.

Fig. 7-8. Strange place for an exhaust gas analyzer probe! Combustion gases can enter the cooling system through a blown head gasket(s), a cracked cylinder head or a crack in the block. With the engine idling at normal temperature, an exhaust infrared tester can sniff cylinder gases just above the radiator filler neck.

Automatic Transmission Load On Cooling

An automatic transmission can overtax your engine's cooling system. Automatic transmissions operate hot, well in excess of normal engine coolant temperatures, and the truck's radiator is often the only source of cooling for the transmission. As a result, a heavily worked transmission can actually cause an engine overheat.

Borg-Warner and Ford automatics run fluid lines to the radiator for cooling. On downflow type radiators, the

Fig. 7-9. An add-on auxiliary transmission cooler takes a tremendous load off the engine's cooling system. Install an auxiliary transmission cooler if your plans include trailer pulling or rock crawling in the off-pavement environment.

lower tank of the radiator harbors a separate cell for circulating automatic transmission fluid (ATF). Crossflow radiators incorporate the transmission cooler in one of the side tanks. Engine coolant, moving around this cell, draws off heat from the scorching ATF.

One of the best solutions for better engine and transmission cooling is an auxiliary transmission cooler. Some Ford trucks feature an optional original equipment (OEM) transmission cooler, which is usually part of a heavy duty/air conditioning or trailer pulling package. Aftermarket manufacturers build units that work either in-line with the radiator or independently.

The auxiliary transmission cooler resembles an air conditioning or refrigeration condenser. Air, either from vehicle movement or from the engine's fan, moves past the fins on the transmission cooler, drawing heat away from the transmission fluid.

If you install an aftermarket transmission cooler, position it carefully. Since so much heat passes from its surface, placing the unit in front of the radiator core is not always wise. Pre-heated air can raise the temperature of the radiator fins and tubes. Often, a better approach is to place the transmission cooler safely behind the radiator, or somewhere in the vehicle's air stream, without restricting the flow of radiator air.

Keeping Late Model Engines Alive

Late model light truck engines operate hot. More thorough combustion, better fuel economy plus lower CO and HC emissions result from lean fuel mixtures and higher thermostat settings; the side effect is more heat. Years ago, a truck engine came from the factory with a 180° winter thermostat. It was common practice to install a 160° thermostat in the summer months.

Today, due largely to cooling system controls and emission restrictions, engines run at 195 to 205° F thermostat settings. Normal operating temperature can range to 240° F—well past the boiling point of water.

One way to compensate for high operating temperatures is by using the correct radiator cap and coolant mixture. A radiator pressure cap of 15 psi can raise the boiling point of a 50/50 anti-freeze and water mixture to

265° F, while a 60/40 coolant mix is good for 270°. Each pound increase in radiator cap pressure raises the boil over point by 3°. Make sure the cap pressure rating is right for your engine.

Also, while anti-freeze/coolant seems the cure-all for raising the boiling point, remember that there's a limit to its use. The expansion rates differ between water and anti-freeze/coolant. An excessive amount of ethylene glycol limits the solution's ability to expand within itself. Running pure anti-freeze can cause boil over—expansion right out of the system!

Too much anti-freeze/coolant also affects the freezing point. At -8° F, pure ethylene glycol anti-freeze will actually freeze, resulting in broken engine castings and/or a cracked radiator core! Never mix ethylene glycol solutions richer than the 68% maximum ratio recommended by most vehicle manufacturers. (The minimum recommended mix is usually 44%.) A 68% anti-freeze/32% water solution should provide engine protection to -90° F.

A mix of at least 40% water is considered practical in an ethylene glycol anti-freeze/coolant solution. This can be confirmed by either mixing the solution from scratch or testing the cooling system with an anti-freeze hydrometer. Make sure that the coolant has circulated (through the heater system, too) before you attempt to check its specific gravity with a hydrometer.

When To Use An Aftermarket Electric Fan

It takes far less to cool a low compression inline six-cylinder engine than a high compression V-8. The earliest Ford F-truck sixes cranked out a modest 95 horsepower, while a late EFI V-8 can produce over 200 net horsepower. A modified or supercharged V-8 engine, or a heavily built up 460 Ford V-8, could easily range from 250 to 500 horsepower.

You can now find auxiliary electric fans in OEM truck applications. They typically serve as factory add-on devices for a heavy duty cooling or tow package. The engine driven fan assembly still provides primary cooling. Factory auxiliary electric fans meet engineering guidelines for a particular cooling system, GVWR rating and engine package.

For the conversion engine in a tight chassis bay, there's a temptation to use an electric fan in place of an engine driven fan. On many large V-8 conversions, the engine's mechanical fan is difficult to fit within the confines of a smaller engine bay or will not line up easily with the center of the radiator core. Fortunately for F-truck owners, even the original 1948 chassis will accommodate a V-8 engine. '53–up models have huge engine bays that easily accommodate large V-8 engine swaps.

Some custom street rod builders believe that the mechanical (engine driven) fan is unnecessary and that a heavy duty electric fan system, alone, can cool the engine. As a former truck fleet mechanic and long standing four-wheel drive user, I am not a supporter of aftermarket electric fans and am especially disappointed with electric fans that rely on the radiator fins for support. (These kinds of assemblies are held in place by plastic ties through the radiator core.) With enough vibration, a fin mounted electric fan can severely damage the radiator.

A mechanical fan, if centered reasonably well and shrouded properly, proves superior in all cases. A heavy-duty truck fan or any of the better aftermarket flexible (engine driven) cooling fans provide far more pitch and air draw than the typical electric fan.

An electric fan may provide adequate cooling for light load highway use where cruise speed air flow meets the majority of cooling needs. I once tested a "high output" aftermarket electric fan on a 4x4 truck with a high horsepower conversion engine. The electric fan was the sole source of cooling air. At crawl speeds or traffic light stops, the engine heated up as if the cooling system was under sized. When the vehicle reached 25–30 mph, the engine cooled rapidly, even with the fan turned off.

The real test of truck cooling is a high noon rock crawling episode on a mid-summer trip through the desert—or pulling a 30-foot travel trailer up a six-percent, twelve-mile-long grade out of El Centro, California in August—or getting stuck in the Los Angeles freeway interchange with a sailboat in tow and the ambient temperature around 100° F. Here, when used as the sole source of air flow, a heavy duty engine driven fan serves far better than any aftermarket automotive electric fan.

I would consider using an aftermarket electric fan to cool an auxiliary engine oil cooler or a transmission cooler. These devices often rely on the engine driven fan for air flow, which places an added burden on the engine's own cooling system.

Fig. 7-11. Factory electric fans are an auxiliary source of air flow for cooling. A cooling system's principle source of air flow is still the heavy duty engine driven mechanical fan (shown). An OEM auxiliary electric fan meets a special cooling need and works in conjunction with (not in place of) a heavy duty radiator and high output engine driven fan system. This seven-blade mechanical fan could serve a high GVWR package that wrestles with an automatic transmission, an air conditioner and a large displacement V-8 engine.

Fig. 7-10. Follow factory belt tightening procedure whenever possible. If data is unavailable, adjust a V-type belt to 1/2" deflection midway between the generator/alternator pulley and fan pulley. Measure this deflection while applying firm downward thumb pressure to the belt. Correct tension will rotate generator/alternator pulley slightly as you apply pressure.

Fig. 7-12. Even a defective spark advance mechanism or vacuum unit can cause engine overheating. The State of California once advocated a retrofit smog control that eliminated vacuum spark advance under most driving conditions. Engine overheat damage was so prevalent that California abandoned the measure.

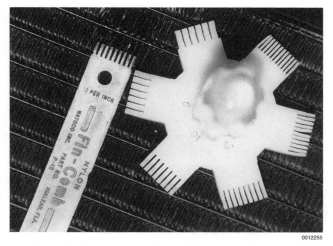

Fig. 7-13. Fin design makes a difference, with serpentine-type fins generally better for the off-highway environment. Overall, whether your oversize radiator is a downflow or crossflow design, quality construction and adequate air flow are more important than whether coolant moves horizontally or vertically.

Tenacious Overheat Problems

Cooling problems can go beyond the radiator and fan. A dirty or corroded engine block, obstructions in the block, the wrong cylinder head(s), an improperly installed head gasket or excessive internal friction can each cause overheating. Faulty ignition timing or spark advance, excess carbon, valves ground too thin, a defective thermostat, the wrong intake manifold, cross-firing spark plug wires and an overly lean or rich carburetor mix can also cause an overheat.

Water pump defects are a common cause of trouble. The most obvious pump problem is a leaking seal. Worn pump bearings allow pulley and fan blade runout, usually visible when looking sideways at the idling engine. Improper gaskets, corroded impeller vanes or a missing water pump backing plate can also cause coolant circulation problems.

A plugged exhaust system or a stuck heat riser valve will quickly overheat an engine. Pinched or air-blocked cooling hoses, excessively hot spark plugs or a loose fan belt(s) can also cause trouble. Avoid using flex type hoses, as they can collapse or place excess stress on radiator inlet and outlet sleeves. Wherever possible, use OEM type molded hoses with wire reinforcement.

An older radiator may need boiling and rodding. This process involves removing the top and bottom tanks, boiling the radiator in caustic, then running rods through the scaly tubes. Reassembly and pressure testing complete the job. Pressure testing assures a margin of safe operation. Late model truck cooling systems operate at higher pressures, which, in conjunction with antifreeze/coolant, raises the boiling point.

A clean, pressure tested radiator, with adequate flow rate and the proper fan cooling, should keep your truck's engine running at normal temperatures. Most radiators that test leak free at 20 psi in the shop will offer long service. A 17-psi cap affords a 260-plus° boiling point with a 50/50 mixture of high grade antifreeze/coolant and water.

Fig. 7-14. Check radiator solder seams and joints for coolant seepage. Have weak or loose brackets repaired by a radiator shop.

A heavily modified engine, however, may require a special radiator. Especially challenging are the big V-8s. Here, a custom down-flow or cross-flow type radiator must have a large flow capacity. Also consider a heavy duty OE replacement radiator. Often, a radiator specialist can mount your original radiator tanks and brackets to a much larger new radiator core.

As for specialty radiators, don't rush to buy a NASCAR or SCCA aluminum road racing radiator. Such a unit may rely on high speed air flow for cooling, a nonexistent commodity when your 4x4 shares a desert floor with the lizards or your fifth wheel dualie lugs four horses over the Grapevine.

2. WATER PUMP SERVICE

Eventually, every engine's water pump will fail or wear out. Although water pumps often last between engine overhauls, the load and stress placed on a hard working truck can cause earlier failure. If you periodically pressure check the cooling system, maintain an adequate amount of coolant/anti-freeze and keep proper tension on the drive belts, you will decrease the likelihood that a failed water pump will leave you stranded.

Fig. 7-15. *Water pump failure seldom occurs instantly. Signs of weakness, like coolant seepage or a wobbling shaft bearing, give forewarning. Watch bleed hole at base of pump. When the seal fails, coolant will leak from bleed hole.*

On that note, like an extra fan belt, a bottle of radiator stop leak solution is a smart accessory for your truck's toolbox. Often, if the leak has just developed, stop leak can get your truck home or to a service garage. For the water pump in good condition, a water pump lubricant additive is of some value.

As a precaution, pressure check your cooling system regularly. Often, a water pump will only leak when under pressure. Also, with the engine shut off, rock the fan blade to test the water pump shaft bearings.

Fig. 7-16. *In an emergency, you can change the water pump yourself. Make sure the engine is completely cool before attempting to drain coolant, and use a drain pan. Avoid prolonged skin exposure to anti-freeze, sealants or parts cleaning agents. Use adequate ventilation as indicated.*

WARNING —
Be extremely careful when handling an aftermarket stainless steel fan. The edges are often as sharp as a knife.

At the first sign of water pump seepage, replace the pump. Don't take chances or attempt a permanent fix with a liquid or powder stop leak. A weak pump will likely fail at a critical time, such as when the engine is under load and pulling hard.

General Guidelines For Water Pump Replacement

Prior to the advent of engine driven power options, water pump replacement was relatively easy. For later models, depending upon equipment and how many engine accessories stand in the way, this task can vary. In general, Ford trucks with inline sixes and small-block V-8s have open engine bays and ready access to the water pump.

Power steering and other engine driven accessories can make the water pump more difficult to access on any engine. If your truck's engine has an alternator, power steering, air conditioning and an air injection pump(s), allow plenty of time to complete the water pump replacement.

Although the steps discussed should assist in your water pump removal-and-replacement (R & R), the job may require additional measures for your particular year, model or accessory package. If you find areas not discussed and have doubts about what steps to take, consult the Ford factory service/shop manual for your specific F-truck year and engine application.

Fig. 7-17. *Crowded engine bays, large engines, and a multitude of driven accessories can make water pump removal difficult. In many cases, removing the radiator makes the job easier and protects the radiator core from damage.*

Before tackling a water pump change on a Ford truck engine well-loaded with power accessories, consider the scope of the project. If you decide to proceed, outline on paper the steps and position of parts as you go. This sequence is crucial to correct reassembly. To avoid a "sour" job or the ultimate frustration of re-doing the project, take time to observe how these many pieces come apart.

General Replacement Procedures

Begin any water pump replacement by placing a large pan beneath the radiator drain cock. With the engine cool, loosen the petcock and allow coolant to drain into the pan. (You may find that removing the radiator cap allows faster draining.) Unless this coolant is relatively new and very clean, discard it at your local recycling outlet.

Disconnect the battery ground cable if your engine requires removal of the generator or alternator and its mounting bracket. With the battery ground cable disconnected, loosen the generator/alternator belt, whether serpentine or V-groove type. For serpentine belts, make careful note of belt routing.

Fig. 7-18. Serpentine belts have unique routings. Note the engine equipment and match to your Ford workshop manual chart or the decal beneath the hood of your truck. Many later fans are reverse rotation design.

Unbolt and lay the generator/alternator aside, with its wires still attached if possible. Do not stretch these wires. Support the alternator or generator properly.

On all engines other than the early flathead V-8s, remove the radiator fan shroud, fan and fan clutch where applicable. If you have not already done so, you will need to loosen and remove the generator/alternator belt or serpentine belt to perform these steps. When the engine drives power accessories, other belts may also need removal. Note their location and routing so that you can reinstall them in the proper sequence.

If you are not removing the radiator but need to remove the shroud, reinstall one screw at each side to support the radiator as the shroud is detached. On some trucks, the space between the radiator and engine is enormous, so you can replace the water pump by just removing the shroud. Take care not to damage radiator fins when removing the fan, pulley or water pump.

Fig. 7-19. If the air conditioner interferes with pump removal, you must follow necessary steps to move the compressor and access the water pump. Power steering pumps, air injection pumps and even electronic ignition components may interfere with water pump removal.

If the lower radiator hose attaches to the water pump, you will need to disconnect this hose at the water pump. (On some engines, you may want to remove the upper hose to allow more room to work.) Now loosen all other hoses attached to the water pump.

All water pump installations require wire brush cleaning of bolts and fasteners and close inspection of hardware and fittings for corrosion damage. Carefully scrape old gasket material from the water pump mounting surface. If surfaces are aluminum, use extreme caution when scraping to avoid nicking soft alloy.

Years ago, water pump rebuilding kits were available. Today, the local parts outlet supplies complete new or rebuilt replacement pumps. Make certain that the new or rebuilt pump is identical to the pump you have removed, and inspect the new gasket(s).

As required, transfer any reusable fittings or pipes from old pump to new pump. If fittings show excessive wear, replace with new parts of like kind and coat threads with a film of liquid Teflon sealant. Evenly coat both sides of new gasket(s) with a suitable gasket sealant. Apply sealant or liquid Teflon to bolt threads before installing the new water pump.

Find an appropriate coolant-resistant sealant approved for water pump installation. Avoid using too much sealant on gaskets, as excess sealant finds its way into the radiator tubes. On very late model engines, anaerobic sealers sometimes take the place of a conventional gasket.

With the odd routing of serpentine drive belts, some late model engines have either forward or reverse rotation water pumps. Make note of which way your water pump and fan rotate. Be certain that the new pump's impeller vanes match the original pump's direction of rotation.

If electrolysis or erosion has weakened your water pump bolts, discard them and replace with new, properly graded hardware. Always be certain that bolts are of the same thread pitch, thread length and overall length as original hardware. Use hardware gradings equal to or better than those indicated on the heads of OEM bolts. Install new lock washers of the same kind as the

Fig. 7-20. Use the specified gasket sealant when installing a water pump. Proper sealant is both oil and coolant resistant. Place a thin coat on each side of the gasket. Thoroughly clean bolt threads and pipe fittings, and apply thread or pipe sealant before assembly.

original hardware, and apply coolant-resistant sealant to the bolt threads.

WARNING —
The running fan and water pump contain a lot of energy. One of the worst possible accidents is a fan coming loose and either driving through the radiator core or flying in lethal fashion from the engine bay.

When a specific torque setting is not available, torque bolts according to their thread size and grade standards. Many non-factory service manuals neglect the torque settings for water pump and engine accessories hardware. If you cannot find a torque setting, see the appendix of this book for a general purpose torque/tightening chart and an explanation of grade markings. Be aware that aluminum castings generally use different torque settings than iron castings.

Reinstall and torque power driven accessory hardware to the settings found in your factory or professional level shop manual. Much of the hardware that you remove during a water pump installation supports components that are under stress when the engine is running. Setting proper torque is essential.

Unless otherwise specified, after tightening the water pump bolts, other parts go back in place by simply reversing the step sequence used for removing the old pump. Once you've safely secured the water pump, pulley and fan, install a new fan belt or serpentine drive belt if the old one is worn, and adjust belt tension.

Avoid damaging your new water pump or the alternator/generator by following the factory belt tightening

Fig. 7-21. These bolt markings represent different grades of USS and SAE hardware. Three marks is Grade 5. Six marks is a Grade 8 bolt, a much higher tensile strength than the general purpose Grade 5.

procedure. In some cases, a special belt tensioner or a torque wrench is necessary to meet OE requirements.

If no data or special tools are available, a V-groove belt should deflect about 1/2" when you apply heavy thumb force midway between the pulleys. (The alternator or generator pulley should rotate very slightly as you press firmly on the belt.) Serpentine belts require a large amount of tightening force. Adjust to factory specification.

With coolant drained, this is also a good time to replace the thermostat. During replacement, carefully scrape old gasket material from the manifold, taking care not to scrape gasket material into the cooling ports. (If old gasket material circulates to the radiator tubes, it can restrict coolant flow and inhibit cooling.)

Examine the radiator for rust and scale, seepage at solder seams and signs of corrosion. Consider sending the radiator unit for a boil out and pressure testing, even if no leaks are apparent. You only want to do this job once, so consider any parts that could fail in service.

Put a light coat of suitable pipe or hose sealant on the inner ends of hoses or outside the hose fittings. Install hoses with new clamps centered carefully. (Where applicable, make sure the coil of wire is in place within the lower radiator hose, if so equipped. This prevents the hose from collapsing.) Tighten clamps securely.

Make certain the radiator draincock is shut snugly. Pour anti-freeze/coolant and correct water mix into the radiator. Allow the coolant to settle, and keep filling until liquid reaches full level. Top off as necessary. On closed coolant systems with an overflow tank, fill radiator to the top of the filler neck, then seal with the radiator cap. Add coolant to the overflow tank's COLD line.

Install the radiator cap, turn the heater controls to HOT, and start the engine. Let the engine reach operating temperature, then turn it off and allow to cool completely. Once cool, slowly open the radiator cap.

Since the coolant has circulated thoroughly with the heater on, you can check coolant mixture with a hydrometer. This will help you decide whether to top off with straight coolant, water or a mixture of both. Unless your climate has arctic temperatures, strive for a 50/50 coolant/water ratio, which will read around -34° F protection. Now is a good time to recheck torque on all hardware and the hose clamps. Also check closely for leaks. If you suspect a leak, pressure check the system.

Water Pump R & R Notes For Specific Engines

Water pump installations differ by model, year and engine application. For later trucks, the Ford F-Series Light Truck Shop Manual is available through the local Ford dealership, along with any specialty tools needed for service operations. If your truck is older and the factory manual is no longer available through Ford, see the appendix at the end of this book. I have provided some sources for new and used factory manuals and service books.

The following descriptions give additional details for each engine. Look closely at your engine and its accessories. If you see distinct differences, refer to the Ford F-Series factory shop manual that covers your specific year and model.

1948–51 226-H flathead six: Four bolts secure the water pump to the block. On installation of new pump, torque bolts in gradual cross sequence to a maximum of 32 ft/lbs.

1948–53 239 flathead V-8s: Since each of the two water pumps double as the front engine mounts on many of these models, you will need to support the engine with a jack. (Protect the oil pan with a block of wood between the jack and pan.) Raise the jack just enough to unload engine weight, then loosen necessary engine support bolts. There are three upper water pump bolts plus a bolt inside the hose inlet, which often gets overlooked. Torque the water pump bolts in gradual cross sequence to a maximum of 28 ft/lbs.

1952–64 215/223/262 inline sixes: There are two pump types, one with a pressed on fan pulley, the other has a removable pulley. Disconnect fan belt, fan and pulley if removable. There are three bolts that secure the pump to the engine block. Torque bolts in gradual cross sequence to a maximum of 35 ft/lbs.

1954–64 239/256/272 and 292 OHV Y-Block V-8s: The pump is bolted to the engine's front timing cover. (Various Y-block truck engines use "high fan" and "low fan" mounts. High fan engines require removal of the fan mount bracket to access the water pump.) The by-pass hose is hard to access once the pump is installed, so now is a good time to replace it. Torque 5/16" diameter mounting bolts (1/2" wrench size) in gradual cross sequence to maximum of 15 ft/lbs. Check the tightness of 3/8" diameter (9/16" wrench size) timing cover bolts, which call for a maximum of 28 ft/lbs.

1965–up 240 and 300 (4.9L) inline sixes: Early 240/300 engines use a one-piece gasket from the timing cover to the water pump. Trim off this old gasket carefully and squarely at outer edge of timing cover and install the new water pump gasket that comes with pump. Install new pump, torquing bolts in gradual cross sequence to a maximum of 18 ft/lbs.

1965–up 352/360/390 FE V-8 Engines: These engines have more complex accessories and brackets. In many cases, you need to loosen the air conditioning compressor and power steering pump or detach the alternator and brackets. If you remove these parts, leave their hoses or wires attached, and set the device safely aside without stretching or damaging wires or hoses. On many FE engines, you will find a radiator tank that may need to come off with the water pump. Loosen the fan shroud and lay it toward the engine. Torque water pump bolts in gradual cross sequence to a maximum of 28 ft/lbs.

1968–up small-block V-8s, including the 302 and 351W, and the 351M/400: You may need to remove the air cleaner assembly on your engine. Drain radiator and loosen the fan shroud. Place the shroud toward the engine block and remove any idler or power accessory brackets and pulleys that stand in the way. Some later engines have ignition components and brackets that must be loosened. Note that the water pump has a large steel plate at its back side. The pump mounting gasket, coated on each side with sealant, goes between this plate and the engine timing cover. (If the plate is loose or not included in the water pump kit, read instructions carefully. The installation may require reuse of the original separator plate, which means you need to thoroughly clean and inspect the plate. You may need to coat both sides of plate-to-pump and pump-to-timing cover gaskets during assembly.) This type of water pump and timing cover arrangement is common to all small-blocks and the 351M/400 (6.6L) engine as well. U Torque pump mounting bolts in gradual cross sequence to a maximum of 18 ft/lbs.

460/7.5L V-8: Although water pump installation for a 460 is much like the small-block Ford engines, the amount of accessory and bracket obstacles make this job a nightmare for the ill-prepared or disorganized mechanic. On some applications with air pumps, you must remove the air pump pulley and belt from the air pump plus the pump pivot bolt. Note that the pump comes with a separator plate at its backside. Take note of the separator plate and its mounting gasket. Many 460 water pump installations will reuse the original plate, so you may need to thoroughly clean this part and prepare new gaskets for each side of the separator. Coat the clean bolt threads and both sides of the two gaskets with suitable sealer that is coolant and oil resistant. Carefully install the pump, torquing bolts in gradual cross sequence to a maximum of 21 ft/lbs.

6.9L and 7.3L Navistar V-8 diesels: The factory manual outlines approximately twenty steps for the removal and installation of the water pump on these engines. Two Ford specialty tools (T83T-6312-A and -B) are necessary for removing the fan clutch assembly. (This investment in tools could make the job less than cost effective, so price the tools first.) The fan clutch assembly attaches with a left hand thread, which confuses many mechanics. If you want to tackle this job, a major service task, invest in the manual and read instructions carefully.

Chapter 8

Engine Tune-Up and Emission Controls

T
UNED CORRECTLY, a fully loaded Ford F-Series Camper Special pickup can tow a weighty trailer over Colorado's Old Loveland Pass. At construction sites and timberlands, Ford 4x4 work trucks spend the bulk of their service life hauling maximum payloads over bad roads and up severe grades. For top performance, dependable service and decent fuel economy, your Ford truck's engine requires routine tune-ups and preventive maintenance.

Tuning demands have changed dramatically since the first F-truck rolled off the line in 1948. Until 1974, all Ford light truck engines had breaker point ignitions. Beginning

in 1974, electronically activated spark has gained prominence, with enhanced and more complete ignition plus lower maintenance requirements. Beginning in 1986, Ford engines have benefitted from electronic fuel injection, oxygen-sensor-feedback fuel ratio adjustments, and instantaneous computer controlled spark timing.

Earlier mechanical and vacuum advance ignition distributors and carburetor fuel systems often require tuning or adjustments for altitude changes and lower grade fuels. Later Ford engines with electronic fuel and spark management automatically adjust for altitude, poor fuel grades and a wide range of loads and driver demands.

Fig. 8-1. *Engine tune-up has changed dramatically since this early L-head engine. On the 226H F-truck six, a tune-up means changing the spark plugs, breaker points, condenser, and rotor. You must adjust point dwell, re-set spark timing, and adjust carburetor idle mixture as well. This engine has no emission controls.*

As an avid outdoorsperson, I have always owned 4WD trucks. Whether living at sea level or near 5,000 feet elevation, I condition for hiking, hunting, cross-country skiing and fishing at much higher elevations. Likewise, I tune my trucks for hard work and expect them to perform reliably from sea level to over 10,000 feet elevation.

If your truck's engine has carburetion and a breaker point or conventional spark advance electronic ignition, precise tuning can make a difference. Understanding your truck's tune-up needs, including the fuel, spark and emission control systems, will also improve your skills at troubleshooting and field repairs. Moreover, tune-up skills provide a cornerstone for off-highway survival.

Emission Controls and Tune-up

Emission control service, which has become an increasingly larger part of engine maintenance, also affects your truck's performance. For EPA (49-State) purposes, emission regulations become important with 1968 and newer vehicles.

California still requires a closed crankcase retrofit on 1955–up vehicles and biennial smog inspection on many model years of light trucks. Other states and local areas, designated as non-compliant or poor in air quality, now have similar annual or biennial inspection requirements.

To pass a visual inspection in California and the many other states and local areas that require emission compliance and testing, all OEM (factory) emission controls must be in place and operative. Your truck can fail a smog test for simply not having the flexible aluminum heat tube between the exhaust manifold and air cleaner intake!

For basic tuning, the exhaust gas recirculation (EGR) circuit and closed crankcase ventilation (PCV) system are primary concerns. Other emission devices can also affect engine tune.

The closed crankcase ventilation system requires routine care. Ford light trucks began using closed crankcase devices in the early 1960s. Always service or replace the positive crankcase ventilation (PCV) valve when tuning your truck's engine. The idle, manifold vacuum and general performance depend upon a clean and functional PCV system.

Assuming that your engine is in good condition, a tune-up will assure compliance and help pass the smog test. V-8 engines, especially 1971 to mid-'80s carbureted models, have given up a good deal of horsepower to comply with Federal and California emission standards.

Reclaiming such latent horsepower is possible, in some cases, through the use of aftermarket performance parts that have California E.O. (exemption) numbers. (See the performance chapter.) As a rule, however, if you want your truck to comply with emission laws and contribute to clean air, you need to preserve OEM emission controls. Emission control maintenance helps assure a successful tune-up.

Later in this chapter, you will find details on emission controls and service. If you intend to service a 1965 or newer engine, familiarize yourself with the emission control section before attempting a major tune-up.

Fundamental Engine Requirements

The best tune-up cannot compensate for internal engine defects, wear or damage. As an adult education automotive and diesel mechanics instructor, I fielded many questions about engine needs and tuning. In response, I devised a simple formula called "The Four Basics." An engine must meet these requirements before tuning can be a success. The Four Basics are:
1. Normal compression
2. Correct valve lift and valve opening duration
3. Correct valve timing
4. Normal oil pressure

Additionally, the engine must operate at its normal coolant temperature.

Normal compression depends on proper piston ring, valve and gasket sealing. The valvetrain and camshaft condition determine proper valve lift, valve opening duration and valve timing. Valvetrain troubles include wear at camshaft lobes, the timing chain, the timing sprockets or gears and the valve springs. Oil pressure relies on good engine bearings, polished and true bearing journal surfaces, a sound oil pump and unobstructed oil passages.

For tuning purposes, you can add steady vacuum to the checklist. If your engine meets the four basic requirements and has no vacuum leaks, your tuning efforts will be successful.

1. ENGINE APPLICATIONS

L-head (Flathead) Six and V-8s

Ford's F-1, F-2 and F-3 light trucks offer two L-head engines, the 226H six and the 239.4-cubic-inch V-8. The six-cylinder inline engine has an easily accessible ignition distributor, as does the '48–'53 flathead V-8. (Ford designed the 1948 R V-8 truck engine with service in mind. Earlier truck models, and even the 1948 Ford passenger car V-8s, had a distributor mounted at the front of the camshaft/timing cover, much more difficult to access.) Flathead engines have provided the perfect training ground for budding mechanics. Routine tune-ups take a minimum amount of time and parts.

OHV 215/223/262 Inline Sixes

The 1952 F-1 to F-3 trucks introduced the 215 overhead valve (OHV) six. This roguish, high torque engine is very easy to tune and provides the prototype for the more powerful 1954–64 223 and 1961–64 262-cubic-inch versions. These are four-main bearing, one-barrel carbureted engines that appreciate a good tune-up.

239/256/272 and 292 Y-block V-8s

The torque of these OHV engines, built during the years 1954–64, is impressive, yet tune-up is more complex than later V-8 engines. A rear distributor will have you crawling way over the fenders, while the periodic valve adjustment turns out far more oily than with the early OHV sixes. Once tuned, the Y-block will return your consideration with lots of energy, more pulling power and less appetite for gas.

Fig. 8-2. *The 239-cubic-inch flathead V-8 changed little between 1947 and 1948. Most noticeable on the 1948 F-Series light truck R engine was a more modern distributor location for easier maintenance.*

Fig. 8-3. *Ford's first OHV sixes were four-main bearing types. In 1965, the seven-main bearing 240- and 300-cubic-inch sixes came on line. Well suited for truck service, the 300/4.9L design survives to the current MFI era, remaining a favorite choice for economical pulling. For MFI/EFI, routine maintenance consists of periodic spark plug changes and filter replacement.*

240/300 Inline OHV Sixes

These two engines provide a great opportunity for learning tune-up basics. The 300 six survived the breaker point era, served through the breakerless distributor years and responded readily to computer controlled electronic fuel and spark management. From one-barrel carburetion to electronic fuel injection (EFI), the 300 six remains a highly reliable, low maintenance engine. No periodic valve adjustment required!

Fig. 8-4. *Y-block OHV V-8s launched Ford F-trucks into the modern era. Found in many 1954–64 models, these engines deliver the kind of power that traditional truck owners want. Reliability is exceptional, and tune-up is relatively easy, despite rear location of ignition distributor.*

352/360/390 OHV V-8

Today known as "FE" engines, we called them big-blocks in the Sixties. They were closely akin to Ford's 406, 427 and 428, and even the Lincoln 430. These engines can make brutal torque when properly tuned. Front distributor location is a welcome sight, a major breakthrough for easier tuning. Spark plugs are relatively accessible, except when power accessories take up space. Once tuned right, hold onto your hat, partner.

302/351W/351M/400 Small-block V-8s

Although individual engines have distinct tuning needs and specifications, these small blocks tune easily and feature a front mounted distributor for easy access. Like the FE and big-block truck engines, no valve adjustment is necessary, making the job easier and quicker. Smaller engines in a large engine bay mean ready access to spark plugs and other tune items. You'll appreciate the difference if you compare your small block to a 460 big block.

460 Big-block V-8

Tough and brutish, the 460 tunes much like an FE or a king size version of the Ford small-block. Despite its immense size, which makes some spark plugs more accessible from the bottom of the truck, the 460 features an easy-to-tune front mounted distributor. After tuning the big 460, your reward will be better fuel mileage.

6.9L/7.3L Navistar V-8 Diesel

Who said diesels were exempt from tune-ups? Fuel filters, O-ring seal leaks, air cleaner service, injector cleaning and glow plug/controller repairs will keep your garage light burning on occasion. Fuel savings and overall reliability remain tops, however, so the trade-off is worth it.

Fig. 8-5. Ford FE truck engines were well tested in passenger cars before 1965. The 352, 360 and 390 are related to the formidable 406, 427 and 428-cubic-inch passenger car engines. One version of the 406 rated 405 horsepower, while the dual four-barrel 427 was a conservative 425 horses.

Fig. 8-6. Small-block V-8s also originated in passenger car lines, beginning in 1962. Ford did not use a small-block in light trucks until the late 1960s, although the '67 Bronco models piloted use of a two-barrel 289 V-8 version. The high performance 302-4V has become a popular engine swap for early F-trucks.

NOTE —
Although in-depth repair on your Ford/Navistar diesel V-8 is beyond the aims of this book and many home-based mechanics, there are several routine services that you can perform.

Filter changes are very important with your diesel engine, especially fuel filters. Diesel fuel has a very high water content, and this leads to everything from corrosive damage to the actual emergence of living bacteria cultures in your fuel.

Frequent fuel filter changes and use of a quality water trap filter will help preserve your diesel V-8 and ensure good performance. Become familiar with service on the water trap filter. Anti-fungal agents are available for your truck's fuel system if you suspect that a culture is alive and growing within the system. (See your local diesel/truck stop.)

NOTE —

At this time, the reduction of diesel fuel sulphur content to lower tailpipe pollution is a topical issue for Navistar engines. The lack of lubricity found with the fuel hydrogenation process (one method of eliminating sulphur) can lead to injector O-ring damage and mechanical fuel pump diaphragm failure on a higher mileage engine.

An area that sometimes requires attention is the glow plug system. Failure of the glow plug regulator/controller can cause excessive glow plug operation expensive glow plug failure. Whether you service your Navistar diesel yourself or not, make certain that the glow plug relays and regulator/controller are operative and functioning properly.

Beyond these concerns and occasional replacement of leaky injector O-ring seals, the Navistar diesel V-8 is content with regular oil changes and filter service. The Ford F-Series shop manual devotes good space to other service operations, and if you intend to work more deeply on your Navistar engine, invest in the Ford factory shop manual or a Navistar service guide.

A Closer Look At EFI/MFI Engines

Ford trucks began using electronic/multi-point fuel injection (EFI/MFI) with the 1986 5.0L/302 V-8. By 1987, the 351W/5.8L and 460/7.5L V-8s gained MFI, along with the 4.9L/300 inline six. Although the unique skills and requisite tools for servicing MFI have kept many consumers from servicing their own engines, you can work on various aspects of this system.

NOTE —

Failure of an EFI/spark management system is covered under the manufacturer's product warranty and also under Federal pollution control laws. If your truck has received proper routine maintenance (replacement of serviceable parts like spark plugs, filters, etc.) and is within the time frame or mileage for coverage, see your Ford dealer if troubles develop. You may have warranty against some or all of the repair expenses.

Professional mechanics often lament new technology. When the electronic (transistor) ignitions came into vogue in the 1960s and early 1970s, a trip to the parts house invariably turned up a seasoned mechanic who complained about the "lack of reliability" and huge expenses involved with electronic ignition parts—not to mention that these mysterious solid state devices would surely fail when we least expected and leave us stranded!

Today, few argue that archaic breaker points make more sense than a high voltage, precisely timed and fully electronic ignition system. I can recall working with exotic dual point high performance distributors that required constant tinkering with dwell angle, followed by the mandatory re-timing of the engine on every occasion that the breaker points needed "minor" adjusting.

Yes, there was a time when some electronic ignitions had marginal components, and the repair and maintenance of electronic fuel injection once meant the equivalent of a monthly vehicle payment for owners of high mileage cars. That has changed.

The current generation of Ford EEC-IV is a true marvel. Engine sensors take all climate, altitude, engine temperature, cargo loads and the driver's throttle input into account. In the exhaust stream, an oxygen sensor performs much like an infrared scope analyzer, noting oxygen content in the burned fuel and instantly telling the engine's computer the air-fuel ratio. The computer, in turn, instantaneously adjusts fuel flow to maintain air-fuel ratio constants. The result is precisely metered fuel and optimally timed spark for better power output, fuel economy and a clean tailpipe.

For mid-'80s and up Ford truck owners, EFI/MFI has meant huge savings in fuel, precise startup in the coldest weather conditions and the ability to pull a load without stressing the engine. Smooth travel at any altitude, plus successful use of the current rash of low octane fuels, are major accomplishments. The fact that horsepower and torque output have increased, along with greater fuel efficiency, says much for electronic fuel and spark management systems. Moreover, EFI has enabled the internal combustion piston engine to meet the challenge of higher air quality standards.

Newer Ford F-trucks with EFI/MFI emit less than 1/20th the tailpipe pollution of their counterpart 1968 light truck engines. And these newer EFI/MFI engines require no periodic adjustments or tinkering. Routine tuning is obsolete.

Although all ignition and fuel adjustments are pre-set at the factory, the EFI/MFI engine does have needs. Air cleaner changes and periodic fuel filter changes are crucial to performance and quality service from these engine designs. The most common fuel injection troubles involve the fuel filter(s).

Aside from the more accessible inline fuel filters, Ford EFI/MFI engines also use a pickup (venturi) filter in the fuel tank. If you know the tank has corrosives and debris that could plug a pickup screen, the Ford F-Series truck shop manual describes service steps for the MFI fuel system and its Fuel Delivery Module (FDM).

Despite the high level of reliability of modern electronic components, parts failures and some adjustment needs do occur. The idle speed controls, secondary ignition pieces (distributor cap, rotor, spark plugs and spark cables), even the injectors and their O-ring seals, can require attention. Beyond this, EFI/MFI components either work properly or they don't.

Before condemning expensive EFI/MFI parts, check the simpler possibilities. Wiring, ground leads and vacuum hose leaks cause a variety of problems. Make a systematic check of the wire leads. The fuel pump mounts in the fuel tank. During start-up, you should hear the pump operate. If the pump is not active, check the fuel pump relay, fuses and wiring. Component connectors often become faulty or create too much resistance, which can radically distort the computer's sensory signals.

Fig. 8-7. Before condemning EFI/MFI parts such as the idle air bypass valve, check harness connectors and wiring integrity.

Fig. 8-8. This commercial tester plug is a necessity with high energy electronic ignitions. Never create a spark arc to ground. Ignition damage could result.

When bad tune or poor engine operation occurs, you can perform necessary troubleshooting, replace faulty sensors or repair those parts that test as defective. You may earnestly want to understand, diagnose and repair your Ford truck's EFI/MFI and spark management system. The best way to increase your diagnostic skills to the level of a professional EFI/MFI mechanic is through carefully reading the Ford F-Series shop manual that covers your truck.

An additional aid and excellent instructional guide for 1980–up EEC-IV EFI/MFI Ford systems are the *Ford Fuel Injection & Electronic Engine Control* books by Charles O. Probst, SAE, available through the publisher of this book.

Equipped with these two books and the necessary testing tools and specialty products for EFI/MFI service (which these two books outline thoroughly), you can become competent at modern EFI/MFI service. For me, the only limiting factors are availability of specialty tools and whether I care to invest in the expensive diagnostic equipment required for troubleshooting and testing some circuits and devices. As these books describe the tools needed for each procedure, you can make an informed decision about whether or not to have the work done by a Ford dealership or shop. Acquiring such skills and insights could pay for the two books many times over.

2. IGNITION TUNE-UP

Spark plugs, the distributor cap, rotor, coil and plug cables make up the ignition's secondary circuit. The rotor and spark plugs require periodic service. Less frequently, the distributor cap and spark cables will need replacement.

The primary spark circuit consists of the breaker point set and condenser, if so equipped, or the module on an electronic ignition. During routine tune-up service, the breaker points, condenser and rotor require replacement. Inspect the distributor cap for corrosion at the contacts. If you believe the wires have wear, an ohmmeter can test individual plug wires for end-to-end resistance.

When testing the output of a Ford Dura-Spark or electronic ignition, use a commercial tester plug or fabricate a similar device. The idea is to keep the plug shell grounded to the engine block and not allow any spark wire to arc directly to ground. This tool is also handy for back country troubleshooting, enabling a fast and graphic look at spark output.

If you test spark with a plug wire removed, the misfire of one cylinder creates a rich mixture in the exhaust stream. On late engines, this can send a confusing signal to the oxygen sensor and also load up the catalytic converter with raw fuel. Do not test ignition spark output for long.

Spark Plug Service

Begin an engine tune-up by cleaning debris from the area around the spark plugs, then remove the wires. Use a clean socket to avoid dropping grit into the cylinders. A flex handle spark plug ratchet serves well with awkward spark plug locations.

Fig. 8-9. Use of a spark cable pliers is always wise. Grip the plug insulator firmly. Avoid tugging on the wires, as carbon-core will separate easily.

Fig. 8-10. Spark plug condition provides a clue to engine operation. Plug cleaning machines were once very popular. However, you need a spark plug tester or engine oscilloscope analyzer to verify a used spark plug's ability to fire. Avoid trouble. Replace your spark plugs with each tune-up.

On engines with carbon-core spark plug wires, use a spark cable pliers to prevent damage when removing the wires. Grip the insulator, not the wire section.

Use an air compressor and nozzle to blow debris away from the base of the spark plugs. Remove spark plugs carefully.

WARNING —
Wear protective goggles when blowing debris from the spark plug area.

"Read" the spark plugs. Fouled spark plugs provide a valuable insight. Oily plugs generally mean worn valve guides or piston rings. A sooty black or wet plug surface indicates gasoline fouling, unless ash from burnt oil is also present.

NOTE —
Oily plugs on a Ford flathead six or V-8 usually mean worn piston rings, since valve heads face upward (valve stems face downward), and all valve guides are relatively low in the block.

If caught quickly, gasoline fouling is less ominous than oil fouling. Gas fouling of one or a few cylinders usually indicates a worn spark cable(s) or ignition system problem (a defective rotor, distributor cap, breaker points, condenser, coil, electronic ignition module or faulty wiring).

If all spark plugs appear gas fouled, yet the ignition tests okay, suspect a carburetion or fuel injection problem. The plugs may also show other kinds of damage, including broken porcelain. When this occurs, check for detonation or pre-ignition. On unleaded fuel engines, overly advanced spark timing or the use of very low octane (highly volatile) fuel can also cause plug damage.

Before installing new spark plugs, verify that each plug has the correct part number and heat range for your engine. Especially on pre-electronic ignitions, a slightly hotter (stick within one heat range) spark plug may work

better during extremely cold weather, when long warm-up periods tend to carbon foul plugs.

On engine designs with high-energy ignition systems and stringent emission standards, the correct spark plug heat range is crucial to engine survival. For many engines, the underhood emission control decal provides tune-up data and spark plug information.

Check each plug gap carefully. I prefer a plug gapping tool that provides a flat and parallel gap surface. Many home mechanics, however, achieve good results with a round wire gauge. Bend the side electrode strap carefully. Never attempt to move the center electrode.

In the heyday of the flathead engines, it was popular to clean and reuse spark plugs. Most mechanics have abandoned this practice. Clean plugs may look good, but they may also have lost their firing capability. The only way to test a used plug is with an oscilloscope or plug tester. New plugs eliminate costly troubleshooting problems.

If you have limited experience at tightening spark plugs, use a torque wrench. Too loose and the plug could

Fig. 8-11. The spark plug gapping tool assures a parallel firing surface.

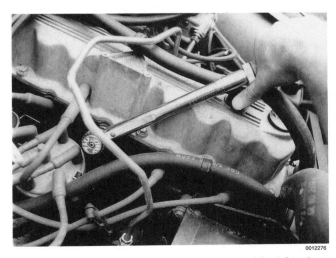

Fig. 8-12. If you have limited experience with tightening spark plugs, use a torque wrench. Overtightening can distort the spark gap or damage the plug or cylinder head.

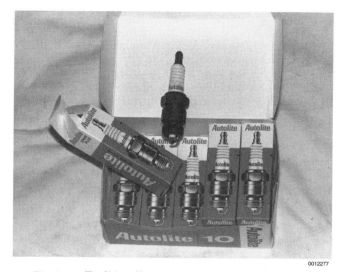

Fig. 8-13. *Traditionally, Autolite and Motorcraft spark plugs have been OEM in Ford light truck engines. Bosch platinum plugs have been added to very late model engines. Note tapered seat on this spark plug. Ford was an early advocate of tapered seat plugs, and for many years the principle user of large 18-mm thread types.*

unscrew and blow out. Over-tightening may distort the spark gap or damage the plug.

Prior to the introduction of electronic ignitions in the mid-'70s Ford F-Series trucks, spark plug gaps and torque settings were very consistent. Here is a quick reference chart for 1948–73 Ford light truck spark plug gaps and torque settings:

Engine	Plug Gap (in.)	Torque (ft-lbs)
Flathead 226 six / V-8	0.025–0.028 (some references call for 0.030)	30 max.
OHV 215/223/262 sixes	0.028–0.032	20 max.
OHV Y-block V-8s	0.028-0.032	20 max.
OHV 240/300 sixes	Light duty engines with BTF-42 Autolite plugs: 0.034 Heavy duty engines with BTF-31 spark plugs: 0.030	20 max.
302/351W/351M/400 small-block V-8s	0.034	20 max.
352/360/390 FE V-8s	0.034	20 max.

'74–up high voltage electronic spark systems require much wider plug gaps. Your underhood decal furnishes information on tuning the engine, including the type of spark plug recommended and its proper gap.

If your Ford engine has the older 18-mm thread, tapered seat spark plugs, the torque setting is a maximum of 20 ft-lbs. From 1974 onward, however, small-block V-8s changed spark plug design, and many of the newer spark plugs torque to a maximum of 15 ft-lbs.

460 V-8s have used both the older 18-mm thread type and a newer spark plug design. Note your engine's plug thread size, and set the torque according to your Ford

shop manual specifications. (Most Ford light truck V-8s call for 10–15 ft-lbs torque from 1975 onward, while only the 4.9L six remains at a maximum torque of 20 ft-lbs.)

NOTE —
If you have a 1974 or later F-truck, consult your underhood decal and the F-Series shop manual for the correct spark plug gap and torque setting.

Wires and Distributor Cap

Because modern spark cables have a carbon core, your truck's ignition wires require periodic testing for ohms resistance and shorts. The simplest volt-ohmmeter comes in handy here, providing a quick means for checking resistance between the ends of each lead. As a yardstick, the longer leads require a minimum resistance of 4,000 ohms and maximum of 15,000 ohms.

Fig. 8-14. *Check plug wires with a volt-ohmmeter. Attach leads to each end of the wire and read resistance.*

As you check the spark cables, twist and coil each wire gently. This will reveal opens or defective segments of wire. Also look at the insulation. Carefully route wires to prevent nicks and melted insulation.

CAUTION —
Never puncture carbon core wire insulation or use a pinpoint probe.

A quick preliminary test of plug wire condition is possible with a strobe timing light—preferably the induction type. Hook up the timing light lead to one spark cable at a time. With the engine idling, observe the consistency of the spark while also listening to the smoothness of the engine. Ideally, the spark should appear steady, without misfire, pause or interruption.

There are other causes of misfire, including lean or rich fuel mixtures, a fouled spark plug, a defective dis-

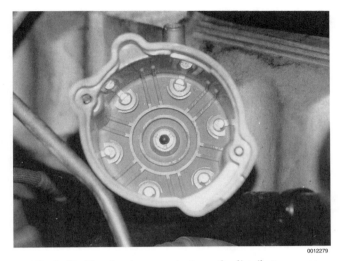

Fig. 8-15. The aluminum contacts on the distributor cap can oxidize and corrode. Replace distributor cap when corrosion or arcing causes damage.

tributor or a worn ignition coil. Remove the suspected wire and test it with your ohmmeter before investing in an expensive set of spark cables.

The spark plugs and cables are part of the secondary ignition circuit. In addition to these components, the distributor cap and rotor require attention. Replace the distributor cap when you see wear, cracks, carbon tracking (a cause of cross-firing between cylinders) or corroded electrical contacts. During routine service, I usually inspect the cap for cracks, examine the rotor contacts and clean the cable sockets with a distributor brush.

On Dura-Spark and other Ford high energy ignitions, high voltage will eventually erode the rotor. If not corrected, electricity can even short to ground through the distributor shaft. Inspect the rotor carefully. Replace the rotor if arcing, heat damage or wear is evident.

Fig. 8-16. High voltage output of Dura-Spark and electronic B/L ignition can burn a hole from center contact or rotor to top of distributor shaft. Spark arcs to ground, shorting out ignition. Check rotor periodically.

Primary Ignition System

On earlier non-electronic ignition systems, the points and condenser require periodic replacement. As for when you should replace the breaker points, consider several symptoms: point misalignment, severe rubbing block wear, pitting, arcing, blue discoloration, or contact surfaces showing a peaked buildup of metal on one side (which can also mean condenser trouble).

When I entered the field of automotive mechanics, ignition point service was still popular. Light contact filing, performing spring tension tests and re-adjusting the breaker gap were routine procedures.

Today, we regard breaker points as a disposable item. At routine intervals, usually 8,000–12,000 miles, most mechanics simply install a new set of points and a condenser. Years ago, if the condenser tested okay and the points showed even wear, reuse was an acceptable practice. In fact, if the condenser tested within specification, it was often better than many new ones out of the box.

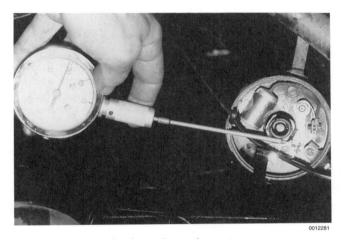

Fig. 8-17. This breaker point spring tester was once a very popular tool. Filing and regapping ignition points extends parts life and service. Use a special file, and clean all filings away with an electrical contact cleaner.

Better engineered breaker point sets have eliminated the need to adjust point spring tension. However, setting the breaker point cam angle or dwell remains crucial to peak performance. Proper dwell allows full coil saturation for a hot, crisp spark and also assures good engine starts, smooth performance and long point set life. Dwell is the number of distributor cam degrees between the spot where the breaker points close and just where they begin to open again.

A prominent source of ignition trouble is defective primary circuit wiring. Especially on early F-trucks with 6-volt systems, cloth wire can fray and short to ground against the engine block or distributor housing. Insulators on the distributor wire terminal block also wear, allowing the stud or wires to short.

Take care when installing the points and condenser. Failure to fully isolate the point spring from the distributor housing can cause hard starts, misfire or total shorting out of the ignition.

Fig. 8-18. *Loose, frayed or broken primary wires will cause ignition trouble. On earlier six-volt electrical systems with cloth wire insulation, shorts to ground become common as the wires age. Wire leads through the distributor housing wear and deteriorate. Shorts cause engine misfiring and ignition failure. Check leads whenever you service the distributor.*

Fig. 8-20. *Ford's use of a closed (no points adjusting window) distributor cap makes dwell setting more difficult. Best method is with distributor cap removed and engine cranking. Adjust points, secure screws and verify dwell once you start the engine.*

Route and attach primary wires and spark plug cables securely. Imagine your truck jostling in rough terrain. Will the breaker plate move with the vacuum advance and cause a wire short to ground? Will wires stay in place, come loose or short to ground? Before condemning your coil or other parts, look for wiring problems.

Remove the distributor cap to service the primary ignition parts (points and condenser) and the rotor. For Ford ignition distributors equipped with a centrifugal advance mechanism, the centrifugal weights and springs mount beneath the breaker plate on breaker point distributors and beneath the pickup plate on electronic units.

Beginning with the first F-truck sixes and V-8s in 1948, Ford uses the Loadamatic distributor with a spark advance that relies strictly on engine vacuum. In 1957, Ford introduced a combination centrifugal/vacuum spark advance system on F-truck V-8 engines but retained the vacuum-only advance distributors on all sixes until 1965. (From 1965 forward, some sixes continue to use fully vacuum advance type distributors.)

If spark timing tests reveal a sluggish or erratic mechanical/centrifugal spark advance, you may need to remove the distributor for disassembly and overhaul. While some distributor vacuum advance units are adjustable or replaceable with the distributor still mounted in the engine, you will find that centrifugal advance mechanism repairs are more easily done on your work bench.

When you suspect spark advance troubles with any of these distributor types, consult your Ford F-Series shop manual for repair and rebuilding procedures. You may decide to overhaul your distributor. Perhaps wear is so severe that installing a rebuilt or new distributor assembly makes better sense or will prove cost effective.

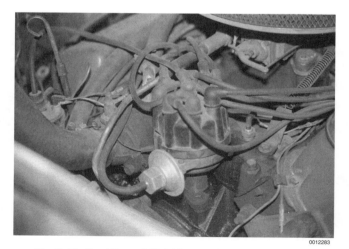

Fig. 8-19. *Ford F-truck V-8s from 1965 onward have a more readily accessible distributor. You can easily tune an FE, small-block or 460 big-block Ford engine. The tougher job is a breaker point and condenser change on the '54–'64 Y-block V-8, with its distributor at the rear.*

Fig. 8-21. *Place cam lubricant in this recess. As this counter-clockwise-rotation distributor cam turns, grease will press against the rubbing block. Grease applied to the opposite side of the rubbing block will pull away, possibly fouling the points. Note direction cam rotates before applying grease!*

Fig. 8-22. *Place the point/condenser set carefully on the breaker plate. (Be careful not to drop screws, or you will be fishing for hardware.) A spring loaded screw holder helps.*

Fig. 8-23. *A dwell meter measures the cam angle from breaker point closure to reopening. Check the dwell angle specs for your engine, and use a dwell meter for best results.*

During breaker point installation, wipe old grease from the cam and apply a thin film of fresh lubricant. Use a special point rubbing block lubricant, applied to the thrust side (toward the direction of the distributor cam rotation) of the rubbing block.

NOTE —
When you apply the grease correctly, the rotation of the breaker cam will push the grease into the rubbing block, rather than pull it away and scatter it.

Dwell Meter and Setting Points

When installing or adjusting breaker points, a feeler gauge is far less accurate than a dwell meter. Using a dwell meter to adjust the breaker points will assure adequate coil saturation for high speed operation plus enough spark for easy starting. Use of a dwell meter will also extend breaker point life.

Use the ignition feeler gauge to set the points for initial start-up. Once the engine starts, you can take a dwell reading and readjust the points as needed. Since Ford engines require removal of the distributor cap to readjust points, you will want to make accurate changes based on your dwell meter reading.

If the engine will not start with a feeler gauge setting, check all wires and connections. (Check insulators where wires attach to the points and be sure you installed these insulators in correct order.) If necessary, have an assistant crank the engine with the distributor cap removed and your dwell meter turned on. Observe spark across the points and read dwell during cranking. No spark across the points and no dwell meter reading mean either a bad electrical connection or a defective condenser. Correct this problem before setting or changing the point dwell.

WARNING —
Do not open the points with a non-insulated screwdriver, or you may get a severe electrical shock from the condenser.

By tightening the mounting screws just enough to allow movement of the breaker set, you can adjust the points as the engine cranks. You can move the point set (change gap) by rotating a screwdriver either clockwise or counter-clockwise at the adjusting slot. Once you adjust the dwell to within specification, tighten the mounting screws securely and confirm that dwell is still correct.

Many years ago, mechanics removed the distributor from the engine and used a stroboscopic distributor machine as a testbed for routine service and repairs. You may want to send your distributor to a shop that has such a machine. They can test and restore the advance mechanism(s), install new points and set dwell. You then re-install the distributor unit and set the base timing. (See timing section for instructions.)

Watch carefully for distributor shaft bushing wear. If your distributor shows a dwell variance of more than 2° cam angle, check the shaft bushings. With the rotor removed and points open on a cam lobe, press gently against the shaft. Note the point gap. Now pull on the shaft lightly. Again measure the point gap.

The difference between these figures helps indicate distributor shaft bushing wear. When your distributor shows wear, you need to overhaul the unit or install a new or rebuilt distributor. (See performance chapter for aftermarket replacement/upgrade distributor units.)

For the benefit of 1948–73 Ford F-truck owners with engines that have breaker point distributors, I have constructed the following chart with point gap and dwell angle settings. As noted earlier, while gap settings will start the engine and provide adequate service, accurately setting the dwell angle will gain even better performance and longer service from your tune-up. For 1970–up engines, confirm specifications on the underhood emission/tune-up decal.

Engine	Point Gap (in.)	Dwell (deg.)
1948–51 L-head 226H inline six	0.025	35–38
1948–53 R Flathead V-8	0.015	26–28-1/2
1952–64 OHV 215/223/262 inline sixes	0.025	35–38 through '59 37–42 '60–up
1954–64 Y-block V-8s	0.015 through '59 0.017 '60–'64	26–28-1/2 through '59 26–31 '60–'64
1965–73 240/300 inline sixes	0.025-inch to '69 1970–73 either 0.025 or 0.027	37–42 to 1969 '70–up, different dwell settings of 37–42, 33–38, 35–40, or 34–39*
FE 352, 360, 390 V-8s	'65–'70 0.017 '71 CA 0.021 '72–'73 0.017	'65–'70 26–31 '71 CA 24–29 '72–'73 24–30
Small-block 302/351W and 400	0.017, 0.020, or 0.021 (check underhood decal or your shop manual)	24–29, 26–30 or 24–30 depending on distributor and emission package

*If uncertain, consult your Ford F-Series shop manual or a professional service guide

Fig. 8-24. *Beginning with B/L electronic distributor in 1974, all later Ford V-8s and sixes have simple tune-up requirements. Spark plugs, cap, wire, rotor and new fuel filters are the customary fare.*

NOTE —

Always reset the ignition timing after you install new points or make a dwell adjustment. Any change in the point gap or the point set's location on the breaker plate will alter the spark timing.

Electronic Primary Ignition System

On 1974 and later Ford F-truck engines, removing the distributor cap provides access to the electronic ignition parts. The Ford electronic ignition systems begin with the Breakerless or B/L, then Dura-Spark (called Dura-Spark II in later versions) and, more recently, the TFI-IV (Thick Film Integrated) and DIS (Distributor Ignition System) distributors.

The TFI-IV and DIS systems are easy to recognize, as there is no vacuum advance diaphragm on these fully electronic units. By contrast, Dura-Spark distributors work much like a traditional breaker point type, with a vacuum advance unit and even a centrifugal advance mechanism.

On later electronic ignition systems, like TFI-IV and DIS, the EEC-IV engine computer controls all timing functions. Even many Dura-Spark II engines rely on the computer for spark timing input and adjustments. You will find that from the early 1980s onward, Ford truck engines have no provision for moving the ignition distributor housing to adjust spark timing. Once properly installed, the unit remains in a fixed location.

Several components are replaceable. These include the rotor, distributor cap, plastic cap spacer, magnetic pickup/stator assembly, armature, wiring and the vacuum advance diaphragm unit (on models so equipped). The distributor cap looks much like any conventional type, although Ford uses a big diameter cap on these high energy ignitions to prevent the possibility of cross-fire or arcing between spark lead contacts.

The ignition coil mounts externally. Vacuum and centrifugal advance units are also accessible with the distributor cap removed, although you may find that repairs are easier with the distributor unit removed and on your work bench.

An important part of the electronic ignition system is the module. Ford B/L, Dura-Spark and DIS units have a familiar externally mounted module, usually away from the engine on the fender well. On TFI-IV ignitions, the module is a smaller unit that attaches to the distributor.

The electronic ignition module or ICM (Ignition Control Module), working with the distributor's stator and armature magnetic pulses, could be considered the contemporary equivalent of breaker points. The module is a primary troubleshooting spot when the ignition fails.

Testing electronic ignition components requires use of a sensitive digital volt-ohmmeter and other equipment, including an oscilloscope in some instances. For service and repairs beyond basic tuning, refer to either your Ford F-Series shop manual or the *Ford Fuel Injection & Electronic Engine Control* manual by Charles O. Probst, SAE.

Before condemning a module or any other electronic ignition component, check all wiring circuits and connections. Wires can fray, short and develop loose connections. Module leads can wear out, especially on vacuum advance equipped distributors. Check your engine's wiring carefully, and replace defective wires or plug connectors as needed.

The externally mounted module is easy to replace on most Ford trucks. This component, however, is also highly suspect when the engine fails to start, especially when hot. If your engine suddenly stalls when completely warmed and won't re-start, or if it cranks but won't start unless the engine has cooled down completely, check the module.

NOTE —
Distributor modules mounted near hot engine components and on the distributor housing usually require a special silicone heat insulating gel supplied with the new module. An even coating on the back of the module helps isolate this sensitive component from engine heat.

Spark Timing

Before you start the engine to verify spark timing, check the tightening torque on fan and water pump mounting hardware. Make sure the water pump shaft and bearings do not have play or wobble. When timing your engine, stay away from moving parts.

WARNING —
Do not race the engine, as the fan is more likely to come loose on a stationary vehicle than when air is moving through the radiator. Make sure your hands, clothing and tools are well away from moving parts. Never operate the engine beyond 2,500 rpm during service work.

Fig. 8-25. *Timing lights with built-in advance will check performance of the spark advance mechanism. If you add initial timing degrees to the specified distributor advance degrees for a given engine rpm, the adjusted strobe light should index with the 0 (TDC) mark.*

Always perform initial or base spark timing with the engine at its curb (fully warmed) idle speed. This means the choke is fully open, and the engine is running slowly enough to prevent the centrifugal/mechanical advance from altering the reading.

Even a slight opening of the throttle will cause the vacuum advance to operate, so verify from your underhood tune decal which vacuum line(s) to the distributor must be disconnected and taped to prevent loss of vacuum. Some engines with dual vacuum lines require that you disconnect and tape off only one line.

Fig. 8-26. *Rotate the distributor housing with the ignition switch ON, making sure your hand is away from the primary wire or stud terminal. First rotate in direction of shaft rotation, then reverse toward #1 cylinder firing position.*

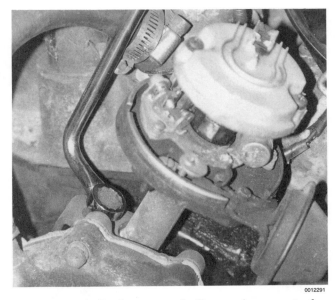

Fig. 8-27. *A distributor wrench allows easier access to the adjuster clamp nut. The moveable distributor housing permits timing corrections. On later engines, the distributor clamps in a fixed location for emission compliance. Here, timing changes come from the computer.*

On pre-emission era engines (1948 to the mid-1960s), disconnect and tape the vacuum advance line(s) before setting or checking base timing. Most emission era engines also require that you disconnect and tape the vacuum advance hose(s), and if this is the case with your engine, you will find details on your underhood emission and tuning decal. If still in doubt, consult your Ford F-Series owner's handbook or shop manual, or verify the timing procedure in a professional level service guide.

Use a stroboscopic timing light for best results. I like the latest induction type lights for their ease of hookup and brightness.

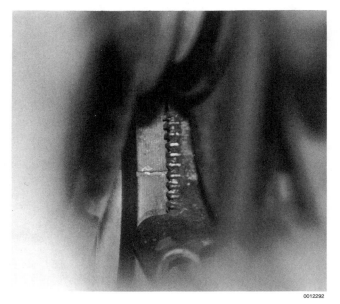

Fig. 8-28. *You will find timing marks at the engine's front timing cover. The tab is likely dirty from road debris and engine grease. With the engine safely shut off, carefully wipe the tab clean. You will index the correct marker point with the correct crankshaft line.*

Fig. 8-29. *Most settings call for the engine at an idle with the distributor vacuum line disconnected and plugged. Your timing light attaches to #1 cylinder. Disconnect and plug or tape off vacuum advance line before verifying base timing.*

Fig. 8-30. *Even big 460 V-8 distributor housing clamp is easy to reach with a special distributor wrench. Loosen the bolt slightly, just enough to move the housing.*

Fig. 8-31. *If the mark is difficult to distinguish, clean the timing tab and notch thoroughly before starting the engine to verify timing. A dab of white or yellow indelible paint helps locate the mark with your timing light.*

Static Timing

If you need to service your engine in the wilds, I have a static timing technique that can prove very useful on breaker point type distributors. (Electronic ignitions cannot be static timed, due to the need to generate signals with a rotating distributor armature.)

Begin by locating the distributor wire lead to #1 cylinder. Remove the distributor cap and spark plugs. Manually turn the engine over in its normal direction of rotation. Watch the rotor as it approaches the #1 cylinder firing position.

Rotate the crankshaft slowly, and stop exactly where the timing marker indexes with the correct initial advance mark. On your truck's engine, the marks and pointer will be visible at the crankshaft damper/pulley and timing cover. You may need to wipe grease off the pointer or pulley to clarify the marks.

Turn the ignition switch to the ON position. With the distributor clamped loosely, move the housing in the direction that the distributor shaft normally rotates during cranking.

> NOTE —
> Some Ford truck distributors rotate counter-clockwise. Observe which way the shaft turns during cranking.

Move the housing well past the #1 cylinder distributor lobe. Now, very slowly rotate the housing in the opposite direction of the distributor shaft rotation, toward the #1 cylinder firing position. Watch the point contacts carefully.

> WARNING —
> *Avoid electrical shock by keeping your hand away from the primary coil wire. When the condenser unloads, the primary wire receives a good voltage spike. Make sure your hand isn't the ground source.*

At the exact moment the points arc, you will have set timing at the number of advance degrees indicated on the pulley and timing marker. When you start the engine and verify the timing with a timing light, you may find a slight difference. This is due to camshaft and distributor drive gear lash. For start-up purposes, however, this method serves well. (When I rebuild an engine, static timing assures an immediate start-up.)

A variation on static timing also works well. With spark plugs removed from the engine, rotate the crankshaft to locate the timing marks as before. Now, reinstall the distributor cap. Place an old spark plug on #1 plug wire and ground the plug's metal shell carefully. Loosen the distributor housing clamp.

Turn the ignition switch to ON. Rotate the distributor housing in the same direction as the shaft rotates, well past the #1 cylinder firing point. Then, slowly rotate the housing in the opposite direction of shaft rotation until a spark fires across the test plug. If you tighten the distributor at this exact point, accurate static timing results. If you pass the firing point, repeat the procedure.

By rotating the distributor first in the same direction as shaft/rotor rotation, and then in the opposite direction, you will prevent the advance mechanism from distorting your static timing results. If you overshoot the firing point, repeat the process to assure an accurate setting.

When you need to remove the distributor, carefully note the rotor position and scribe the distributor housing location before pulling the unit. Upon reinstalling the distributor, immediately verify timing with your induction timing light.

Use Of Timing Light With Built-in Advance

An easier approach to spark timing is possible with a timing light that has adjustable advance. Simply dial the advance until you index the timing cover marker with the 0, TDC or dot/groove on the crankshaft pulley. Read the timing light's scale. If the reading equals the correct timing specification, the engine's spark is in time.

The built-in advance light is ideal for verifying spark advance mechanism behavior. For engines with a centrifugal and/or vacuum advance system (without electronic computer overrides), you can use an advance timing light much like a stroboscopic distributor test machine.

You can quickly test the vacuum advance unit with a vacuum pump. (In your Ford F-Series shop manual or a professional service book, you will find specifications for the vacuum and centrifugal advance units.) With the engine idling, disconnect and plug the vacuum line and read the degrees of spark timing advance.

Hook the vacuum pump to the advance unit and apply the number of vacuum inches (in/hg) described in the service guidelines. Note the degrees of timing advance that now appear at the crankshaft pulley/damper and timing marker. When assessing the results, note whether the service book describes distributor degrees or crankshaft degrees.

Distributor Degrees Versus Crankshaft Degrees

Your professional service manual has specifications on where the vacuum or centrifugal advance unit should just begin to move and how many total degrees it should advance at full apply vacuum or a given rpm. Be aware that most service guidebook distributor specifications read in distributor rpm and distributor degrees.

These figures are exactly one-half the number of engine crankshaft degrees and one-half the crankshaft/engine rpm. When you read degrees of timing advance at the crankshaft, what you see is twice the distributor degrees, plus the number of degrees of initial spark advance. Likewise, engine speed is twice that of distributor rpm.

Example 1: Initial timing calls for 0 or TDC. Centrifugal advance specifications call for 5° (distributor) of spark advance at 1250 distributor rpm. With vacuum advance hose disconnected and taped off, timing will read 10° (crankshaft) of spark advance at 2500 crankshaft/engine rpm.

Example 2: Vacuum advance specifications call for 8 degrees of distributor advance at 13 in/hg vacuum. With the engine at an idle, you apply 13 in/hg vacuum to the vacuum diaphragm. Timing should increase 16° (crankshaft), (possibly a bit more if the engine rpm rises enough for the centrifugal advance to swing).

Consider sending the distributor for testing if you suspect an inoperative centrifugal advance mechanism. Mark the distributor housing and rotor location. Remove the distributor. Have a shop test the advance mechanism(s) in a distributor test machine. Although these machines have become somewhat rare in this era of rebuilt/exchange parts, they were popular during the breaker point distributor era.

Vacuum Versus Mechanical/Centrifugal Advance

Many of the Ford F-truck engines from the breaker point era have vacuum actuated spark advance. Some Ford truck distributors use a very slow or mild centrifugal advance curve and rely heavily on vacuum advance for extra spark timing and power at low engine speeds.

The reason vacuum advance works well for truck engines is that under severe loads, the engine needs spark advance quickly. A centrifugal advance requires engine speed in order to work, and that's not often easy when the truck lugs a heavy load. Vacuum advance brings a brisk and immediate increase in spark advance, just as the throttle tips open.

Vacuum provides the necessary spark advance for low speed power. As speed increases, a centrifugal (weight and spring) advance unit can offer an engine speed related advance. At this stage, as the throttle opening widens and neither engine vacuum nor ported carburetor vacuum can assist, engine speed alone can regulate the degrees of centrifugal spark timing advance.

Ported Versus Manifold Vacuum

When a distributor uses ported vacuum, the vacuum source is a channel just above the carburetor's throttle plate. As the throttle valve begins to open, this port becomes exposed and receives a high rate of engine vacuum, causing the spark timing to advance substantially. Ported vacuum declines gradually as the throttle valve opens further.

Manifold vacuum, which is sometimes used in a single or dual diaphragm vacuum advance system, is the vacuum from within the engine's intake plenum. Manifold vacuum is highest at an idle, remains relatively high at light loads and throttle settings, and drops as the throttle opening and engine load increase. At wide open throttle under load, manifold vacuum reaches its lowest point.

Fuel economy is best at higher manifold vacuum readings. Sluggish spark timing advance reduces manifold vacuum. Adequate spark timing advance, whether vacuum or centrifugal, maintains the best manifold vacuum. This contributes to better performance and optimal fuel economy.

Initial Spark Timing and Firing Order Chart

Initial spark advance settings are generally with the vacuum advance hose(s) disconnected and taped and the engine at its recommended curb (warm) idle speed. On emission controlled engines, read the underhood decal carefully, as you may need to use special procedures or keep certain vacuum lines connected as you adjust base timing.

NOTE —
Emissions law requires that an engine operate at the vehicle manufacturer's recommended setting. When you tune your engine for an emissions test, be aware that many states and local areas require a check of spark timing. Set the timing correctly to avoid failing a smog test.

Engine	Firing Order	Timing
1948–51 L-226H inline six	1-5-3-6-2-4 (front to rear)	Groove or ball on pulley
1948–53 Flathead R V-8	1-5-4-8-6-3-7-2 (right bank 1-2-3-4, left bank 5-6-7-8)	Dot on pulley
1952–64 OHV inline six	1-5-3-6-2-4 (front to rear)	215: Groove on pulley 223, '54–'56: 5° BTDC 223/262, '57–up: 4° BTDC on M/T, 6° A/T (TDC is the long line on pulley/damper. Lines before TDC are 3, 5, 7 and 9° advance.)
1954–64 Y-block V-8s	1-5-4-8-6-3-7-2 (right bank 1-2-3-4, left bank 5-6-7-8)	239/256: timing at groove on pulley 272, '56: 10° 272, '57ECR-Y: 10° BTDC ECW engine: 8° BTDC
240/300 inline sixes	1-5-3-6-2-4 (front to rear)	6–12° BTDC Check underhood decal
1965–up FE 352, 360 and 390 V-8s	1-5-4-2-6-3-7-8 (front-to-rear right bank 1-2-3-4; left bank 5-6-7-8)	Usually 6° BTDC Check underhood decal
Small-block 302	1-5-4-2-6-3-7-8 (right bank 1-2-3-4; left bank 5-6-7-8)	Some earlier 302s call for 6° BTDC Check underhood decal
Small-block 351W and 351M/400	1-3-7-2-6-5-4-8 right bank 1-2-3-4; left bank 5-6-7-8	Check underhood decal
460 V-8	1-5-4-2-6-3-7-8 (right bank 1-2-3-4; left bank 5-6-7-8)	Check underhood decal

If unsure about timing, try a conservative setting, then alter it to achieve a balance between no spark knock (ping) and decent performance

3. CARBURETOR TUNE-UP

Carburetor adjustment is another aspect of your tune-up. Before setting the idle mixture, make certain that the fuel pump provides an adequate supply of gasoline. Change the disposable filter(s) on later models and clean the fuel pump's sediment bowl filter on earlier engines.

WARNING —
During many fuel system procedures fuel will be discharged or exposed. Do not smoke or work near heaters or other fire hazards. Have a fire extinguisher handy.

A plugged fuel filter will restrict fuel flow and affect engine idle. When your truck's engine floods with gasoline or bucks during high speed runs, check the carburetor float setting. Also check the float drop setting.

Altitude changes will alter the idle mixture. If you plan to operate an older Ford carbureted truck at a higher or lower altitude than your home, for an extended period of time, expect to re-adjust the idle mix.

Ford F-trucks use a variety of carburetors. The list and description of specific carburetors would make a full

Fig. 8-33. *Change fuel filter elements as part of routine service. On engines with a carburetor inlet filter, change this filter annually or at a maximum of 15,000 miles. Filters are available at the local dealership or a reputable aftermarket parts source. Filters provide cheap insurance against engine breakdown and high fuel bills.*

Fig. 8-32. *Earliest F-truck inline six uses this basic one-barrel carburetor. Ease of service is apparent in adjustable needle/seat height and cable-controlled manual choke. Single idle mixture screw makes this the simplest of carburetors to tune.*

length service guidebook in itself. Rather than writing a second volume to this book, I recommend that you seek out a quality resource such as Motor's *Truck* and Mitchell's *Domestic Light Truck Tune-up Manual*, or the Ford F-Series truck shop manual for a specific year.

CAUTION —

Overhauling and repairing some of the later Ford truck carburetors require expertise and special gauges, an accurate vacuum pump and exacting service data. Unless you have a good background in carburetor overhaul, either send your carburetor to a specialist or purchase a rebuilt/exchange or new unit. (See performance chapter for tips on replacement carburetors.)

NOTE —

If your truck's engine runs roughly or responds poorly under acceleration (has a flat spot), suspect dirty carburetor jets, a defective accelerator pump or an ignition mis-fire. Once you rule out ignition problems, vacuum leaks, low compression or a worn timing chain, consider a carburetor overhaul.

NOTE —

Consult a factory or professional service book before adjusting or servicing a closed calibrated carburetor. The system may include a vacuum actuator and idle solenoid that interact with your truck's electrical accessory circuits, such as air conditioning. The curb idle speed and fast idle may be adjustable. Use your emissions and tune-up underhood decal as a guide for these rpm settings.

Before seeking specifications to reset the float or adjust any linkages, solenoids or the idle mixture, verify your carburetor's type and its list or tag number. For later vehicles from the emissions era, the underhood emissions/tuning decal is also a reliable tuning aid.

You cannot correct some types of carburetor wear. Consider the age of the carburetor and its general condition. Check for throttle plate wear at the throttle shaft, corrosion in the float bowl area, and warpage of main body parts. Also look for missing linkage pieces or loose and worn components. A new or rebuilt replacement carburetor can often prove practical.

On later emission control era truck engines, the carburetor has no provision for adjustment. Such closed-loop feedback carburetors usually have stepper motors for the main fuel mixture control. Idle mixture is nonadjustable unless emission standards cannot be met.

NOTE —

Generally, when these carburetors function correctly and the idle is still poor, other problems exist, usually a vacuum leak, low compression, late valve timing (bad chain) or ignition defects.

Fig. 8-34. Troubleshooting your electronic fuel and spark management system requires a precise digital volt-ohmmeter. For feedback/closed-loop carburetors and EFI/MFI, tenths and hundredths of a volt make a difference.

There is a factory service procedure for accessing the adjuster screws on some engines. However, these steps must be followed in strict accord with Federal laws. No tampering with these design features is allowed, and "by the book" tuning is crucial to proper engine operation. (See performance chapter for legal replacement carburetors that can restore performance.)

The mechanical fuel pumps on earlier Ford F-truck engines are either single or dual diaphragm types. Single diaphragm pumps serve only as a fuel supply for the carburetor. A dual-diaphragm fuel pump functions as

Fig. 8-35. This fuel pump pressure gauge verifies volume and pressure. During tests, route fuel away from the engine's spark and heat sources to avoid a fire.

both the fuel supply and as a vacuum source for the windshield wipers. Early Ford F-trucks have vacuum powered wipers.

Before condemning either the carburetor or fuel pump, check the bolts that secure these parts to the manifold and engine block. Also check the manifold mounting hardware and for possible vacuum leaks. Look for kinks in the fuel pipes and hoses. On early fuel pumps with a glass sediment bowl, tighten the bail nut carefully to avoid breaking the glass bowl.

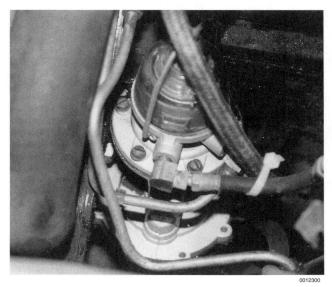

Fig. 8-36. Early F-truck engines feature a sediment bowl on the fuel pump. The serviceable sediment screen traps debris and functions much like a contemporary fuel filter. During service, avoid exposure to gasoline.

Fig. 8-37. Many carburetor pieces can wear to excess. If your older carburetor has a warped or corroded body, or a loose throttle shaft, consider a new or rebuilt replacement unit.

Float Settings

Your Ford F-Series shop manual or a professional service guide give float specifications. If the carburetor has a removable air horn, like the popular Ford truck Motorcraft/Autolite units, you likely need to loosen the fuel pipe for access to the carburetor air horn and float(s). Loosen the air horn screws, then remove and invert the air horn. Hold it level as you measure the float height.

Fig. 8-38. Holley 2300-Series two-barrel and 4150/4160 and 4180-Series four-barrel carburetors have served many Ford F-Series truck V-8s. End float design provides easy method for checking and adjusting float(s).

The exceptions to this procedure are Holley carburetors with end float(s). Many Ford trucks use Holley carburetors. Checking the float settings on an end float type Holley unit is very easy.

Fig. 8-39. Motorcraft/Autolite and Carter carburetors require removal of air horn for adjusting float. Invert the air horn and check height. Turn air horn upright to check float drop. Compare measurement against specifications found in your Ford F-Series shop manual or a professional guide.

On Holley end float models, a check plug at the bowl(s) allows looking at the fuel height without removing a single carburetor component. For 2300-series two-barrel types and the similar four-barrel carburetors, correct fuel height is usually within 1/16th inch (check your shop manual) of the check plug's lower edge with the truck on a level surface.

To adjust the end bowl float's height, use a large straight blade screwdriver, and loosen the fuel valve seat lock screw. Using a box end wrench, turn the adjusting nut clockwise to lower the fuel level or counter-clockwise to raise the fuel height.

Tighten the lock screw, start and idle the engine, then shut it off. Again check the fuel level at the sight plug. The 2300 and four-barrel 4150/4160/4180 Holleys are popular for their tuning flexibility and ease of service.

On some Holley one-barrel carburetors, you can also check the float height without removing major pieces. On these carburetors, you can remove the economizer diaphragm and measure the fuel level with a depth ruler. The correct fuel level is usually 3/4" below the machined surface. (Set the gauge's cross rail just flush with the opening in the casting. Use the height specification found in your shop manual.) The engine should be level and idling.

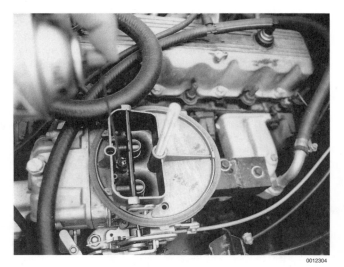

Fig. 8-40. *Most Holley 2300 series and some four-barrel idle mix screws are at the sides of the main metering block. This is a rugged and easy carburetor to repair, with service parts and upgrades available readily. (See performance chapter for details on this carburetor.)*

To reset these one-barrel floats, however, requires removal of the float bowl and careful bending of the float adjusting tab. Refer to your professional level service manual for float adjustment specifications.

> *CAUTION —*
> *Take care not to press the float needle into its seat. Damage could result, causing erratic performance.*

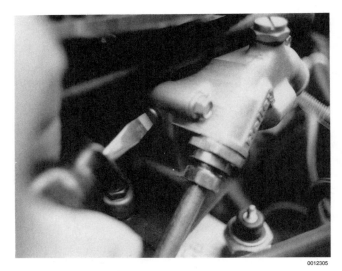

Fig. 8-41. *Measure Holley 2300 series fuel level at the sight plugs. Have the truck level and engine idling as smoothly as possible. Fuel should just reach the lower edge of the plug.*

Fuel Pump Pressure/Output

If the float level is correct and fuel starvation persists, check the fuel pump output. Correct pump pressure varies between models and pump designs. Verify your engine's requirements in a factory-level service manual. Before suspecting fuel pump pressure or volume troubles, check all fuel lines from the tank forward, and also the dual tank switching valve/solenoid if your truck is so equipped. Look for leaks, loose connections or kinks.

Fig. 8-42. *The mechanical fuel pump can wear over time. More often, a defective or clogged filter will cause trouble, mimicking the symptoms of a worn fuel pump. Change filters before condemning the pump, especially on applications where the unit is difficult to reach.*

The fuel pump is a common trouble spot. Some early Ford truck fuel pumps are rebuildable. Repair kits were once a common item at the local retail auto supply. Today, however, rebuilt or new replacement pumps are available. It is wise to carry an extra fuel pump and needle/seat kit on extended trips into back country.

When testing fuel pump volume, make certain that your container is safe and able to catch all of the gasoline. Route gas away from spark sources or hot engine parts. Spark from the ignition or engine heat could ignite fuel and cause a serious fire.

An older, fatigued fuel pump diaphragm will stretch or rupture. Look closely for fuel dilution in the engine's crankcase or leaks around the pump. If the cause of low pressure/volume is unclear, remove the pump and check the condition of the camshaft lobe or eccentric disc that operates the pump arm.

Idle Mixture Setting

Before adjusting the carburetor, look down its throat for carbon and debris. A spray type carburetor and choke cleaner can remove accessible varnish and carbon. Short of an overhaul, these solvents work well for periodic cleaning. If dust or grime is present, suspect an inadequate air cleaner seal. Correct the problem.

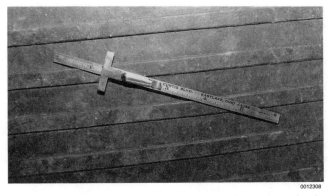

Fig. 8-44. *T-gauge rule is a common carburetor overhaul tool. Better quality overhaul kits come with detailed instructions for your carburetor model and a plastic gauge for setting the float.*

Fig. 8-43. *A quality spray carburetor cleaner will remove accessible debris. Try to wash exposed bleed holes and spray cleaner into the air horn vent. This will allow cleaner to work inside the float bowl.*

A professional service guidebook will describe overhaul procedures and give the preliminary idle mixture settings for your carburetor. If your engine has run reasonably well, turn the engine off and carefully screw the mixture adjusters clockwise while counting each turn carefully.

Fig. 8-45. *Idle mixture screws are easy to identify. For the later emission control era, many carburetors have limiter caps on their adjuster screws or depend upon electronic controls for adjustment. On emission carburetors, cleanliness and frequent filter changes make a difference.*

Turn the mixture screw/needle gently. Over-tightening the screw can seriously damage the needle end. If no lean mis-fire occurs as the mixture screw reaches its closed position, suspect dirty carburetor air bleeds or other woes.

See how close your current adjustments come to the preliminary settings recommended in the service guidebook. If there is a large discrepancy, suspect a vacuum leak or other problems. Return the idle mixture screw(s)

to their original setting, and correct any vacuum leaks. Tighten loose carburetor air horn screws and the bolts or nuts at the carburetor base. Readjust the idle mix.

Before adjusting the idle mixture, run the engine until completely warm, watching the choke through its whole opening cycle. Make sure the heat riser valve also opens properly, along with the coolant thermostat. Bring coolant to normal operating temperature—and make certain that the choke valve is fully open before adjusting the idle mix.

Always be certain the choke remains fully open while adjusting a carburetor's idle mixture. Do not allow the engine to idle for long periods during adjustment, or the spark plugs may foul and distort engine performance.

If you have difficulty judging the engine's smoothness, use a tachometer and vacuum gauge while you set the carburetor mixture screws. Strive for smooth running and the highest vacuum reading at a normal curb idle speed.

Try to adjust the engine to a "lean best" setting to help meet clean air standards. This is the leanest point for each adjuster screw that still allows the engine to run without mis-firing or stumbling.

Fig. 8-46. *Holley end-float type carburetors have an external float adjustment for each float bowl. Sight plugs on the bowls permit quick fuel height checks without removing the bowl.*

Fig. 8-48. *Loosen and tighten V-8 fuel pump bolts evenly to prevent binding of the long fuel pump arm. Damage to the pump or misalignment with the lobe/eccentric will otherwise result.*

Fig. 8-47. *Both two-and four-barrel V-8 carburetors have twin idle mixture screws, while one-barrel unit (shown) has only one screw. Clockwise leans mixture; counterclockwise enrichens. Adjust one screw at a time.*

On a fully warmed engine, begin the idle adjustment by turning the idle mixture screw(s) slowly clockwise. (One at a time in the case of two-and four-barrel carburetors.) A noticeable lean misfire should occur. Stop here.

Slowly back the idle mixture screw out (counterclockwise). Just when a smooth idle occurs, the setting is correct unless your emission decal calls for a "lean drop setting." (Lean drop means to turn the screws inward, toward a leaner mix, dropping the rpm a specific amount.) If the idle speed is incorrect at this point, reset the throttle or curb idle stop screw, then repeat the idle mixture adjustment if necessary.

Mechanical Fuel Pump Installation

Fuel pump installation begins with cleaning the area around the fuel pump. Carefully detach the fuel lines at the pump. Safely cap the fuel inlet line to prevent fuel leakage during service.

Loosen the fuel pump mounting bolts evenly and remove the pump and gasket. Look closely at the eccentric

cam that operates the pump arm. Make certain a worn lobe or loose eccentric cam is not the problem. On some Ford F-truck engines, a bolt holds the eccentric in place.

Clean the gasket surface on the engine block thoroughly. Do not allow debris to fall into the engine. Rotate the engine to place the pump's camshaft lobe or eccentric on the lowest (heel) side to reduce pressure.

Use a suitable gasket sealant, applied to both sides of the new gasket. Put sealant on the mounting bolt threads. Insert the bolts into the pump. Set the gasket, pump and bolts in place.

Carefully place the rubbing surface of the pump arm against the lobe. Start the bolt threads with caution, holding the pump squarely toward the block surface. Tighten the bolts evenly until the pump is secure.

> **CAUTION —**
> *Make certain the fuel pump arm remains in place and straight during installation. Wedging the pump to one side can damage the lever or housing.*

Fuel System Footnotes

Routine service of the fuel system helps prevent problems. Before considering an overhaul, change the fuel filter and air cleaner. Try spray cleaning your carburetor with a commercially available carburetor and choke cleaner.

Refer to the emission control section for insight into the many emission control defects that cause rough idle and other troubles. For example, an EGR valve that cannot seat properly creates symptoms just like carburetor trouble—so can the simple PCV valve, an inexpensive and routinely replaced item. Even a plugged exhaust system can be easily overlooked.

> **CAUTION —**
> *Make sure your spray carburetor cleaner will not damage the sensitive oxygen sensor. Read labels and use these products sparingly.*

4. MAJOR ENGINE DIAGNOSIS

If you suspect major engine trouble or your fuel and spark tune-up has little effect on performance, perform further diagnosis.

On emission era engines (approximately 1966 forward), the emission controls can cause trouble. A defective EGR valve, for example, often creates the same symptoms as carburetor and fuel supply problems. Defective electronic closed-loop carburetion sensors or fuel/spark management components can also mimic these kinds of symptoms.

Although PCV and air injection came on some of the early emission engines, the emission control packages were simple and not likely to cause much trouble. From the late 1970s onward, emission controls play an increasingly larger role in engine performance and tune.

After years of exposure to tune-up and engine overhaul diagnostics, I use a compression gauge only for quick referencing. A low reading usually requires squirting motor oil into the cylinder to distinguish piston ring wear from valve troubles. I go further than this and use a leakdown tester for pinpoint diagnosis.

A leak of more than 10% in any cylinder raises questions of wear, although most engines will still offer reasonable service at 20% leakage. High performance demands, such as turbocharging, require 10% or less leak in any cylinder.

Compression Seal and Testing

For quick diagnosis, a compression gauge is very handy. I prefer a threaded hose gauge, which allows one-person operation. Clean the spark plug areas, then remove all of the spark plugs. Screw the gauge end into #1 cylinder's spark plug threads. With the gauge secure, visible and lying away from rotating engine parts, open the throttle wide.

Consult your service manual for normal cranking compression readings. Crank the engine several revolutions, until the highest stable reading occurs. Record the reading. Repeat these steps for each cylinder.

If you get a low reading and want to pinpoint the problem with a compression gauge, squirt a tablespoon of oil in the spark plug hole for that cylinder and crank the engine again. If compression comes up to normal, you likely have an engine with defective piston rings. If no change occurs, valve or head gasket leakage is likely.

Assessing Compression Readings

According to current guidelines, engine balance depends upon a maximum variance of 25% between the highest and lowest cylinder. I believe this is too great for satisfactory performance and fuel economy. Smooth operation, especially off-highway or when pulling a heavy trailer or load, demands better balance than this. A more traditional factor, 10% difference between the highest and lowest cylinder, still serves as my standard.

Higher compression readings mean carbon buildup. Excess carbon is very hard on the piston rings and valves. At its worst, carbon buildup contributes to deadly pre-ignition, the premature ignition of fuel by glowing material in the cylinders. Pre-ignition can break pistons and bend connecting rods.

0012313

Fig. 8-49. A cylinder leakdown test of this freshly rebuilt engine reveals normal seal. A compression gauge reading is nowhere near as accurate. Leakdown tests foretell trouble long before a compression gauge.

Low compression readings indicate either worn rings, valve wear, a blown head gasket or cracked castings. Improper valve clearance also causes low readings. Although most service guidebooks list valve adjustment as a possible cure for low compression, this is very seldom the case.

After more than twenty-five years of exposure to engine repair and machine shop work, I find that running an engine with valves that do not seat completely will cause permanent damage to valve faces and seats. If valve clearances are so far out of adjustment that compression is low, damage has likely occurred already.

A valve adjustment cannot remove hard carbon build-up, pitting and burnout from valve faces and seats. For these problems, only a valve grind or cylinder head rebuild can restore performance. If adjusting valves does not restore compression, assume that the valves need repair.

Tight valve adjustment is a product of normal wear on engines without hydraulic valve lifters. As the valve faces wear into their seats, a process called valve seat recession occurs.

Valve clearance should remain stable between major overhauls on all Ford truck engines equipped with hydraulic lifters. The lifters, set to proper clearance upon assembly of the engine, can compensate for normal valve seat wear between engine rebuilds or valve grinding.

NOTE —
1948–53 flathead V-8s have non-adjustable mechanical (solid) tappets with running clearance. There is no provision for valve adjustment between engine overhauls or valve grinding jobs. Consult your professional service guidebook for valve grinding procedures on this engine.

Cure For Unleaded Fuel

Unleaded fuel aggravates this wear, especially in engines designed during the leaded gas era. Older, more heavily leaded fuels lubricated the valve seats, faces and stems. Complete phaseout of leaded fuel is currently underway, and all U.S. pump gasoline will soon have no lead. This leaves valves and valve seats of older leaded-gas engines at greater risk.

For older leaded fuel truck engines, the problems of unleaded gasoline and valve seat recession have a remedy. An automotive machine shop can retrofit hardened steel (replacement) exhaust valve seats into the head(s) of OHV engines or into the block of early flathead sixes and V-8s. Hardened exhaust valve seats will offset the effects of heat and reduce valve wear caused by the use of unleaded fuels.

The octane requirements for an engine are also crucial to the prevention of detonation (ping). Under current fuel standards, your engine may need high test fuel. If you must run your truck on 87–88 octane fuel, retard the timing a few degrees if harmful detonation occurs. Power may suffer some, but the engine will survive longer.

Re-torque The Cylinder Head

When you find a low compression reading, re-torquing cylinder head bolts may help remedy slight gasket seal or head warpage problems. Re-check cranking compression when you finish. (See illustrations for cylinder head tightening sequences.) If compression is still low, suspect head or gasket damage—or other low compression related problems.

Since you are re-torquing a head that has already been in service, one pull at the full torque setting should be enough. I like to go through the sequence a second time, as bolts will often yield slightly.

If you remove a cylinder head for service and install a new gasket with proper sealant on both the gasket and freshly cleaned bolt threads, follow the three-step torque method: In sequence, 1) you will bring all bolts up to a snug setting, 2) advance to a firm setting just below final torque, and 3) finish with your final setting. Some gaskets require re-torquing after the engine warms. Instructions with the gasket set will often indicate whether re-torquing is necessary.

Engine	Head Bolt/Nut Torque (ft-lbs)
1948–51 L-226H inline six	70 max.
1948–53 Flathead R V-8	70 max.
1952–64 OHV inline six	up to 1960: 65–75 1961: 95–105 1962–64: 105–115
1954–64 Y-block V-8s	2-barrel: 65–75 1961–up 4-barrel: 70–85
240/300 inline sixes	to 1975: 70–75 1976–up: 70–85
1965–up FE 352, 360 and 390 V-8s	to 1974: 80–90 1975–up: 90
Small-block 302	65–72
Small-block 351W	105–112
351M and 400	95–105
460 V-8	130–140

NOTE —

Three-stage torque figures are found in your Ford F-Series light truck shop manual. If unavailable, they usually run as first stage: 2/3rds of final torque; second stage: 5/6ths of the final torque figure; third stage: final torque. Let the engine set for a while after final torque, then re-tighten again at the final torque setting. Always tighten bolts in sequence.

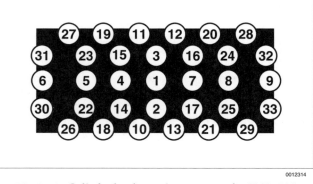

Fig. 8-50. *Cylinder head torquing sequence for 1948–51 L-226 H engine.*

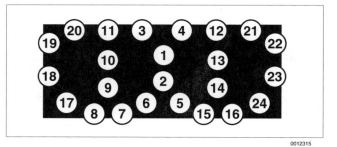

Fig. 8-51. *Cylinder head torquing sequence for flathead R V-8 engine.*

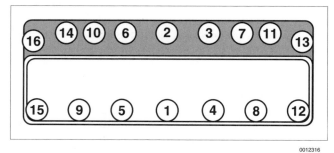

Fig. 8-52. *Cylinder head torquing sequence for OHV 215/223/262 inline six.*

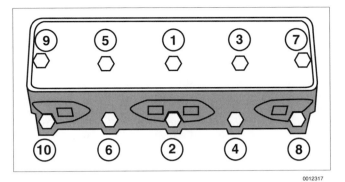

Fig. 8-53. Cylinder head torquing sequence for OHV 239/256/272 and 292 Y-block V-8s.

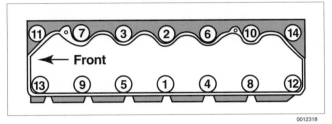

Fig. 8-54. Cylinder head torquing sequence for 240/300 (4.9L) six.

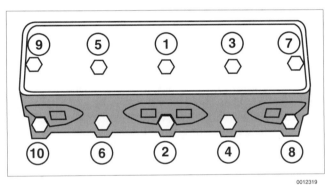

Fig. 8-55. Cylinder head torquing sequence for FE 352/360 and 390 V-8s.

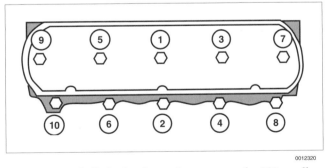

Fig. 8-56. Cylinder head torquing sequence for 302 small-block V-8 and 351W small-block and 351M/400 V-8.

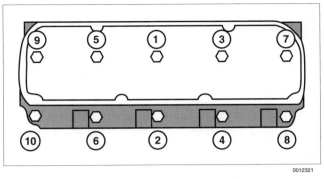

Fig. 8-57. Cylinder head torquing sequence for 460 V-8.

5. VALVE ADJUSTMENT

Once the head is re-torqued, you can adjust the valves on mechanical tappet engines. If the camshaft lobe profiles are normal, a valve adjustment of just a few thousandths of an inch will restore valve lift and valve opening points. Valve adjustment can reduce noise and improve engine performance.

The Ford light truck L-head 226H six, early 215/223/262 OHV sixes and all Y-block V-8s require periodic valve adjustment. On the 1948–51 226H engine, the exhaust and intake valves are in the block. Periodic valve adjustment protects the valves and maintains peak performance.

> **NOTE —**
> Normally, hydraulic lifters eliminate the need for a valve adjustment between engine overhauls. If your engine has noisy hydraulic lifters, suspect poor oiling, a defective lifter(s), improper valve clearances or a camshaft with worn lobes.

226H Six

Before you adjust the valves on the 226H six, allow the engine to cool completely, then remove the tappet side cover. This provides access to the intake valves and rocker arms. Remove spark plugs so the engine can rotate easily.

You must index the camshaft during valve adjustment. I find that using the distributor cap/rotor and timing mark helps eliminate guesswork. Begin with #1 cylinder, setting the pointer on the timing mark. If #1 cylinder is ready to fire, both the intake and exhaust valves will have clearance. The distributor's rotor should point to #1 cylinder's wire. If not, rotate the crankshaft one full revolution (360°).

Adjust the valves, using two thin tappet wrenches. (These are thin open end wrenches sold through professional tool sources.) Turn the self-locking adjuster while sliding the feeler gauge between the valve stem end and the tappet adjuster. The correct thickness blade gauge should fit this gap with just the slightest amount of drag.

Fig. 8-58. *On six-cylinder engines like this 223 inline type, #1 and #6 cylinders both align with TDC. For this reason, you must look at the rotor and distributor cap alignment to see which cylinder is up to fire.*

Fig. 8-59. *L-head sixes require special tappet wrenches for valve adjustment. These are thinner than regular open ended wrenches.*

NOTE —
Distinguish carefully between intake and exhaust valves. You need two feeler gauges for setting valve lash. If in doubt, look closely at the intake and exhaust manifolds to identify exhaust and intake ports and valves.

You will find clearance specifications for the original camshaft in the chart. However, there is a chance that your engine has a replacement camshaft, stamped O or B toward the front of the shaft. If so, the cold clearances are 0.014-inch intake/0.018 exhaust for this replacement camshaft.

Set the tappet clearance for #1 cylinder's two valves, then rotate the engine, by hand in its cranking direction, until #5 cylinder (next in the firing order) is up to fire with the distributor's rotor pointed toward #5 spark wire. Check and set the tappet clearances for #5 cylinder.

Repeat this process for #3-#6-#2-#4 cylinders, in the sequence of the 226's firing order. You will know that your alignment is right if the heel (opposite the lobe crown) of the camshaft is facing toward the valve tappet's foot. Insert the correct thickness feeler gauge between each adjuster bolt's head and valve stem.

If you plan to use an original equipment type cork gasket on the side cover, soak the gasket in water for some time (preferably overnight or at least while adjusting the valves). Once saturated, the gasket is more pliant and less likely to tear. Using Permatex High-Tack or an equivalent adhesive, coat one side of the gasket thoroughly.

Fig. 8-60. *Cork gaskets often shrink and distort in storage. To restore a side cover or valve cover gasket, soak in water until completely pliant.*

Allow the sealant/adhesive to set up, then attach the gasket to a thoroughly cleaned side cover surface. Carefully place the gasket and cover in position and secure the hardware. On other engines with cork valve cover gaskets, perform this procedure with the valve cover gasket as well. After starting the engine, check closely for oil leaks.

215, 223 and 262 OHV Sixes and Y-block V-8s

For the 215, 223 and 262 OHV sixes and all Y-block V-8s, the valve adjustment procedure is on a hot engine. You can take one of several options when adjusting the valves. One method is much like that described for the 226H six: turning the engine with the spark plugs removed, following the firing order, and making sure each cylinder is at its firing point when adjusting the valve clearance.

This static method, or even the two- or three-crankshaft position method, requires removal of the spark plugs. The process of hand cranking is slow, and by the time you approach the last cylinders, the engine has cooled down considerably.

I prefer a hot running set, despite the oily mess. Although hard on tappet gauge blades, the results reflect your engine in its running mode, which is far more reliable than a static adjustment. The main advantages of hot adjustments are: 1) a better feel for valve action and lift under real operating conditions, and 2) an end to tedious hand rotation of the engine while you set the valves. You must guard your knuckles from bruising on moving parts. (Wearing work gloves makes sense here.)

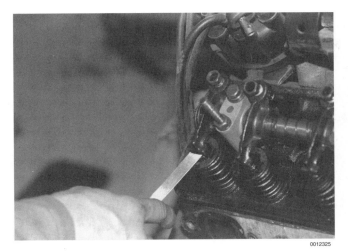

Fig. 8-61. Flat blade tappet gauges have various thicknesses. Some Y-block V-8 intake and exhaust valves call for 0.019" clearance—hot. Make certain the blade lays flat and squarely between the rocker arm end and valve stem tip. Although rougher on gauges, adjusting valves on a running engine produces best results.

Fig. 8-62. The easiest way to identify intake and exhaust valves is by looking at the manifolds. Note which ports lead to which valves. For static valve adjustment, follow the distributor rotor and firing order sequence. Watch rocker arm movement. If the piston is at or near TDC on its firing cycle, both valves will be completely closed. Here, valve clearance is at its widest point.

With the engine warmed completely, my method involves slowing the idle speed to the minimum point that the engine will continue to run. This reduces oil spray and difficulty when handling the moving parts. If possible, shield the engine bay from oil spray.

> **WARNING —**
> *Keep cloth and covers away from the hot exhaust manifolds, or a fire could erupt. Remove the valve cover carefully, without burning your fingers and hands.*

Shut off the engine and check the cylinder head bolt and rocker shaft support bolt torque. Then, with your valve adjusting tools ready, start the engine.

Identify the intake valves by looking at the intake manifold ports. Check the intake tappet clearances by inserting the feeler gauge between each intake valve stem and its rocker arm.

Start the engine. While the engine ticks over slowly, lay the clean gauge flat and squarely between the valve stem tip and the rocker arm end. Correct settings will allow a very slight drag as you gently pull and push the feeler gauge. (You are actually feeling for the moment of widest tappet clearance.)

There is a point at which the gauge blade can slide freely. If you are uncertain what this feels like, loosen the rocker adjuster (self-locking type), or the lock nut and adjuster (non-self locking type), very slightly. Slide the gauge in and out again.

Once you can feel where the gauge measures clearance, unaffected by the opening and closing movement of the valve, you can easily determine whether the setting is tight, loose or just right.

When right, the screw-and-lock nut adjusters require that you tighten the lock nut while holding the screw. You will find that by tightening the nut, the adjuster screw may move or pull up slightly in its threads.

This could be enough to distort the setting and require re-adjustment of the valve. If so, re-adjust the clearance, compensating for the distortion, and tighten the lock nut. Again check the clearance. When intake valves are all adjusted, move to the exhaust valves with your other tappet gauge.

On those OHV Ford engines with self-locking adjusters, the job is faster and easier. For screw-and-lock nut adjusters, a valve adjusting tool is available that both secures the lock nut and provides a screw driver.

Such tools were popular during the era of adjustable tappets and come in different nut sizes for various engine applications. K-D Tools or Eastwood Company are good sources for these kinds of specialty items.

Valve Clearance Chart

All of these Ford truck valve settings are for a fully warmed up engine, with one exception: the 1948–51 L-head 226H inline six requires a cold engine setting. 1965–up 240/300 inline sixes and FE 352, 360 and 390 V-8s, small-block 302 and 351W, 351M and 400, and 460 V-8s all have hydraulic lifters; no adjustment needed between engine overhauls.

Engine	Valve Clearance (in.)
1948–53 flathead V-8	non-adjustable valves except during valve job (grinding) operation
1948–51 L-226H inline six	0.010 intake/0.014 exhaust (cold)
1952–64 OHV inline six	1952–53 215: 0.015 intake/0.015 exhaust 1954–55 223: 0.015 intake/0.019 exhaust 1957–64 223 and '61–'64 262: 0.019 intake/0.019 exhaust (hot)
1954–64 Y-block OHV V-8s	1954–55 239: 0.019 intake/0.019 exhaust 1954–55 256: 0.016 intake/0.018 exhaust 1956 272: 0.018 intake/0.018 exhaust 1957–up 272, all 292 V-8s: 0.019 intake/0.019 exhaust (hot)

TUNE UP SPECIFICATIONS FOR MY FORD
TRUCK ENGINE

IDLE SPEED_____

INITIAL (LOW SPEED OR IDLE) SPARK TIMING @
_____RPM:_____-DEGREES

HIGHER SPEED (2500 CRANKSHAFT RPM) SPARK
TIMING_____-DEGREES

CARBURETOR IDLE MIXTURE ADJUSTMENT
PROCEDURE (IF ADJUSTABLE)

_____

AIR FILTER PART NUMBER_____

FUEL FILTER(S) PART NUMBER_____

SPARK PLUG TYPE AND NUMBER_____

BREAKER POINT OR
MODULE PART NUMBER_____

DISTRIBUTOR CAP PART
NUMBER_____

ROTOR PART NUMBER_____

Fig. 8-63. Sample of a quick reference chart for tuning your truck engine. Keep a copy of these specifications with your on-board tool kit or in your glovebox.

6. EMISSION CONTROLS

All manufactured motor vehicles must comply with federal and state tailpipe emission standards. Since the 1960s, Ford truck engines have required factory installed emission control devices, designed to combat air pollution. Some emission control devices help the engine achieve more complete combustion, while others work directly at reducing tailpipe pollutants.

Emission control components vary, depending upon the model year and requirements. Your truck's emission control package may include the ignition spark timing, the carburetor or EFI and a series of devices to reduce three major exhaust pollutants: 1) the poisonous gas, carbon monoxide (CO), 2) raw, unburned hydrocarbons (HC), and 3) oxides of nitrogen (NO_x), the building block of visible smog.

Many engine emission controls focus on peak performance, fuel efficiency and longer engine life. The care and maintenance of these devices remains an important part of servicing your truck. Even tuning your engine requires a working knowledge of emission control components, as the idle, acceleration, gas mileage and overall performance depend upon a fully operational emission control system.

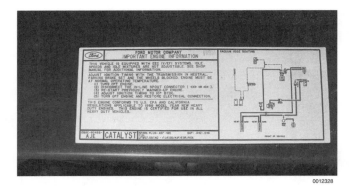

Fig. 8-64. The underhood emission and tune-up decal is important. It describes the standards for tuning your truck's engine and also the emission control package assigned to the vehicle. The decal often describes smog devices and vacuum hose circuits.

Emission Control Basics

In the early 1960s, U.S. vehicle manufacturers began installing Positive Crankcase Ventilation (PCV) systems on engines. The simple concept aimed at purging the engine crankcase of combustion blow-by and fumes.

Prior to 1961, most engines vented blow-by to the atmosphere through a road draft tube. These devices were simply open pipes with their tips cut on an angle toward the rear of the vehicle.

The road draft tube relies on low pressure vacuum, created as the vehicle moves forward, to purge the crankcase. Primitive and inefficient, an engine with a road draft tube pollutes the environment and permits condensation and corrosive agents to build sludge in the crankcase.

Fig. 8-65. The simple PCV valve contributes to engine longevity by fighting sludge and crankcase condensation. Additionally, a closed crankcase prevents water from entering the engine during stream fording. The PCV system requires the simplest of maintenance: periodic replacement of the valve. Change the PCV valve with each spark plug replacement (30,000 miles maximum for late engines). On some engines, the spark plug and PCV interval is 12,000 miles. Also make sure that hoses and grommets seal properly.

Fig. 8-66. This clean-air filter lies just inside the air cleaner canister on most closed crankcase engines. Manifold vacuum through the PCV valve creates low pressure in the crankcase. Clean air enters the engine from the filter. Without an adequate source of fresh air through the breather filter, PCV vacuum could damage engine seals and gaskets.

The modern PCV system allows manifold vacuum, regulated by a spring-balanced valve, to draw crankcase blow-by back through the intake manifold. This closed crankcase system continuously removes and recycles harmful combustion by-products. A PCV valve and closed crankcase contribute to better performance and longer engine life.

Air Injection System

The most visible emission control device is the air injection pump system. Found as original equipment on many truck engines since the mid-1960s, the smog pump's ungainly physical features and maze of plumbing have attracted unwarranted criticism.

Fig. 8-67. The air injection pump lowers tailpipe emissions. The diverter/bypass valve (small canister to left) directs air away from the exhaust stream during deceleration. This pollution control prevents an over-rich mixture of unburned fuel from igniting and damaging the exhaust system.

Air injection is an external emission control. It has no effect on either the fuel/induction or ignition system and creates a negligible amount of exhaust back pressure. Although the engine drives this pump, power loss is less than one-half horsepower—hardly noticed by a V-8 or six-cylinder truck engine. Since the air injection system is relatively passive, removal of the pump system does not improve performance.

The principle of air injection is simple: Inject oxygen into the exhaust stream near the engine exhaust ports and/or directly into a catalytic converter. Given this fresh source of oxygen, the combustion of unburned hot hydrocarbons and carbon monoxide can continue.

Your truck engine's air injection system requires little maintenance. Pump bearings are permanently lubricated, and the drive belt seldom requires adjustment. The rest of the air injection system consists of a diverter/bypass valve, anti-backfire check valves, and manifold or cylinder head distribution tubes.

Fig. 8-68. One-way or anti-backfire check valves prevent hot exhaust from reaching the air injection pump and hoses. Distribution tubes direct clean air into the exhaust manifold(s) or the cylinder head exhaust ports. Dangerously charred hoses and a burned pump can result from a defective check valve.

Fig. 8-70. An EGR valve can lower upper cylinder temperatures by as much as 2000° F. Lower temperatures reduce oxides of nitrogen (NOx) emissions, the key component in visible smog. The EGR valve, effective from off-idle through cruise rpm, typically operates via a ported vacuum source.

Fig. 8-69. The air pump drive belt requires periodic adjustment and replacement. Relatively light load of this device assures long belt life. Check the vacuum line to the diverter. On a fully warmed engine, snap the throttle open and shut and observe whether air exits the by-pass/diverter valve under deceleration. If the valve functions properly, air should by-pass.

Air Bypass Systems

The diverter or bypass valve receives a high manifold vacuum signal during engine deceleration, as carburetor venturi effect causes an over-rich fuel mixture. The valve opens, allowing pump air to vent into the atmosphere. Without a diverter valve, air pumped into rich, unburned exhaust stream gases would cause spontaneous combustion. The exhaust system could be severely damaged.

Additionally, the engine's exhaust valves, manifold(s) and even the air injection tubes rely on pump air for cooling. When an air injection system is defective, or a mechanic disables the engine's emission devices, melted injection tubes, damage to exhaust valves or a cracked manifold often result.

Exhaust Gas Recirculation

Lean fuel mixtures reduce CO and HC emissions. These lean fuel mixtures, however, also increase combustion temperatures and raise NOx emissions. In the early 1970s, engineers applied a simple, effective means for lowering combustion temperatures: recycle the exhaust gases.

Recirculating exhaust through the intake stream dilutes fresh fuel mixtures yet has little effect on the air-fuel ratio. These cooler combustion temperatures also enhance performance.

The exhaust gas recirculation (EGR) system permits the use of leaner air-fuel ratios without compromising cyl-

Fig. 8-71. EGR valve inspection is simple. Attach a vacuum pump to the valve. With the engine idling, unseat the valve by applying vacuum. Idle should get rough, often enough to stall the engine. Watch the gauge to be certain the EGR valve diaphragm holds vacuum.

inder temperatures. EGR valves serve a useful function on any engine that runs low octane fuel, requires a mild spark advance curve or operates with lean air-fuel mixtures.

Unfortunately, ill-informed mechanics see the EGR as a source of trouble or a horsepower thief. This false reasoning overlooks the EGR system's ability to lower scorching combustion temperatures (which in some high compression Muscle Era engines could create temperatures as high as 4800° F without an EGR system) to below 2500°! Operating properly, the EGR system eliminates most detonation or ping.

If, after tossing the EGR valve in the dumpster, your truck's engine now suffers severe ping, look here for the problem. Lean burning, low-octane fueled engines need an EGR system to prevent detonation, poor combustion and damage to internal engine parts, including the rings, pistons and cylinder walls.

Catalytic Converter

Another anti-pollution device, found on many light truck engines since 1975, is the catalytic converter. Simply a muffler-like device, the converter operates a small chemical processing plant in your exhaust system.

Oxidizing catalysts (usually platinum and palladium) in the converter react with carbon monoxide and hydrocarbons. The by-products of this catalyzing process are harmless carbon dioxide and water. Reducing catalysts also take the oxygen out of NOx, leaving harmless free nitrogen to pass out the tailpipe.

Although the catalytic converter emits sulfuric acid and an annoying rotten egg smell during rich fuel conditions, the only cost in performance is exhaust system back pressure. Aftermarket high performance catalytic converters are now available to reduce this back pressure. (See the performance chapter of this book). They reduce pressure yet still contribute to clean tailpipe emissions.

Fig. 8-73. An emission-legal aftermarket high performance exhaust system can reduce back pressure. But do your share for clean air, even if high performance is your goal. Be sure your exhaust system complies with federal and state emission regulations.

Fig. 8-72. Catalytic converters resemble a muffler. These small chemical processing plants reduce carbon monoxide, hydrocarbon and oxides of nitrogen. Consider the very high temperatures generated by a catalytic converter. Avoid touching the converter during service work, and never park your truck in tall, dry brush.

Fig. 8-74. The conventional choke, either manual or automatic, must open quickly to maintain low tailpipe emissions. Spray all carburetor linkages with a quality cleaner. Clean the choke valve, choke housing and vacuum piston if there is any evidence of choke stickiness. (See your truck's underhood emission decal, the factory shop manual or a professional service guide for proper settings.)

Cold-start and Warm-up Devices

All gasoline engines require cold start systems. For the light truck engine that operates in the most extreme climates, our very survival may depend on proper start-up. A carburetor's choke or an EFI engine's cold start enrichment cycle must meet both cold start-up and emission control needs.

For low tailpipe emissions, the choke should open as quickly as the engine can accept leaner air-fuel mixtures. To accomplish this, a number of devices come into play. The air cleaner assembly doubles as the thermal air system to direct heated air from the outside surface of the exhaust manifold into the intake inlet of the air cleaner.

Light truck engine chokes come in a variety of shapes and sizes. Early F-models rely on manual, cable controlled choke valves. Later carbureted engines feature either an electric or engine-heated bi-metallic spring automatic choke.

Fuel injected (EFI) engines benefit from a computer controlled cold start enrichment system that maintains precise air/fuel ratios and driveability during the entire engine warm-up cycle.

Additionally, carburetors rely on a vacuum signaled choke pull-off to allow quicker vehicle operation during warm-up. The choke pull-off unit consists of a vacuum diaphragm and choke release linkage, usually operated

Fig. 8-75. *Many chokes, such as those on Motorcraft, Holley and Carter carburetors, open electrically. Others rely on engine coolant for heat. Check the coolant or current flow to the choke unit. Chokes quickly become too hot to touch. Take care not to burn your fingers.*

Fig. 8-76. *The modern carburetor is plumbed for emission devices. Several vacuum sources (manifold or ported) may be built into an OEM carburetor.*

by ported vacuum. (Ported vacuum originates just above the carburetor's throttle valve to provide high vacuum just as the throttle opens and very light vacuum at an idle.) On many emission engines, a thermal air cleaner (TAC) provides a vacuum-actuated warm air valve. The vacuum motor receives signals from a thermal vacuum switch and/or bi-metallic valve. The motor opens and closes the warm air door at the air cleaner intake.

When the engine warms sufficiently, the vacuum motor closes the warm air door, permitting cooler, fresh air to enter the air cleaner. Your engine's thermal air cleaner allows quicker choke opening and better driveability as the engine warms.

Exhaust Heat Riser

The heat riser, usually eliminated with the installation of aftermarket exhaust headers, also serves a vital function. Heat risers can have one of several power sources. For inline sixes, sometimes an electric heating unit mounts in the plenum area of the intake manifold. Early designs use a bi-metallic spring that simply expands and opens with engine heat. Another style is vacuum operated, using engine coolant temp and a TVS to apply vacuum.

During cold start-up, the riser valve stays closed, which redirects hot exhaust through a passage in the intake manifold of V-type engines or to the base of the intake manifold on an inline engine. This heated section of the manifold sometimes houses a stove well for the choke.

The intake manifold heat passage warms the area under the carburetor, permitting better atomization of fuel and more thorough combustion. It is important that the manifold heat passage remain clear. Often, especially on V-type engines, the passage clogs as carbon builds up.

A heat riser stuck shut creates severe back pressure and reduces engine power. A heat riser stuck open causes the choke to stay on too long, affecting performance and fuel economy.

Fig. 8-77. *The heat riser valve plays an important role during engine warmup and choke operation. To service, on a cold engine, spray the heat riser valve with a suitable penetrant oil. Make certain that the valve moves freely and the bimetallic spring or vacuum diaphragm is intact and functional.*

Switches, Valves and Vacuum Controls

Your truck engine's emission control devices must know when to work and usually require energy to work. A variety of electrical and vacuum switches help meet those requirements.

The ignition switch often serves as the trigger for a fuel shut-off solenoid. Other switches, such as the thermal vacuum switch (TVS), control vacuum to the distributor spark advance or an EGR valve. Most TVS switches rely on the engine coolant temperature to expand an enclosed wax pellet, which opens one or more vacuum ports.

On your truck's engine, vacuum serves as a very powerful and economical source of energy for switches,

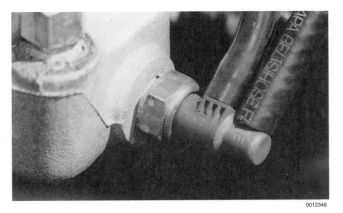

Fig. 8-78. *Thermal vacuum switches (TVS) are useful. On many truck engines, they activate the thermal air cleaner or EGR valve. At a preset temperature, the valve opens ports, directing vacuum to devices. Check your engine's vacuum circuit diagram to determine the role of the TVS switch.*

Fig. 8-79. *Some emission carburetor designs rely on a vacuum-actuated throttle positioner. Vacuum often provides ignition spark advance. Emission service always includes inspection of vacuum hose circuits that operate devices like this bypass/diverter valve.*

valves, and motors, like those that open and close the thermal air cleaner intake flap.

Vacuum- or electrically operated throttle positioners serve a variety of roles. Some raise the idle speed to compensate for extra loads like the air conditioner. Others serve as a dashpot, relying on a spring and resistance diaphragm to slow the throttle return. On carbureted engines, a dashpot helps reduce over-rich fuel flow (venturi effect) during deceleration.

Fuel Tank and Carburetor Fumes

The raw fumes from gasoline are another source of air pollution. To contain these vapors, light trucks have incorporated evaporative emission control devices since the early 1970s. Although storage methods vary, vacuum helps capture float bowl, crankcase and fuel tank fumes, eventually recycling them through the engine's intake system. These passive systems, still in use today, have no impact on performance.

When servicing or repairing your truck's fuel system, you must route vacuum and ventilation hoses very carefully. Follow a factory or professional level guide for your model.

WARNING —
Gasoline fumes are highly volatile. Use extreme caution when working with the evaporative emission control system. All parts must fit according to design, including the gas cap.

Fig. 8-80. *Evaporative emission controls include a vapor canister. Typically, the replaceable canister is plastic with a granulated carbon element inside. If the canister smells heavily like gasoline or feels weighted with liquid, safely drain the gas and replace the canister with a new unit. Evaporative canisters have check valves and for performance and safety require careful routing of hoses to the carburetor/EFI unit, the vacuum source and fuel tank.*

Conversion Engines and Emissions

Many earlier F-Series light trucks have conversion engines. The low horsepower output of early six-cylinder and flathead or Y-block engines has encouraged swapping to larger, more powerful powerplants. Since the late 1950s, a number of manufacturers have produced parts for engine and transmission swaps into Ford light trucks.

Engine conversions come under Federal emission control compliance laws and statutes in many states. Whether your truck now has a conversion engine or you plan such a change, be certain of emission control laws. (You will find further information on engine conversions and emission control compliance in the performance chapter.)

Passing An Emission Test

Although California has the strictest motor vehicle pollution laws in the United States, many vehicles that fail California's smog tests have sufficiently low tailpipe emissions. They fail the visual inspection portion of the test.

During the visual inspection, before the engine has a chance to show how cleanly it burns, the inspector takes a close look at the emission control system and vehicle chassis. Any missing or modified parts are cause for failure.

This is a tough test. All vacuum hoses, flexible heat tubes, the smog pump drive belt, vacuum switches, the EGR valve (if required) and closed crankcase devices must be intact and function properly. The inspector, using

Fig. 8-81. OHV V-8 transplants into an early truck chassis became a popular practice in the 1960s. An entire industry developed around improving the performance level of light trucks. By California and U.S. EPA standards, this engine, despite a closed crankcase, EGR valve, enhanced ignition and precise tuning, is not legal. Handsome aftermarket chrome air cleaner, without a thermal air system, would immediately fail visual smog inspection.

Fig. 8-82. Use of this Edelbrock Performer intake manifold is acceptable. The dual-plane design, provision for an EGR valve and no increase in tailpipe emissions help determine compliance.

a detailed manual and the emission decal found under your truck's hood, checks your engine and chassis equipment against the OEM requirements.

The vehicle can fail visual inspection for something as simple as a missing two-dollar section of aluminum flex hose at the thermal air cleaner. Although many aftermarket performance parts immediately fail the visual test, some pieces comply with California Air Resources Board standards.

Fig. 8-83. Many 1975 and newer U.S.-sold light trucks require unleaded gasoline. Note that this truck's fuel filler neck has a restrictor. In California and other states, smog inspection includes a look at fuel filler.

Approved aftermarket parts bear a special number allowing your truck to be inspected at a regular California smog station. Such products even include the retrofit superchargers built by Vortec and Paxton for Ford light truck V-8 engines.

Increasing numbers of aftermarket high performance engine components, including intake manifolds and a number of ignition devices and exhaust pieces, also meet CARB standards. (Lists of these devices are available from the California Department of Consumer Affairs, Bureau of Automotive Repairs.)

NOTE —
Aftermarket components described as "not legal for use on California highways," hold a good chance of getting your engine an F on the smog test. California has essentially become a model for Federal and 49-State emission control policy.

The cold start circuit is among the many items considered on the visual inspection. Although this system operates for only minutes during the warm-up cycle, every component is essential.

A hand choke retrofit kit to replace an automatic choke, a missing vacuum hose or a discarded thermal air cleaner are each cause for failure. Even raising the air cleaner bonnet with a thicker filter element results in an F, as the open canister compromises both the cold start and closed crankcase systems.

Well tuned and running properly, your engine will meet hydrocarbon, carbon monoxide and NOx standards at both an idle and the currently required 2500 rpm. Bonafide defects, such as vacuum leaks, carburetor flooding, bad ignition cables, fouled spark plugs or a defective EGR valve, will result in a tailpipe test failure. Ignition timing must match OEM specifications for the engine.

When a California Smog Chek inspector suspects that the wrong engine is in a chassis, he or she may examine the block and/or cylinder head casting numbers. If determined that your engine is not original for the truck, you'll receive a non-compliance certificate and referral to a referee.

The referee station identifies the engine by casting or serial numbers, determining the age and OEM emission requirements for both the engine and the chassis. (You may need sales documentation for the engine.)

The referee compiles a list of necessary emission control devices for both your truck's chassis and the conversion engine. A visual engine and chassis inspection confirms whether the needed devices are in place. If not, the referee recommends which devices will bring your truck into compliance.

After meeting compliance, the vehicle receives a certification tag noting the required emission control devices. Currently, this enables the owner to take the truck to any Smog Chek station for biennial or a change of ownership inspection. If the truck complies, you only need to see the referee once.

For emission compliance by California legal criteria, your engine must fit a given range of years (be the same year or newer than your truck's chassis), and meet either OEM or state-approved aftermarket parts requirements. The chassis requires such original equipment as the catalytic converter(s) and the gas tank unleaded fuel restrictor if so equipped.

Lastly, your engine must meet specific tailpipe emission standards—equal to or better than the truck's original engine in good operating condition.

Exhaust System

A truck's exhaust system is subject to severe abuse. Off-highway debris, harsh climates, corrosion, freezing, scorching temperature extremes and a variety of other hazards impact your truck's exhaust system. Aside from emission related components, like the catalytic converter, the system has several other replaceable components.

The exhaust system begins at the exhaust manifold flange and heat riser (if so equipped). The exhaust pipe leads from the manifold to either the catalytic converter or a muffler. If your truck requires a catalytic converter, a pipe exits the converter and connects to the muffler. After the muffler, a tailpipe continues to the rear of the truck.

> **NOTE —**
> Pre-1975 trucks have no catalytic converter. Some light trucks through the mid-'80s have no required cat system, either. These cat exempted trucks have heavier chassis ratings. You can determine this requirement by looking at the underhood decal for the terms CAT, catalyst or catalytic converter.

Fig. 8-84. *Dual exhaust system conversions for V-8 engines help reduce back pressure. Better economy and performance result. A correct installation has tailpipes exiting at the rear of the truck, just like original equipment system. Keep exhaust fumes away from the cab and bed areas. Check state and federal requirements before converting to dual exhausts on catalytic systems.*

The majority of Ford light trucks use a single exhaust system. V-type engines use a Y-shaped exhaust pipe that leads to the catalytic converter or muffler. These single exhaust systems restrict the flow of gases on V-type engines, and many owners of V-8 powered trucks have converted their exhaust systems to dual exhaust.

The obstacle to a dual exhaust conversion is legality. In states like California, splitting the exhaust system allows one bank of a V-type engine to by-pass the catalytic converter. On some trucks, it's acceptable to split the exhaust system and install a second catalytic converter.

Interpretation of the 1990 Federal Clean Air Act has varied. One view states that if your cat-controlled truck has a single exhaust system, you cannot convert to dual exhaust—period. Under this judgement, no muffler shop can install a two-cat, dual exhaust system on a single exhaust equipped truck. If the truck were converted before the 1990 revision of the act (and receipts are available to prove this fact) a shop can service and repair the two-cat, dual exhaust system.

If your state requires visual inspection of the emission control system, discuss the dual exhaust option with an emission control inspector or contact the state bureau. When periodic inspection is necessary, make sure your new system is smog legal as well as functional.

Always replace any worn or damaged exhaust parts. Your exhaust system inspection should take place with each lube job. Especially on short wheelbase models or those equipped with a bed cap or camper unit, a safe and leakproof system is a must. Backflow of exhaust and seeping fumes present a health hazard to vehicle occupants.

By design, light truck tailpipes have always exited to the rear of the truck. This is important for health and safety, as it allows fumes to flow away from the truck's body. Some owners, however, choose to shorten their exhaust systems, thinking that less length will improve performance. Such pipes usually exit just forward of the rear wheels. This is a significant health hazard, as exhaust fumes roll upward from the sides of the truck and into the cab, especially on shorter wheelbase models.

If a muffler shop suggests short dual exhaust pipes that exit out the truck's sides, insist that the tailpipes continue to the rear of the truck. An experienced muffler technician can bend and twist pipes to fit the contours of your truck's chassis. Dual tailpipes can always exit the rear of the truck—even if both pipes must fit along the same side of the chassis.

Routine Emission Control Service

At regular intervals, your truck's emission control system requires attention. Consider emission control service an important part of tuning your engine.

Fig. 8-85. *A very popular tool with emission control specialists is the hand vacuum pump and pressure tester. Use the tester to check EGR valves, vacuum diaphragms, vacuum hose circuits and thermal vacuum switches.*

Fig. 8-87. *Inspect the warm air vacuum motor on the thermal air cleaner. Make certain this device works properly. If the flexible heat tube shows evidence of leakage or poor fitup, replace tube.*

Fig. 8-86. *Inspect the vacuum hoses. A principle energy source for emission control switches is vacuum. Hose routing and quality are critical to peak performance. Leaks reduce performance and create tune-up problems.*

Fig. 8-88. *Check electrical connections at switches and solenoids. Watch the solenoid as someone activates the ignition switch and air conditioning. An idle control solenoid has been popular on engines since the 1970s.*

Clutch and Transmission Service

CLUTCH AND TRANSMISSION PROBLEMS are sometimes difficult to separate. The high cost of a clutch replacement or transmission overhaul makes diagnosis very important. Transmission wear is often mistaken for a bad clutch and vice versa. As troubleshooting skill is the best mechanical resource you can muster, I'd like to help you understand various clutch and transmission problems.

Troubles first appear as driving quirks. As an accurate troubleshooter, you must isolate each symptom and determine its cause.

1. CLUTCH AND TRANSMISSION TROUBLESHOOTING

> **WARNING** —
> *The clutch disc may contain asbestos fibers. Asbestos materials can cause asbestosis. Always wear an approved respirator and protective clothing when handling components containing asbestos. Do not use compressed air, do not grind, heat, weld or sand on or near any asbestos materials. Only approved cleaning methods should be used to service the clutch disc or areas containing asbestos dust or asbestos fibers.*

Clutch Chatter

You release the clutch pedal, and the powertrain shudders, sometimes violently, as clutch engagement begins. If the problem has developed suddenly, especially after an unusually hard day of trailer pulling or pounding a rocky trail, examine the engine mounts and, on 4x4 models, the transmission/transfer case mount. (On some models, a torque arm helps limit transfer case torque twist. Check this bracket along with the mounts.)

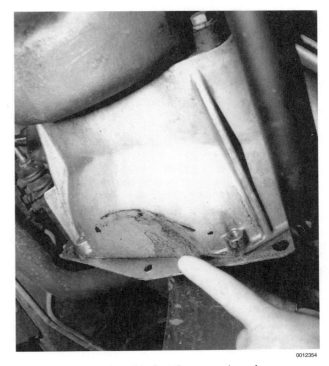

Fig. 9-2. *An engine oil leak at the rear main seal or pan gaskets can cause clutch damage. Oil saturates the clutch disc and causes chatter, slippage and failure. The only cure is clutch replacement.*

If none of these points appear troubled, look to the clutch unit. Disc wear, clutch damage or oil on the disc are common causes of chatter. Especially with 4x4 trucks operated at odd angles, an engine oil leak from the rear main seal or pan gasket can find its way into the clutch assembly and saturate the disc.

An attempt to burn off the oil by riding the clutch to generate friction is a waste of time and could prove dangerous. Clutches can explode under extreme stress or from over revving. There's no sure way to clean the disc in the truck, either. If oil has entered the clutch housing and soaked the disc, the disc is ruined.

Another source of oil on the clutch is from the transmission. The front bearing retainer seal is responsible for

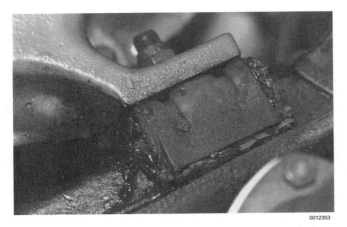

Fig. 9-1. *Worn or loose motor mounts and transmission mounts can create clutch chatter symptoms, especially on suspended pedal models with mechanical clutch linkage. Inspect all mounts before condemning your clutch assembly.*

keeping oil within the gearcase. These seals wear, and on rare occasions, the retainer may crack or leak around its sealing gasket(s). Gear oil, acidic and tenacious, has a devastating effect on a clutch disc.

A common cause of clutch chatter is a distorted clutch cover or broken springs. Excess heat and overworking the clutch can warp a clutch cover. Springs break from fatigue or abuse. Heat also weakens springs, making them exert uneven force. Simply put, clutch chatter results from uneven application of pressure. Loose clutch cover bolts, broken torsional springs in the disk hub or a warped disc will cause chatter.

Fig. 9-3. *As the clutch disc wears thin, clamping force decreases. (The clutch cover springs compress less, which reduces their apply pressure.) This is why a high mileage clutch cannot deliver the same performance as a new assembly.*

Clutch slippage symptoms are obvious. In gear, the engine revs up, yet the truck does not accelerate. Slippage and chatter often have common causes. In either case, clutch cover apply pressure cannot hold the disc firmly. Slippage results from oil saturation of the disc or extreme wear of either the friction disc or clutch cover springs. The faintest sound of rivets grating on the flywheel face or pressure plate is a sure sign of major wear. Replace the clutch before irreparable damage to the flywheel results.

Unwanted Clutch Noises

Truck owners become accustomed to particular powertrain and geartrain noises, the rhythms and pitches of whirring machinery that accompany us on long interstate pulls and dusty trails. An abnormal sound from the clutch area immediately draws attention.

A defective clutch sends a clear message. A warped or severely worn disc will grate or transmit a metallic sound as the disc engages. Broken torsional springs around the disc hub also transmit noise. The more common clutch noises, however, are bearing defects.

The pilot bearing supports the forward end of the transmission input shaft. Pressed into the center bore of the crankshaft flange, the pilot bearing allows the clutch or input gear to rotate independently of the crankshaft during clutch disengagement. Ford trucks use needle and caged ball-type pilot bearings and also bronze bushings.

Fig. 9-4. *There are three types of pilot bearings and bushings available for various Ford truck applications: the solid bronze bushing, a needle bearing assembly and a caged, permanently lubricated ball bearing. In some cases, you will have a choice of designs. Needle and ball bearings offer less friction, while bronze bushings have a reputation for long, trouble-free service.*

While some pilot bearings have permanently sealed cases, others require lubrication during installation.

> **CAUTION —**
> *A needle or ball bearing should never be used with an input gear designed for a bronze bushing. Heat treatment of gears differ, and needle bearings will damage a shaft end designed for use with a bronze bushing.*

The pilot bearing or bushing should only need service during clutch replacement. A dry pilot bearing, however, is common to trucks that perform "submarine duty." Running in surf or stream crossings and other water traps can wash grease from the pilot bearing. Dry, the bearing wears quickly and sets up a howling noise distinct from any other. With the clutch disengaged and the transmission in a gear, pilot noise is obvious.

Loss of lubricant can cause the pilot bearing to seize on the clutch/input gear nose end. This mimics symptoms of a clutch disc and pressure plate that won't disengage properly.

On rare occasions, debris from a backwoods trail enters the clutch housing. Protective plates, tinware and a rubber clutch fork boot should prevent this from happening, but in extreme cases, gravel or other abrasive material seeps through and becomes embedded or trapped in the clutch disc. The symptoms are chatter, clutch slippage and metallic grating. (Twigs or rocks will rake or rattle against the spinning faces of the flywheel or clutch pressure plate.)

A time-honored clutch noise is the worn release or throwout bearing. These bearings often fail before the disc and clutch cover, and the noise is easy to distinguish. First, make certain that the clutch is adjusted properly, as

Fig. 9-5. The dust boot at the clutch fork is a vital part. Water and debris entering your truck's clutch housing can damage parts. Water can wash vital grease from the pilot bearing or transmission front bearing retainer surface. Keep seals, plates and tinware in good condition.

described later in this chapter, and that free-play exists between the clutch release fingers and the throwout bearing. At this point, with the engine running and the pedal fully released, the throwout bearing cannot make noise.

Now apply very light pedal pressure, just enough to bring the bearing against the fingers. The bearing will begin spinning and allow noise to develop. It may require firmer pressure before the bearing transmits sound. Also, to avoid confusing throwout bearing noise with pilot bearing noise, leave the transmission in neutral (with the clutch engaged) so the clutch/input gear can turn in unison with the pilot bearing.

With your transmission in neutral, the clutch fully engaged and the throwout bearing clear of the release fingers, clutch pilot and throwout bearing noise should disappear. If you hear bearing sounds now, look to the transmission for trouble.

Difficulty Shifting Gears

The simpler causes of hard shifting are a maladjusted clutch or insufficient clutch linkage travel. Begin troubleshooting by adjusting the clutch properly and examining linkage from the release fork all the way to the pedal. You need full pedal travel and proper fitup at the various links. If your truck's clutch linkage has a pivoting bellcrank, replace worn bushings and eliminate any excess play. Each link must provide full movement when you depress the clutch pedal.

Any obstacle to complete clutch disengagement will cause hard shifting. This includes a warped disc or pressure plate, a clutch disc bound on the input gear splines, a seizing pilot bearing or debris wedged between the clutch disc and pressure plate or flywheel.

NOTE —
For smooth shifts and complete clutch disengagement, the clutch pressure plate must move away from the disc and allow the disc to rotate freely and independently of the flywheel.

On trucks with hydraulic clutch linkage, look first to hydraulic system troubles. Aside from proper pushrod and pedal height adjustments, the hydraulic system requires a full stroke of fluid to release the clutch completely. This means that the master cylinder piston must retract completely, and the clutch slave cylinder piston must have ample travel in its bore.

The clutch master cylinder piston must return to its stop when you release the pedal. Adjust the pushrod and/or pedal height to achieve correct piston-to-pushrod clearance and travel. Assuming that the master cylinder has a full fluid reservoir (check fluid first!), check the pushrod and pedal height adjustments. (See adjustment section of this chapter.)

If the fluid has run low, the system may require bleeding. Like a hydraulic brake system, the hydraulic lines can trap air, causing a loss of piston movement at the slave cylinder. Flush and bleed the system periodically with clean brake fluid to purge sludge, accumulated moisture and any air. If the system draws air regularly or loses fluid, overhaul the master cylinder and slave cylinder. (See the brake section of the book for tips on hydraulic cylinder overhaul.)

Manual Transmission Troubleshooting

Ford F-Series light trucks have used a variety of manual transmission types. (See earlier chapters.) If you have the skill and tools necessary to overhaul your transmission, your F-Series shop manual provides an excellent, in-depth guide for rebuilding the unit.

CAUTION —
Never work on your truck's transmission without first reviewing a professional level service manual. Subtle differences between synchronizer assemblies and other parts make transmission designs unique. A professional guide will provide correct step-by-step instruction, outline critical clearances and suggest the tools you need. You'll find the job rewarding and a great confidence builder.

As hard shifting is a symptom shared with clutch troubles, take the time to distinguish causes. Begin by adjusting the clutch and transmission linkage, if possible. Although many F-truck transmission shifters are within the control housing and inaccessible to adjustment, many three-speed transmission trucks have column shift linkage.

On three-speed models with column shift, the neutral gate and shift linkage alignment are crucial to shifting ease. (Refer to the shift linkage adjustment section of this chapter.) Periodically clean away all debris and lubricate the linkage.

CHAPTER 9

Hard Shifts, Jumping Out Of Gear and Other Woes

Binding shift linkage is always a concern. Your truck is subject to twisting and off-highway stress, and the effects are often felt at linkages and pivotal supports. Eliminate any binding conditions in the shifter or clutch linkage.

Before disassembling the transmission for a shift problem, take the gear lubricant into account. In many late model trucks, lighter oils, including ATF, have replaced traditional 80- or 90-weight gear lube. Make sure your truck has clean, proper viscosity lubricant. Some synthetic oils, such as Mobil's 75W-90 weight gear lubricant, replace traditional 90-weight, with claims of easier shifts and a multi-viscosity lube that will work at -50° F, allowing one oil to serve year round—from summer heat to extreme winter cold.

If your manual transmission has the wrong gear lubricant and the weather gets cold, expect trouble. The braking action and movement of synchronizers becomes difficult, and in some cases, the effect is so severe that gear clash makes cold shifting impossible.

Perfectly good clutches come under suspicion because a transmission won't shift into the lower gears when cold. The cause is often an improper viscosity lubricant which prevents normal synchronizer action.

Refer to your Ford truck lubrication specifications when selecting correct lube—summer and winter. In extreme climates, it may be necessary to change oil in the fall and spring. If the linkage, lubricant and clutch check okay, look to possible transmission problems.

Hard shifting is rarely a transmission shift fork problem, although you cannot rule out this defect. Broken shift rail detents and other shift mechanism troubles are possibilities, although that likelihood is again slim. The most common hard shift problem is a defective synchronizer assembly.

Synchronizers wear over time. The balky shift common to high mileage transmissions is usually a synchronizer problem. The tendency for a transmission to slide out of second, third or any other synchronized gear is often caused by a synchronizer assembly defect.

Loose transmission bearings, worn synchronizer parts and excessive clearances can cause a transmission to slip out of gear. (Before condemning the transmission on column shift models, check shift linkage adjustment for full travel and smooth operation.) Worn or chipped gear teeth, excessive shaft end play, and drive gear pilot bearing wear are also causes of hard shifting and jumping out of gear. Other possibilities include a loose or misaligned clutch housing, worn motor or transmission mounts, a broken torque brace, or a defective crankshaft pilot bearing. Synchronizer interlock springs, detent keys and shift rail poppet springs each help keep the transmission in gear. Wear or defects here require a transmission teardown.

If you have isolated your trouble to the transmission, prepare for considerable expense. An overhaul must be thorough, replacing all worn pieces. If severe growling or gear whine noises have developed, you may wish to compare the cost of a major overhaul to that of a recycled or new transmission.

Burnt gear oil is a sign of major trouble. If fried oil and various metals come from the drain hole, expect to find heat-discolored shafts, damaged gears and failed bearings.

Transmissions contain hard steel gear and shaft parts, bronze thrust washers and in some later units, nylon shift fork slippers. When you service your transmission, examine the lubricant carefully for the presence of these materials. Powdery bronze thrust washer material, in small quantities, is normal. These washers wear very slowly over time. However, a high degree of bronze, or the presence of harder metal pieces, means trouble.

2. CLUTCH SERVICE

A truck clutch will eventually fail or wear out. Fortunately, a clutch rarely breaks without warning. The key to getting the most from your clutch is to exercise reasonable driving habits, avoiding severe powertrain shock loads or continuous clutch overheating.

Although many accessories speed up clutch wear, oversize tires have the heaviest impact. Light trucks are popular candidates for large tires, as ground clearance and improved traction remain major concerns for off-highway driving. Big wheels and tires, however, have the same effect as installing a taller (numerically lower) set of axle gears. Unless you change axle gearing to match the new tire diameter, the new gearing will take its toll on the clutch.

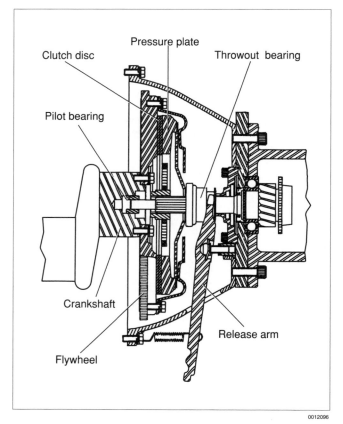

Fig. 9-6. *The spring loaded clutch pressure plate sandwiches the clutch disc face against the flywheel. As the disc's friction material wears, spring apply pressure weakens. This accounts for the slippage common with higher mileage clutch units.*

Clutch Wear

A variety of causes lead to clutch slippage. Maladjusted clearance between the throwout bearing and pressure plate, overloading, slipping the clutch and other bad driving techniques usually speed up the process. Even under ideal circumstances, the clutch disc wears, becoming progressively thinner and seriously weakening the clutch cover apply pressure. In each case, slippage results.

The best safeguard against clutch wear is to reduce the amount of time that the clutch plate slips during engagement. Beyond this, proper use of your gears can help. (See chapter on operating techniques.)

Clutch wear is obvious. Slippage will occur as you release the pedal, when the truck climbs steep inclines and during low speed lugging of the engine. If your clutch isn't noticeably weak, you can push the test further: Place the shifter in high gear at 15–20 mph. Disengage the clutch, and, as you hold the clutch pedal to the floor, bring the engine speed to about 2500 rpm and quickly release the clutch pedal.

Assuming that clutch free play has been adjusted correctly, one of two things will happen. When the clutch is in good condition, releasing the pedal will cause an immediate and noticeable drop in engine rpm, sometimes enough to nearly stall the engine. If the clutch has excessive wear, such as glazed friction lining or weak pressure plate springs, the engine speed will either remain high for several seconds or drop slowly.

Sooner or later your truck's clutch will fail this test. When it does, a variety of rebuilt and new clutch assembly options exist to restore or improve your truck.

An improved aftermarket clutch design can work with no modifications to your truck's existing flywheel, clutch linkage, or other clutch-related parts. (See the performance chapter for details on aftermarket clutch parts.) A clutch replacement offers an excellent opportunity to improve your truck.

Identifying Your Clutch

There are several clutch types used in Ford light trucks: Borg & Beck, Long-type, and several diaphragm designs. All clutch discs have torsional springs and composition friction material.

The earliest Ford F-trucks use Long-type clutch assemblies. Long and later Borg & Beck (B&B) type clutches have a multi-spring clutch cover design with three release fingers. Most later Ford light truck engines use direct pressure, semi-centrifugal and diaphragm type clutches.

Many years ago, Long-type clutches had release fingers with adjusters. It was common for a general repair shop to rebuild a cover or adjust release finger height. Today, neither the three-finger nor multi-finger diaphragm clutches require such field service. Auto parts retailers and your local Ford dealership sell fully adjusted (rebuilt or new) cover/pressure plate assemblies.

When your Ford truck needs a clutch replacement, consider installing the largest diameter unit that will fit your engine's flywheel and within the bellhousing. When seeking such a clutch, you will find that diameter usually increases with larger displacement engines. Light Ford F-

Fig. 9-7. *Early Ford F-trucks use the Long type clutch/pressure plate with three adjustable release fingers. Clutch disc diameter is an indication of stamina and strength. In many cases, your Ford truck flywheel and clutch housing will accept a larger diameter clutch disc and cover. This is a way to upgrade with OEM type parts.*

Fig. 9-8. *Borg & Beck clutches are common to many Ford trucks. This Borg & Beck three-finger release type unit offers good clamping force and smooth operation. These clutches deliver quality service.*

Series trucks commonly use a 10", 10-1/2", 11" or a larger 12" diameter clutch disc. Torque, horsepower, load demands and transmission type will determine the original clutch size.

If you increase the engine performance level or the load placed on the clutch, a heavier duty unit is often necessary. When buying a new clutch assembly, you will need to match your clutch disc diameter (unless a larger unit will fit properly), the hub spline configuration and the clutch cover design. (See also the upgrade chapter.)

Ford trucks have used a variety of manual transmissions. The clutch splines and input shaft diameter can vary between designs. Identify your transmission whenever ordering parts.

Fig. 9-9. *Aside from the clutch diameter, the spline configuration must match the transmission input gear. It's good practice to take your complete clutch unit to the parts house, however, always avoid inhalation of asbestos fibers from the disc. Asbestos is a known health hazard.*

Clutch Adjustment

A manual transmission truck may require periodic clutch adjustment. On later models, the clutch adjustment is automatic, and the hydraulic clutch linkage readily compensates for wear. (Actually, Ford light truck hydraulic clutch linkage dates back to the 1957–60 models, although these early trucks do require periodic clutch adjustment.) Other models use mechanical linkage to actuate the clutch.

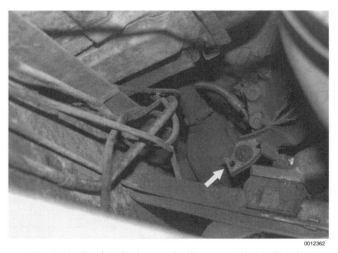

Fig. 9-10. *Ford F-Series trucks first used hydraulic clutch linkage in 1957. Shown here (arrow), the early hydraulic linkage was popular from 1957–60, then replaced in 1961 by mechanical linkage. Ford reintroduced hydraulic clutch linkage in the mid-1980s. '57 was also the first year for firewall-mounted, suspended pedals.*

WARNING —
Always block wheels and set the parking brake before adjusting the clutch.

Since the hydraulic linkage slave cylinder mounts firmly to the clutch housing, smooth clutch engagement is possible under all operating conditions, a distinct advantage over mechanical linkage. With mechanical linkage, engine torque can twist and shake the release rods, and this translates as jerky clutch engagement. Especially for trucks that operate with heavy loads or off-pavement, hydraulic clutch linkage is superior to mechanical designs.

On models with adjustable linkage, inspect the clutch linkage and clutch adjustment when service needs take you beneath your truck. Always begin your clutch adjustment by checking freeplay at the release arm.

Although proper clutch operation demands sufficient pedal travel and free play, release arm movement provides the only true measurement of the throwout bearing-to-clutch clearance. Maintaining the required gap between the clutch release fingers and the throwout bearing face assures full engagement of the clutch and a long life for the throwout bearing.

Fig. 9-11. *Always check clutch free-play at the release arm (arrow). Note relationship of throwout bearing and clutch release fingers. Linkage wear can make free-play measurement at the pedal inaccurate.*

On models with adjustable clutch linkage, normal clutch wear will decrease the clearance between the clutch release fingers and the throwout bearing. If wear becomes excessive, the throwout bearing will actually ride on the fingers. This can cause premature failure of the clutch release bearing or damage to the clutch release fingers.

If wear continues beyond the point of contact, the throwout bearing will not allow the clutch to engage completely. Slippage occurs, resulting in heat buildup and friction. The clutch will wear rapidly when adjusted too tightly and ruin a perfectly good clutch unit or release bearing.

Late model F-trucks use hydraulic clutch linkage. From mid-'80s onward, there is no need to adjust the clutch. However, you should check fluid level regularly and change the fluid at appropriate intervals.

Fig. 9-12. While newer Ford trucks have self-adjusting hydraulic clutch linkage, the '57–'60 release rod is much like mechanical linkage. You need to periodically adjust the clutch on these earlier hydraulic systems (arrow).

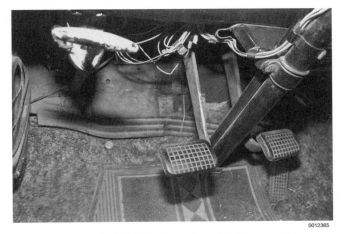

Fig. 9-13. Pedal height is often adjustable. If you need to confirm or adjust pedal height, dimensions are available in an F-Series shop manual and sometimes in other professional level service guides. Unless damage or wear has occurred, adjusting the pedal height is usually unnecessary. If you need to make this adjustment, check and reset clutch free-play as required.

NOTE —
Your truck's clutch can be costly and difficult to access (especially 4WD models), taking considerable labor to replace. Avoid trouble. Inspect clutch linkage and check the clutch adjustment periodically.

Minor Adjustments: Early Models

The earliest Ford F-trucks have through-the-floorboard pedals. On '48–'56 light truck models with 10-and 11-inch clutches, the adjustment is 1-1/8" to 1-3/8" free play at the clutch pedal. This assumes the linkage is in good condition and the return springs pull the pedal to the top of its travel.

You will find that pedal free-play figures strive for clearance between the pressure plate fingers and throwout bearing face. Despite the pedal travel specifications, make sure that at least 1/16" of free-play exists between the release bearing and clutch release fingers.

Fig. 9-14. Clutch linkage on early F-trucks is through-the-floor pedal type. Release rod (arrow) requires periodic adjustment. Watch for wear at pivots and rod fatigue, especially on '48–'56 models, where more friction applies.

You will need to crawl under the truck with appropriate wrenches to adjust linkage at the clutch release arm or rod. Remember to loosen locknuts before attempting adjustments. Tighten lock nuts when done.

Check for throwout bearing movement by moving the release arm and observing the bearing-to-finger relationship within the bellhousing. Early Ford F-truck designs have one of the return springs at the throwout bearing collar. Later models use a return spring on the release arm.

Proper clutch adjustment and a functional return spring eliminate risk of the bearing dragging on the clutch release fingers. Adjustment differs depending on years. C levis/pin-type on '48–'52 model adjust at the release rod linkage near the clutch bellhousing. '53–'56 models adjust (lock nuts) at end of the release arm.

On '57–'60 model F-trucks with hydraulic linkage, the adjustment is more involved. Make sure the master cylinder is full and bleed any air from the slave cylinder. The clutch pedal should be even with brake pedal in fully retracted position. (Adjust pedal stop if necessary.) Disconnect the clutch release arm spring, and do not touch the pedal at this stage of adjustment.

Push the release rod and slave cylinder pushrod forward until the piston bottoms in the slave cylinder bore. Now pull the clutch release arm until the throwout bearing touches the fingers of the clutch cover/pressure plate. Adjust the play between the adjusting nut and the release arm seat to a minimum of 1/4". Tighten the lock nut.

Now you can adjust the eccentric bolt at the clutch pedal pushrod until there is 3/16–3/8" of pedal travel from the pedal's fully retracted position until the pushrod contacts its seat in the clutch master cylinder piston. (This translates as only a small amount of clearance between the pushrod tip and clutch master cylinder piston.)

You now should have 1-5/8" pedal free travel, measured from the center rib of the pedal pad. Again, with the release arm's return spring connected, there should be clearance between the throwout bearing and clutch fingers when the pedal is fully released. Secure each locknut with each adjustment, and always recheck the release bearing-to-clutch finger clearance after driving the truck.

Clutch Linkage Minor Adjustment: 1961–up

Ford light trucks returned to mechanical clutch linkage in 1961, and this type of linkage carries through 1983. From 1984 onward, hydraulic linkage once again takes the place of mechanical clutch linkage. These later type hydraulic systems, however, do not require periodic clutch adjustment.

For mechanical linkage models, the general rule applies: Always make certain enough freeplay exists between the release bearing and the fingers of the clutch when the pedal releases completely. For 1961–83 F-truck models, the two concerns are proper pedal height and correct clearance between the release bearing face and the fingers of the clutch cover/pressure plate.

If the pedal height is correct and linkage is in good shape, your main concern is the clutch release rod-to-release arm clearance—which translates, again, as clearance between the throwout/release bearing and fingers of the pressure plate with the clutch pedal fully retracted.

The specification for Ford F-trucks of this era is approximately 1/4" free play between the release arm's seat and release rod adjuster nut. If the release arm can move this distance (without the return spring attached) before the throwout bearing touches the clutch release fingers, you should have the 1/16" or more of clearance needed between the throwout bearing face and clutch fingers. Always reattach the release arm return spring after adjusting the clutch.

Later hydraulic clutch linkage designs omit the use of a release arm spring. This design relies on the rotational force of the clutch to thrust the release bearing slightly away from the clutch fingers when the driver releases the pedal. These systems self-adjust, requiring no type of adjustment between clutch replacements. Check clutch reservoir fluid with regular maintenance.

Hydraulic systems occasionally need bleeding, and a periodic bleed/flush will provide fresh fluid and remove moisture or other contaminants. (Bleeding procedure is much the same as for hydraulic brakes.) Always use fresh DOT 3 or better grade brake fluid and maintain cleanliness. Keep all contaminants out of the system, as damage to the hydraulic cylinders will otherwise result. Clean fluid will help protect the release mechanism from premature failure.

> *CAUTION —*
> *As with a brake system, clean debris from around the fluid reservoir before removing the cap. Prevent contaminants and dirt from entering the hydraulic clutch system. Always use clean brake fluid.*

Clutch Replacement Tips

Replacing your truck's clutch is a major job. Before condemning your clutch, try a simple adjustment first. Also, clutch wear or failure symptoms are often mim-

icked by other troubles, like loose or broken motor mounts, a worn axle limited slip unit or binding clutch linkage. When a clutch failure or diagnosis like "worn out" seems premature, consider other possibilities.

> *WARNING —*
> *The clutch disc may contain asbestos fibers. Asbestos materials can cause asbestosis. Always wear an approved respirator and protective clothing when handling components containing asbestos. Do not use compressed air, do not grind, heat, weld, or sand on or near any asbestos materials. Only approved cleaning methods should be used to service the clutch disc or areas containing asbestos dust or fibers.*

Fig. 9-15. Examine motor mounts and other areas before condemning the clutch. Mounts sag, break, loosen and become oil saturated. A 4x4 Ford truck clutch job is a major task, done only when necessary.

When your truck requires a clutch replacement, the factory shop manual for your model will clearly outline the steps. Rather than provide step-by-step instructions for the clutch replacement, this section provides the footnotes that factory workshop manuals often omit while serving the professional mechanic.

The clutch in your truck mounts on the flywheel, at the back of the engine and in front of the transmission.

On 4WD equipped trucks, the removal of the transmission involves far more work than on a 2WD truck.

2WD trucks require driveshaft and transmission removal for a clutch replacement. On a 4x4, the front and rear driveshafts attach to the transfer case. Clutch replacement on a 4WD model means removing the transfer case, plus numerous components that connect to the transfer case, before removing the transmission.

Obviously, if you have any good reason to remove the engine, consider performing a clutch replacement at the same time, especially on 4WD trucks. This is simply good insurance.

Fig. 9-16. A massive truck four speed, coupled to an iron transfer case, can weigh in excess of 250 pounds. Separate these components and use a special transmission jack to remove and install the sub-assemblies. Here, transfer case has been removed with a transmission jack. Floor jack shown supports engine and transmission.

Clutch replacement can be done in concert with other repairs. For example, if your 4WD's radiator needs repair when the clutch also begs attention, consider doing both jobs simultaneously. Once the radiator is out, you have added engine bay space. This could make it possible to separate the engine from the bellhousing and, with a safe engine hoist, partially remove the engine to access the clutch. If changing the clutch in this manner makes sense, securely support the transmission before moving the engine forward. This method is an alternative to the customary routine of removing the two drivelines, the transfer case and the transmission assembly.

The choice is yours. First read the factory procedure for removing the engine, then the steps for replacing the clutch. Depending upon the model, you may spend a lot less time on the cold ground by partially removing and then installing the engine than if you remove the driveshafts, transfer case and transmission. Assess your truck, the available tools and your working conditions. Some later model engines have a mass of accessories and confusing A/C plumbing, special wiring considerations and a maze of vacuum hoses that could make engine removal less practical.

Fig. 9-17. A 4x4 Ford truck clutch replacement calls for transmission and even transfer case removal. In some cases, it may be easier to remove the radiator, detach and move the engine forward, and leave the rest of the powertrain in place. Support the transmission/transfer case carefully.

When removing and installing powertrain components, understand that they are very hefty and cumbersome. Use appropriate jacks and any other safety equipment to protect yourself from injury. If you cannot afford a transmission jack, rent one. This will save time, make the job easier and prevent damage to vital parts. Aligning the transmission and transfer case with the clutch is an awkward job, even with a special jack.

A T-18 or NP435 truck four-speed gearbox and NP205 iron transfer case weigh near 250 pounds—enough to pin you to the garage floor for good! Use extreme caution with this type of bulk, as no clutch job is worth a permanent injury. Use a hoist, hydraulic transmission jack or special lifting devices.

For saving time and protecting vital parts, always use clutch aligning tools. More trouble occurs during attempts to align the transmission with the clutch disc hub than any other operation. To avoid clutch disc damage, never hang weight off the clutch hub.

Take care to tighten clutch cover bolts gradually, evenly and in cross sequence, following factory guidelines. Warping a brand new clutch cover can ruin the whole job, plus require a teardown to correct the clutch shudder!

Inspect the flywheel surface for heat cracks, glazing and possible warpage. Again, with the magnitude of this task, don't try to cut corners. Mark the flywheel's location on the crankshaft and remove the flywheel. Send the flywheel to a quality automotive machine shop. Let them inspect the flywheel and resurface its face. If the flywheel's starter ring gear shows any damage, replace either the ring gear or the entire flywheel.

Fig. 9-18. *Check the flywheel for heat cracks, blue discoloration and glazing. If you find any of these symptoms, send the flywheel to an automotive machine shop for service.*

Flywheel thickness is important for normal clutch operation, engine balance and correct positioning of the release bearing. Make sure flywheel thickness is within specifications.

The Parts List

The job is tough, and you don't want to do it over. When you make your list of necessary parts, begin with the clutch cover (pressure plate), clutch disc and throwout or release bearing. Closely inspect the crankshaft pilot bearing and clutch release arm for wear. If in doubt, replace these parts.

On most F-trucks, weather and age have taken their toll. The release arm sealing boot has deteriorated. Replace it now. Any saggy return springs need replacement. Look closely at the clutch linkage; inspect for wear, fatigue and life expectancy. Inspect the front bearing retainer of the transmission that supports the throwout bearing. If galling or wear exists, toss this part and replace with a new one. The retainer helps maintain release bearing alignment and must be straight and true.

Replace all seals that are leaking or could leak. This includes the front bearing retainer seal, control housing shift rail plugs and felt wick seals used with early-model front bearing retainers. Use your imagination; visualize where a leak could develop and which parts would be especially hard to access.

Toss out any worn fastening hardware and replace with equivalent grade bolts, nuts and locking devices. Know your grading (see appendix charts) and upgrade if necessary. If you remove the flywheel, install new original equipment (OE) type replacement flywheel bolts. The same with the clutch cover. Replace all locking hardware and/or washers, and clean or chase threads to assure proper torque settings.

WARNING —
Use properly graded hardware, identical to OE design. Engineers often design bolts to serve a particular function. Match hardware perfectly, and do not install generic hardware in place of specially configured bolts. Always replace hardware with identical parts. Match bolt shoulder length, thread pitch, grading, lock washer design and other details. Do not replace specialized hardware with generic fasteners.

Tools

For a quality job, you'll need several specialty tools. Removal of the pilot bearing generally requires a special puller. For solid bushing type pilots, you might try this alternative, which I learned from a Model A era mechanic: Pack the pilot cavity with grease. Find a steel shaft or an old transmission input gear with the same diameter nose as the pilot bushing bore. Tap the shaft into the pilot bore.

WARNING —
Cushion your blows with a block of wood or a plastic hammer, and wear eye protection.

The shaft acts like a hydraulic ram. As you tap, grease will create impact force at the back side of the pilot bushing and drive the bushing out. This only works with bronze bushings, not with bearings, and the driver shaft must fit snugly into the bore.

A clutch aligning tool is a must. An old transmission input gear with the same splines will also serve to align the clutch disc as you secure the clutch cover to the flywheel.

Over the years, I have accumulated a drawer full of alignment dowels for the two upper bolt holes of various clutch housings. To make your own transmission alignment dowels, simply cut the heads off long bolts of the proper thread size. For simpler removal, make a screwdriver slot at the end of each dowel and keep threads clean.

By installing dowel pins, you can keep the transmission aligned and on center as you slide the assembly into position. Once you've installed the lower transmission bolts, unscrew one pin at a time and replace each dowel with a transmission mounting bolt. Tighten all bolts in sequence, and establish final settings with a torque wrench.

Prevent damage to the transmission case, bearing retainer, clutch hub and pilot bearing. Carefully maintain transmission alignment during installation. Always support the transmission with a jack until all upper and lower mounting bolts are secure.

Fig. 9-19. *A clutch disc aligning tool is a must when fitting a new disc. Always install a new pilot bearing/bushing and clutch throwout bearing when replacing the clutch disc and pressure plate.*

You will want some high melting point grease for the inside collar of the throwout bearing. Some manufacturers package the bearing with grease. Never clean a new throwout bearing in solvent, as this will remove grease.

Make sure you have proper sealant if you intend to remove the front bearing retainer and install a new gasket. As I commented earlier, transmissions like the NP435 four-speed have selective fit bearing retainer gaskets (shims) for precisely adjusting the end play of the input gear and bearing.

> **CAUTION —**
> *Don't alter the thickness of selective fit shim/gaskets! If necessary, use a micrometer to confirm the original thickness and match this figure with the new gasket stack. The NP435 calls for a dial indicator check of end play, then use of proper gaskets to restore or correct end play.*

Be sure you have plenty of parts cleaner and shop towels. This is a very messy job, especially on a 4x4 or truck that runs off-pavement. (Before you start work, thoroughly clean the chassis and powertrain.) You will also need the best hand cleaner available. You'll be very oily when this job is done!

Clutch Linkage Repairs

Many Ford trucks have mechanical clutch linkage. These systems require periodic service, as bushing wear leads to unwanted play. The rods and levers that actuate the clutch will wear and fatigue at the pivot points. Nylon bushings wear out, along with the pedal stops and return springs. You must replace parts when wear develops.

Hydraulic clutch systems have been popular on Ford F-Series trucks. These systems, used from 1957–60 and 1985–up, consist of a master cylinder, hydraulic hose and pipe, and a clutch slave (release) cylinder.

Fig. 9-20. *Mechanical clutch linkage requires regular inspection for wear and excessive play. Older models with through-the-floor pedals have the advantage of chassis mounted linkage. This reduces flex, distortion and binding.*

In most applications, the slave cylinder actuates a release fork/arm, much like a mechanical clutch linkage system. (Some contemporary systems use a hydraulically-actuated throwout bearing.) Similar to your truck's braking system, cleanliness and fresh hydraulic brake fluid assure longer service.

Fig. 9-21. *Hydraulic clutch linkage eliminates many problems. Twisting and body/frame flex off-highway can raise havoc with mechanical clutch linkage, especially models with suspended pedals. By contrast, a hydraulic cylinder mounts solidly to the bellhousing, maintaining constant alignment with the release arm.*

When performing work on the hydraulic clutch system, you need clean hands, free of any grease, oils or abrasive contaminants. Repair kits are sometimes available for the master and slave cylinders, or you can replace these parts if they show excess wear.

Judge cylinder wear as you would a brake cylinder. Consult your Ford F-Series light truck shop manual for safe tolerances and rebuilding details. Do not take chances here, as a clutch linkage failure could strand your truck or cause clutch damage.

Look closely at the hydraulic hose. Again, like brake hose, this is a wear item. If embrittlement or dehydration has occurred, replace the hose. Use DOT 3 or better brake fluid. (See the brake section of this book for further details on hydraulic system repairs.)

3. TRANSMISSION ADJUSTMENTS

For Ford truck manual transmissions, linkage adjustments are limited to three-speed column shift models. Other gearboxes feature removable control housing assemblies, generally considered part of the transmission assembly. Rarely does a control housing require overhaul, although you can perform such service without removing the complete transmission unit.

0012374

Fig. 9-22. Column shift linkage will wear, stretch and fatigue, and worn parts require replacement. Periodically clean linkage and thoroughly lubricate this assembly. (See the lubrication chapter.) Normal wear requires periodic adjustment of column shift linkage.

Ford F-1 trucks began using column shift linkage on light duty three-speed transmissions in late 1950. Many F-1, F-2 and F-3 trucks were equipped with floor shifted light duty or optional heavy duty three-speed and four-speed (spur gear) transmissions.

The 1953 introduction of F-100/250/350 models brought the more versatile Warner T-98 option, a floor shifted four-speed gearbox. Ford's T-98 option better served light truck customers in need of a heavy duty transmission. For light service use, the column shift three-speed transmission remained a Ford truck mainstay into the 1980s.

Although the Ford F-Series shop manual provides details for adjusting the column shift linkage on your truck, I will share some basic aims. Two rods reach from the transmission's control levers to pivoting arms at the steering column (just forward of the engine cowl). The driver controlled shifter lever moves fore and aft through a neutral gate. This aligns the shifter lever with one or the other pivoting arm.

One pivot arm works the first and reverse gears, while the other attaches to the second and high gear control lever. Adjustment consists of aligning these two pivoting arms so that the shifter moves smoothly from the first/reverse gear path, then through the neutral gate and into the second/high gear shift path.

You will find specific adjustment procedures in your F-Series truck shop manual or a professional level service manual. Three objectives apply: 1) the rod adjustments should place the steering column pivot arms in perfect alignment through the neutral gate; 2) for driver convenience, the column shifter should swing through a comfortable range; and 3) rods must move freely and permit complete engagement of reverse, first, second and third gears.

This last point is crucial. The only place to verify proper gear engagement is to crawl beneath the truck (with the engine turned off and cold so the exhaust system won't scorch your hands, and with the wheels blocked and parking brake set) and have an assistant move the shift linkage through each gear.

Make sure that the transmission control lever moves completely into each gear position indicated. If you are uncertain, remove the shift rod at the transmission control lever and note whether the lever is completely in gear.

Automatic Transmission Adjustments

Your Ford truck's automatic transmission requires periodic service. Look for fluid leaks, the condition of vacuum hoses to the modulator, if so equipped, and perform periodic fluid and filter changes. Cleanliness in the service of your transmission cannot be overstated— guidelines call for lint-free shop towels when working around an automatic transmission's valve body.

0012375

Fig. 9-23. When servicing your automatic transmission, cleanliness is crucial. Dirt, even lint, in the valve body can cause shifting irregularities and other problems that lead to an overhaul. When changing the filter, use extreme care to keep contaminants out.

There are some basic adjustments for your automatic transmission. Later trucks have sophisticated electrical and electronic controls, yet the rules remain similar. First, the manual (shift) valve requires proper adjustment. This measure cannot be overstated.

A manual valve out of adjustment may direct an inadequate flow of hydraulic fluid within the transmission. In-

Fig. 9-24. A full service on your automatic transmission includes a fluid and filter change, adjustment of the shift and kickdown linkage or electric switch, and adjustment of the neutral/park safety switch.

correct manual valve adjustment can cause weak shifts, incomplete apply pressure, slipping clutch packs and weak band application. Damage or complete transmission failure can result from incorrectly adjusted shift linkage.

The second automatic transmission adjustment is the kickdown or downshift linkage. Mechanical linkage found on Ford and Borg-Warner transmissions, or the electrical switch used on later transmissions, takes a message from the throttle to the transmission (on later models by way of an electronic module/computer). For three-speed automatics, the electrical switch or mechanical linkage causes a downshift from Drive to second gear at full throttle if the vehicle speed is less than the limit set for your truck's axle gearing and tire size.

If your transmission has a vacuum modulator, this can also affect shifts. The modulator helps dictate upshift and downshift points. An automatic transmission that shifts erratically can suffer from either a defective governor or a bad vacuum modulator.

Fig. 9-25. A defective vacuum modulator can cause shifting irregularities that mimic symptoms of more serious problems. If you catch a defective modulator before other damage occurs, the cure is relatively inexpensive. The modulator can be changed easily on most automatics.

On many Borg-Warner and Ford automatics, periodic band adjustment is a requirement. These types of transmissions, described in your Ford F-Series light truck shop manual, depend upon proper band clearances in order to shift properly and hold planetary members securely. If excessive clearance develops, poor shifts and slippage on upshifts will occur. This can rapidly damage the transmission's clutch packs and other expensive parts.

Before condemning your whole transmission, perform a full service. Change the fluid and filter. Adjust the manual linkage, centering the shift indicator for neutral and park. Readjust the neutral safety switch, if necessary, to assure that the engine will start only in neutral or park. On adjustable band-type units, adjust the bands. Adjust carburetor linkage on models with manual detent/kickdown controls. Check the adjustment of electrical kickdown switches on later transmissions. Change the vacuum modulator, if suspect, and make certain that leak-free vacuum signals reach the modulator.

If none of these measures improve your automatic's performance, accept the likelihood that the unit needs in-depth repairs or a major overhaul. Like a manual clutch, automatic transmission parts wear over time.

NOTE —
You can upgrade some automatic transmission components. High performance clutch packs and torque converters are available from aftermarket sources.

4. REBUILDING THE WARNER T-98/T-18 FORD TRUCK TRANSMISSION

The T-98 and T-18 Borg Warner four-speed transmissions represent rugged dependability and real truck stamina. Versions of these transmissions have appeared on medium duty trucks built by Ford, Diamond T, Divco, I-H, Reo, Studebaker and White. I would loosely characterize the T-98/T-18 as a two-ton truck capacity transmission, easily the stuff of Ford F-500 or even the F-600 models.

The T-98 is the original layout, dating back to the late 1940s. So rugged is this configuration that the later T-18 (mid-'60s and newer) follows virtually the same blueprint. Numerous parts readily interchange between these two transmissions, and their overhaul procedures follow similar guidelines.

The most significant design change surrounds the late T-18 reverse shift fork location. Since the overall layout of gears remains virtually the same, however, I will illustrate, step-by-step, how to overhaul the more common (earlier) design.

In the modifications chapter I heavily advocate the use of the T-98 or T-18 in your light Ford F-truck, so you may be seeking a recycled transmission. Perhaps the unit will just require cleaning and inspection. Maybe the rugged gears are in fine shape, but the unit needs fresh bearings, small parts and gaskets.

My goal here is to help you easily identify parts and develop a hands-on feel for properly overhauling the T-98 or T-18 series transmission. This is a tried and proven method of overhaul. May your Borg-Warner T-98 or T-18 truck four-speed enjoy a long service life!

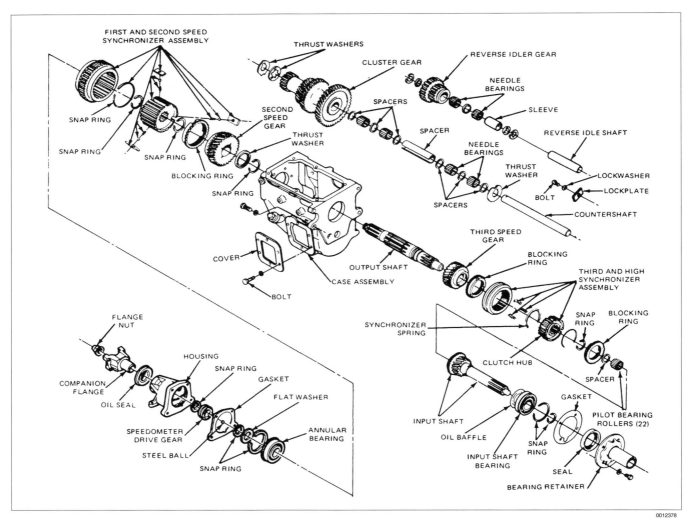

Fig. 9-26. *Exploded view of T-18 transmission provides a detailed sense for parts nomenclature and layout. Use these descriptions when securing parts from your Ford dealer. (Courtesy of Ford Motor Company.)*

Fig. 9-27. *In neutral, with all gear oil drained and the shift cane removed, the overhaul begins. Loosen the control housing bolts and place them in a properly marked container. Grading and sizing of bolts is crucial to the proper function of a transmission. Early on, get in the habit of separating and carefully storing bolts.*

Fig. 9-28. *Lift the shift control housing from the case. Note that the shift forks slide easily from the synchronizer clutch sleeves. On this version, the reverse fork remains attached to the case. (The upper end of the reverse shift fork is seen above the deck of the transmission case.) On very late versions, the reverse shift fork comes out with the control housing.*

Fig. 9-29. *The front bearing cap/retainer comes off next. Four bolts secure the retainer to the front of the transmission case. Note that an oil passage determines the location of the retainer. Gently scribing parts before teardown will assure proper reassembly. If the transmission has been disassembled before, follow these illustrations and comments closely.*

Fig. 9-31. *Here, the 1st/2nd clutch sleeve is gently tapped forward with a weighted plastic hammer. The rear mainshaft bearing is accessible once the sleeve is out of the way.*

Fig. 9-30. *The rear retainer plate serves the same role as a 4x4's adapter to the transfer case. Removal accesses the rear mainshaft and bearing.*

Fig. 9-32. *Wearing safety goggles, use a long and blunt-ended punch to drive the rear bearing loose from the mainshaft. Extreme care must be taken to avoid damage to the mainshaft, transmission case or ball bearing (especially if the bearing may be reusable).*

Fig. 9-33. *The clutch shaft and bearing can be easily accessed once the rear mainshaft bearing has been removed. Although a special puller will aid in the clutch shaft removal, the method shared here works well. Note that the chisel is simply used as a pry lever, with the hammer tapping the chisel end gently toward the case. Take care not to damage the gearcase.*

Fig. 9-34. Once the bearing has moved free of the case, the mainshaft and gear assemblies become accessible. If a special puller is available, the front (clutch shaft) bearing snap ring slot permits easy loosening of the bearing. An oil slinger/spacer fits between the bearing and clutch gear. Do not damage the oil slinger.

Fig. 9-35. Remove tapered pin and then remove the support/pivot for the reverse shift fork. Note that the O-ring seal prevents gear oil from leaking out the case side. The inner groove is where the tapered pin seats. When the transmission is overhauled, replacement of this O-ring is cheap insurance. Silicone sealant assures a positive seal and easy installation.

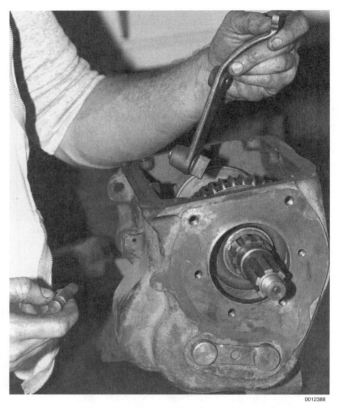

Fig. 9-36. Now the reverse shift fork may be removed. This is the last obstacle before removing the mainshaft and its geartrain sub-assemblies.

Fig. 9-37. Lift the mainshaft from the case.

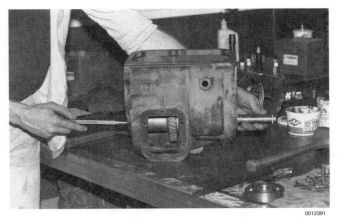

Fig. 9-39. *The countershaft supports the countergear (cluster gear). Two sets of uncaged needle bearings fit in the ends of the countergear. With safety goggles and a blunt punch, the countershaft is tapped rearward from the case. Remove the reverse idler shaft in similar fashion. Now the teardown is complete.*

Fig. 9-38. *Knock out the rear shaft lockplate to access both the reverse gear/idler shaft and the countershaft.*

Fig. 9-40. *The disassembled transmission lies on the workbench. (Note specialty pullers at rear.) Clean all parts thoroughly and inspect closely. Check bearings for roughness and all shafts for nicks or wear. Gear teeth and shafts require close attention. If you heard noises before teardown, find their source now. Replace gears in paired sets. To replace bearings, use proper pullers and a suitable press. If your shop does not include these tools, take the sub-assemblies to a transmission shop or machine shop.*

Fig. 9-41. *Reassembly begins with loading the needle bearings into each end of the countergear. With a clean and lubricated countershaft (use fresh chassis or lighter wheel bearing grease), install the full set of needle rollers. Note that the grease and Keystone effect hold the bearings in place. Keystone principle assures that if all bearings are evenly in place, they will not fall inward. The only exception is when the bearing bore is worn to an oversized diameter. During your disassembly, pay close attention to the placement of bearing washer(s). Various applications of the T-98/T-18 have different bearing washer layouts. (Some versions require only one washer per countershaft end.)*

Fig. 9-42. *Continue with the reverse idler gear and outer thrust washer.*

Fig. 9-43. *With all the needle rollers in place, the reverse idler shaft is carefully inserted through the gear. Note that slot at end of reverse idler shaft must face toward countershaft.*

Fig. 9-44. *New thrust washers, snap rings (always measure and match the thickness of the original snap rings) and other hardware are supplied in a small parts kit. Here, a thrust washer is placed at each end of the countergear. A film of grease holds the thrust washer in place. Note the locating tang engaging the notch in the case. (Force should not be required during assembly and installation of the countergear.)*

Fig. 9-45. *The countergear, with needle rollers and thrust washers in place, is lowered into the transmission case. Once the countergear occupies the space between the thrust washers, the bearings and washers will stay in place. Do not install the countershaft at this point.*

Fig. 9-46. This snap-ring begins the mainshaft geartrain assembly. Sequence of assembly is important.

Fig. 9-47. Second gear and the second gear thrust washer are the first parts to be placed on the mainshaft.

Fig. 9-48. 1st/2nd gear clutch hub is a tricky mechanism to assemble. Three shifting plates, stiff springs and poppet balls must each be pressed into the hub at the same time. Four hands are a good idea here! Be careful not to stretch or bind the springs during assembly and watch for pinched fingers! Use of goggles is advised. This is the proper configuration for placing the poppet balls into position and sliding the 1st/2nd clutch sleeve over the hub.

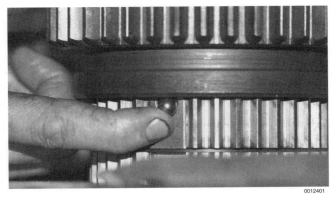

Fig. 9-49. Here's the trick. This poppet ball, and two others like it, must seat in the hub as the sleeve moves into place. Be very careful here.

Fig. 9-50. This is the correct configuration for the hub, three plates and the outer sleeve. Note the machined gear tooth ends on the outer sleeve and the direction in which the hub faces.

Fig. 9-51. Look closely at both the outer gear tooth ends and the hub configuration. This is the proper relationship of parts. The rounded teeth on the 1st gear sleeve denotes the non-synchromesh design of compound low gear in these transmissions.

Fig. 9-52. With the brass synchronizer ring in place, the 1st/2nd gear assembly slides down the mainshaft splines.

Fig. 9-53. This is the mainshaft taking shape. Here, the 1st/2nd gear assembly has moved as far as possible without persuasion.

Fig. 9-54. A little help from this driver tool will seat the hub. Stay aware of the brass synchronizer ring position as the hub is driven into place.

Fig. 9-55. This snap ring is the lock for the 1st/2nd gear assembly. Always install new snap rings of proper thickness. Tolerances are noted in your OEM level shop manual. Experience dictates the use of this style snap ring tool.

Fig. 9-56. *The second speed gear easily fits into place. Note the use of grease on all friction surfaces of the gears. This is a precaution to prevent scoring or damage during initial run-in.*

Fig. 9-58. *A detail of the assembled 3rd and 4th gear synchronizer. A hub, three plates, and two retaining rings fit inside the outer clutch sleeve. Note that the spring end is not inside the plate. When properly installed, the spring will place equal pressure on all three plates. The opposite spring captures all three plates in the same manner.*

Fig. 9-57. *The completed mainshaft assembly is the major part of a T-98/T-18 overhaul. At this point, the 3rd and 4th gear synchronizer assembly is all that remains.*

Fig. 9-59. *Note direction of the hub flange. The raised center of the hub faces forward. This snap ring completes the assembly of the mainshaft. All that remains is fitup of forward synchronizer ring. If this ring falls off as mainshaft assembly is laid into the case, no problem. Simply hold it in place as you install the clutch shaft.*

Fig. 9-60. *Mainshaft pilot bearing roller spacer must be installed before clutch shaft is fitted. Grease again holds the piece in place.*

Fig. 9-61. Drop the rear end of mainshaft assembly through the bearing bore at the rear of the case. The mainshaft assembly rests atop the loose countergear at this stage.

Fig. 9-62. Here the pilot needle rollers fit snugly in the bore of the clutch shaft. Keystone effect is apparent, with the complete circle of rollers creating outward pressure. This holds the rollers in place and serves as a reminder that the full set is present. Recall that the thrust washer rests on the nose end of the mainshaft.

Fig. 9-63. With the brass synchromesh ring in place, the clutch shaft is carefully pushed into position. This operation is tricky, as the pilot needle rollers must stay in their bore. Also, the brass synchronizer ring must fit up properly with the three plates.

Fig. 8-64. With the front bearing installed, you can now slide the rear bearing into place. The bearing is an interference fit on the mainshaft and requires some light encouragement to install. With its outer snap ring in place, the rear bearing is tapped forward. Front bearing retainer/cap is not in position at this point. It's necessary to watch the clutch gear. If the clutch shaft shows a tendency to move forward, place the pilot end of the shaft against a firm wood post. Drive the rear bearing until its outer snap ring seats against the rear of the case. Note that the inner collar of the bearing is the only area where force is applied.

CAUTION —
For any tapping, use a suitable driver tool and plastic hammer to protect bearing from damage. Do not beat on outer bearing race, as this could damage bearings.

Fig. 9-65. Here the rear bearing is seated. Note that on this application, no snap ring is required on the mainshaft. (Outer snap ring is still used.) When the U-joint yoke is installed, the bearing will be squeezed between a shoulder on the mainshaft and the yoke. (Your OEM shop manual will have details of your transmission's design and whether snap ring is required.)

Fig. 9-66. Now that the mainshaft/clutch shaft assembly is completely installed, the transmission case may be turned over. The countergear, floating in the bottom of the case, will easily align now with the countershaft bore.

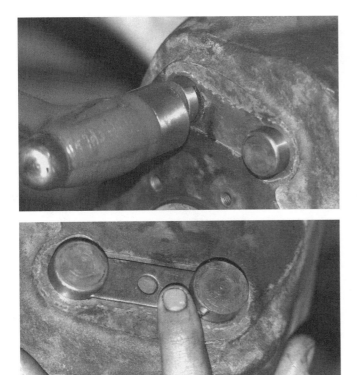

Fig. 9-67. Using care, fit the countershaft through the thrust washer, roller/needle bearing assembly, the countergear, the opposite roller/needle bearing assembly, the opposite thrust washer, and the opposite end of the case. Before seating the countershaft in the case, be certain that the notched end faces the reverse idler shaft. Then tap the lock plate into place. This will align the two shafts.

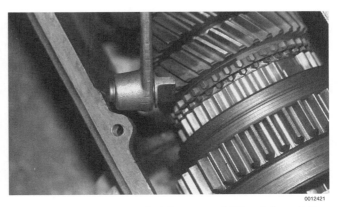

Fig. 9-68. You can now feed the reverse shifting fork carefully into the case. It may be necessary to move the 1st/2nd gear clutch sleeve slightly to ease installation. Don't move the sleeve too far!

Fig. 9-69. The reverse fork pivot pin taps into place. A new O-ring and film of silicone sealant around the O-ring groove complete the effort. Then insert the tapered lock pin to secure the reverse fork pivot pin. Tap the small end of the taper into the hole and set the pin firmly with your hammer.

WARNING —
Wear goggles when driving the tapered lock pin. This steel is very hard.

Fig. 9-70. Install a new seal in the bore of the front bearing retainer/cap. Be certain to index the oil return passage with the case oil hole. A new gasket, coated with a thin film of Permatex Ultra Blue (or its equivalent) is good assurance of leak proof service. Protect the new seal with a thin coat of grease on its lip. Make sure that sealant is used evenly and sparingly. The retainer fits easily over the clutch shaft. Sealant on threads of front retainer/cap bolts is a wise precaution. Torque these to a maximum of 15 ft-lbs or as specified.

Fig. 9-71. If required, the mainshaft rear retainer seal is easy to replace. This is good insurance. Apply a thin film of sealant to the outer rim of a new seal, and use a seal driver or suitable technique to drive in the seal. As with the front bearing retainer seal, these parts should be handled carefully to ensure a permanent repair.

Fig. 9-72. Coat this new paper gasket with a thin film of Ultra Blue or equivalent. Adapter plate bolts, clean and coated lightly with sealant, are tightened evenly. Final torque setting is a maximum of 35 ft-lbs (3/8″ threads) or 50 ft-lbs (1/2″ threads).

Fig. 9-73. The control housing is the last item. Before installing a gasket and bolts, make certain that the forks align with the synchronizer clutch sleeves. This measure is easy but highly important. The reverse slot in the shift mechanism must also be in alignment before the cover falls into place. Use a light coat of sealant on a new gasket to prevent nuisance oil leaks.

Fig. 9-74. The finished assembly is easy to view through PTO outlet. Install cover plate with a new and sealant coated gasket. Coat bolt threads lightly with sealant and torque to specification. (Most Ford applications call for 35 ft-lbs, but verify the figure in your OEM-level shop manual. If you use a PTO drive mechanism, always apply the higher torque setting.)

Chapter 10

Transfer Case, Driveshafts, Axles, and Hubs

FORD TRUCKS have a strong work ethic. Whether moving a loaded fifth wheel travel trailer or hauling supplies to a minesite or logging camp, an F-Series truck will earn its keep. The rugged four-wheel drive models, once the beasts of burden for primitive worksites, have gained popularity among suburban and urban non-commercial users.

Ford 4WDs can grapple with mud and snow, inch their way up steep grades and slosh through swampy bogs. A wide variety of chores requires auxiliary gearsets, and the two-speed transfer case provides the solution. 1965–76 F-100 models with the single speed Dana 21 power divider are the only Ford 4x4 F-trucks that have not featured a two-speed transfer case with provision for 4WD low range mode.

1. TRANSFER CASES

The Ford transfer case mounts to the rear of the transmission and divides power between the front and rear axles. A two-speed transfer case offers low range, essentially an extra gearset available for four-wheel drive mode and heavy off-pavement pulling chores.

On F-truck 4WD geartrains, the transmission output shaft drives the transfer case input. Some units mount the transfer case separately, which requires a short driveshaft between the transmission and transfer case. Other versions attach the transmission to the transfer case via a cast adapter housing, which doubles as a pedestal for the transmission and transfer case mount.

Beginning with the earliest Spicer/Dana Model 24 transfer cases, the rear driveshaft's output yoke is in line with the transfer case input shaft. Power within the transfer case flows downward to the intermediate gearset and power take-off (PTO) gear, then to the front output shaft, which rides low in the case.

Known as a through-drive transfer case design, these auxiliary gearboxes have a driver operated shift lever that engages 2WD High, 4WD-High, Neutral (PTO mode) and 4WD Low ranges. Two sliding forks provide the necessary power flow and engagement of the front axle output shaft (four-wheel drive), low range and a neutral mode for PTO use.

For rock crawling or heavy off-pavement pulling in low range, the Spicer/Dana 24, Dana 20 and the gear drive New Process transfer cases accomplish speed reduction through engagement of a gear on the intermediate shaft. When the operator moves the lever toward low range, a sliding gear or sliding clutch releases the high-range gear, then moves further to engage the low-range gear.

CAUTION —

These units have no synchromesh between high range and low range. You must stop your truck before engaging low range, although most transfer cases can shift from 2WD High to 4WD High modes without stopping the truck. (For details, see earlier chapter on operating your truck.)

The gear drive transfer cases and even the optional 1973–79 NP203 chain drive transfer case can easily meet the requirements of Ford F-truck users. A through-drive transfer case proves superior to side drive types like the Spicer Model 18 unit found in pre-1972 Jeep CJ and earlier Willys truck models.

As Ford four-wheel drive trucks evolved from utility vehicles into multi-purpose vehicles, the transfer case design also changed. As 4x4s spent more time on the highway than off, simultaneously facing stiffer emission and fuel economy standards, Ford reduced the two-wheel drive mode wear and frictional losses by changing to chain drive part-time 4x4 transfer cases.

In 1980, Ford F-trucks began using the New Process NP208 and Warner 1345 transfer cases. Although these units definitely reduce friction, with planetary gear systems acting in place of hefty gearsets, many buyers regretted the passage of iron cased gear drive units.

Fig. 10-1. 1959–64 Ford 4x4 F-trucks all have divorced transfer cases. The F-250 keeps this arrangement through 1977 models. First Spicer, then Dana and finally the New Process transfer cases carried Ford into the early 1980s, when F-trucks switched to chain drive style NP208 and Borg-Warner (shown) transfer cases that attach directly to the transmission via an adapter.

For stamina and a remarkably long service life, there is no substitute for a pre-1980 gear drive (iron case) transfer case. In particular, the industrial strength New Process 205 unit is my number one choice of all light truck transfer cases built to this date. Ford began using the NP205 in 1973 and stopped after 1979, although versions of the unit appear in Dodge and GM heavy duty 4WDs (one-ton rated models and Dodge/Cummins diesel powered trucks) into the 1990s.

Full- vs. Part-time Four Wheeling

During the '70s, a series of chain drive full-time transfer case systems appeared. Jeep used Warner's Quadra-Trac, while Dodge, Ford and GM trucks adopted the massive chain-drive, full-time New Process 203 unit.

A full-time four-wheel drive transfer case prevents use of front locking hubs and provides four-wheel traction at all times. These systems use an internal differentiating system which allows proportional power flow to the front and rear axles.

On the early types, the differential system is similar to a spider gear arrangement in a drive axle assembly. The design continuously delivers power to both the front and rear axles. A hefty chain connects the two drive outputs, while a gearset provides low range. High and low range lock mode overrides the transfer case's differential system for off-pavement or loose traction driving.

Excess parts wear and poor gas mileage encouraged most light truck manufacturers to abandon full-time four-wheel drive by 1980. The return to part-time four-wheel

Fig. 10-2. This variety of New Process transfer case units serve early 1980s Ford F-trucks and other makes. They are lightweight, easy to shift and feature chain drive.

drive, however, did not signal a change back to the rugged NP205 or Dana 20 and 24 gear drive units. Instead, most American manufacturers of full-size trucks switched to the New Process 208 chain drive part-time unit.

The NP208 transfer case and Warner's 1345 unit that Ford utilized are lightweight aluminum-cased transfer cases. An NP208 design allows quick, easy shifting (on-the-fly) between 2WD high and 4WD high ranges. Although some assume that drive chain life is a weakness with these designs, chains and sprockets are, in fact, very durable.

> **NOTE —**
> On early NP208 transfer cases, wear is most often at the shifting forks and nylon fork channels. As many of these units use thin ATF for a lubricant, seal and case leakage is another area of concern.

Lightweight Part-time Systems

Chain drive transfer cases have proven far less durable than earlier iron cased Spicer/Dana and New Process gear drive transfer cases. Shift mechanism failures and leaks plague many aluminum chain drive transfer case units. A major overhaul is necessary to correct these problems.

The 1973–79 New Process 205-equipped Ford F-Series trucks still offer the best stamina. Iron cases and durable gear drives have proven superior to all other designs. For years, my magazine tech columns and technical features have challenged the use of lighter duty transfer cases with chain drive and planetary gearsets.

The vehicle manufacturers argue that weight savings and reduced friction encourage the use of lighter transfer units. A Spicer/Dana 20 or 24 and the New Process 205 gear drive transfer case mechanisms could easily be fitted within a high-strength and lightweight alloy case.

Most four-wheelers are fully capable of pulling a lever, twisting a manual hub or reading an instruction decal. Overall reliability and off-pavement survival suggest the need for heavy duty factory options—choices like a bulletproof New Process 205 transfer case that can give trouble-free service in excess of 150,000 miles.

Transfer Case Troubleshooting

Overhauling your truck's transfer case is a job much like a manual transmission overhaul. If you need to do such work, you will find step-by-step overhaul procedures in the factory or professional level service manual for your truck.

Within the scope and aims of this book, I am outlining some general troubleshooting guidelines for common transfer case problems. This should help you determine what measures to take. Your Ford F-Series shop manual or a professional level service guidebook can help with step-by-step removal/installation ('R&R') and overhaul procedures.

The most frequent transfer case trouble is hard shifting. Often, the remedy is really simple, requiring nothing more than cleaning the linkage and properly lubricating these parts. Sometimes the problem is bent or damaged linkage, the result of off-pavement abuse.

If external linkage is not the problem and your transfer case slips out of gear or front wheel drive, anticipate more serious trouble. Before condemning the transfer case, check the transfer case-to-transmission attaching hardware. A loose transfer case housing can cause gear binding and internal side loads or pressure on the gears.

Deeper Troubles

Service manuals list the shift mechanism among the possible causes of transfer case problems. Poppet balls and springs are of concern in earlier transfer case shift mechanisms, but noises, jumping out of gear and difficult shifting usually indicate more serious troubles.

Before removing the transfer case from your truck for overhaul, it's always prudent to check the condition of the shift rail springs and poppet balls. There are instances when a worn or broken spring does cause trouble, but more likely the culprit is bearing damage, a bent shift fork or other internal defects.

If your high-mileage transfer case has never been through an overhaul, suspect bearing fatigue at the very least. Although gear-drive transfer cases have a solid record for longevity, you should always replace worn bearings, as excessive gear clearance and poor tooth contact can quickly cause gear failure and expensive parts damage.

Chain Drive Transfer Case Troubles

Failure of a fork or shift mechanism can leave your 4x4 stranded. With the NP208 or Warner units, trouble symptoms include jumping out of gear, failure to engage the low, high or neutral range, or noisy operation. Before tearing into the unit, however, check the easy possibilities.

Fluid deserves a look. (Various applications use ATF or motor oil, so check your truck's requirements.) Leaks develop at seals, case halves, and castings. Pay close attention. Shift linkage sometimes needs adjustment or alignment. Make certain the linkage does not bind or interfere with the body parts. When these simpler cures fail, plan to remove the transfer case unit for overhaul.

NP208 "R&R"

The NP208 transfer case is usually simple to remove. General procedure includes placing the shifter in 4H and draining the fluid. Disconnect all cables, linkages and driveshaft joints.

Drain all fluid, then separate yokes from the input and output shafts. See whether the exhaust pipe or brake cable interferes, and check the top of the transfer case for switch wires.

Once you have disconnected all external parts, place a transmission jack beneath the transfer case. Now unbolt the case from the transmission adapter. In minutes, with the use of a floor jack or the help of a stout friend, you can free the transfer case from the adapter.

Keep all parts level until the input shaft completely clears the transfer case. Place the transfer case on your workbench. Level the ends, and lay the unit with the case's split lying parallel to the benchtop.

Remember to replace all seals, including yoke seals. Always refer to your OEM level service manual for de-tailed procedures on the removal, overhaul and reinstallation of your transfer case.

Late Electronic Shift Transfer Cases

Ford 4x4 trucks, bending to the new consumer's clamor for simpler shift mechanisms, has adopted an electronically shifted transfer case. Later model trucks offer two versions of Warner's Model 13-56 transfer case.

The conventional version of the 13-56 has a reputation for reliable service and offers a fundamental design that affords ease of operation, quick troubleshooting and the ability to tow the vehicle at highway speeds without disconnecting drivelines. A rear output shaft operated pump within both the conventional and electronically shifted 13-56 units supplies lubrication in tow mode.

CAUTION —

When towing any 4x4 truck, consult your glovebox owner's handbook for special towing instructions that apply to your model and transfer case design. Severe geartrain damage can result from failure to observe the manufacturer's requirements.

Currently, an optional version of the basic 13-56 unit features a dash switch controlled electronic shift mechanism. Electronic shifting operation involves a driver activated (via manual dash switches) magnetic clutch mechanism within the aluminum transfer case housing.

This clutch has an important job. It spins the front drive system to the speed of the rear output system, facilitating a synchronous and smooth transitional shift from 2WD to 4WD in high range. By design, this clutch should engage in milli-seconds, and once synchronous speed has been reached, a mechanical (spring loaded) collar will engage, thus locking the mainshaft's hub to the chain drive sprocket for power flow to the front driveline and axle.

As with older 4x4 transfer case designs, this shift mechanism still does not engage low range unless the vehicle is near a stop (maximum of 3 mph). This aspect of the electronic shift system is excellent, as the dash control switches cannot be over-ridden, and the driver cannot affect a low range engagement with the vehicle at speed.

However, the overall design of this system raises questions about the very essence of four-wheel drive utility. Since this shifter technology is dependent upon electronic modules, speedometer signals, an electro-magnetic clutch mechanism and a plethora of control switches, relays and wiring, I wonder whether the system's vulnerability outweighs its benefits. Do you want to depend on such technology many miles from nowhere with the nose end of their truck hanging precariously near the edge of a cliff? Fortunately, the electronic shift transfer case is currently an option. This leaves room for many of us to take the standard transfer case with a manual shift lever.

And I'll take a pair of manual locking hubs while we're at it. (The electronic shift transfer case is only available with automatic locking hubs.) When my truck's four wheels claw through 18 inches of snow on a Search-and-Rescue mission, I'd rather stay on the helping end rather than the receiving end.

Chapter 10

2. Driveshafts

A light truck's driveshaft(s) take tremendous punishment. On 4WD models, excessive suspension travel, weighty loads, radically changing driveshaft angles and modifications like an overly zealous suspension lift kit can tear your U-joints and driveshafts to pieces.

Often, the cause of a U-joint failure is misconstrued. Sure, wear takes a rapid toll on trucks that ford streams, flex their springs to the maximum and crawl through tortuous rocks with massive torque applied through low range gears. On 2WD models that pull trailers or campers, the loads on drivelines also become excessive.

Poorly fitted driveshafts, however, also provide a major cause of failure. Shafts pieced together out-of-phase or badly angled are the worst culprits. Wear in the rear

Fig. 10-5. Longer wheelbase trucks use a mid-shaft bearing. Wear here will cause severe driveline vibration.

Fig. 10-3. A variety of U-joint failures directly relate to poor maintenance, loss of grease, worn seals, or bad driveshaft angularity.

Fig. 10-4. Trent Alford at M.I.T. in El Cajon, California aligns hefty replacement parts for a heavy duty rear driveshaft that will increase a truck's stamina.

driveshaft slip yoke, stub spline or mid-shaft bearing can produce an unusual vibrating sound during a float condition (period between acceleration load and deceleration). This is especially noticeable on very early trucks with driveline-mounted parking brakes, as the brake drum amplifies the noise.

A driveshaft's U-joints must also be in phase with each other. As a simple maintenance concern, proper grease intervals and grease gun pressures contribute to driveshaft longevity.

Beyond these factors, driveshaft survival depends mostly on torque loads. These include the weight placed on the vehicle, the amount of engine torque applied to the joints and also the departure and receiving angles between the driving and driven yokes of the driveshaft.

A common problem with trucks that have a suspension/spring lift kit is too much angle on the joints. This results from the radical difference in height between the axle pinion shafts and the transfer case output shafts.

Rotating the axle pinion shaft upward is a shoddy method that some lift kit installers use to reduce U-joint angles. This approach can lead to another crop of problems, those caused by unmatched U-joint angles. U-joints rotating on widely dissimilar arcs can create enough rotational vibration and stress to break a gear case housing!

Driveshafts Under Construction

Your truck's driveshaft survival depends upon joint size, tubing diameter and wall thickness, plus the ability of the assembly to compensate for speed, length and angle changes. Often, a driveshaft that worked perfectly well in its original mode cannot handle a chassis lift or increased horsepower loads. Here, a custom heavy duty driveshaft is necessary.

U-joint Service and Repair Tips

U-joint replacement always begins with driveshaft removal. Before loosening a driveshaft, mark the shaft's order of assembly. Drivelines must be in-phase, with couplers kept in line with their original splines.

Fig. 10-6. *Although they look similar, replacement U-joint at left fits one-ton trucks. Middle joint is size found in most half-and 3/4-ton models. At right, the small size joint fits driveshaft of compact 4x4. Bigger is better.*

Fig. 10-8. *Dramatic difference between an OEM front driveshaft tube section and a replacement heavier wall thickness tube is obvious.*

Fig. 10-7. *Use of a hefty custom built driveshaft assures resistance to torque loads. With a truck-type four speed and low gearing, reduction ratios in excess of 70:1 are possible! Such torque is tremendous.*

NOTE —

If your driveshaft has two pieces, scribe an indexing line on each section. Reassembly in the original position will assure satisfactory service, alignment, and balance.

Fig. 10-9. *This step is critical during driveshaft construction. Proper driveshaft phasing requires that U-joint cross yokes are absolutely in line. Before welding, a spirit level or protractor and a perfectly flat benchtop assure alignment.*

Fig. 10-10. *Before MIG wire-feed welding, the shaft is carefully tapped into alignment. The builder will work this section until total runout is less than 0.005-inch! Such tolerances are necessary for vibration-free results and illustrate the importance of protecting your driveshafts from bashing.*

Proper Lubrication

U-joint survival depends upon correct lubrication. Stream crossings, wintry highways and sandy deserts take their toll. Assuming that U-joint dust seals are in top shape, you can follow Spicer's on/off highway lubrication guidelines: 5000-8000 miles or every three months (far more often if your truck is subject to either severe service or exposure to water). A high-quality lube gun is a prerequisite to preserving U-joints and their delicate seals.

When selecting U-joint and driveshaft greases, follow Spicer's guidelines. Use only National Lubricating Grease Institute (NLGI) Extreme Pressure Grade 1 or 2 greases. Avoid heavier greases. Severe service requires lithium soap base or EP grease with a temperature range of +325 to -10° F.

Cleanliness is essential, regardless of the locale in which you make the repairs. (I and others have replaced U-joints on the tailgate of a pickup and even atop granite boulders!) If the work area is particularly gritty, beware. New U-joints, freshly coated with grease, attract dirt like a horseshoe magnet draws pig iron from beach sand. Assuming that the shaft isn't damaged, you can make a permanent U-joint installation in the field if you approach the job with professional expectations.

The tools needed to remove and replace a U-joint are minimal. In the field, a good mechanic's hammer, solid punch, blade screwdriver, a variety of sockets and a set of pliers can handle the job. Specialty or homemade tools can ease the job further, although the principles remain the same.

If your technique is correct, even the most trying environment will not prevent a quality job. Find a solid surface to work on, preferably steel plate (the bumper, a front winch mounting plate, or a hefty wooden board in a pickup bed). Get out of the weather if gale winds prevail, and plan on several minutes of painstaking work.

Fig. 10-11. *Coupler types and U-joints vary. Double Cardan (constant velocity) joints have become common on 4x4 driveshafts. Joint to yoke attaching methods also vary.*

Fig. 10-12. *Disassembling a joint requires few tools. On Spicer-type U-joints, you must remove two external snap rings.*

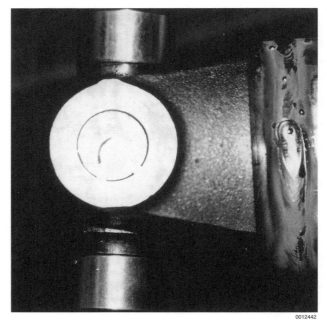

Fig. 10-13. *Clean the driveshaft for close inspection and reassembly. This will assure proper fitup of parts.*

Driveshaft Angularity

Angles and rotational arcs make or break U-joints and driveshafts. While torque load determines the proper size U-joint to use, engineers design driveshafts for an 85% efficiency factor. To understand the highest load placed upon your driveshafts, the formula is: Lowest Gear Torque = Net Engine Torque X Transmission Low Gear Ratio X Transfer Case Low Range Ratio (if a 4x4 with low range) X 0.85.

Two angles affect a driveshaft: side-view drop and plane-view shift. Side view is simply the angle that the driveshaft slopes downward from the transfer case to each axle's differential. Plane view is the lateral angle of the driveshaft, viewed from directly above the frame.

For your truck's driveshafts to live, the angles on each end of the driveshaft (the side-view drop combined with the plane-view shift) must create as little non-uniform motion as possible. U-joint angles, in simple terms, must rotate on nearly identical arcs, with the vertical faces of the U-joint flanges nearly parallel. (Spicer/Dana recommends that the limit of inequality must not exceed that of a single U-joint operating at a 3° angle.)

The included U-joint angles should remain identical on each end of the driveshaft. When the shaft rotates, joints should move in similar arcs, with bearing cross shafts each running at the same tilt.

Speed dictates maximum allowable driveshaft angles. A driveshaft rotating 5000 rpm (somewhat obscure for a 4x4 truck unless flat out in a desert race) tolerates no more than 3 degrees, 15 seconds of operating angle, while the same shaft spinning 1500 rpm will work at an 11 degree, 30 second angle. Driveshaft length affects this formula, too, with longer driveshafts tolerating more operating angle.

Owners who lift their trucks with shackle kits or springs must also consider that a 3/4° change in the differential pinion angle will change the U-joint operating angle about 1/4°.

Shimming the axle housing at the spring perches is a common method for restoring the pinion angle and U-joint operating angles. Driveline specialists insist that appropriate steel shims be used or, if the angle is radically off, cut the spring perches from the axle housing, reposition to the correct angle, and re-weld the perches in place. Brass and aluminum shims tend to pound flat during off-road bashing.

Before hybridizing your engine, transmission or transfer case angles, take accurate measurements of the shaft angles. When lifting a 4x4, the side angles of the driveshafts also change. Small changes are acceptable, as long as the axle swings up and down on its original arc of movement. Problems begin when the side angle becomes excessive.

An excellent source of information, including formulas and professional driveshaft service tips, is Spicer/Dana's *Trouble Shooting Guideline*, available through Spicer distributors or Dana Corporation, Drivetrain Service Division, P.O. Box 321, Toledo, Ohio 43691. This quick reference guide and the Spicer *Universal Joints and Driveshafts Service Manual* are the last word on professional driveshaft service, maintenance and construction techniques.

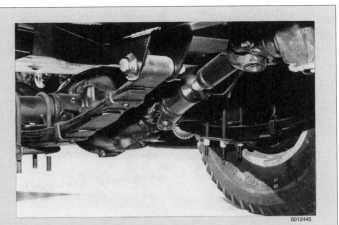

Looking upward from below the rear driveshaft, the line between the U-joint flanges is evident. A short shaft demands precise side and plane angles.

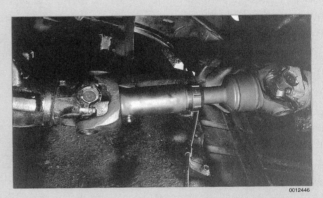

Side view angle shows the relationship between the sloping driveshaft and the U-joint flanges. Note that flange centerlines are parallel.

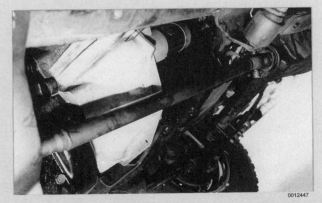

Short wheelbase 4x4s sometimes boast a long front driveshaft with very slight slope (side view angularity). As length reduces torque load, this heavy duty replacement shaft will easily handle the chores.

Fig. 10-14. *Once both bearing caps are free of the driveshaft, you can separate the U-joint.*

Fig. 10-15. *Protect these snap ring grooves during service. Striking a groove with a hammer or punch could cause permanent driveshaft damage.*

U-joint Installation

Although an arbor press or specialized U-joint tools are helpful, don't be misled. Some of the best craftsmen in the automotive repair industry still replace U-joints with basic hand tools. The reason? U-joint bearing caps fit precisely into their saddles and bores, and the slightest cocking of a cap during installation can ruin a driveshaft. Presses and hefty tools eliminate the feel of the cap moving into its bore. Hand tools maintain your awareness of fit.

Once you have completed the U-joint replacement and reinstalled the driveshaft in the truck, grease the U-joints. Do not grease a U-joint before bolting it into the yoke, as you will force the bearing caps out of position. (See your factory service manual for torque specs.)

If you left the grease gun home, new joints usually contain enough grease for the drive back. Permanently sealed joints, have very high quality grease and seals, and require no further greasing. Other joints, equipped with grease fittings, require periodic lubrication.

Fig. 10-16. *Install the first bearing cap. Use the hammer carefully and support the bearing needles with the cross section of the U-joint. If you doubt your hammer skills, use a socket to drive the bearing cap into its recess. Install the cap far enough to insert the snap ring. Install the second cap. Again, carefully keep the cross section centered to hold needle bearings in place. If all needles remain intact, the second bearing cap will just clear its snap ring groove. Install the snap ring. Make sure snap rings seat completely.*

Fig. 10-17. *New U-joints come with snap rings and a grease fitting. Make sure needle bearings stay in place during assembly. Always align the grease fitting to permit easy access and service. Field lubrication of double Cardan joints requires special grease gun tip.*

Fig. 10-18. A constant velocity, double Cardan U-joint has a precise assembly sequence. Be aware of the spring, which must be in place when installing the new joints. Reassemble in exactly the reverse sequence of disassembly.

Fig. 10-19. By contrast, Detroit type U-Joints utilize internal snap rings. Straps hold the joint to the yoke.

3. AXLE ASSEMBLIES

The mysteries within the axle housing, the maze of gears and bearings, are responsible for turning horsepower into motion. How that happens is as significant as any other aspect of your truck's powertrain. Although axle overhaul is beyond the scope of this book, your knowledge of tell-tale wear signs could prevent serious trouble, reduce damage and contain the repair costs. Let's begin with some axle basics.

Engine power flows through the clutch or torque converter, transmission, transfer case (4WD models) and driveline(s). The driveshaft rotates the axle's pinion shaft/gear (attached to the U-joint companion flange) to carry power into the axle. Supported by bearings in the axle housing, the pinion shaft's bevel gearhead transfers power to a matching ring gear, which changes the direction of the power flow by 90°.

Together, the ring and pinion gears serve two functions: 1) changing the power flow direction, and 2) increasing torque, proportionally, by reducing the rotational speed of the axle shafts. A 4.10 gear ratio (41 teeth on the ring gear and 10 on the pinion) rotates axle shafts with nearly four-and-one-tenth times the torque of the driveshaft—and at slightly less than one-fourth of the driveshaft's speed.

Fig. 10-20. Comparison of ring and pinion gears says it all. Top row, left to right, is a Spicer 27, a light duty Dana 28, and a WWII vintage Jeep MB Model Spicer 25. The bottom row of Dana gears shows the 60, 44 and 70 sets. The 44 is a popular front axle on full-sized 4x4 1/2-tons and some 3/4-tons, also used at the rear of pre-'57 1/2-ton pickups. The two larger gearsets fit 3/4-ton and one-ton trucks.

Fig. 10-21. *This early Spicer integral front axle housing features pressed-in and welded axle tubes and closed steering knuckles. An integral axle overhaul takes place in the chassis.* The job requires a special spreader to remove the differential carrier from the axle housing.

Fig. 10-22. *Compare the Dana 70 differential side gear with that of the 44. Note the axle splines inside each gear, indicating the size difference between a one-ton truck's axle shaft and that of a full-sized 1/2-ton.*

The ring gear bolts to a case, generally called the differential carrier. Bearings support the differential carrier in either the hypoid axle housing or a removable third member housing. (Ford trucks use both the integral-type hypoid axle housing and a separate carrier assembly, most notably like the one used in the 9-inch Ford axle.)

NOTE —
The earliest F-trucks with higher GVW ratings had oddball spiral-bevel rear axles that feature a two-piece, vertically split housing.

If the axle shafts were connected directly to the ring gear's case, both wheels would spin continuously at the speed of the ring gear. Such a locked rear end or spool, although maximizing traction, is incapable of adjusting for the vehicle's left or right turns.

All four-wheeled vehicles require unequal wheel speed to negotiate a turn. The inside wheels rotate slower than the outside wheels. If all four wheels turned at equal speed, serious trouble would result. Tires would skid and axle shafts would work against each other.

Here the differential becomes important. We need to vary the speed of the right side wheels from those on the left. In a straight ahead mode, the ring gear turns both shafts at equal speed, that speed determined by the axle ratio and engine rpm. For turns, however, the individual axle shaft speeds adjust for smooth traction at each wheel.

Imagine your truck's driveshaft(s) rotating at 2000 rpm. With ten teeth on the pinion gear and forty teeth on the ring gear, the axle shafts will spin at 500 rpm. Although useful for illustration purposes, an axle ratio of 4-to-1 would cause the pinion gear teeth to continuously find the same ring gear teeth, an undesirable tendency. Instead, engineers devise ratios like 4.10, with a 41/10 tooth arrangement that constantly renews tooth contact.

Differential Action

As your truck enters a corner, the inside wheel turns slower than the outside wheel. The speed at each wheel must differ. To allow for the speed change, the differential contains a series of gears inside the rotating carrier case. While ring and pinion speeds are constant, the differential gears allow axle shaft speeds to vary.

The differential carrier housing is hollow, and the axles slide through the space in the housing, entering from each side. Splines on the inner ends of the axle shafts engage the differential side gears. These side gears, in non-locking differentials, also have bevel teeth, meshing with two smaller gears, called pinions or spider gears.

The spider gear teeth, facing inward toward the center of the carrier case, engage with the side gear teeth.

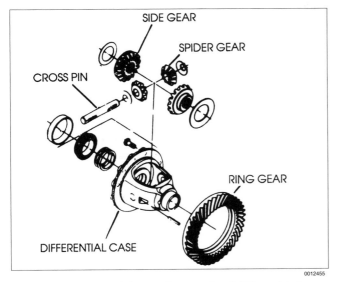

Fig. 10-23. Exploded view of conventional differential shows gear locations.

The spiders float on a pinion shaft, which mounts rigidly through the center of the carrier case. Effectively, the four gears can move independently of the carrier.

The result: 1) If road speed at both wheels remains the same, the gears all rotate like a solid unit in unison with the differential carrier case; 2) when turning a corner, the four gears can rotate at the speed necessary to apply more rpm at the outside wheel and proportionately less at the inside wheel; and 3) at times, discouragingly, the conventional differential mechanism directs power to the wheel with the least resistance. This last point remains the primary shortcoming of conventional, non-locking differentials.

When watching a 2WD truck negotiate rocks, sand and loose terrain, it's easy to distinguish the conventional rear axle. One wheel will often spin furiously, while the opposite wheel, with solid traction, stands still. Four-wheel drive models, even with conventional axles, fare much better than a 2WD truck.

Controlling Wheelspin

Traction loss is a serious problem. The other extreme is damage caused when no differential action takes place. A truck's handling with a permanently locked rear axle is very dangerous, too. For this reason, we depend upon systems that provide more positive traction but still allow differential action.

Ford F-Series light truck limited slip differentials enjoy a variety of trade names. Several aftermarket performance systems have also been developed, many suited for street, drag strip and off-pavement use. (See the performance section of the book for detailed information on aftermarket traction devices.)

Typically, a limited slip unit is built around a clutching mechanism within the differential. Simply put, the clutching device enables torque delivery to the axle and wheel with traction. The basic difference between factory limited slip and aftermarket locker differentials is the design of the clutching or lock-up mechanism.

By design, the clutch type limited slip unit can still allow variance of wheel speed on corners. The differential behaves in much the same manner as a conventional unit, permitting the inner wheel to rotate slower.

> **WARNING —**
> *Use caution with any limited slip or positive traction differential. Your truck will tend to go sideways when both wheels of an axle lose traction at the same time. On ice or slick pavement, locked traction at both wheels of an axle can cause sideward motion of the vehicle, most often toward the low side of the road. (See chapter on driving techniques for details.)*

Axle Types

Although integral housing hypoid axles require more tools for disassembly, they generally provide substantial ring and pinion support. Spicer's integral-type axles have served many Ford F-Series trucks. The Spicer/Dana 44, 60, 60 HD and the Spicer/Dana 70 have been popular rear axles over the years. Light F-truck 4x4 front axles include the Spicer/Dana 44, IFS-44, IFS-50 and Dana 60 units.

A similar integral rear axle design is the late Ford F150's 8.8-inch (ring gear diameter) Ford unit. This axle has replaced the rugged non-integral type 9-inch Ford carrier unit that served from 1957 to the mid-1980s, first in F-100s and then in F-150 models.

Semi- vs. Full-floating Axles

Semi-floating axles offer less safety margin than full-floating axles. On the semi-floater, a single outer wheel bearing supports the axle shaft, while the splined inner end of the axle shaft relies on the differential side gear for support. A broken axle shaft can cause real trouble.

Most semi-floating axles rely upon bearing retainer plates at the outer bearing to hold the axle in place. If the axle shaft should break in the wrong place, the broken axle shaft, hub and wheel can slide right out.

Some semi-floating axles use a C-lock at the inner end of each axle shaft, but the risk of losing an axle remains. C-locks and the inner axle shaft end can wear out, or the axle shaft could break and come loose, much like an axle shaft without a C-lock.

Full-floating axle shafts, by contrast, act simply as a drive bar. The wheel and hub ride on bearings much like on the front end of a conventional 4x4 truck. A retaining nut provides for hub bearing adjustment and also holds the wheel hub on the spindle.

The spindle is a component part of the axle housing, and the axle shaft fits through the spindle's bore. Engaging the side gear at its inner end, the axle shaft's outer flange bolts to the wheel hub. If an axle shaft breaks, the hub and wheel continue to rotate safely on the spindle. To remove the broken shaft, you unbolt its flange from the wheel hub and fish out the broken section. The wheel and tire remain on the ground, supported by the wheel hub bearings, so there is no need to even jack up the truck.

NOTE —
Since a broken front axle shaft or steering knuckle joint could impair steering and cause further axle damage, it's best to remove the axle shaft assembly before moving the vehicle.

To date, all Ford F-Series 4x4 light trucks have featured full-floating type front axles. Half-ton (F100/F150) 2WD and 4x4 models all feature semi-floating type rear axles. Until 1980, all F-250 and F-350 models use full-floating rear axles. Since then, however, only the F-250 Heavy Duty models and the more rugged one-ton F-350 have continued to use the full-floating rear axle design. For truck use, especially hauling cargos, carrying a fifth-wheel trailer or working off-pavement, the added stamina and safety of a full-floating type axle is significant.

NOTE —
Ford has kept full-floating 4x4 front axles longer than the competitive models from GM and Dodge. As of the 1994 model year, full-floating front axle wheel hubs still prevail in F-150, F-250 and F-350 4x4s. Manual locking hubs are still available for these trucks. Consider this a virtue. A full-floating front axle with free wheeling hubs provides the only means for completely eliminating front axle and driveline wear.

Ford 4x4 Front Axle Types

Two primary changes have occurred in F-truck 4x4 front axles. The shift to open steering knuckles with ball-joints began in 1966, when Ford's F-100 models and the new Bronco pioneered use of this design. The change to independent front suspension (IFS) on F-150 and F-250 4x4s came in 1980. All F-250 4x4 live front axles remained closed knuckle type until the gradual changeover to open knuckles began with 1973 light duty rated F-250 front axles.

Closed knuckle front ends use kingpin bearings (tapered roller type) or conical bronze bushings. Open knuckles use ball-joints or pivot pins and bushings. Prior to 1966, all Ford 4x4s featured closed front steering knuckles.

The closed knuckle axle system features fully enclosed front axle shaft joints (Spicer cross type) that receive grease from the sealed knuckle cavity. The later open knuckle axle joints are also Spicer-type U-joints, permanently sealed with grease.

NOTE —
Permanently sealed joints are easy to distinguish. They have no provision for a grease fitting. Always replace these joints with a sealed joint of the same OEM design.

Drive Axle Troubleshooting

Before suspecting trouble with your truck's axles, check the fluid levels and also the type of gear lubricant required. On limited slip differentials, special lubes prevent multi-plate clutches from sticking together. If you introduce a non-specified oil to these axles, symptoms of differential trouble can result.

Try to isolate the noise. Tire sounds, front or rear wheel bearing noises, engine and transmission troubles and even the type of road surface can confuse the situation. Especially with oversize tires, light trucks often develop noises that have nothing to do with the differential or any other axle component, yet the sound comes from that area. Check each of these other possibilities before condemning your axle(s).

A clicking or patterned ratcheting noise at the rear wheels is a possible wheel bearing problem. By supporting the rear axle safely on jack stands, you can rotate each wheel by hand and feel for bearing roughness. (See other chapters of the book for front wheel bearing inspection and service.)

If you detect an actual wheel bearing problem, consult your Ford F-Series truck shop manual or a professional level service manual for details on axle shaft removal and wheel bearing service.

Differential side gear and small pinion (spider) gear noises are most often heard when the vehicle turns. If your truck has a conventional or limited slip rear axle that makes noises as the vehicle negotiates a corner, suspect differential trouble. Similar front axle noises, especially with the hubs engaged and the transfer case in 4WD, also suggest differential trouble, although a defective axle shaft joint can mimic these sounds.

A continuous grating noise that varies with vehicle speed suggests pinion bearing failure. Trucks that run in deep water without frequent changes of gear lubricant are vulnerable to ring gear, pinion gear or bearing failure.

Ring and pinion noise is distinguishable under various driving conditions: coast, drive or float. Deceleration creates coast noises. Drive noises are detectable as you accelerate the truck. Float noise occurs under light throttle situations and easy loads that keep the ring and pinion gears spinning with the least amount of pressure.

When your truck's axle gear lubricant smells badly burned, remove the inspection cover and examine the gear teeth and bearings. Blue discoloration usually indicates extreme heat, fatigue and poor lubrication.

CAUTION —
If lubricant is very low for any length of time, the axle is subject to major parts damage. Always watch for seal leaks or other symptoms of fluid loss. Proper fluid levels are crucial to axle survival.

Seal Leaks

Seal failure is a primary cause of fluid loss on truck axles. Look closely for fluid loss at the axles whenever you service your truck, and watch for oil drips when you park the vehicle. The locations for axle seal leaks are easy

Fig. 10-24. A pinion seal leak is easy to spot. Loss of lubrication can lead to expensive parts damage.

Fig. 10-25. This tool, fabricated twenty years ago with simple materials, holds the U-joint flange. The pinion shaft nut torque is very high, and heavy leverage is necessary. Today, the option for most mechanics is an air impact gun. Always set and check final torque with a torque wrench.

to monitor, beginning with the pinion shaft seal, the ventilation valve (if so equipped) and the axle shaft seals.

The pinion shaft seal is very easy to locate. Follow the driveshaft to the U-joint flange, then note the point at which the pinion shaft enters the axle housing. The seal that surrounds the shaft at the entrance to the axle housing is the pinion shaft seal.

Axle shaft seal leaks appear as oil dripping from the bottom of the rear brake backing plates or at the steering knuckle on an open-knuckle front end. Axle seal leaks on closed-knuckle front ends can lead to dangerously diluted wheel bearing lubricant. Often the closed knuckle system's large diameter inner axle housing seal will leak visibly. (See brake section for details on parts damage from leaking axle seals.)

When a seal leak occurs, first check the lubricant levels. Overfilled steering knuckles or differentials will cause leaks and can even dislodge a seal by hydraulic pressure. Again, a common leak on all closed-knuckle front ends is the large inner oil seal. This seal at the inner side of the steering knuckle will leak grease from the knuckle cavity. You can replace this seal without removing the entire steering knuckle.

Axle Seal Installation Tips

Front drive axle seals are difficult to replace. Rear axle seals are also a handful. You'll want to do the job right the first time. Axle pinion seal replacement requires a holding tool to keep the U-joint flange from rotating while you loosen its nut. As an option, mechanics usually use an air impact gun.

Before installing a pinion seal, clean the housing bore thoroughly. Be certain to apply a thin film of gasket sealant to the outer edge of the seal. Coat the inner lip of the seal with light grease. (Early models use leather seals that require soaking the seal in oil before installation. Neoprene replacement seals are now available.)

Tap the seal gently and evenly in cross. I like to use a rubber or plastic sand head hammer to avoid damaging or distorting the steel portion of the seal. Although I've always had access to special seal drivers, I feel that carefully placed hammer taps can produce the same results—and often better. Without a solid driver, you can maintain the *feel* for what you're doing by using a soft headed hammer and a light touch.

Coat the backside of the pinion flange washer with a thin film of gasket sealant, and install a new self-locking nut if required. Torque the nut to OEM specifications found in your Ford F-Series shop manual or a professional level guidebook.

Other seals, including the front and rear axle shaft seals, are more difficult to access. Fortunately, seal replacement is relatively easy on Ford 9-inch axles and earlier semi-floating Spicer type axles found in light duty half-ton trucks. Later models with C-locks can be a much messier job. Follow the F-truck shop manual when servicing the axle.

Front Axle and Knuckle Seals

By careful seal placement and use of sealant, you can change a closed knuckle inner split ring seal and felt without removing the steering knuckle. The closed-knuckle inner felt seal can be carefully cut on a diagonal. (See my step-by-step illustrations or your OEM shop manual for details.)

After carefully sliding the split seal/wiper into place, the sealant, cut felt and retainer halves can also fit around the axle housing's tube and against the ball end. Follow the illustrations for this procedure.

> **NOTE —**
> When servicing the closed knuckle front end, be aware that spindle bolts have a nasty habit of loosening on the steering knuckle and shredding the spindle gasket (if so equipped). Once loose, a very unsafe condition exists, with the risk of shearing the bolts or threads that attach the spindle to the knuckle casting.

Fig. 10-26. *An early closed-knuckle front axle trait: the spindle's six bolts have ripped cleanly from the threaded holes in the steering knuckle.*

Some remedies for this chronic spindle bolt problem include 1) drilling and wire tying the bolt heads to aircraft standards, 2) replacing the bolts with Grade 8 studs secured with thread locking compound, then using aircraft Grade 8 self-locking nuts to secure the spindle, or 3) installing special aftermarket buttonhead (aircraft tensile strength) studs that have a serrated shoulder and compact round head. The studs pass from inside the knuckle through the thread holes and face outward to receive the spindle, looking much like the later open knuckle type. The spindle then attaches with self-locking aircraft nuts.

NOTE —
While some Spicer/Dana OEM spindles attach with bolts and split lockwashers, others use conical washers. I prefer the conical washer for its full locking surface and long service life, plus a dose of Loctite 242 on cleaned threads to provide added insurance.

Closed-knuckle Steering Rebuild

The original 4x4 live front axles all had closed-knuckle steering mechanisms. A popular Ford 4x4 F-truck axle was the closed-knuckle Spicer/Dana 44, used from 1959 into the 1970s. A traditional Spicer full-floating design, these closed-knuckle units now have many miles on them, and most have fallen victim to fatigue and wear.

Before the ball-joint or open-knuckle era, these axles provided the rugged service and stamina that a 4x4 needed. In the interest of your truck's steering safety and for a leak-free closed-knuckle system, here is an illustrated restoration/rebuild that I performed on a common closed-knuckle Dana 44 front axle.

Individual model years require different specifications. This how-to provides an overview of the closed-knuckle Spicer/Dana axle's steering wear points, repair needs and general overhaul requirements. See your OEM shop manual for specifications and recommendations for your truck's live front axle. Remember, when done right, this job should last for 100,000 miles or more.

Fig. 10-27. *Closed knuckle steering served Spicer live axles from 1941 until mid-1970s. Knuckles pivot on pins and tapered roller bearings or bronze conical bushings. Wear occurs at pivot pin bearings or bushings, seals and steering linkage. Axle U-joint is within the spherical housing end, enclosed by steering knuckle casting.*

Fig. 10-28. *Rebuild begins with removing tie-rod assembly and drag link. Inspect for wear and replace any worn pieces.*

Fig. 10-29. *First part of this job resembles wheel bearing repack. Remove brake drum and free wheeling hub. In applications where time has frozen parts together, it will be easier to remove drum-and-wheel hubs as an assembly. (Closed-knuckle live front axles have drum brakes.)*

Fig. 10-30. *Some wheel bearing applications use double hex nuts and a lock plate, others use two special nuts with a locating pin and indexing lock ring. Consult your service manual for details on wheel bearing service and adjustment.*

Fig. 10-31. *Disconnect brake pipes or hoses before removing brake backing plate. Use a flare nut wrench and be sure to keep debris out of the brake system. Seal pipe end with a clean cap.*

Fig. 10-32. *Unbolt wheel hub spindle and remove the brake backing plate and spindle. Avoid getting grease on brake lining. Axle shaft will slide easily from housing.*

Fig. 10-33. *Remove retainer plates, felt seal and rear knuckle seal. Plates, felt and large steel reinforced neoprene seal will come loose once you remove these screws.*

Fig. 10-34. *With seals loose, remove lower bearing cap bolts. Keep cap and shims together, as these shims are selective fit and set the proper preload on pivot pin bearings.*

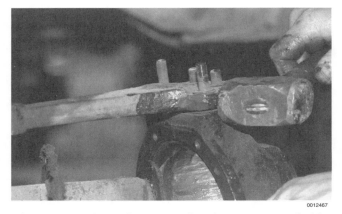

Fig. 10-35. *At steering arm, studs and nuts are centered with split ring cone washers. Tap at side of arm with a plastic or brass hammer to unseat cones. Pry cones out before attempting to remove arm. Knuckle is now free. (Axle shaft will slide easily from the housing once wheel spindle is removed. Slide shaft very carefully to avoid damage to axle shaft seals.)*

Fig. 10-36. *Clean and inspect all parts. Replace worn or damaged bearings and castings. Check for cracks and fatigue. Take this opportunity to repaint outer hub, knuckle and brake drum's outer surface with high temp engine paint.*

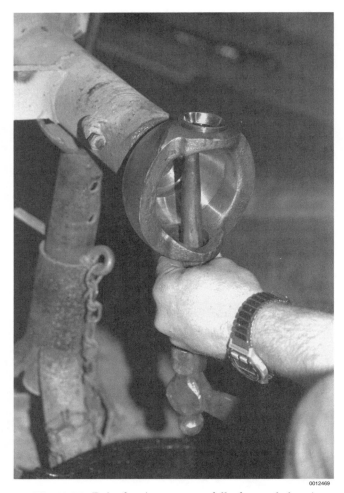

Fig. 10-37. *Drive bearing cups carefully from axle housing seats. Avoid damage to axle casting and inspect housing ends for cracks or damage. Clean housing end and use crocus cloth to eliminate burrs or scratches to machined ball-shaped seal surfaces. Install new cups squarely with a cup driver.*

Fig. 10-38. *Bearing cups show reason for sloppy front knuckle and excessive play. This 44 application uses conical bushings at top pivot pins and tapered roller bearing cones at bottom. Conical bushings wore, and lower bearing rollers pounded bearing cups. (Some applications use tapered roller bearings at both upper and lower pivot pins.)*

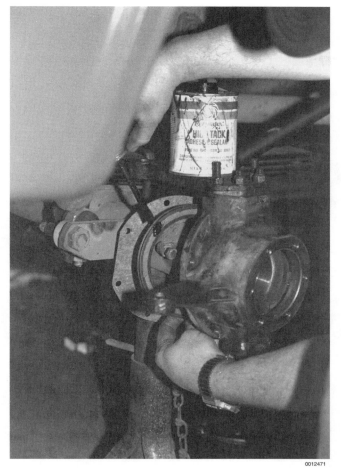

Fig. 10-39. *Although some cut felt seal straight for installation, I make a diagonal cut and place split at top of knuckle with Permatex High Tack sealant applied at cut point. Diagonal cut resists moisture penetration at the split.*

Fig. 10-40. *Carefully spread neoprene seal, just enough to twist sideways around inner side of axle spherical end. Once walked around housing tube, seal can be straightened for seating at back of knuckle. Apply High Tack at split.*

Fig. 10-41. *Straighten tin plates where bolts attach. Do not overtorque these bolts. (See your manual for tightening specifications.) Plates secure felt and large neoprene seal.*

Fig. 10-42. *Packed with grease, upper conical bushing fits into newly installed bearing cup. Conical bushings need light coaxing (plastic hammer or wood block) onto pivot pin. Make certain bearing cups are firmly seated into axle housing for accurate preload adjustment. Hand pack tapered roller bearings with grease before installation.*

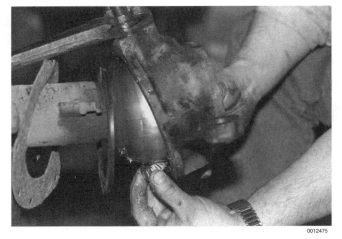

Fig. 10-43. Set top shim(s) into place and attach upper bearing cap or steering arm. (You may need to tap bronze conical bushing onto pivot pin before installing cap. If this design, carefully align teeth or locating key during installation.) Set grease-packed lower bearing into its bearing cup. Slip knuckle onto upper bearing cup. Swing knuckle over lower bearing.

Fig. 10-45. When upper and lower bearing cap fasteners are torqued to specification, you can check steering knuckle drag (bearing preload). Rotate knuckle at bearing cap studs and read torque. Note that inner seal and steering linkage are not attached during this check. Your service book will give required torque specifications. As an alternative, some Spicer axles call for spring scale test. Hook scale into tie-rod socket and move knuckle. Read amount of pull required to keep knuckle moving through its arc.

Fig. 10-44. Use the original shims between lower bearing cap and knuckle. Tighten slowly, moving knuckle as you attempt to seat bolts. Stop if knuckle will not move, and increase shim pack thickness. Too loose, you will need to decrease shim thickness. Check your shop manual for recommendations on the placement and thickness of upper and lower shims.

Fig. 10-46. Oil the felt lightly with a quality penetrating oil. You should apply Permatex High Tack to split at upper end of felt seal and carefully align the split during its assembly. Apply High Tack to split in neoprene seal. Install felt and retainer plate halves carefully, making sure neoprene seal and felt each seat properly into place. Torque bolts to specification or snugly, in a manner that will not warp plates or distort the felt seal.

Fig. 10-47. *Grease or oil splined inner end of axle, and carefully keep axle shaft centered during installation to avoid damaging axle shaft seals within housing tubes. Backing plate and spindle will slide into place. Bolts that retain backing plate and spindle to knuckle housing have a habit of loosening. Some replace OEM hardware with pre-drilled aircraft Grade 8 bolts and wire ties. I opt for heavy duty OEM-type conical washers and Grade 8 bolts, cleaning threads with Loctite Kleen & Prime, then applying liberal amount of Loctite 242 onto bolt threads.*

Fig. 10-48. *Always tighten spindle bolts in cross, then set final torque with a torque wrench. See your shop manual for correct tightening specifications. Final step is to refill knuckles with recommended lubricant or grease, the type noted in your shop manual or owner's handbook.*

4. FREE-WHEEL LOCKING HUBS

Free wheeling hubs stretch drivetrain component life by thousands of miles. Manual or automatic locking hubs eliminate front axle shaft rotation during two-wheel drive operation. Hubs save wear on front axle joints, seals, the differential assembly, and front driveshaft components. Drag, especially in cold weather, translates to added engine wear, increased clutch effort, and a loss of fuel economy.

On most 4x4 full-floating front wheel spindles and hub castings, you can install retrofit manual or automatic locking hubs. By design, a full-floating system affords safe operation and rotation of the wheels, with or without an intact axle shaft. This type of spindle and hub flange also allows use of free-wheeling hubs.

Full-floating wheel hubs, supported by inner and outer wheel bearings, ride on the spindle. The axle shaft fits through the hollow recess of this spindle, and the spindle attaches to the steering knuckle.

At the splined outer end of the axle shaft, a drive flange attaches to the wheel hub casting, much like the systems found on older 3/4-ton and larger truck rear axles. Here, the axle delivers its rotational force to the wheel hub, wheel and tire.

Fig. 10-49. *Aftermarket free-wheeling hubs have existed since the 1940s. Hubs come in many shapes and sizes to fit various axle splines and wheel hub flanges.*

All early 4x4 locking hub systems were manual. Highly dependable, manual hub designs survive to this day. Although locking mechanisms differ between manufacturers, each design disconnects power flow from the axle shafts to the front wheel hub flanges. Providing a means to disconnect rotational force, free-wheel/locking hubs allow the wheel hub, wheel and tire to free-wheel on the spindle.

Automatic locking hubs came in the wake of troublesome 'full-time' four-wheel drive. The full-time 4x4 systems, which proved costly to maintain and taxing to fuel economy, eliminated free-wheeling hubs.

While many owners appreciated the convenience of having no hubs to operate, they were glad to see an end to full-time 4x4. Bridging the gap, automatic hubs pro-

Fig. 10-50. This very early Warn system was clearly manual. The hub cap bolted in place of an OEM drive flange and permitted wheel hubs to rotate without turning the axle shafts. By 1959, when Ford introduced its first factory 4x4 F-trucks, Warn hubs had evolved far past this design.

vide easier operation for a part-time four-wheel drive system. I still prefer manual locking hubs, despite the inconvenience. (See chapter on vehicle operation for tips on making manual hub use easier.)

Maintaining Your Locking Hubs

Many four-wheelers wrestle with their front wheel locking hubs. Some go to extremes, fabricating special tools for muscling the manual hub knob. Whenever more than light hand force is necessary, there's something wrong with the hub mechanism or its installation.

Laid out, the parts of a locking hub can include a clutch mechanism, springs, locking clips or drive plates. Manual hubs utilize sleeve bushings, needle bearings, ball or roller bearings. Periodic bench stripping and service of the front hubs will assure free movement and proper lubrication of all parts.

Free-wheeling hub bearings and bushings cannot tolerate the rotational loads of parts running at speed. If pressed into such service, as when one hub is accidently left in LOCK while the other is on FREE, a free-wheeling hub assembly will quickly fail. Periodic disassembly and cleaning help reduce the risk of dragging hubs.

Servicing hubs is relatively simple and should accompany every front wheel bearing repack. Repeated or prolonged submersion of your 4x4 truck in deep, fast-running water requires immediate hub disassembly and inspection for water damage. The sealing areas of hubs deteriorate over time, another reason for periodic inspection and service.

Service Work

Servicing front wheel locking hubs is well within a competent mechanic's ability. Hub disassembly requires basic handtools, including a torque wrench and snap ring pliers. As always, seek out a service guidebook. A detailed schematic of the hubs will eliminate guesswork as you inventory parts.

Servicing hubs requires cleanliness and order. Remove parts carefully, noting their relationship to each other. Lay pieces on clean newspaper or shop towels. Clean pieces carefully in solvent. (Avoid harsh cleaners that affect plastic parts.) Clean grease will not adhere properly to solvent coated parts. Rinse away solvent with a dish detergent solution and a clean water rinse, then air dry (preferably with compressed air) before regreasing parts.

CAUTION —
Never spin a bearing with compressed air. High speed, friction and stress could score the bearings or cause the assembly to explode.

Use a grease recommended for your hubs. If wheel bearing type is acceptable, use the same grease that you use for your front wheel bearings. This often falls into the category of high temp wheel bearing grease, recommended for disc brake equipped applications. Such greases have excellent heat resistance yet afford the viscosity needed for free hub movement on those -40° F mornings in North Dakota. Avoid mixing unknown grease types—perform a major wheel bearing repack at the same time.

Service kits are inexpensive and provide cheap insurance against hub sealing problems. The O-ring or paper gasket that looks marginal is a risk. For a few dollars, new seals and other hardware will keep water out of your hubs and wheel bearings. Properly and sparingly applied, a silicone compound like Permatex Ultra-Blue can provide additional protection in areas that require gasket sealant.

As with any mechanism, inspect parts carefully. Look for bushing wear, galling, scoring and binding of parts. Include emery cloth in your service tools for light touch-up of rough or scratched pieces. Clean thoroughly after sanding. Dry before repacking.

Fig. 10-51. For ease of maintenance, most hub manufacturers offer service kits for their hubs. Warn's kits consist of paper gaskets, snap rings, O-rings, new Allen head screws, and bolt lock tabs if required.

Fig. 10-52. First step in overhaul of Warn hub is removal of free-wheeling hub unit from the wheel hub flange.

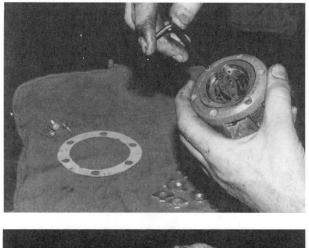

Fig. 10-53. Disassembly begins with clutch mechanism flange screws.

Fig. 10-54. Drive hub rides in needle bearings on this early Warn hub design. Watch out for falling needle bearings!

Fig. 10-55. Spring roll pin locks clutch unit to flange.

Fig. 10-56. Mark or scribe location of plate to flange.

Fig. 10-57. *Now remove the spring clutch mechanism.*

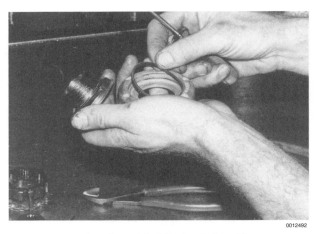

Fig. 10-60. *Another critical O-ring is found here.*

Fig. 10-58. *Snap ring holds hub knob to flange.*

Fig. 10-61. *Scrape gasket material from surfaces before thoroughly cleaning parts.*

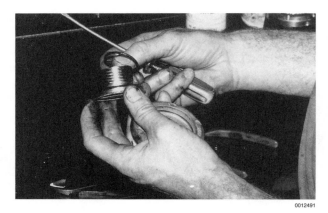

Fig. 10-59. *With knob removed, important O-ring is accessible. Here's where water often seeps into hub units.*

Fig. 10-62. *After a hot tank dip, thorough rinse and air blow drying, these clean pieces can go back together.*

Fig. 10-63. Pack the cavity of the needle bearing bore with a compatible wheel bearing grease. Needles are carefully replaced. Last bearing holds set together by keystone effect. After a hot tank dip, thorough rinse and air blow drying, these clean pieces can go back together.

Fig. 10-64. Drive hub, with proper spacer/thrust washers in place, goes easily into bearing bore.

Fig. 10-65. Snap ring secures drive hub.

Fig. 10-66. Install new O-rings, greased lightly, to base of brass knob assembly and to cover.

Fig. 10-67. Install the hub knob and place in FREE position.

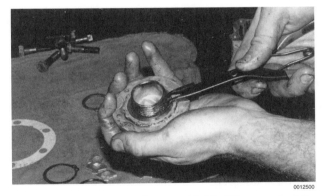

Fig. 10-68. New snap ring, provided in Warn service kit, fits at base of knob.

Fig. 10-69. With clutch spring mechanism screwed into place, reinstall spring roll pin.

Fig. 10-70. Check clutch movement by rotating hub knob to LOCK, then slide clutch mechanism into the clean, lightly greased hub body bore. Careful fitup, torquing bolts, and bending lock tabs will help assure proper operation.

Once clean, the hubs reassemble easily on the workbench. After putting each unit back together, make certain that the finger control works freely and smoothly. Hubs that test friction-free on the bench should provide easy operation on the vehicle.

Before reinstalling the hubs, carefully inspect the wheel hub mounting flange. Internal splines must be free of debris, rough edges or galling. High-grade hardware, specified for this installation, is necessary. The mounting bolts are subject to tremendous stress, so tighten them in sequence. Recheck final torque before securing new lock tabs. Some bolt applications require wire tying, Loctite Threadlocker or special lock washers.

Suggestion: Hub mounting bolts on some applications may loosen or even shear. One remedy is the installation of Grade 8 studs set with thread locking compound and using aircraft grade self-locking nuts. In severe operation, this has prevented many hub and casting failures.

Lastly, especially if your 4x4 truck was purchased used, be certain that all locking hub parts are present. Often, after several services, small pieces get lost. Find a blow-up schematic in a service guide, parts catalog or manufacturer's literature. Compare your pieces with those required, and restore the hubs accordingly.

Retrofitting New Hubs

Eventually, your truck's free-wheeling hubs will wear out. The effects of weather, age and abuse take their toll. (Late model automatic locking hubs may simply fail to meet your requirements.) Fortunately, you can retrofit a set of quality manual hubs.

A variety of new hubs are available through aftermarket suppliers. When selecting new hubs, consider your driving habits and intended use of the truck. Although price often influences your decision, weigh the cost against the inconvenience of walking home from a remote mountain range or the desert.

Since free-wheeling hubs require the same stamina as the differential, transfer case or transmission, consider upgrading your equipment. The controversy around automatic locking hubs continues. I maintain a singular view on the subject: Unless you need automatic hubs to offset a physical disability or other medical problem, forget them!

Whenever possible, I request new test vehicles with manual hubs or a delete-automatic-hubs option. I always retrofit manual hubs if I buy a used 4x4 equipped with automatic hubs. To me, stepping from the truck to twist manual hubs into LOCK mode is worth it. At least I'm certain the hubs have engaged. Uphill or down, I know that positive engine power and compression braking will assure safe four-wheeling.

Chapter 11

Suspension and Steering

SEVERAL YEARS AGO, my journalist's duties had me interviewing Jim Sickles at Downey Off-Road. When my questions shifted to worn suspension parts, Jim commented, "Springs are a perishable commodity." No vehicle proves this point better than a light truck, whether 2WD or a 4x4!

Fatigue, owner upgrades and modifications limit the life-span of springs, shock absorbers, shackles, bushings and steering linkage. Changes in tire diameter or the need to carry an extra load can also demand more body clearance. For serious off pavement use, special spring rates can offer an advantage.

1. SPRINGS

On F-trucks with leaf spring suspension, three criteria govern suspension height and spring rates: 1) the necessary eye-to-eye length of leaf springs, 2) arch of leaf springs, and 3) plate thickness for each spring leaf. Leaf spring arch also affects your truck's ride height, while leaf plate thickness and taper control the spring rate.

On models with coil springs, like those found on front ends of 1965–up F-100 4x4s, F-150 4x4s and 2WD light F-trucks built from the mid-'60s forward, wire diameter and free length/height determines suspension height and spring rate. Another factors is coil spring length.

For light truck trailer pulling, heavy cargos or off-pavement four-wheel drive use, custom springs and shock absorbers can remedy a multitude of quirks. Often you can order such products with your new truck. In other cases your truck may need special suspension products, available through aftermarket vendors or a custom spring shop.

Although inexpensive modifications meet some tire clearance and ride height needs, the right springs offer a much better solution. For oversized tire clearance, a properly engineered lift spring set or custom coil spring and radius arm kit can raise chassis/body height without compromising axle caster or pinion/driveshaft angles. When age and fatigue become a problem, a traditional spring/blacksmith shop can also fabricate stock-type replacement springs that will improve both the suspension longevity and ride quality.

WARNING —
Front axle spacer blocks and homemade lift kits are not only unsafe but also illegal in most states. F-100/F-150 4x4 models with radius arms are especially vulnerable to handling quirks when lifted incorrectly. See the suspension upgrade chapter for details on safe kits and what to seek when modifying your truck chassis.

Fig. 11-1. Ride or suspension height is determined by springs (leaf or coil) and how they are mounted. Rear leaf springs are common on all Ford light trucks. Support for working on the truck would be a set of 5-ton (per stand) rated jackstands. Don't compromise here. Your life and limbs are at stake.

Fig. 11-2. Twin I-Beam suspension came on line in 1965, giving Ford F-trucks their first independent suspension system. Twin I-Beam incorporates the durability of a conventional I-beam axle with the independent movement and more pleasurable ride quality of coil springs.

Installing New Leaf Springs

Leaf spring replacement is relatively simple. Unlike torsion bar and coil spring installations, there is no threat of a loaded spring flailing out of its socket like a missile. If you keep the axles safely away from the springs until all spring mounting hardware is attached, there's very little risk of injury. Although awkward, truck leaf spring replacement is reasonably easy.

When aligning the parts, mount the spring in the frame anchor first, then secure the hardware. Attach the shackle assembly at the opposite end of the spring, tightening all hardware to specifications found in your OEM shop manual.

You may find it easier to bend out a slight amount of arch from the spring before clamping the axle U-bolts into place. (Compress the spring slightly with a safe garage-type floor jack beneath the axle, just enough for the axle's spring pad to drop into place at the spring center bolt.)

> **NOTE —**
> Especially with new lift springs, spring compression may be necessary to achieve spring conformation at the original axle center point. Use a garage-type floor jack, which will place you safely away from the axle and the loaded spring.

Attach the U-bolts carefully, tightening U-bolt nuts uniformly. Watch the exposed thread lengths to determine equal tightening. Torque nuts in sequence. (See your Ford F-truck shop manual for tightening specifications.) Gradually tighten each nut until you have reached full torque value and the bolt threads extend evenly past the nuts. Properly installed springs often live well past 100,000 miles, depending on how and where you drive your truck.

Fig. 11-3. When installing U-bolts, tighten nuts evenly and in a cross pattern. At final torque, all exposed threads should be of equal length. Re-check torque periodically.

> **NOTE —**
> After driving a few miles, re-torque these spring U-bolt nuts. It's also a smart policy to re-check U-bolt torque periodically, especially on 4x4 models.

Shackles and Their Bushings

The leaf springs on your truck move in a shackle. Early models use bronze bushings and serviceable shackles. Later models use low-maintenance rubber bushings. Eventually, either type of shackle bushing will wear out.

Always replace the shackle bushings when noticeable wear develops. Even with proper lubrication, the earliest (1948–56 light F-truck) bushings will wear out. Often, if the bushings have not received grease for a long time, wear occurs. A grease job often turns up loose and worn parts.

> *CAUTION —*
> *Spring bushings and frame hanger designs vary. Each type requires specific torque settings for both the pivot bolts and shackle nuts. Refer to your F-Series truck shop manual for further details on spring assembly methods and torque settings.*

Coil Spring Front Suspension

Ford introduced independent coil spring front suspension with the 1965 F-100 (2WD and 4WD models) and the F-250 2WD truck. In 1967, the 2WD F-350 models also changed from a single I-beam front axle with leaf springs to the newer coil spring Twin I-Beam front suspension system.

In its essential form, Twin I-Beam coil spring suspension survives at the mid-1990s on all 2WD light F-trucks. Only the F-350 Super Duty models use an I-beam axle and leaf front springs, a rugged design that mimics systems found on medium duty F-trucks.

The F-150 4x4 pickups also feature coil spring suspension similar to the 2WD models, with the addition of a Twin Traction-Beam front axle design in 1980. Ford 4x4 half-ton trucks have used coil spring suspension since 1965.

By basic structure, the twin-beam coil front spring chassis has changed only slightly since 1965. Key components include 1) the radius arms for fore and aft support of the twin axle beams, 2) two pivoting axle beams on 1980–up F-150 4x4 Twin Traction-Beam axles and all 2WD Twin I-Beam models from 1965–up, 3) the chassis/frame towers for supporting the coil springs and 4) steering linkage that accommodates the movement of two axle beams. These beams pivot from bushings mounted at frame supports on both the 2WD Twin I-Beam models and Twin Traction-Beam 4x4 trucks.

The 1965–79 F-100 4x4s and '76–'79 F-150 4x4 models have a non-independent type solid front driving axle. However, these trucks share many chassis features with 2WD Twin I-Beam models and the later Twin Traction-Beam F-150 4x4 trucks. From a maintenance standpoint, several of the items that require attention on the 2WD

Fig. 11-4. *2WD Twin I-Beam and 4WD Twin Traction-Beam suspension incorporates coil springs and radius arms as part of the front end system. Solid strength of I-beams or* *hefty traction-beams offers truck stamina with a bonafide independent ride quality.*

Twin I-Beam and later 4WD Twin Traction-Beam suspension systems also apply to these 1965–79 1/2-ton Ford 4x4s.

Twin-beam Wear Points

The Twin I-Beam, Twin Traction-Beam and 1965–79 1/2-ton 4x4 front axle suspension systems have several wear points. Radius arm bushings and axle beam C-bushings deteriorate over time, a factor that affects wheel alignment, handling and safety. Steering linkage wear is also a trouble area.

Two-wheel drive Twin I-Beam front ends originally used kingpins and greaseable bronze bushings at the steering knuckles, a tradition that carries forth from the earlier I-beam axle F-trucks. Beginning in 1980, kingpins were abandoned on some F- and E-trucks (light duty models), replaced by upper and lower steering knuckle ball-joints.

These ball-joints, fitted at the ends of 2WD Twin I-Beam axles, look much like the ball-joints on open knuckle 4x4 steering systems. (The likeness suggests that this is the origin of the design.) Into the 1990s, Ford F-models use either ball-joint or kingpin type steering knuckles.

Whether your 2WD F-truck has kingpins or ball-joints, either design is prone to wear and requires replace-

Fig. 11-5. *Radius arm bushings and C-bushings wear and cause looseness in front end. This affects wheel alignment and safe handling. Always consider these wear points when your Ford F-truck wanders or tracks poorly.*

ment service at high mileage. The Ford F-Series shop manual describes the procedure for replacing kingpins, which requires access to a machine shop for pressing the bushings in and out. Reaming/fitting new bushings is also a machine shop procedure.

CAUTION —

You will find that an older or high mileage truck's kingpins are likely frozen in the axle beam. Use caution and protective safety eyewear when driving old kingpins from position. The kingpin is exceptionally hard steel. Avoid flattening its end—use a plastic head hammer if possible. Most truck owners prefer to send this job to a well equipped front end alignment and frame shop.

The procedure for changing ball-joints on 2WD and 4x4 models, plus information about minor camber corrections, is within your Ford F-Series Truck Shop Manual or a professional level service guidebook. Review this task before proceeding. You may decide that sending out such work is appropriate. (Also see illustrations for 4x4 ball-joint replacement in this chapter.)

Frame Damage

Off-pavement pounding and heavy hauling can damage your truck's frame. All Ford F-Series trucks feature a drivable chassis or ladder frame. Subject to severe twisting and overload, frame damage is possible.

During routine service, inspect your truck's frame. Look closely for tears, cracks, wrinkles, loose rivets or damaged fasteners. Inspect axle housing mounts and spring hangers. All pivot bolts and other friction points require a close look. Make certain crossmembers are intact. On 4x4 models, consider the skid plates and transmission crossmember an integral part of the frame. Structural support and frame stiffness depend on intact crossmembers.

A common area of frame fatigue on earlier truck models with leaf springs, especially rigs with histories of hard use off-pavement, is just behind the front spring anchor points. The anchor (rear) end of the springs receives a great deal of punishment, as road and trail obstacles want to drive the front axle from beneath the truck. The frame, sadly, receives the brunt of the punishment and often cracks.

Under the most severe service, spring shackles on a leaf spring 4x4 can break, along with the front spring shackle upper frame supports. When such a truck twists in the off-pavement environment, harsh push and pull on the upper shackle supports can break the bracket or frame rail. (See suspension upgrade chapter for more details.) Also watch the steering gear mount on integral power steering models.

WARNING —

Fatigued or stress damaged spring shackles, frame brackets or spring hangers pose a safety hazard. Broken leaf springs can cause complete loss of vehicle control. Inspect your truck's frame and spring supports regularly.

2. SHOCK ABSORBERS

Single, dual and gas shocks...The market seems glutted with shock absorbers. What do you need? Which shock design works best? Is there a formula for choosing the right shock absorbers? You bet!

Shock absorbers make a major contribution to your truck's handling, ride, braking and safety. As shocks wear and fatigue, they lose their effectiveness. On most off-highway vehicles, the original shock absorber set fails before any other chassis item. Shocks deteriorate rapidly under excessive heat, friction and overwork.

Anatomy Of A Shock Absorber

All shock absorbers meet the same goals: 1) damping the oscillating motion of the vehicle frame and body, 2) limiting the rebound effects as uneven loads affect each wheel, and 3) keeping the wheels safely on the ground when suspension moves violently, like over rough washboard roads.

Your safety depends upon adequate shock absorbers. Off-pavement, your truck's suspension travels constantly, from full extension to pounding compression. Damping such forces, the shock absorbers pay the price, often succumbing to leakage or faulty performance. A bone jarring ride, squeaks and rattles develop when shock absorbers fail.

Of the two common shock absorber designs, single tube and twin tube, most truck manufacturers install the lighter duty single tube types, avoiding the more expensive and dependable twin tube or gas filled designs. Original equipment shocks concentrate on highway ride and driver comfort.

A single tube shock absorber has a machined steel cylinder and a rod/piston assembly. The body of the shock absorber holds an oil (plus freon or nitrogen on gas filled types) that resists the force of the moving piston. Precise valving in the piston controls the flow of oil, which helps regulate the movement of the rod.

Twin-tube shock absorbers provide the added benefit of a second valving and reservoir system. Beyond the valves on the piston head, these shocks provide a bottom

Fig. 11-6. Laid out, twin tube shock absorber components consist of an outer tube, inner tube and cylinder, plus the rod and valve assembly. Fluid fills the reservoir of this sealed Doetsch Tech unit.

Fig. 11-7. Piston head and cylinder have valves and precisely metered orifices. Doetsch Tech's Pre-Runner shocks boast progressive valving.

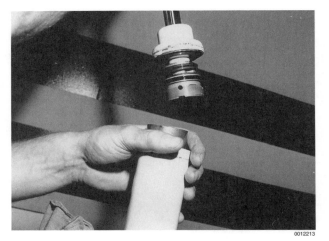

Fig. 11-8. O-ring sealing on these valves is sign of better quality.

check valve, permanently affixed to an inner, machined cylinder. Valving in the piston head allows fluid to bypass during shock absorber compression and rebound. The second, fixed valve enhances damping sensitivity. Located between the inside cylinder tube and outer shell reservoir of the shock absorber body, this valve enables fluid or gas pressure to act as an additional damping force.

When resistance against the piston is too great, the suspension cannot move. Too little damping will cause serious handling and ride problems. Therefore, the most important job for your truck's shock absorbers is to sense road forces and continually work to control them. The heat generated during rapid movement of the piston compounds that task by weakening the damping ability. Fluid fade directly corresponds to the velocity of the piston.

Shock absorber valving faces its greatest challenge when your truck tackles a washboard road. The better shock designs, which boast as many as ten stages of valving, compensate for the varying fluid velocities and heat demands found in severe off-pavement conditions.

Gas Shocks

Foaming (aeration) of fluid inhibits shock absorber action by creating gaps that cause erratic shock behavior or fade. The best counter measures employ gases such as freon (now outlawed as an environmental hazard) and nitrogen. These substances offset many of the troubles associated with hydraulic oils, including heat buildup.

> *WARNING —*
> *Freon is no longer used in gas shock absorber assemblies. Freon has been classified as an environmentally harmful (ozone depleting). Do not intentionally vent or cut open a freon charged shock absorber.*

When high performance and constant pounding demand real shock action, gas shocks do the job. Non-gas shocks suffer from oil thinning. They operate best under moderate piston velocities. By contrast, nitrogen gas keeps shocks cooler and foam-free, allowing valves and fluid to continue working, even at extreme piston velocities.

Popular nitrogen gas shocks come in two varieties: low and high pressure. As gas filled shocks place high loads on the rod and piston, many recreational and off-pavement users prefer low pressure gas shocks. (By contrast, desert racing demands high pressure, 200 psi-plus nitrogen gas damping.)

Selecting A Quality Shock Absorber

Most OEM shocks feature one-inch to 1-1/8" piston diameters. I feel that the minimum piston size for overall good performance should be 1-5/16". Popular for many years, the even larger 1-3/8" piston head satisfies all but the most brutal off-pavement maulers and heavyweight haulers.

> NOTE —
> Some Ford F-Series trucks come with optional gas-filled or heavy duty shock absorbers. If your truck is so equipped, be certain to replace these shocks with a similar type at replacement time.

A typical high performance shock is Rancho's RS 7000 series, a gas cell design with 1-5/8" piston diameters. The operating pressures of these shocks hover around 200 psi with chrome-hardened 17.3 millimeter rods. Sealing ability contributes to the life expectancy of shock absorbers. (See suspension upgrade chapter for additional details on performance shock absorbers.)

Pistons should be O-ring sealed, and the cylinder requires a tough double wall. Oversize fluid reservoirs provide better cooling and more resistance to fading. Refinement of the valve mechanism, that ability to sense terrain and load demands, will determine a shock absorber's worth. Proper shock damping serves as a primary element in a truck's suspension system.

Lastly, shock mounting grommets and eyes must hold up to road and load demands. A shock absorber is useless when detached or loose. A weak set of grommets allows wasted movement and undamped travel.

CHAPTER 11

3. 4X4 STEERING AND FRONT END

Off-highway driving can punish your truck's steering and suspension components. On 4x4 trucks, the live front axle design, especially with full-time 4x4, adds extra wear to the steering knuckle ball joints (open knuckle models) or kingpin bearings (earlier models).

Replacing a steering knuckle ball joint is a major job, requiring removal of the wheel hub assembly, spindle, axle shaft and steering knuckle. (For repairs on your live front axle unit, including axle shaft removal, refer to your factory-level service manual.)

Rebuilding A Battered Ball-joint Steering Knuckle

My friend Greg Williams is a veteran race truck suspension mechanic with a wealth of front end and suspension experience. At his East County Alignment day job, Greg rebuilds popular 4x4 steering and suspension systems regularly.

As an enhancement for this chapter, Greg helps illustrate repairs on a Dana 44 open-knuckle front axle. Here, a U-joint has blown apart, and Greg's work includes straightening the frame before making axle repairs. After removing the automatic locking hub and the rotor/wheel hub and bearing assembly, Greg tackles the steering knuckle removal.

WARNING —

Do not re-use any fasteners that are worn or deformed in normal use. Many fasteners are designed to be used only once and become unreliable and may fail when used a second time. This includes, but is not limited to, nuts, bolts, washers, self-locking nuts or bolts, circlips and cotter pins. For replacement always use new part of OEM grade and quality.

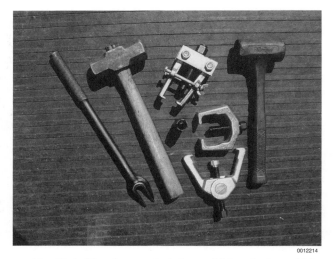

Fig. 11-9. *Use of proper tools is crucial to safe, dependable work. Steering knuckle replacement requires each of these tools. A spring scale is also necessary.*

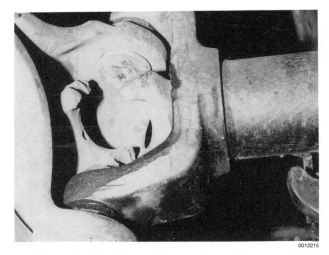

Fig. 11-10. *This Dana 44 front axle provides an excellent example of U-joint failure. The steering knuckle now needs replacement as a result of the damage.*

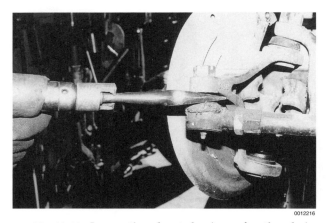

Fig. 11-11. *Loosen tie-rod nut, leaving a few threads in place to prevent tie-rod from falling. As joint will not be reused, insert a pickle fork between tie-rod joint and steering arm to separate the ball stud from its tapered seat in the arm. (Never use pickle fork if you plan to reuse the tie rod or ball-joint.)*

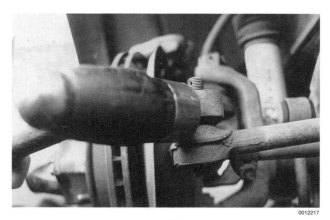

Fig. 11-12. *Alternate method for loosening tie-rods is a pair of hefty hammers. Place one at back of steering arm's tie-rod seat and rap the other hammer on the front of the arm. A sharp rap will dislodge the tapered ball stud from its seat. Take care not to damage the steering arm or tie-rod threads.*

Fig. 11-13. *Another method for loosening ball stud is to simply strike the flange near ball stud. With a few solid blows directed at flange, ball joint drops. (Lower ball joint nut is loose, but still in place to prevent spindle from falling to the ground.) Follow by removing upper ball joint adjusting sleeve using a specially keyed socket.*

NOTE —

Some OEM guides suggest loosening the upper and lower ball joint nuts until the top of the nut is flush with the end of its stud, and then rapping the top of the upper stud/nut squarely with a lead, brass or sand head hammer to unseat both joints. Consult your shop manual for approved methods.

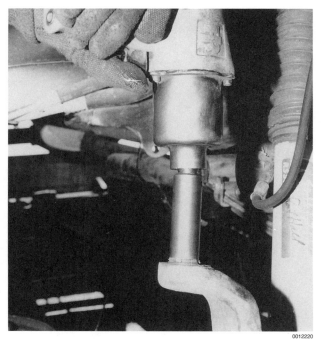

Fig. 11-15. *Installation of a new steering knuckle and adjuster sleeve is straightforward. Install adjuster sleeve loosely to allow tightening of lower ball-joint.*

Fig. 11-16. *Finger tighten the castellated upper nut to hold the knuckle in position while torquing the lower self-locking nut to specification. Now set the adjuster sleeve for proper pre-load on the ball joints, followed by final tightening of the upper nut. The castellated nut requires a new cotter pin. Replace self-locking nuts with new and identical OEM hardware.*

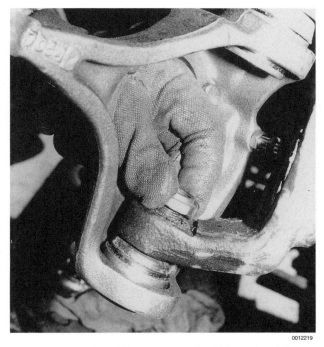

Fig. 11-14. *The self-locking nuts should be replaced during reassembly. Spindle nuts and lower ball-joint nuts are self-locking and should be replaced with new self-locking nuts during assembly.*

Fig. 11-17. *The axle shaft seals must be placed in order on the new axle. Use the original pieces as an example, or better yet, consult your OEM-level service manual's illustrations. Before installing the spindle, repack the needle bearing with fresh grease.*

Fig. 11-18. *Once the spindle is secure on the steering knuckle, proceed with wheel bearing service and assembly. (See next chapter or your OEM shop manual for details.) With wheel hub/rotor assembly installed, mount disc brake caliper and tie-rod. Torque bolts and tie-rod nut to specification, then install new cotter pin at tie-rod nut.*

Knuckle Assembly and Tie-rod Footnotes

The tapered and threaded upper ball joint seat is a critical part, responsible for setting a slight load on the ball joints for steering control and proper wear. Upon reassembly, adjust the new sleeve slightly loose until the lower ball joint is secure. While supporting the knuckle, torque the new self-locking nut to the lower ball joint stud.

Now, torque the adjusting sleeve at the upper ball joint to specification. (Find specs in your OEM-level service manual.) Lastly, torque the castellated ball stud nut to spec, completing the job with the installation of a new cotter pin.

Reassemble the remaining parts in the reverse order of disassembly. This is also a good time for a wheel bearing re-pack. Assemble wheel bearings carefully and adjust to spec. Include new inner wheel grease seals with the bearing pack. Follow the procedures and tightening specs outlined in your OEM-level shop manual.

Always use new self-locking nuts, new lock tabs or retainers and new cotter pins. Cleanly assembly methods during fit-up of parts, proper use of tools, and correct procedures for cleaning, re-packing and adjusting bearings will assure a safe job. If you intend to reuse parts, don't bang directly on the ball joints, tie-rod ends or their studs. Aim your sharp hammer blows carefully and protect the dust boots. Never use a pickle fork if you intend to reuse the ball-joints and their dust boots.

When adjusting wheel alignment or installing new steering linkage pieces, always center the tie-rod ends in the tie-rod sleeve. The ball studs and their sockets should line up evenly before you tighten the sleeve clamps. Make sure each tie-rod end has its full range of motion.

4x4 Closed-knuckle Axle With Kingpin Pivots

Earlier 4x4s with closed-knuckle axles use kingpin bearings rather than ball joints. At the bearing caps, shims control steering knuckle preload. When your early 4x4 truck has high mileage, the kingpin bearing clearance may increase enough to cause looseness at the knuckles or a kingpin shimmy. If inspection reveals excessive play, consider replacing the bearings and their races.

> *WARNING —*
> *When a large amount of kingpin play appears suddenly, suspect that kingpin bearing race or knuckle damage has occurred. Immediately repair the problem.*

You will find additional information on inspection and rebuilding procedures for a 4x4 closed-knuckle steering system in the chapter on axle and 4WD service. I cover routine lubrication service in the how-to maintenance and lubrication chapter.

Steering System

Whether your truck serves utility needs, lugs a travel trailer or plies recreational back country, safe vehicle control depends on a reliable steering system. Ford F-truck steering system layouts differ widely, both in design and function.

Fig. 11-19. Shims beneath the bearing caps on closed knuckles control the steering knuckle preload. Proper placement of shims is crucial. If these bearings need adjustment, use a spring scale or torque wrench as per guidelines found in your OEM-level shop manual. (See previous chapter for more details on closed-knuckle steering rebuild.)

Your truck's suspension and steering linkage design dictate the location of the steering gear, while driving requirements and engineering intent determine the speed or ratio of the steering gear. Responsive handling results from correctly matching the suspension, steering linkage and steering gear, while a chassis lift and other suspension modifications often compromise the steering geometry.

> NOTE —
> Bump steer and other handling anomalies result from the misalignment of suspension and steering linkage. See chapter on suspension upgrades for details.

Production trucks, especially older models with manual steering systems, have slower steering response and less suspension feedback than passenger cars. Concerned about safety and liability, truck manufacturers de-tune suspension to meet a wider audience of drivers. (Later models feature quicker power steering ratios, which gives the light truck a sportier feel, nimbler parking habits and easier trailer backing ability.)

Types Of Steering Gears

Long after the General Motors' switch to improved ball-and-nut gears, Ford's light F-trucks still offered the more primitive worm-and-roller manual steering gear systems. By the mid-1960s, GM's success with recirculating ball-and-nut steering gears encouraged other manufacturers to make the change.

Within Ford's early worm-and-roller steering gearboxes, a machined, spiral groove runs along the steering or worm shaft. This spiral groove meshes with a toothed roller that mounts in the head of the sector (Pitman) shaft. The crude relationship of these parts creates high friction and encourages wear.

The Pitman arm attaches at the outer end of the sector or cross-shaft. Clockwise and counterclockwise rotation

Fig. 11-20. Ford/Gemmer worm-and-roller steering gears produce more friction than later recirculating ball-and-nut types. If your F-truck is a 1948–64 2WD model or 4WD with this steering, keep a close watch on the steering system.

of the sector- or cross-shaft translates as the fore and aft swing of the Pitman arm on earlier Ford F-trucks.

> NOTE —
> A common cause of steering parts damage is from towing a pre-1965 Ford F-truck with a worm-and-roller type steering system. (Construction companies often do this.) The design does poorly with reverse flow of energy, like when the road causes the roller head to turn the worm shaft. If you must transport your earlier Ford F-truck, especially a classic '48–'56 model, use a low-bed car hauling trailer.

By contrast, the manual recirculating ball-and-nut gears drastically reduce friction. A ball nut, machined internally to form the top half of a ball race, rides on ball bearings. These ball bearings run in the worm shaft's precisely machined groove. The machined groove serves as the inner half of the ball bearing race.

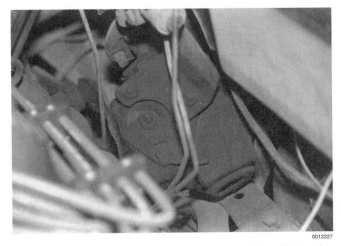

Fig. 11-21. Ford's mid-'60s switch to recirculating ball-and-nut steering was overdue. This improved gear offers a superior service life and much easier action than earlier worm-and-roller gear types.

Machined teeth on the outer surface of the ball nut engage teeth on the Pitman (cross/sector) shaft. Steering wheel/worm shaft rotation translates as up and down movement of the ball nut. This movement of the sector teeth rotates the sector shaft and Pitman arm.

> **CAUTION ──**
> *Service adjustment, although rare with ball-and-nut gears, focuses solely on the mesh between the ball nut's teeth and the Pitman/sector shaft teeth. Worm shaft bearing pre-load is also adjustable, although this procedure is also rare between steering gear overhauls. Signs that the steering gear needs a significant amount of adjustment always suggests internal damage and time for a complete overhaul. Never attempt a steering gear adjustment without instructions from your factory-level shop manual.*

The major gain of newer recirculating ball-and-nut steering gear designs is the reduction of stress and friction. Gliding motion of the ball nut, up and down the worm shaft, takes place with ball-bearing smoothness. Wrist wrenching steering gear kickback is drastically reduced (especially with integral power assist). Moreover, even with severe four-wheel drive use, these gears can survive.

The earlier worm-and-roller gears suffer from tooth and worm gear chipping and, in the worst cases, seizure from jammed tooth debris. Friction and shock loads translate to wear that requires periodic adjustment. Unseen damage often follows hard use; my experience with the Ford/Gemmer worm-and-roller truck steering gears has taught that any steering gearbox with an excessive amount of play deserves a teardown for inspection and replacement of defective parts.

The Power Steering Option

Power steering, once considered a horsepower-robbing accessory for lazy drivers, is now a light truck standard feature. Major design breakthroughs, especially the switch to integral power steering gears, popularized power steering from the mid-1960s onward. Ford's first light truck use of integral power steering came about in 1966 2WD models.

Ford F-Series 4x4 models did not offer power steering until the early 1970s. Even then, the integral type gear was not employed. Instead, Ford used linkage type power steering until the change to integral gears on some 1976 4x4s. All light F-trucks have offered either an optional or standard equipment integral type power steering gear since 1978.

Before integral power steering gearboxes, power steering was a cumbersome affair. Linkage-type power assist, with a hydraulic power ram and an awkward network of hoses, uses a conventional (manual) steering gearbox. A control valve, mounted at the drag link/Pitman arm socket, senses the steering wheel apply pressure. Hydraulic force directs ram pressure for either left or right turn power assist.

Linkage type power steering is an add-on device that simply reduces steering effort. Beyond its negative features, like attracting debris and becoming easily damaged by trail obstacles, linkage power steering offers benefits, particularly driving ease and reduction of road kickback at the steering wheel.

Saginaw Power Steering Gears

The reliability found in GM's Saginaw manual and power gears is legend. Some Ford truck models have used Saginaw units, while other F-truck integral gear offerings draw heavily upon Saginaw's pioneer concepts.

A Saginaw gear provides an excellent example of integral power steering design. For this reason, I am offering a description of the Saginaw integral power gear here, although your Ford F-truck model may use either a Ford, Ross, Bendix, ZF or Saginaw recirculating ball type steering gear or pump components.

The Saginaw integral power gear employs a rotary valve that opens ports and directs high pressure fluid to help during turns. The degree of assist corresponds directly to the driver's steering wheel effort.

Some Saginaw integral units offer a unique variable ratio, produced by using unequal length teeth on the Pitman/sector shaft and rack piston. As you steer full left or right, the Pitman shaft speed increases, quickening the steering. Straight ahead, steering is very stable, with a slower ratio giving more road feel.

Saginaw integral power steering gears are sensitive, precise mechanisms operating under close tolerances and very high fluid pressures. Service on a power gear is rare, but when necessary, requires intricate preload adjustments and special assembly tools. Your safety depends upon proper fit-up of parts.

> **NOTE ──**
> Despite basic similarities between recirculating ball-and-nut manual gears and the Saginaw integral power units, you need much greater skill to service a power gear.

Fig. 11-22. Saginaw's recirculating ball-and-nut technology carries to the integral power steering gears. Every U.S. truck manufacturer has benefitted from the use of these rugged Saginaw power steering gears.

Ford F-truck owners sometimes retrofit Saginaw integral power gears to an early truck. Even a recirculating ball type manual gearbox provides a drastic improvement for an early F-truck. Such a conversion project requires skill, however, plus a thorough knowledge of steering safety and chassis fabrication requirements.

CAUTION —

Do not attempt such a conversion without the requisite skill level. The most common mistakes that inexperienced installers make are 1) misalignment of steering linkage (causing bump steer or limiting travel), 2) failure to make sure that the steering gear is in its center position when the vehicle's wheels aim straight ahead, and 3) not setting the steering knuckle/wheel stops properly, which could allow the steering gear's ball nut to hyper-extend at the extremes of its travel and severely damage the gear assembly.

Advance Adapters and others make conversion kits for retrofitting a Saginaw recirculating ball power or manual steering gear to an earlier truck chassis. (See the suspension upgrade chapter of the book.) The few horsepower lost in running a power steering pump are sometimes worth the trade-off: smooth and easy modern steering.

Steering Linkage And Control

Although lock-to-lock steering ratios affect turning quickness, the true blueprint for off- and on-highway handling is the precise delivery of steering signals. The wheels must respond readily to linkage movement.

Later 4x4 model steering linkage often includes a stabilizer shock designed to eliminate severe road kickback. Although an OE or aftermarket stabilizer is a major asset, it's not a substitute for replacing worn steering components. Before tackling steering wander, eliminate worn or dangerously loose linkage.

If your truck wanders, inspect the wheel bearings, steering knuckle joints/kingpins and steering linkage for excess play. The Pitman arm, draglink, tie-rod ends, steering knuckle ball joints and kingpin bearings are acute wear areas.

Begin your inspection with the wheel bearings and knuckle joints or kingpins. Next, check the steering linkage. Worn tie-rod ends and other joints cause steering looseness, road wander, and the risk of losing control.

Suspension frame mounts, radius arm bushings and spring shackles are also wear points that can cause poor vehicle handling and loss of control. Especially on a 4x4 model or a truck used extensively off-pavement, off-road pounding can stress the steering system to its limits.

Rear spring position also affects steering control. Check for misaligned springs, loose U-bolts, broken spring center bolts, and worn or defective spring bushings. Wander and rear wheel steer can result from rear suspension defects.

Worn steering linkage parts are generally not serviceable. When defective, you must replace them. (The pre-1957 Ford F-truck draglink assemblies are rebuildable.)

Fig. 11-23. *The best procedure for checking steering linkage, ball-joint and wheel bearing play is to shake the tire and wheel assembly. Jack and secure the front end safely off the floor. Grip each front tire at 6 and 12 o'clock to check ball joints and wheel bearings. Lower one tire to the floor, then shake the raised tire from a 3 and 9 o'clock position to note steering linkage wear. Have a partner watch for play at each tie-rod end and the other joints while applying a shaking, back-and-forth force.*

Fig. 11-24. *Excess spring movement contributes to wander. Always inspect spring bushings for wear. OE-type hard rubber bushings can wear over time and leave your front end wobbly and unstable.*

Parts removal requires care and should follow professional service guidelines.

Periodic steering linkage maintenance is simple, consisting of wiping dirt from fittings, then greasing joints with clean chassis lube through a hand grease gun. Safety inspection should include dust boots, joint wear, and straightness of rods. Always replace bent steering linkage components. Straightening a bent tie-rod compromises

Fig. 11-25. *Sway/stabilizer bar bushings are also perishable. On later trucks, inspect these pieces for wear, looseness and deterioration. Too loose, the bar serves no purpose. Control in corners benefits greatly from the sway bar. Here is bushing wear at sway bar link.*

Fig. 11-26. *Inspect ball-joint supported steering knuckles. Excess play here causes kingpin shimmy, characterized by a violent shake of the steering wheel and the entire front end. Kingpin bearing shims on early models and upper ball joint adjustment sleeves on open knuckle axles allow for minor adjustment. Major looseness calls for parts replacement or knuckle rebuilding. (See previous chapter.)*

safety. Stretched one way, then the other, tie-rod tubes and steel rods can weaken and fail.

> **CAUTION —**
> *You may need special tools, including pullers. Cleanliness is essential. Debris must not interfere with the tight fitup of tapered ball studs on tie-rod ends and ball joints. Torque self-locking and castellated nuts to factory specs. Always install a correctly sized new cotter pin on the castellated nut.*

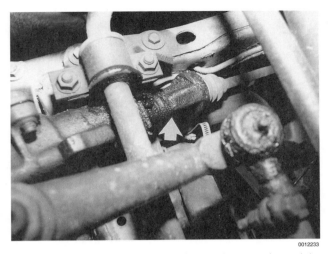

Fig. 11-27. *The coupler above the steering gear (arrow) is also a wear point. An open column and coupler enable a quick check for steering gear damage and excess backlash.*

Inspecting The Steering System

Restoration of steering linkage, knuckle joints, kingpins and wheel bearings usually eliminates steering play. If looseness remains, make certain that the frame, spring bolts and spring attachments are intact and that hardware is secure.

Tires and front end alignment are also a concern, as wander often occurs when tires have abnormal wear patterns. On Ford F-trucks with I-beam front axles or kingpin type knuckle pivots, wheel alignment is simple. Unless you've bent the axle beam/housing or the truck's frame, alignment consists only of setting toe-in.

> **NOTE —**
> As mentioned earlier in this chapter, later 4x4s with open knuckle ball-joint steering do provide for camber adjustment. On leaf spring front suspension 4x4s, you can set caster with wedge shims between the axle and leaf stack.

If steering play still exists, suspect the steering gearbox. For a quick check, center the steering and carefully rotate the worm or steering shaft. (This may require a helper on the early trucks with an enclosed steering shaft/column.) Note the amount of rotational movement necessary to just move the Pitman arm.

On later trucks with exposed steering shafts, this operation is very easy. Park your truck with the wheels straight ahead. Turn the shaft at the input end of the steering gear while holding the Pitman arm with your other hand. It's easy to detect Pitman movement by gently rotating the steering shaft.

Be sensitive to the exact point at which the Pitman arm responds to the steering shaft movement. Rotate the shaft in the opposite direction to determine the degree of play. If wear or play is evident, either steering gear adjustment or overhaul is necessary.

Note that the steering gear must be in its center position when checking for play. Steering gears have a high point in the exact center position that creates a very slight pre-load in the straight ahead driving position. Turned left or right of this point, sector play or backlash will increase. If you suspect a mis-centered steering gear, disconnect the steering linkage at the Pitman arm and very gently rotate the steering to one extreme.

Now count the exact turns back to the opposite extreme, then divide that number by two. Turn the wheel back this amount, and your steering gearbox will be on center. Check for play and over-center (high point) pre-load at this position. (Never turn the shaft hard against its extremes, as damage to ball races could occur.)

Signs Of Steering Gearbox Trouble

Sudden development of steering gear play or symptoms of wander, clicking noises or binding imply internal damage to the gear. Although later steering gears have great resiliency, hard-core abuse or four-wheeling can damage even the best steering unit.

Unless high mileage dictates a minor readjustment to compensate for wear, any more than a slight amount of steering gear play suggests internal gear damage. Since the gear's inner workings are invisible without a teardown, you must make a judgement call here.

CAUTION —
Never adjust a gear that has substantial play. Under such circumstances, removal and teardown of the gear is mandatory.

Before considering a steering gear teardown, review your factory-level service guidebook. Understand the complex tools, close tolerances, and sequence of disassembly and reassembly.

Power steering gears, in particular, require special care, cleanliness and safe work habits. Consider a new, factory rebuilt or undamaged (low mileage) recycled gear. Individual power steering gear pieces get very expensive.

The chance of finding a good used early Ford F-truck worm-and-roller type steering gear is slim to none. Unless you find a recycled truck with under 75,000 original and easy miles on the odometer, the manual steering gear likely has substantial wear. With these 1948–64 steering gear assemblies, always install new parts in a sound housing. Always use new seals, bushings, bearings, a new worm shaft and a new roller/sector assembly. Never mix or fit up old and new parts, especially gear pieces. If you cannot find parts at your local Ford dealer, try for NOS pieces through a vintage truck restorer's outlet.

Steering Linkage And Suspension Damage

Normal wear over time and the common off-pavement use of light trucks can affect wheel alignment. Rough terrain and obstacles like rocks, stumps, slick mud, and streambeds each threaten the chassis and front end system. Damaged steering linkage and badly misaligned front wheels can ruin a brand new set of tires in just a few hundred miles.

Off-pavement pounding can cause serious suspension trouble. Especially sensitive are the leaf spring centering bolts and the spring U-bolts (which shear or break

and allow the axle to shift out of alignment). F-truck coil springs ride above the axle beam(s), and unless stressed to the limit, these coils seldom break, even under tight off-pavement twisting. Coil springs can dislodge, however, from serious suspension bashing.

Steering linkage is a major area of concern. Steering linkage must move with the axle to maintain wheel alignment. Generally, tie rods lie near the axle centerline, making tie rods the most vulnerable steering linkage component. On 4x4 models, the drivetrain layout has the front driveshaft angling from the transfer case to the backside of the front axle. Here, the steering linkage must ride in front of the axle, as it also must do on Twin I-Beam 2WD systems.

Tree stumps can easily damage the tie rod(s) or a steering stabilizer. If the stabilizer shock damper (found on some 4x4 models) becomes bent, steering bind is possible. If obvious damage exists, remove the stabilizer shock damper. Other than some wander and possible shakiness, the truck can get home without this unit. Replace with a new stabilizer shock damper immediately.

4. WHEEL ALIGNMENT

Subjected to normal wear-and-tear or off-pavement pounding, your truck demands regular steering system inspection and front wheel alignment. The longevity of expensive tires and your safety both depend on proper front wheel tracking.

Front end alignment also reveals defective steering and suspension components. Consider wheel alignment an important part of your truck's preventive maintenance program.

Steering Geometry

For the light F-truck, a periodic front end alignment always includes toe-in. Toe-in is the measurement between the centerlines of the tire tread at the tire's horizontal midline.

Imagine lines scribed at the center of your front tire treads, running the full circumference of the tire. Each line references 360° of tire tread surface and offers an easy measurement at the front and rear of the tire. The object when setting toe-in is to adjust tie-rod length to properly distance these two reference points.

Vehicle manufacturers establish toe settings with consideration for rolling resistance and chassis geometry. Generally, older bias ply tires require a slight (1/32" to 1/8") toe-in. Modern radial tires have less rolling resistance and need only minimal inward toe. They often call for a zero-degree/inch toe set, or tires that run perfectly parallel in the straight ahead mode.

Normal steering and reasonable tire wear also depend upon correct caster and camber geometry. Camber is simply the upright angle or tilt of the tire. The camber angle can change when an axle housing, I-beam, steering spindle, or steering knuckle becomes bent or excess wear develops at the knuckle pivots (kingpins, pivots or ball-joints).

Caster is trickier to define. The caster angle is the tilt of an imaginary line drawn through the centerline of the steering kingpins. On ball-joint front ends like 4x4 open-

Fig. 11-28. *Toe-set is a regular part of chassis service. Especially on vehicles subjected to off-pavement pounding, tire life depends on periodic checks of front wheel toe-set. Radial tires have different toe-set requirements than bias-ply types. Adjust toe-in when installing new tires. On solid front axles, toe-in is normally the only adjustment required. Caster or camber changes result from axle, chassis or suspension damage and wear.*

Fig. 11-29. *Note use of a special tie-rod sleeve wrench. After rain, slush, mud, and water crossings, joints require fresh chassis grease to displace water and foreign matter.*

knuckle axles or the late 2WD Twin I-Beam, we draw this line through the orbital centerline of the upper and lower ball joints.

This line's angle tilts rearward (positive caster) or forward (negative caster). Its purpose is to encourage straight ahead orientation of the wheels—the feature that causes the steering wheel to center naturally as we leave a turn. Caster also helps prevent kingpin shimmy, the violent back and forth shaking of the front wheels.

Fig. 11-30. *Caster and camber gauges clamp to the wheel. Once on a center line with the wheel spindle, levels indicate steering and wheel tilt angles.*

The last front end geometry issue is steering axis inclination. Effectively, steering axis inclination is two angles (caster and camber) in one, with the steering spindle angled to maintain a specified arc during turns. Steering axis inclination depends upon the condition and integrity of the steering knuckle and spindle. If axis of inclination has changed, yet the caster, camber and toe-in remain correct, suspect a bent or defective steering knuckle or spindle.

Newer Ford IFS front suspension systems allow for minor caster and camber adjustments by adjusting the kingpin centerline tilt, either inboard (negative camber) or outboard (positive camber) from its vertical axis. Such systems also provide slight fore and aft adjustment of the kingpin centerline for setting proper caster.

Ford's early 2WD I-beam, solid live front axle 4x4s and kingpin-type (non-ball-joint) 2WD Twin I-Beam systems have no provision for camber adjustment. On the twin-beam type of front ends, ride height does affect camber, and proper ride height (i.e., normal spring and frame height) should maintain camber.

Ford's Twin I-Beam and Twin Traction-Beam IFS has only minimal provision for caster adjustment. The radius arms hold caster in a fixed location. On solid mono-beam axles, common to early model 2WD F-trucks and 4x4s with solid front drive axles and leaf springs, caster can be corrected by installing wedge-shaped shims between the axle perch and main leaf of each front spring. Accurately degreed, these wedge-shaped shims restore proper tilt of the kingpin or ball-joint centerline. Make sure that sagging springs are not at fault when caster reads out of specification.

CAUTION —
Caster and camber should never be adjusted by bending the axle beams (hot, cold or otherwise). If these measurements are beyond specification, look for bent, worn or damaged parts.

A major advantage of the ball-joint type knuckle pivots is the use of camber adapters at the ball-stud seats.

Later ball-joint type 2WD and 4x4 front axles have a provision for minor camber corrections by replacing the mounting sleeve at the upper ball-joint with a special sleeve of the proper angle. (Caster, fixed by the radius arm/axle beam position, is slightly adjustable.) Earlier 4x4s with open knuckle ball-joint steering have no such factory service provision, however, aftermarket off-set angle upper ball-joint seats are available for minor caster and camber corrections.

0012237

Fig. 11-31. Late Ford 4x4 front axles have provision for camber adjustment at upper ball-joints. Leaf spring models also provide for caster adjustment by placing properly degreed wedge shims between axle housing and leaf springs.

NOTE —
See a local frame and wheel alignment shop or your NAPA store for leaf spring shims, offset ball-joint mounting sleeves and 4WD spindle shims to correct wheel alignment. Before installing such parts, be absolutely certain that none of your truck's suspension or steering components have become damaged. Never compensate for collision or wear damage with the use of shims or adjuster sleeves. Replacing defective parts should correct the caster or camber error.

Field Fix To Get Home

A front end alignment is a good safeguard after any serious off-pavement pounding or hard bout with washboard. In an emergency, you can restore toe-in in the field—at least close enough to keep your precious tire rubber from peeling away like an apple's skin.

Back woods straightening of the tie rod could save a walk home and allow your truck to track reasonably straight. As for the permanence of such a fix, realize that any straightened steering linkage part should be replaced as soon as possible.

CAUTION —
Many frame and axle specialists can skillfully straighten a slightly bent I-beam or solid axle (and even pull out several degrees of frame kink). No professional, however, will reuse a bent piece of steering linkage.

For just getting back to civilization, be very cautious not to break the parts as you straighten them. Use care to distribute force over a broad area, while centering the pull at the bent section. If the kink is at the threaded portion of a tie rod, leave it alone. Threads respond badly to stretching, and breakage is very likely.

Attach a tow strap to an immoveable object—like the tree stump that caused all this trouble! Use the truck's power to gently pull the tie rod straight.

If your truck has a winch, a tree and a snatch block provide an ideal alternative. Park the truck in low gear or Park with the brake set. Run the cable forward and loop it 180° at the snatch block. Attach the hook to the tie-rod. Use your winch remote control to operate the winch while watching from a safe distance.

CAUTION —
Never use Park mode when winching a heavy load. The small parking pawl of an automatic transmission will break under such stress.

Straighten the tie rod only enough to provide safe clearance for moving parts and approximate wheel alignment. Once you straighten the tube or sleeve, adjust toe-in.

When adjusting wheel alignment or installing new steering linkage pieces, always center the tie-rod ends. The ball studs and their sockets should align correctly before you tighten the sleeve clamps. Make sure each tie-rod end has its full range of motion. Also be sure that each tie-rod end is safely threaded into the sleeve.

A Wooded Backdrop For Your Alignment Shop

Temporary toe-in can be set with a few hand tools, a tie-rod sleeve wrench, a tape measure, and an axle or frame jack. Center the steering (Pitman arm) before beginning. Set the steering wheel for normal, straight ahead driving, then jack one front wheel slightly off the ground. Without a toe adjusting bar and scribe for drawing lines around the tire centerlines, the next best tool for a primitive "get home only" alignment is a piece of chalk.

Carefully note the tread pattern of your front tires. Find reference niches that are easy to identify. Hold the tape measure level, close to the mid-point of each tire's diameter. Make sure that the tape does not interfere with suspension parts, and pull it snugly from the opposite tire's mark.

If you encounter an obstacle while pulling the tape straight, drop the level of the tape, rematch the tread pattern, and try again. Once the tape is level, make an accurate note of the length between your two niche marks.

Perform the same procedure at the rear of the front tires. Again, attempt to draw a level line, close to the tires horizontal mid-line without parts interference. Note the length between these tread pattern niches. (Make sure your chosen tread patterns match those used at the front.)

These two measurements form the basis for your toe-in alignment. For simplicity, use an emergency toe-in spec of zero. Both front and rear measurements should read the same. (Were our goal 1/8" toe-in, the rear measurement would be 1/8" longer than the front. Simple? Well, with practice it gets easier.)

Fig. 11-32. *After straightening the tie-rod with a tow strap, the "Lantern Alignment Shop" opens. Raise the driver's side wheel slightly from the ground and reference mark the front tire tread. Keeping the steering wheel straight ahead, measure between the front treads of the tires and the rear reference marks. This will indicate the degree of misalignment.*

Fig. 11-33. *Loosen the tie rod clamps and stabilizer mount, then turn the tie rod tube or sleeve to adjust its length. The adjusting tube, often stubborn from rust and scale at the tie rod threads, may require a pipe wrench or sleeve adjuster tool to rotate.*

Fig. 11-34. *Safely position the sleeve clamps after confirming the final measurement. Clamps must not interfere with steering linkage movement or other components.*

Fig. 11-35. *Make sure plenty of tie rod thread remains within the sleeve/tube ends. Tighten clamps and make certain that parts move freely as you turn the steering wheel. Envision suspension movement, and make sure of adequate clearance when the chassis or axle beam(s) move.*

A bent tie rod shortens the distance between the steering arms. On a 4x4 truck or 2WD Twin I-Beam model with its steering linkage forward of the axle beam(s), this toes the front wheels inward. Under such conditions, the bend will cause a long measurement at the backside tread. The exact opposite is true of an earlier 2WD I-beam axle model with its tie-rod mounted behind the axle.

To shorten or lengthen the tie rod, loosen the tie rod end clamps to allow rotation of the adjusting tube/sleeve. Note the left-hand or right-hand threads at each end of the tube, and also the amount of thread screwed into each sleeve end. If you must lengthen the tie rod, be careful not to unthread the tube so far that the tie-rod thread fitup becomes too shallow and unsafe.

The tube may not rotate easily. Moisture, rust, and scale cause seizure of tie-rod end threads. A rust penetrant will sometimes help. Rotate the tube, checking the fore and aft tire measurements often. When the measurement is correct, tighten the clamps securely.

Many of us have been fortunate enough not to hit tree stumps or rocks. It's wise, however, to travel prepared. Whether we experience trouble or find ourselves able to help others, survival skills help. A slow drive to pavement with a temporary field fix sure beats walking! Success can sometimes be a twelve-mph trip to civilization—with your truck's heater humming, windshield wipers swishing and headlights leading the way.

Chapter 12

Brakes and Wheel Bearings

Properly functioning wheel bearings and brakes are essential to safe driving. Inspect your truck's wheel bearings and brakes regularly. Perform all brake work with careful attention to cleanliness, correct specifications and proper working procedures.

> **WARNING —**
> • *Brake friction materials such as brake linings or brake pads may contain asbestos fibers. Do not create dust by grinding, sanding, or cleaning the pads with compressed air. Avoid breathing any asbestos fibers or dust. Breathing asbestos can cause serious diseases such as asbestosis or cancer, and may result in death. Use only approved methods to clean brake components containing asbestos.*
>
> • *Brake fluid is poisonous. Wear safety glasses when working with brake fluid, and wear rubber gloves to prevent brake fluid from entering your bloodstream through cuts and scratches. Do not siphon brake fluid with your mouth.*

1. WHEEL BEARINGS

All Ford F-truck front wheel bearings are tapered roller type. Tapered roller bearings provide for slight float. While maintaining the vehicle load, properly adjusted rollers can still move laterally (axially) within the clearances of the inner and outer bearing races. Ball bearings, by contrast, cannot tolerate any axial play and require a pre-load rather than end play adjustment.

Any type of rolling bearing will micro-slip (slide or scuff) slightly, and all bearings suffer chronic wear at their rollers, balls, and races. The most common bearing race, roller or ball steel is a chromium-alloy, usually SAE 52100 bearing race steel.

This is tough, pure stuff (ranging between 60-68 on the Rockwell C scale tests for hardness). These materials furnish high rolling mileage, but the hardness makes races vulnerable to impact damage and pitting from abrasive contaminants. For this reason, thorough cleaning, inspection, and periodic bearing repacking with a suitable grease is necessary.

Front Wheel Bearing Fundamentals

Although wheel bearing service procedures and exact adjusting specifications differ among models, some general points apply to all F-Series light truck models. (Adjustment standards and methods for your truck are available in an OEM or professional service guide.)

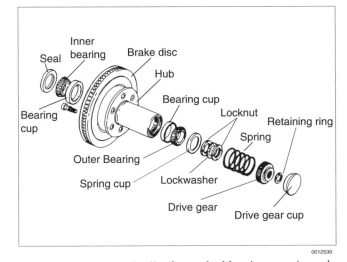

Fig. 12-1. *Tapered roller front wheel bearings require end play adjustment. On your truck, a specified in and out movement of the bearing assembly provides proper running tolerance.*

Fig. 12-2. *The disc rotor and wheel hub rotate as an integral unit. Correct disc brake rotor lateral runout is critical. Trueness of rotor and adjustment of the wheel bearings provides acceptable runout.*

Fig. 12-4. *Dial indicator on magnetic stand measures wheel bearing end play. This measurement addresses the acceptable range of bearing roller movement (axially) on the races. Holding the hub flange at 9 and 3-o'clock, push the hub straight in and pull straight out while measuring end play. Check your OEM-level service manual for proper end play specifications.*

Fig. 12-3. *Inspect the spindle surface where the wheel bearings ride. On both 2WD and 4x4 front spindles, any wear, galling or play will affect the adjustment of the bearings. Check closely for cracks, especially if your truck has overly wide aftermarket wheels and oversize tires. Always replace worn parts.*

Precise wheel bearing adjustment takes end play into account. End play is measurable with a dial indicator attached to the wheel hub, outer brake drum face or rotor. Push the brake drum or rotor straight inward with both hands. (Push evenly to avoid cocking the hub to one side). Take a dial indicator reading, aiming straight toward the spindle.

The dial indicator measures end play when you pull the hub outward. Do not rock the drum or rotor, or a false reading will result. End play is the straight inward and outward (lateral) movement of the hub along the spindle's axis.

Bearing Survival

The two most common causes of bearing failure are poor maintenance and abuse. Poor maintenance includes neglecting periodic cleaning or failure to repack and properly adjust the bearings.

For 4x4 trucks, abuse takes on several additional forms. Such a truck may sport oversized custom wheels and tires, or perhaps a change in weight on the front end, the result of a larger V-8 transplant or a cabover camper. (This can also apply to 2WD trucks.) Operating the truck

with either too much load on the bearings or excessive lateral stress can cause damage.

Often, bearing failure results from using radically offset (reversed) custom wheels. Shifting the tire centerline outboard from the stock location causes vehicle weight to act as leverage against the wheel hub and bearings. With a front mounted winch or a hefty V-8 engine, even more weight bears directly on each wheel hub. If that same weight applies with the tire centerlines located further outboard, the bearings must now resist an added amount of leverage force.

Wheel Bearing Service Notes

Always service wheel bearings with the correct grease. All wheel bearing greases are not the same. Mixing grease types can severely damage parts and compromise your safety.

When repacking your truck's front wheel bearings, begin with a thorough solvent cleaning. Make certain that no solvent residue remains on the bearings before repacking them. Also clean the spindle, inner wheel hub and races. Wash, wipe and dry parts thoroughly to remove any traces of solvent before repacking the bearings with fresh, clean grease.

> *CAUTION —*
> *Use the recommended wheel bearing grease for your model. Disc brake equipped vehicles demand exacting wheel bearing adjustments and highly heat resistant lubricant.*

Wash bearings and other parts in clean solvent. Remove all old grease and any solvent residue. Drying with compressed air is acceptable, however, never spin the bearings with compressed air.

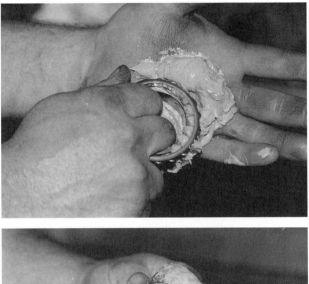

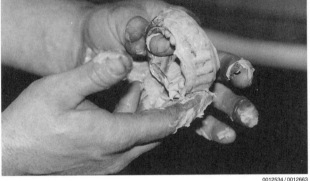

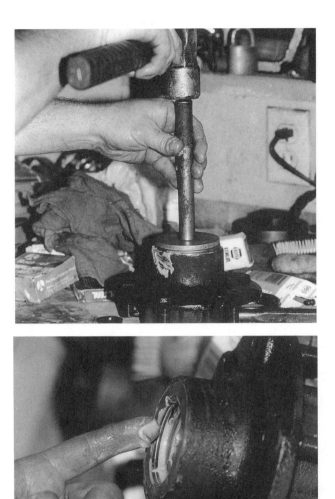

Fig. 12-5. *Wheel bearing packers make this job easy and assure complete grease penetration of the rollers. When hand packing a bearing, squeeze the grease between the wider end of the bearing cage and the inner bearing race. Make sure grease flows out the opposite end of the rollers. Go around the entire bearing assembly at least two full times to assure thorough saturation. Once grease fills all spaces between the rollers, spread a generous film of grease around the outer face of the bearing and cage.*

WARNING —
Severe bodily harm could result from a bearing assembly flying apart at speed.

Fig. 12-6. *After cleaning and thoroughly drying the hub and rotor assembly, swab clean grease against the walls of the hub's inner cavity. Grease should fill the hub's grease recess and provide a dam to prevent hot grease from leaving the inner sides of the bearings. Install the freshly packed inner wheel bearing and a new grease seal. The hub is now ready for installation on the spindle. Keep grease away from brake linings. (Shown here is an early Spicer/Dana-type 4x4 front hub assembly.)*

Always replace grease seals. Do not attempt to reuse them. Installing new front or rear wheel seals lowers the risk of parts failure. At the front wheel hubs, they prevent moisture and dirt from entering the hub assembly. Rear axle seals prevent grease or gear lubricant from ruining brake lining and causing failure of the rear brakes.

Use proper tools, refer to your OEM or professional level repair guidebook, and take your time when servicing your wheel bearings. On early 4x4 models with a bendable locking washer between the two spindle nuts, install a new washer whenever fatigue is obvious. On 2WD models, always install a new cotter pin after adjusting the castellated or adjuster nut and aligning the retainer (if so equipped) with the cotter pin hole.

On later 4x4 spindles with an inner pinned adjuster, a lock washer with indexing holes and an outer lock nut, make certain that the washer seats securely when tightening the outer lock nut. Done properly, a wheel bearing repack and seal replacement will last for many miles. Precise steering, handling, and braking will result, assuring your truck's safety and reliability.

Fig. 12-7. *Install the repacked outer wheel bearing. Build a dam of additional grease between outer side of bearing and thrust face of spindle nut.*

Fig. 12-8. *Thread the adjuster nut carefully onto the spindle. 4x4 front axles require a special spindle nut wrench. (Consult your Ford F-Series truck shop manual for adjustment procedure and torque figures.) Note that later model 4x4 hubs have a small locating pin on the inner adjuster nut. Make sure the pin faces outward to receive the multi-holed indexing washer.*

Fig. 12-9. *Confirm the order of parts assembly in your F-Series shop manual. Carefully install the retaining lockwasher (early 4x4 models) or multi-holed indexing washer (later model 4x4s), then install and torque the outer lock nut to specification before measuring hub end play with a dial indicator.*

Fig. 12-10. *Once end play is correct, bend the early style lockwasher tab (shown here) to secure the nuts. Earlier Ford 4x4 axles with hex nuts use this type of lock washer. Do not bend later style multi-holed index washer.*

CAUTION —
Wheel bearing service and adjustment is a critical part of your vehicle maintenance. Your safety and the truck's reliability depend upon proper bearing adjustment. Always follow the adjusting procedure and specifications described in your Ford F-Series truck shop manual or a professional-level service guidebook. On models so equipped, use the correct size and type of cotter pin, and secure pin properly.

2. THE BRAKING SYSTEM

All Ford F-Series light truck brakes actuate by hydraulic pressure. The basic hydraulic apply system begins with a brake pedal and master cylinder. 1948–56 F-truck brake systems have a single reservoir master cylinder mounted beneath the floorboard. 1957 was the first year that F-trucks had a firewall mounted master cylinder with a suspended pedal.

WARNING —
Brake friction materials such as brake linings or brake pads may contain asbestos fibers. Do not create dust by grinding, sanding, or cleaning the pads with compressed air. Avoid breathing any asbestos fibers or dust. Breathing asbestos can cause serious diseases such as asbestosis or cancer, and may result in death. Use only approved methods to clean brake components containing asbestos.

In 1967, the U.S. Department of Transportation invoked safety standards requiring dual hydraulic circuits on the master cylinder. All U.S.-built trucks from that year forward have separate hydraulic supply lines for the rear and front brakes. If either end of the system should fail, brakes still operate at the opposite axle.

For light trucks, the dual brake system was a major advancement, eliminating the risk of total brake loss in the event of a fluid leak. For the many truck chassis exposed to fallen trees, jagged rocks and raw terrain, the pre-'67 single braking system offers little protection. If a brake hose snaps or a steel pipe tears, the system loses pressure and the brakes fail completely.

Pedal Warning Signals

A spongy brake pedal is caused by air in the hydraulic system or low brake fluid level. This leads to poor braking action and rust within the system. Check for leaks and bleed any air from the system.

> **NOTE —**
> Low fluid can be due to normal lining wear. Periodically verify the thickness of lining, check for proper lining-to-drum clearance, and top off fluid after adjusting the brakes. Make sure that the emergency/parking brake has been released before adjusting the wheel brakes.

0012086

Fig. 12-11. On earlier truck models without self-adjusting brake mechanisms, you must periodically adjust the drum brake lining to avoid a low pedal. Some early Ford F-trucks also have the parking/emergency brake at the rear driveline. The emergency brake drum has openings for inspection and adjustment of the brake. Watch for oil, grit and contaminants that will make your parking brake ineffective. Also check and lube the parking brake cable frequently.

Another sign of trouble is the pulsating brake pedal, characterized by a rhythmical pumping action during braking. On your truck, possible causes include warped drums or rotors, defective brake hardware, a bent front spindle or rear axle shaft and loose wheel bearings. These symptoms can occur suddenly, often following an off-road pounding or submersion in water.

High pedal pressure accompanied by increased stopping distance is brake fade. Fade suggests poor lining quality, drum or rotor warpage, contaminated brake fluid, excessive rotor runout, old brake fluid, or materials that have fatigued severely.

Brake pull, another common trouble symptom, results from contaminated brake lining, misadvised shoes or sticky hydraulic cylinders. If brake pads or shoes require replacement, always change lining at both wheels of that axle to avoid uneven braking. Ideally, you should change lining and renew the brake cylinders at all four wheels (both axles) for optimal braking efficiency.

> **WARNING —**
> *Overheated brakes and old brake fluid make deadly companions. Trailer pullers and those who haul heavy cargos should change brake fluid periodically and avoid overheating the brakes whenever possible. (Recreational or tow vehicles that set for long off-season periods are especially vulnerable to brake fluid moisture contamination.) Always use lower gears on a steep downgrade to relieve the load on your truck's brakes. Let the brakes cool down thoroughly when severe heat-up has occurred. Any pedal fade is a sure sign of trouble.*

Other Brake Woes

Metallic brake noise signals danger. Generally, metal-on-metal sounds imply total loss of lining and the dragging of shoes or pad backs against a drum or rotor. These symptoms quickly degenerate into damaged rotors or drums, often beyond the point of repair.

Periodic inspection of your truck's brakes can help prevent this trouble. Check for leaks, worn lining and heat damage. Look closely at hoses and brake pipes, especially in those areas exposed to debris and trail abuse. Periodically, remove all brake drums to assess lining wear.

Brake Fluid Precautions

Safety is at stake when you replenish brake fluid. Accidental use of mineral-based oils in the hydraulic brake or clutch system can cause swelling of rubber seals and complete failure of the brakes or clutch.

> **WARNING —**
> *Brake fluid is poisonous. Wear safety glasses when working with brake fluid, and wear rubber gloves to prevent brake fluid from entering the bloodstream through cuts and scratches. Do not siphon brake fluid with your mouth.*

> **CAUTION —**
> *Always use DOT 3 or higher rating brake fluid in the master cylinder/braking system or hydraulic clutch system of your truck. Never add motor oil or any substance other than brake fluid to a hydraulic brake system. Do not mix silicone brake fluid with conventional brake fluid.*

Clean, moisture-free brake fluid is fundamental to brake safety. The master cylinder cover must seal tightly. When topping off fluid, use clean brake fluid with the DOT rating specified by Ford Motor Company— or better. Brake fluid, with alcohol as a constituent component, has an affinity for water (it is hygroscopic.) Atmospheric moisture, passing through a cap vent, mingles with brake fluid.

Exposed to the atmosphere, brake fluid has a short shelf life. Keep lids sealed snugly and never store fluid in an open container. DOT 3 fluid, fresh out of a new can, boils at 401° F or higher, while the absorption of only 3% moisture reduces the boiling point to 284° F! This is ample justification for the annual flush and replenishment of clean brake fluid.

As braking is essential to your safety, apply special care when handling brake service parts and brake fluid. The need for cleanliness cannot be overstated, as hydraulic brake cylinders will fail when exposed to abrasive debris or mineral/petroleum based oils, solvents and greases.

Brake Service

Your truck's brakes require regular attention, including checking the hydraulic brake fluid, inspecting hoses and steel pipes for damage, and noting the lining left on disc brake pads and brake shoes. With clean hands and a clean master cylinder cap, check the brake fluid level at each lubrication interval.

> **NOTE —**
> Take care when checking fluid, especially on models with floorboard inspection covers. Make certain that debris and grit cannot fall from the floorboard into the open brake fluid reservoir. Before removing the master cylinder fill plug, clean the area thoroughly.

Fig. 12-13. Before checking brake fluid on a 1948–56 Ford F truck, vacuum or brush dirt away from the inspection plate hole and the master cylinder fill plug area. Carefully remove the plug to verify the correct fluid level, which you will find listed in your F-Series shop manual.

Dusty trails, stream crossings, slush and snow expose various brake parts to water, abrasive dirt and road salts. Older trucks, with master cylinders mounted beneath the floorboard, have atmospherically vented filler caps. These models face the risk of both contaminants and moisture entering the reservoir.

Fig. 12-12. 1967 and newer Ford F-trucks feature tandem master cylinders, mounted high on the firewall, a sensible distance from debris and water. Still, always clean around the master cylinder assembly before removing cap.

The early master cylinder design also raises other service issues. The air vent in the master cylinder cap often draws dust and moisture into the master cylinder reservoir. It is common for abrasive mud to accumulate in the base of the master cylinder reservoir. A complete system flush and overhaul of each cylinder is the only remedy for this problem.

Even more hazardous for the earlier 1948–56 F-truck models with an under the floorboard master cylinder, submerging the chassis in running stream water or driving through a flooded roadway can contaminate the hydraulic braking system.

Most truck owners and mechanics ignore flushing the hydraulic brake system. Years ago, brake parts manufacturers recommended pressure flushing with a special flushing compound (usually containing denatured alcohol) or pumping clean brake fluid through the brake system annually. Replacement of all rubber cups, seals and boots followed. For the early F-truck or any truck that sets for long periods or drives through streams regularly, flushing the system is still a good idea.

At the very least, you should pump fresh brake fluid through the system annually and bleed out all air. Make certain that enough brake fluid passes through to carry away most of the stale fluid. If your truck has an under floorboard master cylinder with a cap that vents the reservoir to atmosphere, periodic inspection and service of your hydraulic system will contribute to the safety and preservation of expensive brake parts.

Newer F-truck braking systems have much less trouble with atmospheric contamination of brake fluid. Later master cylinder covers provide a sealed rubber bellows to accommodate pressure and fluid level changes. This eliminates the need for a vent hole from the reservoir to atmosphere.

For details on servicing, flushing or bleeding the brake system, consult your F-Series shop manual. Ford truck brake systems vary, and modern brake designs, especially the newer Anti-lock Braking System (ABS), call for different service procedures than earlier models.

Brake Service and Overhaul Tips

Avoid introducing contaminants or abrasive foreign material into the hydraulic reservoir(s). Such debris damages sensitive rubber parts within the master cylinder and hydraulic system. Late model trucks with aluminum master cylinder bores are especially vulnerable to scoring.

During brake system overhauls, check the labels on brake parts cleaners. Many contain petroleum solvents or distillates. These cleaners work fine as metal parts degreasers. However, petroleum or mineral-based solvents and oils can cause the wheel cylinder, caliper and master cylinder rubber parts to swell up and fail.

> *WARNING —*
> *Never use mineral or petroleum-based solvents or oils around rubber brake parts.*

Denatured alcohol and automotive brake fluid are among the few substances that will not destroy rubber. The traditional cleaner for critical brake parts is denatured alcohol. (Allow alcohol to evaporate completely be-

Fig. 12-14. Disc caliper piston scoring resulted from the severe heat generated as a rotor disintegrated. Piston seizure can cause brake lockup or severe brake pull.

Fig. 12-15. Wheel cylinders cannot tolerate scoring. If honed, this cylinder will lose too much material. Pitting and scoring result from moisture and wear. Periodic flushing could have prevented pitting.

fore filling the system with brake fluid.) Your F-Series shop manual will indicate which cleaning substances to use. Read safety precautions before handling any of these cleaning substances.

> *CAUTION —*
> *Due to changes in metal types and factory bore finishing methods, manufacturers do not recommend honing certain hydraulic cylinders. Consult a factory workshop manual for recommended service procedures that apply to your model and year vehicle. Follow factory guidelines when servicing a master cylinder, wheel cylinders and disc brake calipers.*

Always inspect hydraulic brake cylinders for pits, scratches, scoring and corrosion. If in doubt, replace the cylinder. If rebuildable, remove the cylinder from the system. When recommended in the factory workshop manu-

Fig. 12-16. *Many late model master cylinders have aluminum housings. Most shops regard such assemblies as a throw away item, finding them ill-suited for overhaul. Deep scratches and scoring, common traits when these parts require service, can render such a master cylinder useless. Never hone an aluminum brake cylinder. Follow factory service guidelines.*

Fig. 12-17. *Overhauling disc brake calipers requires cleanliness, care and proper tools. Here, a new seal seats in a reconditioned, safely sized bore.*

al covering your model and year vehicle, hone the cylinder's bore lightly with a suitable brake cylinder hone.

Hone as described in the factory workshop manual. Be certain not to leave debris or abrasive material in the cylinder. Carefully measure the bore diameter. If within factory tolerance, the cylinder must be thoroughly cleaned in the manner noted within the factory shop manual for your model. Assemble new rubber parts with clean brake fluid or special brake rubber parts assembly lube.

When servicing disc brakes, make certain that floating (self-centering) caliper assemblies and pistons slide freely. If signs of friction exist, overhaul or replace the caliper.

If four-wheeling or off-pavement bashing has caused damage to your truck's hydraulic brake lines or fittings, replace parts only with DOT-approved brake hardware.

Tees, junction blocks, and valving should meet or exceed your vehicle's original equipment brake standards.

Use pre-formed steel brake pipe. This tubing, cut to length and double-flared at each end, comes complete with flare nuts and ready to install. Once you have shaped the new tubing with a tubing bender, use a flare nut wrench to remove and replace the brake pipes. Torque flare nuts to the manufacturer's specifications listed in your F-Series truck shop manual.

WARNING —
Avoid introducing debris or contaminants into the hydraulic system when changing brake hoses or pipes. Always bleed air from the system and check for leaks before driving your truck.

While servicing your brakes, inspect the wheel bearings and axle seals. A leaky rear axle seal can ruin new brake lining quickly. Preserve your truck's braking system. Apply preventive care wherever possible. This is your best safeguard against losing your brakes.

Brake Linings

Whether your Ford F-truck is bone stock or highly modified, brake performance is important. Although we refine our engines, transmissions and axles, brakes often get overlooked.

WARNING —
Brake friction materials such as brake linings or brake pads may contain asbestos fibers. Do not create dust by grinding, sanding, or cleaning the pads with compressed air. Avoid breathing any asbestos fibers or dust. Breathing asbestos can cause serious diseases such as asbestosis or cancer, and may result in death. Use only approved methods to clean brake components containing asbestos.

Improving your truck's brake system begins with brake lining. Organic friction materials use asbestos, usu-

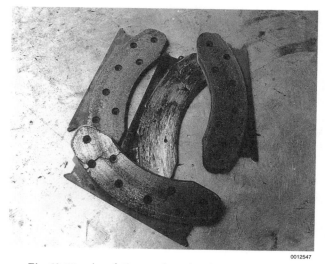

Fig. 12-18. *Age, fatigue and overheating cause brake lining failure. Thinner lining loses heat resistance, as witnessed by these heat-cracked disc brake pads.*

Fig. 12-19. *Thinned brake lining shows heat crack forma-tion. Replace parts now to avoid the risk of lining separation.*

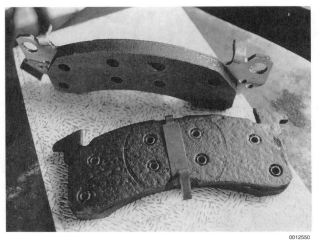

Fig. 12-21. *Coat new pad backs before installation. The special silicone grease dries quickly and helps prevent brake squeal.*

ally in a phenolic-resin compound. Asbestos, an environmental hazard, places the brake mechanic at risk. The brake and clutch industry's attraction to asbestos has been its exceptional heat resistance, low wear and minimal noise. Asbestos health risks outweigh benefits, however, and asbestos-bearing organic friction materials now border on extinction.

Bendix, a respected industry supplier of quality brake parts, advises several precautions when purchasing new brake lining: 1) If your truck has semi-metallic brake pads, always refit with semi-metallic lining; 2) Replace asbestos/organic pads and shoes with comparable lining; and 3) Don't replace OEM organic or organic/asbestos lining with semi-metallic lining— unless sanctioned by the vehicle manufacturer.

Fig. 12-22. *Non-directional finish of rotors assures semi metallic lining break-in. Some manufacturers recommend a brake lathe grinder for this task, while others find a hand held drill motor and disc sander acceptable. Wear an approved particle mask or a federally approved respirator (if you suspect presence of asbestos) and safety goggles.*

Fig. 12-20. *New brake lining has code marks. Many states require edge coding, to help a consumer determine lining type and quality.*

As of this book's publication, asbestos is still legal for some applications. All manufacturers, however, will stop using asbestos as suitable non-asbestos products become available. Stay informed on this issue, and avoid using asbestos products whenever possible.

Semi-metallic brake lining, suited for front disc pad material, provides cooler operation. Under severe braking conditions and heavy loading, semi-metallic lining rapidly draws heat away from the rotors. Excessive heat, the cause of fade and pad/rotor damage, is less likely with semi metallic brake materials.

Manufacturers recommend that replacement brake lining match the OEM material standards. Poor braking, short pad life, and rotor scoring or warping will otherwise result. From a safety standpoint, fade leads to complete brake failure. If you have questions about your truck's original equipment brake lining, consult your local Ford dealership or a brake parts supplier for guidelines.

Semi-metallic Brake Pad Break-in

Semi-metallic pad replacement always includes rotor resurfacing— even if very minor work is necessary to true the rotor and condition the surfaces. Bendix recommends a satin-smooth final cut, followed by a non-directional finish. The final non directional finish assures quieter operation and quick seating of pads.

Like engines and other automotive components, brakes require break-in. For semi-metallic brake pads, Bendix recommends light use of the brakes for the first 150–200 miles. When pads are new, avoid panic stops if possible. Instead of hard burn-ins, Bendix suggests 15–20 slow stops from about 30 mph. Use light to moderate brake pedal pressure and allow at least 30 seconds of recovery between each stop.

As another consideration, semi-metallic lining requires heavier pedal pressure when cold or wet. Some disc brake trucks with heavier (integral with the wheel hub) front rotors will dissipate heat so effectively that a semi metallic retrofit lining cannot work at peak efficiency.

Reciprocally, a less expensive organic lining will overheat and wear rapidly when installed on a late model, lightweight rotor system designed for semi-metallic lining. This is one more reason to stick with original equipment recommendations.

Drums and Rotors

The trueness of a rotor or drum is essential. Drums and rotors should be checked for scoring, hard spots, warpage and proper inside diameter (drums) or thickness (rotors). Micrometers for this task are common to brake shops and automotive machine shops. If the rotor or drum surface is at all suspect, resurfacing on a brake lathe is necessary.

Fig. 12-24. *Read the thickness and wear of the rotor with an outside micrometer. Determine whether to cut the rotors or buy a new pair. Better ventilated, lightweight rotors are often candidates for semi-metallic pads. Your local Ford dealership's parts department can verify which type of lining is acceptable.*

Fig. 12-25. *A badly scored rotor cannot be reused. Here, disc brake pads and rivets wore into the rotor, destroying its surface. One shoe absorbed gear oil from a leaky rear axle seal. On another, riveted lining has simply worn out.*

Fig. 12-23. *Before disassembly, check your truck's hub/drums or disc rotors for lateral runout, warpage and thickness variance.*

Rotors, drums and lining are expensive. Care should be taken to tighten each set of lugs gradually and in cross. Whenever possible, use a torque wrench for final tightening.

Always recheck air gun tightened lugs when you have new tires mounted commercially. If too tight, jack up the wheel, loosen the whole set of nuts, and retightened properly. If too loose, bring nuts to specification in cross sequence.

Fig. 12-26. *Resurfaced rear brake drum assures a quality brake job. Lining will wear-in better and offer complete contact with the drum surface. For safe braking, opposite-wheel brakes should be serviced at the same time; all four wheels on a four-drum braking system.*

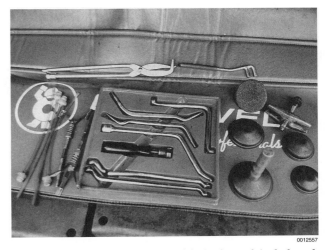

Fig. 12-28. *Specialty tools used for brake work include seal drivers, piston removal tools, adjuster spoons, bleeder wrenches, spring pliers and retainer/removal tool. Seen also is a set of master cylinder bench bleeding hoses.*

Fig. 12-27. *Professionals install hardware kits with every brake overhaul. Old springs and retainers fatigue from heat, while new pieces contribute to proper shoe alignment and action.*

CAUTION —

A common cause of disc brake rotor damage is over-torquing the wheel lug nuts. Wheel lugs too loose or tight, or tightened out of sequence, can warp a rotor. Use of an impact gun is the easiest way to overtighten lug nuts. Aside from the risk of breaking lug studs, overtightening enlarges wheel holes and warps disc rotors. Improperly torqued lugs can warp a rotor enough to cause pulsation of the brake pedal and premature pad wear.

Fig. 12-29. *Wheel cylinder cups and dust boots are available in a variety of sizes. Replace these parts at each brake overhaul. Older trucks called for an annual brake system flush and replacement of these cups and boots. Your Ford F-Series light truck shop manual describes the service requirements for your model.*

Fig. 12-30. Other damage, like these over-torqued and broken wheel studs, adds to restoration cost. Broken studs usually result from overtorquing during wheel installation.

Fig. 12-31. Here is a common cause of premature rear brake lining failure. This semi-floating axle's bearing seal has leaked. Gear oil saturated the brake shoes and rubber dust boots.

Fig. 12-32. Resurfacing the brake drums is an important part of a brake job. Your Ford F-Series light truck shop manual provides safe machining limits. Rivet heads, steel pad backings and metal shoe backs cause the worst damage.

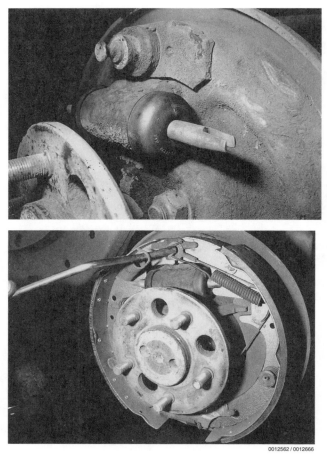

Fig. 12-33. New wheel cylinder boots protect against moisture and debris. Once the cylinder overhaul is complete, new brake shoes and hardware fit into place.

Chapter 13

Body and Detailing

HARSH CLIMATES, BRUSH SCRATCHES and off-pavement bashing tear unmercifully at your truck's body. Over the years, a truck also accumulates its share of oxidation. The battle against rust is an endless vigil. You must watch constantly for fresh scratches and exposed metal. In salt air regions, including areas with corrosive salt spread on winter roadways, truck bodies are especially vulnerable. Bright metal, chrome and painted surfaces can oxidize rapidly.

1. BATTLING RUST

Sadly, hundreds of thousands of otherwise restorable Ford F-Series trucks have wound up as rusty hulks at recycling yards. Rust is a chronic problem for any truck, even more so for 4x4 models.

In addition to environmental hazards, some truck bodies have weak sheet metal areas or a section that provides very poor water drainage. Mid-'80s and newer models, with more extensive use of galvanized (zinc treated) metals, plastic and rubberized trim, can resist rust much better than older trucks.

Ironically, rust was not a major issue with the earliest 1948–56 F-trucks. Many restorers discover these early models still much intact, with a minimal amount of rust. Despite their age, the oldest F-trucks with separate running boards feature strong gauge sheet metal and few body areas that collect mud or road salt.

By contrast, the most susceptible models for rust are the '57–'60 and '61–'66 series F-trucks, the first two body designs without running boards but with door sill step areas. Recycling yards, body shops and sheet metal parts

Fig. 13-1. *Proper care and detailing has kept this 4WD F-truck in showroom condition. Periodic detail work helps pre-vent paint oxidation, rust, and road salt damage. Protect your truck's value—clean and detail on a regular basis.*

vendors have done a thriving business around replacement body panels for these trucks and others. The more persistent rust areas are the front fenders, door sill/step areas, the tailgate area and the bed.

Rust forms at hood hinges and any other part of the body where paint can wear thin. Bare metal on inner fender panels, the cowl, floorboards, grill shell and front fenders will rust quickly in corrosive or moist air.

One of the most common haunts for rust lies behind the front fenders and around the four wheel openings. Especially on '57-up models, styling makes these areas a natural catch basin for debris. Over time, this trapped debris and water will erode the paint, find bare sheet metal and begin the rust troubles. Another trouble spot is the floorboards.

With the body and chassis thoroughly cleaned, inspect your truck for rust. Pay close attention to areas with add-on accessories, which can expose bare sheet metal. Look for poor sealing and exfoliation (bubbling), an indication of rust formation beneath the paint.

If you suspect rust, remove the accessory and treat the area with thorough sanding, primer/sealing and paint as needed. When damage is excessive, consult a local body shop.

Fix It Yourself

The flatter panels on a truck body make a good place to enhance your metalwork and painting skills. Restoration and maintenance can include sealing, priming and painting your truck.

Fig. 13-2. *When the carpet rolls back, so can the metal! A small bulge at the outer body surface never suggested this major rust. On older F-Series trucks, floorboard and door sill rust is a major problem. If your truck or a prospective buy needs restoration, look closely. You must always seal around any drilled holes. Carpets may hide an area where water can accumulate and menacing rust forms. Always take rust bubbles or exfoliation seriously.*

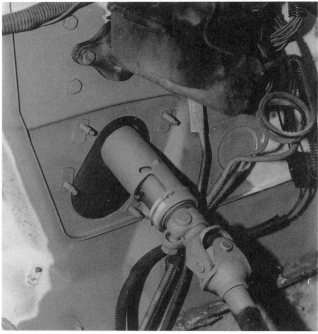

Fig. 13-3. *Surface rust on firewall, although unsightly, does not effect the integrity of base sheetmetal. A professional body worker sees this as salvageable. Sandblasting reveals that underlying metal is strong and serviceable.*

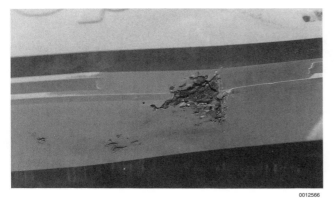

Fig. 13-4. *This is insidious rust. Hidden behind a trim panel, rust now presses through the sheetmetal. Watch for high spots like this.*

Fig. 13-5. *Sandblasting at this metal bulge tells a broader tale. Hidden between an aftermarket trim panel and interior carpet, major rust damage resulted from improper metal seal during installation of the add-on roll bar.*

Ford F-truck frames, although made of metals which resist rust perforation, also build up surface oxidation. Wear a particle mask and safety goggles, and clean rust with a drill-powered wire brush. Prime and paint surfaces to prevent further problems, using a rust inhibiting primer or paint.

Rust Repairs

Louie Russo, Jr., owner of L. J. Russo's Paint and Body Shop at Lakeside, California, is an auto body and paint master. If your truck restoration includes rust removal, Louie's step-by-step rust repair system provides a good lesson. Consider these procedures carefully before tackling your truck's rust. Techniques shown here provide a like-new fix and prepare the truck for a quality paint job.

Fig. 13-6. *Factory rivets drilled, Louie Russo separates floorpan from the interior body brace. Extent of rust is still deceptive at this point.*

Fig. 13-7. *Louie carefully removes rotted metal. Here, a carbide disc cuts quickly through the sheetmetal brace. Structural integrity of the body is a consideration with this repair. Use an approved particle mask or respirator and goggles around carbide grinding.*

Fig. 13-8. *Remove or treat all rust-effected metal. At this point, wire brushing and sandblasting will determine strength of metal and pinholes to fill.*

CHAPTER 13

Fig. 13-9. *Heavy-gauge metal section from a Model A Ford fender has become a replacement piece for the OEM brace. Louie welds the hand-formed repair section into place. Note use of salvageable segment of the original brace. This small portion of metal helps maintain alignment and contours.*

Fig. 13-10. *MIG welded into place, section now fits against the cleaned floorpan. Heat applied to lower bracket flange allows shaping with a body hammer until new brace matches OE fit perfectly. Louie also welded pinholes in floorpan. Surface grinding of welds will restore original appearance.*

2. BODY DETAILING

As a light truck owner, get to know your local self-service car wash. Here, the combination of soap and high pressure spray can transform a mud-caked truck into respectable suburban driveway material. In minutes, pounds of mud and debris will stream from the body, wheel wells, frame, axles and suspension.

Detailing your truck begins with a thorough wash. Many trucks face as much dirt, sun and abrasive wind as a desert camel, yet there's no protective hair or hide to seal the elements from your truck's paint finish. Magnetic abrasives cling tenaciously to the paint pores, while scorching sun and road salts oxidize the trim and rubber. A cleaner must be gentle enough to leave healthy paint intact, yet still cut and flush the grit from the paint.

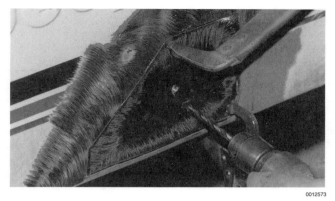

Fig. 13-11. *Louie cuts and forms flat piece of sheetmetal to fit cutout. He purposely keeps the original lower roll of body lip to avoid reforming edge. Drilling and spot-welding outer panel to inner brace duplicates OE engineering. MIG confines heat. Louie strategically lays down welds while carefully quenching hot sheetmetal to maintain shape.*

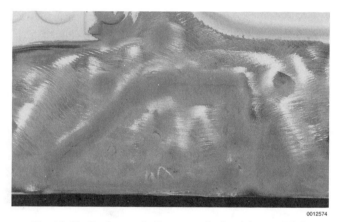

Fig. 13-12. *Surface grinding reveals Louie's careful handling of metal. Masterful heat isolation, shrink/stretch control and correct heat diffusion results in near perfect surface straightness.*

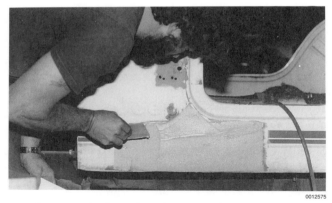

Fig. 13-13. *Louie applies a light coat of plastic body filler to sanding scratches and very slight depressions. Once shaped and sanded, only a tiny amount of plastic will remain. Louie Russo prefers the challenge of metal working to the simpler, plastic fill approach. His work shows good-as-new quality.*

Fig. 13-14. Local car wash or a home pressure washer will remove major debris after a hard day's work or off-roading.

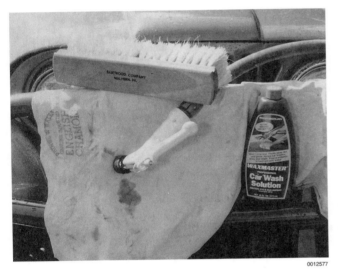

Fig. 13-15. A spray nozzle, car wash solution, horse hair brush and a genuine English chamois are tools for a safe wash job.

Fig. 13-16. Eastwood Company's mail order catalog features products for a show-winning appearance.

There are many commercial car wash solutions on the market. The main objective with any good car soap is to dissolve road oils and gently flush dirt away. Although dishwashing liquids work well, commercial products might be part of a complete cleaning system, chemically engineered to work with specific waxes or polishes.

Even more important is your washing technique. For a safe wash job around grit and abrasives, avoid scratching the finish. A sponge or wash cloth is hazardous. Special car wash mitts work much better, but hand pressure can still cause grit to press into the paint or drag across the surface.

I always begin with a thorough wash-down using a high pressure washer that attaches to an air compressor source and garden hose. This washer can easily clean dirty engine bays, inner fender wells and the chassis.

For hand washing, the gentle bristles and cushion provided by a horse hair brush reduce the risk of scratches yet still massages foaming soap into paint pores. Your truck's panels will cleanse easily, followed by a gentle rinse of clear water. Use a quality, rubber-nosed faucet nozzle, capable of controlling pressure while protecting the vehicle's finish.

Why Fight Your Paint Finish?

Most truck owners can find better things to do with their weekends than wash and polish a vehicle. In recent years, however, professional detailing equipment has drastically sped up detailing work. Shifting away from disc-sander type buffers, the orbital polishers now appear everywhere—and for good reason.

Traditional buffing methods, especially hand or disc polishing, can leave the paint finish full of swirls. Worse yet, the risk of buffing right through the paint edges scares most non-professional detailers from even attempting to use a disc-type buffer. The gentle orbital buffers, by contrast, offer the first-time user a chance to do a professional polishing job without ruining an expensive paint finish.

As for the risk of paint removal from orbital buffing, I once interviewed Loren E. Doppelt, Senior Product Manager for Waxmaster/Chamberlain. Loren noted, "I've buffed and polished a sample hood at car shows. The hood receives 1,000 buffings before we routinely re-paint it . . . Frankly, even then, there's no evidence that the paint is damaged."

Fig. 13-17. .A random orbital waxer/polisher is your best investment and incentive for detail work. The Chamberlain/Waxmaster and other units are available from retail suppliers.

Fig. 13-19. An orbital buffer works with any number of specialized products. Shown are Waxmaster and Mothers brands of waxes and polishes.

Fig. 13-18. This buffer bonnet's grey debris came from a fully cured new paint job after a thorough wash. An orbital buffer, used with a wide range of detailing chemicals, can strip/clean, apply wax or polish and buff the finish to a high luster. Uniform results make hand or disc-type polishing obsolete.

Your First Orbital Buffing Job

When your new paint finish turns dull from road film and caked mud, don't panic. Armed with the right detailing chemicals and a quality orbital buffer, you can produce a professional wax job in less than an hour. Park your truck in the shade, and begin by washing it thoroughly. With the metal cool, apply a smooth coating of wax.

The body contours and accessory hardware on many trucks can pose a nightmare for buffing. A steep sloping cab, trailer pulling mirrors and abutments sticking out everywhere create a real challenge for an orbital buffer. Still, the promise of uniform buffing action, as opposed to sluggish, ineffective hand waxing, will spur your polishing job forward.

Carnauba based semi-paste wax, mixed with a liquid polish, works best with the orbital buffer. Although the buffer easily works with other chemical products, the combination polish and wax allows a faster, more thorough job. Carnauba based waxes provide better paint breathing and protection. I've had good results with waxes such as Eagle 1 and Mothers.

Apply the wax and polish solution simultaneously to the terry cloth buffing bonnet. Movement of the orbital buffer is easy to master. The technique is much like operating a floor polisher. Application of wax/polish will take approximately thirty to forty minutes on a light truck, including the exterior surface of the bed.

The buffer will lay down a uniform blend of wax. Hard to reach and hand applied areas rub easily with the remaining wax/polish on the polishing bonnet. Install a clean cloth and begin buffing. Use a a terry cloth towel to hand buff inaccessible areas.

Orbital buffing leaves your truck's finish with a protective, penetrating coat of Carnauba wax. Surface oxidized material transfers to the buffing pads.

Conventional hand waxing, a tedious, unfulfilling task, is now passe. An orbital buffer produces professional results, the first time out. For a sharp appearance that lasts for years, treat your truck to quarterly polish jobs with a random orbital buffer and a quality Carnauba wax/polish.

Weather-beaten Paint

A grossly oxidized finish may still respond to a finishing compound buff out. Seek a quality compound that lifts dead paint by chemical action, not abrasion, and leaves no swirl marks. Follow buffing with a careful polish and wax job.

Badly oxidized finishes may take a full morning and several orbital buffer pads to fix. Bonnets are washable and reusable if you keep them wet after use.

Finishes raked by disc buffer swirls respond impressively to an orbital buffing with a quality swirl remover. Applied directly to the buffer pad, this non-scratching substance is more like a polish than a rubbing compound. I've played with ultra-fine sanding scratches left by 1200 grit wet-sanding paper and found that an orbital buffer can remove all traces in minutes—without cutting into the finish.

Quick Tips To A Better Detail Job

1) Wash your truck thoroughly. Use bug and tar remover and other specially formulated chemicals to treat problem areas.

2) When using a buffer, make sure your polish and waxes are compatible. Chemical bases differ, and some chemicals react adversely with each other.

3) Use several terrycloth towels when hand waxing. Don't apply towels used for buffing the sides and rocker panels to the upper body surfaces. Avoid introducing road oxidants and corrosives to the upper panels.

4) Wax your truck in the shade. Many polishes and waxes have chemistry that evaporates rapidly in direct sunlight. A hot paint surface is also more vulnerable to damage.

5) Apply polish to the cloth or bonnet. Pouring it onto the painted surface may cause uneven chemical action, including stains.

6) Avoid use of any product that seals paint permanently. Such materials may prevent normal expansion and contraction of paint and seldom offer protection against UV radiation. Auto painters lament the fish-eye effect that results when repainting finishes sealed with permanent protectants.

7) Invest in the miracles of modern science. Special detailing chemicals not only leave more time for recreational drives, fishing and fun, but they often provide superior results.

8) Allow vinyl surfaces to breathe. Most vinyl has a chemically engineered top-coat that needs protection. Choose your vinyl treatment carefully.

9) Use a small detail brush to reach difficult areas. A freshly polished finish draws attention to those small crevices and crannies that you miss. A few extra minutes makes the difference between a show-stopper and a shoddy job.

10) Pay attention to quality. There's a reason for higher priced products, and all waxes are not the same. The longest lasting stuff may not serve your paint finish best. Look for breathable Carnaubas and anti-oxidants. They can extend the life of your truck's finish.

The Rest Of The Details

When your truck's paint finish comes back to life, a sparkling surface with deeply colored lustre, there's a real incentive to complete the detailing chores. Here, too, I recommend fast, high quality chemical products for highlighting the interior and exterior trim.

Flat stainless steel and chrome moldings respond readily to the gentle buffing action of the orbital machine, and the balance of the stainless hardware will polish easily by hand. Rubber and vinyl, the two most vulnerable materials after paint, require a hand-applied combination cleaner/protectant product that will counter oxidation.

The principle cause of oxidation on your truck's paint surface and rubber is sunlight. Use of a protective UV-blocker agent on vinyl, leather and plastic trim extends the life of these materials. I get good results with 303 Protectant.

0012582

Fig. 13-20. The boating and outdoor equipment industries highly recommend 303 Protectant for vinyl and fiberglass. 303 can protect tires, dash pads, door rubber seals and bumper inserts.

0012583

Fig. 13-21. Permatex's Indian Head Rubber Lubricant has a long history. Claims have it harmless to vinyl, rubber and canvas, with many uses around your truck. This substance also works as an emergency tire mounting lubricant. Used regularly on shock bushings, sway bar bushings and other chassis rubber, this lubricant enhances service life.

A gentle cleaner, 303 claims to provide a protective barrier against oxidation without damaging the vinyl's top-coat chemistry. Sensitive vinyl surfaces must flex and breathe. Any coating that either draws away the special surface chemistry or seals the top-coat from breathing will eventually cause embrittlement. According to Orvis, the noted fishing tackle company, 303 will also lengthen your flyline cast as much as 30 feet!

Paint Scratch Repairs

Light trucks and four-wheel drive utility vehicles have close scrapes with trees, limbs and brush. Scratches detract from the appearance of your truck, and brush-on touch up paints often leave ugly scars.

Armed with a random orbital buffer, some brush touch-up paint, a sheet of 1200-grit color sanding paper, a 3M Soft Hand Pad and some swirl remover, here's my formula for a super-fast, professional scratch repair:

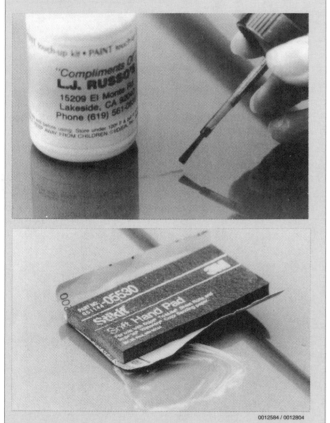

0012584 / 0012804

9:00 a.m.—Slight scratch in hood surface is carefully cleaned and filled with touch-up paint. (5 minutes)

11:00 a.m.—Left in direct sunlight, touch up is completely dry. Move the truck into the shade.

11:30 a.m.—Gently color sand with 1200-grit paper and 3M pad, confining your sanding to the crown of the touch-up paint. Sanding stops when adjacent paint or clearcoat shows signs of ultra-fine, uniform discoloration. (10 minutes)

11:40 a.m.—Swirl remover is applied to orbital buffer pad. Buffing the discolored area, focus directly on the repair. Light use of the buffer edge will concentrate the polishing effort. (2 minutes or less buffing time)

11:48 a.m.—Wipe away remaining swirl remover. Treat the beautifully matched surface to a new coat of wax/polish. (6 minutes)

12:00 p.m.—Load fishing poles into the cab or bed of your truck. Grin broadly and drive to the hottest local angling spot. Catch your limit before heading for camp. (Releasing fish is optional, if such is your ethic.) (Time involved depends on fishing action.)

CAUTION —
Avoid silicone oils and other chemistry that leave a wet look on vinyl.

Wheel cleanup is simple on most truck models. Painted steel rims respond readily to a light coat of Carnauba wax. If wheels are chrome or alloy and dull, hand rubbing with a metal polish such as Simichrome does the trick. If the wheel surface has oxidized, polishing with a die-grinder driven buffer pad will restore its surface.

NOTE —
A light coat of Carnauba-based wax will allow porous surfaces to flex and breathe. This prevents UV absorption and permanent dulling, yellowing or damage.

The final step in detailing your truck is interior clean-up. Professional shampoos, cleaners and specialized chemicals work quickly on the interior. Carpet stains and other tough challenges respond best to professional cleaners.

Stripping Film and Wax Buildup

Improperly applied waxes and polishes, particularly those which seal the paint surface, will permit oxidation and yellowing. The worst example is a dull, sun-bleached truck with a color base coat and a clear-coat finish.

Some aftermarket paint sealant/protectant products also pose a threat to paint. Claiming long term paint protection and ease of maintenance, many of these products actually smother the original paint. Sealed and unable to breathe, the treated paint or clear coat surface succumbs to cracking, weather checking and other damage caused by ultraviolet sunlight.

The most common cause of wax buildup is poor application technique. The paint finish likely had untreated surface oxidation, and uneven hand rubbing has built up successive layers of wax. Although most one-step waxes and polishes employ a cleaner to cut through and loosen the old layer of wax, this chemistry often fails.

After using a random orbital buffer and professional chemical products, it's obvious why hand polishing leads to wax buildup. A truck waxed regularly by hand will turn a terrycloth buffer bonnet blacker than the tire sidewalls. Successive layers of wax simply seal off the paint. Paint cracking or severe fade then develops. A proper wax job should lightly coat the surface and allow paint to breathe.

Use a chemical finishing compound and an orbital buffer to reverse the damage of wax buildup. (Avoid the use of rubbing compounds. They are abrasive and remove paint.) The goal is to eliminate old wax and gently lift oxidized, dead paint from below the wax. (Yellow simply means that oxidation has occurred.)

Once the finishing or cleaning compound has removed wax and oxidized paint, the surface will regain its luster. The fresh finish can receive a coat of quality polish or wax.

3. PICKUP BED AND TUB LINERS

Did your pickup truck go off to work, only to return all bashed and battle scarred? Does your cargo bed rattle with tools, jacks and other menacing items? Forget the dents and raw paint. An aftermarket slide-in bed liner or sprayed-in polyurethane bed coating can prevent utility bed damage. Both the looks of your truck and its resale value will benefit from bed protection.

The traditional plastic tub liners now compete with a new generation of spray-in materials. Advocates of tub liners assert that the liner is replaceable (or removable on resale of the truck), while spray-in materials are permanent.

0012585

Fig. 13-22. Slide-in tub liners have the advantage of easy removal if you sell the truck. If you use this kind of liner, periodically remove the tub and check for rust. A heavy coat of wax on the bed floor can help prevent the formation of rust on sheet metal beneath the liner/tub.

By contrast, a spray-in polyurethane coating will rust-proof far better than a slide-in tub. Polyurethane sprays adhere to every square inch of the pickup bed or the cab's floor, one of the other areas that can benefit greatly from this material.

This last point is important. A major concern with slide-in bedliner installations is that moisture can creep beneath the liner. Once there, collected water waits patiently for bare metal to appear. Hidden rust forms, spreading beneath the bedliner. Often, rust perforation through the bottom of the bed is the first clue that oxidation has occurred.

If a bedliner is installed in a new truck, the odds of rust formation can be drastically reduced. Most rustout develops when owners install bed protection after scratches and seam spreading have already scarred the bed. For a bedliner installation in a used truck, first eliminate all rust, caulk or seal each seam, and prime any repaired or scratched surfaces.

Tub or polyurethane spray-in bedliners offer protection against chemicals, corrosives and denting. For loading and handling materials, however, another factor should also influence your choice of a liner: anti-skid protection.

My choice is a spray-in polyurethane coating that offers a permanent barrier to rust. In many parts of the

"Chemistry 101" For Detailers

Effective detailing is knowing which chemicals to use on a given surface. For washing your truck, look for solutions that prevent streaking. Professional car soaps remove very little wax and allow several cleanings between re-wax jobs. Tar and spot removers are actually high-grade cleaning solvents designed for safe work around interior and exterior finishes.

> *CAUTION —*
> *Although tar and spot remover safely removes grease, gum, most stains, adhesives and undercoating, it may affect the top-coat of some vinyl and plastic items. Read labels carefully. These chemicals are also useful for removing wax and silicone before painting stripes or applying touchup.*

Rubber dressing and protectants generally have a polymer or silicone base. Renewing tires, moldings, floor mats, pedal pads, dashpads, vinyl materials and other items is as easy as applying the right chemistry to the surface. Some materials require slight hand buffing.

Rubbing and finishing compounds meet several uses. Cleaning or cutting into the painted surface, these materials remove dull paint, orange peel and water spots. Often, new paint or even clear coatings require color sanding, which leaves a mildly scratched, dull surface. Power (or orbital) buffing with non-abrasive chemical compounds can make the finish smooth and shiny.

Products like Carecraft's Swirl Remover fit a special niche. Carecraft says it is a buffing cleaner capable of removing fine scratches and oxidation. Swirl Remover contains no wax or silicone, yet it lubricates the buffer pad. As a follow-up to rubbing compound or a poor detail job, Swirl Remover has no harsh abrasives and can be a mild, effective alternative for restoring a slightly oxidized finish.

Additionally, there are treatments and cleaners for upholstery, rugs, chrome, stainless steel and every other material found on a truck. The concern here is chemical compatibility. With questionable materials, always test chemicals first. Discoloration and damage can result from improper use or poor mixing of chemicals.

Let modern tools and chemistry do the work. Save your time and energy for recreational pursuits.

United States, a moist climate or harsh and wet winters make a slide-in bedliner unwise.

By comparison, if the bed is prepared properly and sprayed correctly with a quality polyurethane bedliner material, rust is no longer an issue. An aftermarket spray-in bedliner can preserve your bed and prevent rust formation.

These spray-in bed coatings require special equipment and spray booths for installation. They adhere so well that it would be virtually impossible to remove the cured material without damaging paint—and possibly the bed metal. If damaged, the coating can be retouched.

Fig. 13-23. Spray-in polyurethane bed coatings have gained popularity. This material, applied properly, offers durability and anti-corrosion protection, plus a waterproof barrier against rust. When textured, the coating has anti-skid quality. Color can be added to contrast with your truck's paint scheme.

Fig. 13-24. This bed mat provides ample protection plus an oil resistant surface that has a non-skid texture. Easily removed or exchanged between vehicles, bed mats are practical for many light truck and utility applications.

An alternative to the permanent tub or spray foam installation is a bed mat. Bed mats, custom fitted to cover the entire floor of your truck, provide substantial protection. Better mats offer skid resistance and a cushioned cargo surface.

Mats insulate the bed or floor from cargo damage. Additionally, you can remove a quality mat periodically to thoroughly clean and wax the bed to reduce the risk of rust formation. Better quality bed mats are resistant to oil, chemicals and marring. They provide years of service.

Chapter 14

Electrical System Basics

TRUCK RESTORATION AND MAINTENANCE include the electrical system and wiring. Repair work and routine service frequently mean the renewal of wiring and changing connectors. Often, the frame-up restoration of an older truck chassis (especially six-volt systems with cloth wrapped wiring) requires wiring the truck from scratch.

A successful wiring job can be gratifying. I well remember my first job as a truck fleet mechanic. My employer bought a two-ton capacity '59 Ford F-500 stake truck. The vehicle came really cheap, via a U.S. government surplus source, as someone had cut every wire behind the instrument/dash panel and left the truck paralyzed.

My first task was to re-wire the entire chassis and engine electrical system. Armed with a wiring schematic from the local Ford dealership, I chose the proper wire gauge for each circuit and carefully began routing the scores of new wires.

When I finished and turned the key, the engine started—and the lights, turn signals, wipers, accessories and all instrument gauges worked, too! In fact, everything operated safely, as I had routed all circuits through an OEM fuse panel for reliable service. The truck had a fine six-cylinder engine and rugged geartrain, and we got excellent service from the workhorse chassis.

Your truck works dependably when the lights glow, turn signals flash, heater blows, starter spins, wipers swish, spark plugs fire, alternator charges and electric fuel pump pulses. Understanding the dynamics of a truck's electrical system can enhance your troubleshooting skills, a vital asset when traveling through remote country.

1. THE ELECTRICAL SYSTEM

Light truck electrical systems vary in voltage layouts. Until 1956, all Ford F-Series light trucks had 6-volt electri-

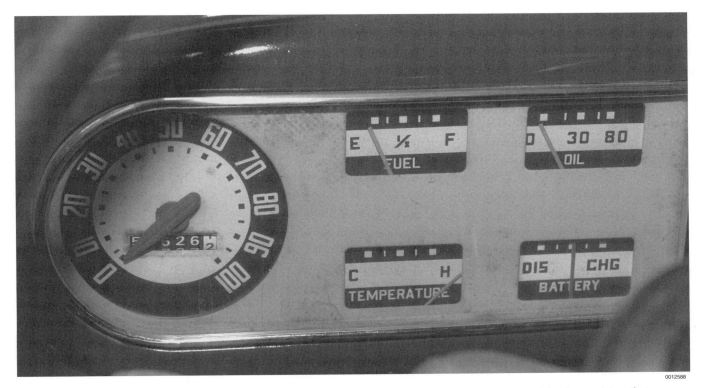

Fig. 14-1. *1948 F-truck dash was simple and functional—so was the wiring to this set of instruments. Unless the cloth insulation has deteriorated, early wiring presents few problems.*

Modern trucks feature computers and intricate wiring that demand a precise voltage supply and exact resistance measurements.

cal systems, positively grounded. Early wiring was the infamous cloth-wrapped design, heavy in gauge and light in lifespan.

Beginning in the mid-'50s, Ford and other vehicle manufacturers switched to plastic wrapped wiring. Ford F-trucks gained their first 12-volt electrical systems in 1956, which improved the performance of accessories, the starting circuit and lighting.

CAUTION —
1948–55 Ford F-truck's with six-volt electrical systems use a positive ground arrangement. All Ford 12-volt systems ('56-up) have the more common negative ground polarity.

NOTE —
Both cloth and plastic wiring insulation deteriorate over time. Trucks used off-pavement, in agriculture, harsh climates or around corrosive industrial settings are ongoing candidates for electrical wire repair.

System Overview

Depending on the chassis year, a 6-volt or 12-volt wet storage battery supplies current for the electrical system. Ford trucks have used a variety of starter motor types, including the early Bendix spring drives, overrunning clutch drive styles and even a few GM Delco-Remy type applications. More recently, permanent magnet starter motors have become popular.

One of the distinct features of Ford starter systems is the fenderwell mounted solenoid switch, which also doubles as a junction block for the main cables of the electrical system. This switch mechanism survives from the earliest Ford electric start systems. During the 6-volt era, some switches even offered a start button on the bottom of the solenoid switch to provide an underhood means of activating the starter—great for service work and tune-ups!

Years ago, Auto-Lite was a mainstay source for many Ford truck electrical components. Generators served battery charge needs into the 12-volt era, and the first models to use alternators were early in 1965, when Ford made sweeping engine changes as well.

What Is An Alternator?

Although alternator designs have evolved since the early '60s, their operation remains much the same. Typically, as the ignition switch turns ON, a wire lead with 12-volt current feeds to the alternator or external regulator. Through transistor and diode switching, current reaches a field coil. While the engine cranks, a high field current is generated to increase available voltage. This is the pre-charging mode.

As the engine runs, the alternator's rotor spins at speed to produce alternating current within the stator winding. Typically, the stator sends AC current to an internal rectifier bridge and diodes, which convert the AC current to usable 12-volt DC current. Diodes also prevent battery current from draining at the alternator.

The battery (BAT) pole on the alternator or regulator can perform two roles: 1) act as a route for charging current returning to the battery, and 2) serve as an information source for the battery's state of charge or electrical loads on the system.

During normal operation, all amperage drains on the battery send a voltage reading to the alternator's regulator. (Later trucks feature voltmeters on the instrument panel. The voltmeter signals the correlation between battery drain and volts.)

While the engine cranks, a 12-volt battery reads approximately 9 or 10 volts. At times, an electric winch load can equal this rating. Headlights, air conditioning or any other electrical demand will also drop voltage at the battery.

How The Alternator Charges The Battery

When your truck's battery has a low state of charge, the alternator returns high amperage current to the battery. Although this current flowing from the battery is actually a quantity of amperage, the battery and regulator interpret the flow in terms of voltage.

Charging a 12-volt battery requires meeting a range of voltages at various temperatures. At very low temperatures, for example, the regulator may test at 14.9–15.9 volts of current. The same regulator at 80° F may operate between 13.9 and 14.6 volts, while 140° ambient temperature produces 13.3–13.9 volts. Above 140° F, the same regulator may offer 13.6 volts.

Since a fully charged battery reads approximately 12.6 volts, the charging circuit must at least maintain that voltage. This requires enough current flow to recharge the battery plus the amperage necessary to operate the entire range of electrical devices, lights, and accessories.

Charge Circuit Routine Service

Battery condition and state of charge are very important to your truck's performance. Later models with electronic fuel and spark management systems depend upon very accurate voltage readings and a strong current supply. All trucks, regardless of the environment in which they operate, require a quality battery in premium condition.

NOTE —
The new generation of high cold cranking amperage (CCA) batteries exceeds older OEM requirements by a good margin. (For details on battery service, see the lubrication/service chapters.)

Early Ford F-truck generators require periodic bearing lubrication. Drive belt condition is always crucial, and a spare belt is a mandatory item for back country trips. All Ford generator systems have external voltage regulators, which are adjustable. Most mechanics, however, prefer to replace a unit that reads out of range.

Polarity is a concern when servicing or replacing either the generator or voltage regulator. You must polarize the generator/regulator to prevent damage and permit charging. As the regulator adjusts current flow back to the battery, correct wiring of the charging system is essential. The different types of automotive regulators (6-volt or 12-volt with either an internally or externally grounded field) require different polarizing procedures.

CAUTION —
Know which type of regulator your Ford truck uses, and consult the Ford F-Series shop manual for instructions on polarizing the generator system when you install a new/rebuilt generator or regulator.

The Lights and Other Circuits

Truck lighting is basic, with current simply flowing through switches, fuses/relays, then to the headlights, tail lamps, turn and brake lights, warning lights and interior lamps. To avoid shorts and unreliable service, your truck's lighting system requires safe routing of wire, correct wire size and secure connections.

Aftermarket accessories pose a challenge. Sound systems, add-on lighting, auxiliary fuel pumps and other additions to your truck's electrical system demand careful consideration. Where should components source their current supply? What wire gauges are suitable? How do you route wires safely? (You'll find more about these issues in the accessory chapter.)

Your truck's OEM electrical system follows a layout common to other U.S. built trucks and cars. Earlier F-trucks have very simple electrical systems, built around common components still available at any auto supply house. Later 12-volt era models boast modern electrical systems, with more complex switches and power accessories. By the late 1970s, the automotive electronic era emerged, introducing the use of modules and computer components that depend on constant voltage levels and perfect wire and ground connections.

The modern light truck electrical system proves very demanding. Air conditioning, closed loop emission controls and electronic fuel, spark and automatic transmission shifting systems create a maze of wires. ABS braking has its own demanding circuits, with speed sensors and other components dependent upon the integrity of the chassis wires.

Work on a late Ford F-truck electrical system involves use of accurate wiring diagrams, an understanding of wire gauge requirements and a clear sense for wire routing. Electrical wire shorts and poor ground connections can leave your truck stranded or cause expensive damage.

Relays

Relays begin to appear with the 12-volt era. The main advantage of relays is that minor amounts of current can control major power flow. For heavy amperage (a measurement of electrical resistance), this is useful. There are two basic relay designs, electro-thermal and electro-magnetic, each with a different function.

Electro-thermal relays receive and delivers current to a bi-metallic contact set. After exposure for a given interval of heat, the switch opens, stopping current flow. As the contacts cool down, the switch closes. The traditional turn signal flasher switch is this type of relay.

Electro-magnetic relays tend to control circuits with larger current flow. Systems like the horn and starter motor can use lighter wiring over several sections. As the smaller gauge wiring from the horn button activates the relay, current flows from a higher amperage (heavier wire

0012589

Fig. 14-2. Relays and fuses come in a variety of sizes and meet various needs. Circuit or reset breakers work well with vehicles that are temporarily exposed to shorts or grounding, especially a 4x4 model that wades through streams.

0012590

Fig. 14-3. This unique fuse/relay holder, available through Wrangler Power Products, features popular ATO-type fuses and circuit breakers that fit ATO sockets.

gauge) battery source lead to the horn. Likewise, a starter solenoid, which must deliver very high amperage battery current directly to the starter motor, also receives its signal via a much lighter gauge ignition/starter switch wire.

Some electro-magnetic starter solenoids also engage the starter's drive teeth with the flywheel ring teeth. Likewise, a fuel cut-off solenoid or similar device uses electrical current to magnetize and move a plunger.

Volt-Ohmmeter: The Perfect Troubleshooting Tool

Of all my automotive testing equipment, one of the most valued tools is a combination volt-ohmmeter (VOM). The ohmmeter can read circuit continuity levels and ohms resistance. A voltmeter reads the actual voltage available at a given circuit. Adjusted for alternating current (AC) or direct current (DC), a voltmeter can measure line voltage between any two points. For automotive electrical troubleshooting, these tools provide a wealth of useful information.

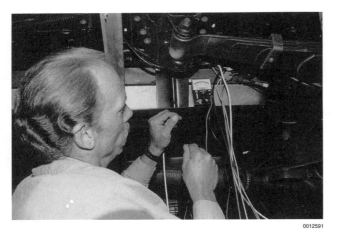

Fig. 14-4. *Grounds are as important as hot sources. Ohm-meters take the guesswork out of testing your truck's engine, chassis and body grounds.*

Fig. 14-5. *Trailer connectors demand more than a test lamp check. You can detect insufficient current flow or resistance at a ground lead with your volt/ohmmeter.*

Ohms, a measurement of electrical resistance, follows an engineering formula: 1 ohm = 1/siemens = 1 volt/ampere. Simply, each ohm is a precise increment of resistance to current flow. Conductive liquids or solids (such as electrical wiring) serve as mediums through which we can measure ohms resistance.

Aside from testing alternator diodes or components in a fuel injection or electronic ignition system, most automotive electrical troubleshooting centers around continuity of current flow and availability of voltage. The ohms segment of a VOM will quickly satisfy a wide range of these continuity checks, helping you find shorts and either partially or fully open circuits.

An inexpensive needle meter can handle basic voltage and resistance tests. For less than $25, you can buy a quality pocket-size tester. (My Radio Shack tester, purchased in 1982 for $10, still functions flawlessly.)

Designed for light use, these handy testers can perform a wide range of effective tests and still fit neatly into your truck's on-board toolbox. For testing fuel injection

and other electronic components, however, you must use a more precise digital volt-meter.

> CAUTION —
> • *Connect or disconnect multiple connectors and test leads only with the ignition off. Switch the multimeter functions or measurement ranges only with the test leads disconnected.*
>
> • *On later model vehicles with sensitive electronic components, do not use a continuity/test lamp with an incandescent bulb to test circuits containing electronic components. Use only an LED (light emitting diode) test lamp. Do not use an analog (swing-needle) volt-ohmmeter to check circuit resistance or continuity on electronic (solid state) components. Use only a high quality digital multi-meter with a high input impedance rating (at least 10 meg-ohms).*

Electrical Troubleshooting

Four things are required for current to flow in any electrical circuit: a voltage source, wires or connections to transport the voltage, a consumer or device that uses the electricity, and a connection to ground. For trouble-free operation, the ground connections, including the battery ground cable and the body ground strap, must remain clean and free from corrosion.

> NOTE —
> Most problems can be found using only a VOM to check for voltage supply, for breaks in the wiring (infinite resistance/no continuity and such), or for a path to ground that completes the circuit.

Electric current is logical in its flow, always moving from the voltage source toward ground. Keeping this in mind, electrical faults can be located through a process of elimination. When troubleshooting a complex circuit, separate the circuit into smaller parts. The general tests outlined here may be helpful in finding electrical problems. The information is even more valuable when used in conjunction with OEM wiring diagrams for your truck.

Testing For Voltage and Ground

The most useful and fundamental electrical troubleshooting technique is checking for voltage and ground. A voltmeter or a simple test light should be used for this test. For example, if a parking light does not work, checking for voltage at the bulb socket will determine if the circuit is functioning correctly or if the bulb itself is faulty.

To check for battery voltage using a test light, connect the test light wire to a clean, unpainted metal part of the truck or a known good ground. Use the pointed end of the light to probe the hot lead of the connector or socket.

To check for continuity to ground, connect the test light wire to the positive (+) battery post or a battery source. (Use the negative (-) post on early F-truck systems with 6-volt positive ground polarity.) Now use the pointed end of the light to probe the connector/socket's ground lead. In either case, the test lamp should light up.

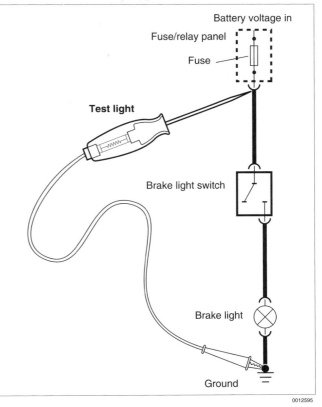

Fig. 14-8. *This is a test light set-up for checking available current. A test light makes a quick check of voltage sources and a complete ground.*

Fig. 14-6. *This 20-amp breaker and a late ATO style Buss fuse each pass the ohmmeter test. Test any suspect circuits and switches for high resistance readings.*

Fig. 14-7. *Test variable voltage devices with the voltmeter. Although most trailer brake controllers are now electronic, they still send voltage signals to the trailer brakes, much like earlier rheostat devices.*

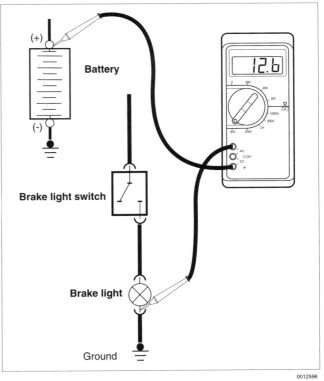

Fig. 14-9. *Here, a voltmeter checks for proper ground.*

CHAPTER 14

WARNING —
Never create electrical sparks at or near the battery. A hot or defective battery emits explosive gases.

CAUTION —
Do not use the pointed end of the test light to pierce through a wire's insulation. This could permanently damage the wire or insulation.

NOTE —
A test light only determines if voltage or a ground is present. It does not determine how much voltage or the quality of the path to ground. If the voltage reading is important, such as when you test a battery or when you need a precise reading of a circuit's voltage, use a digital voltmeter. To check the condition of a ground connection, check for voltage drop on the suspected connection as described below.

To check for voltage using a voltmeter, set the meter to DCV and the correct scale. On 12-volt Ford systems, connect the negative (-) test lead to the negative (-) battery terminal or a known good ground. Touch the positive (+) test lead to the positive wire or connector. (Use the opposite approach with an early F-truck's 6-volt positive ground system.)

Again, on a 12-volt system check for ground, connect the positive (+) test lead to the positive (+) battery terminal or voltage source. Touch the negative (-) test lead to the wire leading to ground. The meter should read battery voltage. (Reverse this approach on an early F-truck's 6-volt positive ground electrical system.)

NOTE —
When using an analog (swing needle) voltmeter, be careful not to reverse the test leads. Reversing the polarity may damage the meter.

Continuity Test

The continuity test can be used to check a circuit or switch. Because most automotive circuits are designed to have little or no resistance, a circuit or part of a circuit can be easily checked for faults using an ohmmeter or a self-powered test light. An open circuit or a circuit with high resistance will not allow current to flow. A circuit with little or no resistance allows current to flow easily.

When checking continuity, keep the ignition off. On circuits that are powered at all times, disconnect the battery. Using the appropriate wiring diagram, a continuity test can easily find faulty connections, defective wires, bad switches, defective relays, and malfunctioning engine sensors.

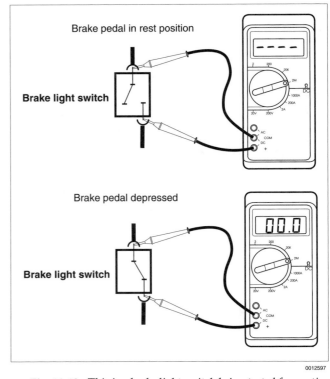

Fig. 14-10. *This is a brake light switch being tested for continuity. With the brake pedal in a resting position (switch open), the test reveals no continuity. With brake pedal depressed (switch closed), there is continuity.*

Short Circuit Test

A short circuit is exactly what the name implies. The circuit simply takes a shorter path than intended. The most common short that causes problems is a short to ground where the insulation on a hot lead wire wears away, and the metal wire becomes exposed. If the exposed wire is live (positive battery voltage on a 12-volt Ford system; negative battery voltage on a 6-volt earlier Ford F-truck system), either a fuse will blow or the circuit may become damaged.

CAUTION —
On circuits protected with large fuses (25 amp and greater), the wires or circuit components may be damaged before the fuse blows. Always check for damage before replacing fuses of this rating. Always use replacement fuses of the same rating.

Shorts to ground can be located with a voltmeter, a test light, or an ohmmeter. However, these shorted circuits are often difficult to locate. Therefore, it is important that you use the correct wiring diagram when troubleshooting your truck's electrical system.

Short circuits can be found using a logical approach based on the path that current follows. To check for a short circuit to ground, remove the blown fuse from the circuit and disconnect the cables from the battery. Disconnect the harness connector from the circuit's load or consumer. Us-

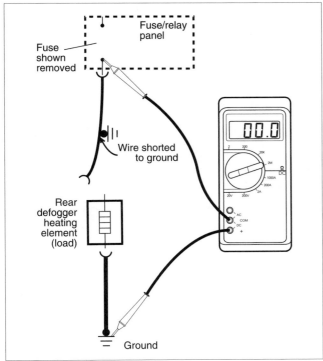

Fig. 14-11. *Ohmmeter being used to check for short circuit to ground.*

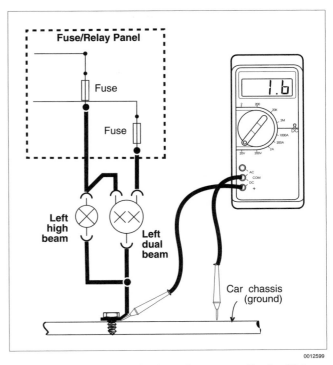

Fig. 14-12. *Example of voltage drop test on dim headlights. Voltmeter showed 1.6-volt drop between ground connector and chassis ground. After removing and cleaning headlight ground, voltage drop returned to normal and headlights gained brightness.*

ing a self-powered test light or an ohmmeter, connect one test lead to the load side fuse terminal (terminal leading to the circuit) and the other test lead to ground.

A short circuit can also be located using a test light or a voltmeter. Connect the instrument's test leads across the fuse terminals (fuse removed) and turn the circuit on. If necessary, check the wiring diagram to determine under which circumstances the circuit should be live.

Working from the wire harness nearest to the fuse/relay panel, move or wiggle the wires while observing the test light or your meter. Continue to move down the harness until the test light blinks or the meter displays a reading. This will pinpoint the location of the short.

Visually inspect the wire harness at this point for any faults. If no faults are visible, carefully slice open the harness cover or the wire insulation for further inspection. Repair the defects to OEM standards.

> **NOTE —**
> On critical circuits, like the EFI system, you will likely need a new harness to ensure circuit integrity and the quality of connections. Consult your Ford F-Series shop manual for recommendations on repairing a particular electrical circuit.

Voltage Drop Test

The wires, connectors, and switches that carry current have very low resistance so that current can flow with a minimum loss of voltage. A voltage drop results from higher than normal resistance in a circuit. This additional resistance actually decreases or stops the flow of current.

A voltage drop produces symptoms and problems ranging from dim headlights to sluggish wipers. Some common sources of voltage drop are faulty wires or switches, dirty or corroded connections or contacts, and loose or corroded ground wires and connections.

Voltage drop can only be checked when current is running through the circuit, such as by operating the starter motor or turning on the headlights. Making a voltage drop test requires measuring the voltage in the circuit and comparing that reading to what the voltage should be. Since these measurements are usually small, a digital voltmeter must be used to ensure accurate readings. If you suspect a voltage drop, turn the circuit on and measure the voltage when the circuit is under load.

A voltage drop test is generally more accurate than a simple resistance check because the resistances involved are often too small to measure with most ohmmeters. For example, a resistance as small as 0.02 ohms results in a 3 volt drop in a typical 150 amp starter circuit. (150 amps x 0.02 ohms = 3 volts).

Keep in mind that voltage with the key on and voltage with the engine running are not the same. With the ignition on and the engine off, full charge battery voltage should be approximately 12.6 volts. With the engine running (charging voltage), voltage should be approximately 14.5 volts. For exact measurements, first measure voltage at the battery with the ignition on, then with the engine running.

The maximum voltage drop, as recommended by the Society of Automotive Engineers (SAE), is: 0 volt for small wire connections; 0.1 volt for high-current connections; 0.2 volt for high-current cables; and 0.3 volt for switch or solenoid contacts. On longer wires or cables, the drop may be slightly higher. A voltage drop of more than 1.0 volt usually indicates a problem.

Testing Battery and Charging System

When checking the battery and charging circuits, be careful and considerate of battery hazards. High amperage applied to a defective battery is, literally, a potential bombshell. When you know your truck's charging system is functional yet the battery acts dead, proceed with extreme caution.

Find a good ground, and attach the correct meter probe (based on your system's polarity). Attach the other probe to the hot wire source and read battery voltage. If you get a reading of 12.30 or less volts on a 12 volt system, with all known current drains (including lights, ignition and accessories) shut off, the battery's state of charge is at 50% capacity or lower. This indicates poor electrical connections, weak alternator output, excessive current drain from accessories or a defective battery.

You can check each of these possible problems with the VOM. Start the engine and begin at the alternator. The battery signal to the voltage regulator should say, "I'm low on voltage, flow some current my way!"

In response, the normal charge circuit will call for a heavy amperage flow. Use the voltmeter mode of the tester, and probe the charge wire at the alternator with the positive lead (F-truck with a 12-volt system). On these 12-volt systems, attach the negative lead to ground. On 6-volt positive ground systems, reverse your DC voltmeter leads.

Charging properly, the alternator should now read well over 12.6 volts on a 12-volt system. (See your shop manual for 6-volt system requirements.) With current flowing toward the battery, voltage could read 14.8 volts or higher, depending upon the parameters of the voltage regulator. If you see no increase in voltage from your static battery test level, the alternator or regulator is not per-

Fig. 14-13. The solenoid junction block and other points that lie well away from the battery provide alternate battery testing sources. Avoid direct voltage checks at the battery, especially after heavy charging from the alternator or a battery charger. Explosive hydrogen gas can surround the battery and ignite from the slightest spark.

forming properly. Before condemning these expensive parts, however, troubleshoot further.

Shut the engine off and leave the meter set for the twelve volt range. Touch the heavy (BATTERY or BAT) lead at the rear of the 12-volt system's alternator with the positive (red) meter probe. Using a quality engine ground for the negative probe, again read available voltage at the alternator. This should be approximately the same as the battery's voltage reading.

If you cannot read voltage here, a wiring or fusible link problem exists. Trace the route of the alternator BAT lead. At the first junction between the alternator and the battery, your ohmmeter test can begin.

Zero the meter and set for DC and K-Ohms. Check the wire for continuity and conductivity by holding a probe at each end of the wire and reading the scale. If no opens or shorts exist, the meter will rest happily at the zero line. If there is too much resistance, as with a slight open in the lead or a poor connection, the needle will read upward on the scale. An actual open in the wire prevents the needle from registering at all.

Repeat this procedure along the wire path toward the battery. Eventually, you will locate the short or open. Resistance readings help locate corrosion within wire leads, too. Battery cables or terminal clamp connections often develop such problems. Unseen in a visual inspection, a current blockage cannot fool your ohmmeter. The force necessary to keep current flowing is measurable.

When the alternator unit is defective, your OEM-level shop manual will provide test information and overhaul procedures. Most bench tests of alternators, generators, starters, coils and ignition modules involve a VOM. You can also test headlight and dimmer switches, relays, breakers, fuses, and turn signal switches with the meter. Tracing poor ground wires, troubleshooting faulty gauges, finding nuisance shorts, isolating worn spark plug cables and most other electrical tests are well within the VOM's ability.

Getting A Charge Out Of Your Alternator

Alternator and generator output tests are similar. (For simplicity, I use the term alternator for this section.) If your earlier truck has a generator, you will find the majority of these troubleshooting and test suggestions useful and applicable.

Any concern about alternator output should begin with checking the drive belt tension. Next, inspect all wire connections. To test the alternator and regulator output, test the current flow from the alternator with an induction ammeter. Compare the ammeter flow to the OEM specifications for your truck, beginning at an idle, then 1500 rpm, then finally 2000 rpm.

> **NOTE —**
> Perform the induction meter test with the battery charge low. You want the alternator near its maximum output.

An induction ammeter, although not as accurate as more expensive test equipment, provides a quick sense for alternator output. These handy tools fit easily in your truck's on-board tool box. Since the meter simply fits over the cable or wire insulation, you can test without removing any electrical component. (Note: Make certain that magnetic interference from adjacent wires does not influence the readings.)

My two alternator (charging) and starter (draw) induction meters have served for over twenty years. If your equipment includes an ohms-resistance meter, you can perform additional field tests. When you suspect an alternator problem but cannot find its source, take the alternator and regulator to an automotive electrical repair shop. The shop can help distinguish regulator troubles from alternator defects.

Note: Your Ford F-Series shop manual or a professional service manual will detail the troubleshooting guidelines for your generator/alternator and regulator. Most public libraries maintain a reference section that contains automotive and light truck service manuals.

Shorts and Voltage Leak-off

If starter and alternator circuits check okay and the battery's cells read normal specific gravity at a full charge, then chronic low battery voltage is still possible. Accessories like the clock or the improper hook-up of an aftermarket sound system can cause the battery to go dead. Be sure to wire your sound system through a fused and ignition switched accessories (ACC) source.

A defect in the ignition switch, air conditioning clutch, lighting equipment, the turn signal switch, a radio, tape deck or hazard lamp can each draw excessive current from the battery. The dome, underhood and hazard lamps operate without the ignition switch on, so check these areas first. When an aftermarket accessory taps directly to a battery source, disconnect the accessory and see if the problem resolves.

If a current drain persists, suspect the ignition switch. A shorted ignition switch can deliver current, even when the key is in the off position. Current may be passing to the coil, ignition module or EFI computer (on later models). You can confirm current flow at each of these areas by taking voltage readings with your VOM.

Testing Ignition and Fuel System Components

Most automotive tool boxes include test lamp type continuity and hot lead testers. The VOM serves far beyond these tools, however, giving precise readings about the underlying condition of your truck's electrical system.

For example, spark plug misfires or engine balking under load are often the result of excessive resistance in the primary or secondary ignition circuits. Here, the VOM can provide an ideal tool for diagnostic work.

Many ignition and late model fuel system parts rely on electrical switches and electronic components. Given the ohms-resistance values for these pieces, you can easily test them with your meter. The troubleshooting and service guidelines in your OEM-level shop manual can provide useful test criteria.

Ballast resistors, spark plug wires and electronic ignition modules each have specified tests. Voltage and ohms-resistance readings at the ends of a ballast resistor can determine whether the unit works properly. Likewise, an ignition coil has a specified resistance in its winding. Ohms resistance tests of a coil can identify most shorts and internal defects.

You can also test spark plug cables with an ohmmeter. Read resistance to identify defective wires or those that demand excessive firing voltage. Continuity/ohms tests can also identify rotor shorts.

> **NOTE —**
> When worn excessively, electronic ignition rotors can short to ground through the distributor shaft. You may experience this problem on a Ford B/L or Dura-Spark ignition system.

Used imaginatively, the tests performed with a VOM often serve the same purpose as diagnostic analyzers that cost a thousand times more. The VOM's simple, pragmatic answers often serve better than expensive and bulkier diagnostic equipment. After all, you can't tow an oscilloscope engine analyzer along a 4x4 trail.

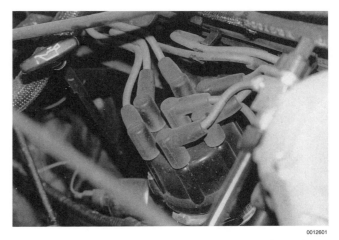
0012601

***Fig. 14-14.** Check your ignition cables periodically with an ohmmeter. Late electronic ignitions with higher firing voltages place more stress on high tension carbon cables.*

2. STARTER MOTOR

Engines resist cranking as compression, valve spring tension and spinning belt-driven components fight the starter motor's efforts. Toss in a bit too much ignition spark advance, and it's clear why some starter drive housings break.

A 12-volt starter is a high torque electric motor, with or without an internal gear reduction drive. Very heavy lock test amperage draw, well in excess of 450 amps on many large V-8 engine applications, is normal.

Such a starter may demand over 100 amps just to spin freely on a bench test. A defective starter motor may draw over 500 amps while cranking the engine, enough to fry both the battery and its cables. The typical engine with a modest compression ratio still requires a starter cranking draw of 150 to 210 amps.

A 12-volt automotive starter motor can spin as high as 8500 rpm on the bench. However, while cranking the engine at 160 crankshaft rpm, with an 18-to-1 flywheel-to-starter drive tooth ratio, this same starter motor might spin 2900 rpm. Considering the amperage necessary to rotate the flywheel or flexplate, the starter motor has a major job.

Brush-type starters consist of typical electrical motor components: an armature, field coils and brushes that ride on the armature's commutator. From a service standpoint, these motors require nothing more than periodic brush changes and replacement of the armature end bushings. There are other wear factors, however, that can also retire the starter motor from service.

Starter Solenoid

For massive current flow to reach the starter, without cooking the wiring circuits, the starter utilizes a solenoid switch. Simply put, the solenoid is an electrical switch that handles heavy current flow. The switch receives its signal from the ignition/starter switch via a small wire. Ignition switch start-mode current magnetizes the load switch inside the solenoid.

Once the load switch closes, heavy battery cable current flows to the starter motor. This sequence works in tandem with a starter drive gear. The gear engages the flywheel or flexplate ring gear teeth during starter operation. To prevent severe clash of teeth or starter motor damage, starter drives have a clutch or over-run mechanism.

Starter Drive

There are two types of starter drives. One design engages when the solenoid switch moves a shift lever. The other starter drive, found on the earliest F-truck starter motors, is a Bendix spring drive.

The Bendix unit has a spring on the head of the starter drive. As the starter spins, centrifugal force launches the drive gear toward the flywheel ring gear. The spring absorbs shock. These Bendix drives were popular on Ford products for years, and they require no shift lever fork.

On large V-8 applications, Ford has occasionally used a starter design similar to popular GM (Delco-Remy) starters. These types utilize a fork attached to the sole-

Fig. 14-15. *Release lever relationship is clear here. The solenoid's magnetic core draws the lever and also closes a high amp current switch. Forward of lever is drive clutch and drive gear.*

noid's magnetic plunger. When ignition switch current flows to the solenoid (mounted astride the starter motor), two events occur: 1) The plunger moves the starter drive toward the flywheel teeth, and 2) just upon engagement, a second phase begins as the solenoid closes the heavy amperage switch and battery current flows to the starter motor.

The most common Ford starter motor for the later 12-volt era has been the Motorcraft positive engagement design. Inside, this starter features a distinct four pole/four brush layout that works with a set of three series coils and one shunt coil.

Significantly, the shunt coil surrounds a floating pole shoe. As current flows to the starter motor assembly, the shunt coil electro-magnetically moves the lever that engages the starter drive. All of this takes place when you turn the key to START, and the fender mounted solenoid switch sends high amperage current to the starter motor.

On these Ford/Motorcraft starters, the drive has a clutch mechanism not much different in concept than the GM/Delco-Remy design. You can rebuild this starter if your soldering skills are good, as the primary wear point is the brushes, followed by armature bushing fatigue and clutch drive failure. In recent years, however, most owners simply exchange their worn or defective starter motor for a relatively inexpensive rebuilt unit.

NOTE —

Your starter motor may spin but not engage the flywheel or flexplate gear properly. This sounds like a high speed electric motor whir without the engine cranking over. (Or perhaps the drive only partially engages, causing a raucous grating noise as the gear teeth gnash.) Usually, the cause is a worn starter drive.

All starters must compensate for drive gear shock. Torque loads at the point of gear tooth mesh is where most starter housing damage occurs.

Starter housing nose end breakage, especially on big V-8s, is often the result of poor starter motor mounting or bracing methods. This problem is less significant on most Ford engines, as the starter motor bolts/studs attach to the clutch or transmission housing face, holding the starter more securely and helping to keep it on a straight plane.

Troubleshooting The Starter Motor

Assuming that your truck's engine won't crank over, you need to answer a few questions. Does the starter solenoid click? Is the starter motor turning too slowly? Can you hear the starter motor spin, but the engine isn't cranking?

If the battery and cables check okay and the solenoid simply clicks, the trouble is either 1) a defective solenoid, or 2) a defective starter motor (bad brushes, armature, or internal windings). Also check the starter drive shift lever or fork.

When the starter motor turns too slowly, you must consider internal engine problems. With the ignition switch turned off and the coil high tension lead disconnected, rotate the engine by hand and observe any friction. If the crankshaft turns okay, the trouble is likely within the starter motor assembly or solenoid switch.

NOTE —

Two exceptions to this conclusion are a jammed starter drive or water in the engine's cylinders (hydro-lock). Either will prevent the engine from rotating. If you suspect water in the engine, remove the spark plugs and crank again. (If you find that internal engine friction keeps the engine from turning freely, refer to the troubleshooting chapter.)

Attach a starter motor induction meter to the heavy starter cable, and observe the amount of current flow necessary to crank the engine. If an abnormally high amp draw is evident (above the level of 150–210 amps), remove the starter motor for a bench test and determine the damage. Should the starter motor spin quickly and loudly, without rotating the engine, suspect a defective starter drive.

On those starters with the solenoid mounted at the motor housing, the starter drive or the starter shift lever could be faulty. Noise also suggests teeth missing from either the starter drive, flexplate or flywheel ring gear. The latter prospect is costly and difficult to repair.

Fig. 14-16. Induction ammeter can check starter current flow. Without removing the starter or any other parts, place the meter over the battery cable's insulation. Used in conjunction with a volt-ohm meter, the induction ammeter can help pinpoint defects and malfunctions by showing excessive current draw while the engine cranks over.

Fig. 14-17. Ford style remote starter solenoid (right) is also common to most winch controls. These solenoids are readily available at auto supply outlets.

Fig. 14-18. worn GM/Delco-Remy type solenoid, sometimes used by Ford trucks with larger V-8s, welded its contacts and kept the drive and starter motor engaged. The motor winding unraveled from the heat—not a healthy prospect for a truck used in back country!

Fig. 14-19. *Crumbliss test bench at North Country Rebuilders tests this V-8 starter motor. If you suspect trouble with your starter, an auto electric shop can assess the unit's performance.*

Replacing a damaged starter ring gear (flywheel or flexplate type) requires removal of the transmission and clutch or the torque converter. In the ranking order of starter motor related repair costs, a solenoid switch is the least expensive item next to brushes and armature bushings.

For popular Ford F-truck engines, rebuilt starter motors are available and inexpensive. However, if you have modified your engine with performance parts, a generic rebuilt starter may not handle the cranking load of a modified engine. You may need an aftermarket high-torque starter.

If the field coils and armature are intact, your starter's overhaul should include new end bushings, properly installed and reamed to fit. New brushes, re-dressing (cleaning and resurfacing) of the commutator, replacement of a worn starter shift lever/fork, a renewed solenoid and general clean-up of components will complete the job.

> NOTE —
> Always check the neutral safety or clutch pedal start switch before condemning the starter motor or starter solenoid switch.

Overhauling Your Starter Motor

Your truck's reliability depends on an engine that will crank and start readily. Especially with an automatic transmission model that cannot be bump or push started, starter performance is critical to safety. Depicted in these photos is a unique starter motor with features common to some Ford F-Series truck starters. For specific details on your truck's starter motor and electrical system, refer to your OEM-level shop manual.

Fig. 14-20. *On this starter design, overhaul begins with the solenoid switch removal. This particular Ford V-8 starter has a striking resemblance to a GM/Delco-Remy unit. The solenoid mounts to the nose section.*

Fig. 14-21. *Brush inspection is possible once you move this shield. You will likely replace brushes during a Ford starter repair.*

Fig. 14-22. *Brushes removed, the end plate comes off.*

Fig. 14-23. *The commutator and armature show wear. Note the angle of the shaft (arrow), an indication of end bushing wear.*

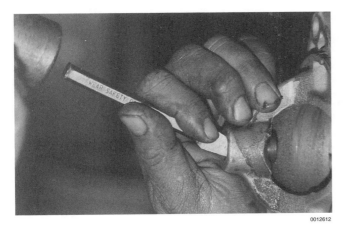

Fig. 14-24. *End bushing replacement is a standard procedure.*

Fig. 14-25. *Loosening brushes precedes field coil removal. An impact driver or special tool is necessary for removing field coil screws (arrows). These screws are really seated firmly and should only be removed if field coils require service.*

Fig. 14-26. *Bench tester charges armature. Time-honored hacksaw blade test indicates shorts or opens. I recall performing this test as a fleet truck mechanic during the 1960s. The procedure was already old at that time!*

Fig. 14-27. *Commutator receives resurfacing in a metal lathe. This operation requires the professional skill of a local starter rebuilding shop.*

Fig. 14-28. *A new or rebuilt drive is a must. This item wears over time.*

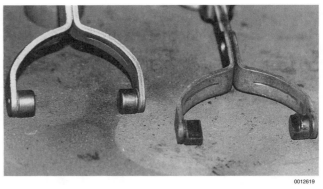

Fig. 14-31. *Release fork wear is evident here. This fork needs replacement to assure starter's reliability.*

Fig. 14-29. *Some Ford starters require soldering new brushes into place. Replacement brush sets have become scarcer, and some parts are often available only through rebuilders.*

Fig. 14-32. *Rebuilt solenoids are not all the same. On the right is a cheap replacement item of approximately 80 winds. 140-wind wire at left is a high quality rebuild, similar to a new OE unit.*

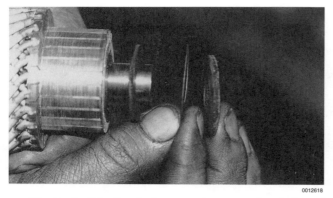

Fig. 14-30. *Selective fit thrust washers control end play of the armature. Consult your OEM-level service manual for end play specifications.*

Fig. 14-33. *This kit will overhaul a modestly worn starter. Brushes, a new drive and end bushings make up the necessary pieces. A new or rebuilt solenoid unit will round out the rebuild unless the coils or armature show damage. If wear shows, turning the commutator is a sublet task.*

Chapter 15

Accessories

AS EARLY AS THE FORD MODEL T ERA, light truck accessories were a booming industry. The original Model T trucks were themselves the product of aftermarket body builders. Rolling out of the Michigan plants in cab-and-chassis form, the earliest T and TT trucks set a precedent for today's Ford F-and E-models with custom utility beds or motorhome coach bodies.

F-truck Accessorization

As the first F-Series light trucks rolled out of the plant in early 1948, buyers immediately began personalizing their vehicles. The WWII years of rationing had encouraged owners to stick with their trucks and make them work better. Spare tire carriers, trailer towing hitches and military-style tow hooks, auxiliary lighting and add-on safety equipment were common products that carried forth into the postwar era. From custom bodies to turn signals and heaters, the new Ford F-models offered plenty of room for accessories. Many items went on a new truck before it left the dealership.

Auxiliary heaters, electric wiper motors, spare gas can holders and power take-off (PTO) driven accessories expanded the versatility of Ford trucks. For specialized off-pavement needs, aftermarket and pre-delivery Marmon-Harrington and Coleman four-wheel drive conversion packages became available in 1950.

Add-on traction devices were popular F-truck improvements, as OE limited slip and locking axles were still a decade away. Postwar suburban consumers found more time and resources for outdoor recreation, which

Fig. 15-1. *The light truck aftermarket has developed along two distinct paths. While commercial fleets create a demand for utility products, a growing number of recreational and multi-purpose users now personalize their trucks with cosmetic and convenience accessories. (Photo courtesy of Warn Industries)*

Fig. 15-2. Early F-trucks had vacuum windshield wipers, driven by a dual diaphragm (combination) fuel pump that seldom provided enough vacuum to operate the wipers under all driving conditions. For better service, the aftermarket provided replacement electric wiper motors. By the mid-1950s, electric wipers were a factory option.

Fig. 15-3. Truck transmissions had PTO drive access. This convenient feature became the power source for mechanical winches and hoists.

created wide interest in camping, amateur mineral prospecting, touring ghost towns, fishing and hunting.

More popular aftermarket items often become original equipment or factory options on later trucks. As a Ford light truck owner, you can select from a huge array of aftermarket upgrades, including safety enhancements, high performance components, specialized wheels and tires, utility products and cosmetic changes.

If your F-truck needs more personality, better on-board work tools, styling improvements or a less spartan interior, there's likely an aftermarket solution. In some cases, an older truck can provide the features and conveniences of a later model by simply adding the right accessories.

1. WINCHES

Nearly as important as optional four-wheel drive systems, power winches have enhanced truck utility for half a century. Pioneered by Claude C. Ramsey, front mounted power take-off (PTO) winches were the first truck designs. By 1948, Ramsey's winch popularity was widespread. A recognized dealer-installed option, Ramsey winch systems were often factory-approved products offered through U.S. truck dealerships.

Early truck winches relied solely on engine power. Many light truck transmissions and transfer case designs feature a power take-off (PTO) drive, and tapping into such a gearbox gives access to all forward speeds and a reverse gear. Power flows to a front mounted winch gearbox via an accessory PTO driveshaft.

Koenig Iron Works also offered PTO winches. In the 1930s, Emil Koenig had furnished oil field trucks with power drive winches. His entry into the postwar power winch field targeted both commercial and recreational users. Koenig's King winches were suitable for front, rear and bed-mounted use, which gave Koenig, like Ramsey, access to the commercial hoisting and tow truck markets.

The Koenig/King and Ramsey PTO product lines drowned in the wave of electric winch sales. By the early 1970s, the bulky PTO winches, with scores of moving parts and a massive installation task, made the PTO winch far less attractive than the growing number of electric winches.

Ramsey Winch Company made a successful transition to electric winches. The respected Koenig Iron Works, however, disappeared from the recreational accessory market. Today, PTO-driven winches are still available, although their use is largely limited to commercial and utility company service.

Electric Winches

Since the late 1960s, a heated debate has waged between PTO winch advocates and electric winch users. PTO buffs argue that battery power limits the usage of the electric winch. Stranded in a stream, will the battery last long enough to pull the truck free? Electric winch advocates counter with the argument that a stalled engine can't spin a PTO shaft. Either way, the operator is in trouble.

Dual battery installations, isolators and high output alternators have virtually eliminated the shortfalls of electric winches. Today, electric winches furnish the quality—and quantity—of service that users demand. Notable manufacturers in the truck mounted electric winch market include Ramsey, Warn and Superwinch. Contemporary winch marketing emphasizes gear and motor design, integrity of components, amperage draw, load capacity and utility.

Determining Your Winch Needs

Electric winches have a variety of ratings. Speed (defined as feet-per-minute or fpm spooling) results from the gear reduction ratio and electric motor speed. Popular electric winch designs feature worm, spur or planetary gear systems.

The vehicle's battery (and/or an auxiliary battery) powers the winch motor, which basically resembles the motor portion of an automotive starter. In turn, the winch motor spins either a drive gear, worm shaft or sun gear.

Fig. 15-4. Warn's XD-9000 winch is an electric planetary design. Compact and inconspicuous, the unit ranks a hefty 9000 lbs. single line rating. This winch is rated to pull twice the weight of an F-150 4x4 truck. Select a winch rated at least 1.5 times the GVWR of your truck.

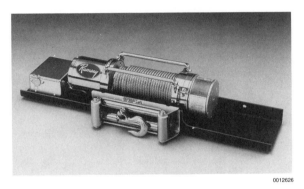

Fig. 15-5. Ramsey REP 8000 is a popular winch unit. Optional roller fairlead is shown. This is Ramsey's heaviest duty planetary gear model, weighing 61 lbs. RE 8000 and heavier RE 10000 or 12000 models feature worm gear drives and choice of Hawse or roller fairleads.

Worm-and-gear systems rotate the worm gear inside a bull gear. Typically, the bull gear attaches to the cable spool drum. A major advantage of the worm drive is its ability to stop abruptly or load-reverse when power flow ceases. Planetary and spur gear arrangements, by contrast, require a brake mechanism to prevent reverse rotation when the motor stops spinning.

Worm gear systems have a low efficiency factor (the ability to transmit energy from one gear to another). By contrast, if a winch gear system could develop 100-percent efficiency, it would spool in either direction with equal ease, whether loaded or unloaded.

Gear efficiency of less than 45% creates a self-locking capability. Here, the relationship and ratios of the gears create a lesser incentive for free-spooling, even with a load on the cable. Worm gear systems, although extremely strong, offer only 35-40% efficiency, and hence need no brake.

Spur gear drives like Warn's Model M8274 work at 75% efficiency. This requires a braking mechanism to prevent load-reversal. Similarly, the popular planetary gear systems offer 65% efficiency. One variation, the compound planetary gear, produces 40% efficiency, which provides for self-braking action. The compound planetary gear system requires a high speed motor, generally in the 4000-5000 rpm range.

The planetary systems provide both strength and smooth operation. Compact planetary winches have good resistance to torque loads. Direct power flow through the sun gear permits lighter weight, a low profile and high output.

Winch Motors

At present, the heaviest duty winches feature series wound motors. These provide maximum torque with a price: maximum amperage draw. The series wound brutes demand a heavy duty battery or the use of an auxiliary battery.

Permanent magnet motors require far less amps, draw less battery power, and save weight. On light and medium load winches, these motors work fine. After all, many newer autos and trucks feature permanent magnet starter motors. These motors serve well here, as engine cranking takes a short time and seldom generates excess heat.

The arguable disadvantage of permanent magnet motors is overheat. Under sustained and heavy loads, the permanent magnet motor tends to overheat. The operator needs to monitor the winching effort and time involved, allowing the motor to cool at safe intervals. (Most winch motors have circuit breaker protection against extreme overload.)

Winching and R.V. Batteries

Modern batteries offer higher cold cranking amperage or CCA. These types of batteries are far more practical for series wound motors. A dual battery system, once mandatory for high output winch systems, remains an option.

If your truck's battery rates above 650 CCA (preferably 850 CCA or higher), the normal needs of a high output series wound winch motor could be met with a single battery. For extreme duty use or very long winch pulls, consider a second battery and an automatic battery isolator. The isolator prevents draining your main battery below the level necessary to start the engine.

Selecting A Winch

Determine your truck's gross vehicle weight (GVW) before choosing a winch. This is the combined weight of the truck, your cargo, fuel, oil and any other items on board. Include your spare tools, the mounted winch and any accessories attached to the truck.

Also account for the other guy. As a rescue or emergency tool, your truck (especially a 4x4 model) has a wide range of uses. Consider not only your GVW but also the weight of other vehicles that you might assist.

Engineers compute the winch safety factor at 1.5 times the working GVW of your truck. Working GVW is the real world, loaded version of your vehicle. If in doubt, take your fully loaded vehicle to a local truck scale, and

Fig. 15-6. *A snatch block and 180° reversal of the cable can reduce load on the winch motor by nearly one-half. Always allow a 15% safety margin.*

have it weighed. Multiply the amount of working GVW by 1.5. Example: If your fully loaded truck weighs 4000 lbs., the minimum winch capacity should be 4000 x 1.5, or 6000 lbs. Remember, this rating applies to the inside wraps of the wire and decreases as the wire spools onto the drum.

Many buyers, even those who own lighter half-ton rated trucks, seek 8000-pound or higher capacity winches. The added margin of safety is obvious with a high output winch. A winch motor rated to pull heavier loads than you have planned will last longer and hold up better when worked hard.

Also be clear of a winch's rating method. "Single-line pull" or "double" makes a major difference. Applying the physics of a snatch-block (making a 180° turn of the cable and coming back to a tow hook near the winch) provides almost twice as much pulling strength and far less strain on your winch unit.

Although doubling and even tripling the cable is possible, the cable length eventually becomes an issue. Also, it is very hard on larger wire cables to bend them 180° around a snatch block pulley. Even with a high output winch, conservative loads make a good strategy.

> *CAUTION —*
>
> *Although physics shows nearly a doubling of pulling power, engineers advise a 15% safety factor. If your winch's single line pull is rated 6000 lbs., a 180° turn of the cable should increase pulling power by 85% or 5100 lbs. This would make your total pull rate 11,100 lbs for the first few wraps of the cable. Any deviation from the 180° pull angle will reduce load capacity. Also, always consider the cable's load limit when using a snatch block.*

Mounting A Winch

Mounting position is important. Winches that mount at or above the frame/bumper height seem better suited to off-pavement use. Often, when you most need a winch, the front of the truck is low to the ground. If above the bumper height, the cable and spool will still be easy to reach.

In the worst instance, a below bumper mount could actually become buried in snow, mud or a creek. As with any front bumper extension, the truck's approach angle may also suffer from a below-the-bumper mount. A winch near the ground increases the likelihood of dragging the cable during pulls.

Fig. 15-7. *This Warn Industries winch mounts low and features a sturdy bumper assembly. Roller fairlead and brush guard are smart accessories. Cable pulls in-line with the truck's frame, placing far less stress on the chassis.*

Many truck owners, however, prefer hiding the winch behind the bumper. An open grill frontal area is important. In very hot climates, under severe loads, a high mount winch may compromise the truck's cooling system. Decreased air flow over the radiator core can reduce radiator efficiency.

Options are another factor when selecting your winch. Winch manufacturers frequently offer extra equipment. A roller fairlead, winch cover, remote controls, a portable/receiver mount, handtools or a wiring harness may be items you'll want—either when you purchase your winch or later.

Mechanical engineers design winch mounts to match a given winch installation. As life, limb and expensive property are at stake, proper installation is a necessity. Your safest strategy is a manufactured winch mount. Installation kits available from the winch manufacturer will fit the frame and vehicle requirements of your truck. Mount kits address load points, the strength of frame attachments and the ease of access to the winch. Engineers take the rated load capacity of the winch and apply that force safely to the truck's frame.

Sadly, operators often underestimate the load forces involved with winching. A cable drawn to maximum load capacity must transfer force safely to the frame. This concern goes beyond the winch mount and hardware. If the winch attaches to the OEM bumper or brackets, that hardware must also be at factory standards. If the bumper has been removed, make certain that the attaching bolts and nuts meet or exceed OEM standards for your truck. Winch kit engineering assumes that the truck meets or exceeds OEM guidelines.

Portable Winches

A recent development in winch mounting is the portable winch receiver. Recognizing the versatility of a detachable front or rear mounted winch, manufacturers now build winches and winch frames that fit a Class III (2" square) trailer receiver.

Using a quick disconnect electrical cable and pin-type receiver hitch, these winches install and disconnect in minutes. The main advantage of a quality portable winch is out of the way storage. Protected from theft and foul weather, the winch can stow in a covered pickup bed or bed tool box. Ready for an emergency, the winch assembly is free of ice, mud or rusted cable. Additionally, the portable winch is useful at either end of the vehicle.

Portable winches rely on the safety of your truck's receiver mount or hitch kit. Commercially made, most frame mounted hitches that have a two-inch receiver rate

Fig. 15-8. *Portable winches allow quick removal. A Class III or stronger frame mounted receiver serves at either end of your truck. The portable winch is highly versatile for recovery work.*

as Class III or higher. The load capacity of a properly installed Class III hitch is 5000 lbs., with a maximum tongue weight of 500 lbs. Graded bolts and reinforcement plates generally accompany a frame mount hitch kit.

Winch Controls and Installation

Winch installation kits offer either direct or remote controls. The remote cable allows control of the winch feed from twenty or more feet away, well away from the cable, spool and gearworks. This gives an optimal view of the pull without your standing in line with the load.

When mounting the control box, follow the suggestions of the manufacturer. Since distance equates to amperage loss and resistance, many control units have a specified location. The switch box should be easily accessible, in an airy space, preferably out of the weather.

Modern electric winch controls include solenoids, breakers or relays. In most instances, the control box is a plastic case, sealed from the weather. Since relays and/or solenoids flow constant battery current, you must isolate them from moisture. If ice, snow or sleet were to freeze inside the switch box, a current drain could sap your battery. Likewise, operating the winch under such conditions could create a short circuit.

A properly grounded electrical system is fundamental, and the issue becomes more critical with a winch. A 400- to 600-amp resistance load, even for a brief time, will tax your truck's electrical system to its limit. Poor grounding is a fast way to establish a power robbing voltage drop.

Winch Wiring

As a guideline, the best ground system takes the battery negative cable directly to the engine block. Next, the alternator housing, or its ground post, connects to the

Carry-on Winch Accessories

Once you've mounted and wired your new winch, it's ready for work. A few accessory items, handily stored in your truck, will help your winch perform at maximum capacity. These devices enhance performance and provide a better margin of safety.

Accessory kits offer compact storage for important winching gear. Warn's kit includes a snatch block, forged steel shackle, tree protector, leather work gloves and a carrying bag. Ramsey and other winch manufacturers also offer such kits.

An industrial or logging supply provides an excellent assortment of high grade snatch blocks, pulleys, shackles and swivels. Swivels protect cable from twisting under load, a major source of damage. Load rated assortments of hooks are also available. Watch for rough inner edge of hooks. Protect your nylon tree saver and recovery straps by carefully bevelling forging scars with a grinder or file.

Recovery Strap—Quality winch accessory kits always include a recovery or tow strap. Often, you can free a stuck vehicle with a tug rather than setting up your winch. Many strap designs provide controlled stretch, which reduces shock loads.

Snatch Block—Known in other circles as a pulley block or block and tackle, the snatch block is an anchor plate with a pulley inside. Attached in front of the truck with a 180° return of the line, the snatch block offers 85% (with safety factored) load reduction when the cable hook attaches near the winch.

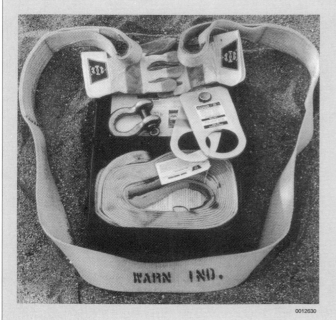

0012630

Choker Chain—A term familiar to woodsmen and loggers, the choker is a high tensile strength link chain with hooks at each end. The chain is very versatile, acting as a vehicle recovery tool or reinforcement between two an-chor points. You'll find it handy for wrapping around huge rocks, truck frames or other anchor points. You can easily store a six-to ten-foot choker in your truck.

Tow Hooks—Factory or aftermarket front and rear frame mounted tow hooks require high tensile strength bolts and self-locking aircraft quality nuts. Attaching points and hardware must meet OE frame requirements. Never mount a tow hook directly to the bumper. Hooks are available with spring clips to prevent straps from slipping off. These are especially useful for one-person operation. Mounted upward, downward or sideways, tow hook bolts should align in the direction of pull. Mount the hook(s) at frame height and remember that the safest pull is a straight line. If possible, avoid welding tow hooks into place. These hooks may need replacement at some time.

D-Shackle—Most popular winch accessory kits include a D-shackle and pin. This is a highly versatile device for attaching and joining straps, rings, chain and even cable. When using a D-shackle with straps, make certain that nylon material rubs against the smooth looped end. Otherwise, fraying and damage to the strap will result. Tighten the threaded bolt, then back it off 1/4 turn to prevent thread seizure during heavy pulling.

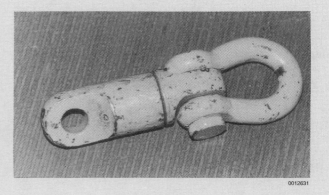

0012631

Gloves—Every accessory kit should include a pair of hefty (preferably leather) work gloves. These gloves must resist weather, cable friction burns, scraps and abrasions. Frayed cable and sharp sheet metal edges can cut fingers to the bone. Wear gloves.

Tree Saver Strap—This is vital. For attaching a winch cable or anchoring your vehicle to a tree, the tree saver strap protects the bark and live sections. The eyes of the saver strap provide an attachment point for your D-shackle, which in turn becomes the snatch block anchor.

Shovel and Hand Tools—A simple, often overlooked tool is the folding shovel. Vital hours are wasted when shovels, handyman jacks and proper handtools stay at home. Many winches provide the framework for a shovel/axe/jack mount. Also, bring along strong wire cutters, as a broken cable can easily wrap up in the winch or the truck's chassis.

Note: The MAX multi-purpose tool kit and a Hi-Lift or Handyman jack are must items for serious off-pavement adventures.

Fig. 15-9. A heavy duty engine, alternator, frame and winch ground system assure full power. Here, 1/0 welding cable supplies both positive and negative battery cables and the complete ground circuit.

engine, with a ground strap from the engine block to the frame completing the circuit. (To assure a good body ground, add a strap from the frame or engine to the cab.) The winch system may now ground directly to the block or frame.

Each manufacturer furnishes specific electrical requirements for its various winch models. Consult your kit instructions for details. As an additional item, consider an accessible master disconnect switch. Mount the switch in an easy to reach place, out of line from the winch.

If your winch electrics interface with a complex electrical system (sound system, lights and an extra battery), you may need a complete, high amperage cable and wiring harness.

Using A Winch

Before operating your winch, raise the hood. A broken winch cable is potentially lethal and could easily break your truck's windshield. (For this reason, a brush/grill guard makes a smart addition to a winch mount.) Make sure that the cable can spool evenly onto the drum, and attach the hook to a substantial anchor point.

If possible, stand far to the side when winching, well outside the cable's path. Many operators lay a blanket over the cable, assuming that this will reduce recoil if the cable breaks.

Although a cover or blanket may help contain the cable, no cloth blanket can absorb the immense force of a snapping cable under load. Pull as straight as possible, and always use leather work gloves when handling wire cable.

For safety sake, always leave a reasonable length of cable on the winch spool. Your winch manufacturer has guidelines for the necessary length. Paint the cable red from the starting wrap to the length specified. This will signal when the maximum length of cable has spooled out.

WARNING —
A loaded winch cable is dangerous. Imagine the path a snapped cable might take. Stay out of that space. Also, remember that the winch's maximum load rating only applies to the inner few wraps on the spool/drum.

Safely freeing a vehicle often will require more than one run of the cable's length. If the vehicle wants to roll faster than the cable spools, apply slight brake pressure. Many winches operate at both a minimum and maximum operating load. Proper cable spooling depends upon working within this load range.

Fig. 15-10. The remote winch control is a must. Never stand in the line of a winch cable. If the cable breaks and recoils under load, severe bodily injury could result.

0012634

Fig. 15-11. *Loads on cables are fully capable of launching a tow hook, clevis, snatch block, bumper section, bumper bracket or frame piece through the windshield of a vehicle. Never stand in the line of a loaded cable. Many truck owners raise their hoods to protect the windshield in the event of a cable failure. Use your remote winch control to keep clear of the cable.*

0012635

Fig. 15-12. *A sensible anchor point for your tow chain or strap is the receiver of a safely mounted hitch. (Place hitch pin through strap end.) A Class III hitch/receiver rates 5000 lb. load capacity and will withstand the stress of moving another light vehicle. Avoid use of elastic or bungie cord recovery straps. The load of a stretched cord places far too much stress on tow hooks and attachment points.*

Preventive Maintenance For Your Winch

Your winch is a safety device and lifeline. When a four-wheeling trip requires the use of your winch, you're way out there. A secluded box canyon or a muddy creekbed is no place for winching errors or a poorly maintained winch.

The modern electric winch is easy to maintain. Unlike PTO winches, with their oil-filled transmissions and mechanical driveshafts, the electric winch requires simple service.

Cable Inspection—The major wear item is the cable. Properly used, the wire winch line will last for years. One careless moment, however, can weaken or kink the cable. If a night-time or blizzard winching episode leaves your winch cable coiled wrong, free-spool the cable entirely and check for damage. Kinks, broken outer strands and twists that leave the cable distorted are all signs of weakness. Clean the cable thoroughly to allow close inspection.

Lubrication—Your winch may have grease fittings and require periodic lubrication. If you have an oil bath drive (usually on PTO winches), the gear oil must be clean and up to the full level. Check for seal leaks. If your winch operates in a dusty and wet environment, always wipe zirk fittings clean before greasing. Use the manufacturer's recommended grease or a water-resistant chassis/bearing lube. Cable friction leads to fatigue and unnecessary stress. Many users lube the cable.

Note: As greases often attract unwanted dirt and dust, special lubricants are available for use on cables. Industrial supplies sell chain and cable lubricants that cure like cosmoline. This reduces messy handling and resists dirt accumulation. Such lubes also work well on clevis pins, hook pivots and the snatch block. They provide a good moisture barrier against rust, too.

Mounts, Hooks, Pulleys and Straps—Inspect your hooks and straps. Make certain clevis pins are free of moisture and lubricate them lightly. Dry out your nylon straps before storing them. Check tow hook and winch mount bolts and nuts for tightness and signs of fatigue. Inspect parts closely for bending or possible fatigue cracks. Clean and lubricate pulleys and the snatch block at regular intervals.

Electrical System—Inspect your remote control cable, control box and all cable leads to the winch. Insulation on these leads must be in good condition and free from nicks. Amperage passing through the winch motor cables is high enough to weld metal. If a hot cable shorts to ground, a fire or severe damage might result. Inspect the cable routing to make certain no cable lays across sharp metal edges. You can reduce the effects of moisture through the use of silicone sprays and dispersing chemicals. Make certain that the control box and remote connectors are free of debris and corrosives.

2. ELECTRICAL SYSTEM UPGRADES

Automotive electrical wire must meet various current loads. Amperage requirements determine the proper wire gauge for each area of your truck. Since resistance increases with distance, longer runs of wire require heavier gauge sizes.

Wire for 6-volt accessories and components is substantially heavier than wiring found in later 12-volt systems. This is an advantage when converting an early F-truck's 6-volt system to 12-volts. Factory wires, if in good condition, are usually more than ample.

For rewiring and repair work, safety standards must apply. Heavy duty devices demand more amperage draw and larger wire sizing. OEM standards assume a specific distance between the current source and each device.

As a rule, 12-volt ignitions draw between 1.5 and 3.5 amps. A pair of horns draw 18–20 amps, while electric wipers demand 3–6 amps. A pair of back-up lights drain 3.5–4 amps, while an air conditioner drains 13–20.

On a 12-volt and four-lamp system, headlights demand 8–9 amps on low beam and 13–15 additional amps for high beam operation. Assume slightly less draw if your truck has a two-headlight system.

The cigar lighter, often used for plug-in accessories, drains 10–12 amps from the battery. A radio draws up to 4 amps (tape decks more), while power antennas drain 6–10 amperes. Instrument lamps, engine gauges, a clock or dome light each pull from 1–3 amps, a relatively mild load. Wire type ranges accordingly, and gauge size increases with wire length.

By contrast, the 12-volt starter motor, requiring an arc welding size lead from the battery, draws 150–450 amps during cranking. (This is a generalized range for modern engines. An OEM level shop manual offers specific data for your truck's engine and starter.) These amperage requirements demand safe wire sizes.

Determining Wire Gauge

Distance also fits into the wiring equation. A device demanding 10 amperes of current requires a minimum 18-gauge wire for a seven foot flow. The same device needs a heavy 10-gauge wire at 75 feet.

NOTE —
When choosing wire, the higher the wire's AWG number, the smaller the wire size.

Undercapacity wire creates an excess voltage drop (the inherent loss of current due to a wire's resistance), causing lights to burn dimly, motors to turn slowly or accessories to operate below capacity. If the wires are grossly undersize, resistance rises to the point that the insulation melts, usually followed by a short to the closest chassis or body ground.

For auxiliary lighting (lightbars, emergency lights, floods, halogen lamps and such), look closely at the Watt ratings. Manufacturers list the Watt output, and there's a simple formula for converting watts to amperage: Wattage divided by voltage = amperage.

Example: On a 12-volt electrical system, a 100W lamp equals 100W divided by 12, or 8-1/3 amps. Therefore, a string of ten 100-Watt lamps draws 83.3 amps.

For computing your electrical needs, consider the typical amperage draws for various accessory and OEM items on your truck. Add up the on-line components, and build your charging and battery system around these guidelines.

Wire, available at local auto supplies, usually comes in spool lengths of 25–100 feet. Once you determine the proper amperage draw for each electrical component in your truck's system, select wire by gauge size.

Carry the amperage needs through the fuses and relays, those safety devices that will prevent wires from frying in the event of an overload or short. When matching fuses to electrical components, each fuse should allow little more amperage flow than the device requires. Allow a slight margin for upstart surges and hot operation (when amperage draw increases slightly).

CAUTION —
Never install a higher amp fuse as a cure for an OE circuit that keeps blowing fuses. Find the reason for the overload.

Fuses blow for valid reasons: a defective electrical component, a bare wire short in the circuit, a weak ground, loose connections, or a charging circuit defect. Resolve the problem and install the correct fuse. A small volt-ohmmeter makes the ideal tool for troubleshooting resistance and the continuity of wiring circuits. (See chapter on electrical system.)

The backside of an early Ford F-truck dash is readily accessible. Later model (approximately 1967–up) electrical systems become increasingly more complex and difficult to access.

Matching Accessories and Wiring

When selecting the right wire gauge for your add-on accessories, make note of the relationship between amperage draw, watt ratings, candle power and length of the wire runs.

Auxiliary lights, a sound system or a winch each have an assigned amperage draw. Cover that rating with a safety margin. You can always go bigger and be safe. Wherever possible, use fuses or circuit breakers. Protect higher amp items with reset breakers. Protective devices are available from 1.0 amp to 250 amp ratings and higher.

The winch current draw is similar to a starter motor. Route cables very carefully to avoid high amperage shorts and possible fire. Review the winch manufacturer's guidelines for circuit protection and cable routing.

Remember, longer wire runs mean added resistance. Resistance raises amperage. Note the length of wire feeding each accessory. Select the recommended amperage ratings from an automotive wire manufacturer's guidebook, and match wire size accordingly. For safety's sake, account for the entire distance that current will flow, from the battery source to the accessory.

If your truck has a camper or aftermarket fiberglass body panels, you must run a ground wire to any accessory mounted on non-conductive material (fiberglass, plastic, wood, etc.). In this case, choose a wire gauge that satisfies the total length of the power lead and ground wire. A ground lead must always match the gauge size of the power lead.

High Work Standards

Safe routing of the long wires that run from the front to the rear of your truck is essential. A quality wiring job ensures that vibration and road shake will not separate or damage wires.

> *CAUTION —*
> *Improperly installed plastic wire ties, clamps and straps have a nasty habit of wearing through wire insulation.*

A yardstick I like to apply is the worst case scenario. (Some call this Murphy's Law, but I don't believe Murphy or anyone else can stake sole claim to the concept.) Assume that the wire you're routing will face tension, heat and friction. Are there metal edges just waiting to whittle at your vital wiring loom? Can engine heat melt the plastic off wires? Will chassis movement tear a crucial connection apart?

You must depend on your wiring in blizzards, on remote desert moonscapes, atop craggy, windswept mountains and even in the fast lane of the freeway during rush hour. Take the time to route, shield, tape and secure all wires.

Wire Looms and Connections

For assuring quality work, use universal plastic wire shielding, quality wire connectors, ties and straps. Rewiring and repairs often involve use of insulated, solderless connectors. These connectors match wire gauge sizes. When using solderless connectors, be certain to select the correct size for the wire involved.

Fig. 15-13. Wrangler Power Products at Prescott, Arizona offers this crimping tool for the do-it-yourselfer. These crimps in heavy duty copper battery terminals offer maximum conductivity and a long-lasting cure for resistance problems.

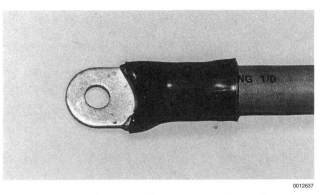

Fig. 15-14. This is a quality wire connection. After crimping, the copper terminal receives a coating of special adhesive-lined heat shrink tubing.

Fig. 15-15. Various types of battery attachments are available. Shown are two crimp type terminals and a unique compression nut clamp. Each meets high industrial/automotive standards and feature durable, high quality copper.

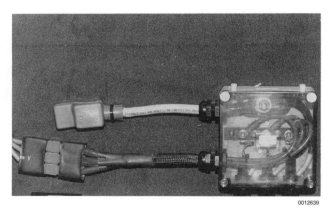

Fig. 15-16. This arrangement from Wrangler Power Products offers major protection and a high quality appearance. Imagine these junction boxes beneath the hood of your truck.

Color coded solderless connectors have become popular over the last two decades. They are easy to fit, quick to secure in tight places and offer long service life. A special crimping pliers is necessary for installation. Don't cut corners when buying this tool. Tight, neat connections depend on professional caliber tools. Expect to waste a few connectors practicing your crimping skills. Too tight or loose won't do. On connectors and crimp terminal ends with seams on the metal sleeves, make certain your crimp is on the solid side, not the seam.

The factory (OE) wire connections are often solder type, with molded insulation. In some cases, aftermarket pigtails are available to restore OE integrity to electrical connections. Some fitups, however, benefit from the use of an entire OE wiring harness, tailored to your truck's needs. Pre-formed harnesses, insulated properly, provide the best connections possible.

> **NOTE —**
> Late model Ford F-Series trucks with electronic/solid state components depend upon proper circuit resistance and voltage signals. On such a system, it may be necessary to repair damaged wiring with the installation of a complete new harness assembly. Consult your Ford F-Series shop manual before attempting wire repairs on a late model truck.

Some forethought and a factory schematic of your truck's electrical system will contribute to a quality wiring job. Electrical work, done properly, is very gratifying. It also provides a better understanding of how your truck operates. Armed with this knowledge, you'll feel more confident about traveling to isolated regions.

Consider The Load

When amperage load rises, so does the need for a high performance electrical system. Light trucks, and especially four-wheel drive models, offer more room for accessorization than any other vehicle. These trucks press their electrical systems to the limit.

Installation of an aftermarket high output alternator can serve your high amperage charging needs. Along with high amps from the alternator, you must consider the wiring and safety devices needed to support such a high output charging and accessory system.

Protecting Your Electrical System

Once you've selected the right alternator to meet your amperage needs, heavy duty wiring can begin. In external regulator systems, wiring starts with the alternator-to-regulator harness. Needs here include proper wire sizing and use of quality terminals. If the alternator unit has an integral regulator, an adequate charge wire, routed directly to the battery, is necessary.

If your alternator delivers 130 or less amps, the appropriate (minimum) requirement for a 10-foot or less length alternator lead is 4-gauge wire. A positive battery cable with the proper ring size end for the alternator output stud is more than adequate. (Protect this lead with a 150-amp circuit breaker or fusible link.)

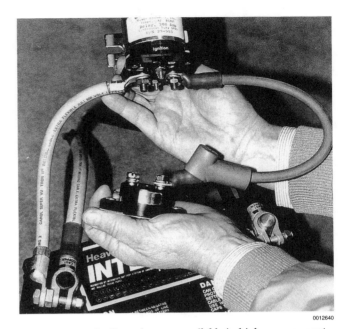

Fig. 15-17. In-line relays are available in high amperage ratings. These devices service heavy accessory circuits.

For a battery cable or a higher output alternator, premium 1/0 size copper welding-type cable is more than adequate. Unlike battery cables, which are relatively rigid and of lower grade, fine-strand welding wire, with quality crimped or compression clamped ends, meets the highest industrial standards for carrying amperage. Welding wire permits oversizing without excess resistance, voltage drop or false battery/current signals to the voltage regulator.

When building the charging/battery wiring with 1/0 welding cable, make sure you also use 1/0 cable for all grounds, including the engine-to-frame and battery. The 6- or 12-volt battery system of a Ford F-truck is direct current (DC), and this means the ground circuit wire gauge must match both charging and starter draw demands.

Dual Battery Electrical Needs

Many truck owners with heavy duty electrical winches add an extra battery to their system. For electrical systems with auxiliary batteries, I recommend use of Wrangler Power Products' Battery Management System.

The system provides an automatic low voltage battery response designed to disconnect the current flow from the auxiliary battery when voltage drops to a critical level. This prevents abuse of your truck's expensive accessories and also protects the auxiliary battery from severe discharge. Upon recharging the battery to a full state of charge, the system reconnects the circuit.

A quality dual or auxiliary battery management system performs two functions: 1) delivers maximum battery current for starting, and 2) charge system protection. In the event that the chassis main battery(s) become low, a management system reads the voltage level of the auxiliary battery and brings that current on line to help start the engine.

The system monitors the two batteries once the engine starts, applying current solely to the main battery

Fig. 15-18. *Dual batteries require a quality management system. Wrangler Power Products' Battery Manager System is a driver switched dual battery circuit controller. The reliable battery isolator and switching components make it virtually impossible to get stranded by a discharged battery. Wrangler also offers a Heavy Duty Steel Dual Battery Tray kit for installing a second OEM-size or other group size batteries.*

until it reaches a full charge state. Then the management system reads the charge state of the auxiliary or winch battery and feeds current to both batteries as required.

Other types of battery isolators are also available. Both electronic and electro-magnetic/mechanical relays, ranging in amperage limits from 100 to 200 amps, can handle major current flow chores. A hefty 250-amp battery switch will also meet heavy current requirements.

Circuit breaking relays, gaining popularity over traditional fuses, work very well on truck electrical systems. In environments where temporary shorting is likely, such as submersion in a running stream of water, a circuit breaker will reset when the hazard passes and the components dry—a helpful prospect.

Circuit breakers range from huge devices to small two-spade ATO fuse size relays. The latter conveniently fit in place of the original fuses in later model F-trucks.

Assessing Your Electrical System's Reliability

Building a first class wiring system involves use of high grade copper terminals and wire products. Regardless of style, judge switches by two criteria: amperage load capacity and a switch's designated number of service cycles.

> **NOTE —**
> Better quality switches have amperage load and service cycle ratings. You will find these switches listed in automotive and electrical/industrial parts catalogs.

If you want maximum performance from your truck's electrical system, each piece of hardware, including crimped and compression terminals, should bear either a military, commercial or industrial (UL) rating. The switches found at discount outlets seldom have these ratings.

For heavy duty purposes, be suspect of any electrical component without a recognizable rating. When in

doubt, seek out an industrial/commercial supplier or high quality automotive sources like NAPA's Belden line or Wrangler Power Products. (See appendix for parts sources.)

High grade hardware, including both brass and copper battery attachments and wire terminals, eliminates trouble in heavily worked electrical systems. Protection from battery acid and the corrosion of salty winters is a must. Underhood heat becomes your nemesis in desert climates, gnawing away at wire insulation and taxing the voltage regulator and other relays. Quality electrical hardware is the best protective measure.

Some Unusual Electrical Hardware

Among the electrical specialty items that fit a light truck owners' needs is a battery jumper system that mounts permanently to the front or rear of your truck. Quick connect cables can serve easily in emergencies, enabling your truck to park nose-to-nose with a stalled vehicle.

Quick disconnect jumper cables help you avoid the hazard of hanging your truck out in the road or running over a cliff while trying to pull alongside a vehicle. The best system I've found yet comes from Wrangler Power Products. These kits feature 1/0 welding cable, copper terminals and industrial grade connectors.

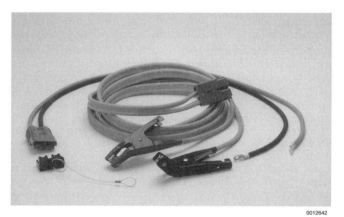

Fig. 15-19. *This is the best way yet to jump batteries: Warn's special quick-connect system that terminates at front bumper.*

Selecting A Battery

Each battery has an ampere hour rating and cold cranking capacity. The engine and electrical system dictate their needs, with air conditioning, power options, the engine size and compression ratio determining the necessary battery group size.

An under-capacity battery will discharge quickly and require excessive, high amperage recharging. Such recycling leads to short battery life. If your truck has a heavy electrical load, or has been hybridized with an engine transplant, battery selection should favor the engine.

Find a listing for a car or truck equipped with your engine and approximately the same accessory package, and note its battery size. Select a similarly rated battery that will fit your battery box, if possible, or change boxes to an adequate size. Secure the battery safely, and use the best battery cable connections available.

A 12-volt battery will operate best above 12.3 volts. (A full state of charge is 12.6.) When you crank the engine for several minutes or leave the headlights burning without the engine running, the battery voltage drops below 12 volts. Healthy batteries will recover some voltage if left alone for awhile, however, to completely restore a battery's state of charge, the generator or alternator must flow amperes.

Maintaining and Monitoring Battery Charge

Earlier Ford F-truck charge systems (both generator and alternator versions) have ammeters to read the actual amperes of electrical current that flow either toward or away from the battery. Later trucks have voltmeters instead of ammeters.

An ammeter tells only the flow of current necessary to restore battery voltage. Voltmeters, by contrast, show the battery's actual state of charge, or the charge state while current flows from the alternator to the battery. Most truck owners prefer a volt-meter and find it more useful. I certainly do.

A worn battery with bad cells loses more voltage while spinning the starter motor. This may bring the battery's volt reading down to 10 volts or less. When this occurs, the alternator floods the battery with heavy amps of current, and a vicious cycle begins. The already tired battery suffers from this fast charge, which heats the battery and reduces its life even further. Soon, the worn battery is nothing more than a source of lead for recycling.

Likewise, an engine rebuild or performance modifications may finish off a lighter duty or worn out battery. Heavy voltage depletion followed by maximum charging after each engine start-up will quickly ruin any battery. Battery drain from heavy lighting or an electric winch can also create a high-rate charging situation. This can quickly destroy the battery.

High Performance Charging System

A high output alternator can restore the battery's state of charge in minutes. OE alternator output usually improves with power options like air conditioning, electric door locks and power window lifts.

Even with a high output factory alternator, however, truck owners find ways to overwhelm their electrical system. Auxiliary lighting, an electric winch, high watt sound systems, and dual-battery installations leave the alternator with a heavy burden. Worse yet, high amp draw auxiliary lighting or a winch often operate with the engine either idling or stopped.

The alternator's strongest advantage over older generator designs is its ability to produce a higher charge rate at slower speeds. Alternators can meet the demands of a vehicle that idles in traffic with air conditioning and other luxury accessories gnawing at the battery.

Late OEM alternators have outstanding charge rates at an idle. By comparison, trucks built before the 1980s, even with high output factory alternators, lag at lower rpm. The typical high output alternator of early '70s vintage produces 55 amps @ 6500 alternator/rotor rpm but only 9 amps at an engine idle. In fairness, this alternator

at 1500 engine rpm jumps to a 44-amp output, but the message is clear: At a curb idle, or when you're crawling off-pavement in the desert, the older alternator has limited output.

As a high output OE alternator retrofit for your truck, consider the features of later factory alternators. By 1982, a popular 80-amp Delco-Remy alternator produces 55 amps at 2000 engine rpm. The newest Delco high output units produce in excess of 60 amps at a 675 rpm idle. Now that's progress! Ford's F-truck alternators have achieved similar performance gains.

An On-board Welder

We were five tortuous, rock crawling hours into the Rubicon. In our whole group, only one rig had given us mechanical trouble. Compared to the two guys now standing in the trail, the trip was a breeze.

A powerful Saginaw power steering gear, manhandled by two burly arms, had ripped out the section of frame rail that supports the steering gearbox. In three hours time, the CJ model Jeep had moved only a couple of healthy stone's throws.

As much as we wanted to help these guys, our tools fell short. What we really needed was an alternator powered frequency welder. Such a device takes a fabrication welder wherever your truck goes. Mounted either underhood or in the bed, the compact unit is powerful stuff.

Better frequency welders perform serious welding, including the use of 5/32" rod on heavy steel plate. Since the principle is frequency, not amperage, cable length is no barrier. Some designs provide a 110-volt D.C. outlet with enough wattage to run brush motor power tools or a string of camp lamps. A battery booster mode can assist stranded vehicles in minutes.

A high-output alternator is at the core of a high frequency welder. At 1500 engine rpm, a high output alternator can reach 135 or more amps, enough to deliver peak welding voltage.

Options include all welding accessories and even TIG (heliarc) or MIG (wire weld) equipment. Most frequency welder kits are easy to install. From my view, this is the ultimate tool for the serious outback traveler. (See Appendix for sources.)

Always upgrade your battery size when installing a high output alternator. Running a winch from a single, low ampere hour battery is dangerous. Completely draining a battery then forcing massive current back into it (which is the voltage regulator's normal response to a fully discharged battery) will heat up the battery plates and cause their failure. Weak batteries produce gases that can explode violently under such conditions.

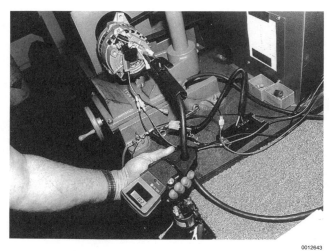

Fig. 15-20. OEM GM CS-130 style alternator is potent. This Delco-Remy unit, capable of 100 amps at an equivalent of 1500 crankshaft rpm, has a top end output of 103 amps. Characteristic of many late model alternators, the CS-130's most impressive attribute is 61 amp output at an engine idle.

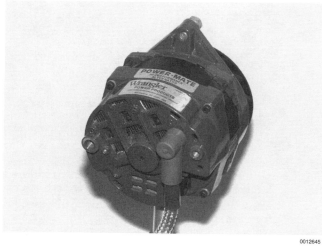

Fig. 15-21. Upgrade your wiring system when you install a high output alternator. A heavy duty solution is 1/0 welding wire with custom crimped ends. Wrangler's 160-amp Ford-type alternator fits late Ford trucks.

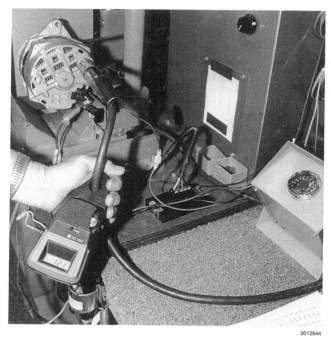

Fig. 15-22. Wrangler Power Products tests a GM factory CS-144 alternator, which stormed to a 121 ampere output by 5000 rotor rpm. Idle speed amperage read 61! Wrangler builds the GM CS-133 or CS-144 alternators into even higher output 140 and 160-amp systems. A full line of Ford alternators can also upgrade your F-truck's charging capacity.

Fig. 15-23. Here are high quality components for building longevity into a charging system. Your new alternator is just the beginning. Shown is a junction block for high amperage, battery size leads.

3. ROLL BARS

By design, light trucks need ground clearance, which means that your truck has a higher center of gravity than modern passenger cars. Concerns about a hazardous rollover are valid, with taller 4x4 models especially vulnerable.

> *WARNING —*
> *A cabover camper raises the vehicle's roll center and its center of gravity. When you carry such a load, your truck should have stabilizer bars and other devices to offset the risk of rollover. Wheel and tire width also play a role here. For ideas on how to reduce risk, see the chapter on chassis/suspension upgrades.*

It's unnerving when a trail or roadway shifts off-camber and your truck's tilt meter runs off the safe zone. When you drive in these kinds of environments, the best protection against bodily injury and major vehicular damage is a roll cage and ample seat belt/harnesses.

Greater concern for product liability has encouraged aftermarket manufacturers to classify cab bars and other steel tubular assemblies into distinct classes: the bonafide roll bar (chassis or cab mounted) and a group of lighter weight, largely cosmetic tube or bed bars.

Cab cages, built for light trucks and multi-purpose sport/utility 4x4s, resemble race truck protection. The critical differences between a hard-core Baja race truck cage and a manufactured cab cage are the bracing and attachment methods.

A Racing Roll Cage

Off-road racing is the best test for roll cages. The standards set by the High Desert Racing Association (HDRA) and SCORE say a lot about our safety needs. Whether you are building your own truck roll cage or shopping for quality aftermarket rollover protection, racing requirements offer the highest standards.

Fig. 15-24. *Where does the roll cage/frame end and the suspension begin? On desert race trucks and stadium race trucks, the line is thin. Bracing angles reflect Nature's strongest design, the triangle. This shape repeats itself throughout the chassis and cage.*

Fig. 15-25. *Roll bars require padding. If your bars are shaped oddly or you want a custom pad, Bar Glove by the Off-Road Factory is one such accessory.*

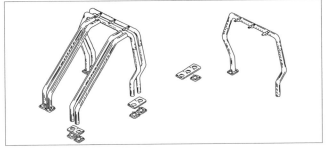

Fig. 15-26. *Many manufacturers make truck bars for pickup beds. These bars provide mounts for lighting and minimal protection. Mounted to the bed sheet metal, they do not qualify as bonafide roll bars. More protective are cab cages for pickups.*

For racing, the minimum tubing size for a 2000–3000 lb. truck is 1-3/4" diameter for open cockpits and 1-1/2" for closed cabs. Tubing wall thickness is minimum 0.120". A 3000–4000 lb. race vehicle requires 2" x 0.120" for open cockpits and 1-3/4" x 0.120" for a closed cab. In trucks over 4000 lbs., tubing size increases to 2-1/4" x 0.120" for open cockpits and 2" x 0.120" for closed cabs.

Materials and construction follow strict guidelines. HDRA/SCORE recommends CRW, DOM, WHR, or WCR mild carbon steel or 4130 Chromoly steel. Light weight and high strength make 4130 popular.

According to official rules, "All welded intersections should be stress relieved by flame annealing. Welds must be high quality with good penetration and no undercutting of the parent metal. No oxy-acetylene brazing on roll cage tubing is permissible. No square tubing is permitted. Use of other materials is subject to prior HDRA/SCORE approval."

Along with these minimum material standards, HDRA/SCORE has strict construction guidelines. The cage must mount securely to the frame or body. All intersection points must have gussets and bracing.

Officially, "Cab or body mounted cages must not be attached to the body structure by direct welding, but must be bolted through and attached by the use of doubler plates (one on either side) with a minimum thickness of 3/16". Roll cage terminal ends must be located to a frame or body structure that will support maximum impact and not shear...."

The required tubing sizes apply to front and rear hoops, front and rear hoop interconnecting bars, rear down braces and all lateral bracing. Minimum bolt size for any attachments is 3/8", with Grade 5 or better strength. A minimum requirement for HDRA/SCORE racing is a roll cage with one front hoop, one rear hoop, two interconnecting top bars between the hoops; two rear down braces and one diagonal brace.

NOTE —
Gussets are mandatory at all welded intersections on the main cage and down braces. Fabricators must also use gussets at any single weld where a fracture could affect driver safety.

Triangular gussets at the top corners may be halves of a 3" x 3" x 1/8" flat plate. Another approach is split, formed and welded corner tubing, or tubing gussets the same thickness as the main cage material. When making the rear down braces and diagonal bracing, the angle cannot be less than 30° from vertical.

HDRA/SCORE rules provide another valuable insight. If a race truck has no steel doors to protect the driver and co-driver, side bars are mandatory. A minimum of one bar per side, as near parallel with the ground as possible, must provide protection yet allow the driver and co-driver (i.e., passenger) to get in and out of the vehicle quickly.

The side bars, formed from the same tubing as the roll cage, must attach to the front and rear hoops of the cage. Gussets and other such braces are also necessary. Sure, it might be tougher to crawl in and out of such a truck, but if rough terrain—or even city traffic—are part of your game plan, the added protection could prevent severe injury in a rollover or T-bone accident.

Racing rules also state that the roll cage bars must be at least 3" in any direction from the driver or co-driver's helmets while in their normal driving positions. Poorly constructed cages have many back country four-wheelers knocking themselves silly against their roll bars.

In addition to the roll cage requirements, HDRA/SCORE requires head and neck restraints to minimize whiplash. The restraint is usually 36 square-inches with at least 2" of padding. Rules also call for padding at all areas of the roll bar or bracing that the occupants' helmets might reach. For an off-pavement or race truck, full padding of the whole interior cage is practical.

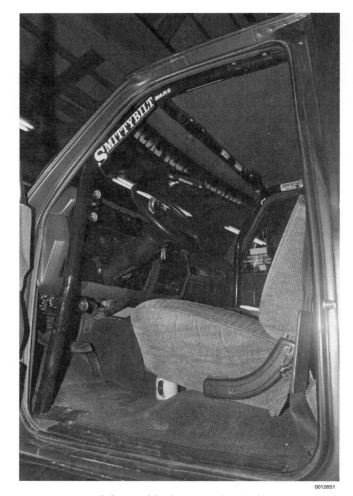

Fig. 15-27. Cab cages like the one in this Ford F-150 4x4 can serve well in a crisis. Quality Hobrecht or Smittybilt kits make installation easier, with minimal amount of assembly time. Carpeting and seat removal are part of the installation.

Practical Alternatives

Few drivers will ever experience a rollover at high speed or the catastrophic impact forces that regularly threaten desert racers. An alternative to a racing-specification cage is a manufactured cab cage system. Better manufactured kits have the advantage of pre-fabricated pieces, with all necessary bends in place. Manufacturers like Smittybilt and Hobrecht work hard to assure proper fitup and ease of installation.

While HDRA/SCORE standards assure maximum protection, less elaborate designs can serve most off-highway situations. At lower speeds, especially while rock crawling, a rollover is generally the less extreme matter of slowly laying a truck on its side. Here, a quality roll cage with side protection, proper seat mounts and secure belts can meet most needs.

WARNING —
An often overlooked issue is flying objects, like tool boxes, metal jacks and jack handles, which can become lethal weapons during a rollover. A latched or locking box to contain these pieces is a very important off-pavement or 4x4 accessory.

4. SEAT BELTS AND SAFETY HARNESSES

Rough terrain driving means odd angles and plenty of bounce. Vehicles can roll over, even at a snail's pace. With very few exceptions, an occupant is safest when safely seat belted within the truck.

If, however, your truck faces a situation like rolling off the edge of a ledge above a steep cliff or into a deep and swift running body of water, consider getting out. (The same rule applies if you might be crushed or impaled by an object in your path as the truck heads for a very low speed rollover.)

WARNING —
Faced with such a foreboding choice, exit your truck as safely as possible, at the point furthest away from the hazard. Avoid being crushed or trapped by your vehicle as it rolls over. Use extreme caution if you choose to jump from the vehicle. This is always a tough call to make — and on extremely short notice.

Beyond these kinds of situations, you're better off seat belted within the protection of your cab and, optimally, a roll cage. That's why you have one!

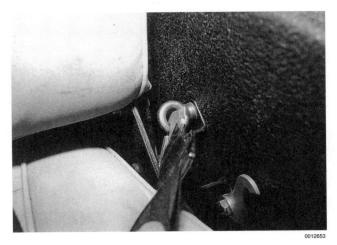

Fig. 15-29. *Grade 8 or better quality hardware, including this eye loop anchor from Filler Safety, assures safe seat belt and harness attachments. A 3" square reinforcement plate backs up sheet metal where harness tail strap attaches.*

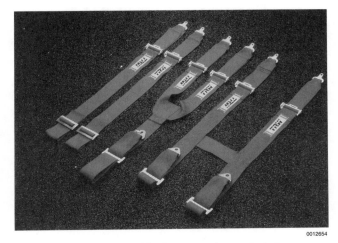

Fig. 15-30. *TRW shoulder harnesses demonstrate two popular styles: H and Y types. TRW is popular in off-road and other forms of sanctioned racing.*

Fig. 15-28. *Factory seat belt anchors are quality attachment points for lap belts. OE engineering accounts for high strength and proper angles.*

The Racing Harness

HDRA/SCORE racing standards provide an excellent yardstick for measuring seat belt and harness quality. The minimum standard for racing is a five-point fast release seat belt and shoulder harness assembly. Buckles must be metal-to-metal, with the single anti-submarine strap attached "as close to the front edge of the seat as practical so that it will exert maximum restraint to the upward movement of the belt and harness."

Seat lap belts are 3" width, the submarine belt 2", and shoulder straps must be 2" to 3". Harness materials must be Nylon or Dacron Polyester and in new or perfect con-

dition with no cuts or frayed layers, chemical stains or excessive dirt.

HDRA/SCORE recommends that belts be changed after one year of use. They must be changed three years from the date of manufacture. The mounting position of the shoulder harnesses is approximately 4" below the top of the driver and co-driver's shoulders. This issue is critical, as severe injury can result from poorly positioned belt anchor points.

By HDRA/SCORE guidelines, "Lap belts should be kept at a minimum at least 2-1/2" forward of seat and backrest intersection. All belts must be mounted directly to a main structure member with the strength at least 1-1/2" x 0.090" tubing with gussets." HDRA/SCORE also recommends keeping adjustment buckles a minimum distance of 1-1/2" from the seat to prevent accidental loosening or chafing.

CHAPTER 15

Avoid Submarining!

Submarining is your body sliding beneath the lap belt during a frontal impact. In desert racing, submarining also occurs when a truck or buggy flies over a rise and lands nose first in a silt bed or the edge of a streambed.

Spinal and head injuries can result from submarining. By sliding down into the seat, the body's alignment during the recoil phase (when the body slams rearward after impact) is awkward. Your head may hit the space between the headrest and seat back, causing severe neck injury.

A series of factors cause submarining: poor design of the safety-belt, bad location of the belt's attachment points, and the wrong seat configuration.

Many shoulder belt designs actually pull the lap belt up during a collision. Schroth, a major producer of rally and racing seat belts, discovered that evenly distributed loads on the shoulder belts were more likely to pull the lap belt up and cause submarining.

As a remedy, Schroth's ASM (AntiSubMarining) system is designed to allow one shoulder belt to readjust very slightly on impact, turning the body a few degrees. The slight shift in body position causes the lower body to press into the lap belt earlier (approximately 20 milliseconds sooner). This tiny delay before the shoulder belts begin to pull is just enough time to tighten against the lap belt.

Using a precalculated energy change also cushions head and shoulder force as the belts begin to tighten. An additional benefit, Schroth notes, is that the design prevents hard pressure on the sternum and breastbone.

WARNING —
Like all other seat belts or harnesses, once the ASM shoulder belts have experienced a heavy frontal impact in an accident they require replacement.

Filler Safety Products, very popular with racers, also stresses the importance of proper seat belt mounting. On 5- and 6-point harnesses, Filler recommends that lap belts angle 45–55° to the tangent line of the thigh. Filler shoulder harness tailstraps require a 45° angle from the seat top, tying to a roll bar cross brace four inches below the shoulder line.

The lap belt anchors two inches forward of the point where the driver's back line and the floor intersect, or 2-1/2" forward of the intersect point of the seat and backrest. Belts should attach to the floor at the same width as the occupant, with brackets aimed in the direction of belt pull. The crotch strap should anchor in line with the driver's chest. Filler's guidelines comply with HDRA/SCORE rules.

Engineers work continuously to improve seat belt and roll bar systems. Light truck and four-wheel drive users have a lot to gain from that effort. If you and your truck have an appetite for the rough stuff, give yourself a fighting chance.

5. TRAILERING AND WHEELBASE CONSIDERATIONS

For towing stability, I always choose a hefty, long wheelbase truck chassis. My experience includes testing and operating many makes and models of two-and four-wheel drive light trucks and SUVs. In my experience, any truck with a wheelbase under 110-inches makes a poor candidate for pulling a sizeable trailer.

As a rule, short wheelbase vehicles don't track well in front of long framed trailers. Even without a trailer, a short wheelbase vehicle can be a handful on ice, slick pavement or when turning at excess speed.

The shorter the wheelbase, the tighter the turning radius, though, and that's where some mini/compact 4x4 pickup and sport utility (SUV) models reign. These shorty SUVs and light 4x4 trucks are often ideal for a tight, twisty off-pavement trail. Once such a vehicle crosses up or skids sideways on a firm roadway surface, however, they're in big trouble.

WARNING —
When a short wheelbase truck starts to skid, directional stability has already been lost. Events happen very quickly with a shorter wheelbase and frame. A full spinout or rollover is possible.

When towing a trailer, steering control is the main drawback for a short wheelbase vehicle. Most trucks under 110" wheelbase have insufficient frame length for absorbing the side sway and whip of a trailer. Additionally, a lightweight truck chassis is easily overrun by a bigger trailer during braking.

A truck's higher center of gravity adds to the short wheelbase problem, making risk of a rollover even greater with a trailer out of control. A two-ton load pushing at the rear bumper centerline of a light duty truck will tax both the vehicle's design and intent.

For the truck better suited to towing, a set of beefier springs, heavy duty shock absorbers, sway controls and an increased tread width can help add stability. A wider-than-stock tread width, accomplished with appropriate wheel rims and oversized tires, can improve the vehicle's directional control. (See suspension/chassis upgrade chapter for details about wheels and tires.)

Use A Stable Hitch Assembly and An Equalizer

Equalizers have revolutionized trailer towing. An equalizer is the ultimate torsion bar suspension system, designed to neutralize chassis load on the tow vehicle.

The equalizer apparatus looks inconspicuous enough, basically two unassuming bars that trail rearward from the truck hitch's ball mount. They swing in their hitch mounting sockets, attached by link chains to brackets that mount on the trailer frame. The adjusting links of the chain are significant, actually loading tension between the truck's hitch and the trailer frame.

The theory is ingenious. As you load the bars, the tongue weight that would otherwise push downward at the rear of the truck becomes equalized by the torsion bar

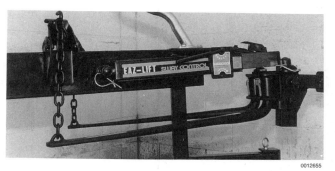

Fig. 15-31. *Drawtite equalizer and EAZ-Lift Sway Control provide ingenious means for stabilizing a trailer in tow. The trailer and truck chassis move in unison, offsetting road forces while distributing the load.*

Fig. 15-32. *Receiver ball mount adjusts horizontally and also for tilt angle. Note massive sockets for equalizer torsion bars. The welded miniature ball bracket holds a sway control ball head. Sway control and equalizer assemblies make the whole package work.*

tension. When properly adjusted, the trailer's weight becomes distributed over the entire length (each of the axles' spring sets) of both the trailer and truck frames. Incredibly, your truck can set almost exactly at its unloaded ball height with a thirty-foot travel trailer attached.

Now visualize pulling such a trailer without the equalizer. Imagine hard braking with a 3500-lbs. trailer rocking forward. Consider the interaction between the two chassis when your truck encounters dips. Picture the truck loaded with additional gear in the back, its front tires too light to steer and the rear springs slamming against the bump stops.

The equalizer apparatus attacks each of these problems, allowing the truck and trailer chassis to move together. These torsion bars aren't just responsible for balancing the load, they also exert a counterforce as they flex.

An equalizer assembly works effectively to counter uncontrolled chassis movement. With an equalizer hitch assembly, the truck and trailer frames can move closely together on nearly the same plane.

Big League Trailering

If a 1500 pound or larger trailer fits your vacation or utility needs, consider towing with a Ford F-Series truck of 117" or longer wheelbase. (I prefer the 131-inch and longer F-250 and F-350 chassis.) The strikes against shorter wheelbase models are not only the wheelbase but also their lighter duty braking capacity, weaker axle sizing and lower spring rates.

A Class III fabricated hitch rates strong enough for a 5000 lbs. load. These hitches accommodate Warn and Ramsey portable winches. Similar hitches are available from Ford truck dealerships and RV outlets.

Good trailer brakes, a frame-mounted Class III or better hitch and an equalizer assembly can help bring your truck and trailer to a quick, straight and safe stop. Add a sway control (basically a friction brake mounted between the trailer tongue and hitch) to reduce the effects of cross winds and whip on curvy roads. Most trailer whip can be controlled with a matched equalizer and sway control.

Sturdy Trailer Hitches

Pre-fabricated trailer hitches are available for all popular light truck models. Your local Ford dealership or a trailering/RV center can supply a bolt-on assembly that meets a wide range of needs and load ratings. In some cases, however, a custom hitch will better suit your trailer or the truck's needs.

A capable shop can build the right hitch for your truck. When choosing a custom trailer hitch, look carefully. You want a well-equipped shop, with all the necessary tools, welding apparatus, and quality steel for building a good hitch.

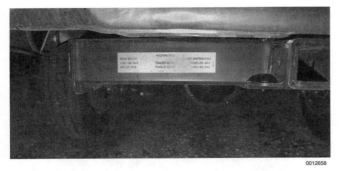
0012658

Fig. 15-33. This platform hitch rates 10,000 pounds only when used with a weight distributing (or equalizing) hitch assembly. For serious trailer loads, you should use an equalizing hitch and frame-mounted platform.

The highest grade steel, 1/4" thick, should be used for braces and gussets. 2-inch square, 0.188" wall thickness rectangular tubing is best for the hitch framework. To prevent stresses inherent to heat-and-bend methods, tubing bends should be made on a press. Likewise, all construction welds and actual frame attachment welds should follow rigid standards for reducing heat stress to frame members and other vital parts.

Trucks and 4x4s used off-pavement occasionally bury their rear bumpers in the dirt. For this reason, a receiver-type hitch, tucked in close to the rear frame member, works well.

You can remove the detachable ball assembly when the trailer is not in use. This will reduce rear departure angle hang ups and also discourage theft of expensive pieces. Use of a pin-and-clip disconnect on the ball mount, with a nut welded to the side of the receiver for an anti-rattle bolt, provides for quick installation and removal of the ball mount.

Years ago, when doing a magazine assignment on safe trailer hitches, I met Rick Preston, owner of Rick's R.V. Center and Hitch Shop at El Cajon, California. Rick is one of the best hitch fabricators around, an experienced and innovative designer of safe, custom built towing hitches.

When Rick's crew builds a custom hitch, they often incorporate two rearward facing side gussets, triangular in shape. Safety chain-holed plates brace the receiver. The trailer's safety chains, which can route through the hitch and index with chain slots, help meet the legal safety requirements.

Final fitup includes strategically placed welds for the frame mounts, then installation of cross-bracing and support. (Added braces can raise the class rating of the hitch.) A trailer electrical connector bracket and glossy black engine enamel complete the job.

Before towing any trailer with your truck, get an expert opinion about the vehicle's towing equipment. Shops like Rick's R.V. Center know the requirements and can quickly identify unsafe hitches.

Chapter 16

Ford Engine Performance: Mild to Wild!

1. ENGINE PERFORMANCE AND SMOG LEGAL MODIFICATIONS

THE UNITED STATES CLEAN AIR ACT of 1990 was a watershed measure to curb environmental pollution. "This landmark bill will result in deep and lasting reductions in acid rain, of toxic industrial air pollutants and urban smog," President George Bush noted. "It also will limit U.S. greenhouse gas emissions and sharply reduce our potential contribution to climate change."

The President expressed this nation's commitment to protect the environment and added, "While national governments have an important role to play, progress in protecting our environment is also made community by community, street by street, person by person..."

Targeting engine modifications that defeat pollution controls, the U.S. Environmental Protection Agency (EPA) has given aftermarket performance manufacturers a higher level of accountability. Product disclaimers that read "off-highway use only" are no longer enough.

The Message Is Clear

The California Air Resources Board (CARB) and EPA mean business. Cars and trucks manufactured and licensed for public road use must comply with clean air standards and emission control guidelines.

An EPA letter addressed to automotive parts manufacturers, distributors, retailers and installers clarifies the amended government policy: "The Clean Air Act now prohibits any person from manufacturing, selling, offering for sale, or installing any part or component intended for use with, or as part of, any motor vehicle, where a principal effect of the part or component is to bypass, defeat, or render inoperative any device or element of design, and where the person knows or should know the part or component is being put to such use."

As an example, the letter notes, "...EPA has determined that a catalytic converter replacement pipe, also known as a test pipe, is a part or component intended for use with a motor vehicle for which a principal effect is to bypass, defeat, or render inoperative a vehicle's catalytic converter...EPA believes it is illegal for any person to

Fig. 16-1. *High performance for the '90s takes emission requirements into consideration. "50-state legal" supercharger systems, like this centrifugal blower, provide substantial increases in torque and horsepower without a negative impact on tailpipe emissions. Look for "50-state legal" labels on upgrade parts.*

CHAPTER *16*

manufacture, sell, offer for sale or install a catalytic converter replacement pipe...The penalty for violations is up to $2500 for each such device which is manufactured, sold, offered for sale or installed."

Ignorance is no excuse. Simply saying that the pipe cannot be used on pollution controlled vehicles won't satisfy the law. The manufacturer of such a device must now take full responsibility for the actual use of the product. The EPA warns, "We intend to focus our enforcement efforts not only on the manufacturers of these defeat devices, but also on auto parts houses and repair facilities who stock, sell or install such devices."

Taboos Under The Law

How does this new policy affect your F-truck? Using the catalytic converter as an example, you cannot remove it for off-road driving. According to the EPA, "The federal tampering prohibition pertains to motor vehicles, which are defined by section 216(2) of the Act as 'any self-propelled vehicle[s] designed for transporting persons or property on a street or highway.'"

EPA emphasizes that in each model year, vehicle manufacturers certify engine-chassis configurations to meet certain emission standards. Under 1990 mandates, "...it is not legal for anyone to de-certify a motor vehicle for off-road use." This means that Ford Motor Company has certified your vehicle model. You cannot compromise any part of your truck's pollution control system.

This same law says that swapping an earlier non-catalyst engine into a later, catalytic-equipped chassis is illegal. The chassis still requires the use of a catalytic converter, and the engine must be either the same year or newer than your F-truck. Shops are now held accountable for knowing whether a vehicle originally required a catalytic converter.

Importantly, a muffler shop cannot install a non-certified (termed non-exempt in California) dual exhaust system in place of a single exhaust system—even if the shop installs dual catalytic mufflers. If your truck was originally a single exhaust model, certified by Ford in that mode, the new EPA law restricts any kind of non-certified modification by a muffler shop.

So strong is this ruling that the only current exception is a vehicle already converted to dual exhausts with double catalytic converters. Although the EPA encourages a shop to retrofit an OEM style single exhaust system in such cases, the agency currently allows shops to install replacement catalytic converters and pipes on a previously retrofit dual exhaust systems. The shop must be able to prove, however, that they did not replace the OEM single system with a dual exhaust setup.

Catalytic converter rulings are just the beginning. EPA has adopted California's standards for exemption or certification of aftermarket engine parts. Components that CARB finds acceptable also earn a federal stamp of approval. An Executive Order (EO) number from California indicates that an aftermarket part has undergone the testing necessary to meet or exceed OEM tailpipe emission standards.

Legally Exempted Components

Before you limit the utility of your smog-compliance Ford truck, consider the legal alternatives. The EPA and CARB each approve (exempt) many engine components that meet clean air requirements. There are also legally recognized components that have no impact whatsoever on tailpipe emissions. A high output water pump, an improved cooling system, a high capacity charging circuit or chrome valve covers will not fail your truck's emissions test.

Equally important, engine rebuilding can legally include many upgrade parts that will increase the reliability of your engine. Components like stronger pushrods, hardened exhaust valve seats, better bearings, improved piston rings, quality (stock compression ratio) pistons and a heavy duty timing chain have no effect on tailpipe emissions.

The point here is tailpipe emissions. Changing the camshaft to a long duration grind for maximum mid-range and top end power is a sure way to raise measurable hydrocarbon and carbon monoxide output at lower engine speeds. (California-type biennial smog inspection tests traditionally have taken place at an idle and 2500 rpm.) Likewise, a non-approved high performance retrofit carburetor could raise your truck's tailpipe emissions.

> NOTE —
> A non-approved replacement carburetor will immediately fail the visual portion of the California-standard smog inspection test.

Many aftermarket manufacturers have taken their components through the California emission certification process. Some performance items qualify as OEM replacement parts. Most of Edelbrock's Performer dual-plane manifolds, for example, provide a mount for the EGR valve.

Although these Edelbrock manifolds improve flow and engine efficiency, they will not increase tailpipe pollution. Several exhaust header and ignition component manufacturers have also passed the CARB tests and received EO numbers for their products.

For electronic fuel injected and turbocharged engines, a variety of aftermarket improvements in air flow and induction tuning parts have met certification standards. If a part has an official California exemption number for use on your specific engine, you can install these parts without violating the law.

Clean Air High Performance

Under the amended Clean Air Act of 1991, aftermarket manufacturers must certify any induction system component, ignition system piece, performance camshaft or exhaust device that differs from the OEM design or engineering standards. Additionally, each state has statutes or regulations that prohibit defeating or tampering with pollution control equipment. The EPA emphasizes, "Vehicle owners who tamper with their own vehicles may be subject to substantial penalties under both federal and State law."

These laws, however, encourage lower tailpipe emissions. For this reason, California has no objection to replacing the carbureted 302 V-8 in your 1979 F-100 chassis with a late model Ford MPI 351W V-8. Despite the increase in horsepower and torque, the tailpipe pollution from a late EFI engine is a fraction of that allowed for 1979 vehicles.

> **NOTE —**
> A late EFI conversion engine must include its OEM computer and all factory engine sensors. You must swap all parts that make up the OEM engine/emissions package.

Buy Legal Performance

A wide range of aftermarket parts have California EO exemptions (50-State legal status). When you find EO exempted parts, make sure that pieces have approval for use on your particular year and model engine. Some parts might fit your engine but still do not meet the emission requirements. EO exemptions apply to a specific year/model, chassis type and engine application. There are a variety of devices that have EO numbers. Currently, the EPA accepts CARB tests and exemption criteria. Parts that have California exemption status also meet Federal/EPA standards.

> **NOTE —**
> A complete list of California exempted components is available from the California Air Resources Board or local motor vehicle emissions testing stations throughout the State of California.

A Bright Future

Improvements in engine technology means more likelihood of swapping late EFI engines into earlier F-truck chassis. Electronic fuel injection overcomes sidehill flooding and the negative effects of altitude. Also, without exception, later EFI engines have lower tailpipe emissions and potentially better fuel efficiency than earlier carbureted versions of these same engine designs.

California has provided a referee program for smog certification of vehicles with engine conversions. Referees determine whether you have made a complete conversion, including all necessary emission equipment.

> **NOTE —**
> Tailpipe emissions from your new, upgraded engine must not exceed those of your original Ford truck engine in good operating condition. For details, contact the California Consumer Affairs Department for referral to your local Bureau of Automotive Repairs referee station.

Imagine the performance of a late Paxton or Vortech (50-State legal) supercharged 351W MPI V-8 in place of the 302 V-8 in a 1971 F-100 pickup. How about a stout 460 MPI/EFI V-8 engine in place of a 1980 351M/400 V-8 smog motor in an F-350 4x4 Camper Special model? Your earlier Ford F-truck would gain both torque and fuel efficiency, yet produce far less tailpipe pollution.

Aftermarket manufacturers have responded to the EPA requirements. Crane Cams has tested and received California Air Resources Board EO numbers for several camshaft profiles. Crane camshafts with EO numbers have 50-State legal status when used in specific engines. Gene Ezzell, President and CEO at Crane Cams, credits the Specialty Equipment Market Association (SEMA) for encouraging the aftermarket to build California/EPA legal products. SEMA's effort helps assure the stability and future of the automotive performance aftermarket.

As an active supporter of TREAD LIGHTLY! and the Clean Air Act standards, I encourage you to protect the environment. Use those aftermarket performance parts with California EO numbers or EPA/50-States Legal status. At the very least, make sure that your truck is emission legal.

2. FORD F-TRUCK POWER: AN OVERVIEW

Building a truck engine strictly for horsepower, a valid goal for desert racing, may actually inhibit low speed torque output and diminish trail running and rock crawling ability. Careful planning and selection of components can give your engine more usable torque, better breathing characteristics and greater stamina for tortuous off-pavement lugging and climbs.

> *CAUTION —*
> • *Many engine modifications are illegal for street or public highway use. If your truck must comply with vehicle registration and public highway requirements, make certain that aftermarket parts have California and federal EPA approval. It is illegal to remove, modify or degrade pollution control devices on vehicles licensed for use on public highways.*
>
> • *When making major engine modifications, the rest of the truck's powertrain must be able to withstand the added torque. A light duty transmission, transfer case and drive axle(s) often fail when subjected to great increases in horsepower. Beware. You may need a host of powertrain modifications.*

Begin With The Valvetrain

The typical valve-in-head (OHV) engine's valvetrain consists of the camshaft, camshaft followers (lifters), pushrods, rocker arms, valve springs and valves. 1948–53 flathead V-8s and early F-truck L-head sixes use only a camshaft, tappets, valve springs and valves.

On OHV Ford engines, the valves and springs fit in a removable cylinder head. Camshaft followers or lifters ride on lobes of the camshaft. Pushrods link the lifters to the rocker arms, which pivot and press against the valve

CHAPTER 16

stem ends. The intake and exhaust valves open and close the ports, allowing gases to enter and leave each cylinder.

The camshaft has an important job. Lobes, carefully shaped to open and close the valves at precise times, rotate at one-half the speed of the crankshaft. Each two turns of the crankshaft, the camshaft will open and close each valve, doing so for the entire service life of the engine.

The tension at the camshaft and lifter contact point is the highest pounds-per-square-inch load within your truck's engine. Hardness of the camshaft material and its compatibility with the lifter will affect the overall reliability of the engine. The severity of lobe contours or profiles also dictates the degree of stress placed upon pushrods, rocker arms and valve springs.

Camshaft Lobe Profiles and Valve Timing

Each truck engine type requires a camshaft of unique dimensions. Lobe profiles vary, and careful engineering determines the correct shape from low point (heel) to peak lift. Lifter design limitations also influence the lobe ramp shape.

CAUTION —
Radically tall lobe contours increase stress and wear between the lobe and the lifter base. Very tall valve lift requires roller lifters, special valve springs and other valvetrain upgrades. (See camshaft manufacturer's recommendations.)

The three basic elements in camshaft design are the total valve lift (over the full range of lifter movement), valve opening duration (the number of crankshaft degrees that the valve stays open) and valve timing (essentially the opening and closing points for the valves). The correct replacement camshaft will have proper valve lift and opening duration with the right valve timing.

Selecting Your Camshaft

Some general rules apply when meeting off-pavement and heavy duty pulling chores. For general four-wheeling and trailer towing, your engine will operate over a broad rpm range, needing power from just off idle to at least 4000 rpm. Here, the long duration performance-street camshaft is incorrect, as valve timing has excessive overlap.

Valve overlap is the exhaust valve still closing while the intake valve has already begun to open. Excess valve overlap creates two fundamental problems for an off-pavement 4x4 or towing engine: 1) rough idle and poor low speed throttle response, and 2) low manifold vacuum at slower engine rpm.

Manifold vacuum is crucial to truck pulling power, proper combustion, and fuel economy. In effect, an automotive gasoline engine is a vacuum pump. Your truck engine's operating cycle begins with the vacuum characteristics of the intake stroke.

If you plan serious rock crawling and trailer pulling, or want low speed economy and good throttle response, high manifold vacuum will be on top of your priority list. Especially at higher elevations, engine breathing depends upon efficient manifold vacuum.

Off-pavement and Towing Camshaft Profiles

The back country truck engine needs a camshaft that works well at highway cruising speeds (generally 2000–3000 engine rpm) and still can crawl through your favorite rockpile. Likewise, a truck that tows a trailer or carries heavy loads will require strong low speed performance and low-to mid-range strengths.

If light duty use, highway cruising, occasional trailer pulling and modestly good fuel economy are your goals, a camshaft close to the OEM specs will likely work fine. The formula for hardcore off-pavement or trailering success, however, requires more low-rpm torque response and a relatively low speed horsepower peak. This typically requires more valve lift than the older OE truck camshafts provided.

Most early camshaft grinds were much the same as passenger car profiles. The last decade of engine/camshaft development has produced higher torque and more horsepower at lower engine rpm. This is a substantial improvement.

Controllable power in an off-idle rock crawl situation relies more on torque than horsepower. (Good low speed torque is often the product of increased valve lift and a mild valve opening duration.) As lugging the engine can prevent wheelspin, the engine must have good low-end torque at very light or tip-in throttle. (For driving details, see the chapter on operating your truck.)

Traditionally, gasoline engines have realized their full horsepower potential in the mid-to top-end rpm range, speeds upward of 3500 rpm. However, when your truck's tires need a solid grip and rock shale threatens the sidewalls, running the engine at 3500 or more rpm is not only unsafe but also abusive to the engine and geartrain.

Low rpm control requires immediate off-idle torque, the product of healthy valve lift. I always use manifold vacuum as a guide for selecting a real truck camshaft, looking for a grind capable of delivering at least 16 (preferably 18) inches of manifold vacuum at an idle.

Such an RV, trailer towing or economy camshaft grind will work well with milder carburetion or MPI/EFI. Four-wheeling and trailer towing always benefit from the strong torque characteristics of a camshaft that delivers good idle and low speed vacuum.

In general, I look for a camshaft with slightly more valve lift than the OEM profile. (OE specifications are generally available in your factory level shop manual.) I keep both the valve opening duration (total degrees) and valve timing conservative.

Aftermarket Camshaft Options

For high torque within a reasonable rpm range, several camshaft profiles have worked well in Ford engines. For the ever popular 300-cubic-inch six, a real torque monster with seven-main-bearing crankshaft support and a healthy stroke, it's easy to extract serious stump pulling power.

For 240/300 inline Ford sixes, a hydraulic cam of approximately 0.444 inches gross lift and 264 degree duration will work well. Assuming that your Ford six has a reasonable compression ratio (9.2:1 or less), the idle with this kind of camshaft is smooth, and your engine can develop usable low-end torque and respectable mid-range

(2000-3500 rpm) horsepower. Expect this type of camshaft's power curve to drop abruptly above 4500 rpm.

For Ford carbureted V-8 engines like the 302, 351W, 351M/400 and even the big block 460, lift is again useful. Two camshafts that I like for true towing power are Competition Cams' High Energy 252H or 260H.

The 260H has more multi-purpose and light duty uses and would also satisfy the 302 builder or others who want low (numerically higher) axle gearing. Similarly, the Competition Cams 268H can work well for a 460 big block trailer puller with low axle gearing, although fuel economy will suffer.

A 252H and proper gearing will deliver exceptional fuel economy and lugging power. For a 351W or 351M/400 travel trailer puller, I like this camshaft with 4.10:1 axle gearing and a 31-inch diameter tire. The 252H produces great low end torque, high manifold vacuum and good horsepower at cruise rpm. Expect a noticeable power drop above 4200 rpm.

> **NOTE —**
> Whenever you upgrade the camshaft, install new lifters and make certain that the valve springs are in top shape. The valve lifts I recommend here are relatively mild, and they require only that your OEM components, including valve springs, be in good condition. Install a high quality roller timing chain and sprocket set, and carefully follow the camshaft manufacturer's recommendations for setting camshaft/valve timing.

Camshafts of this type satisfy rock crawling needs, help pull a light trailer and deliver good gas mileage. On a pre-EFI/MPI engine, you can use OEM-type carburetion or an improved carburetor with near stock cubic-feet-per-minute (CFM) flow rate.

For carbureted engines, my manifold of choice for a 4200 rpm ceiling and 351 or larger V-8 is either a stock OEM four-barrel design or Edelbrock's Performer dual-plane design. (Most Performer applications are emission legal.) For the older 302 carbureted engines, a two-barrel 2300-series Holley or even the Motorcraft 2100-type carburetors work well.

The Ford OEM camshafts found in early F-truck flathead engines, the Y-block OHV V-8s or even the early FE 352 and 360 engines will work fine for trailer pulling and overall performance. An aftermarket camshaft grind for any of these engines would enhance highway performance but not necessarily improve economy or trailer pulling power. If you rebuild an engine of this type for towing or hauling, consider a stock truck replacement camshaft grind.

Variable Duration Lifters

Few camshafts can satisfy a truck owner's every need. Some cams deliver strong bottom end power but weak performance from 3600 rpm upward. Others offer more mid-range and top-end power while sacrificing crucial idle and low speed power. For some engine designs, the solution is a set of variable duration valve lifters.

Jack Rhoads pioneered such a hydraulic lifter. The Rhoads lifter bleeds down at low rpm and allows valve lift to drop 0.020–0.030" with milder valve opening duration. The precisely metered bleed down essentially makes several camshaft profiles out of one. Rhoads, Crane and others now offer variable duration lifters for many engine designs.

The reduction in lift and duration creates a tolerable idle and good low speed response, even with a slightly racy camshaft. A popular V-8 performance camshaft of 270 (total) degrees or more duration can now be acceptable for many truck uses.

Similarly, valve lift can be extended to 0.435" or more. Better low-end torque, reasonable manifold vacuum at low speeds and great mid-range and top-end power are all possible from the same camshaft grind. The only downside to variable duration lifters is noise. They often create more valvetrain sound than stock valve lifters.

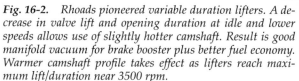

Fig. 16-2. Rhoads pioneered variable duration lifters. A decrease in valve lift and opening duration at idle and lower speeds allows use of slightly hotter camshaft. Result is good manifold vacuum for brake booster plus better fuel economy. Warmer camshaft profile takes effect as lifters reach maximum lift/duration near 3500 rpm.

Axle Gearing For Your Camshaft Choice

When making a camshaft selection, consider your axle gearing and tire diameter. These two factors determine the cruising rpm and low-speed responsiveness of your truck's engine.

Unless the tire diameter is oversize, very low axle ratios (like 4.27:1 to 5.38:1) will substantially raise the highway cruising rpm. Likewise, mid-'70s and later trucks often have taller axle ratios (3.08:1 to 3.73:1).

Taller axle ratios or oversize tires can drop the truck's highway/cruising rpm range to below 2000 rpm. This will not work with a mid-range or top-end camshaft grind. You would need a milder camshaft or lower axle gear ratios.

Tall gearing (numerically low) and oversize tires require a camshaft that delivers plenty of low end torque. Forget about 5000 rpm performance. For a truck with 3.08:1 gearing, 33" diameter tires and a non-overdrive transmission, the engine spins 1,882 rpm in high gear at

60 mph. For the engine that develops peak torque at 3,000 rpm or maximum horsepower around 5,000 rpm, this could impede performance and hamper fuel economy.

By dramatic contrast, a truck with 5.38:1 gears and 30" diameter tires would have the engine spinning 3617 rpm at 60 mph. Making an engine's horsepower available and useful is the primary concern of axle gearing and tire diameter choices. With careful planning, your truck can make substantial performance and fuel economy gains off-pavement or at highway cruise speeds.

Hot and Reliable Ignition Spark

A high performance or working truck engine requires top ignition performance. An excellent source for late Ford electronic ignition enhancements is Ford's own SVO program. Ford experts offer enhanced ignition coils, complete distributors, rev limiters and interface devices that will not compromise even the latest electronic fuel and spark management system.

Accel Performance Products also offers a wide range of high performance ignition components. Racing Coils, the Super Coil and HEI intensifier kits are designed to work in conjunction with various OEM Ford ignition systems. Super Stock Coils also replace several Ford OEM types.

Electrical accessories, including ballast resistors and coil brackets, round out the OE replacement components. Accel is also serious about racing, and a number of all-out performance distributors are available. A 37-Series Dual-Point provides performance to 9000 rpm. The 43-Series Magnetic NASCAR-developed distributor has an adjustable spark curve, making the unit useful for many applications. Accel's 44-Series Direct Drive distributor, with rigid timing, ranks well as a sand drag or mud bog ignition.

Crane's Emission Legal EFI/MPI Performance Camshafts

Since the early-1980s, EFI and carbureted high performance engines owe their much improved performance levels to the wizardry of electronic fuel and spark management. Factory engines meet stringent tailpipe emission and fuel economy standards while horsepower increases have continued.

Rather than pursue computer modifications, like other aftermarket performance researchers, Crane (a prominent camshaft builder since the dawn of high performance) went after improvements in camshaft valve timing, lift and duration.

Focus On What You Know Best

Crane believed that camshaft changes could take advantage of factory programmed spark and fuel variables. The OEM computers produced reasonable performance, driveability and fuel economy. Why mess with a good thing? Crane also discovered that the factory computers could compensate for minor camshaft changes.

One of the secrets to Crane's success is high manifold vacuum. Manifold pressure sensors, which heavily influence computer decisions, need a strong vacuum signal at engine idle and low speeds. Crane worked with this need, not against it. Instead of overloading the feedback loops with low manifold vacuum readings and overreach signals from the oxygen sensor, Crane designed the cam lobes to provide even more lift and a larger flow area.

Center Of The Action

Crane determined that if intake valves lifted from their seats more quickly and seated at a faster rate, valve timing improvements were possible—without a sacrifice in necessary manifold vacuum.

Crane tightened the camshaft lobe centerlines. On the average, a Crane CompuCam 2000 profile has a 4-degree tighter lobe center than the factory camshaft. Coupled with a mild lift increase of around 0.030" at each valve,

these Crane camshafts deliver increased low-end to mid-range torque and more horsepower at a higher rpm. The CompuCam 2000 also retards exhaust valve timing slightly, yet holds exhaust valves open slightly longer. Better exhaust scavenging results.

The intake lobe, meanwhile, advances valve timing very mildly. This usually requires more intake/exhaust lobe center spread, but here the key to this design's success is quicker ramp action to accelerate the intake valve from its seat faster. The effective lift and duration give much better performance, yet the computer believes that all is normal. The OEM shift to roller lifter camshaft profiles pursues a strategy similar to Crane's CompuCam 2000 designs.

Compucam For Late Ford Engines

The multipoint injected MPI 302 put power and reasonable economy back on the American road. These engines, stock, act much like a 351 Windsor of a bygone era. The H.O. version even brings back memories of high performance mid-'60s Ford small blocks. If your F-truck 302 with MPI lacks mid-range performance, Crane's #36111 CompuCam 2020 grind camshaft can help. Best of all, they are 50-State emission legal.

For H.O. 302 MPI engines, the #444112 CompuCam 2020 matches low-end and mid-range torque with tall (2.73 to 3.50:1) axle gearing. Models with Mass Air Flow sensors can deliver more mid-and upper-rpm performance with the #444122 CompuCam 2030 camshaft. The CompuCam 2030 aims at cruise speeds above 2400 rpm, which is common to many F-trucks. (Other modifications, including a 3.08 or lower gearset and a higher stall torque converter may be necessary with this cam profile. Crane requires special valve springs, steel retainers and valve locks with any of the Ford 302 V-8 camshafts.)

As for dyno measured improvements, an '87 Mustang GT HO engine gained 8 horsepower and 16 lbs-ft of torque. 0–60 time dropped nearly 0.4 seconds. Torque peaked at the same rpm as the stock engine, while the horsepower peak occurred at 300 extra rpm (4800).

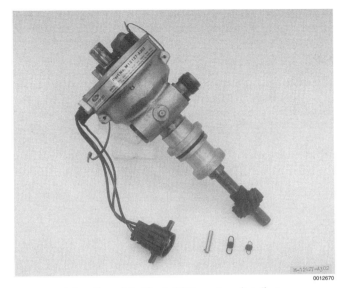

Fig. 16-3. *Complete Ford SVO racing distributor assemblies fit all popular small-block and big-block Ford engines. Mechanical tach drive units are available. Custom drive gears, advance spring kits, spark cable kits and special distributor caps are also in Ford's SVO/Motorsport program.*

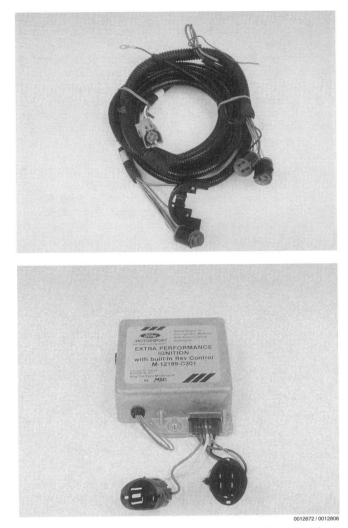

Fig. 16-5. *"Extra Performance" self-supporting ignition system by Ford SVO consists of ignition control module, a high output coil and complete wiring harness. Designed for use with Ford Motorsport or Dura-Spark II distributor (without EEC), this kit enhances ignition performance. Rev control is included, and a similar system is available for use with Dura-Spark III/EEC ignition components.*

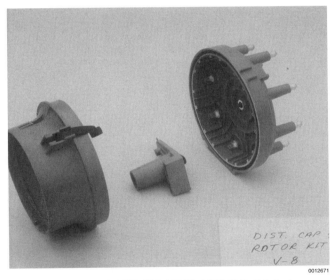

Fig. 16-4. *Ford SVO #M-12106-A302 V-8 distributor cap and rotor kit fits all 1957–93 Ford V-8 ignition distributors except EEC types. (This is actually a replacement for '77–'93 style cap and rotor.) Wider cap prevents ignition spark crossfiring with a high output ignition. Similar cap is also available for six-cylinder Motorcraft distributors.*

Accel Crankshaft Trigger Kits for high performance V-8s are designed to afford greater accuracy, while milder needs revolve around the 34-Series Super Stock dual point distributors. Less racing oriented, the 34-Series units offer a vacuum advance option.

Off-pavement truck users find the Accel 41-Series electronic distributor attractive and available in optional vacuum mechanical/vacuum advance form. In an off-road emergency, a common GM HEI module and Chrysler distributor cap can bring your rig home.

Allison, which is now a division of Crane Cams, has a long record of quality ignition products. Popular is the 50-State legal XR-700 electronic ignition conversion for older breaker point ignitions. This system allows use of your stock distributor with all the benefits of an electronic high energy spark. For many older (pre-electronic) Ford ignitions, the XR-700 kit can upgrade ignition performance while eliminating breaker points.

Allison claims performance and mileage gains, along with easier starting than the original breaker points. The XR-700 kits are about as simple to install as OEM breaker points. In addition to a lifetime warranty, the XR-700 conversion offers the ideal off-pavement backup system: an OE set of points and condenser. If the electronic parts fail in the field, simply reinstall the OE ignition pieces.

Mallory pioneered high performance ignitions, primarily around Ford engines. Racing and high performance distributors, coils, electronic conversion kits, modules, rev limiters and much, much more make Mallory a strong choice for your spark needs. The Mallory catalog covers OE replacement upgrades, computer chips and a traditional line of accessories that distinguish this company from its competition. The popular Unilite breakerless distributors or a Unilite conversion kit provide plenty of dependable spark. Racing dual-point and Unilite units are also popular.

MSD is distinguished by a full line of ignition distributors and all-out racing hardware. Many MSD electronic devices interface with OEM, aftermarket or the complete MSD ignitions. Adjustable timing controls provide more complete combustion and a cure for high altitude and poor fuel grades. Want to compensate for thin air or Mexican gasoline? The MSD timing controls place spark timing at your fingertips.

Performance Distributors provide completely reworked OE-type units that wield a whopping spark. Performance Distributors claim nearly twice the fire of a magneto, reach the 9000 crankshaft rpm range, offer a custom spark curve to meet your exact engine needs and undergo thorough pre-testing before shipment.

Running 0.050–0.055" recommended spark plug gaps, these new distributor units yield tremendous gains from idle through high rpm. A bronze terminal cap and racing coil accompany each distributor. Performance Distributors can rework a popular Ford electronic distributor unit to meet high performance standards.

Performance Carburetion

Ford trucks have used Holley carburetors for many years. Y-block truck engines introduced the use of the popular 2300-series two-barrel design, while passenger car and larger V-8 truck engines have benefitted from Holley square-flange four-barrel carburetors.

The 2300-series two-barrel and square-flange four-barrel carburetors offer a wide range of interchangeable parts. You can upgrade most Holley two- and four-barrel carburetors with readily available Holley performance parts.

Spark Knock Cures

Trailer pulling and hauling heavy loads can stress your truck's engine to its limit. This kind of use boosts cylinder pressures and creates risk: Running hot, at extremely high cylinder pressures, your spark-ignited engine's worst enemy is detonation. Detonation is far more than an annoying rattle or ping. If severe enough, it can damage pistons, piston rings, valve faces and even the crankshaft.

The most advanced engines with fuel and spark management (like Ford's EFI/MPI system for F-trucks) meet low emission standards and cope with low octane fuel by using an engine-mounted knock sensors. The sensors "listen" for spark knock, then the system electronically retards spark timing for all cylinders until the noise disappears. The system then advances spark just to the point of detonation, giving optimum performance.

Aftermarket Knock Fix

Aftermarket devices can now rival or exceed the performance of OEM systems. I have tested one such device on several engines and can say that this is probably the most significant breakthrough in aftermarket ignition engineering.

Built by J&S Electronics, the 50-State legal Safe Guard ignition retard system senses spark knock and then seeks out the individual culprit cylinder(s). A pre-programmed computer/module draws down the spark advance in small-degree increments until just the point that detonation disappears.

As an option, the kit offers a Retard Display monitor that reads the number of spark retard degrees necessary to stop engine ping and piston rattle. The monitor also features an Air-Fuel Ratio Display that interprets signals from an oxygen sensor mounted in the exhaust stream. The various Safe Guard kits can interface with a conventional, fully electronic or even an older breaker point ignition.

Hook-up requires few tools and only a basic understanding of automotive wiring. My installations, which involve extra care when routing wires and mounting hardware, have taken a maximum of 3-1/2 hours. Drilling and welding for the oxygen sensor plug takes some additional time. The simple sensitivity adjustment, which requires driving your truck under load conditions, takes an extra half hour.

Safe Guard is capable of twenty crankshaft degrees retard per detonating cylinder. Aside from dramatic gains in fuel economy and performance, Safe Guard has a distinct advantage over many OEM spark management systems. OEM systems pull back on timing for all cylinders. Safe Guard, by retarding spark for individual cylinders, keeps the other cylinders developing peak performance.

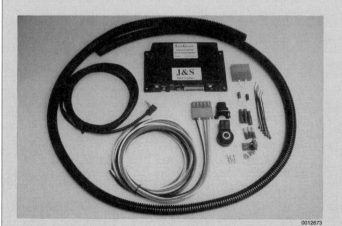

0012673

J&S Electronic's Safe Guard retards spark enough to stop detonation. Under load, it retards spark only on individual cylinders that knock. Other cylinders remain just below their detonation threshold, where optimal power and economy occur. Safe Guard is 50-State legal, has sensitivity adjustment, and includes an rpm limiter.

Engine Tuning With An Oxygen Sensor

A number of aftermarket engine tuning devices use an exhaust system mounted oxygen sensor to indicate the air-fuel ratio or mixture. Sending a signal to LED display lights, such an instrument can provide an instant account of the carburetor's air-fuel ratio delivery and jetting.

Deviations from the ideal 14.7:1 (stoichiometric for gasoline) air-fuel ratio are easy to detect. Tuning an aftermarket fuel injection system or jetting a carburetor is simple with such a device. As a skilled engine tuner, I find that road tuning with an exhaust stream (oxygen sensing) air-fuel ratio meter is much like using a wheel dynamometer. Equipped with this technology, you can quickly become a proficient engine tuner.

Few out-of-the-box aftermarket carburetors or EFI systems will produce exactly the right air-fuel ratios for your performance engine buildup. By using an air-fuel ratio meter, you can analyze the engine's performance over the entire span of fuel circuits—from idle to the full-on power cycle, from partial throttle response to cruising mixture.

Detonation results from premature ignition or rapid burning of volatile fuel. Current fuels, with limited octane and anti-knock capacity, have faster burn rates, increasing the risk of detonation or annoying ping.

Engineers and chemists work hard to reduce detonation in engines, yet the only reliable means is to delay the point of fuel ignition. While late (more retarded) spark timing does decrease detonation, it also lowers horsepower and torque, and gives poor fuel economy.

The gains of tuning with an air-fuel ratio meter are better fuel economy, maximum performance and the assurance that the engine will not be over fueled. Over-fueling of a newly rebuilt engine can damage the cylinder walls, pre-

J&S Electronic's SafeGuard (shown here), K&N's air-fuel meter and a similar device from Edelbrock and MSD can each indicate approximate air-fuel ratios across the rich to lean scale. This is a tremendous tuning tool for carburetor jetting and troubleshooting fuel and spark system problems. While some later engines may have an extra oxygen sensor port, exhaust tubing or a header set can be easily retrofitted with a common oxygen sensor. You can perform real world exhaust analyzer simulations at a fraction of the cost of an infrared tester and dynamometer.

vent piston ring seating and radically shorten engine life by fuel diluting the lubricant in the crankcase.

Threaded plugs are available for simple oxygen sensor installation into an exhaust pipe or header collector. If a muffler shop positions the plug to match the heat requirements of the oxygen sensor, the meter will offer concise and quick response.

Holley carburetors offer simple tuning and ready availability of parts. If you rebuild your engine and increase the flow requirements of your existing Holley carburetor, proper jets and other upgrade parts are available at automotive performance shops and Holley carburetor dealers.

Later Y-blocks, the small-block and FE Ford V-8s use either a 2300-series two-barrel or a square-flange Holley four-barrel manifold as OEM equipment. Often, you will find that a four-barrel carburetor version of the engine was only available in passenger cars. (Aftermarket four-barrel manifolds are also available for all FE, small-block and big-block Ford V-8s.) Most carbureted 460 engines use the Holley square-flange pattern intake manifold.

Most aftermarket V-8 performance intake manifolds offer the popular square-flange four-barrel Holley carburetor mounting pattern. Six-cylinder two-barrel performance manifolds, like the Clifford Performance or Offenhauser manifolds for Ford 240/300-cubic-inch inline sixes, offer the Holley carburetor mounting patterns.

Clifford offers either the 2300 two-barrel or a four-barrel Holley option for the 300 Ford inline six. The four-barrel package performs very well with a smaller 390 cfm Holley square-flange four-barrel carburetor.

Many Holley carburetors use side-hung float bowls. Holley offers both center-hung bowls and off-road racing

side-hung bowls that help offset starvation and flooding tendencies. These bowls replace a standard side-hung assembly in minutes. The center pivot or special side-hung racing float will also tolerate the jostling and angles of off-pavement rock crawling.

When selecting a carburetor for a modified engine, I often begin with an OEM carburetor application for a larger stock engine. For example, if I were to modify a 360 FE engine with a performance camshaft and other changes, the Holley four-barrel for a stock 390 Ford FE truck engine could provide a good start. (The 390 four-barrel manifold would fit the 360 FE, too.) I would still verify air-fuel ratios and fine tune the new carburetor if necessary.

CAUTION —
Installation of a non-exempted aftermarket performance part on your truck's emission certified engine may violate Federal, State and local pollution control laws.

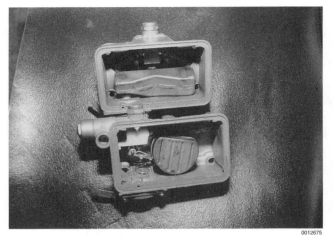

Fig. 16-6. *Center-hung floats fit a variety of two-and four-barrel Holley end float carburetors. Holley recommends a side hung racing bowl and high pressure needle/seats for desert racing and hard off-pavement pounding.*

Fig. 16-7. *Jack Clifford explains strategy for inline six performance. A single-outlet header and ram-tuned four-barrel intake manifold combination can increase available torque and horsepower on popular F-truck inline sixes.*

Fig. 16-8. *Clifford intake manifold also makes ideal foundation for a retrofit TBI or MPI system. Clifford's EFI systems with multi-point injection have yielded a 28% increase in rear wheel horsepower and torque when used with a performance camshaft, header, and proper spark tuning.*

Fig. 16-9. *Clifford's off-highway retrofit TBI uses a four-barrel intake manifold and 2300-series Holley two-barrel adapter. This Clifford/AirSensors TBI package shows a strong resemblance to Ford's OEM CFI system.*

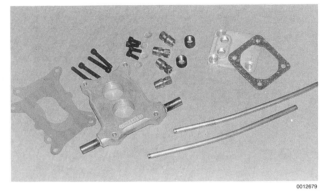

Fig. 16-10. *These Clifford heaters operate with hot engine coolant or exhaust heat. The hot water type spacer features a cast-in, wraparound steel pipe and could fit an F-truck two-barrel V-8 with the Holley 2300 series carburetor flange pattern. (Such a device, if regulated by a manual coolant shut-off valve, could enhance engine warmup and improve performance when using an exhaust header set.) These systems were designed for Clifford's inline six cylinder manifolds.*

Fig. 16-11. *A spreadbore four-barrel carburetor adapter enables use of GM Quadrajet or Carter Thermo-Quad as an alternative to Holley square flange unit. Quadrajet can be fitted to any Clifford in-line six manifold, including the 240/300 Ford F-truck engine—or even the Hudson in-line six shown.*

Fig. 16-12. Holley performance parts availability is perfect for serious carburetor tuning. Note the available center hung float and optional electric choke assemblies.

Lubrication and Engine Oil Cooling

Internal combustion engines depend upon heat as hot, expanding gases move the pistons. However, thermal loss from the cylinders is tremendous, as heat dissipates throughout the engine. The cooling system must draw this excess heat away. A radiator, the engine fan and coolant play a key role here, yet there's far more to cooling an engine.

Oil, expected to lubricate and battle friction, is a major outlet for heat. On later truck engine designs, emission control and fuel economy standards lean the fuel mixes and advance the spark timing. As smaller engines do bigger jobs, upper cylinder temperatures increase.

The buildup of engine heat also increases the oxidation rate and acid content in the oil. Oxygen combines with oil hydrocarbons, producing easily recognizable sludge. This sludge may include varnishes, waxes, corrosive acids and the water of hydration compounds. According to Hayden, a respected manufacturer of engine

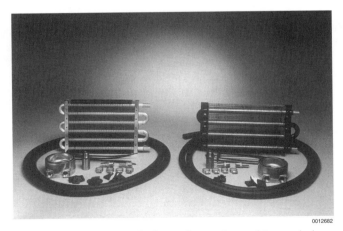

Fig. 16-13. OEM and aftermarket engine and transmission oil coolers make a good investment. Oil plays a crucial role in cooling your truck's engine and transmission. Cooling the oil can extend engine and transmission life. (Photo courtesy of Flex-A-Lite)

and transmission oil coolers, each 20° F of excess oil temperature doubles the oil oxidation rate and bearing wear.

Launching A Second Front Against Heat

Traditionally, water/coolant circulation and dissipation of heat through a fan assisted radiator have provided reasonable cooling for trucks. Porsche and Volkswagen, however, proved the effectiveness of direct oil-to-air cooling. The Porsche and VW air-cooled engines have survived in desert dune buggies and Baja racers, illustrating that enough air, moving through the right oil cooler, can offer sufficient engine cooling.

Sceptics of air cooled engines need only look at their own water cooled truck engine. Outside the block's water jackets and cylinder head coolant ports, your entire engine is oil cooled. The valves and valvetrain, including the camshaft and timing chain or gear mechanisms, the connecting rods, pistons, rings, all bearings, and even the crankshaft rely on the oil's ability to continuously carry heat away.

For many years, truck and industrial users have recognized the effectiveness of engine oil coolers. Newer trucks have optional OEM engine oil coolers, an obvious choice for the aware buyer. Mini-cooler/radiators also appear on other automotive systems, including the power steering unit of many trucks.

Aftermarket automatic transmission coolers, offered since the 1960s, have drastically extended transmission life. Despite OEM radiator cooling, in-line automatic transmission fluid coolers and engine oil coolers are a must for trailer pulling and other heavy duty uses.

Subjected to loads, hills and towing, oil heat rises rapidly. The best radiator and fan can only address coolant temperature, while oil temperature continues to increase. An add-on, external oil-to-air cooling system could prove vital to your truck's engine. If hot climate driving, off-pavement four-wheeling or travel trailer pulling fit your plans, aftermarket engine and transmission oil coolers add practical protection.

Engine Oil Cooler Installation Tips

Like any other accessory, an engine oil cooler requires careful fitup. Mounted improperly, the cooler may actually inhibit air flow through the radiator. Most oil cooler kits provide detailed instructions. Necessary hardware should include quality hose and fittings, designed for exposure to high temperature oil under pressure. Usually, an oil filter spacer/adapter provides the attachment point for both pressurized oil and the return flow.

Many aftermarket kits include quality coolers and adapters, but they fall short with attaching hardware. For simple installation, manufacturers have resorted to through-the-radiator plastic ties to secure the cooler. For off-pavement use and situations where vehicles jar, vibrate and twist, plastic ties lead to trouble.

I agree with radiator experts who suggest fabricating a lightweight metal framework for the oil cooler. The cooler may still mount in front of the radiator, isolated from the expensive fins and tubes of the radiator core. Also route hoses carefully, and consider potential road hazard damage or any risk of chafing on body or chassis edges.

Supercharging

Aftermarket retrofit superchargers (blowers/turbochargers) now fit a wide range of popular engines. By the late 1990s, in step with demands for greater fuel economy and performance, most domestic and import trucks will offer models with OEM supercharging.

Acceleration, mid-range power, and volumetric efficiency improve drastically with supercharging, yet a sensibly staged blower or turbocharger usually has no impact on engine start-up, idle quality or off idle tip-in performance. As rpm rises, the supercharger boosts both manifold and cylinder pressures. The higher the speed, the greater the performance and efficiency.

Fig. 16-14. *When boost is controlled properly, a supercharger retrofit is the quick route to high performance, and many kits are emissions-legal for EFI engines. For time and money invested, this is the biggest gain per dollar.*

Blower Basics

Mechanical superchargers or blowers receive power directly from the engine via a belt- or gear-drive mechanism. Altering the blower shaft speed regulates air displacement. Fitted to a gasoline engine, a blower increases torque, mid-range and top-end power. There are five popular mechanical blower designs: Roots-type, sliding-vane, spiral, centrifugal and rotary piston.

GM's Detroit diesels popularized the Roots-type blower. Plentiful and relatively inexpensive, the 6-71 and 4-71 blowers have served the racing community for over three decades.

The Roots-type blower, like other positive-displacement superchargers, provides smooth volumetric flow rates and high pressures—even at relatively low blower speeds. Although some pressure loss occurs through backflow, Roots-type superchargers provide useful boost over a wide speed range.

In the Roots-type blower, two rotors spin in a blower housing/cavity. (These twin rotors never touch each other or the housing.) The close tolerance fitup between the rotors and housing create high boost pressures.

Other mechanical superchargers share a common theme: timed phases first draw air then squeeze, forcing air into the plenum. (Centrifugal superchargers compress air within the blower rather than in the intake plenum.) On OEM diesels, injectors spray pressurized fuel into each combustion or pre-combustion chamber as compression peaks.

When retrofitting Roots-type blowers to gasoline engines with carburetion or throttle body injection, fuel passes through the compressor chamber. Tuned port (TPI) or multi-point (MPI) injection requires a different approach, as injectors spray fuel directly into the intake ports. For TPI and MPI, the high speed, close tolerance centrifugal blower has become popular, as fuel does not pass through the compressor. (Centrifugal blowers work well for late Ford gas truck engines equipped with MPI.)

Exhaust Turbocharging

Turbochargers receive their power from the exhaust gas exiting the engine. The exhaust spins a turbine mounted on a shaft. On the other end of the shaft, in the intake, is a vaned wheel. As the vane turns, it compresses the intake air flow. The result is an energy gain, as boost occurs when engine rpm (i.e., exhaust pressure/turbine speed) reaches a suitable level.

Turbochargers are usually of single-flow turbine design, and deliver a slight excess of boost. Excess boost bypasses through a wastegate system. The wastegate prevents cylinder overcharging and minimizes the energy spent spinning the turbine/compressor.

> **NOTE —**
> High intake manifold vacuum reduces exhaust pressure and also the demand for boost. Reciprocally, low manifold vacuum (heavy loads) increases exhaust pressure and creates turbo boost. The adjustable wastegate sets a ceiling on boost pressure.

Intercoolers provide a major breakthrough for turbocharging. Compressing air generates heat. This heat expands the air-fuel mix and absorbs vital space. Cooling the air between the turbo unit and the intake plenum provides a denser air-fuel mass (and more power) for each cylinder.

Aftermarket Blowers

B&M Products: B&M has put years of product development into a complete line of blowers and an extensive blower accessory line. B&M focuses on both street and off-highway applications, ranging from streetable boost to the highly acclaimed and popular MegaBlower, a 6-71 size unit made completely from new materials. A small-block V-8 with 7.5:1 compression ratio and a Mega Blower is claimed to produce 540 horsepower at 6500 rpm. Torque peaks near 520 ft./lbs. at 4500 rpm. Maximum boost for such a dual 750 Holley carbureted system is 12 psi at 6500 rpm.

B&M also offers much tamer superchargers for milder engines. Kits permit use of stock factory accessories, which can be a real savings in cost and time. B&M engineering also offers an impressive 144- or 162-cubic-inch blower kit for the flathead Ford V-8s. The milder 144 CID kit would even fit the R engines found in '48–'53 F-trucks.

Camden Superchargers: John Camden began supercharging Chevrolet V-8s when Ford trucks were in the Y-block era. Camden's Road Warrior blowers pioneered several design features, including a highly efficient pressurized lubrication system with insert-type rotor shaft bearings.

Low profile for underhood clearance, the Camden street unit claims a 30% horsepower increase for engine compression ratios up to 8.5:1. Six-pound maximum boost helps assure engine longevity for stock, low compression engine applications. Camden offers kits for Ford V-8s and sixes.

Paxton: 302 and 351W MPI V-8 Ford truck owners rejoice! 50-State street-legal supercharger systems are available for your engine. Paxton, well known for its OEM factory automotive superchargers, has linked up with Roll-A-Long. The joint effort has produced an exciting advance in streetable blowers.

Actual gains for these applications are notable. In street form, Roll-a-Long tested the Paxton kit in a 351W powered F-150 truck and claimed a 48% increase in both net flywheel horsepower and torque. At 4000 rpm, horsepower jumped from 214 to 317. Torque climbed from 280 lbs-ft to 416. This is with a mild, 5-psi limit boost, ideally suited for making major performance gains on a stock EFI engine.

Belt-driven, the unique and reliable Paxton planetary ball drive supercharger package has lead the industry into the blown street legal V-8 era. An Al Unser Ford Signature Series Hi Tech Truck has already dazzled fans with a 0–60 mph run at 5.8 seconds and nearly 100 mph quarter mile speeds.

Vortech Engineering: Vortech has also developed 50-State legal centrifugal blower kits for Ford V-8 engines. The Gearcharger blower is a high rpm design that provides the mild boost needed for maximum power and engine life.

Vortech has focused on late F-truck needs with both these blower kits and also Shift Command electronic shift improvement kits for late E4OD Ford F-truck automatic transmissions. (See chapter on geartrain modifications and upgrades.) Like Paxton, the Vortech kits offer all hardware necessary for a quick blower installation. Many Ford F-truck owners with MPI V-8 engines have installed the Vortech system.

Supercharging Compression Ratios, Camshafts, Air Filtration

Supercharging a gasoline engine requires compression ratios of 7:1 to 9:1 on engines with good cylinder sealing (10% maximum leakdown). Blower drive ratios determine the boost levels. Forged aluminum pistons, quality stainless valves, and hard steel valve seats are minimal requirements for higher boost pressures.

Weiand, a highly reputable manufacturer of automotive, marine, racing and pro-street type blowers, has found that high performance camshaft grinds for blower use feature 112- to 114-degree lobe centers, 0.450–0.500" lift and 220–234 degree valve opening duration at 0.050" lift (272–288 degrees gross duration). (Logically, the exhaust valve must remain closed while the intake valve is open to prevent pressurized air-fuel charges from racing out the exhaust port.)

Fig. 16-15. *Paxton has built automotive blower assemblies since 1951. The 50-State legal centrifugal blower kit for small-block Ford F-truck V-8s is a quick way to make major horsepower gains and additional torque. Paxton 351W blower kits come complete with all mounting hardware and instructions for a tidy installation.*

True blower grinds also have slightly longer duration on the exhaust side to totally clean out cylinders during the exhaust cycle. For mild or street-legal supercharging, a stock or RV camshaft grind works fine.

Air-fuel ratios are critical with blowers, so carburetor jetting and adequate air flow are essential. K & N Filtration and similar filtration systems provide the protection needed for expensive, close-tolerance blower systems. Although carburetor flow or cfm requirements may rise above stock demands, many OEM air cleaner assemblies still provide ample flow capacity when used with a K & N-type element.

Engine Modifications For Supercharging

Before considering a blower installation, assess the condition of your engine. Weiand, with extensive experience in this area, offers some general recommendations. To begin, the optimal engine compression ratio for a street blower installation is 8.5-to-1. This works nicely for '71–up smog engines, but inhibits blower usage on Sixties muscle engines that sport 9.5:1 and higher compression ratios.

If pistons are of cast design, the boost limit should range from 4–7 psi, with an engine rpm ceiling in the 4500–5000 range. Regardless of piston type, detonation should be avoided. Lower boost levels, a milder spark timing curve and/or a boost in fuel octane will help offset detonation.

CAUTION —
Uncontrolled detonation is the number one cause of damage in a supercharged engine.

Fuel leanout or starvation, an additional cause of detonation, can be avoided through use of larger fuel supply lines and a higher volume fuel pump. Attention to detonation cannot be overstated, as broken pistons, burned valves and crankshaft damage result from sustained periods of detonation.

An engine overhaul should be performed if excess wear exists on an engine intended for supercharging. Forged pistons, moly rings, close attention to tolerances and a general blueprinted philosophy should prevail. The blown engine produces far more cylinder pressure, and valve and gasket sealing become critical.

Although the Weiand and other blower kits will work with a street engine in good operating condition, any effort to improve engine stamina and longevity will also enhance performance. Select block and valvetrain parts with a known ability to last longer than OEM pieces.

Weiand has emphatic suggestions about carburetion and jetting, recommending that primaries be opened 5–10% and that secondaries provide 10–20% extra flow. For those contemplating a carburetor switch, the stock size carburetor works adequately with Weiand's Pro-Street Supercharger kits or a similar mild boost (street) system.

For the typical V-8 street blower installation, a 600–750 cfm flow rate with vacuum secondaries seems appropriate. A Holley double pumper may be needed for a more modified engine. Weiand's massive 6-71 Supercharger works best with a pair of 600 cfm vacuum secondary carburetors on a small-block V-8 engine, while a big-block may require a pair of 750 cfm carburetors.

Aside from a healthy cooling system, increased fuel supply network, and tight sealing air cleaner to prevent debris from ruining the rotors and blower housing, the ignition spark timing is critical. Initial, static spark timing should fall within 6–10 crankshaft degrees advance, with the curve swinging to a combined static and mechanical maximum spark advance of 32 crankshaft degrees by 3400 rpm. Weiand notes that no more than 38 total crankshaft degrees of spark timing advance should be attempted under any circumstance.

The late model electronic spark control and closed loop carburetor/EFI engines may create an obstacle. If such a computer-operated system prevents accurate control of spark or air-fuel ratios with a blower installed, Weiand recommends replacement with a conventional electronic ignition and carburetor.

NOTE —
Removal of any emission control components or the electronic fuel and spark management system is for off-highway/racing use only and violates Federal/EPA, state and local laws for vehicles driven on public roads.

When installing a blower, large tubing headers provide the best exhaust flow. Turbo-type or other low restriction mufflers also enhance performance. Proper tuning, including use of the correct spark plugs, will assure desired results.

Supercharging: High Performance For 6.9L/7.3L Navistar Diesel V-8

The Navistar 6.9L/7.3L V-8 diesels found in Ford F-trucks respond well to exhaust turbocharging. This is a rugged engine design, fully capable of withstanding the reasonable boost levels found in several aftermarket blower systems. If you intend to keep your diesel F-truck for a long time, the investment will amortize as major fuel savings and additional satisfaction when towing loads.

Many Navistar turbo-diesel users have discovered that both performance and engine longevity improve with the installation of a properly calibrated exhaust turbocharger. Having operated heavy equipment with Detroit, Caterpillar and Cummins engines, I would agree with these findings. A diesel engine labors far less with turbocharging, and substantial gains in fuel economy (especially under load) indicate that the engine enjoys its boosted power.

Fig. 16-16. ATS served as engineering consultant for the official Ford OEM turbocharger system found on 1994 and newer Navistar 7.3L diesel V-8s. Craftsmanship of ATS retrofit kits meets OEM quality standard. Navistar diesel responds readily with a substantial performance increase and major fuel economy gains.

The appeal of aftermarket turbo systems has encouraged Ford to offer a factory turbo kit, beginning in 1994. This OEM kit, the product of a joint engineering effort with Advanced Turbo Systems, has encouraged greater interest in Ford's F-truck diesel engine option.

For owners of pre-'94 diesel powered Ford F-trucks, the aftermarket offers several kits for turbocharging your engine. I am familiar with the kits from Banks Engineering, Hypermax, and ATS and would use any of them. Each has unique features and particular performance/fuel economy claims.

3. FLATHEAD TO FE F-TRUCK POWER

Beginning with the Model T and TT models, Ford trucks offered reasonable performance. The early flathead V-8 brought a real boost to Ford light truck and commercial car performance. Notably, John Dillinger, the Depression Era criminal, thanked Ford Motor Company for the quick response of his Ford V-8 getaway car.

When the F-Series models came on the scene in early 1948, Ford flathead sixes and V-8s were busy building legends in racing circles. Ford's compact V-8 60-horsepower engines powered many midget racers. L-head sixes made records in sleek racing boat hulls.

The 239.4-cubic-inch flathead Mercury and Ford V-8s, modified in every way known, had become a hot rodding mainstay for setting dry lakes speed records. Radically modified 59A and similar flathead V-8 designs were the inspiration behind a new phenomena called drag racing.

The newer R V-8 in the F-trucks also received attention from performance enthusiasts, and soon the 8BA-type passenger car and R truck engines earned their share of high performance accessory items: triple carburetor manifolds, hot ignition systems, special camshaft grinds and dual exhaust header pipes.

Flathead Warm-up

The flathead V-8 has a following to this day. If your F-truck has its original '48–'53 V-8 engine and you have no desire to install a later OHV-type V-8 engine, consider the many aftermarket parts that can enhance your early engine's performance.

Edelbrock Corporation and others have kept the flathead V-8 alive. Vic Edelbrock, Sr., was among the legendary pioneers and innovators of flathead Ford racing technology, a tradition that has carried forward for over fifty years by the Edelbrock family. Available today are the famous Edelbrock cylinder heads, now made of 356/T-6 aluminum and boasting 8:1 compression ratio.

Also in the marketplace are custom camshaft grinds and valvetrain components by Iskenderian, Crane and others. Many of the camshaft lobe profiles originated in the post-WWII era of racing and street hot rodding. Along with camshafts, adjustable tappets and other useful aftermarket parts can still be found.

For ignition and fuel system improvements, you can find Offenhauser and Edelbrock multiple carburetor manifolds. A classic Mallory dual point distributor is also popular. You may find some components new. Otherwise, try performance parts sources like an early Ford vehicle restorer's outlet or a vintage car parts swap meet.

The 8BA passenger car and R truck engines were Ford's final evolution of the flathead V-8. Traditional flathead V-8 racers prefer the 1948 and earlier 239.4-cubic-inch 24-stud cylinder head Mercury and Ford passenger car engines with the distributor mounted at the front of the timing cover. 1948–53 F-truck and '49–'53 passenger engines remain plentiful, however, and they have much the same performance potential as the earlier flathead V-8s.

A factory stroker version of the late flathead engine is the '49–'53 Mercury 8CM 255.4-cubic-inch engine. The 1/4-inch longer crankshaft stroke produces more horsepower and torque than the Ford 239.4-cubic-inch passenger car and light F-truck V-8s.

An 8CM long block will fit your '48–'53 truck chassis without modifications. (The carburetion is different, so you may prefer using the Ford truck manifold and carburetor.) Stock, these 8CM engines boast 125 horsepower at 3800 rpm in their most refined 7.2:1 compression ratio version. The longer stroke also raises torque to 218 lbs-ft at 1700 rpm.

Thunderbird Special Y-block V-8

When Ford introduced the new generation of Y-block V-8s in 1954, the flathead V-8 era came to an end. Light F-trucks first came on line with smaller Y-blocks of 239- and 256-cubic-inch displacement. These engines, despite their strong torque and obvious edge over a stock flathead V-8, were too small in displacement to gain much attention.

The 272 Y-block V-8, first offered in 1956 model F-trucks, was another story. Already proven in Ford and Mercury cars, the 272 developed enough torque to offer respectable stoplight-to-stoplight performance against the new Chevy 265 small-block V-8. When Ford F-trucks gained the larger 292 V-8 option in 1958, the Y-block's inherent torque advantage was even more apparent.

For enthusiasts wanting a classic street truck profile, the high performance 292 and 312 Y-block V-8s found in 1955–57 Ford, Thunderbird and Mercury passenger cars provide great swap material for 1954–64 F-trucks. By changing the oil pan, oil pickup and, in some applications, the front timing cover casting, these engines provide a simple bolt-in swap. A high performance 292 or 312 can deliver big horsepower dividends at a reasonable fare.

> **NOTE —**
> The 292 and 312 V-8s were produced after 1957, however, the introduction of the bigger FE engines reduced the 292 and 312 to standard V-8 status with lower performance components. The last 312 passenger car engine was in a 1960 Mercury, while the 292 continued through 1964.

My favorite Y-block V-8, and the only one I would consider for a high performance buildup, is the 1957 312 prototype equipped with factory ECZ casting cylinder heads. These engines pioneered the use of Holley's square flange four-barrel 4150-series carburetor. In Holley 4150 four-barrel form, one factory high performance version of the 312 rates 300 horsepower. A factory supercharged 312, found in rare 1957 F serial number Thunder-

Fig. 16-17. Zenith of hot Y-block V-8 performance was 1957 Ford passenger car and Thunderbird V-8s. Supercharged 312 and a 300 horsepower four-barrel engine topped the option list. Ford won big in racing that year.

birds, has become the highest valued '55–'57 T-Bird collectible car.

When it comes to 312 Y-block performance, hold onto your hat! In 1968, I took a ride in a '57 Ford two-door sedan that had a built 312 (Jahns racing pistons, Iskenderian camshaft, headers and a dual-point Mallory ignition). Tuned to perfection by a Ford fanatic with a penchant for beating 327 Chevy V-8s, that car remains one of the most impressive near stock vehicles I've known.

I had gone through high school with a parking lot full of '55–'57 Chevys and '60s Muscle Era high performance cars, including Ford 406s and 427s, Mopar wedgehead big-blocks and the Fairlane/Comet 390s, 396 Chevelles, Olds 4-4-2s, Pontiac GTOs and Buick GS intermediate models. Yet in a drag race that '57 Ford Custom two-door would easily have beaten our best 327-powered '55 Chevy Bel-Air coupe.

Although Y-block 272, 292, and 312 speed parts were once common, the popularity of later Ford FE engines, the big-block (429 and 460) and the 289, 302 and 351 small-block V-8s has softened the Y-block performance market. Most F-truck performance enthusiasts prefer converting to one of these later engine types. The truck engine bays, especially 1953–up models, will easily accommodate a large engine.

Some loyal Y-block fans remain. If you take this route, improved performance means the customary camshaft and compression ratio changes. Seek a set of 312 ECZ-casting number cylinder heads, as they offer massive intake valve sizing for higher compression ratios and a more radical camshaft. My intake manifold choice is the four-barrel square flange version that will accommodate the popular Holley carburetors.

Despite the cumbersome weight of the Y-blocks and their bulky and sluggish rocker arm/rocker shaft valve trains, these engines make impressive torque. In a '54–'64 light F-truck, the 312 can deliver real performance and offer a touch of period nostalgia. For more modern power and a relatively easy conversion, however, the 351W V-8 would be my alternative choice.

Ford FE V-8: Brutish Power

My folks bought our first upscale family car in the fall of 1960, when a light metallic green Ford Country Squire station wagon, loaded with options like power steering, power brakes, a deluxe radio and power operated tailgate window, caught my father's eye. So did the all new 390 V-8 Thunderbird Special engine option.

Our previous pre-owned cars had included a '41 Buick Special and 1950 Packard Clipper sedan, each with straight eight engines, plus our current commuter car, a one-year-old '56 Volkswagen with a 36-horsepower air-cooled powerplant. The only other new car my folks had purchased was a grossly underpowered and stripped '58 Plymouth two-door sedan with an archaic L-head inline six-cylinder engine and a column shift three-speed manual transmission.

Never to be slighted in the performance realm again, my father found the all-new 390-cubic-inch FE engine just right. Not only did the 390 V-8 fill the engine bay completely, the four-barrel Thunderbird Special version produced a whopping 300 horsepower.

Although its curb weight exceeded the unladen weight of a 1961 3/4-ton Ford F-truck, the Country Squire wagon was a stormer. A set of secondary throats on the carburetor and passing gear of the Cruise-O-Matic transmission gave the powertrain its edge, and that two-tons plus of iron could hurtle across the Mojave Desert in record time. Moving from 60–90 mph in just seconds was the engine's favorite trick. When the engine was barely broken-in, we moved to Nevada, one of two states that enjoyed a basic speed law. Brute torque and horsepower apparently had no bounds, as the 390 withstood over one-hundred thousand miles of high speed driving.

FE engines came into the F-trucks with the 1965 352-cubic-inch V-8 option. Developing plenty of torque in detuned two-barrel form, the 352 and later 360 V-8s satisfied many owners. Ford even used the 390 for a brief time as an F-truck engine option (ideal for Camper Special packages), but the truck version never rivaled the horsepower or torque rating of a 1961 Thunderbird Special engine. Most obvious was that the lowered compression ratio caused a decline in the 390 V-8's horsepower.

When building a high performance FE engine for a pre-smog controlled F-truck, my choice would be the 390, 406, 427 or 428-cubic-inch versions. Like all other Ford FE engines, these designs feature a very heavy intake manifold that partially overlaps the block deck. My first goal with aftermarket parts, intended to raise performance while reducing the hefty engine weight, would be an aluminum intake manifold and a set of tubular exhaust headers.

The legendary 425-horsepower 427 V-8, with its cross-drilled main bearing caps, or a later 428 Cobra Jet (CJ) engine, would be my top choices for drag racing type performance. A Thunderbird Special four-barrel 390 or the modestly tuned four-barrel 428 would make good truck performance for pulling a trailer or hauling severe loads.

Fuel economy with any FE buildup would depend upon a quality dual plane intake manifold (like the Edelbrock Performer), good exhaust flow and the vehicle's transmission and axle gearing. For a pro-street truck, drag racing or heavy towing uses, a C-6 automatic transmission performs admirably, offering good ratios and the stamina necessary to handle high engine torque loads.

Fig. 16-18. *Top dogs of all FE-based engine designs were the side-oiler 427 (shown) and the exotic 427 OHC (overhead camshaft) NASCAR racing versions. A built up 390, 406, 427 or 428CJ engine is still highly competitive today, easily capable of meeting one horsepower per cubic inch standards.*

No 390 or larger FE engine (nor the later 429/460 engine types) will deliver exceptional fuel mileage in a weighty F-250 or F-350, especially when towing heavy loads. From my experience, a properly geared 390 FE or 460 powered F-250 carrying a large cabover camper (or pulling a twin-axle travel trailer) will range between 7–10 mpg under the best conditions.

If towing or heavy cargo power is desirable, consider an RV type camshaft with good lift and a mild valve opening duration. I like Competition Cams' 252H grind for an automatic transmission application or the 260H grind when using a manual transmission and lower (numerically higher) axle gearing.

These two camshafts will set a lower ceiling on rpm. However, a non-racing or relatively stock FE engine works best to a maximum of 5000–5500 rpm anyway. The correct tow vehicle camshaft will peak horsepower around 4200–4600 rpm, provide massive low end torque and lugging power, plus offer considerable manifold vacuum at low speeds.

For towing, camper loads and cargo hauling, select a compression ratio around 8.5:1, no higher than 9:1. At these compression ratios, your FE engine will work well with a milder RV camshaft grind. Fuel economy will also benefit.

NOTE —

As Ford racing buffs recall, the 390, 406, 427 and 428 CJ High Performance FE engines tolerate far more valve opening duration and valve lift than an RV camshaft provides. However, in order to make 300 to 425 horsepower, as Ford's mammoth Muscle Era engines produced, you need a compression ratio in excess of 10:1. Today's low octane fuel will not support such ratios.

Y-block and FE V-8 Valvetrains

While detractors consider the Y-block and FE Ford engines overly heavy, even boat anchors, an aftermarket aluminum intake manifold (available for FE engines) and tubular steel headers can slim these engines down to fighting trim.

Valvetrain of Y-block and FE Ford V-8s uses a rocker shaft/rocker arm assembly. Y-block valve lifters are mechanical (solid) type of the mushroom variety. Changing Y-block valve lifters requires removal of the camshaft (while holding all lifters up with clothes pins) plus the engine's oil pan. Lifters exit only through the bottom of the block.

The real limiting factor, for those who want a high speed racing engine and ultra high compression ratio, is the rocker shaft-and-rocker arm valvetrain. These rocker shaft assemblies present a lot of mass and inertia—not a problem for a lower speed truck engine, but certainly an obstacle for drag racing and high rpm operation.

Although the factory 406 and 427 high performance engines spun to 6,000 rpm, they did so under duress. The 1963 factory dual four-barrel (eight venturi) 427, with its 12:1 compression ratio and mechanical lifter high performance camshaft, reached a peak horsepower of 425-plus at exactly 6,000 rpm. While this feat proved worthy of drag racing and NASCAR victories and records, such engineering would work poorly in a trailer pulling F-truck.

Built around a 4000–4600 rpm horsepower peak, a Y-block or FE truck engine will last a long time. Such a powerplant will reach top torque at 2000–2600 rpm, the range where most trucks operate best. This kind of truck engine will deliver top performance and wear well. At these speeds, a rocker shaft assembly, with its ability to stabilize the alignment of pushrods and rocker arms, is an asset and not a liability.

4. 460 V-8: THE ULTIMATE RACING AND TOW ENGINE

When Ford's Lincoln-Mercury Division abandoned Lincoln's massive 462 FE-type engine in 1968, few realized the significance of its replacement, the 460 V-8. By 1972, the 460 had developed an excellent reputation in the larger Mercury and Lincoln car models, followed the next year by its introduction into Ford F-trucks.

For high performance and racing, GM and Mopar had concentrated on their big-block engines during the mid-'60s. Until 1968, Ford's primary big block focus had been the 427 FE engine. When the new 429 and 460 engine designs emerged, Ford moved away from the FE powerplants, leaving behind their weighty valvetrain mechanisms and massive intake manifolds.

The comparatively lighter, large displacement 429 and 460 engines helped Ford compete strongly against the high output Chevrolet 454 and Mopar 440, and even the Mopar 426 Hemi engines. Before heavy emission constraints dampened the horsepower ratings in 1972, Ford 429 Cobra Jet engines and the high output 460 V-8 had proven their worth in racing and passenger car service. The superior durability of these engines was already apparent.

Building The High Performance Street 460 V-8

The 460 V-8, popularized as the heavy duty option in Ford F-trucks, has tremendous performance potential. Building on the inherent reliability of this engine, custom street truck builders use many of the same techniques as drag racers to create an impressive and racy 460 powerplant.

On an engine of this size, a high performance street buildup often begins with light upgrades. For the low budget builder, simply choosing the right camshaft can transform a staid Lincoln or stock F-truck 460 into a high torque pavement scorcher.

Other affordable street improvements include Edelbrock's Performer intake manifold, a set of Ford SVO #M-9430-A75 or Doug Thorley Tri-Y headers, Crane's rump idle #353941 or SVO #M-6250-A442 camshaft, and Ford SVO Multi-Index timing chain set #M-6268-B429.

Further tricks for street warm ups include Crane valve train upgrades and a rocker stud conversion kit to accept adjustable rocker arms. For the budget conscious, Ford D00Z-6A528-B floating fulcrums with Manley Poly-locks will provide adjustable rockers at much lesser cost. SVO or Crane's 1.73 ratio roller rocker arms are optional.

A valuable aspect of Ford big-block engines is their responsiveness to valvetrain/camshaft changes. Cylinder head work, including exhaust porting, polishing chambers and a competition valve grind (three angle seats, flow contours, trick chamfering, etc.), also brings big results.

460 Pro-street Engine Lessons

Although relatively few F-truck owners will build a pro-street truck, many of the techniques racers and performance enthusiasts apply to the Ford 460 V-8 engine can help enhance longevity and durability of a basic tow engine.

0012689 / 0012807

Fig. 16-19. Ford's own Special Vehicle Operations (SVO) program offers a special 429/460 cast iron four-bolt main engine block that will handle bores from 4.360" to 4.625". SVO part #M-6010-A460 uses stock 3" main journal size and will accommodate strokes to 4.5", allowing 600-plus cubic inch displacements! 265 pound block, approved by NHRA as a legal service replacement part for the 429 or 460 engine block, is radically reinforced for high performance stresses. All stock and SVO cylinder heads will fit.

On the 460, a hotter camshaft and valvetrain kit requires cutting for dual valve springs. During head machining, install screw-in rocker studs, pushrod guide plates and PC type valve guide seals to reduce the chance of oil seepage past the valve guides. Ford's SVO or ARP NASCAR 7/16" rocker studs, Manley guide plates and Crower's Chromemoly pushrods can further enhance the buildup.

A beefed C-6 automatic works great with a built 460. With the right axle ratio and stall converter, the hotter SVO #M-6250-A443, Crane #354551, or Competition Cams' 34-331-4 hydraulic camshafts work well in the 2000 to 5800 rpm range. For solid lifters and an all-out competition engine, Competition Cams' #34-340-4 or Crower's #22355 cams make impressive horsepower.

The Edelbrock Victor Jr. or SVO #M-9424-G429 intake manifolds with either 4010 or 4160 series Holley carburetion can deliver a major induction gain. Again, SVO, Doug Thorley Tri-Y or Hooker headers aid in engine breathing.

If the block assembly needs attention, there's room for major improvement. SpeedPro's Hypereutectic alloy pistons with Plasma-Moly rings and SpeedPro rod bearings can keep pace with the high performance and racing big blocks. SVO offers a complete short block assembly (#M-6009-C460) that includes hypereutectic pistons and the hot #M-6250-A443 camshaft.

Hot tanking and magnafluxing precede the usual block machining. Before cylinder honing, main caps should be installed. This method, plus the use of torque plates during the power hone operation, will assure concentricity of bore diameters and each cylinder's squareness to the crankshaft.

Many 460 engine builders recommend the internally balanced pre-1979 460 crankshaft. Customary crankshaft service includes magnafluxing, inspection, index grinding, polishing and chamfering at oil holes. Stock main caps undergo deburring, chamfering, and align honing. The goal is a fitup that will assure firm bearing crush.

SpeedPro full groove main bearings, Fel-Pro Wire Encased Seal head gaskets, and either the SpeedPro or Ford SVO press-in or bolt-on oil pump pickup help assure proper oiling. A nine-quart rear sump oil pan, Ford SVO's #M-6674-A460 is an option if there is chassis clearance.

Most block build-ups involve resizing the connecting rods and fitting them with high strength ARP bolts. A stock 460 cast crankshaft demands balancing, and most racers turn to the SVO #M-6316-A460 or Fluidampr harmonic balancer to protect the crankshaft from vibration. Massive torque is a chief characteristic of the Ford 460.

NOTE —
Be careful when balancing a 460. 1979 and newer externally balanced crankshafts use a neutral balance damper and the Ford #D9TZ-6359-A external counterweight. All 460 engines require use of the correct flexplate or flywheel, the right vibration damper/harmonic balancer and crankshaft pieces that match. Considering the mass of a 460 crankshaft assembly, this issue is critical to engine smoothness and longevity.

Parts List For 460 Pro-street Engine

Block: 4-Bolt 429 CJ #DO0E-A, DOVE-A, SVO # M-6010-A460 or production 2-bolt 429/460 machined web block

Crankshaft: Pre-'79 casting 460 crankshaft (internally balanced); for racing, avoid use of the 3Y 79 crankshaft and later castings

Rods: Any stock 460 or the preferred 429 CJ DO0E-A football head rods will work; use ARP AR307 bolts

Harmonic Balancer: SVO #M-6316-A460 or Fluidampr #712510

Flexplate: Ford truck D1SZ-6375-A solid center type. Be certain of the crankshaft casting type (whether externally or internally balanced) before choosing a flexplate or flywheel. For long life, always balance these assemblies.

Pistons: Lower compressions run SpeedPro Hypereutectic Alloy pistons #6009-P series; For hot street run 7065P series forged pistons with domes relieved

Rings: SpeedPro Plasma-Moly file-fit rings R-10246 series

End Gaps: Gap to SpeedPro specifications based on usage

Main Bearing Set: SpeedPro Full Groove 360-7161

Rod Bearings: SpeedPro 363-6141

Cam Bearings: Childs & Albert C-4290 (standard size) or Durabond F-30

Oil Pump: Ford/SVO #M-6600-B4 High Volume

Oil Pump Shaft: Ford SVO #M-6605-A429

Oil Pump Pickup: Included with Canton T-Pan; avoid use of perforated metal sump pickups

Oil Pan: JBA/Canton #1576 8.5" deep, 8-Quart T-Pan with built in slosh baffle (F-trucks generally require an OEM or aftermarket truck-type rear sump oil pan and pickup to clear steering linkage or the front axle)

Camshaft: SVO #M-6250-A442, Crane #354551, or Comp-Cam #34-331-4 hydraulic grind

Pushrods: Crower Chromemoly hardened 3/8"

Rocker Arms: SVO #M-6564-A460, JBA #2332, or Crane #27750-16 (1.73:1) roller rockers

Rocker Studs: Ford SVO 7/16" #M-6527-A311 or ARP 7/16" #RRS4-DR

Guide Plates: Manley 3/8" #42160

Timing Chain: Ford SVO Multi-Index #M-6268-B429

Cylinder Heads: Ford #DOVE-C or equivalent, small chamber 429 design (good torque); #DO0E-R 429 CJ heads for larger displacement; best iron head is #DO0E-R 429 CJ type; SVO aluminum CJ heads #M-6049-A429 are an upgrade aftermarket equivalent

Chamber Volume: CJ Heads = 72cc; early 429 = 77cc; late 460 = 92cc or 97cc, depending on year and casting design

Head Gasket: SVO #M-6051-A441 or Wire Encased Seal Fel-Pro #1018

Compression Ratio: 7065P with dome removed yields 9.25:1 with largest chamber heads and 11.5:1 with small chamber heads

Head Bolts: OEM-type Ford replacement

Valves: Manley stainless intake #11800 2.19"; cut down to 2.082" for heads with smaller valves (high torque); Manley exhaust #11529 (1.76") dia.; SVO CJ stainless intake #M-6507-A429 (2.25" dia.) and stainless exhaust #M-6505-A429

Guides: Silicone/bronze type; verify compatibility with stainless Manley valves

Retainers: Crane #99953-16 steel, or SV0#M-6514-A50

Locks: Crane #99097-1, or SVO #M-6518-A351

Springs: Crane #99893-16 dual valve springs, or SVO #M-6513-A351

Valve Seals: PC-type SVO #M-6571-A221

Manifold: Edelbrock Victor Jr. or SVO #M-9424-G429 for use with square flange Holley

Carburetor: Holley 750 or 850 cfm, flowed and modified

Distributor: Recurved OEM Dura-Spark II unit

Ignition Control: Ford SVO M-12199-C301 unit with M-12029-A302 coil

Wires: MSD #3119 magnetic suppression wires

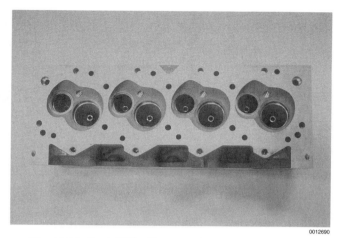

Fig. 16-20. Ford SVO offers several varieties of racing application cylinder heads for the 429/460 engine. Aluminum modified port head designs and matching intake manifolds can reduce weight dramatically and serve race truck or all-out drag car demands. Heads are available in four- and six-bolt-per-cylinder designs. Various valve sizes contribute to either maximum horsepower or superior torque. Shown here is Ford/SVO Pro-Stock head, available through your local Ford/SVO dealer.

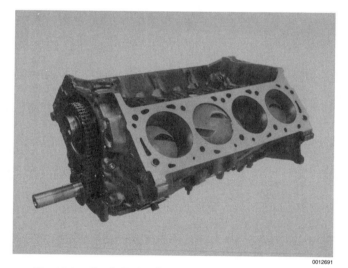

Fig. 16-21. Ford SVO offers the 460 short block assembly (#M-6009-C460) with forged aluminum pistons, heavy duty forged steel connecting rods, a nodular iron crankshaft, the hot SVO hydraulic camshaft, a roller timing chain and optional SVO #M-6049-A429 aluminum Cobra Jet (CJ) cylinder heads. Use of CJ heads (11.5:1 compression figure at 72cc combustion chamber volume) will net in excess of 500 horsepower and 500 ft-lbs of torque.

460 Exhaust Tuning

For the typical 460 powered multi-purpose truck or tow vehicle, I recommend Doug Thorley's street legal Tri-Y type headers engineered for your F-truck chassis. A low restriction dual exhaust system with 2-1/4-inch exhaust piping from the header collectors rearward will also help

considerably. (See guidelines on emissions law at the beginning of this chapter.)

Despite the huge bore size and long stroke of a stock 460 V-8, this engine offers exceptional durability. Power boaters, automotive drag racers, F-Series trailer toters, and scores of other users depend upon the reliability and remarkable versatility of Ford's 460 big-block.

5. 351 WINDSOR V-8 BUILDUP

I feel that the 351 Windsor is an overlooked gem. While the Ford Cleveland blocks (including the 351-C and the 351M/400) have thin cylinder castings, a heavy timing cover casting in the block, and poorer water circulation, 351 Windsors have thicker cylinder walls yet a light block. This yields a superior engine, capable of meeting reasonable hauling needs while delivering decent fuel economy. Modified 351W blocks fitted with Cleveland-style cylinder heads now power NASCAR's winningest machines.

Larger main bearing journals make this engine far better than a 302 for stamina, and the torque available with the 351W's longer stroke design is ideal for F-truck use. A four-bolt main bearing cap conversion kit is available for pre-'73 engines, or you can use Ford/SVO's 351W four-bolt main block. Unless you need big-block 460 muscle for severe hauling chores, consider the 351W a wise multi-purpose light truck choice, especially for an F-150 or F-250 2WD or an F-150 4x4 model.

The 351W design emerged at an awkward historical crossroad—smack between the Golden Age of Muscle Cars and our current climate of tough emission constraints, low octane ratings and high fuel costs. The 351W first appeared in Mustang and other car models. At the time, Ford's higher horsepower small-block engines were the Boss 302 and the newly unleashed 351-Cleveland. Somehow, through the irony of historical timing, the 351W gained little recognition for its performance potential. Even the Ford F-trucks, which today flourish with 351W multi-point EFI engines, featured the cumbersome 360 FE big block engine in 1969.

Overlooked in the 351W was its dynamic block, made of iron and fully capable of sustaining high torque output. The 351W also offers tremendous crankshaft stamina. Although a cast crankshaft falls short of the forged steel found in high output performance engines, the 351W boasts 0.250" more crankshaft main bearing diameter than the hot Cleveland engines. The 351W main bearing diameter is approximately 0.750" larger than the standard 302/5.0L V-8.

Although the standard cylinder bore diameter of the 302 and Boss 302, 351C and 351W are common at 4.00", the 351W offers a larger main bearing surface than any other small block Ford. In common with the 351C, the Windsor has a 2.3103-2.3111" rod journal size. Both of these engines, and even the 351M/400, offer much larger diameter rod journals than the standard and Boss 302 V-8s.

The stock 351W winds up with a strong overall reliability factor. Of interest, the 351W shares the firing order of the Cleveland 351 and late (1982–up) 302 H.O. engines: 1-3-7-2-6-5-4-8. This measure reduces main bearing and cylinder block loads at the front of the crankshaft.

If the standard 302 firing order were used (1-5-4-2-6-3-7-8), #1 and #5 cylinders would fire in sequence, resulting in high torque loads at the front main bearing area. Although a Ford small-block 221/260/289/302 (non-H.O. type) camshaft will fit the 351W engine, it requires changing the firing order to 1-5-4-2-6-3-7-8. Crane notes that in a high output engine, this firing order change creates unwanted loads at the front main bearing and block web when number one and five cylinders fire next to each other in sequence.

NOTE —
High performance 302 cylinder heads can be fitted to a 351W block with some minor machining and an intake manifold adapter kit from aftermarket sources.

Fig. 16-22. *Out-of-the-box 351 HO Ford SVO Aluminum Head Engine Assembly #M-6007-A351 pounds out 377 ft-lbs torque at 4500 rpm and 385 horsepower at 5750 rpm with a 780 CFM Holley carburetor and aftermarket headers. (Engine is completely assembled with all parts except carburetor, headers and wiring.) Built around rugged two-bolt main Marine block, 351W design features high performance components throughout, an ideal bolt-in for a classic Ford street truck or VORRA-level desert race truck. (Requires installation of F-truck oil pan and oil pickup.)*

Discrete oiling of the main bearings distinguishes the 351W from the 351C powerplants. With discrete oiling, the main bearings receive oil before the lifters. The hotter 351C actually oils the main bearings and lifters simultaneously, a risky prospect for any racing or high performance engine.

In other areas of commonality, the flywheel of the 351W interchanges with other Ford small blocks. Like the early 289/302 V-8, 351 Windsors require external balancing. Small block 289/302 engine builders find the 351W very familiar and similar in design.

351W engines are readily available. In its passenger car and more recent (1981–up) F-truck form, the engine

has survived a quarter century of emission constraints, the transition to unleaded fuel, and the change to high technology EFI/MPI. In the process, the 351W has built a fine reputation among those in the know: machinists, performance engine builders and truck fleet operators.

For the high performance enthusiast, the 351W has real potential. J. Bittle American (JBA) has proven this point. Through years of Ford racing experience, JBA has developed several stages of 351 Windsor engine buildups. Beginning with its Pure Stock prototype, JBA offers much of the reliability discovered through racing and high performance street successes. Let's look closely at the engineering of JBA's mild-to-wild Windsor buildups.

JBA'S Stage 1: Inexpensive Pure Street Power

For the budget-conscious builder, there's room for major horsepower gains in the 351W. Beginning with the customary disassembly, hot tanking and magnafluxing of the block and heads, the block must be examined for core shift. A cleanup rebore to 0.030" is typical. For reboring beyond 0.030", sonic testing of the cylinders is advisable. JBA notes that local overheating in the water jackets becomes a concern when reboring to 0.060" on a production 351W block.

Cylinder walls should be bored and finish honed on a CK-10 Sunnen machine or its equivalent. JBA insists that a torque plate be used with all Ford V-8 reboring. Cylinder head bolt layout is only four bolts per cylinder, and the later 351W head bolt torque is 110 ft-lbs. This pressure, applied to only 10 head bolts, can distort the block deck and cylinder walls, thus the need for torque plates to prevent cylinder distortion upon final assembly.

Always install new cam bearings. JBA recommends SpeedPro Plasma Moly (standard tension) piston rings for better sealing and oil control. On the street, oil consumption is a real issue, and a good piston match is SpeedPro's Hypereutectic design, which clearances more like a cast piston but has the high strength of a forged type piston.

Compression ratios of 10:1 with 60cc heads and 9.1:1 with 69cc heads promise plenty of air-fuel squeeze. Domed high compression forged pistons remain an option, providing ratios to 11:1—or you can have the piston crowns milled to achieve lower ratios for the street.

The crankshaft regrind must include careful radius work and chamfering of the oil feed holes. JBA recommends grooved main bearings, matched to the oil hole chamfers. For engines working at sustained speeds above 6500 rpm, cross drilling of the crankshaft oil feed holes will provide a margin of safety and continuous oil supply.

Line honing the main bores is a per case decision. Your machinist can judge whether the main saddles and caps need cleanup. Clearances are critical, so line boring is necessary whenever the fitup is questionable.

Connecting rods require magnafluxing, shot peening, sizing and truing. New high performance rod bolts complement the rod reconditioning, while balancing and weight matching all reciprocating pieces is always advisable.

Iron cylinder heads, vintage '69–'70, provide good street or multi-purpose service. A rugged, closed chamber design, these 60cc (combustion chamber volume) heads allow retrofitting with screw-in studs, guideplates and adjustable rocker arms.

The desired heads are C9 or D0 castings and feature 1.54" exhaust valves and 1.84" intakes. This is streetable, and the same heads allow retrofitting of the 1.60"/1.94" GT-40 SVO valves. (The optional SVO/Y303 aluminum cylinder heads offer 1.94" intake and 1.54" exhaust valve sizes.) When using larger valve heads, JBA recommends that you clearance the valve to piston eyebrow areas.

Heads require dual valve spring cuts and hardened pushrods with guideplates to handle the valve lifting chores. The last, and perhaps most important, performance measure is cylinder head porting. Exhaust ports, especially, require opening.

According to JBA, extensive exhaust porting creates no great risk to the 351W's low-end torque. Port matching also helps, while the use of a Ford/SVO 9424-Z351 dual plane manifold will easily handle 5500 rpm. An Edelbrock Torker II or Victor Jr. (SVO #M-9424-V351) is the hotter option, although for multi-purpose F-truck use, this would be excessive. The Performer or Performer RPM (SVO #M-9424-Z351) manifold and carburetor or a factory MPI/EFI system make more sense.

Use tuned headers like the proven JBA designs for the 351W V-8. Also install the high volume SVO oil pump and a roller timing chain set that allows sprocket indexing. The newer 4010-Series Holley (vacuum secondary 600 cfm) square flange carburetor works well with the dual plane manifold and JBA's recommended camshaft choice.

A camshaft of 220 degree @ 0.050" ramp intake/225 degree exhaust @ 0.050" ramp can provide substantial horsepower gains. A gross valve lift of 0.480–0.500" with stock ratio rocker arms works fine for the street truck. 112-degree lobe centers offer the best street driveability, better mileage and maximum idle vacuum.

Net performance gains from JBA's most common pure street configuration equal a highly respectable 330 lbs-ft torque @ 3500 rpm and 325 horsepower @ 5200 rpm. Great stuff for a classic street truck like the lightweight '53–'56 Ford F-100 short bed chassis.

6. 302/5.0L V-8 TIPS

The later MPI 302 Ford V-8, due largely to its success in the Fox-bodied Mustang/Capri, Bronco and light duty F-truck applications, has become an affordable performer. Excellent cylinder wall strength and a strong crankshaft assembly keep these high revving engines together.

If your lighter weight late F-truck or classic street truck has a 302 V-8 ready for a rebuild, experts recommend torque plate honing the cylinders to eliminate oil consumption. Total Seal rings also work well.

Another recommendation is TRW forged aluminum pistons. (Avoid use of low tension piston rings.) A complete engine builder's kit typically includes fly-cut pistons, custom parts fitup and modifications to meet your specific needs.

Valve sizes of 1.94"/1.60" generally do not require piston fly cutting until valve lift reaches 0.500". However, always check piston-to-valve clearance with clay and a trial fitup.

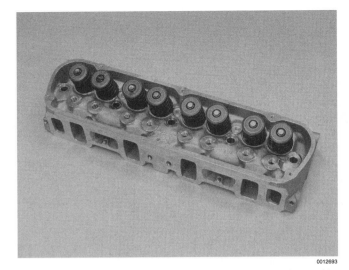

0012693

Fig. 16-23. *Ford SVO cylinder heads include mild-to-wild versions. SVO #M-6049-Y303 aluminum design for 289, 302 and 351W engines provide from 30-120 additional horsepower, depending upon other components used in conjunction with these cylinder heads. Pair of SVO heads shave forty pounds of engine mass and come with 1.94" intake and 1.54" exhaust valve diameters. This is bolt-on boost for Ford smallblocks. (May require use of SVO intake manifold, valve timing components, and other hardware.)*

Improving The MPI/EFI System

You will find that the late EFI engines are sensitive to modifications. Some modifiers have has discovered that by reducing coolant temperature and increasing fuel pressure, you can offset the quirks caused by a heavy overlap camshaft or induction system modifications.

The stock speed-density type EFI computer, anxiously compensating for erratic oxygen sensor readings, most often will create a lean and unstable mix during closed loop operation.

Experts have also found that the Mass Air Flow (MAF) system is easier to tune and more tolerant of camshaft changes. These systems also reduce tailpipe emissions. By contrast, pre-MAF speed-density EFI systems rely on manifold vacuum and a throttle position sensor (TPS). On these engines, the only compensation for camshaft and other changes is through increased fuel pressure to increase fuel flow through the injectors, resulting in a richer overall mixture.

An F-truck 302 speed-density type EFI system can also benefit from the MAF conversion kit available through Ford SVO.

On Mass Air Flow (MAF) and speed-density EFI systems, a 160° F thermostat permits more timing advance. These engines rely on engine temperature to dictate timing settings. Lower engine temperatures mean a higher detonation threshold. This allows the computer to apply more spark advance without causing detonation, which translates as increased horsepower.

The weakest links in Ford's EFI hardware are the temperature sensor and throttle position sensor (TPS). I recommend that you know how to troubleshoot these components. For racing purposes, you must be able to

Fig. 16-24. 351 GT-40 EFI V-8 engine assembly from Ford/SVO (#M-6007-L58) is among several "crate" engines that are rarin' to go right from the manufacturer. 240 horsepower @ 4200 rpm and 340 ft/lb of torque @ 3200 are on tap. Add an SVO # M-6250-B351 camshaft and gain an additional 70 horsepower on the dynamometer.

adjust the TPS at trackside. Invest in a good digital voltmeter and familiarize yourself with the Ford factory shop manual procedures for adjusting the TPS.

High Performance 5.0L Induction And Manifolds

Factory speed-density type EFI hardware will sometimes handle the Ford Motorsport GT-40 manifolding. Production Trick Flow Specialties (TFS), JBA, and similar design iron heads produce 260–270 CFM flow, and a ported GT-40 manifold yields 260 CFM. More radical 302 heads, such as those equipped with 2.080" intake valves, will easily flow 310–320 CFM. Here factory EFI components may fall short.

Use of a TFS fuel injection top manifold will bump flow to 400 CFM. (Stormin' Norman, a prominent and successful Ford racer, has relied upon a TFS 5.0L induction system that flows 430 CFM.) For F-truck owners, TFS has modified the stock 302 EFI truck lower manifold for flow rates to 350 CFM.

Overall, a ported GT-40 manifold is a must for maximum performance. According to the experts, a set of TFS cylinder heads and a ported GT-40 manifold can deliver at least 80 extra horsepower from an otherwise stock 302 engine.

Cylinder Head Recommendations

Economical 302 iron heads work okay for the street, while premium heads have aluminum castings. Iron heads permit decking, porting and multiple exhaust flange sizing. Exhaust flow for the street (iron castings) or SVO heads is approximately 200 CFM with 1-3/4" header tube sizes. Custom exhaust porting, intended for competition, can produce up to 240 CFM flow and generally requires 1-7/8" headers.

High performance exhaust valve staging for 302 heads (aluminum or iron) include 1.60", 1.625" and 1.650". Intake valve sizing ranges from 1.94", 2.02" 2.055", 2.080", 2.100" to the massive 2.120" intake valves.

For 302 engines, high performance SVO valve springs for use with a hydraulic roller camshaft can tolerate a maximum lift of 0.600". 0.050" longer valve stems are necessary for such high lift. On aluminum heads with dual springs and dampers, most builders recommend seat pressures of 130 pounds. Iron heads with single springs and dampers require 110 pound seat pressures.

For ultra-high performance, use severe duty stainless valves, SVO valve locks, retainers, and valve seals. Iron heads call for iron valve guides and hardened steel insert exhaust seats. Aluminum heads rely on hardened steel intake and exhaust seats. Alloy heads typically use manganese/bronze valve guides.

Quality aluminum heads will have 3/8" deep valve seats. An interference fitup of 0.006" assures tight seats that won't loosen under severe service. As a caution, experts note that OE iron heads require a minimum of 0.060" wall thickness after porting. Most prefer a minimum of 0.100".

Do heads make a difference? At 9.5:1 compression ratio on a stock late Mustang 5.0L short block, aftermarket heads produce phenomenal gains. Motorsport iron heads, a bigger performance camshaft and the SVO GT-40 manifold deliver 300 ft-lbs of torque and 290 horsepower. The AR-1 Aluminum Motorsport/SVO heads yield 305 ft-lbs torque and 305 horsepower with the same camshaft.

A set of bigger valve aluminum heads and a custom ported GT-40 manifold can produce clean tailpipe emissions yet still make 340 ft-lbs of torque and as much as 375 horsepower.

While much of the SVO 302 V-8 technology serves bracket racing Mustangs, some components would work well in a 302 powered classic Ford F-100 street rod, a lighter weight pro-street pickup or even a small displacement V-8 race truck. (See your local Ford/SVO dealer for details.)

Intake Plenum: Enhanced EFI/MPI Performance

JBA, TFS, Kaufmann Products, Ford/SVO and others have unleashed plenty of latent horsepower in the late 302 H.O. V-8 Ford engines. Adding cylinder heads with bigger valves, a set of matching exhaust headers, an SVO mass air flow sensor and a hot camshaft can provide big gains for the Ford 302/5.0L EFI V-8.

An additional and often overlooked area for performance gains, however, is the air intake flow. Research by TFS on the effects of intake plenum and manifold modifications noted the large increase in cylinder head flow that Ford's multi-point EFI computer can tolerate. Armed with this data, TFS went to work on the MPI induction manifolding.

Experimentation resulted in horsepower increases gained strictly through air intake modifications. Exploiting the superior characteristics of Ford's EFI/MPI F-truck manifold design, TFS focused on truck engineering, modifying this plenum for both underhood clearance and better flow.

The initial TFS manifold kits capitalized on readily available truck parts, although the plenum is highly modified. When installed on a 5.0L Mustang H.O. engine, changes include new fuel rails, custom fuel supply lines, redesigned heater hose fittings, a truck-type EGR valve and Air Bypass Valve, electrical wiring modifications, and the use of TFS's transition casting.

The transition casting and its rubber connectors provide the link between the truck-type intake throttle body and stock air box. Repositioning the PCV valve is necessary, since the original HO Mustang intake manifold provides for the valve, while a truck lower manifold has no such outlet.

If big valve heads and a hot camshaft grind have your late EFI 302 near its peak output, your engine is very likely breathing poorly or hiding extra horsepower and torque. A custom intake plenum/lower manifold or careful custom manifold porting may unleash the horsepower you've been looking for.

Dyno Buildup Of An F-150 302 V-8

Every F-truck owner knows the engine's horsepower rating. Horsepower ratings also play a major role in our decision to buy a new truck. Brake horsepower (bhp), SAE (net) horsepower and other rating methods, however, can obscure data.

On the other side of the horsepower issue are more realistic questions like, What does the rated horsepower mean when my two-horse trailer nearly pulls the tow hitch off the back of our F-250? Or perhaps, What kind of power will get my Ford F-150 4x4 through the perils of a rock pile and back home again?

The real test of usable horsepower is at your truck's drive wheels. For this data, a wheel dynamometer provides the best results. To illustrate the value of a dyno, I will share a research and development project that J. Bittle American (JBA), a Ford specialty outlet at San Diego, California, conducted, using a wheel dynamometer and a new F-150 Ford 4x4.

The Test Truck

Equipped with a Federal emission 302 (5.0L) V-8 and multi-port electronic fuel injection, the 1989 truck was ideal for JBA's current research. Curious about the performance potential of full-size Ford F-trucks, and highly experienced with the 302 H.O. Mustang V-8, JBA accepted the task.

To quantify gains made during the engine buildup, JBA enlisted the assistance of Gene Green, a dynamometer expert and manager of nearby SAMCO at San Diego. JBA began the project with nothing more than an oil, tune and air filter check on a bone-stock engine, mainly to establish an accurate wheel horsepower baseline figure for the 302 V-8.

The F-150 was just past break-in, with slightly over 8000 miles on the engine. A short wheelbase pickup, rated 6100 lbs. GVWR, the rig featured a truck-type four-speed manual transmission, 32x11.50R15LT tires, 3.55:1 axle gearing and some aftermarket upgrades. The powertrain was completely stock.

0012695

Fig. 16-25. In a preliminary warmup, stock 1989 302 F-truck MPI V-8 registered 80 horsepower @ 60 mph as the engine climbed up the rpm scale. A full throttle run to 95 mph @ 4500 rpm in fourth gear produced unstable readings. Gene Green, an expert dyno operator, then coaxed an honest and steady 124 horsepower at 4000 rpm and 90 mph.

The Initial Dyno Run

Primarily, a wheel dyno monitors power under simulated road conditions—the energy available to maintain wheel speed on a good traction surface. Paired rollers provide the testbed/cradle for the drive wheels.

A wheel dyno measures torque (twisting) force produced at the wheels, and SAMCO's Clayton dynamometers determine net wheel horsepower produced by the engine. In the case of the Ford F150 4x4, an arbitrary engine speed limit (under load) was set at 4000 rpm, estimated as the realistic ceiling for any of the truck's off-pavement uses. This standard prevailed throughout the test series.

Manual transmission vehicles are often more predictable on the dyno. Once in gear, they offer lower friction losses than automatic transmission models. Gene Green has found that an automatic transmission vehicle will net 2/3 of the total crankshaft horsepower at the drive wheels. By contrast, the average manual transmission car or a truck in two-wheel drive mode delivers approximately 3/4ths of the crankshaft horsepower.

> **NOTE —**
> Since a 4x4 truck has one more driveline and axle/differential assembly to create a frictional loss, the wheel horsepower figures would be slightly lower with the truck in four-wheel drive mode.

Why does horsepower decrease between the crankshaft and the wheels? Because friction in the geartrain is a major energy eater. Transmission gears, old style side-drive transfer cases, axle differentials (two in the case of a 4x4) and automatic transmission planetary gear systems each contribute to frictional loss of horsepower. Interestingly, although logic might suggest otherwise, the weight of the vehicle, tire diameter and transmission gear selected for a wheel dyno test have only a negligible effect on the results.

In street form, the stock F-150's 302 V-8 engine felt strong. SAMCO's dyno results showed why: At 4000 rpm in fourth gear, with a road speed of 90 mph, the stock truck powerplant produced 124 honest horsepower at the rear wheels. That may not sound so hot, but for a late model emission control engine of 302-cubic-inch displacement, it really is! The success of Ford's multi-point EFI systems has established major horsepower gains for F-truck owners.

With baseline dyno figures, the modifications to the F-150's 302 V-8 could begin. JBA went to work, attempting to fill in the engine's performance gaps.

Bolt-on Horses: Improving The Exhaust Headers

The engineering of tubular steel headers is a JBA specialty, as they are thoroughly versed on Mustang H.O. 302 V-8 technology. In this case, however, the performance goals differed slightly, skewed more toward truck power and good street performance.

For testing purposes, JBA wanted to isolate the gains made by its prototype header set. Rather than eliminate the factory single exhaust, catalytic converter or any other OEM device, JBA built a header set that fit exactly in place of the stock manifolds. By outward appearance, the installed exhaust system looked bone stock. Ford couldn't make the fitup any neater, and every factory emission control and EFI component remained intact.

JBA staff felt certain that the headers would make a difference. The one drawback, of course, was the restrictive nature of the factory single exhaust system. JBA, accustomed to high performance Ford cars, had never addressed a 302 V-8 with a single exhaust system. The dyno would determine whether JBA technology was on track.

0012696

Fig. 16-26. JBA steel tubing headers provide a neat OEM appearance. Fitup is exactly like factory single exhaust system. Stock exhaust pipe flanges work perfectly, and remainder of exhaust system is bone stock. All emission control and computer components have been maintained. Two dyno runs verified an honest 130 wheel horsepower @ 90 mph, a six horsepower gain over stock 5.0L truck V-8 output.

A Trip Back To SAMCO's Dyno

After checking the oil and warming the engine completely, we began the first of two tests. (Two tests balance any error factor.) Gene carefully noted each change that appeared on the Sun gauges. JBA's Doug Baker and I stood by in suspense, watching the dials.

Gene, a specialist with a wheel driven dyno, cautiously avoids false readings that can result from "flying" runs up the rpm scale. Gene opened the throttle slowly, bringing rpm up gradually as he selected the right gear. Again, we used fourth gear of the truck's manual gearbox, aiming for approximately 90 mph at 4000 rpm.

After two runs, the data was conclusive. The header set, alone, added six rear wheel horsepower, up to 130, a major gain for a single, bolt-on component change.

Normal factoring would translate as a gain of 10-plus crankshaft horsepower, even with a restrictive single exhaust system. This is substantial and verified horsepower, tested the hard way, under professional methods. Considering the size of the engine, JBA had accomplished a major feat.

302 Gains: Where To From Here?

The shift to dual exhausts was next. JBA decided to capitalize on the exhaust flow gains by focusing on the 302's valvetrain and cylinder heads. Doug Baker selected the camshaft and valvetrain components. Mike Salyer went to work on a complete off-highway (non-emission compliant) exhaust system. Switching to tri-Y headers, Flowmaster mufflers, and mandrel bent 2-1/2" exhaust pipes would help a hotter 302 breath.

John Elderhorst performed the engine work, with the largest task centered around cylinder head removal and porting. A performance camshaft change completed the upgrade, with a complement of JBA valvetrain hardware.

Doug Baker knew just the right camshaft for a healthy 302 V-8. Although the majority of upgrades at JBA focus on street and automotive racing paradigms, Doug felt that the 302's off-highway torque could benefit from better valve lift—which could also complement the porting.

At the time (1989), the 302 Ford truck engines used non-roller lifters. Doug added a set of Ford/SVO rollers #M-6500-R302 to enhance the valve opening action. Several other stock HO 302 pieces fit nicely: lifter guideplates #E5ZZ6K512A and the retainer #E5ZZ6C515A. So did a set of roller tappet pushrods, which are shorter in length than the stock truck items.

NOTE —
During the time that JBA built and tested the 1989 F-150 4x4, Ford used the same block design for both roller hydraulic and flat tappet (truck) engines. This makes a roller/hydraulic valve lifter conversion much easier.

With extensive porting and polishing of the stock iron heads, Doug knew the engine would breathe and wind up well. His camshaft choice followed these parameters, a special grind aimed at more mid-range and top end performance than the stock Ford camshaft offered.

CHAPTER 16

His design provided a gross valve lift of 0.514" on both intake and exhaust valves plus 258 degrees of running duration (lobe centers spaced at 110 degrees)—quite substantial, even for a roller/hydraulic camshaft. Doug wanted even more lift, though, and he changed the rocker arms to fully adjustable 1.70:1 ratio JBA roller rockers. (The stock 302 arms approach 1.60:1.)

This valvetrain required heavy duty valve springs with inner dampers. In addition to JBA's H014 head porting, a super modified prototype that relies on the stock 302 valve head diameters, the valve springs and spring heights also met careful tolerances. Porting consisted of a one-inch match-and-blend of the intake runners and heads, with precision polishing of the combustion chambers.

These combustion chambers feature a slightly rougher finish around the intake valve area and a sleek surface flowing into the exhaust ports. With such improvements in flow, Mike Salyer switched to a 1-1/2" exhaust exit tube for each cylinder, funneling into 2-1/8" Ys, then collecting before entering the low restriction 2-1/2" exhaust system.

Despite nominal 1.78" diameter intake valves and 1.45" diameter exhausts, the engine would now produce higher volumetric efficiency. A lower temperature 180° F thermostat, in compliance with the horsepower jump expected, was an added item. Felpro high performance gaskets completed the parts list.

Dirty Hands: Installing Horsepower In An F-truck

John Elderhorst mapped the job out thoroughly before starting. The F150 4x4 boasted a modest lift and a Warn winch/bumper out front. This would present a slight barrier, encouraging John to perch in the engine bay with the majority of his tools nearby.

Most late model F-trucks have plenty of hardware. With air conditioning, power steering, and a host of emission control pieces, the removal of cylinder heads took a while. Access to both heads and the timing cover were reasonable, however, and John pulled the camshaft forward without hitting the grill, an impossible feat with 460 V-8s.

Doug Baker indexed the valve timing with a dial indicator and degree wheel, aligning the camshaft straight up in this case (neither advanced nor retarded from the stock valve timing location). The rest of the components went together smoothly.

CAUTION —

The cylinder firing sequence with an H.O. 302 camshaft is like the 351W (1-3-7-2-6-5-4-8). This is different than the stock 302 F-truck firing sequence. You must reroute spark cables to the H.O. 302 firing sequence when using an H.O. 302 camshaft. Otherwise, the engine will never start—or worse yet, it might backfire severely and cause serious damage.

NOTE —
Unlike stock Ford 302 rocker arms, the JBA roller rocker arms require adjustment.

Fig. 16-27. JBA dug deeper for horsepower. Heads, camshaft and valvetrain came under scrutiny. John Elderhorst carefully removes factory flat base lifters. He keeps them in order for possible reuse with original camshaft.

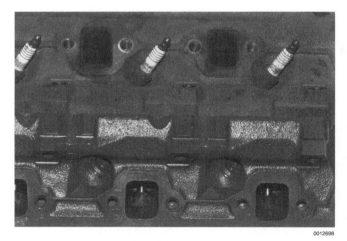
Fig. 16-28. Original head (top) shows smaller exhaust ports than cast iron replacement head (bottom). JBA offers these modified cylinder heads on an exchange basis.

Fig. 16-29. Intake ports show exceptional porting work. A one-inch blend with intake runners is highlight of JBA's HO14 (super modified) 302 porting package.

Fig. 16-30. JBA high performance valve springs and inner dampeners make a major difference in higher rpm range. 1.70 ratio roller rockers and a camshaft with increased valve lift dictate use of these springs.

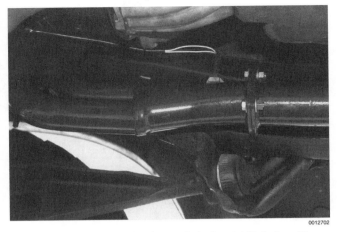

Fig. 16-32. Exhaust headers switched to tri-Y design. Oxygen sensor fits at right bank header collector. Data for MPI computer now comes solely from right cylinders. Mike Salyer performs a clean fitup for dual exhausts. Pipes bend to right side, flow smoothly through a pair of low restriction Flowmaster 2-1/2" diameter inlet/outlet mufflers, then exit to right rear of truck. Resonators fit into tailpipe tips to reduce exhaust decibel levels.

Fig. 16-31. Stock camshaft (top) had flat based lifters. New JBA grind camshaft has SVO (H.O. 302) roller tappets. Installation of roller/hydraulic tappets requires guide plates, pushrods and a spring retainer.

Back To The Dyno

Gene Green at the SAMCO shop was surely in for a surprise. Our previous dynamometer testing had focused on street legal changes and subtle modifications. Even now, all but the F-150's exhaust system looked stock. The exhaust note, however, sounded very throaty.

John set the base timing at the stock specification. The fuel injection was neither modified nor adjusted, and now the single oxygen sensor fed the right engine bank's exhaust data to the computer. After preliminary safety checks, Gene insisted that he drive the truck before putting it on the dyno (allegedly to be sure it was ready to test, although we knew better—Gene wanted to feel the throttle response firsthand!).

The earlier tests were at 4000 rpm, a figure that respected Ford's truck engine dynamics. We'd do that number again, but also push to 5000 rpm for the sake of evaluating the camshaft's potential and the value of precision cylinder head porting.

A tiny crowd had gathered around the dynamometer as Gene prepared the truck for its earlier test sequence: 90

mph in high gear. The truck snapped up the rpm scale, a high pitch whine echoing the torque increase from the performance camshaft and increased head flow. At a minimal exhaust restriction, the entire shop, despite its huge bays, resonated with the 302's power. Near 4000 rpm, Gene stabilized the throttle, assuring maximum traction as the rollers raced in the floor.

"144 horsepower!" he exclaimed, as the engine rpm dropped to an audible level. "Not bad for rear wheel horsepower on a 302."

The rest of us grinned, anticipating the 5000 rpm readings. We knew from the H.O. 302 experience that the engine was just hitting its stride at 4000 rpm. That was a truck-type rpm ceiling. Cautiously, Gene cooled the engine and exhaust for a few minutes. The crackling exhaust pipe paint now scented the entire shop.

Gene peered intently through the driver's window at the Sun tach and dyno gauges. 5000 rpm near 110 mph rattled the shop floor. The astonishing result: 172 horsepower. We speculated for a moment that the engine might do even better at 5500 rpm. Here, Gene drew the line. All-terrain tires on hot steel rollers set poorly with him, a risk compounded by the 120-mph limit of the equipment.

Up The Learning Curve

Considering the number of engine modifications, we expected 160 rear wheel horsepower. The actual results, with plenty of room left for finer tuning, were well beyond our expectations. At this point, we even debated whether the 1.70 ratio rocker arms were necessary.

The test proved a number of concepts. Despite the hot street performance, the high rpm horsepower gains would do little for a rock crawling four-wheel drive situation. A different camshaft, with less duration and milder lift, would serve better there. Also, Gene Green recom-

0012703

Fig. 16-33. SAMCO's Clayton dynamometer and Sun gauges got a good workout with the F-150 Ford 4x4. Here, back tires spin their way toward 110 mph, where rear wheels read a steady 172 horsepower at 5000 rpm.

mended an H.O.-type mass air flow sensor retrofit, and John Elderhorst agreed. Mike Salyer made notes as we left SAMCO.

> **NOTE —**
> Ford/SVO's MAF sensor retrofit kit has since become a smart add-on for 302 MPI performance. MAF tends to stabilize high speed performance and improve idle quality.

7. ENGINE OVERHAUL

As your truck engine reaches the upper end of its service life, you have two options: an in-the-chassis ring-and-valve job (overhaul) or a complete, out-of-chassis engine rebuild.

An in-chassis overhaul is relatively easy with many truck engines. Following your factory-level service guide, you'll remove the cylinder head(s), oil pan and timing cover, ream the cylinder ridges before removing the rods and pistons, fit new rod and main bearings, along with new piston rings, a timing chain/sprocket set and a new or reconditioned oil pump.

Most likely, you will send the cylinder head assembly to a machine shop for reconditioning, then carefully hone the cylinder bores (protecting the crankshaft bearing journals from any debris or abrasive materials and restoring cleanliness throughout the engine). A new or reground camshaft and lifters and a new oil pump round out the job.

Overhauls work on mildly worn engines and those having hard, durable cylinder walls. An overhaul buys extra miles of driving yet falls short of a complete rebuild. Restricted by the chassis and body, many rebuilding steps are neglected during an in-the-frame overhaul. By contrast, a complete, professional engine rebuild involves re-

placement or precision machining of every moving part in the engine.

The Real Engine Rebuild

Emission control hardware and a maze of carburetor plumbing overwhelm most 1975–85 Ford light F-truck engines. The basic long-block engine assembly, however, remains relatively unchanged. Once out of the chassis (see your F-Series shop manual for removal procedures), your six-cylinder or V-8 engine can undergo a thorough rebuild.

A quality rebuild will virtually remanufacture your engine. Caustic block and head cleaning, replacing hard-to-reach freeze plugs and installing camshaft bearings are just a few of the procedures.

Unless run on a high grade synthetic oil from day one, the typical 120,000-plus mile Ford truck engine will have 0.006" or more cylinder taper. (A simple ring-and-valve job overhaul would serve little purpose here, as rings cannot seal properly against a tapered cylinder wall.) Restoration to OEM tolerances takes place during a machine shop remanufacture of your engine.

Some Engine Assembly Survival Tips

Sometimes it is easier to have the machine shop completely assemble your long block (cylinder head(s) and block parts). If, however, you plan to assemble your newly machined engine parts, you will need to follow some important guidelines. Although your F-truck shop manual can help with step-by-step procedures, there are some fundamental concerns that I will share.

For example, never fill hydraulic lifters with oil. Hydraulically pumped-up lifters can cause valve-to-piston interference during initial cranking of the engine. (You should, however, coat the lifter bases and bores with engine assembly lube.) After the engine is completely assembled and the valves are adjusted to specification, you can prime the engine's lubrication system before start-up.

Fortunately, most Ford F-truck engines have what I consider reasonably low compression ratios and can tolerate today's lower fuel octane ratings. For the purpose of rebuilding your engine, a compression ratio of 8.0:1 to 8.7:1 works very well on a carbureted V-8 or six. I've found that longer stroke engines, like the carbureted 300 inline six or a 351W V-8, can survive nicely on 8.7:1 compression.

Usually, spark timing changes (like a mild initial spark advance and limited spark curve) will permit use of a higher compression ratio. Some '60s engines had 9:1 or higher compression, and surviving with such a ratio may be possible by simply retarding the spark timing slightly to prevent detonation. The yardstick that I use for truck purposes is to be able to run 87–88 octane fuel without detonating, damaging pistons or pitting valve faces.

On an older Ford engine with 9:1 compression ratio or higher, one means of lowering the compression is to replace the factory shim-type or thinner head gasket with a thicker (Detroit or similar) composition type gasket. Apply sealant and install the gasket according to the manu-

Fig. 16-34. *Valve timing is a critical part of engine performance. When you install a new camshaft, sprockets and chain (or gears), set the valve timing accurately and according to the camshaft grinder's specifications.*

facturer's guidelines. Use Permatex's Teflon Thread Compound on head bolt threads that enter water jackets.

During an engine overhaul or rebuild, you can upgrade performance with high-quality aftermarket parts. Speed-Pro Performance recognizes the potent Ford truck engines and offers race-quality Plasma Moly file-fit gap piston rings. For the less stressed engine, another approach is TRW or Sealed Power high grade or Premium OEM replacement rings.

After refinishing and measuring each cylinder wall, wash your bores thoroughly and coat them with clean oil. Many shops recommend Speed-Pro/Sealed Power rings, fitted to the stock or OEM type cast alloy pistons, to help provide greater durability. Likewise, a full set of Speed-Pro valves and a three angle valve seat grind will assure consistent cylinder sealing and longevity.

Fig. 16-35. *Valve timing is critical to proper engine performance. Aftermarket roller chain sprocket has three keyways for varying camshaft timing. The engine builder has choice of normal (straight up) and an advance or retard of four degrees in either direction from stock alignment.*

Fig. 16-36. *Another function of most camshafts is to drive the ignition distributor gear. Mesh of these gears is critical, as the oil pump may drive from the base of the distributor shaft. Make certain that your new camshaft's drive gear material is compatible with the distributor drive gear. Often, a bronze or specialty distributor gear is necessary. Follow your camshaft grinder's recommendations.*

Fig. 16-37. *Chamfer oil holes during machining. At Sweetwood & Sons Machine Shop in Lakeside, California, crankshaft receives polishing and chamfering of oil feed holes.*

Fig. 16-38. Stock rods and OE replacement Badger cast pistons are one option for a mild performance hop-up. Racing or high performance calls for forged pistons. Cast rings, fitted to cast pistons, serves milder applications. Thin iron cylinders tolerate mild overbores, especially when core shift applies. Sweetwood & Sons and other shops restrict many rebores to a maximum of 0.030" oversize.

Fig. 16-40. Flywheel shows normal scoring for 120,000 miles of service. Re-surfacing and balancing are in order here to restore smooth clutch action. On Ford engines, the OEM method of crankshaft balance (internal or external) will determine which balancing technique to apply.

Fig. 16-39. Checking ring gap is a standard blueprint procedure. This verifies proper cylinder diameter and piston ring fitup to assure good compression seal and oil control.

Fig. 16-41. This inline six cylinder head reveals early signs of oil seepage past rings and valve guides. Note dark areas at cylinders where oil has entered combustion chambers. Burning oil from worn rings appears as blue smoke exiting tailpipe under hard acceleration. Valve guide and guide seal wear shows as blue tailpipe smoke upon startup.

Fig. 16-42. *Ford Y-block cylinders reveal scoring and taper. Cylinder reboring, honing and fitting of new pistons is necessary.*

Fig. 16-45. *Boring bar creates a new cylinder surface. On this engine, Sweetwood found that a 0.030" (diameter) rebore will make an ideal size. Power honing on CK-10 Sunnen machine is best assurance of true, concentric and long-lasting cylinder bores. Machinists use a bore gauge regularly during finish honing. Exactitude pays off in years of rugged, reliable performance.*

Fig. 16-43. *Engine reveals piston wear and signs of ring blowby. Here, oil consumption was a quart in 250 miles. Sludge and slight bearing wear are common at this mileage. A simple in the chassis ring-and-valve job overhaul, common during the flathead and Y-block engine eras, would neglect many of the engine's needs.*

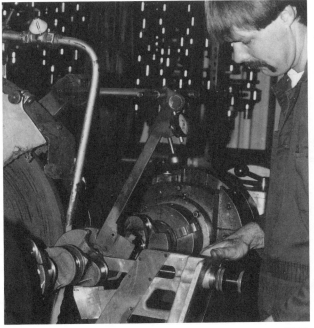

Fig. 16-46. *Here, Gary Sweetwood operates the crankshaft lathe. Relatively light wear on this six cylinder crankshaft required the minimum 0.010" undersize regrind.*

Fig. 16-44. *Timing chain wear causes late valve timing and poor lower speed engine response. A truck engine suffers drastically from late valve timing, as idle and low-speed manifold vacuum drop.*

Fig. 16-47. *Resizing and truing each connecting rod restores new performance to a seasoned set of rods. All critical parts undergo magnafluxing for cracks. Once re-machined, rods can undergo balancing for added performance.*

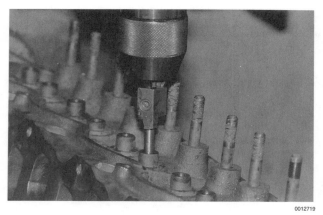

Fig. 16-49. *Clean cylinder head receives new iron valve guide inserts. Fitting new guides and seals will restore manufacturer's tolerances, uniform compression and proper oil sealing ability.*

Fig. 16-48. *Out of CK-10 machine, hot tanked block looks far better than greasy engine that came from chassis. Note uniform and precise cross-hatch finish on each cylinder bore, a necessity for proper ring seating and seal.*

Fig. 16-50. *Machinist carefully machines three-angle seats during cylinder head reconditioning. After cutting valve seats, cylinder head is resurfaced. Head gasket seal and straightness of head are primary goals.*

Fig. 16-51. *Resurfaced or new valves assure compression seal. Here, Clifford's 264-degree duration inline six cylinder camshaft comes with heavy valve springs and inner damper springs.*

Fig. 16-52. *Machinist closely checks valve stem heights after grinding new valve seats. Since many Ford engines have non-adjustable rocker arms and fitted length pushrods, precision cut of valve stem ends can restore proper hydraulic valve lifter clearance. For some engine applications, aftermarket adjustable pushrods or adjustable rocker arms provide an alternative.*

Fig. 16-53. *Heat machine takes load off pistons and pins during fitup. Heating small end of rod expands bore temporarily to accept the new piston pin.*

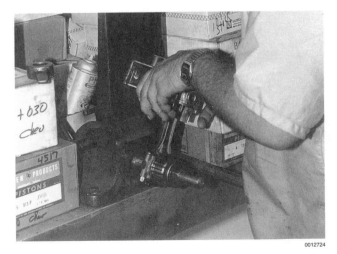

Fig. 16-54. *Once pistons are installed, machinist checks rod/piston alignment. At a quality machine shop, every step is taken to assure close tolerances and true alignment of all parts.*

Fig. 16-55. *Camshaft bearings are installed first since machinist wants a correct cam fitup before fitting any other parts. New bearings fit precisely, with oil feed holes aligned carefully. This is critical to proper engine oiling.*

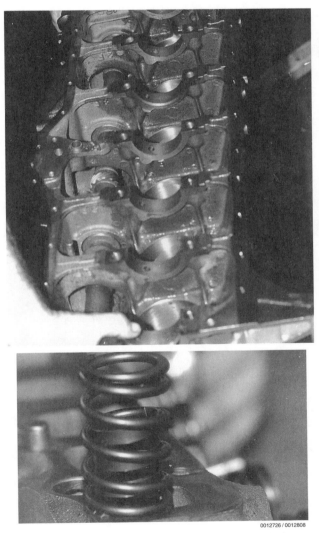

Fig. 16-56. *For an inline six, a 264-degree (gross) duration camshaft will enhance mid-range and top-end performance. Engine balancing and improved valve springs help assure smooth operation at higher rpm. Inline sixes respond exceptionally well to balancing.*

Fig. 16-57. *Oil check valve is an often overlooked item. On engines so equipped, Sweetwood always replaces this valve after hot tanking and age reduce its reliability. New valve is inexpensive insurance.*

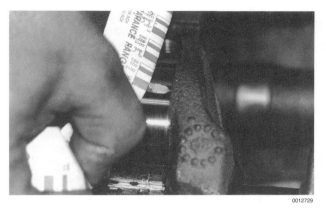

Fig. 16-59. *Plastigage of main bearings is last assurance of correct fitup. After confirming fit, main cap bolts receive final torque in sequence and to specification.*

Fig. 16-58. *Main bearing halves are fitted to spotless block saddles. Every piece is thoroughly lubricated with special assembly oil.*

Fig. 16-60. *New crankshaft sprocket is tapped gently into position.*

Fig. 16-61. *Timing sprockets align to specification. This step is crucial to proper performance and engine survival.*

Fig. 16-62. *New rings mate carefully to new pistons. Note 030 (0.030") on crown of piston, a common oversize. With protective plastic caps on rod bolts, pistons are readied for installation. Sized ring compressor eliminates risk and struggle during piston installation.*

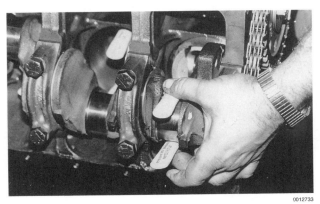

Fig. 16-63. *Carefully, assembler slides each rod into proper position. Rod bearings lubed, matching rod caps fitted, torquing nuts is the final step.*

Fig. 16-64. *New brass freeze plugs resist corrosion and premature failure. Shops like Sweetwood use OEM or better quality pieces during a major rebuild.*

Fig. 16-65. *Bases of new lifters and lifter bores are lubed before installation of the lifters.*

Fig. 16-66. *Head installation brings engine to complete form. A rebuilt long block assembly includes remachining or replacement of all moving and critical parts.*

Fig. 16-67. *High-volume oil pump, remachined crankshaft and new rod and main bearings help keep your truck engine alive under severe loads. After normal break-in, use a high grade synthetic oil to lengthen your fresh engine's lifespan.*

Fig. 16-68. *Pushrods installed, new rocker arms will complete engine assembly. Valve adjustment is not required with this particular engine design. For this engine, simply tighten all rocker pivot hardware to OEM specification, then prime oil system before starting engine. Always follow OEM procedures.*

Fig. 16-69. *When your engine only requires cylinder head work, Eastwood Company's Velcro and Scotchbrite pads leave an ideal finish on block deck and cylinder head. Clean away all abrasive before reassembling the engine. Always protect your engine's crankshaft from abrasive contamination during an in-chassis overhaul or cylinder head work.*

Adjuncts To An Engine Rebuild

Your newly rebuilt engine will produce more horse-power and greater torque. The engine now needs proper break-in and care. This requires adequate cooling, good water pump circulation and a working fan. A marginal OEM radiator, defective fan clutch or worn water pump becomes a glaring problem when new found horsepower places higher demands on the cooling system.

Protect your newly rebuilt engine, with its hot tanked, scale-free block and cylinder head. Have the radiator hot tanked, rodded and pressure checked to assure clean and adequate coolant flow.

Plugged, soldered and damaged radiator cores, or a radiator filled with rust and scale, will prevent your new engine from cooling adequately. Engine break-in heavily taxes the cooling system. If in good shape, your truck's cooling system helps the engine meet the variety of challenges that the vehicle will face.

In addition to installing a new water pump and reconditioning the radiator, pay attention to all hoses, clamps, the thermostat and drive belts. New parts here are cheap insurance. Test the fan clutch and replace if necessary.

Any transmission or clutch parts that were sub-standard before the overhaul now need attention. The new engine will place a higher load on worn geartrain parts, especially when you drive in the off-pavement environment. Replace the clutch assembly (if necessary, re-surface the flywheel), service the transmission, and be certain that the gear assemblies work well before installing the fresh engine.

Precision Engine Balancing

Your truck's engine may face the perils of towing, off-pavement pounding, the extremes of heat, stress, sustained rpm and sporadic runs up and down the rpm scale. Fortunately, a Ford F-truck engine can take this punishment and more. For the sake of smooth engine operation and longevity, however, a rebuild should include balancing of critical reciprocating parts. Careful matching of connecting rod and piston assembly weight, which involves a concern for weight at each end of the connecting rod and other match-weight techniques, will deliver smoother engine performance.

Balancing translates as a margin of safety when you subject the engine to severe duty service—just like using a quality synthetic motor oil and improving the cooling system. When you plan hard work for your truck, the token expense of balancing will return big dividends.

Precision balancing and match-weighting of rod/piston assemblies is a practical element of your engine buildup. Maximum engine smoothness and reduction of stress are the notable gains, as balancing brings the weights of pistons, rods, rings and bearings to blueprint tolerance. The machinist then follows by spinning and balancing the crankshaft, pulley/damper, flywheel (or flexplate) and clutch cover assembly. Fully balanced, your truck's engine will enjoy vibration-free, effortless performance.

Chapter 17

Drivetrain Upgrades

FORD F-TRUCK TRANSMISSIONS AND AXLES span several engineering epochs. The earliest light truck transmissions had either three forward speeds with synchromesh on second and third gears only or the archaic spur gear four-speed with no synchromesh on any of the four forward speeds and reverse. Axle designs range from primitive split-housing types to drop-in carriers and integral housing hypoid units.

The original and popular synchromesh three-speed transmission survived in a relatively common form from 1948 to the mid-1960s. At that time, Ford turned to its own all-synchromesh three speed, a durable design that was a substantial improvement over the earlier one.

For sheer ruggedness, however, 1952 was the light F-truck milestone year, when Ford introduced a version of Warner's T-98 four-speed synchromesh gearbox. The T-98 units were already tested in larger Ford, I-H, Studebaker, Diamond-T, Divco, Reo, and White trucks.

The T-98 later evolved into the T-18 four-speed, and the basic design has now served Ford F-trucks for over four decades. The T-18, T-19, and even larger New Process 435 four-speeds have provided an excellent service record in F-models. As for durability, I believe that the Warner T-98/T-18 design and the New Process NP435 exceed all other Ford light truck transmissions to date.

0012742

Fig. 17-1. *I took this photo years ago to make a graphic statement about truck transmission stamina. Massive unit at left is GM's 465 Muncie box, which dwarfs a compact truck T-5 overdrive. Three-speed Borg-Warner T-14 and T-90 (with V-8 adapter attached) set in middle, while huge T-18 Ford truck box rests to right. In foreground is an early (pre-1968) GM Muncie SM420 truck four-speed. Rugged iron-cased T-18 and earlier T-98 design have been Ford F-truck mainstays.*

Fig. 17-2. *As a truck fleet mechanic, I could remove, completely rebuild and reinstall these popular Ford three speeds in less than two hours. 1953–64 model light F-Series trucks were the easiest to service, with clutch/bellhousing supported by rear motor mounts. You can remove this '57 F-100 transmission in less than twenty minutes.*

Fig. 17-3. *Transmission countergears show the relationship between a real truck four-speed and lighter duty OEM offerings. Left to right, the T-18, T-90, T-14, and T-5 gears stand next to GM's 465 Muncie countergear.*

Fig. 17-4. *Here is a Ford 2WD version of the New Process NP435 truck four-speed transmission ready for a hybrid 4x4 installation. Note size of this transmission, the largest cast iron case unit ever used in a light Ford F-truck.*

Early on, light Ford F-trucks turned to Spicer axles for stamina. The Model 44 became a light duty F-1/F-100 mainstay and survived until Ford introduced its rugged 9-inch banjo removable carrier design in 1957.

While the F-2/250 and F-3/350 stayed with the older split housing (full-floating style) axles for several years, the more modern and popular Spicer/Dana full-floating 60, 60HD and 70 type units eventually prevailed. Until the 1980s, all F-250 and F-350 axles were full-floating types. Since 1980, only the heavier duty F-models still use a full-floating rear axle assembly.

All Spicer axles are integral designs, with the differential carrier bearing saddles built into the axle housing assembly. Unlike the 9-inch Ford or other removable carrier housings, overhaul of an integral axle is usually in the chassis. Ford's own 8.8" ring gear integral unit has become a light duty F-truck standard since the 1980s. Current F-150 models use the 8.8" axle.

1. PERFORMANCE TRANSMISSIONS

Aside from the virtually indestructible nature of a cast iron four-speed gearbox, these units feature extremely low ratios in compound low (first gear). The most common first gear ratio for a New Process 435 is 6.69:1. Typical Ford truck applications of Warner's T-18 offer a 6.32:1 first gear ratio.

For 4x4 trucks with a two-speed transfer case and relatively low (like 4.10 or 4.56:1) axle ratios, the overall reduction ratio is enhanced further. Final drive crawl ratios of 70:1 or lower in first gear/low range are attainable. Taller, more economical axle gearing (3.55 or 3.73:1) can still yield a compound low, low range final driving ratio of over 60:1 when coupled to a transfer case that offers lower gearing in low range.

Some Ford 4x4 transfer cases have less gear reduction than others. Most '65–'76 F-100s have only a single speed power divider and no low range at all. Here, a truck four speed can provide enough gear reduction in first gear for handling typical off-pavement and heavy pulling situations.

> **NOTE —**
> If your '65–'76 F-100 4x4 has the single-speed Dana 21 power divider, consider retrofitting a two-speed Spicer/Dana 20 (Bronco type) or F-100/F-150 NP205 transfer case.

Compound low gear gives a 4x4 truck both crawling and pulling advantages. Such low gearing can save your chassis and powertrain. In hardcore rock-crawling, your truck can inch its way through the roughest terrain, with light use of the brakes, less tire spin and less skidding.

Stalled on a precarious slope, you can engage the clutch with the transmission in compound first gear and the transfer case in low range four-wheel drive. The 12-volt starter motor can pull the truck up a steep incline while firing the engine.

Unless your truck has a load, little starter drag will occur. The low-low gearing will afford a smooth chug forward as the engine catches (providing you have your foot very lightly on the throttle).

NOTE —
Know how your truck will respond to a start-up in gear. Practice this technique before traveling dangerous terrain. Be aware that you cannot start your truck with the clutch engaged if the truck's starter wiring includes a neutral or clutch pedal safety switch.

Installing a four-speed truck box eliminates chassis abuse in rough terrain. Tall geared trucks bend springs and twist their frames as they bash and skid their way through rockpiles. Your Ford 4x4 F-truck with a two-speed transfer case and compound low truck four-speed will perform far better, as ultra-low gearing yields great dividends in extending chassis parts life, vehicle safety, and driver/passenger comfort.

High output engines have great difficulty breaking an iron truck gearbox in good condition. A Warner T-18, T-19, T-98A or New Process 435 can easily handle 300-plus horsepower. A truck four-speed's second gear has a lower ratio than the first gear of most three-speed transmissions. With synchromesh down to second gear, three-speed driving is the norm until you need heavy crawling power. Trucks equipped with correct axle gearing rarely use compound low gear.

Truck-type Manual Four-speed Changeover

For all F-trucks equipped with a light duty three-speed or five-speed overdrive transmission, a four-speed changeover is possible using factory/OEM parts. Begin by finding a truck similar to your chassis that has a four-speed unit, and note all of the components that your truck currently lacks. If you select the right parts for your truck's chassis, a stock truck bellhousing can mate the correct gearbox type behind most Ford F-truck engines.

Example: Although 1948 F-trucks offer a non-synchromesh type four-speed, 1952 models were available with the T-98 Warner gearbox. You could use 1952 parts to couple your 1948 flathead V-8 to a T-98 four-speed. (Ford quit using the L-head six after 1951, so a 226H six to T-98 conversion could present a problem.)

Similarly, the T-98 was available during the Y-block V-8 and 215/223/262 inline six era. The T-18 and NP435 have been available during the 240/300 inline six, small-block V-8, FE and big-block V-8 eras. Determine which four-speed transmission options were available when your truck was built, and seek out a recycling yard truck with those components.

NOTE —
Recycling yards have interchange manuals that can determine year, make and model sources for transmissions, axles and related parts.

Some street truck builders opt for passenger car four-speed transmissions like the all synchromesh Borg-Warner T-10 or Ford rock-crusher. These gearboxes can handle horsepower but not severe loads. For hauling, towing or carrying a cabover camper, stick with truck-type four speed gearboxes that offer a compound low gear. The passenger car four-speed might better serve in a lightweight street truck project like a classic '48–'56 F-1 or F-100.

A transmission changeover may also require use of a larger diameter flywheel, different bellhousing and starter change. Truck four-speeds have high torque ratings and usually come with a larger diameter clutch assembly. You will want this added stamina when you make a four-speed transmission changeover.

CAUTION —
Use the correct flywheel for your engine. Ford crankshafts have either internal or external balancing, and crankshaft and flywheel type differs. Be sure your flywheel selection matches the engine's balance method.

I encourage the use of a cast iron bellhousing if available and suitable for your application. Four-speed truck transmissions are very heavy and hang a massive amount of weight off the rear of the bellhousing. Late model trucks use aluminum alloy housings, and the stress to bolt threads can become an issue. Often, there is a cast iron counterpart housing available from an earlier application.

CAUTION —
When selecting a bellhousing, be certain the index hole that centers the transmission is of the correct diameter to accept the four-speed's front bearing retainer collar. This bore helps keep the transmission in alignment and also centers the input shaft with the crankshaft pilot bearing. The fit should be nearly snug, and the housing bore must index on center.

NOTE —
Aftermarket formed steel racing bellhousings are available, often with universal bolt patterns and detailed instructions for custom fit machining.

Extra Considerations

When planning a transmission swap, determine the driveline length required. You may need to find a driveshaft of the correct length or U-joint type. An alternative is to have a driveline constructed. (See earlier chapters for driveline details.)

The new four-speed transmission may come with a speedometer gear assembly that served different axle gearing or tire diameters. Check your speedometer error, and secure the correct drive gear from your local Ford dealer or another recycled transmission. If you have difficulty with this detail, consult a speedometer shop. They can install a speedometer speed correction kit if necessary.

CHAPTER 17

Fig. 17-5. *Advance Adapters offers the two-speed underdrive or overdrive Torque Splitter gear unit. Mounted between the clutch/bellhousing and transmission, this auxiliary truck transmission provides a durable synchromesh shift mechanism and an extra range of forward and reverse gears. I tested such a unit behind a 280 horsepower engine, pulling heavy loads and a travel trailer. If you want a rugged overdrive for your F-truck, here is my pick.*

For early F-truck upgrades, Warner T-18s share the same gearcase length as the T-98 transmission (11.87 inches). You must also account for the transmission input shaft length. This relates to the distance from the crankshaft pilot bearing to the front face of the transmission. Here, Ford truck four-speeds streamline the engine-to-transmission distance.

Clutch linkage may also differ between transmission types. Release fork or throwout bearing designs for heavy duty transmissions may be different than those parts used with lighter duty transmissions. When securing parts, make sure to include all four-speed pieces, and note their assembly order. Be sure of the clutch arm and linkage return spring types and how they attach.

Why Not An Overdrive Five-speed Conversion?

Light truck five-speed (overdrive type) transmissions reduce fuel consumption and engine wear. Many late Ford F-trucks have five-speed manual transmissions, and earlier truck owners often consider retrofitting such a unit.

I am not an advocate of manual overdrive transmission conversions for several reasons: 1) These transmissions fit only a limited number of Ford engine types; 2) they use hydraulic clutch linkage and have other features that could make a retrofit complicated; 3) the service record of aluminum housed transmissions is questionable, although later units have overcome many of the design flaws of earlier types; and 4) repair parts for overdrive transmissions are very costly, with special tools required for disassembly and fitup work.

Used aluminum case five-speed overdrive transmissions, although increasing in availability, are often defective or in need of overhaul. I would opt for a truck four-

speed conversion. If economy is your conversion goal, consider either a tall (numerically low) axle gear ratio or install an add-on overdrive unit, like Advance Adapters' Torque Splitter.

2. THE CLUTCH

Eventually, your truck's clutch will fatigue and fail. When it does, the aftermarket clutch industry offers a variety of rebuilt and new clutch units to restore or improve performance. You can select a clutch that will handle your engine's torque and horsepower demands.

Traditionally, a high performance clutch was a non-diaphragm design. Two varieties include a centrifugal arm/fulcrum arrangement (Long) and a high spring rate type.

Centrifugally weighted clutch fingers allow two distinct clutch behaviors. To ease take-off and reduce shock loads to the transmission, transfer case or axle, the initial squeeze or clamp pressure is lower. As engine rpm increases in each gear, the centrifugal weights move outward. At speed, the fingers' fulcrum leverage applies increasingly more pressure to the clutch disc.

The complaint with older centrifugal clutch designs is high pedal pressure at higher rpm. In racing and high performance activities, applying the clutch pedal at high revs with hydraulic clutch linkage can actually blow out the slave and clutch master cylinder seals. Under these same circumstances, mechanical linkage will place an overwhelming load on the driver's clutch foot. Reciprocally, relatively low apply pressure often allows damaging clutch slippage.

Borg & Beck Type Clutch

An alternative design, the non-centrifugal, three-finger clutch popularized by Borg & Beck, eliminates guesswork about apply pressure at any given rpm. Spring pressure clutches apply the entire force of the pressure plate at one time. This means that the spring rate built into the clutch cover unit is exactly the rate sandwiching the clutch disc against the flywheel face.

Accurate clutch pressures can be set for vehicle weight, engine power output and the vehicle's usage. In heavy duty towing and 4x4 applications intended for brute work, the clutch apply pressure (static) is 2200 pounds or better. Users choose a non-centrifugal clutch of 2200–2400 pounds clamping force for heavy hauling or a large increase in horsepower.

In a lighter duty vehicle, say a Ford F-150 with a 302 V-8 or 300 inline six, the maximum pressure demands could seldom require more than 2000 static pounds. While adding static pressure will decrease the chance of slippage, it increases the shock to vital geartrain parts during initial clutch engagement.

Diaphragm Clutch

The third common clutch design is the multi-fingered diaphragm type. General Motors popularized the use of diaphragm clutches many years ago, and early high performance enthusiasts discarded these types of clutches regularly in favor of Borg & Beck and Long type clutches. Diaphragm clutches were unable to handle high performance demands and offered few means for increasing apply pressures. Worse yet, overheat quickly damages the flat diaphragm clutch springs.

A diaphragm clutch has two advantages, however. The pedal pressure to disengage the diaphragm clutch is minimal, as sixteen fingers apply leverage instead of three. The long spring fingers allow relatively high apply pressures with minimal pressure at the clutch pedal. Pedal take-up distance is relatively short with a diaphragm design, and clutch engagement occurs very smoothly.

Aftermarket Clutches

Thanks largely to aftermarket innovation, several performance clutch designs are available for your truck. One of the more exciting options is Midway's Centerforce clutch. A diaphragm clutch with unique centrifugal weights, the Centerforce unit uses the best features of each popular clutch design.

Borrowing from the diaphragm unit, the Centerforce clutches have low release pressure, short pedal effort and

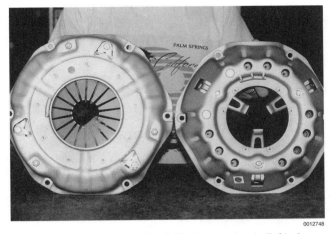

Fig. 17-7. *OEM-type Ford diaphragm clutch (left) shows multiple spring/lever design. Spring tension alone squeezes the disc between the pressure plate and flywheel. At right is a common Borg & Beck OEM replacement clutch.*

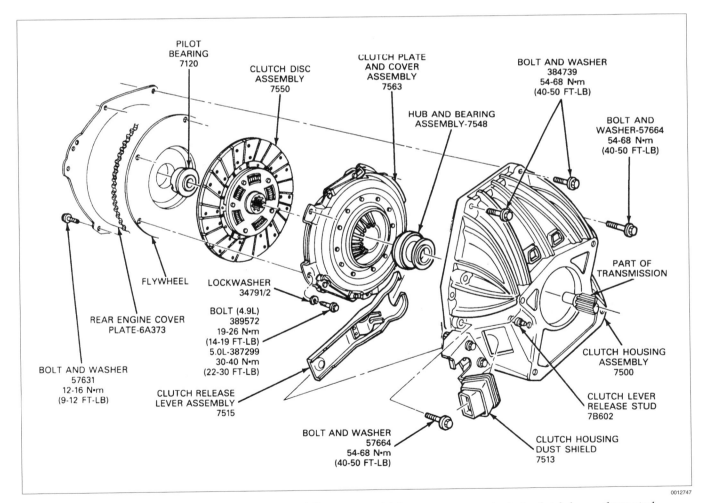

Fig. 17-6. *These 1993 Ford factory shop manual guidelines prevent trouble. Note model application and emphasis on critical measurements and proper tightening techniques to prevent warpage of a new clutch cover. (See your Ford F-truck shop manual for specifications that apply to your model.) Apply high temp grease sparingly to clutch lever release stud and crankshaft pilot bearing (if bronze bushing type) bore. Diaphragm type clutch affords smooth engagement and immediate application of full spring pressure. (Courtesy Ford Motor Company.)*

Fig. 17-8. *Midway's Centerforce clutch unit is a firm clamping diaphragm design with the advantage of centrifugal weights for high clamp pressures as rpm increases. Centrifugal weights apply tremendous pressure at higher rpm.*

Fig. 17-9. *Factory hydraulic clutch linkage (cylinder at right) like this system on a 1957 Ford F-100 pickup works very well. Used from 1957–60 on all F-trucks, hydraulic clutch linkage offers less pedal pressure and smooth clutch engagement.*

smooth take-up. Drawing on centrifugal principles, the Centerforce clutch cover design incorporates an ingenious weighting of the diaphragm fingers to allow higher apply pressure as clutch rpm rises. Centerforce claims increased disc and pressure plate life, and weights can be designed to accommodate a variety of user needs.

Although many clutch manufacturers build healthy aftermarket replacement clutches, Midway's Centerforce II and Dual Friction designs have a wide reputation for their rugged performance, reliability and light pedal apply pressure. For multi-purpose truck usage, I prefer the Centerforce centrifugal weight clutch assembly over all other choices.

Clutch Linkage

Ford F-truck models can develop clutch linkage trouble. If you have plans to upgrade your powertrain, don't overlook the clutch linkage.

The more troublesome Ford F-truck systems are 1965 to mid-'80s mechanical linkage types. Here, the engine mounting system changed to a single rear mount under the transmission and two engine side mounts. Engine movement with this layout contributes to linkage wear, and loose mounts can cause clutch engagement roughness.

Often, a mechanic suspects clutch wear when the real trouble is loose motor mounts, a worn transmission mount or fatigued clutch linkage and bushings. The '61–'64 F-truck models, despite their more rigid motor mount system, also develop clutch linkage wear.

Ironically, the often cursed '57–'60 F-truck adjustable type hydraulic linkage is one of the best designs around. When this hydraulic system is in good working order and adjusted properly (see service chapter), the linkage works fine. Later model F-trucks with hydraulic clutch linkage are also reliable, although I prefer the durability of the older style system with its cast steel cylinders.

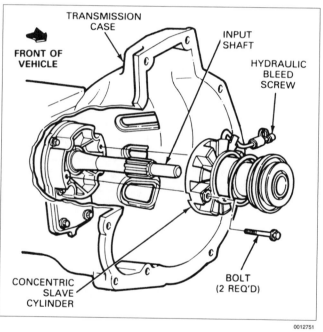

Fig. 17-10. *Ford now offers a hydraulically actuated clutch release bearing assembly on some engine/transmission applications. Although this design eliminates mechanical clutch linkage, a release assembly hydraulic leak could ruin the clutch disc and require a major amount of labor to repair—especially on a 4x4 model.*

CAUTION—
Later Ford F-truck hydraulic clutch cylinders have aluminum housings. The bores of such cylinders can easily become damaged if abrasive contaminants enter the system. Use care and cleanliness when inspecting clutch fluid or servicing the system.

Inspect all mechanical linkage parts when changing or upgrading the clutch. As interior bellhousing parts are difficult to reach, I highly recommend the use of a new, high quality throwout bearing. Install the best pilot bearing type available, and make sure it fits the crankshaft and transmission input gear properly. Look closely for release arm/fork and pivot stud wear.

NOTE —
Aftermarket hydraulic throwout/release bearings are available, and some OEMs have turned to this design. I avoid such systems, especially on 4x4 models. This is a poor concept, as the simplest leak repair or seal replacement could require removal of two driveshafts, the transfer case, the transmission and other parts.

3. TRACTION DIFFERENTIALS: CONTROLLING WHEELSPIN

4x4 F-trucks prove their worth battling climate extremes, stretching over rocks, clawing at mud in fast flowing streams and pulling through deep snow on barren winter paths. Four-wheelers, seasoned by unruly trails, argue that there's no such thing as too much traction.

A factory/OEM positive-traction or limited-slip differential helps deliver traction yet still provides vital differential speed between the axle shafts. Factory traction axles have a variety of trade names. New vehicles can be ordered with Trac-Lok, Posi-Traction, or Power-Loc units. A number of aftermarket performance systems, well suited for severe on-and off-pavement traction demands, are also available.

The typical Ford posi-traction or limited slip unit features a clutching mechanism within the differential. Loss of traction at one wheel reads as no resistance in the differential unit. By design, the clutching device then continues to operate the axle shaft with more resistance, i.e., the wheel with more traction.

Most OEM limited slip units incorporate a multi-plate spring loaded clutch assembly and a standard spider and side gear arrangement. Under normal driving conditions, these differentials flow power through the spider and side gears in the conventional manner. They can also direct power from the differential case directly to the side gears when the clutches apply.

When one tire loses traction and spins, the clutches within the differential provide power to the other wheel by directly driving its side gear. The spider gears, driving through beveled teeth, want to separate or spread the side gears. As the side gears move apart, they exert force on the clutch plates. When the load increases, so does the side gear pressure against the clutch plates. This directs more power to the wheel with traction.

While part of the load on the clutches comes from springs in the differential assembly, the majority of the force is from spreading the side gears. Torque load acting as the decisive factor, this explains why slight application of the brakes will cause a limited slip differential to direct more power to the wheel with good footing.

Fig. 17-11. *The Dana Power-Loc is a limited slip aftermarket differential engineered for light truck applications. Dana 44, 50 (IFS) and 60 front axle units are popular in Ford 4x4 light truck front ends. Users find that OEM style limited slip units deliver high traction without severe shock loads.*

The clutch type limited slip unit, which retains the standard spider gears and side gears, still allows wheel speed to vary on corners. Varied wheel speed under normal load causes the clutches to slip, which allows the spider gears to perform their function. Applying heavy power in a turn, however, can load the clutches enough to lock the side gears against the differential case, causing both wheels to turn at the same speed.

Although various clutch styles exist, the principle remains the same: provide a direct flow of power from the differential case to each of the side gears and wheels rather than only to the wheel with the least traction. Although their method of delivery is entirely different, aftermarket lockers also accommodate this need.

Fig. 17-12. *This 9-inch Ford axle spool is the ultimate traction device. Axle shafts fit directly into spool splines, eliminating the differential completely. Spools serve strictly for sand drags, pulls and other forms of racing.*

Which Differential?

Your highway driving environment or off-pavement tastes dictate which traction differential to buy. Yes, there is such thing as too much traction, and driver caution is a must with any traction differential. A truck with a limited slip or locking differential can go sideways when both wheels lose traction at the same time.

WARNING —

On ice or slick off-camber pavement, torque application at both ends of an axle assembly can create unwanted trouble. If your truck has a traction differential(s) and you're traveling on ice, be very careful. The truck could easily slip sideways if both wheels spin at the same time and the road camber is steep.

As an expert on differentials, Tom Reider, president of Reider Racing Enterprises notes, "While differential choices vary enough to satisfy most everyone's needs, the differential that satisfies everyone's wants still hasn't been invented. For most highway situations, an open differential is all that most people need and is, therefore, found in 90% of all vehicles. Its ability to move the vehicle, however, is limited by the minimum traction available to any of the driving wheels. When operated in slippery conditions or with minimum weight on any of the drive wheels, it often causes the vehicle to become a land-locked barge.

"The alternatives available to us are to install limited slip or locking type differentials which will then provide the type of power flow to the ground that we expect out of our vehicle. Benefits and drawbacks exist for both types of differentials."

While manual and automatic lockers have the advantage of providing 100% traction to the opposite wheel when an axle shaft breaks, if you break a semi-floating axle shaft, or if you snap a 4x4's front axle shaft anywhere near the steering knuckle, you cannot drive safely.

Full-floating rear axles, like those commonly found on older F-250 3/4-ton models and the larger F-350

Fig. 17-13. Multiplate OEM style differential provides power to the axle with traction. The spider gears press the side gears against the clutches to deliver more torque to the wheel with traction.

trucks, will continue to operate with a broken axle shaft if the differential has limited slip or a locker unit. If possible, remove the broken axle section to protect other parts. Reinstall the outer flange to keep debris out and prevent gear oil loss. You can make it home for repairs. Firewood haulers might find this reassuring.

Fig. 17-14. Safety tire chains are a primary traction device. Meeting needs of over-the-road truckers for nearly half a century, Burns Bros., Inc., also owns Security Chain Company, the largest safety chain plant in the United States. Innovative Z-Chain cable design works well with latest ABS braking systems and is officially rated as a high speed safety chain. Easy to install in a blizzard, Z-Chain devices complement a limited slip differential.

Traction Guide

A variety of aftermarket and OE-type traction differentials are available for your truck. The need for these devices depends upon your driving environment and the importance of delivering maximum torque or traction at each wheel. (On some 4x4 applications, this could mean a traction device at both the front and rear differentials.) Several manufacturers offer traction differential kits for improving your truck's axle(s).

Detroit Locker/NoSPIN: A highly respected differential unit that has stood the test of time is the Detroit Locker or NoSPIN unit, built by Tractech, Inc., a subsidiary of Dyneer Corporation. The NoSPIN was offered as a Ford truck option (often dealer installed) for many years.

Speed sensitive, the NoSPIN allows your truck to maneuver corners and operate over irregular terrain. The unique design offers the equivalent of a completely locked differential (similar to a spool) during straight ahead driving conditions.

For differential action, the NoSPIN has a central spider assembly with dog teeth on both sides, two driven clutches (one for each axle shaft) with dog teeth to engage the spiders, and a pair of side gears. This spider assembly fits in the middle of the differential case. The case drives the spider assembly, while the driven clutch assemblies ride on splines machined on the outside of the side gears. Coil springs keep the clutches engaged with the spider assembly. This directs power from the spider to the side gears.

Fig. 17-15. *The Detroit Locker/NoSPIN has a loyal following. The Detroit Locker features positive engagement to the wheel with greater traction. Cutaway display model shows high quality and simplicity of mechanism. Display model has survived years of customer abuse on this parts counter.*

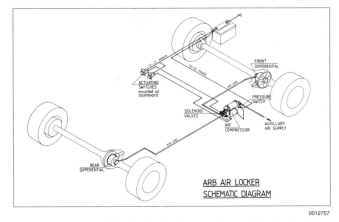

Fig. 17-16. *ARB's Air Locker leaves the traction to the driver. With the push of a switch, the differential locks up and both axle shafts rotate in unison, much like a spool. When disengaged, Air Locker provides the smooth highway operation of a conventional axle.*

As the truck corners and the outside wheel speeds up, cam ramps on the inside edges of the spider unit cause the clutch assembly for that wheel to disengage from the spider. The wheel now coasts freely. As with conventional or factory limited slip differentials, NoSPIN also prevents axle binding on turns. The method differs, however, as NoSPIN completely disconnects the power flow to the outer wheel as the vehicle makes a turn.

When wheel speeds are again equal, the free-wheeling clutch engages with the spider. Power now flows evenly to both wheels. The unique factor with this differential is that power flow is either equal at both wheels or going to the wheel with the greater amount of traction.

If one wheel hangs in the air, the NoSPIN unit stays locked, providing as much power to the wheel on the ground as traction will allow. If you spin the inside wheel on a turn, once the inner wheel's speed reaches that of the outside wheel, the unit will return to a locked position.

ARB Air Locker: After seven years of use in Australia, the ARB Air Locker hit the U.S. market by storm several years ago. This differential locking system now has a loyal following among those who prefer manual control of the differential(s). Winner of the coveted 1989 SEMA Best Product Award, the ARB Air Locker is a popular item with hard-core off-pavement users.

By design, the Air Locker provides conventional open differential operation for normal driving conditions. When your truck needs power to both wheels, Air Locker has a pneumatically operated shift mechanism for completely locking the spider gears and side gears within the differential assembly.

Inside the differential case, the Air Locker has a slider shift mechanism, much like sliders found in manual transmissions or a transfer case. The outside of the slider has splines. They engage and slide inside the differential case.

The slider also attaches to a hollow piston which surrounds the spider and side gears. Actuated by pressurized air, the piston moves the slider. Teeth on the inside of the slider match a set of teeth on the outside of one side gear. When the piston moves the slider over the outer teeth of the side gear, the side gear, slider and differential case lock up as a single unit. The locked side gears and spiders rotate both axle shafts at the same speed as the differential case.

An ARB Air Locker can engage solid power flow to each wheel, much like a racing spool. This is unsurpassed tractability, however, the driver now bears full responsibility for locking and unlocking the unit.

For durability, most ARB Air Locker applications have four spider gears, compared to the two spiders found in most OEM conventional axle designs. An Air Locker installation is much like changing a ring-and-pinion gear set and requires use of a dial indicator for setting up the ring and pinion gears, plus blue dye to perform tooth contact tests. It takes time to fit and route air hoses carefully and mount the compressor. Wiring, which features nicely made harnesses, also requires effort to assure a neat and reliable installation.

From my experience with a common truck axle, the task should take the reasonably equipped home mechanic from 10 to 16 hours to perform. Although installation is more involved than other traction devices, each kit includes instructions and all necessary parts.

Auburn Gear: For truck owners looking for a high-quality limited-slip differential, Auburn Gear provides a smart alternative. Although Auburn focuses mainly on the high-performance automobile market, its heavy duty limited-slip design has applications for popular light truck axles.

Like OEM limited-slip designs, Auburn Gear delivers power to both wheels through a clutching mechanism. However, instead of using clutch plates with high frictional loads, Auburn Gear uses a cone type clutch system. (A cone attaches to the back side of a side gear and nests inside a matching machined surface in the differential case.) When loaded by either the differential springs or the spider gears, the side gear wedges itself within the differential case.

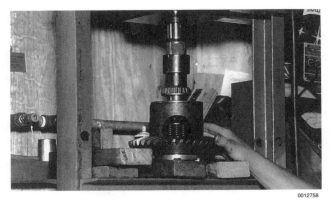

Fig. 17-17. *Auburn Gear's SureGrip is a rugged, heavy duty limited slip. Ford/SVO offers these units.*

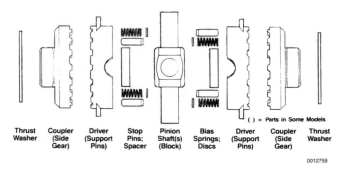

Fig. 17-18. *LA Locker Lock-Right diagram shows differential components. Cam teeth on each coupler allow overrun and disengagement when the axles rotate at uneven speeds.*

By design, much less force is necessary to lock the side gear to the differential case. Since there is direct steel-to-steel contact without clutch plates to wear out, peak performance can last much longer than with other units. Auburn traction differentials also boast large spider and side gears that deliver exceptional strength and durability for a limited slip type differential.

Torque delivery to the wheel with traction is superior with this design. If I were to consider a limited slip traction device, the latest Auburn design would be my choice.

LA Locker/LOCK-RIGHT: LA Locker's differential functions much like the NoSPIN/Detroit Locker. Originally designed for military Dodge trucks and larger W300 civilian Power Wagons, this design has gone widely civilian since 1986. In addition to larger truck axles, LA Lockers fit the popular Spicer 44 unit and Ford's popular 9-inch type.

The dramatic difference between LA Locker and other traction devices, including the NoSPIN, is its quiet operation during clutch lockup. Like the popular NoSPIN, LA Locker delivers 100% of available power to the traction wheel(s) at all times. This design offers a very simple cam action and lockup, shifting smoothly enough for use at rear or front (4x4 model) axles.

WARNING —
Although many four-wheelers use an LA Locker at both the rear and front axles, this design exaggerates the usual understeer associated with running a four-wheel drive truck on a hard surface with the front hubs engaged. Unlock your front hubs as you normally would for driving in 2WD mode on hard pavement. An LA Locker up front will not affect steering in 2WD with the hubs unlocked. Always follow the traction device manufacturer's operating guidelines for using two-or four-wheel drive.

The LA Locker installs in the existing differential case, which saves considerable cost. During installation, there's no need to remove differential bearings, so resetting ring gear backlash is often unnecessary. The LA Locker/LOCK-RIGHT is a tough, military-proven design. If you're attracted to the no-nonsense traction of a Detroit Locker/NoSPIN or ARB Air Locker, this quiet and rugged automatic locker deserves a look.

Spicer and Other OEM Limited Slips: Many trucks have factory-installed limited slip differentials. Spicer has supplied OEM traction differentials since the 1950s, and

Rating Differential Traction Devices*					
Differential style	Smoothness of operation	Tractability	Adverse effect on tires/driveline	Cost	Used for
Conventional (open)	Excellent	Poor	None	Lowest	Highway
OEM Limited slip	Very good	Good	Very little	Modest	Modest off-road
Aftermarket limited-slip	Good	Very good	Modest	Moderate	Modest off-road
Automatic lockers (LA and Detroit)	Good to poor	Extremely good	Modest	Higher	Heavy off-road
Manual locker (ARB)	Good to excellent	Excellent (locked) Poor (unlocked)	Poor (locked) None (unlocked)	Highest	Heavy off-road
Spool/welded diff.	Poor	Excellent	Poor	Modest	Racing

*Source: Tom Reider, Reider Racing Enterprises

satisfied users often restore their worn differentials with Spicer replacement parts.

Spicer traction units also work as retrofits for conventional Spicer/Dana axles. Since all Ford 4x4 light trucks have used Spicer/Dana axles in the front (many models use them at the rear, too), a Spicer Trac-Lok or Power-Loc unit is an option.

> **NOTE —**
>
> Users who prefer a milder application of power and subtler traction at the front axle choose the Trac-Lok. A Trac-Lok front and Detroit or LA Locker at the rear is a popular combination for four-wheelers seeking maximum off-pavement traction.

Fig. 17-19. *Ford OEM style 9-inch axle Traction-Lock unit shows stout ring gear flange. This is a very durable and simple assembly.*

Traction Differential Footnotes

Installing a differential carrier assembly involves close tolerances. Ring gear backlash settings require a dial indicator and patience. Before buying a traction differential, read the installation instructions carefully. Decide whether to send the job to a capable shop or tackle the work yourself.

Give the broader traction issue some thought, too. Consider tires, traction bars and shock absorbers. Added traction to the wheels means a greater challenge keeping traction on the ground. Expect more wheel hop and spring wrap up, especially with large tires.

4. CONVERSION AXLE ASSEMBLIES

To date, all Ford 4x4 light F-trucks have featured Spicer or Dana live front axles. Many Ford F-truck rear axles are also Spicer designs with notable exceptions like Ford's own 9-inch and later 8.8-inch rear axles.

Although Spicer/Dana is one of the most respected names in the automotive industry, the use of a

Dana/Spicer axle is no pat assurance that your truck's axle is bulletproof. The size (capacity rating) or application of the axle determines its stamina.

Fig. 17-20. *Currie Enterprises specializes in high quality performance 9-inch Ford racing and conversion axles, most equipped with some type of traction differential. Here is a hybrid Currie Enterprises front axle with custom steering knuckles for a one-off 4x4 application.*

One example of how this works is the pre-1977 F-250 4x4 models that have the lighter capacity (3300 or 3500 pound rated) Dana 44 front axle. These applications often break under severe duty four wheeling or when carrying a weighty cabover camper. (See comments in early chapters.) Here, a heavy duty 44 (3550 pound rated) or the rarer Dana 60 (3800 or 4500 pound rated) solid live front axle can make a big difference.

Ford F-truck rear axles, with the exception of early split housing types, are common and durable. For 1/2-ton capacity F-trucks, the Spicer 44 and Ford 9-inch axles are best. The late 8.8 integral design axle, although adequate for most F-150 chores, has not earned the respect of Ford's 9-inch design. Service access for the 8.8-inch differential also falls short of the earlier 9-inch axle with its removable center section (third member/carrier housing).

> **NOTE —**
>
> When making an axle swap, be certain to take track width under consideration. Match wheel spacing at front and rear axles carefully. Match OEM standards.

For earlier F-100 and later F-150 trucks, some builders install a 9-inch Ford axle in place of a Spicer or Dana 44 type or the later 8.8-inch Ford integral unit. If you plan such an approach, make sure you match brake sizing and install the correct length driveline. Compatibility with the ABS braking system is a concern on later F-trucks. Some fabrication work (such as spring perch relocation) is usually required.

F-250 models benefit from the Spicer/Dana 60 series axles. The full-floating (pre-1980 style and later heavy duty application) axle design is superior to the 1980–up semi-floating versions.

The heavy duty F-250 and F-350 models use the full-floating Spicer/Dana 60 or 60HD (heavy duty) rear axles, and these types can tote a load. An even heavier duty Spicer or Dana 70 full-floater is available in F-350 models, while Ford Super Duty/F-350 applications often use the massive Dana Model 80 rear axle.

If you own a 1980 or newer F-250 with the semi-floating axle and want to carry a travel or gooseneck trailer with 1500 pounds resting on the bed-mounted fifth wheel, consider retrofitting a full-floating axle unit into your truck. Find an application compatible with your truck's chassis. Make sure of the new axle's braking capacity and be certain your axle choice will interface safely with OEM ABS or any other braking devices. Match U-joint requirements and be certain the driveline length is correct. Axle retrofits usually require some fabrication work.

5. DRIVESHAFT FOOTNOTES

The common 1310 size Spicer U-joint used on many light Ford F-trucks (F-1/100 and F-150 models) is sufficient for most engine types. 1310 series U-joints fit trucks through 1/2-ton capacity and even some 3/4-ton models. They handle reasonable power.

> **NOTE —**
> Your driveshafts must be straight, within close tolerances and in balance. The driveshaft built to a high level of straightness requires very little, if any, balancing.

If your truck is a hardcore off-pavement runner, low driveshaft speeds and twisty, constantly changing driveshaft angles require stronger tubing sizes and a heftier rear coupler/splined shaft. A competent driveline shop can build a shaft with an increased tube diameter and wall thickness.

When driveshaft parts must handle more than 300 horsepower, you need heavy duty 3/4-ton or one-ton truck size U-joints. This is also necessary for a custom street truck that runs a high output powertrain, a pickup pulling a massive trailer or the 4x4 desert race truck prototype. For a radical 4x4 chassis lift, double Cardan type CV-joints will help reduce vibration caused by steep driveshaft angles.

A complete U-joint conversion can include heavier driveshaft tubing and larger U-joint flanges. For most light F-truck owners, the 1350-series Spicer joints can handle severe loads. Dana/Spicer 44 and 60 axle units, common to a wide range of Ford F-trucks, can be fitted with 1350 size replacement flanges. These larger yokes are also available for popular transfer case inputs and outputs plus the live front axle on a 4x4 model.

Steep driveshaft angles reduce the load capacity and safety of driveline assemblies. Speed also determines safe driveline angles. Modified trucks often violate both of these considerations with steep driveshaft slopes and lower (higher numerically) axle gear ratios. (See chapter on driveshafts for more information.)

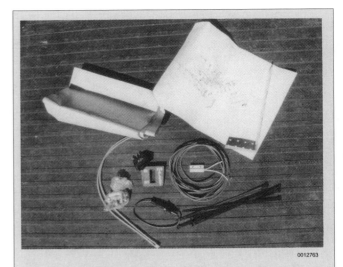

0012763

Hub-A-Lert: Watchdog For 4x4 Front Hubs

Knowing whether your truck's hubs have engaged or disengaged depends on more than the 4-Wheel Drive light on the console or dashboard. In most applications, the OEM 4x4 indicator lamp signal originates at the transfer case and simply indicates that the shifter/fork has moved to 4-High or 4-Low.

This means that power is flowing to the front axle, but if the hubs are not completely engaged, torque cannot turn the front wheels. Similarly, with automatic locking hubs, simply backing the truck up is no guarantee that the automatic hubs have disengaged. Dash lights cannot see inside the front hub mechanisms.

There's a better way to monitor front axle activity. Hub-A-Lert, an easy-to-install device built by 4x4 Specialty Products, can read front driveshaft rotation. The device sends a signal to an LED dash lamp and takes the guesswork out of hub disengagement.

During normal two-wheel drive operation, no shaft rotation (other than the minor lubricant spin common to some gear-drive transfer cases) will display on the LED lamp. If a defective hub begins to drag, however, the front driveshaft will spin and flash a signal at the dashboard.

Simple and designed by a savvy victim of several automatic hub and consequent transfer case failures, Hub-A-Lert is automatic hub insurance—at a fraction of the cost for a damaged front axle, transfer case or hub assembly.

> *CAUTION —*
> *Be certain to use OEM replacement U-joints at the front axle steering knuckles. These permanently sealed joints have no grease fitting and offer more strength than a U-joint cross yoke that is drilled for a grease fitting.*

> **NOTE —**
> In four-wheel drive, the torque splits between front and rear axles, reducing overall load on each U-joint. Two-wheel drive mode is actually much harder on U-joints than running a truck in four-wheel drive.

Chapter 18

Chassis and Suspension Upgrades

MOST STATES now have mandates setting limits on vehicle chassis height and body modifications. Motor vehicle safety administrators, law enforcement agencies and a wary citizenry have targeted unsafe customized street trucks and poorly modified off-pavement prototype pre-runner and 4x4 trucks registered for public road use.

Evidence of sensational accidents and senseless traffic deaths supports this sentiment. The more reputable aftermarket suspension manufacturers share many views with the state legislators. Increasing a truck's height, for example, raises issues like correct safety engineering versus a homespun botch job to achieve a particular look.

Teams of factory engineers work endlessly at improving the ride, handling, safe steering and brakes of Ford F-Series trucks. These mechanical engineers, versed in chassis dynamics and equipped with elaborate computer and laboratory equipment, build trucks to comply with known standards of safe handling and braking.

WARNING —

Any suspension modification will affect the handling characteristics of your truck. Poor braking, risk of a rollover, loss of vehicle control, chronic failure of driveline parts and marginal braking each can result from improper modifications. Before you consider any modification to your truck's chassis or body height, make safety a priority. Take extreme care when modifying the suspension. When in doubt, always follow OEM standards or the information furnished by a reputable aftermarket equipment manufacturer.

1. CHASSIS MODIFICATIONS

Chassis and suspension engineering provide a challenge with any multipurpose truck. Highway driving,

Fig. 18-1. *Suspension lift kits enable the use of bigger tires, which in turn provide more ground clearance and greater wheel travel. The foremost consideration when "lifting" a truck chassis or body is the change in center-of-gravity and the roll center. These safety issues must be addressed; safety is far more important than looks.*

Fig. 18-2. *Custom fabrication work on this race truck reveals serious engineering and ultra-heavy duty components. A homespun look-alike cannot duplicate the stamina and materials displayed here. For high performance driving, safety must be your ultimate consideration.*

trailer pulling, trail running and hardcore desert racing each call for different chassis dynamics.

Visualize your truck sweeping through corners, fighting a crosswind with a trailer in tow, braking hard, bracing against a loose traction surface or negotiating a precarious, off-camber sidehill. The interaction of the springs, shocks, stabilizers, brakes and tire/wheel mass is a blur. An automotive engineer or race truck fabricator must address each of these conditions.

On the test course or skidpad, a safe truck meets many criteria. Along with center of gravity, terms like Ackerman steering angles, lateral acceleration, roll axis, roll center, roll couple distribution, roll steer and toe change; roll stiffness, shock damping, spring/wheel rate,

Fig. 18-3. *No nonsense in the front suspension department on this Ford F-truck off-road racer. For racing purposes, custom four-link suspension works with Ford OEM 4x4 IFS components to provide 20 inches of wheel travel. This truck, under construction by Mike Scheele at Northwest Off-Road Motorsports, will compete in terrain similar to Baja racers. Engineering is similar to competitive desert race truck systems.*

and vertical load transfer each apply to handling. The frame, suspension and axle design (Hotchkiss, solid hypoid, Mono-Beam, Twin I-Beam or Twin Traction-Beam) also enter the equation.

At speed, aerodynamics and road load add to the burden. Braking is critically dependent upon load distribution and the anti-dive/anti-lift characteristics of the overall chassis design. Tire slip angle also becomes a factor, and the safest truck chassis balances each of these demands into a reasonably compliant package.

Modifying Your F-truck's Chassis

Changes in front end geometry, roll center, center of gravity, unsprung weight and tire design each have an effect on your truck's handling. Ford F-truck engineers generally set up a chassis for good ride, safe steering control and manageable braking. Aftermarket components often meet the additional needs of special terrain, loads and driving conditions.

The better engineered aftermarket spring and shock absorber kits offer substantial improvements for your truck. Additional clearance for specialty tires, improved spring rates, massive shock absorbers and a stouter steering damper shock can make our vehicles far better suited for off-highway perils. Many of these parts enhance the truck's handling and control under a variety of driving conditions.

For some light F-truck owners, trends and fads also motivate chassis modifications. Achieving a certain status may override safety concerns. Poor braking, risk of a rollover, loss of vehicle control, chronic failure of driveline parts and marginal braking characterize the worst modifications.

The Culprits

Unfortunately, some truck owners go far beyond the OEM and aftermarket parts sources, seeking to establish their own records for the highest, biggest, fastest and fattest truck. Without the benefit of engineering credentials or a sense for chassis dynamics, builders of homespun, radically lifted trucks have encouraged the wrath of motor vehicle and public safety administrators.

A large number of improperly modified trucks sport crude and unsafe spacer block lifts, disfigured springs, bound up steering linkage, stretched brake hoses and pipes, overheight bumpers and ridiculous headlamp angles that glare menacingly into the eyes of oncoming drivers.

These same trucks, with massively oversize tires creating an unsprung weight imbalance, have overtaxed brake systems that prevent safe stops. Radically sloped steering linkage and drag link angles, common to poorly constructed chassis lifts, create bump steer. The slightest blip in the road can cause the truck to veer uncontrollably.

Many law enforcement officers are also light truck owners and recreationalists, yet most have a profound bias against radically lifted trucks. Each state's motor vehicle safety offices has files on highway mayhem caused by poorly crafted, radically lifted 4x4 trucks. Horror stories of homespun junk run the gamut, including cases of monstrous 4x4 trucks rear ending other vehicles—with

Fig. 18-4. *Here's an illegal setup by many state standards. Two sets of stacked spacer blocks make up this rear lift. Shifting of blocks and failure under load are possible. Never stack rear spacer blocks. Never install spacer blocks at the front springs.*

Fig. 18-5. *The ride height may look hot, but this front end geometry is unsafe. Note the radical slope angle on the drag link. As springs compress and the solid axle rises, bump steer shifts the wheels to the right.*

the lower edge of the front bumper overrunning the entire trunk of the car!

Equally appalling, some of the homemade street truck chassis systems include hastily slammed or lowered suspension and marginal steering hardware. Personal expression is a fundamental human right; highway safety, however, is a collective responsibility.

State Lift Laws And Accountability

Although a few states have no current laws directly regulating chassis lift or excessively oversize tires, a trend is clear. Federal safety laws, interstate highway funding, and the issues of public liability make each state accountable to the same issues.

The aftermarket suspension and body lift manufacturers have similar accountability. For a reputable company to survive, product liability insurance is essential. The cost of this insurance can become prohibitive. Here, the incentive is a safely engineered kit. A good safety record can effectively reduce product liability and operating overhead.

OEM standards remain the best baseline for safety, as Ford Motor Company and other new vehicle manufacturers must comply with U.S. Department of Transportation (DOT), Society of Automotive Engineers (SAE) and other professional engineering guidelines when constructing their vehicles.

Vehicle lift results from changes in tire size, suspension modifications and installation of body mount spacers. Before investing time and money either raising your truck's body or mounting a set of expensive oversize tires, review the laws for your state.

> **NOTE —**
> If you've heard rumors of a height limit change, consult your nearest state police or highway patrol office for the new rulings. These agencies will prove very helpful. Their primary concerns are public safety and compliance with motor vehicle regular off-pavement Suspension Tuning

2. OFF-PAVEMENT SUSPENSION TUNING

Suspension tuning can enhance off-pavement performance. An upgraded spring and shock absorber package transforms a multipurpose 4x4 into a highly versatile trail machine. The right handling, suspension travel and shock damping provide better vehicle control, stability and greater utility.

Several factors determine the need for spring rate and chassis changes. Conversion to a heavier engine, the addition of a hefty front mounted winch or installing a protective front bumper/brush guard each place a load on the front springs. An oversize fuel tank, heavy duty truck-type manual or automatic transmission, a trailer towing package or heavy fuel and water containers can weight the rear springs.

When your fatigued OEM shocks and sagging springs need replacement, an upgrade spring and shock absorber package can improve your truck's performance. Sagging leaf springs allow the axle housing(s) to rest close to the rubber bump stops. Weak front coil springs (F-100/F-150 models) create more bounce, sagging and loss of steering precision.

Loss of suspension travel means that your truck will have difficulty negotiating twisty terrain. Traction off-pavement becomes poor, with body roll and steering con-

Fig. 18-6. *John Maine's Northwest Off-Road Motorsports produced this Rancho Suspension-based F-150 4x4 pre-runner for the street and fast track desert scene. An H.O. 302 EFI/MPI V-8 and built up C-6 automatic deliver power to the oversized wheels and off-pavement tires. This is as close to street/racing multi-purpose use as you can get.*

Fig. 18-7. *In some suspension kits, wedge-shaped caster shims for the front or rear leaf springs can restore pinion, driveshaft or caster angles. These wedges are sometimes made of aluminum alloy. Steel wedges serve better and are available from NAPA and wheel alignment shops.*

Massachusetts' Suspension Modification Formula

Here's an example of a current lift law as it applies to 4x4 (and other) vehicles and their modification. Massachusetts has devised a formula for allowable mechanical (body and suspension) lift that accounts for both vehicle stability and safe handling: Wheel base multiplied by Wheel Track (the tire tread center-to-center measurement at the wider axle) divided by a factor of 2200. The wheel track width may be increased up to four inches—by way of rim offset only; no wheel spacers allowed.

The test is relatively easy. Suppose your Ford F-truck has a 117" wheelbase and wide rims that provide a 68" tread centerline width (four inch increase over OEM tread width of 64-inches). 117" x 68" = 7956 divided by 2200 = 3.6" lift. Under Massachusetts' Sections 6.04 and 6.05, the tire diameter (based on the largest size available as an OEM option) may also be increased the same amount as the mechanical lift.

Simply, the Ford truck could have tires up to 3.51" larger diameter than stock plus a 3.51" mechanical lift by way of chassis and/or a body lift kit. Accordingly, the body/door sill height could set a total of 5.26" over stock with installation of these wide rims, oversized tires and the mechanical (chassis or body) lift.

Example: If the OEM maximum tire diameter was 31", you could install 34-1/2" diameter tires on a wide offset rim size (two inch wider track/wheel centerline measurement per wheel) and add a 3-1/2" chassis lift kit for tire clearance. Within the Massachusetts formula, the added track width restores the center-of-gravity when you increase suspension height and tire diameter.

All parts must be equal to or better than OEM standards, and the vehicle safety cannot be compromised. Massachusetts has addressed OEM vehicle design, roll center, center-of-gravity and all other handling concerns with this statute. Other equipment on the truck must comply with general safety standards. This is a sound approach, allowing reasonable lifts for both off-pavement and highway usage.

---

trol problems. If the springs and shock absorbers now show these symptoms on your truck, or if modestly oversize tires create tire-to-body interference, consider an aftermarket suspension package.

Aftermarket Suspension Improvements

Your goal should be a reasonably firm spring rate and solid traction—without unduly harsh rebound and overly stiff leaf stacks. Spring rebound damping and deflection control remain vital to maximum traction, yet timid shocks lose effectiveness in just a few miles of trail pounding. The best all around kits have easy ride springs and quality shock absorbers.

From my experience, a mild lift/soft-ride suspension package provides several benefits. Once installed, these kits maintain a legal frame/front bumper height when used in conjunction with 31- to 33-inch diameter tires.

The truck now has greater tire-to-body clearance, a much improved spring rate and better handling, both on-and off-pavement.

> *WARNING —*
> • *Use extreme caution when installing a lift kit or otherwise working under your truck. Always support the truck's frame on jackstands rated for the load. Do not rest the vehicle only on a jack, on cinder blocks or on pieces of wood.*
>
> • *Limit your truck's lift to just that amount necessary for safe tire installation and a full range of suspension travel. Select your tire size with care. Follow practical and safe tire and chassis guidelines, and make certain the wheel rim size is correct for your tires.*

Axle Trusses

Pounding off-pavement can bend or break axle housings. Often, 4x4 owners add stiff spring rates and hefty shock absorbers without concern for the axles. If serious trail running or high performance driving is your truck's lot, consider axle trusses as part of your suspension buildup.

Bill Broyes at Autofab in Santee, California has built a show winning truck. Bill likes Rhino's combination rear axle truss/skid plate, which doubles as a shock mount. Rhino clamps provide a simple installation. Although some axle tube support results from this design, its stronger point is skid plate protection.

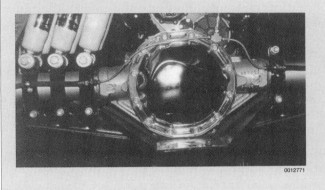

Dana 44 open-knuckle front axle (top right) receives Rhino truss and skid plate combination. Open-knuckle support at axle housing end generally holds up without bracing. This truss design focuses on tube bracing.

Here is a combination skid plate/truss on a 4x4's rear axle. Low running clearance benefits from protection.

NOTE —
Before considering a suspension lift kit, consult your state's lift laws on height and track width limits. Select your chassis lift and tire size accordingly.

Shock Absorbers

Shock absorbers wear out. For some light trucks, the shock absorbers fail fast. Why? Shocks deteriorate from high heat, excess friction and overload—symptoms common to driving on washboard roads and off-pavement poundings.

Most truck shock absorbers look similar, and despite different designs, they each meet the same goals: damping the springs' oscillating motion, limiting the effects of uneven loads transferring to each wheel, and keeping the wheels safely on the ground when the suspension moves violently. This translates as better steering control and an easier seat-of-the-pants ride.

Off-pavement, your truck's suspension travels constantly, with full extension and pounding compression. Damping such forces, the shock absorbers pay severely, often succumbing to leakage or ineffective performance. Driver discomfort and unnecessary chassis or body rattles will usually follow.

Due largely to their off-pavement superiority, gas-filled shocks have become a popular aftermarket item. Hours of jarring through desert washes or pounding along rutted washboard roads will convince most non-gas shock users to make the switch.

The Right Features

When buying replacement shock absorbers for your F-truck, consider a twin-tube type, preferably gas-filled. Piston head size, rod diameter, seal types and valving design determine the strength, reliability and performance of a shock absorber.

Most OEM telescoping shocks offer meager 1" to 1-1/8" piston diameters. Replacement shocks should have pistons of 1-5/16" or larger size. Popular for many years, the 1-3/8" piston head has satisfied all but the most brutal off-pavement maulers and heavyweight haulers.

Severe Duty Shocks

For heavy duty use, look to a nitrogen gas pressurized shock with a 1-5/8" piston diameter. These brute shocks hover around 200 psi, demanding tremendous piston/rod strength. Where a 9/16" or 14mm chrome-hardened rod will do just fine under most driving conditions, shocks like Rancho's RS7000 and others call for a 17.3mm rod, serious enough for real punishment. Complementing this feature, the RS7000 and similar shocks offer superior sealing ability, which also contributes to the shock's life expectancy.

Pistons should be O-ring sealed, cylinders double walled and tough. Larger fluid reservoirs provide better cooling and greater resistance to fading. Lastly, precise valving gives the shock absorber its real advantage. The

Rancho Suspension's RS9000 Shock Absorbers

Rancho RS9000 shocks offer an optional air-actuated cab control system. Standard valving allows quick five-position adjustment at each shock absorber. Air-actuated adjustment kit allows push button driver adjustment from the dashboard.

The term adjustable shock absorber has a variety of meanings. Non-air adjustable shocks mean crawling under your truck, removing the units from the chassis and rotating their housings a number of clicks. Adjusting these kinds of shocks is such a hassle that most users wind up using only one setting.

Rancho Suspension has eliminated these obstacles with its RS9000 shock absorber system. The five-position adjustable shocks offer an easily accessible manual valve for setting the compression and rebound damping. An air-compressor actuated option is also available for cab control of the settings while you drive.

Position 1 provides a good highway ride; 2 makes for slightly firmer control; 3, programmed much like the classic RS5000 shock, offers versatile on-and off-road performance; position 4 addresses light to moderate off-roading; and position 5 provides the heavy off-pavement pounding or trailer lugging mode.

A pin-and-slider design, the adjustable valve enhances a proven cellular gas shock design that features 15-stage valving and an advanced tri-tube, mono-flow design.

I have tested the RS9000 shock absorbers and optional air-actuated adjusting system. Tests exceeded the point where a standard shock absorber fades completely—challenges like running a truck repeatedly through desert dry washes, whoops and a modest simulation of an off-road course.

valve's ability to sense terrain and load demands will determine the shock absorber's worth. Damping properly, the shock absorbers are a basic element in your truck's suspension system.

Shock mounting grommets and eyes must hold up. A loose shock absorber is useless, and a weak set of grommets permits wasted movement and undamped travel. Proper shock absorber angles (a crucial engineering decision) also contribute to handling.

Single Versus Multi-shock Installations

Show trucks, street trucks, lifted trucks and even some OEM suspensions feature multiple shock absorbers. On factory dual-shock installations, the mounting angle and position of the additional shock is vital to the truck's handling. The shocks must counter jarring, chassis/spring oscillation and friction forces along critical paths of frame motion and suspension travel.

Many homespun, multi-shock assemblies defy logic. Few hobbyists have the engineering expertise to properly reposition shock absorbers. Unless looks override every other consideration, do your homework. If your Ford 4x4 F-truck operates off-pavement, begin your suspension buildup around a healthy set of aftermarket replacement shocks.

Urethane Bushings

Polyurethane, a product of mid-1930s German pharmaceutical technology, meets a wide range of automotive chores. Found in dashboards, arm rests, paints, door panels, foam seats and suspension components, urethane meets a host of challenges.

Urethane suspension and roll cage bushings provide the chassis tuning and durability that many desert racers demand. Recreational four-wheelers and street truck builders also benefit from urethane suspension pieces.

Why is urethane desirable? First, unlike rubber products, urethane resists road salt, ozone, gasoline and automotive oils. Precise hardness control provides a variety of stiffnesses for suspension uses. More importantly, urethane offers high resistance to abrasion, yet engineers can factor elasticity into the product during the molding process. Manufacturers of urethane suspension bushings have a large measure of control over the finished product.

The Right Mix For Your Truck's Chassis

Don Bunker, founder of Energy Suspensions in San Clemente, California, comments on the differences in urethane materials. "Obviously," Don notes, "bump stops have to be somewhat soft to perform their duties, where high performance control arm bushings are generally of a

Fig. 18-8. Greg Williams' pre-runner, a support truck for Nelson & Nelson Racing, features rollbar brackets with urethane bushings. Urethane comes in a variety of colors. The correct hardness of finished bushings, however, is far more important than color considerations.

firmer durometer hardness for maximum control. Urethane can be as soft as the Slime toys that kids buy or as hard as a bowling ball!"

Poor ratio mixes create low quality finished products. Noting the disparity between good and poor product, Don Bunker states flatly, "All urethane is not created equal." He cites the bitter experience of early urethane users who broke eyelets loose from their shock absorbers. Although owners often condemned the shocks, the real problem was the bushings. When excessively hard, the urethane acts as rigid as metal. Shock eyes, which actually travel in an arc, can bind up if the bushings are too hard. Eyelets break from the force.

If you upgrade your truck's chassis with urethane suspension bushings, squeak is not uncommon, especially in twisting situations. Several manufacturers have addressed this problem. Some have graphite-impregnated bushings to counter noise and friction.

Urethane Parts Under Construction

There are two methods of urethane bushing production: injection molding and liquid cold pour casting. Injection molding provides the more precise results. Liquid cold pour castings serve in parts that require less critical tolerances.

Aftermarket urethane producers invest substantially in each bushing mold. Molds determine the fitup and ultimate reliability of the parts. Intricate machining is necessary to produce a quality mold. Correct mixture ratios complete the process, while colorful finishes are merely an aesthetic consideration.

NOTE —
When looking for quality in a urethane sleeved bushing, seek out a product with seamless sleeves.

Where Does Urethane Work Best?

Urethane suspension arm, radius rod and stabilizer bushings are popular. Front and rear stabilizers benefit from polyurethane bushings, which allow greater application of force (unlike the loose action of factory rubber bushings).

Polyurethane mounts offer a major gain over factory rubber cab and body mounts. Unlike aftermarket aluminum spacers, which deliver a rigid and harsh ride, urethane can provide firm yet functional suspension while maintaining the alignment of body panels.

Leaf spring bushings, mounting pin kits and most lift kits offer urethane bushings. The trick is to select the right bushings for your particular driving style. Before grabbing the most colorful set off the shelf, consider options like graphite-impregnated products.

If your truck demands more stamina and a finely tuned suspension system, consider the urethane bushing option. The right bushings can drastically improve your truck's steering control and responsiveness.

Installing An Upgraded Suspension Package

In 1980 Ford introduced independent front suspension (IFS) on half-ton 4x4 pickups. The benefits of a smoother ride, better wheel control and more responsive handling have made these later 4x4 trucks popular. A more sophisticated front end geometry, however, has created several obstacles to lifting these chassis.

Although inches of lift can be achieved with various aftermarket lift kits, major engineering weaknesses have also shown up. Primarily due to incorrect radius arm travel or arc, many IFS lift kits create severe bump steer and other control problems.

After exposure to 4x4 suspension systems for many years, I believe that one of the best lift kits available for a Ford F-150 IFS 4x4 is Rancho Suspension's 6420 Suspension System 44 front axle equipped models. The following is a step-by-step procedure for installing the 6420 kit, but the general approach applies to all kits.

The truck used was an ESPN Bronco support crew truck. The full-size Bronco's suspension is nearly identical to that of an F-150 4x4. Installation was by Greg Williams, a topnotch frame specialist who doubles as crew chief with the Nelson and Nelson Racing team. All work was performed at East County Alignment Shop at Santee, California.

Fig. 18-9.   Stock '88 Bronco is a member of ESPN's support crew. Other than oversized wheels and tires, truck had virtually no modifications. This suspension is nearly identical to F-150 4x4.

Installing The Kit

Rancho's instruction sheet states clearly that this is a major job, requiring 10 to 14 hours for completion and requiring both routine and specialty tools. The Rancho parts are very well constructed and finished in either powder coating or cadmium plating. Plans call for use of RS5000 shocks. Another option, if within budget, would be better shocks. Greg stayed with single shocks at the front to provide a better feel for the suspension when fine tuning the system after installation.

Before following Greg's procedure, it's worth mentioning that Rancho knows the home mechanic's needs. Aside from pointers on the proper tools to use and torque

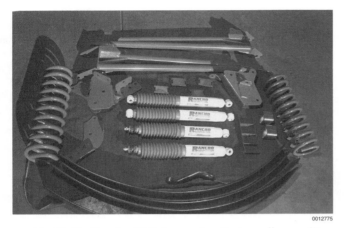

Fig. 18-10. *Rancho 6420 Suspension System offers quality hardware. Long radius arms are an innovative and effective cure for bump steer and other handling quirks.*

settings for every high grade (some beyond Grade 8) bolt and nut included in the kit, safety tips and wheel and tire size requirements are outlined. This was the most thorough installation booklet Greg and I had seen, a real service to the installer.

Necessary modifications to the truck are minimal. Rancho exploits existing holes wherever possible, and the relocated OEM radius arm brackets work well. On other kits that fail to relocate and lengthen the radius arms, off-road bashings often twist the frame rails.

Greg began by supporting the truck's frame securely, with the front wheels suspended slightly. After removing the wheels, he detached and safely tied each brake caliper aside. Although Rancho strongly states that impact tools should not be used for installation of hardware, Greg has found that the severe torque settings on bolts like the radius arm-to-axle housings may require air impact force and six-point impact sockets to avoid breaking your knuckles.

Fig. 18-11. *Greg Williams at East County Alignment begins project by carefully raising the Bronco frame. When removing brake calipers, Greg ties them to spring towers. Protect brake hoses during suspension kit installation. Note short radius arm (arrow) of stock Bronco or F-150 IFS 4x4 suspension. IFS front end has been popular since 1980.*

Greg then detached the steering linkage from the old Pitman arm and steering arms and removed them as an assembly. A special puller can remove the Pitman arm, which Rancho replaces with a dropped arm.

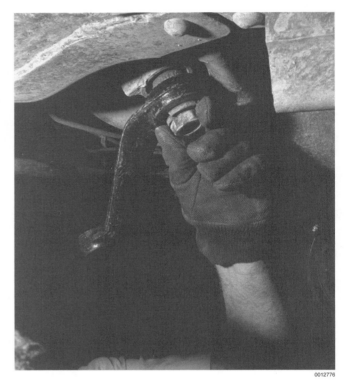

Fig. 18-12. *Rancho provides a dropped Pitman arm. Lower steering linkage will match new position of steering arms.*

Fig. 18-13. *Torque setting on radius arm bolts is tremendous. A six-point impact socket and strong air gun were necessary to safely loosen stud and bolt. Rancho discourages use of air gun for installation of new hardware.*

Fig. 18-14. *Steering linkage may be removed as an assembly. Because this style of Ford tie-rod ends do not use rubber seal-ing boots, Greg could loosen these joints with impact spreader and not damage seals.*

With the stabilizer bar loosened and shock absorbers detached (making certain that all load has been removed from the left spring) Greg unbolted the spring. The left radius arm-to-axle housing bolt, stud and auxiliary shock bracket could then be loosened.

Once he unbolted the shock absorber support bracket, Greg opted to separate the axle assembly. (Rancho instructions had recommended removal of the entire axle subsection, wheel hub to wheel hub, as an assembly.) For many installers, removal of the entire axle assembly as a unit may be practical. Greg, however, is accustomed to working alone, with assistance only when absolutely necessary. The mass of the entire axle assembly is too much for one person to handle.

By disconnecting the front driveshaft and uncoupling the right axle shaft at the sealing boot, Greg was able to detach the left half of the axle. This afforded room for drilling and installing the dropped beam bracket. With the right axle section pulled safely out of the way, the second dropped beam bracket could be aligned, holes drilled, and mounting hardware installed.

NOTE —
In the process of reattaching the power steering cooling tube, Greg fabricated a spacer sleeve to move the tubing away from the new hardware.

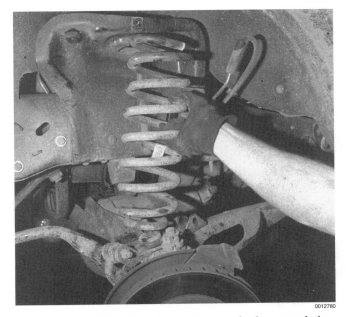

Fig. 18-15. *With coil spring tension completely removed, the spring can be safely unbolted.*

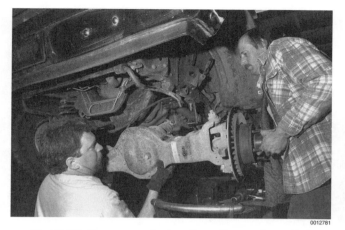

Fig. 18-16. *Two men and a boy time...Greg prefers splitting axle halves and servicing each side separately.*

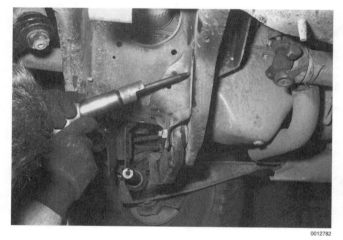

Fig. 18-17. *Removing old axle beam bracket. Air impact tool forces beheaded rivet through the frame. Wear safety goggles when using air tools.*

Fig. 18-18. *Here Greg removes the left radius arm. This part will be replaced with Rancho radius arm.*

While still focusing on the left side of the frame, Greg detached and relocated the left radius arm bracket, following Rancho's measurements precisely. This is the most impressive aspect of Rancho's engineering. By lengthening the radius arms, the arc of travel remains stable and wheel alignment controlled.

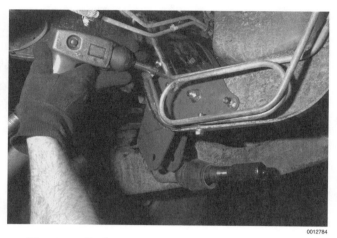

Fig. 18-19. *Replacement radius arm bracket affords lower mounting position. When new bolts interfered with power steering cooling tube, Greg fabricated a spacer to move tube away from hardware.*

Fig. 18-20. *Mounting right side axle beam bracket also requires some drilling. Rancho uses existing holes wherever possible, which eliminates unnecessary drilling.*

Now the left radius arm could be fitted. Here Greg discovered a glitch. Rancho mentioned in their instructions that two radius arm bushing styles exist. The '88 Bronco that Greg had chosen to work on has a shorter radius arm bushing shoulder. Using the original bushings on Rancho's new arms would leave over 1/8" end play in the radius arm.

Greg elected to fabricate a spacer. Using an extra metal cup washer with an inside diameter that clears the bushing step, he added a flat washer that shoulders against the step end (near the threaded section).

Fig. 18-21. Here Greg centers the right axle, then installs pivot bolt.

Fig. 18-22. Top: Be careful when installing new radius arms. Bushing layouts differ, as seen here, and extra space must be addressed. Greg fabricated a step-shouldered pair of washers to eliminate excess clearance. Bottom: Radius arm nut and fabricated step washer viewed from end of relocated frame bracket.

NOTE —

Regardless of installation method, you must address this kind of spacing problem. Otherwise, the radius arms will float endwise, creating less control of the front end and shortening the bushing life. Pay close attention when fitting Ford F-truck radius arms.

Fig. 18-23. Reinstallation of left axle half assembly takes muscle and care. Splined coupler must be reassembled with U-joints in alignment. Coupler seal clamps, removed during disassembly, require replacement.

Now the left axle assembly could be carefully reinstalled. With the right axle pivot bolt in place, two strong men took care to align the right axle shaft U-joints as the splined coupler slid into place. This is an awkward time to align a pair of U-joints, but the job took just seconds. Once the pivot bolt could be installed and the axle secured in the radius arm, the job was well under way.

Next, Greg installed the left spring, a shock absorber, then the brake caliper assembly. (Make sure that the axle's downward travel has been limited before installing

Fig. 18-24. Axle is now free to pivot with new radius arm. Rancho coil spring can be installed easily. Note brake caliper suspended safely to protect brake hose.

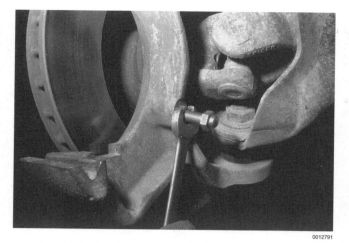

Fig. 18-25. *Steering stops must be changed. Rancho provides two new stops and precise measurements for preliminary adjustment.*

Fig. 18-26. *Steering stabilizer bar links would not fit, so Greg turned each link over and swapped them side to side. The result: Stock appearance and function have been maintained.*

the caliper—Otherwise, you could stretch and stress the brake hose.)

NOTE ——
Longer steering stops, provided in the Rancho kit, are necessary to prevent too much turning arc of the wheels. Greg planned on rechecking the steering limit stops once the wheels and tires could be turned.

With both axle halves secured at their pivots and the left side radius arm and suspension attached, the right side radius arm work was next. Greg unloaded all spring tension, removed the spring, and then the radius arm. Detaching the riveted radius arm frame support, he relocated the bracket rearward. Carefully scribing and drilling the holes for attaching hardware, Greg applied a high speed drill against tough frame steel for the last time.

Once the frame bracket has been installed, the radius arm can be attached at the axle end, then pulled forward for the threaded/bushing end to clear the frame bracket. Greg found the rest of the assembly easy, attaching the new spring, an RS5000 shock absorber and, finally, the brake caliper.

Greg discovered that the stabilizer bar links presented a glaring problem. They would not align with the bar. With his wealth of fabricating experience, Greg quickly sized up the situation. He detached the left and right links, flipped them over, and switched them left side for right. With slight prying to align the attaching bolts, the finished approach took on an OEM look, with the stabilizer bar riding at near ideal height.

WARNING ——
Items like a stabilizer bar are essential to safety and good handling. Be certain to re-use these parts as originally intended. Make sure the fitup allows normal operation, just like before you installed the suspension lift or other modifications.

The last step involved installation of the steering linkage. After securing the castellated nuts, new cotter pins completed the job. Greg smiled and reached for the alignment gauges. With the entire front end completed, his next concern was the effect that the kit had on critical alignment measurements.

Rancho claims that the original alignment settings will be maintained, plus or minus 1/2-degree. This is amazing, considering the inches of lift and alterations that the kit involves. As Greg began taking wheel alignment measurements, he grinned and commented, "Well, they're right on! 8-1/2-degrees positive caster....This ought to handle fine."

In minutes, the toe-in was readjusted slightly and the truck was ready for the rear spring conversion. The rear spring modifications are straightforward, and Rancho's instructions work well here. Add-a-Leaf springs provided with the kit have quite a bit of arch.

Fig. 18-27. *Completed installation, with steering linkage installed, looks ready for a hard day's ride.*

Fig. 18-28. *Caster and camber fell right within factory specs. Toe-in required only minor adjustment. Engineering of this lift kit is tops.*

Greg used all four of the leafs supplied (two per side), but he reduced their arch first to conform to the stock spring contours. Even with a reduced arch, the rear of the truck appeared a bit higher than the front. Greg felt the springs would settle, however, leveling the Bronco.

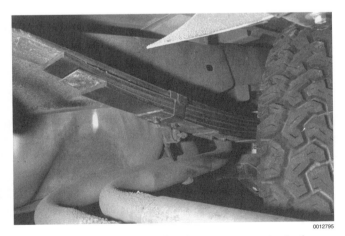

Fig. 18-29. *Rear add-a-leaf springs gave two extra leafs per side. Stock U-bolts could be reused, their threaded sections long enough to compensate for thicker spring stack. When installing U-bolts, tighten nuts evenly and in a cross pattern. At final torque, all exposed threads should be equal length. Recheck U-bolt torque periodically.*

Test Drive

With the rear springs reassembled and new shocks installed, the truck was ready for a run. Immediately clear was the added height. The truck's profile looked great.

Fig. 18-30. Side view of truck with lift kit installed shows slightly extra lift at rear. A few miles of off-pavement pounding reduced the difference as springs began to settle.

Bright red coil springs and radius arms enhanced the appearance as well.

Stepping into the truck, Greg checked the steering wheel position. He made a note to check the centering of the wheel during our test run.

Before the first turn, we realized the improved spring rate. A firmer ride was obvious. After several dips and bumps, Greg commented that a second pair of front shocks would be necessary with the higher spring rate. The Bronco's load capacity had increased with the stiffened springs, and handling was more responsive.

We took the truck through off-road twists and turns, bumps, mild whoops and broad, loose drifts. Greg has pre-run and chased at HDRA/SCORE races (including Baja) for years and is fluent at chassis tuning. He commented that the Bronco worked exceptionally well for an otherwise showroom stock Ford 4x4.

The tractability and steering control felt constant. Firm springs hold the corners at bay, even as the hefty truck pressed into berm edges. On inclines in loose sand, the Bronco resisted wheel hop, its 33" tires holding firmly to the ground.

Greg Williams made this installation look easy, partly because Rancho has done its homework to assure a straightforward installation. Before tackling the job, read the kit's instructions carefully. Decide who's best qualified to install your kit.

3. STEERING GEAR CONVERSIONS

The early 2WD and 4x4 F-trucks offer less efficient worm-and-roller steering gears. Later models use improved recirculating ball manual or power steering gears. The worm-and-roller type steering gears are high in friction and offer shorter service lives than later recirculating ball-and-nut or ball-and-power rack/piston gears.

Ford 2WD trucks changed to recirculating ball steering in the mid-1960s. Within the next dozen years, all 4x4 models made the switch.

NOTE —
Some 4x4 F-trucks offer linkage type power steering assist with a conventional manual steering gear. This is a less desirable means of adding power steering. You could, however, make such a changeover using OEM parts and methods. Many of these service and replacement parts have become difficult to locate.

If your Ford F-truck has worn out another OEM worm-and-roller steering gearbox, you may consider converting to a later integral (recirculating ball-and-power rack/piston) power steering gear. Various retrofit installations have involved passenger car (mostly Lincoln), Ford 2WD F-truck or later 4x4 Ford F-truck steering gear units that will fit the chassis with only minimal fabrication work and also adapt readily—and safely—to your truck's steering linkage.

Your model and year of F-truck will determine which integral power steering gear unit to use. In addition to the steering gear assembly, proper power steering hoses and a matching pump unit with engine brackets and drive pulleys will be necessary.

Retrofitting an integral power steering gear unit may involve welding, fabricating and engineering. If you have limited expertise in this area, do not attempt such a changeover. Seek out a professional shop with experience at this type of conversion, and be sure that they have a working knowledge of the task at hand. Some of the credentials needed for a safe installation include a history of building similar systems on Ford 4x4 F-trucks and also certification as a professional welder. Do not take shortcuts on this kind of work. Safe and predictable steering is a fundamental requirement for your truck.

WARNING —
When converting to modern power steering, do not cut, weld, bend, or otherwise modify steering linkage and other steering components. Find the mix of OEM parts that will enable a safe and straightforward installation.

Choosing The Right Steering Gear

If you make a power or manual steering gear conversion with later OEM steering parts, you must consider the steering gear ratio and related engineering. The quicker (approximately three turns lock-to-lock) gears are entirely too fast for a light truck, and they make a short wheelbase model steer like a sprint race car. Avoid these ultra-quick steering ratios. Follow the ratios offered for a later model F-truck with a similar size chassis.

Length of the Pitman arm or the steering arms also contributes to the final steering ratio. If you have a choice, select a Pitman arm or steering arms that provide good road feel and still offer correct travel of the steering linkage.

CAUTION —

Make sure steering linkage moves freely and on OEM proscribed arcs. Assess how the linkage will react as the wheels turn and as the suspension moves.

When setting up a retrofit steering gear and linkage, keep the steering drag link on a level plane with the tie-rod. This will prevent bump steer. (Check the linkage alignment with the truck setting on flat ground and loaded normally.)

NOTE —

Many 4x4 lift kits contain a raised or dropped Pitman arm (depending on the arm's location and its relationship to the chassis), which can help align the linkage.

Make certain that the steering gear does not reach its full range of movement before the knuckles reach their stops. Hyper-extending the steering gear can severely damage the ball races, nut or power rack. Always make sure that the steering gear is on its center with the front wheels and tires in the straight-ahead position.

CAUTION —

• *Power steering systems require careful engineering. The force of an integral power unit is sufficient to rip a gear loose from the frame. When setting up a power gear and Pitman arm, care must be taken to prevent excess pressure build-up when the knuckles turn against their stops.*

• *Consult factory service manuals for pump and gear pressure specifications. Test your system for correct travel and pressure in all positions.*

4. TIRES

Preparing your truck for a special environment always includes tires. For rock crawling in rough terrain or scaling a wagon road to an abandoned silver mine, you need the right rubber. Ground clearance, superior traction and resistance to rock abrasions each depend on your tire choices.

Wider wheels and oversize tires will affect the handling characteristics of your truck. Take extreme care when selecting your truck's wheels. When in doubt, always follow the recommendations of the manufacturer.

WARNING —

Wider wheels and oversize tires usually require other changes to your truck. Larger tires and wheels may place excessive stress on suspension components, including bearings, hubs, and brakes.

There are mildly and wildly oversize wheels and tires. Oversize tires run anywhere from one or two sizes larger than your stock F-truck rubber to monstrous tires. Concerned with safety and liability issues, the majority of

light truck tire manufacturers limit their maximum tire sizes to 35" diameter.

For highly specialized uses, 36" to 44" tires are available from a small number of producers. An even smaller number of wheel manufacturers cater to the safety standards necessary for handling specialty rubber.

Why is 35" the usual limit? When it comes to mounting massive rubber on a light truck, major tire manufacturers don't have time to conduct safety schools. Product abuse and consumer negligence occur regularly in this realm.

0012797

Fig. 18-31. Wider wheels are necessary with most oversize tires. This 33"x 12.50 x 15 tire mounts on Golden Wheel Corporation's Enkei 89-series one piece alloy rim. Rim bead width is ten inches.

Where Do Monster Tires Serve Best?

Lifted show trucks and boulevard cruisers have monster tires. Are these tires simply an artistic expression? Not always. The 35" to 44" tire is also a workhorse. At highly specialized jobsites, such as logging and mining operations, heavy loads and deep mud packs make a rubber-tire loader cringe. A heavy duty 3/4-or one-ton Ford F-truck, given the unceremonious task of lugging supplies and equipment over miles of primitive road, can benefit from jumbo tires.

Warren Guidry of Interco Tire Corporation comments on the merits of monster tires. "...for 4WD vehicles to obtain their full potential, bigger tires need to be used. Nothing will raise the axles except the tires, which in turn gives greater ground clearance, and this is very important to off-road use."

Fig. 18-32. In the Pacific Northwest logging country, over-size tires have utility value. Here, traction on muddy and rutted roads benefits from large tires, which actually reduce environmental impact when the driver keeps wheel spin under control.

Obviously, there's a limit to monster tire use. These tires, which mount on specially built rims, fit a radically lifted truck. Huge tires require an elaborate spring and body lift for clearance, plus many other modifications to the engine, chassis, geartrain, steering and brakes.

Way Up Has Its Downside

There's a limit to everything. While a certain look and self-expression has its place, mounting huge 100 pound tires on an early Ford F-1 pickup or a '59 Ford F-100 1/2-ton 4x4 overrides all safety considerations. On some light trucks, even a 32" diameter tire can threaten chassis and axle safety and create a precariously high center of gravity.

Making any light truck safe with the mass and unsprung weight of 36–44" tires involves radically altering the track width, brakes, powertrain, steering and suspension. Neither Ford nor any other 1/2-or 3/4-ton capacity light truck builder offers an OEM brake system capable of safely handling the rolling mass of four 44" diameter, 130-pound tire and wheel assemblies.

Furthermore, manufacturers match gearing to their trucks' OE tire diameter. If a Ford F-truck has 30" diameter OE tires and a 3.50:1 axle gear ratio, a switch to 44" tires (if you could ever find a way to fit such a size!)

would require an axle ratio around 5.13:1 to restore the engine's original operating rpm.

The radically lifted 4x4 show trucks have extensive frame, suspension, geartrain and engine upgrades to handle the taller vehicle profile and huge rubber. If you're serious about duplicating this look, don't stop with wheels, tires and a spring lift. Pay attention to the rest of your truck's needs, those engineering measures that will maintain tractability plus safe handling, steering and braking.

Safety First

"The truth is," Warren Guidry notes, "if a vehicle is professionally modified to accommodate larger tires, and if the larger tires are not just taller but also wider, the vehicle can be more stable than when it was stock..."

Guidry concludes, "The wider tire and wheel combination increases the track of the vehicle and adds a tremendous amount of stability. The bigger, wider tires can carry more load with the same air pressure, and because of the greater volume of air are not under the load stresses that the smaller tires have to bear, and are thereby safer."

There's a clear relationship between track width and center of gravity. The savvy state laws, those that aim at restoring a stable center of gravity, suggest the use of a wider track width whenever height changes have been made to a vehicle.

As Warren Guidry suggests, the professional modification of a vehicle takes safety factors into account. If you're unsure of the safety requirements for your truck, consult a race or show truck fabricator who has built his credential around truck safety.

In general, larger tires represent more unsprung weight, which immediately suggests stouter springs, hefty gangs of shock absorbers, added steering stabilization, traction bars or torsion arms and a whole arsenal of heavy duty wheel and brake parts. Oversize brake rotors, pads, rear brake shoes and drums—even heavier drive axles—may be necessary.

CAUTION —
Custom 4x4 trucks that run 39" and larger diameter tires need a full-floating rear axle. The full-floater adds stamina plus better wheel and axle bearing support.

Shock loads transfer back through the entire geartrain to the engine. U-joint upgrades, increased driveshaft wall thickness and/or diameter and other precautions help assure parts survival. Also, by changing axle gearing to restore the original engine speeds, you'll give the manual clutch or automatic transmission a chance to survive. Even so, consider upgrading the clutch or torque converter to handle the extra inertial loads of big tires.

A Tried Trail Running Formula

I've never installed tires larger than 33" diameter on any of my 4x4 trucks, including the 3/4-ton models. I firmly believe that driving skill and a decent tire will handle even the most challenging off-pavement environments. Beyond a mud-bog racer, logging rig or swampland runner, successful traction for your truck is as close as a good tread pattern on a set of moderately oversized tire.

Specifically, I believe that a 31"x10.50x15 tire is plenty for a relatively stock F-100 or F-150 4x4. (This size tire should not require modifying the body or chassis height.) These tires are very popular for this chassis type. Wider and bigger tires, like a 33x12.50x15 will also work on some 1/2-ton 4x4 models, although body clearance does become an issue. At an appropriate load range, these 33" diameter tires will work well on most Ford F-250 or even F-350 4x4s.

The only drawback to a very wide tire on a lightweight truck is the high floatation effect of the wide tire print. Such tires work great on sand, but a narrower tire provides safer traction on ice.

The popular 6.50x16 size tires and narrow wheel rims on early F-100 4x4s teach a good lesson. These trucks, at curb weights of around 4,000 pounds, get exceptional traction in rock and snow. The narrow tire tread places more weight on each tire print. Tread design advantages, a more realistic indicator of traction, have little to do with tire size.

You can choose from a host of tire tread patterns. Fifty years of off-pavement testing, complemented by three decades of desert racing, have produced specialized and multipurpose tread patterns for a wide range of light truck uses.

An extra set of tires, mounted and balanced on spare rims, make a good investment for your truck. Consider a specialized tread pattern that aims at your driving terrain and habits, tires that you can install when you're ready to tackle the rough stuff.

Tire Inflation and Other Safety Concerns

Despite nail holes, rock punctures and other natural hazards of four-wheeling or back country driving, the number one cause of tire blowout is under-inflation. Low tire pressure places tremendous stress on sidewalls and generates unsafe heat levels.

0012799

Fig. 18-33. The B.F. Goodrich Baja T/A tire (right), developed through actual desert racing tests, is an excellent off-pavement performer. Hard compound makes a harsher ride, but sidewall stamina is outstanding in rocky terrain.

Tire Glossary

Bias (Diagonal) Ply—Before radial tires, all trucks rode on bias ply tires. Bias plies run in a diagonal direction to the tire centerline. Plies cross in an X pattern, making a very strong but stiff tire. Today's truck owners demand the better ride and handling of radial ply designs.

Load Carrying Capacity—All highway-legal tires have load capacity ratings (A, B, C, etc.). Inflation pressure, however, affects a tire's load capacity. Ratings apply to each tire size and design. Lower pressures decrease load carrying capacity.

Maximum Inflation—This is a tire's air pressure limit, which influences load carrying capacity. A tire with a load range C and a maximum inflation pressure of 36 PSI may have a 3000 pound rating. This means that the tire can safely support 3000 pounds at 36 PSI inflation. As pressure drops, so does the tire's carrying capacity. Beware.

Ply Rating—Plies are supporting layers of synthetic cord and/or steel built into a tire casing. These layers or belts mold within the tire's rubber. Ply ratings for big radial tires can get confusing. Load range C tires qualify for a traditional 6-ply rating. A closer look, however, may reveal a four-ply tread and two-ply sidewall. Plies also vary in thickness and strength, so evaluate a tire by its load rating, the ply materials and overall construction.

PSI—Pounds per Square Inch refers to the air pressure in your tires. Adding air increases PSI, while airing down reduces pressure. Always maintain your tires at recommended inflation levels. If you drop pressure too low, your tubeless tire may unseat from the rim. Excess air pressure can damage the plies or destroy a bead.

Radial Ply—Belts, whether steel or synthetic cord, circle the tire at a perpendicular angle to its tread centerline. Radial belts flex, allowing the sidewalls to cushion the ride. Tread conforms to the road, providing a better grip. Most new tires, including 36" to 44" monster tires, are radials.

Rim Offset—Wheel rim offset determines track width and frame/tire clearance. Rarely is a wheel's mounting flange aligned with the centerline of the tire. OEM rims offset toward the brakes. Aftermarket wheels should take OEM engineering into account, or stress to wheel bearings, spindles, axle shafts and steering components can occur.

Rim Width—Rim width is the space between the outer faces of the tire beads. This measurement is crucial to safety, and every tire has a rim width requirement. Sidewall and tread shape, the bead angle and even the vehicle's handling depend on rims that correctly match the tires.

Speed Rating—Although most trucks with big tires stay within posted speed limits, speed ratings also indicate a tire's margin of safety. Symbols represent maximum speed: S to 112 mph; T to 118 mph; H to 130 mph; V to 149 mph; and Z over 149 mph. Take heed.

Interco tire, manufacturer of Super Swamper tires, notes, "Do not allow the air pressure to get below 20 PSI regardless of how light the vehicle may be. Pressures below 20 PSI may let the bead of the tire become unseated, especially from lateral forces. An exception is running in soft sand, where you may wish to reduce air pressure below 20 PSI. This should be an emergency procedure only. As soon as possible, pressure must be brought back up. Remember, overloading and/or under-inflation causes excessive heat build up which can cause separation of the tire body."

Like all other tire manufacturers, Interco recommends that you maintain correct air pressure, checking each tire cold at least once a month. (Cold means the truck has parked out of direct sunlight at least 3 hours.)

Match pressure to the weight of your truck and its current load. Remember, maximum load capacity is at the maximum pressure rating for the tire. If you lower the pressure to improve the ride, or for any other reason, load capacity also decreases. Deceptively, big tires stand up easily, so give them more than a glance.

> **NOTE —**
> Invest in a quality tire pressure gauge—cheap gauges seldom read the same pressure twice.

Tire wear depends on proper wheel alignment, inflation pressures, balancing and rotation. Interco recommends tire rotation at 2,500 to 4,000 miles. The traditional pattern of rotation for radial tires has been front-to-rear and rear-to-front. Some manufacturers now recommend a modified cross-rotation method. Consult your tire manufacturer for proper tire rotation procedures.

Many oversize tires benefit from balancing on the truck. When you have your tires balanced with a floor balancer (wheels mounted on the truck), tire rotation involves one more step: Your tires will require re-balancing. Once rotated, or even repositioned on the wheel hub, tire balance changes. Beware!

Installing Your Wheels On The Truck

Your new tires, safely mounted to the correct rim, may be ready to install—but are the OE lug studs and nuts ready? Grossly oversize wheel and tire packages have a lot of mass. Even if your new wheels fit the axle hub flange properly, there's still the matter of stamina. The inertial load may place excess stress on your truck's OE lug studs.

> **WARNING —**
> *Some aftermarket wheel flanges are much thicker than a stock-length OEM lug stud can safely handle. If lug nuts do not fit securely onto the studs, you should install longer lug studs or select another wheel type.*

Ford trucks have used 1/2", 9/16" and 5/8" wheel studs. The typical F-100 or F-150 stud size is 1/2", common to many five-lug light GVWR rated domestic trucks. 3/4-ton and one-ton F-trucks most often use 9/16" and 5/8" thread wheel studs.

> **NOTE —**
> Before mounting a set of monster size alloy wheels and big tires, consider the OEM wheel lug size. Consult your wheel and tire manufacturers for their recommendations. Your tires and wheels may demand an upgrade in either stud diameter or length.

Be sure to tighten the lug nuts securely. Use a torque wrench to prevent under-or over-tightening. Overtorquing is a common cause of wheel damage and stud breakage. Ford and aftermarket wheel manufacturers recommend specific torque settings. (Consult your Ford workshop manual or owner's glovebox handbook for tightening specifications.)

Factory torque settings take load, braking, vehicle weight and stud diameter into account. For safety sake, use a torque wrench whenever possible to verify the torque setting. Always tighten lug nuts gradually and in cross. This prevents distortion of the rim and damage to nut seats.

Choose A Safe Wheel

Big tires increase unsprung mass, raise load capacities and present special mounting concerns. Many OE and aftermarket wheels cannot match the big tire loads. Mickey Thompson/Alcoa and Clement Composite wheels address big tire requirements.

Fig. 18-34. Interco's Swamper series tires make a big impression. The tire has a strong following among 4x4 competition, recreational and show truck users. Traction gains are obvious.

Other wheel suppliers, including Golden Wheel Corporation, Ultra Wheel and American Racing Equipment, satisfy a broad cross-section of user needs. Before selecting wheels, make sure that the load rating and warranty will satisfy your big tire demands.

Sources For Big Specialty Tires

For most four-wheel drive uses, tires built by major tire companies like B.F. Goodrich, Goodyear, General Tire, Michelin, Yokahama or Bridgestone provide excellent selection and tread patterns for back country and multi-purpose use. When your plans lean toward the extraordinary, however, several specialty manufacturers produce 36-44" monster tires.

When shopping for your truck's tires, look closely at construction, ply ratings and the load capacity, not just diameter and price.

Interco's Swamper Tires: The original 78-series Swamper tire has been around for over a quarter century. Originally a 6-or 8-ply bias ply tire, Swamper offers a

Fig. 18-35. Buckshot Radial Mudder provides a high traction option for users who want a narrower wheel width.

Fig. 18-37. The Dick Cepek Radial F-C offers the ride and handling benefits of a radial tire. Radial tires satisfy users who do most of their driving on the highway but still need superior traction off-pavement.

Fig. 18-36. M/T Alcoa aluminum wheels carry a rating for big tires. Load capacity to 3000 pounds and 8", 10", 12" or 14" widths provide margin of safety.

popular tread pattern. Interco also builds grossly oversize tires, including the Super Swamper TSL 36"x12.50-15LT through 18.5/44-15 sizes and a 18.5/44-16.5 tire. These heavy duty bias ply tires with massive lugs and self-cleaning ability meet on- and off-pavement demands for the 4x4 F-truck with an ultra stout, highly modified chassis and appetite for massive rubber.

Super Swamper Radial/TSL tires come in LT315/85R15, 38x15.50R15 and 38x15.50R16.5LT sizes. These are smooth riding, low noise level biggies with a six-ply rating. For severely rugged and rocky terrain, Super Swamper's TSL/SX comes in 36x12.50-15 and 16.5 sizes and rates six plies with a nylon bias body and steel belt reinforcement under the tread. Sidewall lugs protect and add extra traction in ruts and rocks.

Gateway Buckshot and Gumbo Mudders: Campfire talk has the Buckshot Radial Mudder pegged as the hot setup for tall, narrow traction. The QR78-15LT and QR78-16 varieties fit the 36" big tire category, yet they still fit a 7JJx15 or 6.5Hx16 rim. These are tubeless, 6-ply rated tires with a polyester and steel belt cord. Stiff bead areas and provision for studs make the Buckshot a versatile choice, without the need for exotic wheels.

Also available from Gateway are the Buckshot Wide Mudder, Buckshot Metric Radial Mudder and the famed Gumbo Monster Mudders. Gumbo Monster series tires fit the big tire category with easy. These tires begin at 36-inch diameter and grow to 43.6" giants for 15" or 16.5" rims. Tread widths for the 6-ply rated tires range from 10.4" to 14.1", which requires wide rims. For the radial user, the Gumbo Monster Radial Mudder is available in 36–38" sizes with a width of 10.4–10.7" (cross-sections 14.2–15.2"). These radials require 10x15 and 9.75x16.5 rims.

Mickey Thompson Tires/Alcoa Wheels: Mickey Thompson's Baja-Belted polyester and fiberglass belt tires offer an aggressive tread pattern with a soft ride, long wear and Sidebiters for extra traction. The Tall Baja-Belted tire line offers several big tire sizes, including 15/39 and 18/39 for 15" and 16.5" rims.

Mickey Thompson has joined with Alcoa Aluminum to produce the M/T Alcoa Aluminum Wheel. Most wheel manufacturers void their warranties when you mount big tires. Alcoa has engineered these wheels of one-piece forged aircraft aluminum, with a non-porous and leak proof surface. Polished and machined for a 0.020" maximum runout, these wheels have a 2600 or 3000 pound load rating, depending upon application. Available in 15" x 10", 12" or 14" width (3000 pound rated) and 8" width (2600 pound rated), these wheels are available in popular 5- and 6-lug truck patterns.

Dick Cepek Tires: Dick Cepek is a household name among four-wheeling recreationalists. A full line of vehicle and outdoor equipment makes Cepek a one-stop shopping center for four-wheelers. When buyers want tires, Dick Cepek has a full line to match every need.

Radial F-C/Fun Country tires aim at mileage. As a steel belted flotation tire, these tires run quietly, yet the tread design offers self-cleaning. These are legitimate mud and snow tires, much like the popular Fun Country nylon bias-ply design. Dick Cepek's Mud Country I tires can be used for snow plowing or logging trails, while Mud Country II has better flotation characteristics.

Cepek has recently introduced a Super Wide Radial F-C tire available to 38" diameter. These tires concentrate on width, providing all around performance in mud, snow, sand, rock and on the highway. Quietness, an aggressive tread design, steel belts (for a 50,000 mile limited warranty) and tread at least 4" wider than competitors' tires distinguish the Super Wide Radial F-C.

Goodyear—One Big Wrangler RT: Goodyear Tire and Rubber Company is the only major tire producer to offer a tire in the really big category. The Wrangler RT-GC0530 provides a rugged, multipurpose tread design and is available in 36-12.50-16.5 size only. Hummer drivers would recognize this design, as Goodyear developed the tire for military use on this vehicle.

Although Goodyear offers a complete line of Wrangler light truck radial tires, the RT is its only entry in the 36" or larger market. If you're looking for big tires, these load range C biggies may meet your needs. (Order under Goodyear's product code No. 309-552-321.)

Denman Tires Ground Hawg: Denman's line of big tires has a huge following with the 4x4 show truck crowd. The roguish Ground Hawg is a beefy tire, hell-bent on maximum traction. For a flexible tread and superior traction, Denman delivers radial benefits with a deep, self-cleaning tread design. The biggest Ground Hawg tire is 18.5/44x16.5 inches.

5. BRAKE SYSTEM UPGRADES

Years ago, one cure for undersize truck brakes was to retrofit an in-line Bendix Hydrovac booster (common to older medium duty trucks with hydraulic brakes). This fix applies more pressure to the hydraulic cylinders and brake shoes, which also raises the likelihood of either hazardous brake fade or rupture of a fluid seal. This is not the fix for a weak brake system.

Fortunately, even the earliest Ford F-trucks had sufficient brake shoe and drum sizing for their era. In good condition, with the hydraulic system functioning properly and the brake shoe and drum surfaces in top shape, an early Ford F-truck can stop reasonably well.

Before the advent of disc front brakes, a Ford truck with four-wheel drum brakes could match the braking performance of any other light truck in its class. No Ford truck with drum brakes, however, can match the performance of a comparable F-truck with a disc front/drum rear braking system—or better yet, a set of four-wheel disc brakes.

Hydraulic Brake System Improvements

Before 1967, most brake system manufacturers recommended annual flushing and rebuilding of all hydraulic brake cylinders. Although some vehicles tolerate years of neglect without a brake system flush or rubber cup/seal replacement, 4x4s and other off-pavement use trucks are far more susceptible to fluid contamination and parts failure.

Most 1967–up truck tandem master cylinders have air bellows in the master cylinder cap gasket. A bellows gasket completely seals the system and eliminates the need for a master cylinder vent to atmosphere. Problems like moisture, debris, dust and corrosive contamination occur far less often with 1967 and newer Ford F-truck brake systems.

One cure for the early Ford F-truck brake problems is to custom fit a 1967 or newer tandem master cylinder system, including necessary pedal linkage and hydraulic hardware. Such a retrofit could also include a hydraulic clutch master cylinder (if you mount both cylinders on the firewall), a hydraulic clutch slave cylinder and mounting bracket, appropriate clutch linkage and a set of suspended brake and clutch pedals. A modern vacuum brake booster could complete the package.

> **WARNING —**
> *On any hydraulic system modification, make certain that the master cylinder bore and brake pipe sizing can move enough fluid to safely operate the brakes.*

Upgrading or modernizing the wheel brake system of any truck may require special hydraulic system components to meet the demands of a disc brake rotor/caliper conversion or the retrofitting of bigger brake shoes, drums, wheel hubs and wheel cylinders. For baseline engineering, begin with a prototype OEM braking system that will meet your braking demands. Select wheel brake parts and hydraulic components that make up this prototype system. Try to duplicate the complete OEM package to assure a proper match of wheel brake components and hydraulic system parts.

> **WARNING —**
> *Find a safe place to perform braking tests. Determine whether front-to-rear brake system balance (proportioning) is correct. If required, a variety of OEM or adjustable aftermarket proportioning valves are available.*

Manuals and Recommended Books

The Ford Motor Company factory workshop manuals for the F-Series trucks provide official, firsthand information. Highly detailed, with all specifications, the factory workshop manual is your assurance of a professional level, quality repair.

You will find that new manuals are available for more recent year models. The older F-truck manuals cover all body types, powertrains, geartrains and chassis for a given model year. Later factory manuals often require sets, consisting of *Powertrain/Geartrain*, or *Body, Chassis, Electrical*. Models covered in a later factory shop manual usually include the F-150, F-250 and F-350, full-size Bronco and the Super Duty trucks.

See your local Ford dealership's parts department for availability of an F-truck manual. For an older model, you may need to consult a used book source or an automotive literature specialist like Dragich Auto Literature (phone 612-786-3925). Seek out original Ford shop manuals if you want the most accurate and model specific data. Equipped with such a manual, you could confidently rebuild or restore your early Ford F-truck.

Catalogs from Advance Adapters (engine and transmission conversion parts for trucks, including Ford models) serve as useful reference guides for geartrain interchangeability and component applications. Similarly, catalogs from 4-Wheel Parts, Dick Cepek and others offer valuable reference information.

If you want proficiency at pinpoint troubleshooting or upgrading the performance of a later Ford MPI/EFI engine, invest in the Charles O. Probst (SAE) book, *Ford Fuel Injection & Electronic Engine Control* (available through Robert Bentley, Publishers). This text and its useful illustrations takes the earnest lay enthusiast to master technician level at Ford EFI/MPI service and performance. Engineer Charles O. Probst shares his wealth of Ford EFI expertise in an easy to understand format.

For the Ford truck history buff, this ground has been covered best by James K. Wagner in his classic book, *Ford Trucks Since 1905* (Crestline Publishing). Mr. Wagner's work at Ford Motor Company and rich association with Ford truck historians like James B. Bibb has created a sweeping and detailed account of Ford truck product evolution and the company itself. This book is both inspiring and a tribute to Ford trucks of all sizes and shapes. I owe my zeal for Ford trucks to devotees like Mr. Wagner. His *Ford Trucks Since 1905* is must reading for Ford truck loyalists!

Maps And Travel Guides

A variety of map sources and atlas guides serve back country travelers. My favorite references are U.S. Forest Service and B.L.M. topographical maps and the popular state-by-state atlas guides built around these types of maps.

Specialty map sources include the series by Sidekick, which produces a range of maps on California and Baja California four-wheel drive trails. A Sidekick Map details each region, including highlights of local sites, the area's history, minesites, ghost towns, directions from major highways, access costs, camping facilities and public agency offices in the area. Sidekick map/pamphlets are printed on high quality paper stock and include color pictures.

Sidekick
12475 Central Avenue, Suite 352
Chino, CA 91710
714-628-7227

PARTS

Your Ford F-truck is a popular vehicle, and parts availability seldom presents a problem. The local Ford dealer can provide pieces for most 1970s and newer models. Owners of early (pre-1970) Ford F-Series trucks will find a wide variety of parts sources throughout the United States.

In addition to your Ford dealer, retail auto parts outlets can supply tune-up, powertrain and even chassis parts. NAPA provides excellent parts coverage for Ford trucks. Quality filters and oil products are available from NAPA and many other outlets.

For Ford truck geartrain parts sources, Border Parts at Spring Valley, California can supply gear parts for many Ford trucks, including the earliest F-models. 4-Wheel Parts, 4WD Hardware, Inc., Dick Cepek, Inc., and Reider Racing Enterprises also provide geartrain and axle pieces. Each of these outlets can provide OEM-type replacement parts or aftermarket performance components.

Ford truck engine parts are readily available, from the earliest R series 239.4 cubic inch flathead V-8 to the latest Ford MPI powerplants. Popular aftermarket suppliers include TRW, Sealed Power, Dana Corporation, Perfect Circle, Wolverine and Badger.

Axle, Transfer Case and Transmission Service

M.I.T.
1112 Pioneer Way
El Cajon, California 92020
619-579-7727

Holbrook Specialties/4 Wheel Drive Center
115 E. Arlington
Gladstone, Oregon 97027
503-655-4747

Engine/Transmission Conversion Kits

Advance Adapters
P.O. Box 247
Paso Robles, CA 93447
805-238-7000

Engine/High Performance

Advanced Turbo Systems (ATS)
P.O. Box 57547
Murray, UT 84107
801-263-0900
Diesel turbo systems

Camden Superchargers
401M E. Braker Lane
Austin, TX 78753
512-339-4772

Carburetor Specialty Service
P.O. Box 762
Rockwall, Texas 75087
214-722-8333

Clifford Performance Products
2330 Pomona-Rincon Road
Corona, CA 91720
714-734-3310
Inline six-cylinder specialists

Dyers Machine Service, Inc.
7665 W. 63rd Street
Summit, IL 60501
312-496-8100
Superchargers

Edelbrock
2700 California St.
Torrance, CA 90509
213-781-2222
Manifolds, camshafts, carburetors

Flex-A-Lite Fans
P.O. Box 9037
Tacoma, WA 98409
206-475-5772
Engine and transmission cooling

Gale Banks Engineering
546 Duggan Avenue
Azusa, CA 91702
818-969-9605
Diesel/gasoline engine performance

Hypermax Engineering, Inc.
255 E. Route 72
Gilberts, IL 60136
708-428-5655
Diesel engine performance

J&S Engineering (Electronics)
Box 2199
Garden Grove, CA 92642-2199
714-534-6975
Electronic spark retard system

J. Bittle American/Ford Specialists
9630 Aero Drive
San Diego, CA 92123
619-560-2030
Ford performance parts

Jacobs Electronics
500 N. Baird St.
Midland, TX 79701
800-627-8800
Ignition specialty items

K&N Engineering
P.O. Box 1329
Riverside, CA 92502
714-684-9762
Filtration products

Kaufman Products, Inc.
12400 Benedict Ave., #3
Downey, CA 90242
310-803-5531
Motorsport/302/5.0L V-8 specialists

MSD/Autotronic Controls Corp.
1490 Henry Brennan Drive
El Paso, TX 79936
915-857-5200
Ignitions

Motor City Flathead
13624 Stowell
Dundee, MI 48131
B&M flathead V-8 blower kits

Paxton Superchargers
1260 Calle Suarte
Camarillo, CA 93012
310-450-4800

Racer Walsh/SVO Dealer
5906 Macy Avenue
Jacksonville, FL 32211
904-743-8253

Racing Head Service/RHS
3410 Democrat Road
Memphis, TN 38118
901-794-283
Custom engines and buildup kits

Speed-Pro Performance/Sealed Power
100 Terrace Plaza
Muskegon, MI 49443
616-724-5688
OEM/high performance components

Trick Flow Specialties
259 E. Main Street
Smithville, OH 44677
216-669-2838

The Turbo Shop
940 W. Manchester Boulevard
Inglewood, CA 90301
310-215-0147

Vortech Engineering
5351 Bonsai Avenue
Suite 3
Moorpark, CA 93021
805-529-9330
Blower systems

Exterior Trim, Tops, Light Bars,
Roll Cages, Seat Harnesses, Misc.

A & A Specialties
220 E. Santa Fe Avenue
Placentia, CA 92670
714-993-6770
Running boards

Air Lift Company
P.O. Box 80167
Lansing, MI 48908-0167
1-800-248-0892
Air springs

Aris
69045 U.S. 131 South
White Pidgeon, MI 49099
616-483-7631
Running boards

Auto Avionics Instrument Research
P.O. Box 293
Monmouth, NJ 07750-0293
1-800-334-4913
Gauges

Autotech
P.O. Box 4161
San Leandro, CA 94579-0161
510-483-7403
Spare tire covers

Auto Ventshade Company
3571 Broad Street
Chamblee, GA 30341
1-800-241-7219
Protective trim

Beachwood Canvas Works
39 Lake Ave.
Island Heights, NJ 08732
908-929-3168
Restoration canvas and upholstery

Bell Auto Racing
Route 136 East
Rantoul, IL 61866
217-893-9300
Harnesses/safety equipment

Bestop, Inc.
2100 W. Midway Blvd.
Broomfield, CO 80038
303-465-1755
Cab consoles

Bloomfield Manufacturing Company
P.O. Box 228
Bloomfield, IN 47424
812-384-4441
Hi-Lift Jack, tie-downs, ramps

Bushwhacker
9200 N. Decatur
Portland, OR 97203
503-283-4335
Fender flares, protective trim items

California Car Cover Company
21125 Superior Street
Chatsworth, CA 91311
818-998-2100
Car covers

Cargo Trapp Industries
9824 Blackburn
Livonia, MI 48150
313-458-TRAP
Cargo tie-downs

Colorado Consoles
1024 E. Costilla
Colorado Springs, CO 80903
719-528-8190
Cab consoles

Corbeau U.S.A.
4284 Valley Fair Street
Simi Valley, CA 93063
805-582-0517
Custom seats

Country Craft
P.O. Box 62
Norco, CA 91760
714-279-4360
Running boards

Crossville Rubber Products
P.O. Box 729
Crossville, TN 38557
1-800-BED-MATT
Bed mats

Dee Zee Mfg.
P.O. Box 3090
Des Moines, IA 50316
515-265-7331
Running boards

Deflecta-Shield Corporation,
14 E. Jefferson Street
Corydon, IA 50060
1-800-247-2440
Front shields/guards

James Duff Enterprises
P.O. Box 696
Sequim, WA 98382
206-683-2160
Suspension upgrades

Fibernetics
1418 S. Alameda Street
Compton, CA 90220
213-639-9870
Running boards

Filler Products
9017 San Fernando Rd.
Sun Valley, CA 91352
818-768-7770
Racing safety equipment

Forrest Tool Company
P.O. Box 768
Mendocino, CA 95460
707-937-2141
"Max" 7-in-1 tool

Fox Enterprises
P.O. Box 1126
St. Charles, IL 60174
708-513-9010
Fox Weatherboot footwell liners

Gladney Brothers
P.O. Box 2458
Apple Valley, CA 92308
619-240-9500
Cab consoles

Grant Products
700 Allen Avenue
Glendale, CA 91201
213-849-3171
Steering wheels

Hobrecht
15632 Commerce Lane
Huntington beach, CA 92649
714-893-8561
Roll cages/steel tubing products/
running boards

Hoese Corporation
P.O. Box 41
Bulverde, TX 78163
512-438-2211
Cab consoles

Hooker Industries
P.O. Box 4030
Ontario, CA 91761
714-983-5871
Running boards

J & J Enterprises
5498 Mission Blvd.
Ontario, CA 91762
714-628-5679
Running boards

J-Mark
Ranchview Lane
Minneapolis, Minnesota 55447
612-559-3300
Running boards

J.T.M. Industries
Danville, WA 99121
604-442-3031
Steel mesh headlamp guards

Kaddy Shack
2736 Polkville Road
Shelby, NC 28150
1-800-752-7808
Cab consoles

KC HiLites
Avenida de Luces
Williams, AZ 86046
602-635-2607
Adhesive-mount auxiliary lighting

Keiper/Recaro
905 W. Maple Rd.
Ste. 100, Clawson, MI 48017
313-288-6800
Seating

Leer
28858 Ventura Drive
Elkhart, IN 46517
1-800-321-LEER
Truck caps (590 LX)

Lund Industries
9055 Evergreen Blvd.
Minneapolis, Minnesota 55433-6042
612-780-2520
Running boards

Luverne Truck Equipment
1200 Birch Street
Brandon, SD 57005
605-582-7200
Running boards

Mastercraft/Miller Industries
3305 Rio Vista Drive
Bonita, CA 92002
619-472-1954
Seats, off-road accessories

McGard
3875 California Road
Orchard Park, NY 14127
Wheel and tailgate locks

Mercury Tube/Grizzly
1802 Santo Domingo Ave.
Duarte, CA 91010
1-800-253-2859
Steel tubing bumpers/utility
products/running boards

Off Road Performance
10808 Santa Fe Avenue
Lynwood, CA 90262
310-537-2790
Go Rhino! brush guards

Penda Corporation
P.O. Box 449
Portage, WI 53901-0449
1-800-356-7704 (WI is 1-800-362-7611;
Canada is 1-800-343-2469)
Bed liners

PIAA Corporation
15370 SW Millikan
Beaverton, OR 97006
503-643-7422
Auxiliary lighting

P-R, Inc.
6251 Schaefer Unit 1
Chino, CA 91710
714-590-2555
Cab consoles

Premier Power Welder
P.O. Box 639
Carbondale, CO 81623
303-963-8875
On-board Welder

Pull-Pal
P.O. Box 639
Carbondale, CO 81623
1-800-541-1817
Shovel/anchor for winching

Quality "S"
P.O. Box 23910
Phoenix, AZ 85063
Running boards

Schroth (See your local performance
parts outlet)
Safety harnesses/rally belts

Ryken Advance Design
P.O. Box 515
Walled Lake, MI 48390
313-669-3232
Sport bars

Smittybilt
2090 California Ave.
Corona, CA 91719
714-272-3176
Roll cages/steel tubing products/
running boards

SNUGTOP
1711 Harbor Avenue
Long Beach, CA 90801
310-432-5454
Pickup tops

Steel Horse Automotive
1200 W. Walnut Street
Compton, CA 90220
1-800-533-7704
Cab consoles

Stull Industries
1140 California Ave.
Corona, CA 91719
714-371-4561
Running boards

TMI
P.O. Box 7160
Torrance, CA 90504
213-978-2825
Cab consoles

TRW (See your local performance
parts outlet)
Safety harnesses/equipment

Tuff Products
1100 Simms Street, #F
Golden, CO 80401
303-233-5785
Cab consoles, security boxes

VDO Instruments
980 Brooke Road
Winchester, VA 22601
703-665-0100
Gauges

Wolf Automotive
201 N. Sullivan Street
Santa Ana, CA 92703
714-835-2126
Cab consoles

Wrangler Power Products
P.O. Box 12109
Prescott, AZ 86304
602-717-1771
Electrical systems/accessories

Free-wheeling Front Hubs, Winches

HUB-A-LERT
4x4 Specialty Products
P.O. Box 813
Highland, CA 92346

Ramsey Winch Company
1600 N. Garnett
Tulsa, OK 74116
918-438-2760

Warn Industries
13270 S.E. Pheasant Court
Milwaukie, OR 97222
503-786-4462.

Rare, OEM and Restoration Parts

Antique Auto Parts, Inc.
9109 E. Garvey Avenue
Rosemead, CA 91770

Autofab
10996 N. Woodside
Santee, CA 92071
619-562-1740
Body, fiberglass

Archer Brothers
19745 Meekland Ave.
Hayward, CA 94541
415-537-9587

Border Parts
3875 Bancroft Drive
Spring Valley, CA 92077
619-461-0171
Geartrain pieces

Charley's Off-Road Center
14190 E. Firestone Boulevard
Santa Fe Springs, CA 90670
1-800-922-4111
Body panels and more

Dennis Carpenter Ford Reproductions
P.O. Box 26398
Charlotte, NC 28213
704-786-8139

Dick Cepek, Inc.
17000 Kingsview Ave.
Carson, CA 90746

Green Sales Co.
427 W. Seymour Ave.
Cincinnati, OH 45216
513-761-4743

Joblot Automotive, Inc.
Ford Parts Specialists
98-11 211th Street
Queens Village, NY 11429
718-468-8585

Bar S Fiberglas Products
3753 Scripps Way
Las Vegas, Nevada 89103
702-871-1941

K C Obsolete Parts
3343 N 61
Kansas City, KS 66104
913-334-9479

Obsolete Ford Parts Co.
P.O. Box 787
Nashville, GA 31639
912-686-2470.
Coverage from '48-'72 and serves both
the F100 and F250 trucks

Ohio Light Truck Parts Co.
217 W. 3rd Street
Dover, OH 44622
216-343-7791 or 1-800-333-3536

Sam's Vintage Ford Parts
5105 Washington
Denver, CO 80216
303-295-1709

Sarafan Auto Supply, Inc.
23 N. Madison Ave.
Spring Valley, NY 10977
914-356-1080

Vintage Ford and Chevrolet Parts
3427 E. McDowell Road
Phoenix, AZ 85008
602-275-7990

Restoration and Specialty Tools

Eastwood Company Tools
Box 296
Malvern, PA 19355
1-800-345-1178

Easco/K.D. Tools
(Contact Eastwood Company or your
local tool supplier)

Suspension/Chassis

Air Lift Company
P.O. Box 80167
Lansing, MI 48908-0167
517-322-2144
Air suspension kits

East County Alignment
10741 Woodside Ave.
Santee, CA
619-562-4110

Energy Suspension Systems
960 Calle Amanecer
San Clemente, CA 92672
714-361-3935
Urethane bushings

Heckethorn Off Road
P.O. Box 526
Dyersburg, TN 38024
901-285-9000
Shocks/steering stabilizers

JT Industries
8157 Wing Avenue
El Cajon, CA 92020
619-562-3390
Urethane bushings

Rancho Suspension (USA)
6925 Atlantic Ave.
Long Beach, CA 90805
213-630-0700
Complete suspension packages

Rough Country
443 W. Alemeda
Tempe, AZ 85282
602-894-1530
Suspension kits

Rugged Trail/Division of Warn
Industries (See Front Hubs)
Suspension kits

Skyjacker
P.O. Box 1878
West Monroe, LA 71291-1878
318-388-0816
Suspension kits

Superlift
211 Horn Lane
West Monroe, LA 71292
318-322-3458
Suspension kits, traction bars, SEMA
award winning steering linkage system for lifted F-150 IFS 4x4s

Trail Master
649 E. Chicago Road
Coldwater, MN 49036
517-278-4011
Suspension kits

Tuff Country (TCI)
P.O. Box 27944
Salt Lake City, UT 84127-0944
1-800-288-2190 (orders only)
Suspension kits

Tires

Bridgestone Tire
See your local dealer

Dunlap & Kyle Co.
P.O. Box 720
Batesville, MS 38606
601-563-7601

Dick Cepek, Inc.
17000 Kingsview Avenue
Carson, CA 90746

Denman Tire Corporation
216-898-5256

The Goodyear Tire & Rubber
Company
See your local dealer

B.F. Goodrich T/A
See your local dealer

Interco Tire Corporation
P.O. Box 486
Rayne, LA 70578
318-334-3814

Mickey Thompson Performance Tires
P.O. Box 227
Cuyahoga Falls, OH 44222
216-928-9092

Manual Clutch and Automatic Transmission

A-1 Automatic Transmissions
7359 Canoga Ave.
Canoga Park, CA 91303
818-884-6222

Art Carr Transmissions
10575 Belcher River Ave.
Fountain Valley, CA 92708
714-962-6655
Automatic transmission specialists

B&M Automotive
9152 Independence Ave.
Chatsworth, CA 91311
818-882-6422
Automatic transmission specialists

Centerforce Clutches
7171 Patterson Drive
Garden Grove, CA 92641
714-898-4477
Manual clutch and flywheel

Appendix 1: Sources

Regional Four-wheel Drive Associations

Arizona State Association Of 4-wheel Drive Clubs
P.O. Box 23904
Tempe, AZ 58282
602-258-4BY4

California Association Of 4-wheel Drive Clubs
2856 Arden Way, #231
Sacramento, CA 95825
916-974-3984

Colorado Association Of 4-wheel Drive Clubs
P.O. Box 1413
Wheat Ridge, CO 80034
303-321-1266

East Coast 4-wheel Drive Association, Inc.
101 South Miami Avenue
Cleves, OH 45002
513-941-1450

4-wheel Drive Association Of British Columbia
Box 284 Surrey, B.C. V3T 4W8
604-590-1502

Great Lakes 4-wheel Drive Association
13911 Townline Road
St. Charles, MI 48655
517-865-6983

Indiana 4-wheel Drive Association
2203 Osman Lane
Greenfield, IN 46140
317-326-2329

Midwest 4-wheel Drive Association
W 762 State Road 23 and 49
Green Lake, WI 54941
920-748-7852

Montana 4x4 Association, Inc.
516 N. 4th
Bozeman, MT 59715
406-587-8307

Pacific Northwest 4-wheel Drive Association
948 18th
Longview, WA 98632
800-537-7845

Southern 4-wheel Drive Association
Box 3473
Oak Ridge, TN 37831
815-482-6912

Utah 4-wheel Drive Association, Inc.
P. O. Box 20310
Salt Lake City, UT 84120
801-250-1302

Virginia 4-wheel Drive Association
P.O. Box 722
Mechanicsville, VA 23111
804-883-6115

Wisconsin 4-wheel Drive Association
203 Greunwald Ave.
Neenah, WI 54956
414-722-3777

United Four-wheel Drive Associations
105 Highland Ave.
Battle Creek, MI 49015
1-800-44-UFWDA

HARDWARE GRADING

Selecting safe, correct hardware is a vital part of any truck repair. New fastener upgrades and liquid thread locker can affect torque settings. When you follow torque guidelines, clean all hardware thoroughly and note whether the tightening torque is for dry or lubricated threads.

WARNING —
- *Lubricating the threads will alter torque settings. Liquid thread locking compound creates slight drag. You must increase torque settings, using the manufacturer's recommendation, to overcome this drag.*

- *Some automotive assemblies call for high grade steel hardware screwed into softer alloy threads. In such a case, tightening to the bolt's maximum torque allowance may exceed the strength of the casting's alloy threads. This could result in stripped casting threads. Always adhere to the OEM recommended torque settings for such an assembly.*

In your Ford F-truck factory shop manual, "Torque Charts" appear at the end of each repair section. Below is a typical OEM standard torque specifications and bolt identification chart that provides maximum torque settings for bolts not listed in your repair sections.

Unless otherwise noted in official Ford Motor Company references, maximum torque specifications reflect the use of clean and dry threads. Reduce torque by the OEM's recommended percentages when threads are lubricated with engine oil.

Bolt Torque

Bolt size	Grade 5		Grade 8	
	Nm	ft-lb (in-lb)	Nm	ft-lb (in-lb)
1/4-20	11	(95)	14	(125)
1/4-28	11	(95)	17	(150)
5/16-18	23	(200)	31	(270)
5/16-24	27	20	34	25
3/8-16	41	30	54	40
3/8-24	48	35	61	45
7/16-14	68	50	88	65
7/16-20	75	55	95	70
1/2-13	102	75	136	100
1/2-20	115	85	149	110
9/16-12	142	105	183	135
9/16-18	156	115	203	150
5/8-11	203	150	264	195
5/8-18	217	160	285	210
3/4-16	237	175	305	225

Inch		Metric	
5/16 – 18		M8 X 1.25	
Thread major diameter In inches	Number of threads per inch	Thread major diameter in millimeters	Distance between threads in millimeters

Metric Thread and Grade Identification

Metric and SAE thread notations differ slightly. Common metric fastener strength property classes are 9.8 and 12.9 with the class identification embossed on the head of each bolt. Some metric nuts will be marked with single digit strength identification numbers on the nut face.

SAE strength classes range from grade 2 to 8 with line or dot identifications embossed on each bolt or nut head. Markings corresponding to two lines less than the actual grade. For Example: Grade 8 bolt will have 6 embossed lines on the bolt head.

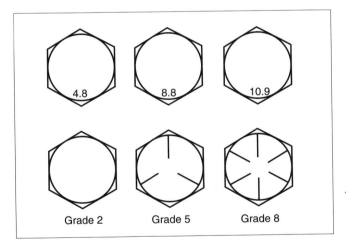

On metric bolts (top), the identification/class numbers correspond to bolt strength. Higher numbers represent an increase in strength. For SAE classified bolts (bottom) markings on top of bolt or nut head indicate grade. More marks or dots represent an increase in tensile strength. The number of marks is always 2 less than the actual grade classification.

APPENDIX 2: HARDWARE GRADING

Metric Hex Head Cap Screws

	Property Class 8.8		Property Class 9.8		Property Class 10.9		Property Class 12.9	
	Suggested Assembly Torques in Foot-Pounds (Inch-Pounds)							
DIA	Dry threads	Lubricated threads	Dry threads	Lubricated threads	Dry threads	Lubricated threads	Dry threads	Lubricated threads
M4	(27.5)	(17)	(30)	(18)	(38.5)	(24)	(53)	(32.5)
M5	(56.5)	(33.5)	(61)	(37)	(78)	(47)	(107)	(65)
M6	(95)	(57.5)	(103)	(61)	(132)	(79)	(180)	(109)
M8	19	12	21	13	27	16	37	22
M10	39	23	42	25	53	32	73	44
M12	67	40	73	44	92	55	127	76
M14	107	64	116	69	148	89	203	122
M16	167	100	181	108	230	138	316	190
M20	325	195	352	211	449	269	617	370
M24	562	337	609	366	775	465	1066	640
M30	1117	670	1210	726	1540	924	2188	1271

Some metric hardware has found its way into late model trucks. Note one hardware manufacturer's maximum recommended torque settings for metric cap screws. By comparing torque limits and load capacities with U.S. graded bolts, you can determine the approximate strength of metric hardware.

The chart lists maximum torque settings for a given bolt, which may not be the right torque for a particular application. Aluminum and other soft alloy threads, for example, tolerate far less tightening torque than cast iron.

If you are tightening bolts into threads in an aluminum alloy casting, use caution. When a torque setting is not available, find specifications for an aluminum threaded parts assembly with the same size threads. It's reasonably safe to follow the torque setting for that component. Tighten all bolts gradually and in cross sequence.

On metric bolts (top) identification class numbers correspond to bolt strength. Increasing numbers represent increasing strength. On SAE classified bolts (bottom) markings on top of bolt head indicate grade. Increasing number of marks represents increasing grade, and number of marks is always 2 fewer than strength classification.

TRAILSIDE TOOLBOX AND SPARE PARTS KIT

Your properly maintained Ford F-Series truck might never break in the back country. Yet for long trips, like the Alaska Highway, Baja California or the Far North, bringing along a full set of tools and spare parts can safeguard your adventure and provide a reasonable level of self-reliance.

CAUTION —
Store your tools and spare parts safely and securely. Take into account the worst case scenario, the possibility that your truck could break in desolate country. Under such conditions, you would need quick access to your winching accessories or tools.

On-board Tools for Remote Trailside Fixes

1. A complete socket set
2. A full set of common hand tools
3. Oil filter wrench
4. Compact volt-ohmmeter
5. Induction ammeter and starter current meter
6. Flare nut wrench set
7. Plumber's small chain wrench
8. Snap ring plier set
9. Front wheel bearing spindle nut wrench
10. Pry bar
11. Vacuum gauge
12. Compact timing light
13. Wire repair kit and crimping pliers
14. Tubing flare tool and repair kit
15. Grease gun with chassis lube
16. Enough tools to break down and repair a tubeless tire
17. Air compressor
18. On-board welder
19. Jacks for tire repairs and transmission/axle work

Spare Parts for the Long Trail

1. Fuses, light bulbs and at least one headlamp
2. 25-foot rolls of 12-, 14- and 16-gauge automotive wire
3. Two rolls of electrical tape
4. Solderless crimp connectors and terminals
5. Roll of duct tape
6. Package of radiator and gas tank repair putty
7. Fuel hose and spare clamps
8. Spare drive belt(s)
9. Upper and lower radiator hoses
10. Thermostat and housing gasket
11. Tubes of silicon gasket sealant
12. Tube of metal mender (Permatex's LocWeld or equivalent)
13. Exhaust system patch kit
14. Thread locker
15. Teflon tape
16. Clean brake fluid
17. A fuel pump and pump gasket
18. Roll of mechanic's wire
19. Spare tire valve stems
20. Patch kit for repairing tubeless (radial or bias ply) tires
21. Spare universal joints
22. Front wheel grease seals (full-floating axles and wheel hubs)
23. At least one oil filter and enough oil for a crankcase refill
24. An oversized and self-tapping oil pan drain plug
25. Two squeeze bottle quarts of gear lubricant
26. Wheel bearing grease
27. Clean rags or shop towels
28. Fuel filter(s)
29. Air cleaner element
30. Spare fuel and potable water (minimum 5 gallons of each), ignition distributor cap, rotor, points or module
31. Ignition spark plug wire set
32. Carburetor float and air horn gasket
33. Water pump and gasket
34. Suitable fire extinguisher(s)
35. Axe, bucket, shovel
36. Backup C.B. radio

CAUTION —
Always carry a quality first aid kit and safety flares. Stow a ground cloth, shelter materials and rope for setting up an emergency habitat. Freeze dried or canned rations will provide a means for survival in the event that your truck becomes stranded.

NEW OR REBUILT ENGINE BREAK-IN PROCEDURE

There is little information available on the proper break-in of a new or freshly rebuilt engine. Your truck engine's performance and longevity depend upon correct break-in. The following procedures are those recommended by Sealed Power Corporation, a major supplier of parts to the engine remanufacturing industry.

CAUTION —

These run-in schedules are good basic procedures to follow for engine break-in. They are recommended as a practical guide for engine rebuilders who are not advised of specific factory run-in schedules. If available, follow OEM guidelines for engine break-in.

Engine Run-in Procedure (engine in vehicle)

Before starting the engine: Make preliminary adjustments to the carburetor or diesel injection system where applicable, adjust tappets and set ignition timing. Always install new oil and air filters. Prime the engine lubrication system before attempting to start the engine. Clean crankcase ventilation components—breathers, road draft tubes or positive crankcase ventilation system. Carefully check coolant and crankcase oil levels.

CAUTION —

When an engine is started for the first time, the most common cause of bearing scuff and seizure is a dry start. This can happen in the short length of time before the oil, under pressure, is delivered to bearings and other vital parts. Pre-priming the oil system can be accomplished with a pressure tank or pre-lubricator attached to the system or by mechanically driving the oil pump to supply the necessary oil throughout all oil passages.

Initial Starting Steps (before run-in schedule)

1) Start engine and establish throttle setting at a fast idle (1000 to 1500 RPM) and watch oil pressure gauge. If oil pressure is not observed immediately, shut engine down and check back on assembly of oil pump and lubricating system. When engine running is resumed, continue at the fast idle until coolant reaches normal operating temperature.

2) Stop engine and recheck oil and water levels.

3) Make necessary adjustments to carburetor (or injectors), ignition timing, tappets, fan belt tightness, etc.

4) Retorque cylinder heads following engine manufacturer's recommendations.

5) Check for oil and coolant leaks, making corrections where necessary.

Run-in Schedule for Light and Medium Duty Trucks

Set engine at a fast idle. Put vehicle under a moderate load and accelerate to 50 miles per hour with alternate deceleration. Continue this intermittent cycling under this load for at least 50 miles. Additional time is desirable.

Note: Harmful Practices

(A) Avoid lugging under any load condition. Lugging exists when the vehicle does not readily respond as the accelerator is depressed. The engine speed being too low, does not allow the engine to develop sufficient horsepower to pull the load. (Keep rpm up.)

(B) Avoid long periods of idling. Excessive idling will drop engine temperature and can result in incomplete burning of fuel. Unburned fuel washes lubricating oil off cylinder walls and results in diluted crankcase oil and restricted (poor) lubrication to all moving parts. The relatively dry cylinder walls depend upon oil throw-off to lubricate them and a speed above a slow idle is necessary for this. Long idling periods produce glazing of cylinder walls, detrimental to ring and cylinder wall seating.

(C) Avoid stopping engine too quickly. When an engine has completed the test run-in schedule or at any time it becomes heavily worked, it is a good policy to disengage the load from the engine and decelerate gradually. Allow it to idle a few minutes before turning the ignition to the off position.

The few minutes of idling will allow the engine to cool gradually and promote a desirable dissipation of heat from any localized area of concentrated temperature. Such good practice avoids the rapid cooling that can cause valve and seat warpage, block distortion, etc.

Engine Run-in procedure (engine on dynamometer)

See chart on next page.

Engine Run-in procedure (engine on dynamometer)

NOTE —

Note: Follow necessary preliminary procedures outlined for engine in vehicle.

Gasoline Engines: Light Truck and Passenger Car

Stage of test	Complete test cycle of dynamometer break-in						
	1st	2nd	3rd	4th	5th	6th	7th
RPM	800—1200	1500	2000	2500	3000	3000	800
Manifold vacuum in inches of mercury	No load	15 in.	10 in.	10 in.	6 in.	Full load	No load
Time limit	Warm-up 10 min.	10 min.	15 min.	15 min.	15 min.	5 min.	3 min.

RULES AND REGULATIONS FOR 4X4 VEHICLE TRIALS

Revisiting the Rubicon in the summer of 1988, I saw many four-wheelers place unnecessary stress on both their machines and the environment. It was clear that these drivers believed a heavy throttle and plenty of power were the only ways to overcome this brutal trail. Believing very strongly that the opposite is true, I sought a useful way to illustrate my point.

In the ensuing months, I carefully drafted a guideline for 4x4 Trials, a competitive event that discredits a driver for displaying wheelspin, misusing power or failing to maintain smooth progress in rough terrain. As the concept unfolded, California Association of 4WD Clubs' Central District (CA4WDC) endorsed the idea of a pilot competition at the 1989 Molina Ghost Run.

I worked with Bruce Swanson and other Central District members at constructing a special course, and we officially established our first 4x4 trials event. The participant drivers and crowd showed real enthusiasm for the project, and we realized that the program could work.

At the 1990 Molina Ghost Run, Bruce Swanson set up an outstanding course. (The low environmental impact of trials competition permits quick course construction, a factor that makes 4x4 trials well suited to clubs with limited space and resources. A large lot and some imagination can produce an event!) Bruce's course was tight and twisty, laced with rocks, and steeper than our first effort.

As Sunday morning's sunlight pierced the deep ravine, each competitor got a first glimpse of the 1990 trials course. The 1989 winners, brothers Harry Hetzer and Alvin Hetzer, Sr., looked over the steep starting bank and shook their heads. "Boy," Harry exclaimed, "my truck's wheelbase is plenty long for this course!"

Minutes before the start, Bruce walked the attentive drivers through the course. For the next hour and a half, seven hard-core four-wheelers battled against the stopwatches as they squeezed through a ravine, inched over two rockpiles, straddled a nasty trench and crept up and down two steep slopes.

These veteran four-wheelers caught on quickly. Few points were lost to tire spin, and high torque again joined forces with driving skill to produce a winning score.

The "Brothers Hetzer," as we now called them, pulled an upset. Alvin, who placed a solid second in the 1989 event, had shown up with a 101" wheelbase '59 Jeep CJ-6. A transplant Chevrolet V-8 with a high carburetor float level (which caused flooding and rough idle) quickly troubled his score.

Harry Hetzer, the 1989 first-place winner with a 103" wheelbase Jeep Scrambler (CJ-8), triumphed once again over nimbler CJ-5s and others. Despite wide skepticism about the longer CJ-8 wheelbase, Harry proved once more that 4x4 trials is a driver's sport.

Creeping and crawling his retrofit T-18 truck four speed and AMC inline 258 six (bone stock with OE carburetion and a maze of California smog hardware!), Harry Hetzer ran to a tight tie with highly skilled Mark Booker from Fresno. Mark and his CJ-5 outperformed everyone except Harry, who racked up another *zero tirespin* score with his CJ-8. In a hair splitting run-off, Harry edged out Mark for first place.

CA4WDC/Central District trophies went to Mark Booker for 2nd Place, and Harry Hetzer took another 1st Place home to Daly City, California. 4x4 trials became a reality at Molina, and these crawl masters now know what it takes to win.

When the course got tougher, the driver skills just came on stronger. Bruce Swanson even hinted about trying a log teeter-totter at a future 4x4 Trials event. Winching skills may also enter into the competition.

I encourage all 4x4 clubs and individuals with a competitive spirit to pick up the trials challenge. A trials course is very easy to construct, and you can spend a fun afternoon competing for trophies or other prizes. 4x4 Trials promotes better driving skills, heightens awareness of the environment and provides a chance to work your four-wheel drive truck through its low-range paces with minimal engine and geartrain stress.

Use these rules and regulations to foster friendly competition—and always remember to TREAD LIGHTLY!

Official Rules and Regulations For 4x4 Trials

In the interest of safe and environmentally sound off-pavement recreation, the following rules and regulations have been established. The sole intent of 4x4 Vehicle Trials is to promote, within a friendly, competitive atmosphere, those driving techniques and skills that minimize vehicle impact upon terrain and natural habitat.

4x4 trials will enhance the off-pavement driving skills of both new and experienced four-wheel drive vehicle operators. The goals set forth for 4x4 trials competition provide a far-reaching model for all off-pavement driving. Safety and preservation of the natural environment underlie these standards, rules, regulations and amendments for conducting trials events.

I. Vehicle Requirements—Any street-legal, four-wheel drive truck or sport/utility model may compete. Engine size, wheelbase and wheel/tire size are optional, providing that 1) the vehicle complies with local, state, and federal regulations for safe use on public highways, 2) tires are of conventional, highway legal "mud and snow" or "highway" tread design, recognized as commercially available, and 3) no aspect of the vehicle has been modified in a manner that would increase impact on the trials road course, terrain or local habitat.

Safety equipment should include, but not be limited to, a Red Cross approved First Aid Kit, a charged and "tagged" fire extinquisher, a four-point (or better) padded roll cage, a properly mounted and operational winch*, minimally of 6000 lbs. (single line) capacity, and an approved "tree saver" strap. Vehicle inspection for operationally safe hydraulic and emergency brakes, lights and brake lamps, and assurances of reasonable operating condition will take place before each event.

(*Events may test operator skills at safely utilizing a winch, with due consideration for trees, fauna and local habitat.)

II. Driver Requirements—Drivers must possess a valid state vehicle operator's license or legally recognized international driver's license. Learner's permits will not be acceptable, and proof of license is a requirement. A valid driver's license with notable restrictions shall not disqualify any driver, unless such restrictions either 1) prevent driving the vehicle during hours in which the trials event has been scheduled or 2) place the driver, passenger/occupants, other drivers/vehicles or spectators at unusual risk.

The driver must be in good physical condition. Use of illegal drugs, alcohol* or medical prescriptions and over-the-counter drugs that impair driving skills shall be cause for disqualification. Reckless, erratic or aberrant driving displays shall be cause for immediate disqualification and removal from the event. In all instances, the officials and judges of the event shall make the final decision regarding qualification and disqualification of drivers.

(*Alcohol at legally acceptable levels for safe vehicle operation on public highways shall be the maximum allowable under any circumstances. Additionally, any driver believed to be adversely influenced or impaired by the use of alcohol must prove his or her ability to compete safely. In each instance, use of alcohol by competitors shall be discouraged. No competitor is to carry alcoholic beverages in or about the vehicle.)

III. The Course—For each 4x4 trials event, the selection of a designated course shall meet with appropriate local, state and federal regulations. Public use permits and use of the 4x4 trials course shall comply with applicable land use regulations. Every reasonable effort shall be made to meet land use regulations. Officials of the 4x4 trials event shall provide participants and spectators with a list of rules, regulations and land use standards for the area assigned for the event. Whenever possible, land use agencies shall be encouraged to assist or participate in the establishment and layout of the trials course. Impact to the local environment will be minimized, and trials event damage to terrain, fauna or local waterways shall be reasonably alleviated by the 4x4 trials organizers or their assignees.

III. Scoring—An ideal score shall be zero ("0"). During the event, each participant will be penalized points according to the methods set forth in Section IV. OBJECTIVES. Penalty points shall be added to the starting score of zero, winners to be the driver(s) with the lowest number of penalty points. Each event's obstacles shall be clearly indicated, and officials will monitor times between course markers in 1/100ths of a second. Penalty points accrue as both the drivers' time errors and technique infractions.

IV. Objectives—There is only one 4x4 Trials winning criterion: TRAVEL THE COURSE IN THE DESIGNATED TIME OR SLOWER, WITHOUT STOPPING AND WITHOUT TIRE SPIN. Trials is not a speed contest, and any exhibition of speed shall be cause for points deduction or disqualification. Points shall also be deducted for running off course or excess abuse of terrain, as determined by the offical(s). Damage to the vehicle or "high centering" on chassis, body or powertrain components shall also be cause for points deductions. The overall winner is a highly competent driver, in full control of his or her vehicle at all times. Such a competitor leaves the least impact upon the course, the environment, his or her vehicle and passengers.

A. Designated Time: Well marked Start and Stop points shall be noted throughout the course. Upon starting from a given marker, the competitor/driver has a specific, minimum time to reach the next stop point. The driver must keep the vehicle moving without leaving the course or spinning tires. (As an option, a co-driver or passenger may assist by keeping time with a conventional stopwatch.)

B. Tire Spin: Each tire of competitors' vehicles shall be marked with one (1) swath of white, washable paint. Paint shall be applied with a 3-inch wide brush, from the wheel center outward to the tread area of each tire. Officials will watch the rotation of tires over the varied course terrain. Points shall be deducted for any occurrence of tire/wheel spin. Spin shall be defined as 1) the rotation of any tire without forward movement of the vehicle or 2) any moment in which one tire/wheel rotates faster than the other three tires/wheels, the one exception being a required, safe maneuver in which a wheel temporarily becomes suspended above the ground. One (1) point shall be deducted for each instance of tire/wheel spin observed.

C. High Center: For the purpose of 4x4 Trials competition, "high centering" shall be defined as interference or contact of vehicle undercarriage components with the course terrain. Such interference refers to, but is not limited to, chassis, suspension, powertrain and body components. Specific course requirements may involve the application of washable paint to undercarriage components. In such instances, officials will judge and penalize drivers for each indication of paint removed by undercarriage interference/contact with terrain. Such a course shall afford sufficient opportunity to avoid high centering.

Water crossings, log climbs, and other obstacles may be designed into any 4x4 trials course. In events with such special obstacles, additional rules and scoring methods shall be thoroughly discussed with all drivers at the "DRIVER'S PRELIMINARY MEETING." To qualify for competition, each driver must attend any and all such meetings. Special obstacles will be clearly marked on course maps and en route.

V. Entry Fees—Organizers of 4x4 Trials events may assign vehicle/driver entry fees for each eligible competitor. These fees shall be clearly designated and posted for the benefit of interested participants. Entry fees must be paid as stated, before each scheduled event. Any eligible competitor who becomes disabled or is unable to participate in an event must notify a designated official one (1) hour before the scheduled start of his or her event. A refund of entry fees or a portion thereof, according to posted and established guidelines, may then be afforded. Any competitor disqualified from competition for any rule or regulation infraction shall forfeit his or her paid entry fees.

VI. Rules Philosophy—4x4 Trials competition is a thorough test of driving skill. Skillful off-pavement driving requires total vehicle control and an awareness of road hazards and obstacles. When driving on off-pavement trails, respect for the natural environment is equally important. 4x4 Trials, conducted over a specified course, simulates the trying situations encountered in serious four-wheeling. Under the watchful eyes of officials and spectators, 4x4 operators can develop and display greater off-pavement/trail driving ability. "RULES AND REGULATIONS FOR 4X4 VEHICLE TRIALS" is for the sole purpose of achieving these goals. Such rules may be changed, amended, or modified to improve this competitive sport. Any changes shall be deemed necessary for promoting safety and sound driving habits on our public lands.

Index

A

Accessories
  bed and tub liners 237
  on-board welder 265
  roll bars 267
  seat belts and safety harnesses 269
  Sources 344
  sturdy trailer hitches 271
  survival 30
  winches, see *Winches*
Air bypass systems, see
  Emission Controls
Air cleaner
  oil bath 79
  paper 80
Air injection, see *Emission Controls*
Alignment, see *Front End*
Alternator, see also *Electrical System*
  basics 240
  high output 265
  overhauling 246
  testing 247
Anti-freeze, see *Cooling System*
Automatic transmission, see
  Transmission, Automatic
Axle
  4x4 front axle types 188
  conversion 321
  front, see also *Front End*
    and knuckle seals 189
    Mono Beam and Twin I-Beam 48
    Twin Traction Beam 49
    wear points 203
  general 185
  rear
    full-floating 21
    full-floating, broken 99
    Semi-floating rear axle, broken 99
    Semi- vs. full-floating axles 187
  ring and pinion, operation 185
  seal installation tips 189
  seal leaks 188
  troubleshooting
    drive axle 188
  trusses 327
  types 187
  upgrades 321

B

Ball Joints, see *Front End*
Battery, see also *Electrical system*
  and charging system, checking 246
  selecting 264
  storing 88
  testing 246
  upgrades 263, 265
Belts, tightening 114
Body and Interior
  detailing
    body, 232
    tips 235
  paint
    repairing scratches 236
    waxing and buffing 233
  rust
    repairing 231
    typical locations 230
Brake fluid
  and moisture 88
  brake lines, flushing 88
  cautions when working with 221
  replacing 223
  requirements 221
  silicone 88
Brakes
  bleeding 223
  brake service 222
  checking drums or rotors 226
  cleaning parts 223
  drum and disc brake systems 50
  emergency/parking brake 51
  general 220
  linings (pads and shoes) 224
  overhauling 223
  pulling 102
  pulsing pedal 221
  semi-metallic pads 225
  troubleshooting 221
  upgrading 342
  warnings for working on 217
Buying an F-Series truck 19
  buying concerns 23
  new truck 28
    1994 Specifications 30
    accessories 30

Buying an F-Series truck (cont'd)
  chassis selection 29
  engine and transmission 29
  factory upgrades 29
  special ordering 30
  models
    F-150 20
    F-250 virtues 21
    F-350, One-ton 22
  used truck
    automatic transmission 27
    body and accessories 27
    chassis 25
    clutch and transmission 26
    drivelines and axles 26
    engine 27
    engine oil 27
    pollution controls and
      registration 28
    Ten Best Picks 24

C

Camshafts
  upgrades
    aftermarket 276, 278
    lobe profiles 276
    off-pavement 276
    performance 276
    performance, and axle gearing 277
    selecting 276
    supercharging 285
    Variable Duration Lifters 277
CARB EO (Exemption Order)
  numbers 274
Carburetor
  feedback, tuning 134, 281
  float settings 135
  idle mixture 137
  performance 280
  tune-up 133
  upgrades 280
Catalytic Converter, see
  Emission Controls and *Exhaust*
Charging System, see *Electrical System*
Chassis
  checking for damage 204
  inspecting 89

INDEX

Chassis (cont'd)
 lift kits, rules for 324
 lubrication, see *Lubrication and Maintenance*
 modifying 323
 overview 48
 springs, see *Springs*
 state lift laws and accountability 325
Clutch
 adjustment 158
  1961-up 160
  early models 159
 aftermarket 315
 alignment 162
 Borg & Beck 314
 centrifugal 314
 diaphragm 314
 freeplay adjustment 158
 identifying 157
 linkage 55
  overview 55
  repairs 163
  upgrading 316
 replacement
  parts required 162
  tips 160
  tools 162
 slippage 93, 157
 throwout bearing, worn 154
 troubleshooting 153, 154
 type identification 157
 upgrading 314
 wear, checking 157
Compression, engine 91
Compression testing, see *Engine*
Cooling system
 and automatic transmission cooler 108
 basics 106
 boil over 97
 coolant (anti-freeze)
  mixing ratios 109
  requirements 106
 cooling fan 96
  air flow requirements 106
  clutch 107
  electric 109
 leaks 108
 overheating 92, 96, 97, 111
 radiator
  boiling and rodding 111
  cap 109, 111
  four-row 96
  size recommendations 106
 safety precautions for overheated engine 105
 service 105
 thermostat 107
 water pump service 112
  general procedures 113

Cooling system (cont'd)
 guidelines 112
 notes on specific engines 115
Cylinder head, see *Engine*

D

Detailing, see *Body and Interior*
Differentials
 traction differentials
 limited slip 187
 operation 184, 317
 positraction 317
  buyer's guide 318
  choosing 318
 ring and pinion, operation 185
 troubleshooting 188
 upgrading 322
Distributor
 see also *Ignition*
 bushing wear 127
 overhaul 126
Distributor Cap, see *Tune-up*
Drive axle troubleshooting 188
Driveshafts
 angularity 183
 assembly pointers 180
 general 58, 180
 installation 184
 lubrication 182
 overview 58
 phase 180
 torque loads 99
 u-joints 180
 upgrades 322
Drivetrain, upgrading 311
Drum and disc brake systems 50
 see also *Brakes*
Dwell, see *Tune-up*

E

EGR, see *Emission Controls*
Electrical System
 amp draw of components 261
 basics 239
 batteries, see *Battery*
 charging system
  troubleshooting 247
  upgrading 265
 fuses 241
 relays 241
 reliability 264
 service 240
 testing Ignition and Fuel System Components 247
 troubleshooting 242
  alternator 246
  battery 246
  charging System 247
  continuity 244

Electrical System (cont'd)
 fuel system 247
 ignition 247
 short circuit 244
 starter 249
 voltage and ground 242
 voltage drop 245
 upgrades 261
  Charging System 265
  Dual Batteries 263
 volt-ohmmeter, using 241
 wiring connections 262
 wiring demands 241
 wiring requirements 261
Electronic ignition, see Ignition
Emergency/parking brake 51
Emission Controls
 air bypass 146
 air injection 145
 and conversion engines 149, 275
 and emissions test 149
 basics 144
 catalytic converter 147
 cold-start and warm-up 145
 controlled gasses 144
 evaporative emissions 149
 Exhaust Gas Recirculation (EGR) 146
 exhaust system 151
 general 144
 heat riser 148
 oxygen sensor, aftermarket 281
 PCV valve 144
 passing an emission test 149
 routine emission control service 152
 service, general 118
 smog inspection, requirements 118
 vacuum switches and valves 148
Engine
 and unleaded fuel 139
 applications 118
 balancing 309
 conversion engines, laws 275
 coolant, see *Cooling system*
 cylinder head
  gasket leak 96
  bolts, retorquing 140
 diagnosis 139
  compression testing 139
  vs. cylinder leakdown 65
 diesel,
  6.9L/7.3L Navistar V-8 55, 119
  glow plugs 121
 L-head six and V-8 118
 overhauling 300
 overview 51
 performance modifications
  50-state legal 274
  302 5.0L 294
  351 Windsor V-8 292
  460 V-8 290, 291

Engine (cont'd)
   and smog laws 273
   camshaft 276
   carburetion 280
   general 275
   FE V-8 288
   flathead engines 287
   ignition 278
   oil coolers 283
   supercharging 284
   valvetrain 275, 289
   Y-block V-8 287
   six-cylinder
      OHV 215/223/262 In-line 52, 118
      226H L-head Six 51, 118
      240/300/4.9L OHV 52, 119
   storing 86
   troubleshooting
      see also *Troubleshooting*
      knock, curing 280
      misfire, causes 125
      overheat 92, 96
      will not crank 94
      will not run 94
   tune-up, see *Tune-up*
   valves, see Valves
   V-8s
      239.4 L-head V-8 52, 118
      239/256/272 and 292
         Y-block V-8s 53, 118
      302/5.0L/351W/351M/400
         Small-block V-8s 54, 119
      352, later 360 and 390, 460FE
         big-block 54, 119
      flathead V-8s 52, 118
      460 big-block V-8 54, 119
      Y-block V-8s 53, 118
Exhaust Gas Recirculation (EGR)
   see *Emission Controls*
Exhaust system 151
   catalytic converter 147

F

Fan, cooling, see *Cooling System*
Ford F-Series truck
   4WD clubs 45

Ford F-Series truck (cont'd)
   how to find 45
   accessories 253
   and your lifestyle 35
   author's trucks 33
   buying 19
      Models 20
      F-1, F-150 20
      F-2, F-250 virtues 21
      F-3, F-350 22
      New F-Series 28
      Ten Best Used Picks 24
   Evolution of
      1942: Ford Trucks Forge Their
         Own Identity 2
      1948: A Truck With A Firm
         Identity 3
      1953–56: A Marque Emerges 4
      1957–64: The Pragmatic Years 8
      1965: The Advent Of Twin
         I-Beam 10
      1967–79: Years Of Bold
         Refinement 12
      1980: An Advanced 4x4
         Chassis 15
      Poised For The Future 17
   storing 86
   troubleshooting, see *Troubleshooting*
   used 24
   washing 233
   working on 47
      Assigning Work To A Shop 69
      automatic transmissions 56
      chassis 48
      clutch 55
      driveshafts 58
      Field Fix To Get Home 215
      transmissions and transfer cases 55
Four-wheel drive
   Driving Though Sand Traps 44
   full-time vs. part-time 178
   learning to drive 35
   operating 36
   SAR (Search and Rescue) 43
   snowplowing with 43
   special uses for 43
   towing, requirements 23

Four-wheel drive (cont'd)
   troubleshooting, see *Troubleshooting*
   two- vs. four-wheel drive 36
   using 38
   when to use 38
Frame, see Chassis
Frame, checking for damage 204
Front End, see also *Steering*, and
   Axle, Front, and *Suspension*
   alignment 100, 213
   ball joints 206
   king pins 208
   shimmy 101
   wander 100
Fuel injection, general 121
Fuel pump 135
   installation 138
   pressure/output 136
Fuel starvation 92
Fuel system, storage 86
Fuses, see *Electrical System*

G

Gear bind 99

H

Hubs 195
   maintaining 196
   rebuilding 196
   retrofitting new 200
   types 195
   upgrading 312
Heat riser, see *Emission Controls*

I

Ignition
   see also *Tune-up*, and
      individual components
   DIS ignition 128
   early systems 125
   electronic (primary)
      problems 128
      testing 128
   HEI systems, rotor problems 125
   performance 278

Ignition (cont'd)
  point and condenser service 125
  tune-up requirements 122
  upgrades
    knock sensors 280
  weak 92
  wires and distributor cap 124

K

King Pins, see *Front End*
Knock sensor, see *Ignition*

L

Lubrication and maintenance
  axles and hubs 83
  chassis 81
  defined 74
  distributor 81
  emission controls 80
  engine oil 75
  engine oil and filter 78
  greases 75
  greasing 82
  lubricants and fluids 74
  oil, synthetic vs. mineral 77
  oil filter, bypass 78
  power steering 81
  schedule 76
  service intervals 75
  springs 82
  step-by-step 78

M

Manual transmissions
  rating 311
  rebuilding 165
  troubleshooting 155
    particles in oil 156
    shifting problems 155
  Warner four-speed transmissions 23
Maintenance, see *Lubrication and Maintenance*

O

Off-road driving
  advanced 43
  airing down 38
  and automatic transmission 41
  environmental impact 41
  hills 39
  sand traps 44
  terrain 39
  Tread Lightly Four Wheeling 41
Oil change, see *Lubrication and Maintenance*
Oil coolers 283
Oil filter, see *Lubrication and Maintenance*

One-ton F-350 22
Overheating, causes 105
Oxygen sensor, tuning with 281

P

Paint, see *Body and Interior*
PCV valve, see *Emission Controls*
Power take-off (PTO) 177
Pads, brake, see *Brake, linings*
Parts, sourcing 68
Points, see *Tune-up* and *Ignition*
Power steering, see *Steering*

R

Radiator, see *Cooling System*
Relays, see *Electrical System*
Repairs on your F-Series truck 59
  flat rate 69
  jacks 59
  miscellaneous 67
  safety and 60
  sending to a shop 69
  sourcing parts 68
  tools 59
  workplace 59
Ring and pinion, operation 185
Rust, see *Body and Interior*
Roll Bars, see *Accessories*
Rotor, Ignition see *Tune-up*
Rotors, see *Brake*
Rust, see *Body and Interior*

S

Seat belts and safety harnesses 269
Selecting the right truck 20
Shock absorbers, see also *Suspension*
  design 204
  gas 205
  general 204
  multiple 328
  selecting 205
  single- vs. twin-tube 204
  upgrading 327
Smog inspection, requirements 118
Spark plugs
  fouled 123
  gapping 123
  service 122
  torquing 124
Springs
  and suspension height 201
  coil applications 202
  general 201
  leaf, installing 202
  leaf shackles, inspecting 204
  shackles 202
Starter
  drive 248
  general 248

Starter (cont'd)
  rebuilding 250
  solenoid 248
  troubleshooting 249
Steering, see also *Axle, front*
  ball joint 206
  general 208
  linkage inspection 211
    damage 213
  power types 210
  steering gear
    and linkage 49
    choosing 336
    conversions 336
    maintenance 81
    troubleshooting 213
  steering knuckles 48
    4x4, rebuilding 206
    rebuilding, closed 190
    maintenance, closed 83
  system inspection 212
  types 209
    closed knuckle with king pins 208
    rebuilding 206
Storage, F-truck 86
Supercharging
  aftermarket 284
  air filtration 285
  and diesels 286
  basics 284
  camshafts 285
  compression Ratios 285
  engine modifications for 285
  turbocharging 284
Suspension, see also individual components
  aftermarket upgrades 326
  modifying 324
  Massachusetts' Suspension Modification Formula 326
  off-pavement tuning 325
  state lift laws and accountability 325
  types 48
  upgrading, installing a kit 329
  urethane bushings 328

T

TFI-IV ignition 128
Thermostat, see *Cooling System*
Tie-rods, off-road damage 90
Timing, see also *Tune-up*
  degrees 131
  ignition 125
  light, see *Tools*
  running 129
  specifications 132
  static 130
  vacuum advance 132
Tires
  Airing down 38
  aftermarket sources 340

> **WARNING —**
> • Automotive service, repair, and modification is serious business. You must be alert, use common sense, and exercise good judgement to prevent personal injury.
>
> • Before using this book or beginning any work on your vehicle, thoroughly read the Warning on the copyright page, and any Warnings and Cautions listed on the inside back cover.
>
> • Always read a complete procedure before you begin the work. Pay special attention to any Warnings and Cautions, or any other information, that accompanies that procedure.

Tires (cont'd)
  balancing 101
  glossary 339
  inflation recommendations 339
  installing 340
  larger 337
  monster 337
  storing 88
  trail running formula 338
  upgrading 337
Tools
  air 63
  books 61
  brake 62
  chassis and powertrain 61
  cooling 66
  dwell meter 64, 127
  emission controls 66
  general 60
  ignition 65, 131
  sealants 67
  timing light 65, 131
  tune-up 63
  volt-ohmmeter, using 241
Towing, requirements 23
Trailering 270
  sturdy trailer hitches 270
Transfer cases
  chain drive, troubles 179
  electronic shift, late 179
  general 57, 177
  lightweight 178
  NP203 and NP205 57
  power take-off (PTO) 177
  troubleshooting 178
Transmission
  automatic
    C-6 23, 57
    and off-road driving 41
    band adjustments 165
    kickdown adjustment 165
    overview 56
  lubricant 156
  manual
    adjustments 164
    gear reduction 312
    hard shifting, causes 155
    jumping out of gear 156
    particles in oil 156
    performance 312

Transmission (cont'd)
  pilot bearing, troubleshooting 154
  rating 311
  rebuilding 165
  shifting problems 155
  synchronizers, worn 156
  troubleshooting 97, 155
  Warner four-speed 23
  upgrades
    four-speed conversion 313
    overdrive five-speed
      conversion 314
TREAD LIGHTLY, Inc. 41
Troubleshooting, see also
  individual components
  alternator 95
  axle 99
  brakes 102
  clutch 97
  cooling system 96
  drive axle 188
  driveshaft 99
  engine 91, see also Engine
    will not crank 94
    will not run 94
  fuel starvation 92
  general 89, 91
  limited slip differential 98
  starter 95, 249
  steering and tires 100
  transmission 97
  vacuum leaks 93
Tune-up
  see also individual components
  engine requirements 118
  fuel injected engines 121
  ignition 122, see also Ignition
    dwell meter and setting points 127
    rotor 125
    timing 129
    wires and distributor cap 125
  tools 63
  tuning with an oxygen sensor 281
  valve adjustment, see Valves
Turbocharging, see Supercharging

U
U-joint
  causes of failure 180
  installation 184

U-joint (cont'd)
  service and repair tips 180
  proper lubrication 182
Used truck, see also Buying
  inspecting 25
  ten best picks 24
Urethane bushings
  choosing 328
  installing 329

V
V-belts, tightening 114
Vacuum leaks 93
Valves
  adjusting 141
    215, 223, 262 OHV Sixes,
      Y-block V-8s 142
    226H Six 142
Valves (cont'd)
  clearance specifications 143
Volt-ohmmeter, using 241

W
Water Pump, see Cooling System
Wheels
  choosing 340
  installing 340
Wheel alignment 213
Wheel bearings
  adjusting 218
  causes of failure 218
  general 217
  servicing 218
Winches
  carry-aboard accessories 258
  controls 257
  electric 254
  electrical requirements 255
  electrical system 257
  general 254
  maintenance 260
  motors 255
  mounting 256
  portable 257
  power take-off (PTO) 177
  selecting 255
  types 254
  using 259

Selected Books and Electronic Editions From Bentley Publishers

Enthusiast

Alfa Romeo Owner's Bible™
Pat Braden 0-8376-0707-8

Chevrolet by the Numbers 1965-1969: The Essential Chevrolet Parts Reference
Alan Colvin ISBN 08376-0956-9

Glory Days: When Horsepower and Passion Ruled Detroit
Jim Wangers ISBN 0-8376-0208-4

Harley-Davidson Evolution V-Twin Owner's Bible™ *Moses Ludel*
ISBN 0-8376-0146-0

Jeep Owner's Bible™ *Moses Ludel*
ISBN 0-8376-0154-1

Toyota Truck & Land Cruiser Owner's Bible™ *Moses Ludel*
ISBN 0-8376-0159-2

Driving

A French Kiss With Death: Steve McQueen and the Making of *Le Mans*
Michael Keyser ISBN 0-8376-0234-3

Going Faster! Mastering the Art of Race Driving *The Skip Barber Racing School*
ISBN 0-8376-0227-0

The Racing Driver *Denis Jenkinson*
ISBN 0-8376-0201-7

The Speed Merchants: A Journey Through the World of Motor Racing 1969-1972
Michael Keyser ISBN 0-8376-0232-7

Sports Car and Competition Driving
Paul Frère with foreword by Phil Hill
ISBN 0-8376-0202-5

Think To Win: The New Approach to Fast Driving *Don Alexander with foreword by Mark Martin* ISBN 0-8376-0070-7

Engineering

Bosch Fuel Injection and Engine Management *Charles O. Probst, SAE*
ISBN 0-8376-0300-5

Maximum Boost: Designing, Testing, and Installing Turbocharger Systems
Corky Bell ISBN 0-8376-0160-6

Race Car Aerodynamics *Joseph Katz*
ISBN 0-8376-0142-8

The Scientific Design of Exhaust and Intake Systems
Philip H. Smith and John C. Morrison
ISBN 0-8376-0309-9

Audi

Audi TT Official Factory Repair Manual MY 2000 Electronic Edition CD-ROM
Audi of America ISBN 0-8376-0758-2

Audi A4/S4 Official Factory Repair Manual 1996-2000 Electronic Edition CD-ROM
Bentley Publishers ISBN 0-8376-0761-2

Audi 100, A6 Official Factory Repair Manual: 1992–1997, including S4, S6, Quattro and Wagon models *Audi of America*
ISBN 0-8376-0374-9

Audi 80, 90, Coupe Quattro Official Factory Repair Manual: 1988–1992 including 80 Quattro, 90 Quattro and 20-valve models *Audi of America*
ISBN 0-8376-0367-6

BMW

Complete Roundel 1969-1998
8 CD-ROM set: 30 Years of the Magazine of the BMW Car Club of America, Inc.
BMW Car Club of America ISBN 0-8376-0322-6

BMW 3-Series Service Manual: 1984–1990 318i, 325, 325e(es), 325i(is), and 325i Convertible *Robert Bentley*
ISBN 0-8376-0325-0

BMW 3 Series (E36) Service Manual: 1992-1998, 318is/iC, 323is/iC, 325i/is/iC, 328i/is/iC, M3
Bentley Publishers ISBN 0-8376-0326-9

BMW 5-Series Service Manual: 1989–1995 525i, 530i, 535i, 540i, including Touring
Bentley Publishers ISBN 0-8376-0319-6

BMW 5-Series Service Manual: 1982–1988 528e, 533i, 535i, 535is *Robert Bentley*
ISBN 0-8376-0318-8

BMW 6 Series Enthusiast's Companion
Jeremy Walton ISBN 0-8376-0149-5

BMW 7 Series Service Manual: 1988–1994, 735i, 735iL, 740i, 740iL, 750iL
Bentley Publishers ISBN 0-8376-0328-5

The BMW Enthusiast's Companion
BMW Car Club of America
ISBN 0-8376-0321-8

BMW Z3 Roadster Service Manual: 1996–1998, 4-cylinder and 6-cylinder engines
Bentley Publishers ISBN 0-8376-0325-0

Unbeatable BMW: Eighty Years of Engineering and Motorsport Success
Jeremy Walton ISBN 0-8376-0206-8

Ford

Ford F-Series Pickup Owner's Bible™
Moses Ludel ISBN 0-8376-0152-5

Ford Fuel Injection and Electronic Engine Control: 1988–1993 *Charles O. Probst, SAE*
ISBN 0-8376-0301-3

Ford Fuel Injection and Electronic Engine Control: 1980–1987 *Charles O. Probst, SAE*
ISBN 0-8376-0302-1

The Official Ford Mustang 5.0 Technical Reference & Performance Handbook 1979-1993 *Al Kirschenbaum*
ISBN 0-8376-0210-6

Saab

Saab 900 16 Valve Official Service Manual: 1985–1993 *Robert Bentley* ISBN 0-8376-0312-9

Saab 900 8 Valve Official Service Manual: 1981–1988 *Robert Bentley* ISBN 0-8376-0310-2

Volkswagen

Battle for the Beetle: The Story of the Battle for the Giant VW Factory and the Car that Became an Icon Around the Globe
Karl Ludvigsen ISBN 08376-0071-5

Volkswagen Model Documentation
Joachim Kuch ISBN 0-8376-0078-2

Volkswagen Sport Tuning for Street and Competition
Per Schroeder ISBN 0-8376-0161-4

Volkswagen GTI/Golf/Jetta Service Manual 1985-1992 Electronic Edition CD-ROM
Bentley Publishers ISBN 0-8376-0759-0

Volkswagen New Beetle Official Factory Repair Manual 1998-2000 Electronic Edition CD-ROM
Bentley Publishers ISBN 0-8376-0760-4

Volkswagen New Beetle Service Manual: 1998-1999 *Bentley Publishers*
ISBN 0-8376-0385-4

Volkswagen Workshop Manual: Types 11, 14, and 15 (Beetle & Karmann Ghia) 1952-1957 *Volkswagen of America*
ISBN 0-8376-0389-7

Eurovan Official Factory Repair Manual: 1992-1999 *Volkswagen of America*
ISBN 0-8376-0335-8

Jetta, Golf, GTI, Cabrio Service Manual: 1993–1999, including Jetta_III and Golf_III
Robert Bentley ISBN 0-8376-0366-8

GTI, Golf, and Jetta Service Manual: 1985–1992 Gasoline, Diesel, and Turbo Diesel, including 16V *Robert Bentley*
ISBN 0-8376-0342-0

Passat Service Manual 1990-1993, including GL and Wagon
Robert Bentley ISBN 0-8376-0378-1

Corrado Official Factory Repair Manual: 1990–1994 *Volkswagen United States*
ISBN 0-8376-0387-0

Super Beetle, Beetle and Karmann Ghia Official Service Manual Type 1: 1970–1979
Volkswagen United States ISBN 0-8376-0096-0

Station Wagon/Bus Official Service Manual Type 2: 1968–1979 *Volkswagen United States* ISBN 0-8376-0094-4

Fastback and Squareback Official Service Manual Type 3: 1968–1973
Volkswagen United States
ISBN 0-8376-0057-X

Fox Service Manual 1987-1993
Robert Bentley ISBN 0-8376-0363-3

Beetle and Karmann Ghia Official Service Manual Type 1: 1966–1969 *Volkswagen United States* ISBN 0-8376-0416-8

Cabriolet and Scirocco Service Manual: 1985–1993, including 16V *Robert Bentley*
ISBN 0-8376-0362-5

Vanagon Official Factory Repair Manual: 1980–1991 including Diesel Engine, Syncro, and Camper *Volkswagen United States* ISBN 0-8376-0336-6

www.bentleypublishers.com

Acknowledgments

My interest in trucks began before kindergarten. As the family tale goes, I could recite the names "Peterbilt," "Autocar" and "K-W" while trucks with these badges rolled past on the highway. That innate curiosity, later fueled by the enthusiasm of peers, co-workers and eventually magazine and newspaper readers, has never waned.

My commitment to detail stems from work with "old-school" professional truck mechanics, desert racers, topnotch parts personnel and truck experts like John Compton, Tom Reider, Doug Baker, Warren Guidry, Jeff Sugg, Tom Telford, Kevin Healey, Greg Williams, Lloyd Novak, Keith Buckley, John Partridge, Richard Corgiat, John Maine, Neal Faught, and Mike Asbahr. Some of my best insights, however, I owe to my students at the San Diego Job Corps mechanics program. They taught me how to convey information in a useful manner.

In assembling archival graphics for the book, I have relied upon the resources of Warn Industries, Ramsey Winch Company and Ford Motor Company. Personnel within these organizations, especially Jim Trainor and Woody Haines of Ford Motor Company and Scott Salmon at Warn Industries, lent considerable support.

I thank Michael Bentley and David Bull for their encouragement and promotion of my work, which has established our enduring and creative author/publisher relationship. Likewise, John Kittredge deserves my profound thanks for his exceptional professionalism and willingness to handle the monumental amount of material, photographs and text that I felt essential for the project.

As a foremost consideration, I thank my wife, Donna, and son, Jacob, for their patience and understanding. My commitment to this book was intensive and time consuming, yet our home remains whole and happy. Thanks, family, for your support, presence and interest in my passions!

About the Author

An avid fly fisherman, hunter, canoeist and four- wheeler, Moses Ludel took his first driver's test in the family 4x4 truck. Two years later, at age eighteen, he drove the Rubicon Trail by the back route (traveling east to west), starting at Miller Lake and tracking the unmarked trail across the Sierra Mountains to Placerville, California.

Moses worked as a journeyman truck mechanic and heavy equipment operator before receiving a Bachelor of Science degree with honors from the University of Oregon. He has taught Adult Education level courses in Automotive/Diesel Mechanics and established himself as an automotive journalist, columnist and photographer, with a specialty in four-wheel drive trucks.

Since 1982, Moses has published over 1,100 technical features and columns. His magazine credits include *OFF-ROAD*, *Four-Wheeler*, *4WD Action/SUV*, *4x4 Magazine (Japan)*, *Trailer Life*, *Motorhome*, *Popular Hot Rodding*, *Super Street Truck*, *Truckin'*, *Sport Truck*, *Fabulous Mustangs*, *Guide To Muscle Cars*, *Super Ford*, *Corvette Fever* and many others. He currently fields three magazine technical columns and also writes the Portland *Oregonian*'s weekly "DriveTime" newspaper column.

In response to his first book, the *Jeep Owner's Bible* (Robert Bentley, Publishers), Moses has been a guest on radio talk shows and has appeared on TNN cable television's "Truckin' U.S.A." He is active with the TREAD LIGHTLY! organization, having served as Media Representative and on the Environmental Relations Committee. He currently conducts 4WD clinics for TREAD LIGHTLY.

Front cover: Photo by Duane Elliott, vehicle courtesy of Kendall Ford, Eugene, OR

Back cover: Clockwise from top: a) F-250 4WD courtesy Tim Luke, photo by Moses Ludel; b) F-150 Lightning, photo by Ron Sessions; c) Ford F-150 pre-runner, vehicle courtesy John Maine, Northwest Off-Road Motorsports, photo by Moses Ludel; d) F-100 hood emblem, vehicle courtesy Bob Frank, photo by Moses Ludel; e) Flareside engine compartment, photo by Ron Sessions; f) 1948 F-1, vehicle courtesy David Lowe, photo by Moses Ludel